# COLLECTED ESSAYS

H. P. LOVECRAFT: COLLECTED ESSAYS

Volume 1: Amateur Journalism (2004)
Volume 2: Literary Criticism (2004)
Volume 3: Science (2005)
Volume 3: Travel (2006)
Volume 5: Philosophy; Autobiography and Miscellany (2006)

# COLLECTED ESSAYS
## VOLUME 1: AMATEUR JOURNALISM

H. P. Lovecraft

Edited by S. T. Joshi

Hippocampus Press

New York

**Library of Congress Cataloging-in-Publication Data**

Lovecraft, H. P. (Howard Phillips), 1890–1937
  [Essays]
  Collected essays / H.P. Lovecraft ; edited by S.T. Joshi. --
1st ed.
    v. cm.
  Includes bibliographical references and indexes.
  Contents: v. 1. Amateur journalism -- v. 2. Literary criticism.
  ISBN 0-9721644-1-3 (v. 1 : hardcover) -- ISBN 0-9721644-2-1
(v. 1 : pbk.) -- ISBN 0-9721644-4-8 (v. 2 : hardcover) -- ISBN
0-9721644-9-9 (v. 2 : pbk.)
  I. Joshi, S. T., 1958–  . II. Title.
PS3523.O833A6 2004b
814'.52--dc22

2004000766

Select unpublished texts have been published by permission of the Estate of
H. P. Lovecraft and John Hay Library, Brown University.

Published by Hippocampus Press
P.O. Box 641, New York, NY 10156.
http://www.hippocampuspress.com

Cover art by Virgil Finlay, used by permission of Lail Finlay.
Hippocampus Press logo by Anastasia Damianakos.
Cover design by Barbara Briggs Silbert.

First Edition
1 3 5 7 9 8 6 4 2

Cloth: ISBN 0-9721644-1-3
Paper: ISBN 0-9721644-2-1

# CONTENTS

# INTRODUCTION

In this first complete edition of Lovecraft's nonfictional writing (exclusive of letters), I have decided that the interests of readers and scholars are best served by a thematic division into seven broad categories: amateur journalism; literary criticism; science; travel; philosophy; autobiography; and miscellany. Lovecraft's essays can, on the whole, fit comfortably within these rubrics, although in a few instances there may be some potential overlap. Given that a majority of his essays were written during his initial involvement in amateur journalism (1914–25), a substantial proportion of them deal at least indirectly with amateur affairs; much of his literary criticism, for example, either focuses on amateur writers or is the product of debates within the amateur press. The editors nonetheless feel that the current divisions will allow for a sound understanding of Lovecraft's nonfictional work within the context of his career as a fiction writer, critic, epistolarian, and thinker.

The present volume includes writings that expressly concern themselves with amateur affairs. This is not the place for a detailed discussion of Lovecraft's participation in the United Amateur Press Association (UAPA) or the National Amateur Press Association (NAPA);[1] but some broad perspectives can be offered here. Lovecraft's entry into the amateur world is sufficiently well known: having published several letters (some in verse) in the letter columns of the *Argosy* and *All-Story*, Lovecraft was invited by Edward F. Daas to join the UAPA, which he did in April 1914. By the fall of that year he had been appointed Chairman of the Department of Public Criticism, and for the next five years he used this forum to express his opinions of the state of amateur writing. By the spring of 1915 Lovecraft had decided to establish his own amateur paper, the *Conservative*, and its run of thirteen issues over the next eight years allowed him to publish his views on a wide array of topics—literary, political, social, philosophical—as well as his unvarnished thoughts on amateurdom. It is only the essays on this last topic that are included here; the others can be found in other volumes in this edition.

Lovecraft, of course, contributed very widely to other papers, as well as to the UAPA's official organ, the *United Amateur*. He was actually called upon to edit the July 1917 issue of the *United Amateur* when the Official Editor, Andrew F. Lockhart, was unable to perform this function. By that time he had been elected President of the UAPA, an office he held until the next July. In the summer of 1920 he was elected Official Editor, serving for the next five years with the exception of the 1922–23 term. On occasion Lovecraft even fulfilled the function of Custodian of the Official Organ Fund, the fund that was collected to finance the publication of the *United Amateur*.

Lovecraft, although professing himself a loyal United man (and, indeed, a devotee of the "Hoffman" branch of the UAPA, which had split from the main body in 1912 as the result of a disputed election), quietly joined the NAPA as early as the spring of 1917; but he restricted his contributions to NAPA papers, rarely contributing anything aside from poems to the *Tryout* and poems and stories to W. Paul Cook's *Vagrant*. Al-

---

[1] See Joshi, *Life* (passim) for more extended coverage.

most none of his writings on amateur journalism appeared in NAPA papers, and he generally reacted with hostility (see "A Reply to the *Lingerer*") when NAPA members criticized the UAPA.

The virtually autocratic control of the UAPA for the period 1917–22 exercised by Lovecraft and his colleagues—including Rheinhart Kleiner, Maurice W. Moe, Alfred Galpin, Verna McGeoch, Winifred V. Jackson, and Frank Belknap Long—eventually engendered a backlash. As early as 1919 Lovecraft is speaking in dire tones of the fate of the UAPA if such perceived undesirables as William J. Dowdell were to gain control of the association; and he must have been mortified when his close colleague Leo Fritter finally turned against him and assisted in the ousting of the Lovecraft faction in the election of 1922. But Fritter's own cadre was unable to counteract the apathy that was overtaking the entire amateur world, and especially the UAPA, at the time, and so it was reluctantly forced to yield the reins back to Lovecraft's group in 1923, although the intransigence of some members resulted in a virtual cessation of official activity until the summer of 1924. By then Lovecraft—now joined by his wife, Sonia H. Greene, who had been elected President—was too preoccupied with his own personal and professional literary concerns to devote the attention he would have wished to the resurrection of amateurdom; perhaps, indeed, no amount of effort would have had any appreciable effect. After shepherding in a new official board in the election of 1925, Lovecraft in effect washed his hands of the UAPA, which in any case folded the next year. (The "other" UAPA—the United Amateur Press Association of America—lasted until about 1939.)

For a period of five years Lovecraft's amateur activity was all but quiescent, aside from the contribution of a small number of poems, essays, and stories to various amateur papers. But his attendance of the 1930 NAPA convention in Boston appears to have rekindled his devotion, and the next year he was persuaded to join the NAPA's critical board, called the Bureau of Critics. For the next five years he wrote tirelessly for this department, chiefly on amateur verse; not coincidentally, he used this forum as a means of expounding his new theories on poetry, so different as they were from the frigid classicism he had embraced in his early years. The progress of Lovecraft's thought in this domain can be charted in Volume 2 of this edition.

Lovecraft found in amateur journalism the ideal haven for the exercise of non-remunerative self-expression. It is likely that he had already arrived at this stance prior to his joining amateurdom—it was probably derived from his absorption of the eighteenth-century notion of art as an elegant amusement for gentlemen—but certainly his involvement with amateurdom helped to foster it and make it a central pillar of his aesthetic thought. In some senses Lovecraft was idealizing amateurdom: there were probably not many even in the amateur world who adhered so rigidly to the non-commercial ideal as he, many of them believing that amateur journalism was merely a training ground for the would-be professional writer. But Lovecraft's need to find in amateurdom an alternative to the money-grubbing world of commerce that he so scorned perhaps explains his fervent devotion to the cause long after it had served its central purposes in his life—of bringing him out of his reclusive shell; of allowing him a means to hone his wide-ranging thoughts into effective prose; and of fostering close friendships with a select few who could bolster his self-esteem by admiring his work and broadening his intellectual and personal horizons—and become thankless drudgery.

Lovecraft also found in amateurdom a venue for education—a point made most succinctly in "For What Does the United Stand" (1920). He understandably felt that he himself would be one of those figures of wide learning who would assist his inferiors in attaining a broad humanistic culture, or at the minimum a modicum of coherence in writing; the claim was not arrogance but plain truth, given Lovecraft's intellectual eminence in the amateur world. His work on the Department of Public Criticism was a significant component of this campaign; and it is no surprise that his career as a professional reviser and ghostwriter emerged from amateur work of this kind. As time passed Lovecraft appears to have exhibited a certain impatience with the slow intellectual progress of other members, and there are times when he seems to advocate a kind of literary fascism (see "Amateur Journalism: Its Possible Needs and Betterment") whereby crude members' work would be improved by main force. But, as the poignant essay "What Amateurdom and I Have Done for Each Other" testifies, Lovecraft was aware that a broader educational function had been exercised for his own benefit.

Lovecraft's involvement in the smallest minutiae of amateur controversies, in conjunction with or in opposition to amateur writers who are in large part nothing but names even to specialists, may seem puzzling or a waste of time that could have been spent better elsewhere; but Lovecraft never regarded his amateur activity as a waste of his time, and the extent to which, over a lifetime, he devoted his energies to it should suggest that its importance in his intellectual and personal maturation has largely been underestimated. This volume will perhaps assist in a revaluation of Lovecraft's amateur work and its place in his literary career.

—S. T. JOSHI

# A Note on This Edition

The editor does not believe that a full-scale critical edition of Lovecraft's essays, with textual variants, is needed at this time. This edition is, however, based upon rigorous consultation of the first publications of Lovecraft's essays as well as of relevant later appearances; the texts are based upon the first appearance unless otherwise specified. At the end of each essay, an editor's note supplies bibliographical and other information that readers might find useful for placing the item within the context of Lovecraft's life and work; footnotes elucidating specific literary, historical, and other data in the essay follow the editor's note.

Abbreviations used in the notes are as follows:

| | |
|---|---|
| AMS | autograph manuscript |
| AT | *The Ancient Track: Complete Poetical Works* (Night Shade Books, 2001) |
| CE | *Collected Essays* (Volumes 1–5) |
| D | *Dagon and Other Macabre Tales* (Arkham House, 1986) |
| DPC | "Department of Public Criticism" |
| DH | *The Dunwich Horror and Others* (Arkham House, 1984) |
| FP | First publication |
| HPL | H. P. Lovecraft |
| JHL | John Hay Library, Brown University |
| Joshi, *Life* | S. T. Joshi, *H. P. Lovecraft: A Life* (West Warwick, RI: Necronomicon Press, 1996) |
| LL | S. T. Joshi, *Lovecraft's Library*, rev. ed. (Hippocampus Press, 2002) |
| LVW | *Lord of a Visible World: An Autobiography in Letters* (Ohio University Press, 2000) |
| NAPA | National Amateur Press Association |
| SL | *Selected Letters* (Sauk City, WI: Arkham House, 1965–76; 5 vols.) |
| TMS | typescript |
| UAPA | United Amateur Press Association |

I am grateful to Captain Victor Moitoret, Michael Horvat of the American Private Press Association, Donovan K. Loucks, and David E. Schultz for supplying some of the texts included in this volume. My research on the text and notes was done chiefly at the New York Public Library, the Fossil Collection of Amateur Journalism (formerly housed at New York University), the American Antiquarian Society, the John Hay Library of Brown University, and the University of Washington Library.

# A TASK FOR AMATEUR JOURNALISTS

It is the fortune of all languages and literatures at first to develop and to flourish, but eventually, if unrestrained, to languish and decay.

While Germany and the principal Latin nations preserve the purity of their respective tongues by means of Academies, or associations of conservative learned men whose decisions in regard to the nicer questions of orthography, grammar, and rhetoric are generally heeded by all authors, our own Anglo-Saxon civilisation has produced no such literary court, and the fate of the English language remains in the hands of the thousands of writers who employ it in their compositions.

Thus unassociated, undirected, and permitted to indulge without supervision the freakish fancies of imperfectly instructed minds, it is not surprising that a numerous horde of loose, popular scribblers and poetasters have in this age of shallow though widely diffused education, begun to destroy our precise, elegant forms of speech, which were evolved and established in the days of superior if less extended culture, and more refined if more restricted taste.

Now if disunion and want of government be the prime cause of the present laxity in writers, then we have in the amateur press association the embryo of improvement. Whilst individuals may not be able properly to sustain the responsibility of preserving the English language, an organization should find it possible to do better, and by the coöperation of its members to serve as a miniature "Academy". The United Amateur Press Association, this month in convention at Columbus, Ohio, could adopt no more beneficial policy than that of encouraging purer and older styles of composition amongst its members. To abjure all distorted or "simplified" forms of spelling, to return to more regular metres in verse, to oppose the modern slovenly employment of nouns as adjectives and verbs, to discourage the use of pernicious recently coined compound words, such as "present-day", "viewpoint", or "upkeep", and above all to lead in a reaction against the prevailing unnatural tendency to select rude, barbaric Saxon monosyllables in place of exact, dignified, and civilised words of Latin derivation, a tendency certainly due to a most lamentable declension of classical scholarship, are labours very appropriate to such an association. To aid so desirable a restoration is well worth the risk of securing a name of pedantry. The amateur journalists of today are the recognized authors of tomorrow, and principles inculcated at this period of their mental development will appear in their later work, affecting thus the future state of literature.

EDITOR'S NOTE  FP: *New Member* No. 7 (July 1914): [3]. HPL's first contribution to the amateur press, and the first of many pleas for literary and stylistic purity in amateur writing. Lovecraft's cause is weakened by the improper use of "declension" (for "decline") in the antepenultimate sentence. He comments briefly on the article in DPC for November 1914 (see p. 16).

# DEPARTMENT OF PUBLIC CRITICISM

*(November 1914)*

The Critical Bureau has lately received a very creditable assortment of amateur journals for review, the papers before us varying from the neat and simple sheet of average quality to the brilliant, artistic, and almost professional product of the experienced writer and publisher. In amateur journalism an inflexible standard of criticism is obviously impossible to maintain, so that we have here attempted to consider each publication independently, making due allowance for the diverging ages and characteristics of the various authors and editors. In the interests of impartiality this collection of journals will be treated in alphabetical order. Many months having elapsed since the publication of the last previous critical article, the present review will include some issues as far back as April and May.

*The Blarney Stone* for July–August is graced by three poetical contributions of unusual merit. In "Ships of the Southland" Miss Edna von der Heide has caught the true spirit of southern languor, producing a lyric of rare beauty. "Cupid's Secret", by Miss Owen, is a delicate bit of fantasy in introducing a multitude of pleasing images. "A Garden of Silence and Roses" introduces to the firmament of amateur journalism a new star, in the person of Miss Annie Vyne Tillery, author of professionally published books and poems. Miss Tillery's style is at once deep and delicate, pervaded throughout with a poetic fervour seldom observed in products of the youthful pen. The green cover of *The Blarney Stone* is a work of art well in keeping with the contents.

*The Blarney Stone* for September–October continues to maintain the position of that magazine among the elite of amateur journals. The issue opens with "The Silent Hero", a deserved tribute to the medical profession which forms the credential of John Burt Stewart, one of the United's latest recruits. Mr. Stewart has a clear and dignified style which will undoubtedly attain an even greater polish with time and repeated effort. "Tempo di Valse" exhibits Miss Mary Bryan Morris as the possessor of considerable ability in the realm of light fiction. Herbert B. Darrow's poem, "Ad Infinitum", shews both crudeness and promise. The author is evidently new to his art, and may therefore be excused for the general stiffness of his expressions, and the employment of such an unpoetical term as "food supply". The sentiment is not new, but yet not inappropriate. Life is, in truth, to most persons just such a monotonous and apparently useless succession of struggles as Mr. Darrow describes. We are pleased to note Mr. Darrow's tendency toward regular metre, and wish he could have made his verse still more regular by dropping the superfluous syllable in line three of the third stanza, and supplying the two missing syllables in the last line of the poem.

Mr. Robbins' sketch entitled "Dit and Dot", and Mr. Hart's bit of dialogue, "Love and the Weather", contain humour of the lighter sort. "Above the Dam and Below" is a truly beautiful allegory by R. W. Rawls. The comparison between the life of man and the course of a river is uniformly well sustained, and the whole is clothed in pure and dignified language. In "The Flirt's Dream", Mr. W. E. Griffin amuses us in his characteristic vein. The piece is a good example of animated conversation.

The Exchange Department is admirably conducted by Mr. H. B. Scott. The want of severity in *The Blarney Stone's* criticisms has been deplored in a previous issue of *The United Amateur,* but the present critic is of opinion that such leniency serves as a useful antidote for some of the captious denunciations which pour forth from other self-constituted reviewers.

Mr. Ronald Germaine's humorous verse is very clever, though we cannot understand how "howl" and "towel" can be made to rhyme.

*The Brooklynite* for October is occupied largely by matrimonial matter. Miss Owen opens the issue with a delightful poem which is marred only by the use of the word "jewel" as a monosyllable. Mr. Kleiner's acrostic lines are very ingenious. Misses Silverman and Carson contribute lighter verse, while Messrs. Adams and Stoddard entertain with prose no heavier in nature. A collection of impromptu quatrains by various members of the Blue Pencil Club exhibit still greater levity. The general frivolity of *The Brooklynite* is doubtless due to the fact that this publication is designed primarily as a relaxation for persons engaged in other and more serious activities.

*The Echo* for June is an interesting individual paper by Leslie W. Rowland. The leading article is a very realistic character sketch entitled "Bob—A Boy", wherein Mr. Rowland displays a fluent, easy prose style and a pleasing power of narration.

*The Forget-Me-Not* for September is headed by a dainty and very meritorious poem from the pen of Carolyn C. McCreary, entitled "My Little House o' Dreams". The metre is as pleasing as the sentiment, and one is inclined to overlook the use of the word "fire" as a dissyllable in the last stanza.

"Neighbors", a short story by Mrs. Florence Shepphird, is very interesting as a character study, but rather vague as a narrative. The want of continuous and gradual development toward the climax is especially noticeable. In a story involving a mystery, each paragraph should have a logical relation to the solution, and very little extraneous matter should be allowed. In "Neighbors" the doubtful parentage of Widow Grey should have been mentioned early in the plot, for as it is, the solution comes upon us unsuggested; not as a revelation, but as a hasty afterthought. More careful treatment would have softened the prevailing effect of extreme improbability.

"Queries", by F. R., is a piece of versified drollery whose humour is somewhat injured by the length to which it is drawn out. It also exhibits the worst aspects of modern irregularity of form. We suppose it is intended to be in iambic octosyllabic couplets, but scarcely see how such lines as

"And was the energetic Eugene"

or

"Always their friends with lemon ice cheer."

can justly occur in a piece of that metre.

*The Inspiration* for September is a typical informal amateur magazine of the better grade. Miss von der Heide's poem "To Forgotten Favorites" is a gem of simple beauty, while Mr. E. H. Cole's brief essay on "The Value of Fraternalism" is an "inspiration" indeed. Miss Dora M. Hepner's lively lines entitled "My Favorite" exhibit much epigrammatic wit, and a very graceful handling of the anapaestic metre.

*The New Member* for April is headed by Mr. J. R. Schaffman's excellent poem, "Because You Tried". The sentiment is so just, and the metre so well sustained, that it is difficult to realise the extreme youth of the author. Mr. Inman Sygman in "War, Must We Have It?" gives with youthful enthusiasm the conventional arguments of the peace advocate. His style is fresh and animated, containing great promise of future development.

*The New Member* for May contains a thoughtful survey of prison conditions by Carrie Jacobs. Miss Jacobs shows much ability, and will doubtless prove a valuable accession to the amateur literary world. "Spring", by O. Henning, is an airy little sketch of considerable merit.

*The New Member* for July opens with "Her First Romance", by Florence M. Ockford. As a specimen of modern verse, this poem is very creditable indeed, though the present critic, being of old-fashioned tastes, cannot but deem it too irregular in construction. This same critic's own contribution to the July *New Member*, "A Task for Amateur Journalists", enunciates the general principles which will guide him in the performance of his duties. Ira A. Cole in simple and pleasing style describes how amateur journalists secure "Something for Nothing".

*The Pippin* for June has a varied and generally excellent contents. Miss Margaret Wilson's pleasing poem, "Latin and 'Deutsch' and Dreams", appears very remarkable when one reflects that the author is a student in high school less than sixteen years of age. With such youthful ability, we have reason to expect much from Miss Wilson's maturer years. "The Little Black Cloud", by Gladys Bagg, reveals another young writer of great promise. This ethereal fairy story of old Ireland is a delightful piece of fancy, and exhibits an excellence which augurs well for the literary future of its author. Lloyd Morris in "Detectives, Ancient and Modern" shews much skill and knowledge of literary history. The heroic verses on "The Club", signed "A. J. Bird", are bright and fairly neat, though rather inclined to slang. The use of the time-honoured decasyllabic couplet is an encouraging sign, and cheers the critic with the thought that his favourite metre is not yet wholly extinct. A line adapted from Dryden's "Absalom and Achitophel" suggests the author's familiarity with the literature of the Golden Age of our language.

*The Plainsman* for November is unpretentious but attractive. Miss Austin's poem "Somebody's Friend" is of excellent quality, though we wish the author had chosen a less halting metre. "Honey", written by Mrs. Florence Shepphird under unusual limitations, is an excellent "problem" story that deserves a sequel. Mr. Ira Cole's editorial comment is instructive, and should excite much interest in the United's Western Manuscript Bureau.

*The Pinfeather* for November marks the first appearance of an excellent and attractive magazine in the field of amateur journalism. In this paper, published by the ladies of the Pinfeather Club of Rocky Mount, we discern little of the painful crudeness which usually characterises a first issue but behold instead a product that will bear comparison with its older brother *The Blarney Stone*. Enclosed in a cover of artistic simplicity is a collection of fact, fiction, and verse whose merit augurs well for the future of the magazine and its club.[1]

"Through the Looking-Glass", which opens the issue, is a clever means of introducing to the amateur public the various members of the club. The mutual descriptions by Misses Finch and Griffin are very creditably and entertainingly written, suggesting those in *The Blarney Stone's* "Hall of Fame".

"Just the Best Emigrant I Ever Knew", by Mrs. L. J. Tillery, is a sketch which exhibits much power of description and insight into human nature. The portrait of a noble character is here painted in vivid and impressive manner. The same author in "Poe and Poesy" displays a familiar knowledge of poetical construction and literary history. Mrs. Tillery's prose style is very pleasing, and promises to attain even greater polish. At present we might suggest slight alterations in the arrangement of the words in certain passages. For example, this extract from "Poe and Poesy": "the music that his wife set his poetry to", would flow more smoothly if written thus: "the music to which his wife set his poetry". It seems best to keep prepositions from the ends of sentences.

Mrs. M. W. Hart in "The Modern Status of Peace" exhibits a sound comprehension of vital economical principles. Her brilliant article contrasts very favourably with some of the miniature defences of peace which have lately appeared in the amateur magazines. Mrs. Hart's style is direct and forceful, but a little wanting in perspicuity. The phrase: "the present war between Austria and Germany and the parties of the Triple Entente and Japan" leaves us somewhat in doubt as to the exact alignment of the belligerent powers, and might thus be improved: "the present war of Austria and Germany with the parties of the Triple Entente and Japan". The expression: "in innovating new methods" is pleonastic. It would be better either to omit the word "new", or to change "innovating" to "introducing".

The anonymous short story "Bread upon the Waters" has a delightfully developed plot, which makes the reader quite forget the slight evidences of immaturity in the style. We wish the writer had not told us quite so abruptly that the book-agent "was canvassing New Market, Mass." This is distinctly an anticlimax, like that famous old couplet held up to us as a horrible example in books on rhetoric:

"And thou, Dalhousie, the great God of War,
Lieutenant Colonel to the Earl of Mar."

A smoother rendering would be to say, that the agent "was canvassing through the busy Massachusetts city of New Market".

Mrs. Bulluck's essay on the war, entitled "Why?" shows much ability, yet might be improved by careful attention. The split infinitive, "to properly understand", and two rather heavy sentences, one concerning Germany's war tax, and the other relating to Germany's jealousy of the Allies' possessions, are the weakest points. These two sentences might respectively be amended to read as follows: (1) "Germany increased her war tax at least a quarter of a million dollars, all this vast amount being raised by special assessment, imposed upon a people already staggering under too heavy taxes." (2) "Germany, with a jealous eye, had been watching Great Britain, France, etc."

The poetry of Anne Vyne Tillery is represented in the November *Pinfeather* by two contributions, "Stranger in the Street" and "We". Any ordinary reviewer's criticism of Miss Tillery's exquisite verse would be as inappropriate as a common stonecutter's opinion on the art of a Praxiteles.

We are pleased to observe that *The Pinfeather* has kept itself free from that annoying evil known as "simplified spelling", whose vagaries appear so offensively in many of the amateur journals.

*The Woodbee* for May is of dainty and attractive appearance both in cover and type. Dora M. Hepner heads the issue with a light poem on "Spring!" While the ordinary grade of "spring poetry" has long been a mere matter of jest, this meritorious bit of verse cannot be classed with the efforts thus ridiculed. The structure is neat but informal, and the language a pleasing modification of rustic dialect. We were especially captivated by the simile which compares the clouds to "down from angel wings".

"The End of the Rainbow" is a mild, well-written short story by Harriet E. Daily. Charles P. Salt in "What Happened to Mary" displays a command of genuine humor rarely found amongst amateur writers. The rapid succession of mirth-provoking images is very ably presented, and the whole shows no trace of the affection, silliness, or buffoonery into which most incipient humorists fall.

"The Convention City" by Leo Fritter is an excellent description and panegyric of Columbus, Ohio. Mr. Fritter has a highly ornamental prose style of almost poetic nature, and is generally judicious in his selection of words and metaphors. If he have any fault at all, it is in being too diffuse; his style might gain strength and force from a more rigid adherence to formal rhetorical models. Mr. Fritter exhibits strong philosophical and idealistic tendencies in his writings, and we believe he is destined to influence greatly the trend of thought in the amateur literary world.

*The Woodbee* for October belongs rather to the Columbus club than to the amateur world at large, being almost entirely occupied with humorous personal accounts of the United's recent convention. Miss Harriett E. Daily furnishes the only bit of verse, a sprightly and clever piece entitled "Just to Laugh", which was recited at the picnic table during the convention. Mr. Fritter, in his attractive prose, convincingly opposes the consolidation of the United and National associations.

EDITOR'S NOTE  FP: *United Amateur* 14, No. 2 (November 1914): 21–25 (signed "H. P. LOVECRAFT, Department of Public Criticism"). The first of many HPL columns of this sort, as he took over the chairmanship of the DPC from Ada P. Campbell. The first paragraph suggests that a DPC column had not appeared in some time—perhaps not since the preceding spring. HPL focuses on relatively mundane literary and stylistic aspects of amateur contributions, not failing to make his own preferences (e.g., for strict rhyme and meter) known but nonetheless striving to say something favorable about each item.

*Notes*

1. HPL contributed the poem "To the Members of the Pin-Feathers on the Merits of Their Organisation, and of Their New Publication, *The Pinfeather*" (AT 335–36) to this issue.

## DEPARTMENT OF PUBLIC CRITICISM

*(January 1915)*

The *Badger* for January is the first number of a strikingly meritorious and serious paper published by George S. Schilling. We here behold none of the frivolity which spoils the writings of those who view amateur journalism merely as a passing amusement. *The Badger* shews evidence of careful and tasteful editorship, combined with a commendable artistic sense in choice of paper and cover.

The leading article, an essay on the minimum wage, is from the pen of the editor, and shews both literary ability and a sound knowledge of economics. "Sister to the Ox", by A. W. Ashby, is an excellent short story whose strength is rather in its moral than in its plot. The editorials are certainly not lacking in force, and seem well calculated to stir the average amateur from his torpor of triteness and inanity.

*The Inspiration* for November is an "Official Number", containing the work of none but titled authors.[1] Rheinhart Kleiner contributes the single piece of verse, a smooth and pleasing lyric entitled "Love Again", which is not like his previous poem, "Love, Come Again". As an amatory poet Mr. Kleiner shews much delicacy of sentiment, refinement of language, and appreciation of metrical values; his efforts in this direction entitle him to a high place among amateur bards.

One of the truly notable prose features of the magazine is Walter John Held's delightful sketch of Joaquin Miller's home and haunts. This artistic picture of Californian scenery exhibits a real comprehension of the beauties of Nature, and stirs to an unusual degree the imagination of the reader. Mr. Held's prose possesses a fluency and grace that bring it close to the professional quality, and its few faults are far less considerable than might be expected from the pen of a young author. However, we must remark some rather awkward examples of grammatical construction. The correct plural of "eucalyptus" is "eucalypti", without any final "s", the name being treated as a Latin noun of the second declension. "Slowly and dignified—it pursues its way", is hardly a permissible clause; the adjective "dignified" must be exchanged for an adverb. Perhaps Mr. Held sought to employ poetic enallage, but even so, the adjective does not correspond with "slowly"; besides, the use of enallage in prose is at best highly questionable. "This free and rank flowers and brush" is another bad clause. But it is not well to dissect the sketch too minutely. A youth of Mr. Held's ability needs only time and continued practice to raise him to the highest rank in prose composition.

*Invictus* for January, the first number of Mr. Paul J. Campbell's new individual paper, is one of those rare journals concerning which it is almost impossible to speak without enthusiasm. Not one of its twenty-six pages fails to delight us. Foremost in merit, and most aptly suited to Mr. Campbell's particular type of genius, are the three inspiring essays, "The Impost of the Future", "The Sublime Ideal", and "Whom God Hath Put Asunder". Therein appears to great advantage the keen reasoning and sound materialistic philosophy of the author. "The Sublime Ideal" is especially absorbing, tracing as it does the expansion of the human mind from a state of the narrowest and most violent bigotry to its present moderate breadth.

The three pieces of verse, "Inspiration", "The Larger Life", and "Down in Mexico", are all of smooth construction and musical metre, though not exhibiting their author's powers as well as his essays. "Down in Mexico", a virile poem in Kipling's style, is unquestionably the best of the three.

Mr. Campbell's comments on amateur affairs are well-written and entertaining, especially his reminiscent article entitled "After Seven Years".

*Outward Bound* for January is an excellent journal edited by George William Stokes of Newcastle-on-Tyne, England. It is gratifying to behold such a paper as this, one of the links between America and the parent country which the United is helping to forge.

Herbert B. Darrow opens the issue with a short story entitled "A Lesson". The tale is of conventional pattern, containing a sound though not strikingly original moral. The language is generally good, except in one sentence where the author speaks of "the vehicles in the street and buildings about him". Surely he does not mean that the vehicles were in the buildings as well as in the street. The use of the definite article before the word "buildings" would do much toward dispelling the ambiguous effect.

"The Haunted Forest", a poem by J. H. Fowler, is almost Poe-like in its grimly fantastic quality.[2] We can excuse rather indefinite metre when we consider the admirably created atmosphere, the weird harmony of the lines, the judicious use of alliteration, and the apt selection of words. "Bird-shunned", as applied to the thickets of the forest, is a particularly graphic epithet. Mr. Fowler is to be congratulated upon his glowing imagination and poetical powers.

"A Bit o' Purple Heather", by Edna von der Heide, is a delightful piece of verse in modified Scottish dialect, which well justifies the dedication of the magazine to this poetess.

Mr. Stokes' editorials, headed "Ships That Pass", sustains the nautical atmosphere of his periodical. We wish he had given his thoughts a larger space for expression.

*The Piper* for December comes as a surprise to those who have known Rheinhart Kleiner only as a master of metre, for he is here displayed as the possessor of a pure and vigorous prose style as well. In this, the opening number of his individual journal, Mr. Kleiner provides us with a pleasing variety of literary matter; two serious poems, two rhymes of lighter character, an essay on the inevitable topic of Consolidation,[3] and a brilliant collection of short editorials and criticisms.

"A Carnation", which begins the issue, is an exquisite piece of sentiment couched in faultless verse. The odd measure of the poem is one peculiarly suited to the author's delicate type of genius; an iambic line of only three feet. The other lyric, "Heart, Do Not Wake", is likewise of excellent quality, though the succession of "again" and "pain" in the first line might suggest to some ears an unnecessary internal rhyme.

"The Rhyme of the Hapless Poet" is very clever, and can be truly appreciated by every author of printed matter. Perhaps the misfortune of which the poet complains is the cause of the extra syllable in the first line of the second stanza; we hope that the following is what Mr. Kleiner intended:

> "I wrote a poem, 'twas a prize".

Otherwise we are forced to believe that he pronounces "poem" as a monosyllable, "pome". "My Favorite Amateur" is a good specimen of light, imitative verse.

The article on Consolidation is cynical in tone, but eminently sensible. It is only too true that our greatest intellectual stimulus is found in controversy and antagonism; we are really quite bellicose in our instincts, despite the utterances of the peace advocates.

Mr. Kleiner concludes his journal with a sparkling epigram on a rather obvious though regrettable tendency in amateur circles.

*The Piper* is in general a paper of satisfying merit, to whose future issues we shall look forward with eagerness.

*The Recruiting Feminine* for 1914–1915 is a publication of unusual worth. "The Rose Supreme", by Coralie Austin, is a delicate little poem in which we regret the presence of one inexcusably bad rhyme. To rhyme the words "rose" and "unclosed" is to exceed the utmost limits of poetic licence. It is true that considerable variations in vowel sounds have been permitted; "come" makes, or at least used to make, an allowable rhyme with "home", "clock" with "look", "grass" with "place"; but a final consonant attached to one of two otherwise rhyming syllables positively destroys the rhyme.

Mrs. Myra Cole's essay on "The Little Things of Life" is well-written and instructive.

"The Dirge of the Great Atlantic", by Anne Vyne Tillery Renshaw, is a grim and moving bit of verse, cast in the same primitively stirring metre which this author used in her professionally published poem, "The Chant of Iron". Mrs. Renshaw possesses an enviable power to reach the emotions through the medium of written words.

"Two Octobers—A Contrast", by Eloise N. Griffith, is a meritorious sketch ending with the usual appeal for the cessation of the European war. We fear that the author cannot quite realise the ambitious passions, essential ingredients of human nature, which render necessary a final decision.

Miss Edna von der Heide, in an able article, rallies to the defence of Mr. W. E. Griffin's now famous "Favorite Pastime".[4] The Modern Lothario is fortunate in having so competent and experienced a champion. However, we cannot wholly endorse the sentiments of these excellent writers. The statement that "all amateur journalists are flirts, more or less", is a base and unwarranted libel which we are prepared completely to refute.

"The Audience", by Mrs. Florence Shepphird, is a masterly defence of those inactive amateurs whom we are all too prone to consider as delinquent. It is indeed true that authors would be useless were it not for some sort of a reading public.

*Toledo Amateur* for December is a wholesome juvenile product. The typography still leaves something to be desired, but the evidences of care are everywhere visible, and we may reasonably expect to see it improve from month to month into one of the leading amateur papers. Credentials form the keynote of the current issue, and a very promising assortment of recruits are here introduced to the members of the United. Miss Sandborn, who is fortunate enough to be one of Mr. Moe's pupils at Appleton, contributes an interesting school anecdote, narrated in simple fashion. Miss Thie gives information concerning the "Campfire Girls". Some new members of adult years are also represented in this number. Mr. Jenkins shews an admirable command of light prose, and will undoubtedly prove one of the United's most entertaining writers. Misses Kline and McGeoch both exhibit marked poetical tendencies in prose, the latter writer having something of Mr. Fritter's facility in the use of metaphor. Mr. Porter's editorials are refreshingly naive and unaffected. His grammar is generally good, except in the one sentence where he speaks of the *Toledo Times*. He should say, "the newspaper which has given me much experience, and to whose publishers I owe a great deal of experience gained."

*The United Official Quarterly* for November marks the beginning of a laudable enterprise on the part of the official board. The magazine is of artistic appearance in cover, paper, and typography alike, while the contents shew considerable care in preparation.

Ira A. Cole's essay on "The Gods of Our Fathers" is the leading feature, and though not of perfect perspicuity nor faultless unity, is none the less noteworthy as a sincere expression of Pantheism. Mr. Cole keenly feels the incongruity of our devotion to Semitic theological ideals, when as a matter of fact we are descended from Aryan polytheists, and his personification of the Grecian deities in the men of today is a pleasing and ingenious conception. We are inclined to wonder whether the author or the printer is to blame for rendering the poet Hesiod's name as "Hesoid".

The metric art is represented by three contributions. Paul J. Campbell's lines on "The Heritage of Life" are smooth in construction and proper in sentiment, though they are far from shewing their author at his best. Mr. Campbell is a supreme master of the philosophical essay and of pointed, satirical prose, being a very "Junius"[5] in bold, biting invective; but is placed at something of a disadvantage in the domain of conventional poetry. Rheinhart Kleiner and ourselves revel in heroic couplets of widely differing nature. Our own masterpiece is in full Queen Anne style with carefully balanced lines and strictly measured quantities.[6] We have succeeded in producing eighteen lines without a single original sentiment or truly poetical image. Rev. Mr. Pyke, the object of the verses, deserves a better encomiast. Mr. Kleiner, on the other hand, uses an heroic metre of that softened type which was evolved at the close of the eighteenth century from the disruption of the more formal style. In this sort of verse the stiff, classic expressions are discarded, and the sense frequently overflows from couplet to couplet, giving the romantic poet a greater latitude for expression than was possible in the old models. "Vacation" is not distinguished by any strikingly novel idea, but is in general a very clever piece of light work. The only substantial defect is in the eighth line, where the word "resort" is so placed, that the accent must fall wrongfully upon the first syllable.

Leo Fritter's article on criticism is timely and sensible. As he justly contends, some authorised amateur critics deal far too roughly with the half-formed products of the young author, while most unofficial and inexperienced reviewers fairly run mad with promiscuous condemnation. The fancied brilliancy of the critic is always greatest when he censures most, so that the temptations of the tribe are many. We are at best but literary parasites, and need now and then just such a restraining word as our counter-critic gives us. Mr. Fritter's style is here, as usual, highly ornamented with metaphor. One slight defect strikes the fastidious eye, but since split infinitives are becoming so common in these days, we shall attend the author's plea for gentleness, and remain silent.

EDITOR'S NOTE FP: *United Amateur* 14, No. 3 (January 1915): 21–25. The column is signed "H. P. LOVECRAFT, Chairman, Department of Public Criticism."

*Notes*

1. I.e., authors holding offices in the UAPA.
2. See HPL's poem "To the Late John H. Fowler, Esq.: Author of Poems of the Supernatural" (*Scot*, March 1916; AT 17).
3. I.e., the union of the UAPA and NAPA. See "Consolidation's Autopsy" (p. 29).
4. The reference is to an article by W. E. Griffin, "My Favorite Pastime—Flirting" (*Blarney Stone*, May–June 1914). HPL responded with two poetic satires, "On a Modern Lothario" (AT 199) and "Gryphus in Asinum Mutatus" (AT 202–4).
5. "Junius" is the pseudonymous author of a series of letters that first appeared in the *Public Advertiser* (London) in 1769–72, bitterly attacking British political figures of the day, including George III. They were published in book form as *The Letters of Junius* (1770–72). Most scholars now believe the author to have been Sir Philip Francis (1740–1818).
6. "To the Rev. James Pyke" (*United Official Quarterly*, November 1914; AT 336).

# DEPARTMENT OF PUBLIC CRITICISM

(March 1915)

*T*he *Blarney Stone* for November–December is dedicated to its contributors and wholly given over to their work. "Did You Ever Go A-Fishin'?", by Olive G. Owen, is a vivid poetical portrayal of that peculiar attraction which the angler's art exerts on its devotees. While the whole is of high and pleasing quality, exception must be taken to the rhyming of "low" with itself at the very beginning of the poem. It may be that the second "low" is a misprint for "slow", yet even in that case, the rhyme is scarcely allowable, since the dominant rhyming sound would still be "low". Miss Edna von der Heide, in "The Christmas of Delsato's Maria", tells how an Italian thief utilised his questionable art to replace a loss in his family. "To General Villa"[1] is a peculiar piece of verse written last summer for the purpose of defying those who had charged the author with pedantry and pomposity. It has suffered somewhat at the hands of the printer; "Intrepido" being spelled "Intrepedo", and the word "own" being dropped from the clause "your own name can't write" in the third line of the second stanza. Also, the first of the Spanish double exclamation marks around the oath "Santa Maria" is right side up instead of inverted according to Castilian custom. Having been hastily written, the piece is wholly without merit. "Señor", in the second line of the third stanza, is placed so that the accent must fall erroneously on the first syllable. The changes of time and revolutions have rendered the last stanza sadly out of date.

The issue is concluded with a beautiful editorial on "The Service with Love", wherein is described the ideal spirit of brotherhood which should pervade amateur journalism. We regret the two blank pages at the back of the magazine, and wish that some talented Blarney had seen fit to adorn them with his work.

*The Brooklynite* for January is of unusual merit, fairly teeming with features of a well-written and substantial character.

The short story by Mrs. Carson is developed with admirable simplicity and ease; the plot not too strained, and the moral not too pragmatically forced upon the reader. The conversation, always a difficult point with amateur authors, is surprisingly natural.

Mrs. Adams' essay on ghosts displays considerable literary knowledge, though the anecdote at the end is rather ancient for use today. We last heard it about ten years ago, with a Scotchman instead of a negro preacher as the narrator, and with the word "miracle" instead of "phenomena" as the subject.

Mr. Goodwin's "Cinigrams" are delightful, and we expect soon to hear the author heralded as the Martial of amateur journalism. "Ford, Do Not Shake", Mr. Goodwin's parody on Kleiner's "Heart, Do Not Wake", is actually side-splitting. The metre is handled to perfection, and the humour is extremely clever.

"Consolidation", by George Julian Houtain, is a fair example of the manner in which some of the less dignified National politicians try to cast silly aspersions on the United. The elaborately sarcastic phrase: "United boys and girls", seems to please its author, since he uses it twice. There is unconscious irony in the spectacle of a National man, once a member of the notorious old Gotham ring, preaching virtuously against the "unenviable record" of the United.

Mr. Stoddard's brief essay, composed at a meeting of the Blue Pencil Club, is excellent, and his concluding quatrain regular and melodious. We wish, however, that he would give us some more of the serious fiction that he can write so splendidly, and which used several years ago to appear in the amateur press.

"Music Moods", by Charles D. Isaacson, is an emotional sketch of great power and delicate artistry. Mr. Isaacson has an active imagination and a literary ability which makes his readers see very vividly the images he creates.[2]

Mrs. Houtain's poem shews great but as yet undeveloped talent. The repeated use of the expletive "do" in such phrases as "I do sigh", or "I pray and do pine", mars the verse somewhat. As Pope remarked and humorously illustrated in his *Essay on Criticism*:

"Expletives their feeble aid DO join."[3]

Mr. Ayres' jocose epic is clever and tuneful. The climax, or rather anticlimax, comes quite effectively.

Mr. Adams, in his brilliant verses entitled "Gentlemen, Please Desist", exposes in a masterly way the fatuity of our loud-mouthed peace workers. Miss Silverman's lines on the same subject are very good, but scarcely equal in keenness of wit. It is all very well to "keep industry booming", but industry cannot take the place of military efficiency in protecting a nation against foreign aggression.

As a whole, the January *Brooklynite* is the best number we have yet seen.

*The Coyote* for March is not a revival of ex-President Brechler's well-known amateur journal of that name, but a semi-professional leaflet by Mr. William T. Harrington, a rather new recruit. The leading feature is a sensational short story by the editor, entitled "What Gambling Did". In this tale, Mr. Harrington exhibits at least a strong ambition to write, and such energy, if well directed, may eventually make of him one of our leading authors of fiction. Just now, however, we must protest against his taste in subject and technique. His models are obviously not of the classical order, and his ideas of probability are far from unexceptionable. In developing the power of narration, it is generally best, as one of our leading amateurs lately reiterated, to discard the thought of elaborate plots and thrilling climaxes, and to begin instead with the plain and simple description of actual incidents with which the author is familiar. Likewise, the young author may avoid improbability by composing his earliest efforts in the first person. He knows what he himself would do in certain circumstances, but he does not always know very exactly what some others might do in similar cases. Meanwhile, above all things he should read classic fiction, abstaining entirely from *Wild West Weeklies* and the like. Mr. Harrington has a taste for excitement, and would probably thrive on Scott, Cooper, or Poe. Let him read the "Leather Stocking Tales" if he loves pioneers and frontier life. Not until after he has acquired a familiarity with the methods of the best authors, and refined his imagination by a perusal of their works, should he make attempts at writing outside his own experience. He will then be able to produce work of a quality which would surprise him now.

We are sorry to note that the *Coyote's* editorial columns are occupied by a mere condensed copy of the United's standard recruiting circular. This space might have been filled much more profitably with brief original comments by the editor on the numerous exchanges which are listed in another part of his paper. The paid advertising and subscription price are not to be commended. Such things have no place in a truly amateur paper. But continued membership in the United will doubtless fill Mr. Harrington with the genuine amateur spirit, and cause *The Coyote* to become a worthy successor to its older namesake.

*Dowdell's Bearcat* for October is a modest but very promising little paper, mostly composed of amateur notes and brief reviews. The editor has interest in his work, and fluency in his language, foundations on which a more elaborate structure may some day be erected. One feature open to criticism is Mr. Dowdell's sudden change in his editorial column from the usual first person plural to the third person singular. It would be better to save "The Old Bear" and his interesting chat for a separate column. The typography of *Dowdell's Bearcat* is not perfect, but may be expected to improve from issue to issue.

*The Emissary* for July is a National paper, but contains the work of several United members. Of the publication itself we need not stop to speak. Mr. Reading, though only eighteen years of age, is an editor and printer of the highest grade, and has produced an issue which will be long remembered in the amateur world.

"Ausonius, the Nature-Lover", by Edward H. Cole, is a pleasing and judicious appreciation of a later Latin poet, shewing how a bard of the decaying Roman Empire approached in certain passages the spirit of modern romanticism. Mr. Cole's translated extracts are beautifully phrased, and his comment upon the subject well exhibits his wide and careful scholarship. Articles of this quality are rarely found in the amateur press, and it will be interesting to note what effect their more frequent appearance would have upon the literary tone of the associations.

"To Sappho", by Olive G. Owen, is a lyrical poem of much merit, yet having a defective line. Why, we wonder, did the author see fit to leave two necessary syllables out of the third line of the opening verse?

"Lamb o' Mine", by Dora M. Hepner, is probably the most attractive bit of verse in the magazine. The negro dialect is inimitable, and the consoling spirit of the old black "mammy" fairly radiates from the lines. Metrically, the piece is faultless, and we wish its author were a more frequent contributor to the amateur journals.

Miss von der Heide's two poems, "The Mill Mother" and "Greeting", express admirably the sentiments of pathos and natural beauty, respectively. Personally, we prefer "Greeting".

Mr. Campbell's lines on "Huerta's Finish" are distinctly below the usual standard of this talented writer's work. The metre is satisfactory, but the humour is somewhat strained, and the pun in the last line based on a mispronunciation of the old Indian's name. "Wehr-ta" is probably the correct sound, rather than "Hurt-a".

The Inspiration for January must be judged strictly by its quality; not its quantity. Pinkney C. Grissom, a very young amateur, cheers us greatly with his article on "Smiles", while Miss von der Heide's microscopic story, "A Real Victory", is indeed a literary treat. We trust that the editor's threat of discontinuance may not be realised.

The Kansan for July reaches us at a late date through the kindness of Mr. Daas. In this magazine the Sunflower Club of Bazine makes its formal debut, being ushered into amateur society by means of a pleasing and well-written article from the pen of Miss Hoffman. The informal "Exchange Comment" is a charitable and generally delightful department, whose anonymity we rather regret. The Editorial pages are brilliant in their justification of the United's sunny spirit, as contrasted with the National's forbidding frigidity.

The Olympian for September–February well sustains the lofty traditions of that magazine. Mr. Cole defines with considerable precision his latest editorial policy and his true attitude toward the United, revealing only the more strongly, however, his remarkable and ineradicable prejudice against our association in favour of the National. "Evening Prayer", by Rheinhart Kleiner, is a poem of great beauty and real worth, couched in the alternating iambic pentameter and trimeter which this poet seems to have made his own particular medium of expression. Mr. Kleiner is rapidly assuming a very high rank among amateur poets.

"The Public Library", by Eloise N. Griffith, is a delightful and appreciative reminiscence of quiet hours of lettered joy.

"The Play Hour", consisting of two clever bits of metre dedicated to a very young amateur, appears in a collection of short and sprightly pieces signed by the Senior Editor himself. It is difficult, nevertheless, to imagine the dignified Olympian Zeus as the author. Though the second of these tuneful rhymes is apparently written in the "simplified" spelling now so popular among certain amateur editors, a closer inspection reveals the fact that the spelling is merely made juvenile to suit the subject. After all, however, simplified spelling and baby-talk are but little removed from each other. The Reviewers' Club is in this issue represented by both editors, whose criticisms are as usual just and illuminating.

Prometheus for September–November is a journal of unusual literary and artistic value, edited by our poet-laureate, Miss Olive G. Owen. The paper well lives up to its sub-title, "A Magazine of Aspirations Dreamed into Reality". Mr. William H. Greenfield, the honoured founder of the United, claims the first page with a graceful Pindaric ode, "To My Friend". "The Weaver of Dreams", by Edna G. Thorne, is a strikingly well-written short story pervaded with a delicate pathos and expressing a beautiful

Christian philosophy. George W. Macauley, continuing to concentrate his narrative powers on the Oriental tale, presents a pleasing fable of Old Moorish Spain, entitled "Ali Ahmed and the Aqueduct". "The Ethics of Stimulation", by Maurice W. Moe, is an eminently sound exposition of the relative evil of coffee and alcoholic liquor as stimulants. "Partners", by H. A. Reading, exhibits great ability on the part of its author, and is well calculated to arouse the emotions of affectionate fathers and sons.

Miss Owen's work, scattered here and there throughout the magazine, is naturally of the very first quality. It is hard to choose between the two poems, "Atthis, I Love Thee" and "To Elizabeth Knopf", but we incline slightly toward the former. The sketches "The Visitor" and "Some Things I Like in New York" are both delightful in their artistic simplicity.

Critically analysed, *Prometheus* may be classed as one of the most varied and generally readable magazines of the season.

*Red Letter Days* for October is the first of an informal individual paper by George W. Macauley, representing the most purely personal phase of amateur journalism. This issue is almost completely devoted to an animated account of the "Red Letter Days" spent by Mr. Macauley last summer with the amateurs who stopped to see him while on their way to the various conventions. The author's style is familiar and pleasing, though rather careless, and slightly marred by defects in spelling and grammar. For instance, we are told of the caution which he and Mr. Stoddard exercised in changing seats in a boat, since neither of "could swim, had the boat DID the usual thing." We are sorry that Mr. Macauley has adopted "simplified" spelling, but it is an evil in which he is by no means alone.

*Red Letter Days*, broadly considered, is a highly commendable paper; its simplicity and lack of affectation are alone sufficient to win general approval.

*Stray Leaves* for May–June is another paper which has arrived late and indirectly. In this publication we note with disapproval some evidence of pseudo-professionalism, such as a subscription rate and advertisements, but we trust that Miss Draper will ere long acquire the perfect amateur spirit. "Love Proved to Be the Master of Hate", a short story by Frances Wood, is handicapped by its unwieldy title. "The Triumph of Love", or some heading of equal brevity, would better suit it. Indications of immaturity are here and there perceptible, and at the very beginning there is an inexplicable mass of hyphenation. However, the tale is undeniably of considerable merit, conveying a pleasing picture of jealousy overcome.

The Editorial department might be improved by a judicious copying of the best amateur models. The reference to Anti-Suffrage and Suffrage as "two vital questions" is hardly permissible; these are the two sides of only one question.

"Thinkers", by G. D., is really excellent as an essay, despite the awkwardness of style.

The Bermuda letter is highly interesting in its descriptions, but painfully unscholarly in its phraseology. We here behold a case of real talent obscured by want of literary polish, and hope that F. A. B., whoever he or she may be, will profit by his or her connexion with the United.

*Stray Leaves* has great possibilities, and will doubtless prove one of the leading papers of amateur journalism in times to come.

*The United Official Quarterly* for January hardly lives up to the artistic standard set by the first number, though it contains much valuable matter. Herbert B. Darrow pleads very ably for the personal acknowledgment of amateur papers received, while Paul J. Campbell writes convincingly on the true value of amateur journalism. Pres. Hepner, in the concluding article, opposes with considerable vigour the Hoffman policy of issuing coöperative magazines.[4] We are not, however, inclined entirely to agree with our executive's conclusions. The coöperative journal is practically the only adequate medium of expression for the amateur of limited means, and most of the later journals of this class, of which the *Official Quarterly* is itself an example, have been of excellent quality. It is perhaps too much to expect the average President, encumbered with a host of other duties, to conduct this work, but in any event some suitable official should be delegated for that purpose. The association should not lightly abandon a policy which made the preceding administration one of the most brilliant and successful in years.

*The Woodbee* for January exhibits amateur journalism at its best. Mrs. Anne Tillery Renshaw opens the magazine with a pleasing poem, dedicated to the Woodbees, which combines simplicity of diction with regularity of metre. These decasyllabic quatrains are a decided departure from Mrs. Renshaw's usual style, which explains the slight lack of fluency. The last line of the third stanza contains a redundant syllable, a defect which might be corrected by the removal of the article before the word "louder", or by the poetical contraction of "sympathy" into "symp'thy". The third line of the fourth stanza possesses only four feet. This may be an intentional shortening to give rhetorical effect, yet it mars none the less the symmetry of the verse.

"The Spiritual Significance of the Stars", by Leo Fritter, is the leading feature of the issue.[5] The inspiring influence of astronomical study on the cultivated intellect is here shewn to best advantage. Mr. Fritter traces the slow unfolding of celestial knowledge to the world, and points out the divinity of that mental power which enables man to discern the vastness of the universe, and to comprehend the complex principles by which it is governed. In the laws of the heavens he finds the prototype of all human laws, and the one perfect model for human institutions. Mr. Fritter's essay is eminently worthy of a place among the classics of amateur journalism.

"A Morn in June", by Harriet E. Daily, is a short and dainty poem of excellent quality, though marred by a reprehensible attempt to rhyme "grass" with "task". As we mentioned in connexion with another amateur poem, a final consonant on one of two otherwise rhyming syllables utterly destroys the rhyme. "We Are Builders All", by Elizabeth M. Ballou, is a graceful allegory based on the temple of Solomon. Edna Mitchell Haughton's character sketch, "The Family Doctor", is just and well drawn.

"A Dog for Comfort", by Edna von der Heide, is a meritorious poem of gloomy impressiveness. We cannot quite account for the defective second line of the fourth stanza, since Miss von der Heide is so able a poetess. Perhaps it is intentional, but we wish the line were of normal decasyllabic length. "My Grandmother's Garden", by Ida Cochran Haughton, is a truly delightful bit of reminiscent description which deserves more than one reading. "A Little Girl's Three Wishes", by Mrs. R. M. Moody, is entertaining in quality and correct in metre. It is a relief to behold amidst the formless cacophony of modern poetry such a regular, old-fashioned specimen of the octosyllabic couplet. "Two Little Waterwheels", by Dora M. Hepner, is an exquisite idyllic sketch. In the second paragraph we read of a channel "damned" up by a projecting root of a tree; which somewhat surprises us, since we did not know that tree-roots are accustomed to use profane language. Perhaps the author intended to write "dammed".

The editorials are brief. In one of them it is stated that the paper is submitted without fear to the critics AND Eddie Cole. In view of Mr. Cole's scholarly and conscientious critical work, we hope that no reflection upon him is there intended.

EDITOR'S NOTE  FP: *United Amateur* 14, No. 4 (March 1915): 61–65. With this column HPL begins what would become a frequent procedure: severe and disparaging comments on his own work, either those published under his own name or under pseudonyms. The article is signed "H. P. LOVECRAFT, Chairman, Department of Public Criticism."

*Notes*

1. By HPL.
2. Isaacson (1891–1936)—who would shortly engage in a feud with HPL (see "In a Major" p. 56)—later wrote two books on music, *Face to Face with Great Musicians* (1918–21; 2 vols.) and *The Simple Story of Music* (1928).
3. Alexander Pope, *An Essay on Criticism* (1711), l. 346.
4. I.e., where a group of members fund a journal by paying a given sum of money (to cover printing costs) for a given number of pages. HPL participated in such a journal, *The United Co-operative* (1918–21).
5. HPL discusses the essay in his astronomy column, "The February Sky" ([Providence] *Evening News*, 30 January 1915, p. 8; CE3).

# WHAT IS AMATEUR JOURNALISM?

Though nearly half a century has elapsed since Amateur Journalism first became a recognised institution, it is doubtful if even the most active veteran amateur can describe the nature and precise purpose of the press associations. Nor can we expect to find a very clearly defined set of ideals in organisations where so little centralised intellectual authority prevails. Amateur Journalism has as many aspects as it has adherents. Each amateur forms his own conception of it; and be that conception high or low, serious or frivolous, he follows it without restraint, and inculcates it in others as widely as he is able; wherefore the institution is today divided into such a multitude of distinct schools, that the faltering recruit scarcely knows what sort of a society he has joined.

Among these divisions, that of petty politics is perhaps the least commendable. The amateur politician, frankly unliterary, and seeking office merely for its own sake, regards his association as a convenient ladder on which to climb upward to the coveted prize. His writing never rises above the level of pamphleteering, and his conduct when in power is invariably that of the boss, not the educator.

Another species of amateur is the purely social member. Though without the vices of the politician, this amiable creature contributes but little more than he to Amateur Journalism, since in his eyes the press association is simply a circle of acquaintances, about whom he may gossip pleasantly and unintelligently. His idea of a paper is a little collection of harmless, insipid chit-chat and society notes, couched in a loose, colloquial style copied from the latest "best seller".

A third kind of member is the person of ability who uses Amateur Journalism as a light amusement. To an amateur of this sort, seriousness is impossible, and he accordingly floods the press with kittenish comment and whimsical impromptu jingles. The associations are obviously nothing to these worldly dilettantes, whose best efforts are all placed elsewhere.

A type which is sometimes combined with one of the preceding types, yet often of loftier aims, is the confirmed club-ite. He may be a litterateur of great accomplishments in his own little clique, but is wholly inactive beyond it, and is scarcely to be classed with the real amateurs. An outsider beholding his work would think that no amateur world existed save within the confines of one local club. The National is especially infested with these narrow folk.

The pedant is fortunately a rather uncommon sort of amateur, but one who makes himself heard very plainly. He is a critic by profession and a cynic by nature, viewing with ill-concealed scorn the immature efforts of the young member. His intentions are obviously well meant, and his acts often prove of great value; which things render him the more difficult to deal with. Like the club-ite, his tribe has generally been most numerous in the National. One modification of this species is the man who becomes so absorbed in the internal workings of Amateur Journalism, that he forgets its connexion with literature.

The typographical enthusiast, purely and simply such, contributes so much to the associations that he must be excused for his failure wholly to embody the amateur spirit. Yet there should be more than mere fine printing in the amateur literary world.

Only partially within the pale of Amateur Journalism is the ten-cents-a-year professional. Usually he is a small boy, but is occasionally an older person engaged in the mail-order business, who sees in the associations a new territory for his cheap advertising. The small boy has possibilities, often of a glorious nature, but the mail-order man is a pernicious parasite.[1]

What, indeed, is Amateur Journalism? Is it not possible to discover amidst this varied assemblage a set of model amateurs whose ideals may be taken as those of the whole institution? I firmly believe that it is. The amateur of earnest literary ambition and true brotherly spirit, who devotes his best energies to the maintenance of a high and dignified standard in the press, who diffuses through his correspondence a mixture of information and good-will, who is kind, appreciative, and just in criticising his fellows, and who shows sincere cordiality and gives sound advice in his welcome of the new member, is the real amateur—the representative amateur. Through him, perhaps, our question shall be answered, for by his ascendancy and influence the associations may some day adopt that one lofty aim which alone is worthy of them; and make of Amateur Journalism an instrument for the development of finished writers from talented raw material by means of pleasurable instruction, fraternal coöperation, and edifying amusement.

EDITOR'S NOTE  FP: *Lake Breeze* No. 18 (March 1915): 127–28 (as by "El Imparcial"). An attempt to distinguish various types of amateurs; HPL's preference is clearly toward the serious literary striver discussed at the end of the essay. This is the first article in which the "El Imparcial" pseudonym (first attributed to HPL by Willametta Keffer in "Howard P(seudonym) Lovecraft: The Many Names of HPL," *Fossil*, July 1958) was used.

*Notes*

1. HPL may be remembering the fact that he himself charged small amounts of money for subscriptions to his own hectographed papers, the *Scientific Gazette* (1899–1909) and the *Rhode Island Journal of Astronomy* (1903–09).

# CONSOLIDATION'S AUTOPSY

The suggestion of our Editor-in-Chief[1] that the troublesome corpse of Consolidation be given an autopsy in order to ensure a permanent burial is one of the wisest yet made concerning this wearying topic. We might also suggest that the coroner's final report be given permanent publication beside the Constitution and By-Laws, lest some future recruit, bewildered by the specious statements of the National, lend his innocent sanction to some piratical enterprise on the part of the latter association. Thus let the autopsy begin.

Though we should first of all endeavour to determine just what element desires an amalgamation of the United and the National, this investigation may be quite properly dispensed with, since the facts are only too well known. The wish for Consolidation is purely a National one, and awakes absolutely no echoes in the younger and more vigorous body. We must, then, seek to discover what hidden reasons could possibly render such a step advisable to us.

Obviously, the membership list of the combined associations would be larger than that of the present United, but do we wish to adopt the fossilised ex-amateurs of which the National is largely composed? The United is growing and expanding; we cannot stop to assume charge of an inactive Old Men's Home. Most of the active members of the National have already found it necessary to enter the United in order to enjoy an Amateur Journalism that is really alive. Why need we sacrifice our identity to gain what we already have?

The financial problem is one upon which many have dwelt with emphasis. Why support two associations, they cry, when one would be sufficient? A close analysis fails to reveal the fact that any association but the United is even now supported except through alms given by former amateurs. The treasury of the National is at present, we believe, practically a zero if not a minus quantity. The independent amateur of today is distinctly a United product, so why should we seek him elsewhere?

Much has been made of the long existence and past career of the "grand old National", and the advocates of Consolidation imagine that the United would consent to a virtual disorganisation merely to secure such a pedigree. But as Thomas Campbell (not Paul J.) remarked over a century ago, "'Tis distance lends enchantment to the view."[2] The National has had as members a considerable number of very accomplished litterateurs, of which the poet Samuel Loveman and the critic Edward Cole are shining examples. But to judge the association by a few men of genius like these is scarcely proper. The National has never more ingenuously confessed its fundamental failing than when referring affectionately to "the small boy with a printing-press". This is the much-vaunted grandeur of the National. Not literary, not educational, grandeur, but a record of mere juvenile typographical achievement; a development of the small-boy ideal. While this may be eminently laudable in its way, it is not the kind of grandeur that our United is seeking, and we would certainly hesitate before bartering our own literary traditions for any print-shop record like the National's. At one time the National had the field for itself, and perhaps made more of the educational element than it now does; but the rise of the United, with its increasingly close relations with the high-schools, has overshadowed the older society in this direction. We have nothing to gain from the "grand old National".

Consolidation, then, would bring us nothing more than a long list of empty names, and an old, boasted title which fails, after all, to do justice to our nobler and more serious aspirations. Let us hope that no further autopsy will be necessary to shew the utter ridiculousness of Consolidation from our point of view. If any shall in future play the part of ghouls above its grave, let them be members of other associations than the United.

EDITOR'S NOTE  FP: *Lake Breeze* No. 19 (April 1915): 133 (as by "El Imparcial"). The article violently opposes the notion of consolidating the UAPA and NAPA, as HPL believed that the UAPA's distinctively literary bent would not mix well with the largely social or political orientation of the NAPA. Only very late in his career with the UAPA (see "President's Message" [May 1924]) did HPL grudgingly come around to the idea, as a means of staving off the collapse of the UAPA.

*Notes*

1. M. W. Hart, Official Editor of the UAPA (1914–15).
2. Thomas Campbell (1777–1844), *The Pleasures of Hope* (1799), Part I, l. 7.

---

# THE AMATEUR PRESS

O*le Miss'* for March is the first number of a paper undoubtedly destined to become an important factor in the literary life of the United. Under the able editorship of Mr. and Mrs. Renshaw, this journal bears the distinctive marks of purpose and intelligence. Joseph W. Renshaw, appearing for the first time as an amateur, proves himself a writer of remarkable attractiveness and satisfying fluency. His opening article, introducing *Ole Miss'* to the United, displays a pleasing sense of affection for his Alma Mater, the University of Mississippi, and for the picturesque old-fashioned Southern atmosphere which he feels to be disappearing with the years. To such a sentiment of regret at the havoc of time, there cannot but be an universal response from those who live in the older states, where the original systems of society are being crushed beneath the pressure of modern commercialism and its unnatural attendant evils. In "An A. J. Suggestion", Mr. Renshaw clearly and forcibly outlines, evidently without having seen Mr. Campbell's original suggestion in *The United Amateur*, the desirableness of obtaining one capable printer for all amateur work, thus securing a uniform good appearance for the various papers, at a very much reduced expense. This article should serve as a final and absolutely convincing argument for the passage of Mr. Daas' amendment creating an "official printer". "The Humble Swallow" is an unsigned article of great sentimental beauty, wherein are celebrated the virtues of a lovely bird, and his wanton destruction condemned. Mrs. Renshaw's article on "A Higher Recruiting Standard" is worthy of long and careful thought. One of Amateur Journalism's weakest points is certainly the freedom with which membership is extended to indifferent persons. That the United can be gradually rendered more select in character is being proved by Mrs. Renshaw herself, whose recruits are almost without exception of a very high order. The poetry, all by Mrs. Renshaw, consists of three short pieces of great merit. Of these, "Man of the Everyday" is perhaps the best. "Night of the Rain" is excellent, though the "mop" simile detracts a little from the general ethereal delicacy of the stanzas. As a whole, *Ole Miss'* has reason to be called the season's best paper.

EDITOR'S NOTE  FP: *Lake Breeze* No. 19 (April 1915): 136–37. A kind of compressed version of a DPC column. HPL wrote only a part of the article (the section here printed is signed "H. P. Lovecraft"); the rest of the column was written by other amateurs.

## EDITORIAL

*(April 1915)*

The Conservative, in thrusting upon an unsuspecting amateur public this first issue of what purports to be a paper, may well adopt that tone of trembling humility which suits the inexperienced beginner.

As another ambitious novice wrote not long ago in rugged verse:

> "Mid amateurs and novices, though oft they are winning,
> Be it ever so humble, there must be a beginning.
> A slap from the critic swiftly brings us to our feet;
> Shakes up our senses, and shakes out our conceit."

Like the poet, The Conservative expects criticism. He does not, however, expressly solicit it; since he is well aware that critics, like the other birds of prey, require but little solicitation before tearing to pieces their latest victim. That his numerous defects and weaknesses will furnish the reviewers' fraternity with a just and ample opportunity for the display of their brilliant superiority, The Conservative is not quite conceited enough to deny; yet he would give warning that he has made a close study of Pope's *Dunciad* and Paul J. Campbell's "Wet Hen", so that he is not altogether defenceless. Reference to "verbosity", "long words", "stilted, old-fashioned style", "dogmatic opinions", and the like will be entirely unnecessary. The Conservative has heard all this before, and is hopelessly beyond reform. Besides, he may never perpetrate another number of this modest magazine.

EDITOR'S NOTE   FP: *Conservative* 1, No. 1 (April 1915): [3–4] (unsigned). HPL's tentative introduction of himself to the amateur world. His editorial in the next issue (see p. 51) is a more forthright exposition of the *Conservative*'s goals and purposes.

## THE QUESTION OF THE DAY

The debate over the propriety of outside matters in the amateur papers, begun in the National association, has quickly spread to the United, where Mr. George Schilling challenges the distinguished exponents of the negative with an able article on the minimum wage. The Conservative, mindful of the nature and aims of amateur journalism, cannot but be opposed to the present attacks on the liberty of the press.

The agitators who would restrict the work of amateurs to subjects immediately connected with the associations base their opinions on ridiculously exalted standards of amateur writing. Endowed with an almost too great refinement of taste, they cannot endure the general article of ordinary merit, but demand that every author become a specialist in his chosen field before he shall so much as dare to express his views in public. While it is easy to imagine the supercilious displeasure with which our faultless critics must examine the average amateur's half-formed views on outside affairs, it is difficult to understand why these impeccable censors should take it upon themselves to stifle the dawning spirit of research in the beginner by suppressing his crude, nascent efforts. The uninspired and unintelligent presentation of a topic may often elicit reams of really valuable discussion, in the meantime forcing the original author to acquire a truer grasp of his subject. It is in this atmosphere of lettered freedom that the educational side of amateur journalism is best developed.

The position of those who favour the exclusive discussion of amateur journalism is peculiarly indefensible. Amateur journalism is like a great machine for the production and publication of literary matter. While it is of course necessary to keep the mechanism in running order, our greatest interest naturally centres on the product. It is only the child who becomes infatuated with the machine for its own sake; who spends all his time in watching the wheels go 'round.

EDITOR'S NOTE FP: *Conservative* 1, No. 1 (April 1915): [4] (unsigned). An article advocating the discussion, in amateur papers, of general matters outside the domain of amateurdom. The point was of importance to HPL in furthering his desire for amateur journalism to serve as an instrument of general literary education.

# THE MORRIS FACTION

Several months after The Conservative joined the U.A.P.A. he received a copy of a strange but excellent paper claiming to be the only real and original *United Amateur*, together with a blank recommending him for membership in "The United Amateur Press Association". Having thought himself already a fully initiated United man, he naturally became rather curious as to the number of times one is supposed to join the same association. Nor has The Conservative been alone in this perplexing experience, which indeed seems quite the rule with United recruits. In time the new member learns of the factional division which has created this confusing situation, and in nearly every case regrets the separate existence of the small branch which, though sadly struggling for its very life, yet refuses to return to the fold.

Whilst the veteran amateur may regard as grave and irreconcilable the differences that cause the Morris faction to stand aloof, the more recent element, already numerous and powerful, cannot help considering them far too insignificant to warrant continued separation. Can no means be devised to effect a reunion? A half-forgotten contest over an office ought not to keep such capable amateurs as Mr. Morris, Mr. Haggerty, Miss Merritt, or Mr. Cook from rejoining the larger, rejuvenated United, and coöperating with its members in the interests of a better amateur journalism.

EDITOR'S NOTE FP: *Conservative* 1, No. 1 (April 1915): [5] (unsigned). One of HPL's many discussions of the split that occurred in the UAPA following the disputed election of 1912, in which a large number of members broke away to form the United Amateur Press Association of America, largely based in Seattle. The title refers to Ernest H. Morris, president of the UAPA of America for 1913–14. See further the essays "The 'Other United'" (p. 160), "The Pseudo-United" (p. 255), and "A Matter of Uniteds" (p. 358). In fact, amateur historians regard HPL's faction as the "rebel" branch of the UAPA.

## FOR PRESIDENT—LEO FRITTER

In the *United Official Quarterly* for February occurs a sentence which may be construed as the launching of a presidential "boom" for Mr. Leo Fritter of Columbus, Ohio. The Conservative, in the best interests of the United Amateur Press Association, desires to be first in seconding such a just and eminently sensible motion. Leo Fritter is of true presidential timber, possessing every qualification which should exist in an executive. He is an attorney of trained legal mind, he is a man of highest culture and real literary taste, he is sincerely devoted to the cause of amateur journalism, he is a despiser of petty politics and factional jealousies, he has a keen feeling of fraternity and good-will, he stands as a champion of the United against the schemers who seek to destroy its identity, and he is not affiliated with any other amateur press association.

The Conservative feels that a rising organisation like the United should have a strong man at its head, and he can think of none stronger or better than Leo Fritter. Mr. Fritter is not an "old-timer" in amateur journalism, which should count much in his favour, since he cannot have absorbed the ancient prejudices which make it so difficult for a veteran amateur to conduct an absolutely impartial administration. No person living is better fitted to aid in a reunion with the disaffected amateurs of the Morris Faction. Wherefore The Conservative again cries, and with redoubled enthusiasm: For President—Leo Fritter!

EDITOR'S NOTE FP: *Conservative* 1, No. 1 (April 1915): [5] (unsigned). HPL's advocacy of Leo Fritter for president of the UAPA. Fritter was in fact elected to the office in the UAPA convention of July 1915, serving for the 1915–16 term. In the early 1920s Fritter broke with HPL and joined a rebellion that ousted HPL's "literary" party (see "Editorial" [January 1922] and "Editorial" [May 1924]).

## INTRODUCING MR. CHESTER PIERCE MUNROE

Visitors at the Slater Avenue Primary and Grammar School in Providence, examining the desks and walls of the building, or the fence and the long bench in the boys' yard, may today discern among the multitude of names unlawfully carved by generations of youthful irrepressibles frequent repetitions of the initials "C. P. M. & H. P. L.", which the vicissitudes of sixteen years have failed completely to efface. The two friends whose initials are thus early associated have not been separated in spirit during the ensuing years, so that "H. P. L.", now become The Conservative, herewith takes pleasure in welcoming to the United as his first recruit Mr. Chester Pierce Munroe, the "C. P. M." of boyhood days.

But while The Conservative has remained in the city of his birth, secluding himself amidst the musty volumes of his library, his friend has been in and of the busy world outside, acquiring a knowledge of men and things instead of mere bookish lore. Wherefore it is no dry replica of himself that The Conservative is ushering into the charmed circle of amateur journalism. Chester P. Munroe was always of literary tastes.

Even in the old Slater Avenue days he used to write short stories in moments snatched from the study of his regular lessons, and in later years he became the author of more than one unpublished novel. His geographical description of Switzerland, composed a few years ago, inspired The Conservative to scribble off some complimentary verses which may one day appear in the amateur press.[1]

Recently, Mr. Munroe has become a disciple of the Muses, and his credential to the United, a delightful little poem called "Thoughts", will soon, it is to be hoped, greet us from the pages of The Blarney Stone. The new member is now a thorough North Carolinian, having established himself at the Grove Park Inn, Asheville.[2] It is therefore possible that he will be in attendance at the coming convention.

In the future politics of the United, Mr. Munroe may play a lively and considerable part, for he comes of a decidedly political stock. His talented father, the Hon. Addison Pierce Munroe, has repeatedly been elected by overwhelming majorities to the Senate of Massachusetts; his uncle, Mr. Oliver Munroe, is Mayor of Melrose, Massachusetts; while his charming younger brother, Harold, is a Deputy Sheriff of Providence County. The Conservative is certain that the rest of the amateurs will join him in making this promising recruit feel at home in the ranks of the United Amateur Press Association.

EDITOR'S NOTE FP: *Conservative* 1, No. 1 (April 1915): [6] (unsigned). HPL welcomes into the UAPA his boyhood friend, who with his brother Harold Bateman Munroe were HPL's closest friends in grammar and high school.

*Notes*

1. See "To Mr. Munroe, on His Instructive and Entertaining Account of Switzerland" (1914; AT 89–90). The poem remained unpublished until long after HPL's death, first appearing in the *Fossil* (July 1979).
2. Presumably Munroe facilitated HPL's writing a series of astronomy articles, "Mysteries of the Heavens" (CE3), for the *Asheville Gazette-News* (February–May 1915).

# [UNTITLED NOTES ON AMATEUR JOURNALISM]

The Conservative desires to apologise for any errors in proofreading which may be found in this issue. Circumstances necessitated a change of printer at the last moment, and an already great delay rendered haste a prime essential.

\*    \*    \*    \*

Ira A. Cole's article on "The Gods of Our Fathers" in the November *United Official Quarterly* is a refreshing departure from the dull, wholly Semitic tone of ordinary theological thought. Like Wordsworth and Schiller, Mr. Cole feels the call of our own ancestral Aryan deities, and revels in the beautiful legends which form so important a part of our racial heritage.

Rheinhart Kleiner, in the concluding paragraph of *The Piper*, refers very wittily to the prevalence of slang in amateur journalism. His epigram on this subject deserves versified form. Here is The Conservative's crude and hasty attempt to set it in metre:

> Slang is the life of speech, the critics say,
> And stript of slang, our tongue would pass away.
> If this be so, how well the amateur
> Takes care that English ever shall endure!

———

Leo Fritter's essay on "The Spiritual Significance of the Stars" in the January *Woodbee* illustrates in a most impressive manner the ennobling effect of astronomical study on the highly organised mind. The boundless heavens have become for Mr. Fritter an enlarged exposition of human life, and a faultless pattern for earthly conduct.

———

In the first issue of *Invictus* Mr. Paul J. Campbell has set a standard for the strictly individual paper which few other amateurs will ever attain. One cannot become too enthusiastic in speaking of this inspired brochure. As a philosophical essayist Mr. Campbell probably has no superior in the United, and his three brilliant homilies, "The Impost of the Future", "The Sublime Ideal", and "Whom God Hath Put Asunder", are notable additions to amateur literature.

———

The Conservative is often inclined to wonder just what methods are used by the United's prominent poets in composing their verses. This curiosity is aroused by the frequency with which gaps and redundant syllables are found in the lines of some of the very noblest bards. Miss Owen, in her Blue Pencil epithalamium, uses the word "jewel" where a monosyllable should be, whilst Mr. Kleiner's "Love, Come Again" in the July *Olympian* contains a line whose harmony is seriously marred by an extra syllable. "A Dog for Comfort" by Miss von der Heide in the January *Woodbee* is supposed to be cast in decasyllabic quatrains, yet the second line of the fourth stanza is woefully defective. The moderns are prone to laugh at the strict regularity of eighteenth-century verse, yet the form of their own compositions would be immeasurably the better for a closer adherence to some of the old-fashioned rules.

———

Since the subject of plagiarism in its varying degrees has been brought to our notice so forcibly by the controversy between Messrs. Edward H. Cole and W. Paul Cook, The Conservative would like to know why the last sentence of his article in the July *New Member* was removed, and placed without credit at the back of the magazine as a motto.

———

It is to be regretted that Edward H. Cole confines his extraordinary talents so exclusively to the treatment of amateur journalistic affairs. Mr. Cole possesses a mind of unusual keenness and a prose style which cannot be approached in quality by that of any other amateur, yet his work is almost provokingly unvaried. It is really the duty of so thorough a scholar to exhibit his powers in matters of wider interest.

Mr. Ernest A. Dench of Brooklyn, a member of the United, and until his advent to America a British amateur of note, is one of the fortunate few who have published books to their credit. His treatise on *Playwriting for the Cinema* is a terse and readable exposition of the motion picture industry which stamps its author as a youth of more than ordinary ability.[1]

The talented Chairman of the Department of Private Criticism[2] writes The Conservative, who has been favoured with the Chairmanship of the other Critical Bureau, that the reviews in *The United Amateur* shew extreme strictness in dealing with the metrical irregularities of the amateur poets. To this charge The Conservative would like to reply, that he is really criticising the whole modern trend in verse-writing, rather than the individuals who exemplify its faults. In the present violent reaction against old-fashioned precision of metre, the art of versification is in danger of expiring. Form, harmony, even prosody itself, alike seem to be ignored by the majority today, so that some counter-reaction seems essential for the preservation of verse as we have hitherto known it. To blame the innocent amateur who merely falls into the errors of his time, the errors which are condoned and practiced by the best writers of the age, is obviously unjust; yet glaring violations of the established principles of prosody cannot be passed by unnoticed.

Wherefore, though The Conservative may appear to be something of a martinet in his conduct of the Department of Public Criticism, he desires to make it very plain that he is opposed not to his fellow-amateurs, but to that insidious breaking down of rhyme and metre which is one of the most regrettable features of contemporary literature.

*Outward Bound* comes to The Conservative as a welcome link with Old England, the land of his fathers. Editor Stokes is to be congratulated on having so talented a contributor as J. H. Fowler, whose fantastic poem on "The Haunted Forest" shews a marvellous and almost Poe-like comprehension of the dark and sinister.

EDITOR'S NOTE FP: *Conservative* 1, No. 1 (April 1915): [6–8] (unsigned). Apparently designed almost as "filler" material to flesh out eight pages of HPL's first amateur journal. In the parlance of today's amateur press associations, the article would constitute "mailing comments"—comments on the contributions of other amateur journalists. HPL's cordial remarks on Ira A. Cole, Rheinhart Kleiner, Edward H. Cole, and Paul J. Campbell foretell his close friendship with these amateur writers in the coming years.

*Notes*

1. Ernest A. Dench, *Playwriting for the Cinema* (London: A. & C. Black, 1914). Dench also published *Making the Movies* (1915), *Advertising by Motion Pictures* (1916), *Motion Picture Education* (1917), and other works.
2. Maurice W. Moe.

# DEPARTMENT OF PUBLIC CRITICISM

(May 1915)

*The Blarney Stone* for January–February is replete with good literature, amidst which may particularly be mentioned Arthur Goodenough's harmonious poem, "God Made Us All of Clay". The theme is not new, but appears advantageously under Mr. Goodenough's delicate treatment.

M. W. Hart's short story, "The Redemption", is intended to portray a righteous transformation from conventional false morality to true Christian life, but in reality presents a very repulsive picture of bestial atavism. The meaner character was not "reformed by mercy", but merely withheld from wholesale vice by isolation. Mr. Hart is so plainly in earnest when he relates this dismal tale as a sermon, that we must not be too harsh in questioning his taste or condemning his free standards of civilised morality; yet we doubt seriously if stories or essays of this type should appear in the press, and especially in the amateur press. Two or three technical points demand attention. The word "diversified" on page 2 might better be "diverse", while "environment" on page 4 could well be replaced by "condition" or "state". On page 5 occurs the sentence "All intelligence . . . were . . . instinct". Obviously the verb should be in the singular number to correspond with its subject. Mr. Hart is developing a prose style of commendable dignity, unusually free from the jarring touch of modern frivolity.

H. B. Scott is proving himself a finished scholar and a thoughtful editor in his conduct of *The Blarney Stone*; his able essay on "Personality" is eminently worthy of more than one perusal.

*The Boys' Herald* for May presents us with a highly interesting account of Robert Louis Stevenson's career as an amateur journalist, together with a fac-simile reproduction of the cover of *The Sunbeam Magazine*, Stevenson's hand-written periodical. The column of reminiscences, containing letters from various old-time amateurs, is extremely inspiring to the younger members, shewing how persistently the amateur spirit adheres to all who have truly acquired it. "Nita at the Passing Show" is a witty and entertaining parody by Mr. Smith, illustrating the theatrical hobby of Miss Gerner, one of the latest United recruits. *The Boys' Herald* discharges a peculiar and important function in the life of the associations, connecting the present with the past, and furnishing us with just standards for comparison.

*Dowdell's Bearcat* for December opens with a Christmas poem of great beauty and harmonious construction from the pen of Dora M. Hepner. The thoughts and images are without exception lofty and well selected, and the only possible defect is the attempt to rhyme "come" with "run" in the last stanza. Edward H. Cole's review of a recent booklet in memory of Miss Susan Brown Robbins, a former amateur, is more than a criticism. It is a rare appreciation of the bonds of mutual esteem and respect which grow up amongst the congenial members of the press associations. Mr. Cole is peculiarly well fitted to deal with his subject, and no praise is needed beyond the statement that the review is characteristic of him.

*Dowdell's Bearcat* for January marks the metamorphosis of that periodical into a newspaper. With youthful ambition, Mr. Dowdell is resolved to furnish the United with the latest items of interest concerning amateurs. While the general style of the paper is fluent and pleasing, we believe that "Bruno" might gain much force of expression through the exercise of a little more care and dignity in his prose. For instance, many colloquial contractions like "don't", "won't", or "can't" might be eliminated, while such slang phrases as "neck of the woods", "make good", "somewhat off", or "bunch of yellow-backs" were better omitted.

*Dowdell's Bearcat* for March is notable for an increase in size. "A Visit to Niagara Falls", by Andrew R. Koller, is an intelligent and animated piece of description, which promises well for the development of its author. What looseness of construction exists may be charged to youth. "An Ambition and a Vision", by Nettie A. Hartman, is a neat and grammatically written little sketch, probably autobiographical, describing the evolution of an amateur. Greater cultivation of rhetorical taste would improve Miss Hartman's style, and we are certain that it possesses a fundamental merit which will make improvement an easy matter. With the usual regret we observe an instance of "simple spelling", which Mr. Dowdell, who does not fall into this vice himself, has evidently overlooked in editing. The news items this month are timely and vivacious, exhibiting "Bruno" at his best.

*The Lake Breeze* for March inaugurates a very welcome revival of the United's foremost news sheet, now to be issued monthly. Mr. Daas is so active an amateur, and so closely connected with the development of the association, that his ably edited journal has almost the authority of an official organ.

The editorial entitled "Ashes and Roses" is a powerful and convincing reply to a rather weak attack lately made on the United by a member of a less active association. Mr. Daas uses both sense and sarcasm to great advantage, leaving but little ground for his opponent to occupy.

"The Amateur Press" is a well conducted column of contributed reviews, among which Mrs. A. M. Adams' eulogy of Mrs. Griffith's essay in *Outward Bound* is perhaps the best. "What Is Amateur Journalism?", by "El Imparcial",[1] is a sketch of the various types of amateurs, with a suggestion of the ideal type. While free from glaring defects, the essay gives no really new information, and brings out no strikingly original ideas. "Some Objections to Moving Pictures", by Edmund L. Shehan, presents a strong array of evidence against one of the most popular and instructive amusements of today. We do not believe, however, that the objections here offered are vital. The moving picture has infinite possibilities for literary and artistic good when rightly presented, and having achieved a permanent place, seems destined eventually to convey the liberal arts to multitudes hitherto denied their enjoyment. Mr. Shehan's prose style is clear and forceful; capable of highly advantageous development.

*Literary Buds* for April is the first number of a paper issued by the new Athenaeum Club of Journalism, Harvey, Ill. Though the text of most of the contributions has suffered somewhat through a slight misapprehension concerning the editing, the issue is nevertheless pleasing and creditable.

"A la Rudyard", a poem by George A. Bradley, heads the contents. While hampered by some of the heaviness natural to authors of school age, Mr. Bradley has managed to put into his lines a laudable enthusiasm and genuine warmth. The editorial column is well conducted, the second item being especially graphic, though the "superdreadnought" metaphor seems rather forced. Clara Inglis Stalker, the enthusiastic and capable educator through whose efforts the club was formed, gives a brief account of her organisation, under the title "The History of an Eight-Weeks-Old", and in a prose style of uniformly flowing and attractive quality. "A Love Song", Miss Stalker's other contribution, is a poem of delicate imagery and unusual metre. "Our Paring Knife", by Gertrude Van Lanningham, is a short sketch with an aphorism at the end. Though this type of moral lesson is a little trite, Miss Van Lanningham shews no mean appreciation of literary form, and will, when she has emerged from the "bud" stage, undoubtedly blossom into a graphic and sympathetic writer. "Co-Education", by Caryl Dempesy, is an interesting but only partially convincing article on a topic of considerable importance. The author, being enthusiastically in favour of the practice, enumerates its many benefits; yet the arguments are decidedly biased. While the advantage of co-education to young ladies is made quite obvious, it remains far from clear that young men receive equal benefit. A desirable decline of cliques and hazing might, it is true, result from the admission of women to men's universities, but the young men would undoubtedly lose much in earnest, concentrated energy and dignified virility through the presence of the fair. The experiment, radical at best, has failed more than once. The style of this essay is slightly wanting in ease and continuity, yet possesses the elements of force. "The Traitor", by Agnes E. Fairfield, is a short story of artistic development but questionable sentiment. The present fad of peace-preaching should not be allowed to influence a writer of sense into glorifying a socialistic, unpatriotic fanatic who refuses to uphold the institutions that his fathers before him created with their toil, blood, and sacrifice. It is not the right of the individual to judge of the necessity of a war; no layman can form an intelligent idea of the dangers that may beset his fatherland. The man is but a part of the state, and must uphold it at any cost. We are inclined to wonder at Miss Fairfield's mention of a king, when the name Phillipe La Roque so clearly proclaims the hero a Frenchman. France, be it known, has been a republic for some little time. "Penny in the Slot", by Vaughn Flannery, possesses a humour that is pleasing and apparently quite spontaneous. We should like to behold more of Mr. Flannery's efforts in this field.

Viewed in its entirety, allowance being made for its present essentially juvenile nature, *Literary Buds* may be regarded as a pronounced success. That it will mature in consonance with the club which it represents is certain, and each future issue can be relied upon to surpass its predecessor.

*Ole Miss'* for March, edited by Mr. and Mrs. J. W. Renshaw, easily falls into the very front rank of the season's amateur journals. In this number Mr. Joseph W. Renshaw makes his initial appearance before the members of the United, producing a very favourable impression with his pure, attractive prose. The introduction, credited in another column to Mr. Renshaw, is of graceful and pleasing character, recalling the elusively beautiful atmosphere of the Old South which is too soon passing away.

"The Humble Swallow", an anonymous essay, praises with singularly delicate art a feathered creature whose charms lie not on the surface. The concluding paragraph, condemning the wanton slaughter of this winged friend to mankind, is especially apt at a time of hysterical peace agitation. While the well-meaning advocates of peace call wildly upon men to abandon just warfare against destructive and malignant enemies, they generally pass over without thought or reproof the wholesale murder of these innocent little birds, who never did nor intended harm to anyone. "A Higher Recruiting Standard", by Mrs. Renshaw, is an able exposition of the newer and loftier type of ideals prevailing in the United. Our association has never lacked numbers, but would undoubtedly be the better for an increased standard of scholarship such as is here demanded. Mrs. Renshaw's work as a recruiter is in keeping with her policy, and this, together with Mr. Moe's work amongst the English teachers, seems destined to raise the United far above its lesser contemporaries. "An A. J. Suggestion", by Mr. Renshaw, deals ingeniously and logically with the always difficult problem of selecting a printer. Though evidently written quite independently, it ably seconds Paul J. Campbell's original suggestion in the *United Amateur*. The advantages of having one printer for all amateur work are many, and the well-presented opinions of Mr. Renshaw should aid much in securing this desirable innovation.

The poetry in *Ole Miss'* is all by Mrs. Renshaw, and therefore of first quality. "Some One I Know" is a lightly amatory piece of tuneful rhythm. "Night of Rain" gives a peculiarly pleasing aspect to a type of scene not usually celebrated in verse. The only jarring note is the rather mundane metaphor which compares the trees to a "beautiful mop". Though Mrs. Renshaw holds unusual ideas regarding the use of art in poetry, we contend that this instance of rhetorical frigidity is scarcely permissible. It is too much like Sir Richard Blackmore's description of Mount Aetna, wherein he compares a volcanic eruption to a fit of colic; or old Ben Jonson's battle scene in the fifth act of *Catiline*, where he represents the sun perspiring.[2] "Man of the Everyday" is a noble panegyric on the solid, constructive virtues of the ordinary citizen, portraying very graphically the need of his presence in a world that heeds him but little.

Considered in all its aspects, *Ole Miss'* is a notable contribution to amateur literature, and one which we hope to see oft repeated.

*The Passing Show* for February is the "second annual production" of an excellent though informal little paper by Nita Edna Gerner, a new member of the United, and the daughter of an old-time amateur. Miss Gerner is an enthusiast on all matters pertaining to the theatre, and has impressed her hobby very strongly on the pages of her publication.

The dominant theme of the current issue is that of amateur romance, exhibiting the press associations in the role of matrimonial agencies. "The Twos-ers", by Edwin Hadley Smith, is a long list of couples who became wedded through acquaintanceships formed in amateur journalism. This catalogue, recording 26 marriages and engagements from the earliest ages to the present, must have cost its author much time and research. "A Romance of Amateur Journalism", by Edward F. Daas, is a very brief statement of facts in unornamented style. "An 'Interstate' Romance", by Leston M. Ayres, is more elaborate in treatment, and displays an easy, colloquial style.

The editorial column, headed "Through the Opera-Glasses", is bright and informal. We note with regret that Miss Gerner has seen fit to adopt the popular mutilated orthography of the day, a fad which we trust she will discard in time.

*Pearson's Pet* for April is a bright and attractive little paper throughout. "Burnin' Off" is a delightful specimen of dialect verse which conveys a graphic image. We have never witnessed such an agricultural function as Mr. Pearson describes, but can gain from his clever lines a vivid idea of its weird impressiveness. "How I Met Elbert Hubbard" is narrated in commendably easy prose, which same may be said of the sketch or editorial entitled "Broke Loose Again". Mr. Pearson is assuredly a competent exponent of amateur journalism's lighter and less formal side.

*The Piper* for May is as pleasing and meritorious as the first number, both in its verse and its prose. "The Modern Muse", exhibiting Mr. Kleiner in a somewhat humorous mood, is very forceful in its satire on the altered ideals of the poetical fraternity, but is marred by the noticeably imperfect rhyming of "garret" and "carrot". It is barely possible that according to the prevailing New York pronunciation this rhyme is not so forced as it appears, but we are of New England, and accustomed to hearing the sounds more classically differentiated. The defect is trivial at most, and mentioned here only because Mr. Kleiner professes such a rigid adherence to the law of perfect rhyming. "The Books I Used to Read" is the most delightful appreciation of juvenile literature that has appeared in amateur journalism within our memory. There are few of us in whom this poem will fail to arouse glad reminiscences. "Spring" is a pleasing poem on a subject which, though not exactly new, is nevertheless susceptible to an infinite variety of treatment. The four stanzas are highly creditable, both sentimentally and metrically. Apart from the poetry, criticism seems the dominant element in *The Piper,* and it would be difficult indeed to find a more lucid and discerning series of reviews. Mr. Kleiner's unvarying advocacy of correct metre and perfect rhyming is refreshing to encounter in this age of laxity and licence. Perhaps he is a little stern in his condemnation of the "allowable" rhymes of other days, especially in view of his recent "garret-carrot" attempt, yet we admit that there is much to be said in favour of his attitude.

The *Plainsman* for February contains a gruesome moral tale by Ricardo Santiago, entitled "The Bell of Huesca". It is proper to remark here, that an important sentence was omitted at the top of page 3.[3] The passage should read "'Sire, thy bell has no clapper!' 'Thy head shall be the clapper,' said the king, and he sent him to the block" etc. Whatever may be said of the aptness of the allegory, it is evident that Mr. Santiago possesses the foundations of a pure and forcible prose style, and a commendable sense of unity in narration and development of climax. This story is undoubtedly worthy of its distinction as winner in *The Plainsman's* post-card contest.

The *Spectator* for June–July, 1914, though somewhat trite in title, is the first number of a magazine notable for its quality. Walter John Held is without doubt one of the most enterprising youths who have ever joined the ranks of the association, though his views on paid subscriptions and advertisements shew his still imperfect acquisition of the true amateur spirit. Mr. Held mistakes commercial progress for artistic development, believing that the aim of every amateur in his ascent toward professional authorship is to write remunerative matter. He therefore considers a publisher's advancement to be best shewn in ability to extract an odd penny now and then from a few subscribers who really subscribe only out of courtesy. We wish that Mr. Held might come to consider amateur journalism in its higher aspects: as a medium for improvement in literature and taste; an aid to the cultivation of the art for its own sake in the manner of gentlemen, not of cheap tradesmen. The selection of commercial prosperity as a goal will ruin any true literary progress, and dull the artistic aspiration of the student as soon as his mercenary instincts shall have been satisfied. Besides, there is really no sound business principle in the so-called "sale" of little papers. No youth could ever found or sustain a real magazine of substantial price and more than nominal circulation. The various ten-cents-a-year journals which some "amateurs" try to edit are no logical steps toward actually professional publishing. The latter comes only after literary skill has been attained, and literary skill must at first be developed without regard for immediate monetary profit.

But the merit of Mr. Held's work is none the less unusual. "The Frank Friend" gives evidence of considerable critical ability, despite the touch of arrogance, apologised for in a latter issue, shewn in imperfect appreciation of Mr. Edward H. Cole's phenomenally pure English. Mr. Held, in his enthusiasm for "local colour", forgets that all the English-speaking world is heir to one glorious language which should be the same from Cape Colony to California or New York to New Zealand.

The only poem in this issue is Olive G. Owen's "How Prayest Thou?", a piece of true sentiment and artistic beauty. The only fault is metrical; the use of the word "trial" as a monosyllable. This tendency to slur over words appears to be Miss Owen's one poetical vice, as exemplified in the imperfect rendering of "jewel", "realness", and "cruelness" elsewhere.

The *Spectator* for August–September is marred by a resurrection of the ever odious topic of Consolidation, but is otherwise of remarkable merit. Elbert Hubbard, a professional advertiser and writer of considerable popularity in certain circles, relates in an interesting way the history of his most widely known literary effort. Mr. Hubbard's prose style is direct and pointed, though rather abrupt and barren. "The Midnight Extra", by Dora M. Hepner, is a humorous short story of unusual merit, leading from a well-created atmosphere of terror to a clever and unexpected anticlimax.

The Spectator for October–November contains much matter of very substantial worth. "Creation", by Edward R. Taylor, Dean of the University of California, is a beautiful bit of poetical sentiment and harmonious metre, while "Half-past-twelve", by Miss von der Heide, is likewise of great merit, both in thought and in structure. We have lately been told that many apparent metrical defects which we have noted are really no more than typographical errors, wherefore we will here content ourselves by expressing the belief that the third line of the second stanza of "Half-past-twelve" was originally written thus:

"Across the dark their shrilling laughter floats."

This rendering would do away with two seeming errors in the printed copy. Olive G. Owen's "Battle-Prayer" is powerful in its appeal and faultless in its construction. Of marked interest is "Divine Self-Tower", a brief essay by Takeshi Kanno, the Japanese philosopher. These words, in a tongue foreign to the writer, contain material for more than a moment's thought.

"The Frank Friend" is in this number as interesting a critic as before. The passage of four months has tempered his undue severity; indeed, we fear that he has in certain cases veered a little too far toward the other extreme. The most ambitious review is that of "Pig-pen Pete", by Elbert Hubbard, which gives Mr. Held an opportunity to display his powers to great advantage. Of the two editorials, that entitled "Life" is the more notable. Though its philosophy must necessarily be rather artificial, considering Mr. Held's age, it is none the less a very artistic and generally creditable piece of composition. The cover of The Spectator would be less Hearst-like if the fulsome announcements were eliminated.

Toledo Amateur for April greets us in altered form, as a two-column paper. Having given over the previous issue to the credentials of new members, Mr. Porter very justly claims a goodly space for himself this month, commenting ably on the affairs and activities of the associations.

"Camp Columbia", by James J. Hennessey, gives an interesting outline of the American army routine in Cuba during the years 1907 and 1908. "Observations of an Outsider", by Mrs. Porter, mother of the editor, sheds light on amateur journalism from a hitherto unusual angle. We note with pleasure that Toledo Amateur remains immune from the destructive bacillus of deformed spelling.

The Woodbee for April contains "The Cycle Eternal", a lucid philosophical article by Samuel James Schilling, wherein is described the dispersal and new combinations of the organic cells that compose the body of mankind. By the perpetual reincorporation or reincarnation of these cells in all other forms of matter, man is shewn to be immortal, and in the closest degree akin to every natural object surrounding him. His outward form is merely one transient phase of a ceaseless rearrangement of atoms; he is simply one aspect of infinite and eternal Nature. Save for a few slight traces of rhetorical awkwardness, Mr. Schilling's expository style is remarkable for its force and clearness; the arrangement of the essay into Prologue, Body, and Epilogue is especially favourable to comprehensiveness.

While Mr. Schilling deals with mankind in the abstract, Miss Mabel McKee, in "A Gift from the City", presents a concrete example of the workings of the human heart. Her subject and treatment are not startlingly original, but such themes lose very little when repeated in pure English and attractive style. The story is distinctly pleasing, and artistically developed throughout.

A notable feature of the April *Woodbee* is Miss Hepner's fervent and unstudied tribute to Mr. Leo Fritter, candidate for the United's Presidency. Though the editorial is bestrown with slang and distinctly familiar in construction, it produces upon the reader an impression of absolute sincerity and intensity of feeling which more elaborate rhetoric might fail so forcibly to convey. Great as is the tribute, however, we feel that Mr. Fritter is worthy of it, and must congratulate him on having such support. Our own efforts for his election, appearing in *The Conservative*, seem slight in comparison.[4] The only verse in this number is "My Shrine", by Harriet E. Daily. Though containing an attempt to rhyme the words "time" and "shrine", this ethereal little poem of spring is of great attractiveness.

*Zeppelin* for March, a publication emanating from the pen of Mr. O. S. Hackett of Canton, Pennsylvania, is scarcely as formidable and menacing as its name, being distinctly friendly and fraternal in its general tone. Mr. Hackett's prose has obviously not received its final polishing, but it is so filled with aspiration, ambition, and enthusiasm for the cause of amateur journalism, that it evidently requires only such development as is obtainable from a closer study of grammar and rhetoric, and a wider perusal of classic English literature. In one matter Mr. Hackett seems to harbour a wrong impression. The name "credential", in the language of the amateurs, is not applied to all literary productions, but only to those which are submitted by the new recruits as evidence of their educational fitness for membership in the association they seek to enter.

Joseph R. Schaffman's poem, "Think of Times Yet Coming", shews the same innate sense of rhyme and metre that has distinguished his earlier work. Only the conclusion lacks perfect ease and naturalness. Mr. Schaffman has so far confined his Muse to optimistic opinions and moral maxims; we hope that in the near future he will vary his efforts and attempt to reflect more of his general reading in his poetry. The field is large for one so happily favoured with the gift of song.

EDITOR'S NOTE  FP: *United Amateur* 14, No. 5 (May 1915): 87–92 (signed "H. P. LOVE-CRAFT, Chairman"). HPL's final column as chairman of the Department of Public Criticism for the present amateur year, although he was reappointed for the 1915–16 and 1916–17 terms.

*Notes*

1. A pseudonym of HPL. See p. 29.

2. The quotation by British poet Sir Richard Blackmore (1654–1729) has not been located. Ben Jonson (1572?–1637), *Catiline* (1611), 5.9.56–57: "The sun stood still and was . . . / . . . seen sweating . . ."

3. The comment suggests that HPL revised the work.

4. HPL, "For President—Leo Fritter" (p. 34).

## FINALE

### Campbell's Plan

As an editorial in the previous *Badger* rather sarcastically implied, amateur journalism has so far proved a practically stationary institution. Despite the customary annual assurances of a "banner year", "unexampled activity", and the like, the press associations have departed but little from a dead level of respectable mediocrity.

While the causes of this stagnation are undoubtedly many and complex, we believe that Paul J. Campbell, with his usual keen reasoning, has probed into some of the weakest spots of our hobby, and given to the amateur world a series of suggestions for improvement which deserve an immediate trial. His article in the January *United Amateur* is based on long experience in both associations, and inspired by a comprehensive knowledge of their ideals.

The United, as always, must act as the leader in the betterment of amateur journalism, so it is that body to which Mr. Campbell looks for the realisation of his aims. He would transform the *United Amateur* into a monthly magazine of from forty to fifty pages, literary as well as official, and having a circulation not only within our ranks, but extending to the high-schools and public libraries as well, thus spreading abroad the all too restricted information which would bring us recruits in immense numbers.

The Associate Editor of the *Badger*[1] can understand very clearly how eagerly many thousand aspiring persons in the outside world would rush into amateur journalism if they but knew of its existence. He himself published an amateur paper from 1903 to 1907 in absolute ignorance of his organised contemporaries,[2] and placed before the indifferent and uncritical readers of rural newspapers and cheap magazines those immature literary efforts of his which might have received a far warmer welcome and a far sounder criticism in the congenial atmosphere of the United.[3] Had he found a copy of the *United Amateur* at the high-school or library, he would certainly have enjoyed the privileges of amateur journalism for more than a decade instead of being at this moment a raw recruit. And how many thousand others have lost a decade or so in this same manner, to say nothing of those who have lived and died unsatisfied! Here, indeed, is an ample opportunity for real progress upward.

A second point touched by Mr. Campbell's able article is the present comparative difficulty of publishing papers. To the average new member, timid in the circle which is as yet strange to him, the issuing of a journal seems a thing of prodigious magnitude. The expense of printing and the difficulty of mailing loom up in terrifying proportions. According to Mr. Campbell's plan, the path would be generously smoothed for the embryonic publisher; his paper would be printed by an Official Printer who could furnish work practically at cost, and the issue would be mailed with the *United Amateur* at the responsibility of the Official Editor and for very low rates. We may safely predict that under these conditions nearly every member would become a rather frequent publisher, and the United attain an activity which might without sarcasm be regarded as new and unprecedented.

## Amateur Journalism and Education

Of immense significance to amateur journalism is Maurice W. Moe's recent campaign for carrying that institution into the high-schools. What he has already accomplished in his own school[4] is one of the brightest chapters of amateur history, and the prospect that this work may be extended to other seats of learning is inspiring in its possibilities. The rise of amateur journalism has always been retarded by the incubus of petty politics. Too often has the United been rent by juvenile dissension, and the National degraded by ring domination. The political element has ever been arrayed against the literary element. But with the entrance of teachers in large numbers on the stage of the associations, the whole atmosphere of amateurdom clears. Cultured persons of mature years and lofty ideals will be brought into contact with the membership at large, and will inevitably make their influence widely felt. Everything will be lifted above the present plane of mediocrity. The Departments of Private Criticism, our most valuable of all features, can be enlarged to pleasing proportions, and assume the additional functions of literary schools, which are now so sadly needed. The younger and cruder members will not be merely censured for their immaturity or crudeness, but will instead be told how to improve themselves; what to study and how to study; what to read and how to read.

An irresistible sentiment against political puerility will undoubtedly develop, and the offices will fall into the experienced hands of professional educators. Above all, the conception of amateur journalism as a light diversion will vanish. Frivolity and insincerity must needs be swept away before such an influx of sober-minded and high-principled scholars. Nor will the beneficial effects be felt by us alone. The advantages are mutual. The friendly and fraternal spirit of associations, particularly of the United, can be used with magnificent success by the teacher in his own life work. The class-room will become the club-room, and advanced English will change from a study to a recreation.

That this glorious dream may some time come true is far from impossible. Throughout the Middle West, that section of great possibilities, a slow but none the less substantial response to the propaganda of Mr. Moe is appearing. Of similar significance is the success of President Hepner in bringing the United to the attention of the Ohio State University's daily publication.

Cynics, particularly in the National, will continue to rail, but the day will eventually dawn when amateur journalism shall take its place of honour amongst the serious branches of education.

## Encouraging Recruits

The recent complaint of a new Providence amateur,[5] that he has failed to receive most of the papers mentioned in the season's reviews, calls the attention of the Associate Editor to the fact that he met with a similarly cold reception on the part of publishers when he joined the United not quite a year ago. Only the *Blarney Stone*, the *Woodbee*, and the *Brooklynite* reached him regularly before his appointment as Chairman of the Department of Public Criticism. As it is, he has received more journals indirectly, through the kindness of Mr. Daas or of Mr. Edward Cole, than he has from the publishers themselves.

This condition ought certainly to be remedied. The National does not profess to encourage recruits, but the United should do better. Who knows how many sensitive persons of real talent have been frozen into inactivity and resignation through lack of proper welcome? Every publisher ought to send every new member the latest number of his journal, and continue to do so unless the recruit shews his indifference by failure to acknowledge receipt. Fraternal spirit is better shewn in acts than in thoughts and words.

EDITOR'S NOTE FP: *Badger* No. 2 (June 1915): 17–16 [*sic*; the magazine was misnumbered, p. 20 being printed as 16]. HPL advocates Paul J. Campbell's amendment recommending a radical increase in the size of the official organ (the amendment did not pass) and again urges the use of amateur journalism as a tool in education. HPL was one of several assistant editors of this issue of the *Badger*, whose editor-in-chief was George S. Schilling.

*Notes*

1. I.e., HPL himself.
2. The reference is to *The Rhode Island Journal of Astronomy*, a hectographed paper. HPL neglects to mention that he briefly revived the paper in January and February 1909, and also that he edited another hectographed paper, *The Scientific Gazette* (1899, 1902–04, 1909), and produced many other juvenile scientific works.
3. HPL's mention of "rural newspapers" refers to his astronomy column for the *Pawtuxet Valley Gleaner* (Phenix, RI) (1906–08?); the mention of "cheap magazines" refers to HPL's letters and poems in the *Argosy* and *All-Story Weekly* in 1913–14, which led to his entry into amateur journalism.
4. Appleton High School (Appleton, WI). See HPL's notices for the *Pippin* (DPC, November 1914, September 1915, December 1915, April 1916, July 1917).
5. John T. Dunn, "On Acknowledgements," *Providence Amateur* 1, No. 1 (June 1915): [8–10].

# NEW DEPARTMENT PROPOSED: INSTRUCTION FOR THE RECRUIT

The swiftly mounting ideals of the United have now attained such a level, that the creation of an entirely novel and distinct department seems to be required. We have hitherto been able sufficiently to benefit our younger and less skilful recruits through contact with the older and more polished members, and through the departments of official criticism; but with our present higher aims and broader ambitions we are very obviously in need of some definite system whereby the elements of literary training may be imparted to the eager and receptive beginner.

A close inspection of the work of our new members reveals the fact that some of the most active and enthusiastic among them are sadly retarded by bad taste and want of scholarship. Not such a slight crudity as that of the high-school boy or college undergraduate, which continued study and membership in the United will smooth out in a year or two, but a fundamental deficiency in rhetoric and good reading. That the possessors of these educational defects are eminently worthy of encouragement, and responsive to friendly instruction, has been proved in nearly every case wherein such a recruit has received advice and suggestions from maturer scholars. They catch avidly at every stray precept which they find in correspondence and in the amateur press, and as Mr. Moe can well testify, they fairly besiege the critics with appeals for assistance.

But willing and earnest as may be these seekers after knowledge, it must be admitted that we have at present no means of adequately satisfying their ambitions. The critical bureaux, even when completely filled, can boast but six members, while very few of the other proficient amateurs have the time to give attention to the development of their less finished brethren. Wherefore it is quite necessary that a suitable "Department of Instruction" be established in the near future; a department which may teach in an easy and gradual manner the basic principles of grammar, rhetoric, and versification, as well as direct the aspirant to a well-graded and selected course of reading in the works of the best authors.

Since the functions of authorship and pedagogy are of an essentially different character, all amateurs not engaged in the educational profession should be debarred *ipso facto* from participation in the activities of such a department, however great their general scholarship. No fewer than six English teachers, with one placed above the rest as chairman, should form the body. The first duty would precede the formal opening of the department, and would consist of the selection of a standard elementary text-book, with suitable commentaries and adaptations to the particular needs of amateur journalism made by the department and enclosed as printed additions in the books. As a commencement of actual instruction, the annotated books should be issued to all applicants, the latter being requested to send in several specimens of their work, and to give details concerning their previous literary education. From this data, the Department of Instruction might be able intelligently to prescribe specific and progressive courses of reading for the individual needs of each aspirant; to discover the especial native talent of each undeveloped recruit, and to foster by careful instruction and advice the latent gifts thus brought to view. The pupils, until greatly advanced in their courses, should be encouraged to send their literary efforts for correction to the Department of Instruction, rather than the Department of Private Criticism, thus relieving the latter of an immense burden, and permitting it to perform its proper function, that of giving the finishing touch to manuscripts of already fair merit. The publication of pupils' efforts should be ensured as far as possible, the corrected manuscripts either being printed in a special paper or placed with the various little journals of the younger publishers.

The formation of the proposed department would undoubtedly be attended by numerous discussions concerning its text-books and general tone, yet after a little argument and compromise it seems likely that a satisfactory medium between ancient precision and modern carelessness could be determined.

The financing of the Department of Instruction would probably present the greatest difficulty of all. The reactionary element in the United might possibly oppose its creation, while the more progressive members, if called upon to support it alone, would rightly deem their burden too great. The question calls for debate, and the substantial benefits of the educational policy should be weighed against some of the less necessary sources of expense.

Several of the most prominent amateurs in the United have expressed themselves in favour of some regular system of literary instruction, and it is hoped that all the members may advance their opinions on this subject, which the steadily rising tone of our Association has brought up for consideration.

EDITOR'S NOTE  FP: *Lake Breeze* No. 20 (June 1915): 143–44 (as by "El Imparcial"). HPL advocates a Department of Instruction to help crude amateurs to develop their literary skills. No such department was ever established. The article is one of many indications that

HPL was already growing weary of the generally slovenly nature of amateur writing; in later years (see, e.g., "Amateur Journalism: Its Possible Needs and Betterment" [1920; p. 259]) he urges actual revision of literarily deficient works prior to publication.

## OUR CANDIDATE

At the meeting of March 24th The Providence Amateur Press Club unanimously endorsed the candidacy of Leo Fritter for President of the United. The reasons for such action are obvious. Mr. Fritter is fitted in every particular to represent the newer, progressive trend of thought in the association, and to assist in its transformation from a mere playground for immature politicians to a serious, dignified means of self-culture and mutual improvement. Our United has already displayed the first signs of the coming change in such ways as the teachers' movement of Mr. Moe, the campaign for high-grade recruits by Mrs. Renshaw, and the thoughtful plans for extending the usefulness of the *United Amateur* by Mr. Campbell. Amidst this era of uplift the need of a strong hand at the helm is great, and of all those qualified to hold this guiding position, none can surpass, and but few equal, Leo Fritter. Mr. Fritter is a thinker and an idealist, yet on the other hand he is a lawyer of trained mind, happily qualified to strike a balance between too much theory and too much "practical politics". The time is ripe to abandon the petty boss type of leader, for his period of usefulness is past. Needing, therefore, a man of dignity and scholarship, with a just appreciation of the epoch-making improvement which it is now undergoing, the United can hardly do otherwise than elect as its next President Mr. Leo Fritter of Columbus, Ohio.

EDITOR'S NOTE FP: *Providence Amateur* 1, No. 1 (June 1915): [3–4] (unsigned). Assigned to HPL on internal evidence. HPL was "Literary Director" of this issue of the *Providence Amateur*, and he and John T. Dunn (the Official Editor) appear to have written the entire 12-page issue.

## EXCHANGES

THE BLARNEY STONE for January–February is a welcome guest. Arthur Goodenough's poem adds the finishing touches to an issue uniformly meritorious.

THE BOYS' HERALD for May gives us an unusually clear perspective of our place in amateur affairs. Such a link with the past is an uncommon but essential element in the life of the association.

THE LAKE BREEZE for March, containing an article by one of our own Providence amateurs,[1] is a newspaper whose revival every member of the United acclaims with pleasure. Mr. Daas is to be congratulated on his able and witty refutation of Mr. Houtain's recent libels on the United.

LITERARY BUDS for April come closely to being blossoms. We have a feeling of particular kindness toward the Harvey amateurs since they sent us such an interesting puzzle picture post-card, containing their signatures and an excellent photograph of their stately high-school.

OLE MISS' for March occupies a high place in the amateur literature of the season. Mrs. Renshaw's plea for better recruits is one we shall try to attend to in our future activities. "The Humble Swallow" is a delightful sketch with a conclusion that ought to be widely heeded.

THE PIPER for May is a delightfully discriminating bit of selected verse and criticism. Mr. Kleiner's remarks on metrical precision ought to attract attention, while his lines on "The Books I Used to Read" brought up tender memories in our hearts.

THE PLAINSMAN for February is notable for Ricardo Santiago's powerful storiette, "The Bell of Huesca". Mr. Ira Cole's editorial ability is great, and we hope in July to see him elected Historian of the United.

THE SPECTATOR is indeed an ambitious magazine, but we wish that Mr. Held might shake himself free from the incubus of pseudo-professionalism.

TOLEDO AMATEUR for April is easily the best of the United's juvenile magazines. The remarks of Mrs. Porter, the editor's mother, are interesting for their point of view.

THE UNITED AMATEUR for March is the best we have yet seen, and a credit indeed to the ability of Paul J. Campbell. We trust that his plans for the official organ's future may come successfully to maturity.

THE WOODBEE for April presents us with a picture of our Presidential candidate that makes us feel better acquainted with him. Miss Hepner's beautiful tribute to Mr. Fritter convinces us that we did right in endorsing his candidacy so enthusiastically.

EDITOR'S NOTE  FP: *Providence Amateur* 1, No. 1 (June 1915): [5–6] (unsigned). Assigned to HPL on internal evidence. Comments on contemporary amateur journals.

*Notes*

1. HPL's "What Is Amateur Journalism?" (p. 28).

---

# FOR HISTORIAN—IRA A. COLE

It is with pleasure that *The Providence Amateur* announces the candidacy of Mr. Ira A. Cole of Bazine, Kansas, for the office of Historian of the United Amateur Press Association. Mr. Cole belongs to the newer, more aspiring element in amateur journalism, and his substantial achievements are eloquently attested by his wonderfully thriving Sunflower Press Club of Bazine, and his tasteful and attractive magazine, *The Plainsman*. As Western Manuscript Manager of the United Mr. Cole has displayed every qualification for the tenure of important office, and the official board would lose much by his absence therefrom. In a literary way Mr. Cole is as promising and energetic as he is in executive matters. His broad, imaginative, and poetic mind has found vent both in prose and verse. His article, "The Gods of Our Fathers", lent distinction to the November *Official Quarterly*, while his long poem, "A Dream of the Golden Age", will soon brighten the pages of *The Conservative*.[1] Mr. Ira Cole's chief interests and sympathies are centred on the growth and development of the United, and Mr. Fritter may be deemed unusually fortunate in finding so suitable a man to run on his ticket.

Both individually and as a club, the amateurs of Providence are unanimous in their endorsement of a candidate so able and earnest.

EDITOR'S NOTE   FP: *Providence Amateur* 1, No. 1 (June 1915): [10–11] (unsigned). Assigned to HPL on internal evidence. HPL's advocacy of Cole for Historian of the UAPA for
the 1915–16 term (he was in fact elected) points to his growing friendship with Cole. Later
HPL, Cole, Maurice W. Moe, and Rheinhart Kleiner formed the round-robin correspondence circle, the Kleicomolo.

*Notes*

1. It appeared in the *Conservative* (July 1915). See HPL's comment in DPC (September
1915) (p. 64).

---

# EDITORIAL

*(July 1915)*

In this, his second issue, The Conservative deems it both proper and necessary to attempt a definition of his journalistic policy, and a forecast of his future endeavours.
Though the title of the sheet affords a general index to its basic character, it is nevertheless well to describe and qualify the exact species of conservatism here represented.

That the arts of literature and literary criticism will receive prime attention from
The Conservative seems very probable. The increasing use among us of slovenly prose
and lame metre, supported and sustained by the light reviewers of the amateur press,
demands an active opponent, even though a lone one; and the profound reverence of
The Conservative for the polished writers of a more correct age fits him for a task to
which his mediocre talent might not otherwise recommend him.

When The Conservative shall have laid down his task, it is his desire that he may
be able to employ with justice the closing words of *The Rambler*, who said, over a century and a half ago: "Whatever shall be the final sentence of mankind, I have at least
endeavoured to deserve their kindness. I have laboured to refine our language to
grammatical purity, and to clear it from colloquial barbarism, licentious idioms, and
irregular combinations."[1]

Outside the domain of pure literature, The Conservative will ever be found an enthusiastic champion of total abstinence and prohibition; of moderate, healthy milita-
rism as contrasted with dangerous and unpatriotic peace-preaching; of Pan-Saxonism,
or the domination by the English and kindred races over the lesser divisions of mankind; and of constitutional or representative government, as opposed to the pernicious
and contemptible false schemes of anarchy and socialism. Though the first named of
these items may superficially appear a rather inappropriate function for a Conservative,
it must be remembered, that he who strives against the Hydra-monster Rum, strives
most to *conserve* his fellow-men.

EDITOR'S NOTE   FP: *Conservative* 1, No. 2 (July 1915): 4–5 (unsigned). HPL's bold and
somewhat smug announcement of his literary and political agenda for the *Conservative*.

*Notes*

1. Samuel Johnson, *The Rambler* No. 208 (14 March 1752).

# THE CONSERVATIVE AND HIS CRITICS

*(July 1915)*

It was remarked by Dr. Johnson in *The Idler,* that "No genius was ever blasted by the breath of criticism; the poison which, if confined, would have burst the heart, fumes away in empty hisses, and malice is set at ease with very little danger to merit".[1] Thus fortified in mind and soothed in temper by the precept of the great lexicographer, The Conservative turns to the sneers of "Bab Bell", whose anonymous remarks against his first effort at publishing appear in *The Lake Breeze* for April. Since the whole principle of anonymous censure is so ignoble, the position of "Bab Bell" robs his "submarine warfare" of its greatest force, and renders further notice unnecessary. If "Bab" has a proper sense of fairness in his composition, he will unmask before committing any more backbiting of this sort.

From such journalistic sneaking it is a relief to pass on to William B. Stoddard's frankly signed and frankly supercilious review in *The Brooklynite.* Mr. Stoddard is a man of intensely negative nature, who cannot bear the positive philosophy and definite dogmatism of The Conservative, and who must therefore be excused for his slighting allusions. However, he is a little premature in predicting the evolution of The Conservative into a careless writer of his own type.

Rheinhart Kleiner is a critic whose keenest censure may be accepted without resentment, since his honest and serious attitude raises him far above the suspicion of petty teasing and attempted cynicism. His strictures on the "art-shot" rhyme in "The Simple Speller's Tale" are just,[2] and the fault is herewith acknowledged by The Conservative. Of Mr. Kleiner's general opinions concerning "allowable" rhymes, more may later be said;[3] yet it must be emphasised that his position, however fundamentally erroneous, has much to sustain it.

It has been asserted by some biographers, that the poet Keats "died of an article".[4] If, however, the contemporaries of The Conservative hope thus to kill off the object of their censure, they sadly mistake their man. As Horace hath it:

> "Fragili quaerens illidere dentem,
> Offendet solido."[5]

To his favourable reviewers, The Conservative must express his sincerest gratitude. They have received in a truly fraternal and wisely lenient fashion the first production of a beginner, and have given him that wholesome stimulation without which the present and future issues would never have appeared. That he may improve under their kindly and encouraging suggestions, and at length become really worthy of their generous commendation, is The Conservative's cherished ambition.

EDITOR'S NOTE FP: *Conservative* 1, No. 2 (July 1915): 5–6 (unsigned). HPL defends himself against comments by other amateur journalists on his first issue of the *Conservative,* in particular his controversial political screed "The Crime of the Century" (CE5).

*Notes*

1. Samuel Johnson, *The Idler* No. 60 (9 June 1759).

2. "Indiff'rent as I was, I us'd his art / Till critics cry'd, 'My printer should be shot!'" "The Simple Speller's Tale" (AT 204). Kleiner (Piper No. 2 [May 1915]: 6) had remarked: "In Mr. Lovecraft's own verses entitled 'The Simple Speller's Tale' the word 'art' is rhymed with 'shot.' This could not be considered 'allowable' even by a very liberal interpretation of the poet's own theory."

3. See "The Allowable Rhyme" (Conservative, October 1915; CE2).

4. Byron wrote of Keats that he was "snuffed out by an article" (Don Juan [1818–24], Canto XI, stanza 60). The reference is to harsh reviews of Keats's Endymion (1818) in the Quarterly Review and Blackwood's Edinburgh Magazine (the latter by John Gibson Lockhart).

5. "[Envy] may think I'm fragile, but she'll find me a tough nut to crack." Horace, Satires 2.1.77–78 (tr. Niall Rudd).

# SOME POLITICAL PHASES

The announcement by The Lake Breeze that it will put forward no ticket in opposition to Mr. Fritter's practically clears the way for the election of The Conservative's candidate. This elimination of political warfare should afford much pleasure to an association whose best energies are dedicated to activities of a more scholarly nature. The United has lately been progressing upward by swift strides and long leaps, so that it is the duty of the members this month not only to place in power without unseemly contests an official board who will ensure a continuance of present activity, but to adopt all constitutional amendments which may facilitate their work.

The dominant ticket, so far as is known at the hour of going to press, is in part as follows:

President, Leo Fritter.
Vice Pres., Mrs. J. W. Renshaw.
Official Editor, George Schilling.
Treasurer, Paul J. Campbell.
Historian, Ira A. Cole.
Laureate Recorder, Clara Stalker.
Directors { Dora M. Hepner. / Herbert B. Darrow. / Mrs. F. Shepphird.

For these capable candidates, all of whom are distinguished by their services to the association, the votes of the amateurs are respectfully solicited. By helping to elect them, each member will assist in that enlargement and elevation of the United which is so ardently desired by all.

We are unusually fortunate this year in having as a Presidential nominee Mr. Leo Fritter, a man animated by the highest ideals, and endowed with the ability to realise them. Here is no petty politician on the one hand, and no mere dreamer on the other; but an active, sensible individual prepared to put into practice the logical principles which he has learnt from a close and discriminating observation of events and trends in amateur circles. The Conservative has no hesitancy in repeating his cry of last issue: FOR PRESIDENT, LEO FRITTER!

The amendments proposed this year are of radical nature, yet so well calculated to further the best interests of the United, that most of them must needs win the favour of a Conservative. They are integral parts of the great progressive movement inaugurated by the Southern and Middle Western members.

Amendment I, creating a laureateship for publishers, is least of all connected with this upward literary trend, yet has much to recommend it. Printing is an art in itself, and one which in its best phases requires far more cultivation and taste than the average person imagines. The typographical achievements of Edward Cole afford almost as much real pleasure to his fellow-amateurs as do his forcefully phrased compositions, and such art as this deserves some form of recognition. The Conservative cannot bring himself to disapprove the amendment as proposed by that energetic young publisher, Mr. Dowdell.

Amendment II would destroy the "cut price of admission" so bitterly ridiculed by partisans of the National; yet as Mr. Daas has pointed out, it might have a tendency to exclude the high-school pupils who are so much desired as recruits. It is doubtful if the increased revenue and increased dignity would repay the United for the decreased number of promising young novices.

Amendment III should be adopted by unanimous vote. The restriction of membership to the North American continent is the summit of folly. Why should we not spread through the whole Anglo-Saxon world, fostering amateur journalism wherever our language is spoken and written? Besides, many Americans and Englishmen residing in foreign countries might be gained, if the United were open to them.

Most vital of all the proposed amendments to the United's immediate progress is the fourth, which provides for a monthly official organ, to be printed uniformly by a regularly established Official Publisher. The adoption of this idea would liberate the Official Editor from his most pressing cares, leaving him free to perform his purely editorial and literary duties in peace. It would likewise eliminate the irregularities in volumes of *The United Amateur*, which arise from the employment of different printers. Mr. E. E. Ericson of Wisconsin, celebrated for his excellence throughout amateur circles, would undoubtedly become Official Publisher, so that nothing need be said concerning the typographical quality of the proposed new monthly organ. Let every member of the United support this extremely desirable amendment.

Amendment V is a solution of the ex-President problem which should have been thought of long ago. The present situation, with half our former executives either indifferent or hostile to the United, yet nominally active, is intolerable. Let the chief officials retire to honorary membership, as Mr. Daas proposes, when they have ceased to participate in the various activities of the association.

Concerning the Convention seat for 1916, The Conservative cannot see what city but Cleveland, active in clubs and publishing, has any valid claim to the honour. Ohio is the logical state, being practically the centre of the amateur world, and Cleveland is the logical city, since Columbus has so lately had a convention. The arguments for Newark are negligible. The Blue Pencil Club of Brooklyn, which would predominate there, is primarily a National body, whilst the Newark boys are all semi-professionals with mercantile rather than literary aspirations.

EDITOR'S NOTE   FP: *Conservative* 1, No. 2 (July 1915): 6–8 (unsigned). HPL recommends the election of selected officers for the UAPA at the coming convention. Of the candidates in question, Fritter became President; HPL himself became First Vice-President, and Anne Tillery (Mrs. J. W.) Renshaw became Second Vice-President; Edward F. Daas became Official Editor, but resigned in the middle of his term and was replaced by George S. Schilling; Ira A. Cole became Historian; the fate of the other candidates is unknown. Of the amendments, the first two failed and the last three passed.

# INTRODUCING MR. JOHN RUSSELL

During the winter of 1913–14 The Conservative was engaged in an extremely heated controversy concerning the merits of a certain author whose work appeared in one of the popular magazines of the day. The letters of the disputants, both in prose and in verse, were printed in the magazine, and among them appeared both the formal heroics of The Conservative, and the neat octosyllabics of one John Russell, Esq., of Tampa, Florida. Mr. Russell and The Conservative, who were arrayed against each other in the metric fray, were each separately invited by Mr. Edward Daas to join the United, but while The Conservative responded eagerly and almost immediately, his opponent deferred action. Meanwhile a peace had been sealed betwixt the contending bards, and a correspondence established, in which The Conservative continued to urge what Don Eduardo had first mentioned; the result now appearing in Mr. Russell's advent to the association.

John Russell, whose present address is General Delivery, West Tampa, is a true-born Scotsman, being a native of Penicuik, near Edinburgh. The patriotism of his family is attested by the presence of his two nephews at the front in Belgium, one with the Gordon Highlanders and the other with a Canadian regiment. Mr. Russell's poetry has appeared in the public press of Scotland, Canada, and the United States, and possesses a tersely epigrammatical and at times brilliant satirical style all its own. Though proficient in classic English, it is in the quaint speech of Caledonia that Mr. Russell chiefly excels. Of this delightful dialect he is a perfect master, and his well-constructed lines are redolent of the atmosphere of North Britain. Upon joining the United, one of Mr. Russell's first acts was to dedicate a poem to the Blue-Stocking Club of Rocky Mount, whose study of Robert Burns at once aroused his interest. This poem, based on the motto of the club, appears in these pages, and affords a striking example of the new member's ability in verse.[1]

We are indeed fortunate in having among us so able a specimen of the race which produced an Arbuthnot, a Ramsay, a Thomson, a Smollett, a Hume, a Blair, a Lord Kames, an Adam Smith, a Campbell, a Scott, a Carlyle, and a Stevenson.[2]

EDITOR'S NOTE  FP: *Conservative* 1, No. 2 (July 1915): 8–9 (unsigned). HPL welcomes his erstwhile literary opponent, who battled him in verse in the letter column of the *Argosy* over the merits of romance writer Fred Jackson, author of numerous romantic serials in the *Argosy*. The incident led directly to HPL's entry into amateur journalism; but whereas HPL joined almost immediately when invited by Edward F. Daas, Russell appears to have waited a full year before joining the UAPA.

*Notes*

1. The poem was not published in the *Conservative* for July 1915, nor in any other issue.

2. HPL refers to a succession of notable literary Scotsmen: John Arbuthnot (1667–1735), physician, essayist, satirist, and friend of Pope and Swift; Allan Ramsay (1686–1758), poet; James Thomson (1700–1748), poet and author of *The Seasons* (1726–30), one of HPL's favourite poems; Tobias Smollett (1721–1771), novelist; David Hume (1711–1776), philosopher and essayist; Hugh Blair (1718–1800), author of *Lectures on Rhetoric and Belles-Lettres* (1784); Henry Home, Lord Kames (1696–1782), philosopher and aesthetician; Adam Smith (1723–1790), political philosopher; Thomas Campbell (1777–1844), poet; Thomas Carlyle (1795–1881), essayist and historian; and Robert Louis Stevenson (1850–1894), novelist.

# IN A MAJOR KEY

It was lately the good fortune of The Conservative to receive from The Blue Pencil Club a pamphlet entitled *In a Minor Key*, whose phenomenal excellence furnishes emphatic evidence that the old National still retains some members who would have done it credit even in its palmiest days. But great as may be the literary merit of the publication, its astonishing radicalism of thought cannot but arouse an overwhelming chorus of opposition from the saner elements in amateur journalism.

Charles D. Isaacson, the animating essence of the publication, is a character of remarkable quality. Descended from the race that produced a Mendelssohn, he is himself a musician of no ordinary talent,[1] whilst as a man of literature he is worthy of comparison with his co-religionists Moses Mendez and Isaac D'Israeli.[2] But the very spirituality which gives elevation to the Semitic mind partially unfits it for the consideration of tastes and trends in Aryan thought and writings, hence it is not surprising that he is a radical of the extremest sort.

From an ordinary man, the acclamation of degraded Walt Whitman as the "Greatest American Thinker" would come as an insult to the American mind, yet with Mr. Isaacson one may but respectfully dissent. Penetrating and forgetting the unspeakable grossness and wildness of the erratic bard, our author seizes on the one spark of truth within, and magnifies it till it becomes for him the whole Whitman. The Conservative, in speaking for the sounder faction of American taste, is impelled to give here his own lines on Whitman, written several years ago as part of an essay on the modern poets:[3]

> Behold great *Whitman*, whose licentious line
> Delights the rake, and warms the souls of swine;
> Whose fever'd fancy shuns the measur'd pace,
> And copies Ovid's filth without his grace.
> In his rough brain a genius might have grown,
> Had he not sought to play the brute alone;
> But void of shame, he let his wit run wild,
> And liv'd and wrote as Adam's bestial child.
> Averse to culture, strange to humankind,
> He never knew the pleasures of the mind.
> Scorning the pure, the delicate, the clean,
> His joys were sordid, and his morals mean.

Thro' his gross thoughts a native vigour ran,
From which he deem'd himself the perfect man:
But want of decency his rank decreas'd,
And sunk him to the level of the beast.
Would that his Muse had dy'd before her birth,
Nor spread such foul corruption o'er the earth.

Mr. Isaacon's views on race prejudice, as outlined in his *Minor Key,* are too subjective to be impartial. He has perhaps resented the more or less open aversion to the children of Israel which has ever pervaded Christendom, yet a man of his perspicuity should be able to distinguish this illiberal feeling, a religious and social animosity of one white race toward another white and equally intellectual race, from the natural and scientifically just sentiment which keeps the African black from contaminating the Caucasian population of the United States. The negro is fundamentally the biological inferior of all White and even Mongolian races, and the Northern people must occasionally be reminded of the danger which they incur in admitting him too freely to the privileges of society and government.

Mr. Isaacson's protest is directed specifically against a widely advertised motion picture, "The Birth of a Nation",[4] which is said to furnish a remarkable insight into the methods of the Ku-Klux-Klan, that noble but much maligned band of Southerners who saved half of our country from destruction at the close of the Civil War. The Conservative has not yet witnessed the picture in question, but he has seen both in literary and dramatic form *The Clansman,* that stirring, though crude and melodramatic story by Rev. Thomas Dixon, Jr., on which "The Birth of a Nation" is based,[5] and has likewise made a close historical study of the Ku-Klux-Klan,[6] finding as a result of his research nothing but Honour, Chivalry, and Patriotism in the activities of the Invisible Empire. The Klan merely did for the people what the law refused to do, removing the ballot from unfit hands and restoring to the victims of political vindictiveness their natural rights. The alleged lawbreaking of the Klan was committed only by irresponsible miscreants who, after the dissolution of the Order by its Grand Wizard, Gen. Nathan Bedford Forrest, used its weird masks and terrifying costumes to veil their unorganised villainies.

Race prejudice is a gift of Nature, intended to preserve in purity the various divisions of mankind which the ages have evolved. In comparing this essential instinct of man with political, religious, and national prejudices, Mr. Isaacson commits a serious error of logic.

The Conservative dislikes strong language, but he feels that he is not exceeding the bounds of propriety in asserting that the publication of the article entitled "The Greater Courage" is a crime which in a native American of Aryan blood would be deserving of severe legal punishment. This appeal to the people to refuse military service when summoned to their flag is an outrageous attack on the lofty principles of patriotism which have turned this country from a savage wilderness to a mighty band of states; a slur on the honour of our countrymen, who from the time of King Philip's War to the present have been willing to sacrifice their lives for the preservation of their families, their nation, and their institutions. Mr. Isaacson, however, must be excused for his words, since some of his phrases shew quite clearly that he is only following the common anarchical fallacy, believing that wars are forced upon the masses by tyrannical rulers. This belief, extremely popular a few months ago, has received a rude blow through the acts of the Italian people in forcing their reluctant government to join the

Allies. The socialistic delusion becomes ridiculous when its precepts are thus boldly reversed by facts. Bryan is out of the way at last,[7] and in spite of Mr. Isaacson and his hyphenated fellow-pacifists, the real American people, the descendants of Virginian and New England Christian Protestant colonists, will remain ever faithful to the Stars and Stripes, even though forced to meet enemies at home as well as abroad.

EDITOR'S NOTE  FP: *Conservative* 1, No. 2 (July 1915): 9–11 (unsigned). HPL directs sharp comments toward Charles D. Isaacson's amateur journal *In a Minor Key* No. 1 (undated, but issued in the early summer of 1915), in regard to both his literary and his political views. Isaacson (and his colleague James F. Morton) battled back in the next issue of *In a Minor Key*; see "The Conservative and His Critics" (October 1915) (p. 73).

*Notes*

1. See n. 1 to DPC (March 1915).
2. Moses Mendez (d. 1758), poet and dramatist; Isaac D'Israeli (1766–1848), father of Benjamin Disraeli and best known for *Curiosities of Literature* (1791–1834) and other collections of literary anecdotes.
3. The "essay" apparently is non-extant. Like Pope's *Essay on Criticism*, it may have been entirely in verse. HPL's lines on Robert Browning (see AT 193) may have been part of the same "essay."
4. *The Birth of a Nation* (D. W. Griffith Corp., 1915), produced and directed by D. W. Griffith; starring Lillian Gish, Mae Marsh, and Henry Walthall. See SL 1.89 for HPL's brief comment on the film.
5. Thomas Dixon, Jr. (1864–1946), *The Clansman: An Historical Romance of the Ku Klux Klan* (1905), dramatized by Dixon as *The Clansman: An American Drama* (1905; not published). HPL owned Dixon's *The Leopard's Spots* (1902; LL 253), another racist novel.
6. HPL may be referring to a book in his library, John C. Lester and D. L. Wilson's *Ku Klux Klan: Its Origin, Growth and Disbandment* (1905; LL 528).
7. William Jennings Bryan (1860–1925) was appointed Secretary of State by President Woodrow Wilson in 1913 but resigned on 8 June 1915 after Wilson delivered a stern rebuke to Germany upon its sinking of the *Lusitania*.

---

# AMATEUR NOTES

Fletcher Otto Baxley's *Alabamian* is assuming an unique and necessary place in the United. Mr. Baxley is devoting his entire time to the encouragement of our poets, who seem rather neglected elsewhere. The amateur world would much appreciate information concerning both the author and translator of the exquisite nature poem "From the Spanish", in the Spring number; though perhaps, like Mrs. Browning's "Sonnets from the Portuguese", this poem is not so foreign as it seems.

In order to satisfy conjecture, The Conservative wishes to state that the peculiar appearance of his preceding issue was wholly unintentional. But for a mistake due to haste and a stupid printer, the paper would have been a conventional 8-page sheet like *The Lake Breeze*.[1]

EDITOR'S NOTE FP: *Conservative* 1, No. 2 (July 1915): 11 (unsigned).

*Notes*

1. The first issue of the *Conservative* was apparently printed locally. It was in fact 8 pages in length, but the pages were unnumbered and were printed in single columns rather than double columns as in the *Lake Breeze* and many other amateur papers.

---

# THE DIGNITY OF JOURNALISM

It is a particular weakness of the modern American press, that it seems unable to use advantageously the language of the nation. While our speech is probably the most forceful and expressive of modern tongues, combining as it does the vigour of the Teutonic with the precision of the Latin elements, the journalistic fraternity have apparently lost completely the art of employing its admirable words and phrases in their compositions. In lieu of correct English, these careless scribes have found it necessary to resort to the jargon of the street, the prize ring, and the bar room, whence they have imported a select assortment of idioms, generically known as "slang"; which, construed in sentences of rustic and plebeian mould, they are endeavouring to foist upon us as a language.

That corrupt forms of speech have existed in all ages and in all countries we cannot doubt. Plautus gives us hints of the idiomatic vagaries of the Roman republic, whilst Petronius Arbiter shews effectively the vulgar patois of imperial Rome. Indeed, the extinction of culture by the Gothic invaders ultimately brought Latin slang to the surface, creating the modern Romance languages. But the plight of America is very different. Here we find no such contempt for the common tongue as existed among the scholars and writers of the Roman period; instead, the pernicious vulgarisms of the rabble are creeping upward into the speech of the most cultured, where they are received with a dangerously increasing favour.

For the use of this barbaric caricature of English, two principal theories have been advanced; first, that it is more conducive to forcible expression and ready comprehension than is correct language; and second, that it lends to reading and discourse an animation otherwise unattainable.

The reason first assigned is, if true, a shameful confession of clownishness on our part. Our language is above all others direct and clear, with the straightforwardness of its Teutonic skeleton and the exactness of its Latin vocabulary. No person in the least familiar with the English classics can justly complain that the language wants force and perspicuity. Nor is the use and appreciation of this excellence necessarily the result of long study. The average man's stock of words includes all that are needed for pure and emphatic expression, were the possessor but free from contaminating familiarity with corrupt diction. There is nothing which cannot be better said or written in good English than in slang, save among the lowest and most vicious classes, which latter scarcely constitute the general reading public.

The idea that slang-infested literature is more readable and pleasing than that which conforms to refined taste is nearly parallel to that of the Italian peasant immigrant, who fondly considers his soiled but flaming kerchief and other greasy but gaudy apparel far more beautiful than the spotless white linen and plain, neat suit of the American for whom he works. While good English may in unskilful hands sometimes become monotonous, this defect cannot justify the introduction of a dialect gathered from thieves, ploughboys, and chimney sweeps. The reader, if disgusted with a dull author's use of the language, should turn to the masters of literature, with whose grace, animation, and general excellence no fault can be found. If any user of slang can excel in fluent ease the sentences of an Addison or a Steele, he does well indeed. As in the matter of clearness, this seeming ease of slang is merely a sign of poor culture. If the public could abandon its indolence long enough to appreciate the artistic possibilities of well-used English, slang would retreat to the slums and low dens whence first it emanated.

The pernicious platitude, 'that the slang of today is the classic language of tomorrow', is best refuted by a perusal of any one of the numerous dictionaries of slang and Americanisms.[1] Therein will be found thousands of colloquial words and phrases, which, though on the tip of the vulgar tongue of yesterday, are today absolutely unintelligible. Many of the old terms and constructions which have been retained are at this moment no nearer adoption than when in their infancy; those which have actually entered the language are few indeed as compared with the whole.

In the United Amateur Press Association the effects of colloquial composition are beheld at their worst. Three-quarters of our writers possess styles so contaminated with deliberate violations of journalistic dignity, that their works send a shudder through the sensitive system. This tendency extends not alone through the domain of lighter literature, but reaches to the serious editorial and even to the weighty official report.

That something must be done to correct the increasing evil is obvious. Amateur authors and editors guilty of consciously bad English must be brought to a realisation of their dereliction, and to an understanding of the vulgar example which they are setting to the younger recruits. In *The Olympian* may be found a model of pure English which ought to be followed with the greatest assiduity. This magazine, apart from its own literary worth, is valuable as a perpetual refutation of the fallacy that amateur papers cannot be made interesting without slang. Not so long as Edward Cole remains in the field of amateur journalism have we the right to plead the necessity, or even the expediency, of debasing the dignity of our art.

EDITOR'S NOTE FP: *Dowdell's Bearcat* 4, No. 4 (July 1915): [6–9]. A screed against the use of slang in amateur writing. For a poetic squib on the subject, see the untitled quatrain in the *Conservative* (April 1915); rpt. *AT* 206. The final sentence has been corrected in accordance with HPL's remark in DPC (September 1915).

*Notes*

1. HPL had such a dictionary in his library: John Russell Bartlett's *Dictionary of Americanisms* (4th ed. 1877; LL 68).

# DEPARTMENT OF PUBLIC CRITICISM

(September 1915)

*T*he *Alabamian* for Spring is a magazine unique amongst the publications of the United. Devoted wholly to poetry, it contains some of the finest short verses to appear this season, whilst even the crudest part of its contents possesses some undoubted merit. The opening poem, a delightful and ornate nature sonnet entitled "The Brook", professes to be a translation from the Spanish, a claim borne out by the use of the word "jasmine" in a place where the metre throws the accent anomalously on the last syllable, as in the corresponding Spanish word "jazmin". The sentiment of the whole is exquisite, and every image exhibits striking beauty. It is to be regretted that both author and translator are suffered to remain unrevealed. "A Poet's Songs", by Miss Owen, is a powerful and well-written tribute to her fellow-bards both ancient and modern. In Coralie Austin's "Tribute to Our President", dedicated to Miss Hepner, we may discern the native talent of the true poet, slightly obscured by the crudities of youth. The opening line appears to lack a syllable, though this may be due only to the printer's omission of the article before the word "laurel". In stanza 1, line 2, the trisyllabic word "violets" appears as a dissyllable. This contraction is a rather natural one, and must not be criticised too sternly. Indeed, there is here a sort of middle zone betwixt error and allowableness, wherein no decisive precepts may be laid down. Words like "radiant", "difference", and so forth, are nearly always slurred into dissyllables, and we were ourselves guilty of an even greater liberalism when we wrote that line in "Quinsnicket Park" which reads:

"The bending boughs a *diamond* wealth amass."[1]

But in Miss Austin's second stanza occur two errors of graver nature. "For only her alone" is a lamentably tautological line which requires the omission either of "only" or "alone", and the substitution of some word to carry on the flow of the metre. The attempted rhyming of "alone" and "home" is obviously incorrect. The dissimilar consonantal sounds render agreement impossible. This "m-n" rhyme, as we may call it, is becoming alarmingly frequent in careless modern verse, and must ever be avoided with utmost diligence. In the third stanza we discover a marked error in maintenance of number. We are told that the "years go" and that at "its end" we will lay trophies, etc. This mistake may be obviated with ease, by changing "years go" to "year goes". Miss Austin's poetic talent is real, but shews the want of precise cultivation. "Mother o' Mine", by Miss von der Heide, is a beautiful piece of anapaestic verse whose metre and sentiment alike attract the reader. "Parsifal", by Miss Owen, shews satisfactory depth of thought, but is rather modern in metre. From the conformation of the last line of the first stanza, we are led to believe that the word "viol" is contracted to a monosyllable, or, to make a rather reprehensible pun, that "vi-ol" has here a "vile" pronunciation. "Frailties of Life", by Editor Baxley, shews a remarkable system of extended rhyming, coupled with a noticeable lack of metrical harmony. Mr. Baxley's technique is such that we believe his improvement would be best effected by a repeated perusal of the older poets, whose classical exactitude of form would teach him rhythm by rote, so to speak. Let him cultivate his ear for metre, even though forced to acquire it through nonsensical jingles. We believe that many a child has obtained from his "Mother Goose" a love of correct rhythm which has later helped him in serious poetical efforts. "Paid Back", a short, powerful poem by Miss von der Heide, concludes an excellent and praiseworthy issue.

*Aurora* for April is a delightful individual leaflet by Mrs. Ida C. Haughton, exclusively devoted to poetical matters. The first poem, "Aurora", is truly exquisite as a verbal picture of the summer dawn, though rather rough-hewn metrically. Most open to criticism of all the features of this piece, is the dissimilarity of the separate stanzas. In a stanzaic poem the method of rhyming should be identical in every stanza, yet Mrs. Haughton has here wavered between couplets and alternate rhymes. In the opening stanza we behold first a quatrain, then a quadruple rhyme. In the second we find couplets only. In the third a quatrain is followed by an arrangement in which two rhyming lines enclose a couplet, while in the final stanza the couplet again reigns supreme. The metre also lacks uniformity, veering from iambic to anapaestic form. These defects are, of course, merely technical, not affecting the beautiful thought and imagery of the poem; yet the sentiment would seem even more pleasing were it adorned with the garb of metrical regularity. "On the Banks of Old Wegee" is a sentimental poem of considerable merit, which suffers, however, from the same faults that affect "Aurora". Most of these defects might have been obviated when the stanzas were composed, by a careful counting of syllables in each line, and a constant consultation of some one, definite plan of rhyming. We must here remark an error made in the typewritten copy of the original manuscript, and reproduced in the finished magazine, for which, of course, neither the poetical art of the author nor the technique of the printer is to blame.[2] In the second stanza, lines 6 and 7 were originally written:

> "How oft I've essayed to be
> A fisherman bold, but my luck never told."

"Anent the Writing of Poetry" is a short prose essay, in which many valuable truths are enunciated. Mrs. Haughton has evidently taken up the poetic art with due seriousness, and considering the marked talent shewn in the first issue of her paper, we may justly expect to behold a wonderfully rapid development in the near future.

*The Badger* for June fulfils the promise of January, and shews us that the present year has given the United a new and serious periodical of satisfying quality. In the "Introductory", Mr. George Schilling discusses in lively fashion the latest topics of the day, thereby atoning for our own tedious "Finale".[3] "Ready Made", by Samuel J. Schilling, is a thoughtful presentation of a lamentable fact. The evil which he portrays is one that has rendered the masses of America almost wholly subservient to the vulgar press; to be led astray into every sort of radicalism through low tricks of sensationalism. Our own poetical attempt, entitled "Quinsnicket Park", contains 112 lines, and spoils three and a half otherwise excellent pages. It is probable that but few have had the fortitude to read it through, or even to begin it, hence we will pass over its defects in merciful silence. "What May I Own?", by A. W. Ashby, is an able sociological essay which displays considerable familiarity with the outward aspects of economic conditions. Mr. Ashby, condemning the present system practiced in the coal and iron industries, declares that on moral grounds he had rather be a brewer or purveyor of liquor than a coal magnate or an ironmaster. In this statement, evidently born of hasty fervour, Mr. Ashby forgets the basic character of the two types of industry which he contrasts. Beneath the liquor traffic lies a foundation accursed by decency and reason. The entire industry is designed to pander to a false craving whose gratification lowers man in the scale of mental and physical evolution. The distiller and vendor of rum is elementally the supreme foe of the human race, and the most powerful, dangerous, and treacherous factor in the defiance of progress and the betrayal of mankind. His trade can never be improved or purified, being itself a crime against Nature. On the other hand, the coal and iron industries are, in their fundamental forms, desirable and necessary adjuncts to an expanding civilisation. Their present evils are wholly alien to their essential principles, being connected only with the uneasy industrialism of this age. These faults are not confined to coal-mining and iron-working, but are merely those possessed in common with all great industries. Joseph E. Shufelt's article on the European war is an amazing outburst of socialism in its worst form. The idea that this shocking carnage is the result of a deliberate plot of the ruling classes of all the belligerents to destroy their labouring element is wonderfully ludicrous in its extravagance. We are led to infer that those best of friends, der Kaiser and his cousins George and Nicholas, are merely pretending hostility in order to rid themselves of a troublesome peasantry! We do not know what Mr. Shufelt has been reading lately, but we hope that time may modify his ideas to such a degree that he will turn his dignified style and pure English to some object worthy of their employment.

Dowdell's Bearcat for July marks the beginning of an unprecedented era of improvement in the quality of that periodical. Having settled down to the conventional 5 × 7 size, it has now acquired a cover and an abundance of pages which the editor informs us will never be lessened. The influence of The Olympian is perceptible in the Bearcat, and for his taste in the selection of so worthy a model Mr. Dowdell is to be commended. "When the Tape Broke" is the first article of the editorial column, and well describes an example of collapsed activity which the United should avoid. "A Runaway Horse", by Mrs. Ida C. Haughton, is a brief and vivid sketch of a fatal accident. "Tragedy", an exquisite poem by Emilie C. Holladay, deserves very favourable notice for the delicate pathos of its sentiment, and perfect adaptation of the measure to the subject. We may discern a few traces of immaturity in the handling of the metre and in the presence of "allowable" rhymes. As elsewhere stated, we personally approve and employ the old-fashioned "allowable" rhyming sounds, but the best modern taste, as exemplified in the United by its Laureate, Rheinhart Kleiner, demands absolute perfection in this regard. As to the metre, we respectfully offer the following amended second stanza as an example. It is absolutely uniform with the original first stanza, which, of course, furnishes the model.

> The summer rains
> And autumn winds
> The snowdrop find yet standing;
> A petal gone,
> And all alone,
> Her tender roots expanding.

The remarkable poetical talent exhibited by Miss Holladay deserves a cultivation that shall invest her productions with a technique of the highest order. "The Dignity of Journalism", by ourselves, may be taken by the reader as a sort of supplement to this Department. We there enumerate in the abstract some of the precepts which we shall here apply to individual writers. There are several misprints, which we hope will not be taken as evidences of our bad spelling, and at the conclusion the word "even" is omitted from the phrase which should read: "the necessity, or *even* the expediency." "June Journals" is an excellent set of short reviews which display very favourably the critical ability of Mr. Dowdell. The concluding notes on "Amateur Affairs" are brief, but very interesting. The general excellence of Dowdell's Bearcat excuses the instances of imperfect proof-reading, which fault we are sure will soon be eliminated.

The Blarney Stone for March–April contains "Thoughts", a meritorious poem by Chester P. Munroe.[4] The tone of the piece is that of sentimental and almost melancholy reverie, hence the metre is not quite uniform; but a commendable absence of rough breaks lends a delightful flow to the lines. We hope to behold further efforts from Mr. Munroe's pen. "The Amateur's Creed", by Mrs. Renshaw, is written in the style of this author's previous and now well-known poem, "A Symphony", and should do much toward lifting the United upward to the highest literary ideals.

The Blarney Stone for May–June has cast off all undue seriousness, and teems with light and attractive matter concerning the recent Rocky Mount convention. Some of the displays of wit and cleverness are very striking and entertaining indeed, while no page departs so far from merit that it may be justly adjudged as dull.

The Boys' Herald for August is an issue of unusual elaborateness, announcing the engagement of its editor, Mr. Edwin Hadley Smith, and Miss Nita Edna Gerner of New York. Excellent portraits of the happy couple follow the formal announcement, and Miss Gerner, now Associate Editor, describes in an excellent prose style the romance which culminated in the engagement. "Gerneriana", consisting mainly of a reprint from an earlier issue, is an interesting account of the late Richard Gerner, an old-time amateur, and father of the prospective bride. This article is well supplemented by the reproductions of parts of old amateur papers which adorn the back cover of the magazine. The remainder of The Boys' Herald is wholly statistical, dealing with the amateur career of Mr. Smith. Few members of the association could produce superior records of activity.

The Brooklynite for April maintains the high standard set by the previous number. "A Miracle", the opening poem, was composed by Alice L. Carson during the course of a meeting of the Blue Pencil Club, yet exhibits all the grace and harmony expected in a carefully planned and laboriously polished work. "Spring Thoughts", by A. M. Adams, is a humorous prose masterpiece by the National's new Critic. Seldom is the amateur press favoured with such a well-sustained succession of brilliant epigrams. Miss Owen's "Ode to Trempealeau Mountain" is a noble specimen of heroic blank verse, containing some very striking antithetical lines. The title, however, is a misnomer, since a true ode is necessarily of irregular form. "Some Late Amateur Magazines", by W. B. Stoddard, is a series of brief, informal reviews. As a critic, Mr. Stoddard shews considerable discernment, though having a rather unpleasant air of conscious superiority in certain places. A little more stateliness of style would add to the force of his criticisms. "Spring" reveals Rheinhart Kleiner in his favourite domain of amatory verse. Mr. Kleiner's tuneful numbers and pure diction render his poetry ever a delight. "Rebellion", by Miss von der Heide, is a metrically perfect piece of verse whose artistry is marred only by the use of the unpoetical philosophical term "subconscious" instead of "unconscious".

The Brooklynite for July is of especial interest as the first paper to print an account of the Rocky Mount convention. This description, from the facile and versatile pen of Miss von der Heide, is of distinctly informal character, yet is none the less interesting as an animated chronicle of an enjoyable event. Rheinhart Kleiner's account of the National convention is more dignified, and may be considered as a model for this sort of composition. Mr. Kleiner shines as brightly in prose as in verse, and each day surprises us with revelations of excellence in various dissimilar departments of literature.

The Conservative for July is notable for Ira Cole's delightfully pantheistic poem, "A Dream of the Golden Age". The unusual poetic genius of Mr. Cole has been revealed but recently, yet the imaginative qualities pervading some of his prose long ago gave indications of this gift. The pantheistic, Nature-worshipping mind of our author lends to his productions an unique and elusive atmosphere which contrasts very favourably with the earthy tone of some of our less fanciful bards. Metrically, Mr. Cole adopts instinctively the regular, conservative forms of a saner generation. In this specimen of heroic verse he inclines toward the practice of Keats, and does not always confine simple thoughts to single couplets in the manner of the eighteenth-century poets. We believe that Mr. Cole is commencing a successful career as a United poet, and await the day when he shall be accorded the honour of a laureateship.

*The Coyote* for July reveals a wonderful improvement over the March number, both in the literary quality of its contributions and in general editorial excellence. Never before have we seen the perfect amateur spirit acquired so quickly as in Mr. Harrington's case. "Night Fancies", by Helen H. Salls, is a sonnet of exceptional power and artistry, whose faultless metre is equalled only by its bold and striking images. Amidst this profusion of excellent metaphor, it is difficult to select individual instances for particular praise, but we might commend especially the passage:

> ". . . the stars still keep
> Afloat like boats that black sky-billows ride."

Miss Salls is clearly an amateur poet of the first rank, and it is to be hoped that she will be a liberal contributor to United magazines. "The Rebirth of the British Empire", by William T. Harrington, is a clear and concise exposition of the virtues whereby Old England maintains her proud position as Mistress of the Seas, and chief colonial empire of the world. The style of the essay is admirable, and well exhibits the progressive qualities of Mr. Harrington. "An Ideal", by Nettie Hartman, is a short poem of pleasing sentiment and harmonious metre. The notes on amateur affairs are interesting and well composed, revealing Mr. Harrington's increasing enthusiasm for the cause.

*Dowdell's Bearcat* for May is another striking illustration of the improvement which can affect a paper within a very short time. Since last October Mr. Dowdell has been progressing swiftly toward journalistic excellence, and even this cleverly conceived and uniquely shaped issue fails to mark the limit of his ambition. "Knowest Thou?", by Mrs. Renshaw, is an expressive tribute to a nation whose recent infamies can never wholly becloud its rugged virtues. "With Nature I Rejoice" is probably the best poem which Joseph R. Schaffman has yet written. As his remarkable talent matures, the didactic element in his verse is gradually giving way to the more purely poetic, and this latest effort is one of which he may be justly proud. Concerning Mr. Dowdell's own spirited prose, we need only repeat the previous suggestion, that a trifle less slang would add much to its force and dignity.

*Dowdell's Bearcat* for May 26 contains another poem by Mrs. Renshaw whose national tone is not likely to be popular just now outside the country to which it refers; in fact, Editor Dowdell has deemed it wise to make an apologetic statement concerning it. However, if we call "Ein Mann" Col. Theodore Roosevelt, and shift the scene to San Juan Hill, we may be able to appreciate the real patriotism delineated.

*Dowdell's Bearcat* for June is wholly given over to notes of the amateur world. Mr. Dowdell is indeed a pleasing young writer, and leaves none of his topics without a characteristic touch of light adornment.

*The Lake Breeze* for April is distinguished by James L. Crowley's poem entitled "April", a brief lyric of marked merit, highly expressive of the season. "Writing Poetry", an essay by Dora M. Hepner, is a clear and tasteful analysis of the poet's art and inspiration. "The Norwegian Recruit", a dialect monologue by Maurice W. Moe, is the leading feature of this issue. This exquisite bit of humour, recited by Mr. Moe at the United's 1913 convention, is a sketch of rare quality. "The Amateur Press", now firmly established as a column of contributed reviews, is this month of substantial size and fair quality. It is needless to say that the news pages are interesting, and that the paper as a whole well maintains the high reputation it has ever enjoyed.

The Lake Breeze for June apparently opens an era of unprecedented improvement, being of distinctly literary rather than political nature. The plea for a Department of Instruction is a just one, and ought to meet with response from some of our pedagogical members.[5] "Broken Metre", by Mrs. Renshaw, is an attempt at defending the popular atrocities committed in the name of freedom by the modern poets. While the article is superficially quite plausible, we feel that the settled forms of regular metre have too much natural justification thus to be disturbed. The citation of Milton, intended to strengthen Mrs. Renshaw's argument, really weakens it; for while he undoubtedly condemns rhyme, he laments in the course of this very condemnation the lame metre which is sometimes concealed by apt rhyming. "Some Views on Versification", by Clara I. Stalker, is an essay written from a sounder and more conservative point of view. The middle course in poetical composition, which avoids alike wild eccentricities and mechanical precision, has much to recommend it, and Miss Stalker does well to point out its virtues. However, we do not see why even the few irregularities which are here said to be inevitable, cannot be smoothed out by the bard without destroying the sense of his poetry. "Disappointment", by Mrs. Maude K. Barton, is a clever piece of light verse whose sprightly humour makes up for its slight metrical roughness. The imperfect but allowable rhyming of "bear" and "appear" in the first stanza is entirely correct according to the old-time standards which we ourselves follow, but we fear that the delicate ear of a precise metrical artist like Rheinhart Kleiner would object to its liberalism. "The Amateur Press" is distinguished by an excellent review from the pen of Mrs. Renshaw. The style is satisfactory, and the criticism just, making the whole well worthy of the prize book it has secured for its author. "'Pollyanna,' the Glad Book", is a meritorious and entertaining review by Mrs. Griffith. "Hope", by Marguerite Sisson, is commendable for its use of that noble but neglected measure, the heroic couplet. Mr. Daas's concluding editorial, "Literature and Politics", is admirable for its concise exposition of the United's new ideals, and its masterly refutation of the common fallacy that political quarrels are necessary to stimulate activity in the press associations.

The Looking Glass for May is a journal unique in purpose and quality. Edited by Mrs. Renshaw in behalf of her many gifted recruits, it reveals a condition absolutely unexampled; the acquisition by one member of so many high-grade novices that a special publication is required properly to introduce them to the United. "To a Critic of Shelley", by Helen H. Salls, is a long piece of beautiful blank verse, marred only by one accidental rhyme. Miss Salls is evidently one of those few really powerful poets who come all too seldom into Amateur Journalism, startling the Association with impeccable harmony and exalted images. The present poem grows even more attractive on analysis. The diction is of phenomenal purity and wholly unspoiled by any ultra-modern touch. It might have been a product of Shelley's own age. The metaphor is marvellous, exhibiting a soul overflowing with true spirituality, and a mind trained to express beautiful thought in language of corresponding beauty. Such unforced ornateness is rarely met in the domain of amateur poetry. We feel certain that Miss Salls has already become a fixed star in the empyrean of the United. Exalted poetry of quite another type is furnished by the work of our new Director, Rev. Frederick Chenault, whose two exquisite lyrics, "Birth" and "The Sea of Somewhere", appear in this issue. With little use of formal rhyme and metre, Mr. Chenault abounds in delicate conceptions and artistic renditions. "Retrospection", by Kathleen Baldwin, is likewise a poem of high order, and of fairly regular metre, evidently following comparatively recent models in technique. "The Faithful Man", by I. T. Valentine, shews growing poetical talent, but is cruelly injured by the anticlimactic line. Not that there is any anticlimax of sentiment, but the colloquial mode of expression shocks the reader who has been perusing the more dignified lines which go before. "The Stonework of Life" is an excellent prose sermon by Joseph Ernest Shufelt, which displays great ability in the field of metaphor and allegory. Mr. Shufelt possesses an admirable style, unusually well fitted for didactic matter of this sort; indeed, it is regrettable that he should ever depart from such congenial themes and turn to the wild sensationalism which he shews in *The Badger.* In demonstrating the beauties of morality and religion, he has few superiors, and a task so appropriate to his genius ought to claim his whole attention. True, his thoughts may follow strange courses in their quest for truth and beauty, but were he always to curb them within the bounds of probability and conservatism, as here, he would never lose the confidence of his public, as he has done with his strange war theories. "The Autocracy of Art", by Anne Vyne Tillery Renshaw, is the leading article of the magazine. Herein the author proclaims the supremacy of spiritual utterance over all restrictions created by the mind, and urges the emancipation of the soaring bard from the earthly chains of rhyme and metre. That the inward promptings of the poetic instinct are of prime value to the poet, few will dispute; but that they may give final form to his soul's creations without some regulation by the natural laws of rhythm, few will agree. The metric sense lies far deeper in the breast of man than Mrs. Renshaw is here disposed to acknowledge. After this article, the perfectly regular stanzas of "Fellow Craftsman", *by the same author,* are refreshing. The typography and form of *The Looking Glass* leave something to be desired, but the riches within make ample compensation for outward crudity.

*The New Member* for May, edited by William Dowdell, contains but one credential, yet doubtless paves the way for a resumption of the enterprise so ably conducted by Miss Hoffman last year. "Melancholy", a poem by I. T. Valentine, shews traces of the beginner's crudeness, yet has about it a quality which promises much for the future of the poet. "Lock-Step Pete", by Miss von der Heide, is an unusual poem with a thoughtful suggestion embodied in its concluding stanza.

*The New Member* bound with the May *Official Quarterly* is a model that should henceforth be followed as the nearest approach to perfection yet beheld. Credentials, lists of prospective members, news of recruits, and accounts of local clubs are here given in just and pleasing proportion. "Bluets and Butterflies", by Carolyn L. Amoss, is a poem of great delicacy and ethereal atmosphere. The solitary, tiny flaw is the attempted rhyming of "Miss" and "yes". "War in America", by Annette E. Foth, is a pleasant juvenile story. E. Ralph Cheyney's extract from his essay on "Youth" is in many ways remarkable, and shews us that we have another recruit of choice quality. His rather peculiar ideas are well expressed, though their soundness is quite debatable. A few abnormal characters like Byron and Shelley doubtless experienced all the adolescent phenomena which Mr. Cheyney describes, but we believe that the average youth is a copyist, and for the most part reflects his environment. Radicalism and novel ideas arise just as much from blasé, elderly cynics, who are tired of sane and sober conservatism. We have been reflecting on Life for about twenty years, ever since we were five, and have consistently believed that the wisdom of the ancient sage is the true wisdom; that Life is essentially immutable, and that the glorious dreams of youth are no more than dreams, to be dissipated by the dawn of maturity and the full light of age. "Flowers on the Grave", a poem by J. D. Hill, has a commendable sentiment, and is remarkable for its possession of only one repeated rhyming sound. Whether or not the latter feature be monotonous, all must admit that the versification is attractive. "We

Are All Desperate!" is a striking philosophical fragment by Melvin Ryder, which first appeared as an editorial in the *Ohio State Lantern*. The conjectures are plausible, and the precepts sound. The news items in this paper are all fresh and interesting, concluding an issue uniformly excellent.

The *Pippin* for May displays very favourably the high school club whose founding and maintenance are due entirely to the genius of Mr. Maurice W. Moe. "The Coasters", by Esther Ronning, is the only poem in the issue, but its quality atones for the absence of other verse. The pleasures and perils of coasting are here portrayed with wonderfully graphic pen, whilst the metre is, so far as technical correctness is concerned, all that might be desired. However, we wish that Miss Ronning were less fond of unusual rhyming arrangements. The lines here given are of regular ballad length. Were they disposed in couplets, we should have a tuneful lay of the "Chevy Chase" order; but as it is, our ear misses the steady couplet effect to which the standard models have accustomed us. "With the Assistance of Carmen" is a clever short story by Gladys Bagg, derived from the same plot nucleus by Mr. Moe which likewise evoked Miss Moore's story in the March *United Amateur*. The structure of the narrative is excellent, but we do not like the use of the plebeian expression "onto" on page 3. There is properly no such word as "onto" in the English language, "upon" being the preposition here required. Webster clearly describes "onto" as a low provincialism or colloquialism. "Little Jack in Fairyland", by Ruth Ryan, is a well-written account of a dream, with the usual awakening just as events are coming to a climax. The style is very attractive, and the images ingenious. "Getting What You Want", by Mr. Moe, is a brief one-act farce illustrating the subtle devices whereby the sharp housewife bewilders the good-natured landlord into the granting of extraordinary favours. Had the heroine kept on to still greater lengths, she might have secured an entire new house. The present number of *The Pippin* is, save for the absence of photographs, quite as pleasing as the previous number. We trust that Mr. Moe's editorial prophecy may be fulfilled, and that we may soon behold another issue which shall make us familiar with the new faces brought by revolving time into the congenial Appleton circle.

The *Plainsman* for July is the best number yet issued, the two eleventh-hour contributions being very cleverly introduced. "Revised Edition", by Mrs. Jeanette Timkin, is a versified piece of keen humour and good metre, well illustrating the opening of the third or aerial element to human travel. "To Bazine, Kansas" is a sprightly prose account by James J. Hennessey of his journey from Boston to Bazine. "An Incident of Early Days", by Mrs. John Cole, is presented in the same attractive reminiscent style which makes her article in *The Trail* so readable and interesting. We are here told of the times when herds of bison were common sights, and are given a pleasing account of the formation of the Bazine Sunday-School. The articles by Mr. and Mrs. Ira Cole shew their appreciation of the amateurs who have visited them, and conclude an issue of thoroughly entertaining quality.

The *Providence Amateur* for June introduces to the United another local press club of great enthusiasm. Owing to some unauthorised omissions made by the printer, this first issue is scarcely representative of the club's entire personnel, but that which still remains affords, after all, a fair index to the character and ideals of the new organisation. The editorials by John T. Dunn are both frank and fearless. We detest a shifty club whose allegiance wavers betwixt the United, the Morris Faction, and the National, and so are greatly pleased at Mr. Dunn's manly and open stand for the one real United. The editor's opinions on acknowledgment of papers is certainly just from one point view, though much may be said for the opposite side. When an amateur journal has been prepared with unusual labour, and mailed conscientiously to every member of the Association, the publisher has substantial reason for resenting any marked display of neglect. We do not blame *The Blarney Stone* for its attitude on this question, and shall probably follow its custom by mailing the next *Conservative* only to those who have acknowledged one or both of the previous issues.

*The Reflector* for June is a British amateur magazine, transplanted on American soil by its able editor, Ernest A. Dench. "Crossing the Atlantic in War Time" is a pleasing account of Mr. Dench's voyage from Liverpool to New York. "Chunks of Copy" forms the title of an excellent though informal editorial department, while "A Brain Tank at Your Service" teems with witticisms concerning various members of the Blue Pencil Club. This magazine has no connexion with any former journal of like title, but seems likely to prove a worthy successor to all its namesakes.

*The Trail* for Spring is a new and substantial illustrated magazine of 20 pages and cover, issued by our well-known Private Critic, Mr. Alfred L. Hutchinson. At the head of the contents are the reminiscences of the editor, which prove extremely interesting reading, and which are well supplemented by the lines entitled "The Tramp Printer". Also by Mr. Hutchinson is the well-written and animated account of Mr. Nicholas Bruehl, whose artistic photographical work adorns the inside covers of this issue. "Pioneer Life in Kansas", by Mrs. John Cole, is a delightfully graphic picture of the trials and adventures of the early settlers in the West. Being written from actual personal experience, the various incidents leave a lasting impression on the mind of the reader, while a pleasing smoothness of style enhances the vividness of the narrative. "Memory-Building" is the first of a series of psychological articles by our master amateur, Maurice W. Moe. It is here demonstrated quite conclusively, that the faculty of memory is dependent on the fundamental structure and quality of the brain, and may never be acquired or greatly improved through cultivation. "Evening at Magnolia Springs", by Laura E. Moe, exhibits the same type of literary talent that her gifted husband possesses; in fact, this sketch may be compared with Mr. Moe's well-known "Cedar Lake Days". The use of trivial incidents gives an intense naturalness to the description. "Caught", by Ruth M. Lathrop, is a brilliant short story whose development and climax are natural and unforced. Fiction is generally the amateur's weakest spot, but Miss Lathrop is evidently one of the few shining exceptions. So thoroughly excellent is *The Trail*, that we hope to see not merely a second issue, but its permanent establishment as one of the United's leading magazines.

*The Tryout* for June belongs to the National, but contains much matter by United members. "Tempora Mutantur", a very meritorious short story by Marguerite Sisson, affords an illuminating contrast between the solid culture of 1834 and the detestable shallowness of the present time. This prevailing frivolity and unscholarliness is something which the United is seeking to remedy, and we are thankful indeed for stories such as this, which expose modern levity in all its nauseousness. It is evident that Miss Sisson is emulating the appreciative Anne Carroll of 1834, rather than her obtuse and indifferent descendant. "The District School", by Edna R. Guilford, describes very vividly the many petty annoyances that beset the average teacher. While the picture is extremely well presented as a whole, certain roughnesses of diction nevertheless arrest the critical eye. "Onto", in the first paragraph, is a provincialism which should be superseded by "to". Further on we hear the teacher admonishing a youth to wash up some ink, and "wash it *good!*" Would a *teacher* thus express herself? "Well" is the adverb here needed. "Too tired *to hardly stand*" is a seriously ungrammatical phrase, which should read: "almost too tired to stand." We note that one of the pupils' names is given as "Robert Elsmere". While it may not be essentially a fault thus to use the name of a famous character of fiction, we feel that the exercise of a little more original- ity might have avoided this appropriation of Mrs. Humphry Ward's celebrated hero.[6] Miss Guilford's fundamental talent is unmistakable, but needs cultivation and practice before it can shine out in full splendour.

*The Tryout* for July contains "Cripple George", a beautiful short story by Mrs. Rose L. Elmore, commendable alike in plot and technique. "A Day in the Mountains", by Harry H. Connell, is a very interesting sketch whose style exhibits considerable promise.

*The United Amateur* for March contains a literary department which will, we hope, remain as a regular feature. "Tobias Smithers, Leading Man" is Miss Ellen Moore's prize-winning attempt at constructing a story from a very brief nucleus given by Mr. Moe. Miss Moore here exhibits a facile pen and a just appreciation of humorous situations. "Ghosts", by Mrs. Renshaw, well illustrates the vague superstitions of the negroes, those strange creatures of darkness who seem never to cross completely the threshold from apedom to humanity. "March", by ourselves, is a gem of exquisite po- esy, etc., etc., which we have here praised because no one else could ever conscien- tiously do so. Line 10 apparently breaks the metre, but this seeming break is due wholly to the printer. The line should read:

> "The longer sunshine, and the shorter night."

"The Unknown Equation" is a love story by Mrs. Florence Shepphird. Though the ma- jor portion is quite polished and consistent, we cannot but deem the conclusion too abrupt and precipitate. Perhaps, being a frigid old critic without experience in ro- mance, we ought to submit the question to some popular newspaper column of Advice to the Lovelorn, inquiring whether or not it be permissible for a young lady, after only a few hours' acquaintanceship with a young gentleman, to encourage him to "put his arm around her yielding form and kiss her passionately"!!

*The United Amateur* for May is graced by "Reveille", a powerful and stirring poem written in collaboration by our two gifted bards, Mr. Kleiner, the Laureate, and Miss von der Heide. "Nature and the Countryman", by A. W. Ashby, is an iconoclastic attack on that love of natural beauty which is inherent in every poetical, imaginative, and delicately strung brain. In prose of faultless technique and polished style, Mr. Ashby catalogues like a museum curator every species of flaw that he can possibly pick in the scenes and events of rustic life. But while the career of the farmer is assuredly not one of uninterrupted bliss, it were folly to assert that Nature's superlative loveliness is not more than enough to compensate for its various infelicities. No mind of high grade is so impervious to aesthetic emotion that it can behold without admiration the wonders of the rural realm, even though a vein of sordid suffering run through the beauteous ensemble. Of all our personal friends, the one who most adores and loves to personify Nature is a successful farmer of unceasing diligence. Mr. Ashby errs, we are certain, in taking the point of view of the unimaginative and unappreciative peasant. This sort of animal interprets Nature by physical, not mental associations, and is unfitted by heredity to receive impressions of the beautiful in its less material aspects. Whilst he grumbles at the crimson flames of Aurora, thinking only of the afternoon rain thus predicted, the man of finer mould, though equally cognisant that a downpour may follow, rejoices impulsively at the pure beauty of the scene itself, a scene whose intellectual exaltation will help him the better to bear the dull afternoon. Is not the beauty-lover the happier of the two? Both must endure the trials, but the poet enjoys compensating pleasures which the boor may never know. The personification and deification of Nature is a legacy from primitive ages which will delight us in an atavistical way till our very race shall have perished. And let Mr. Ashby remember that those early tribes who placed a god or goddess in every leafy tree, crystal fount, reedy lake, or sparkling brook, were far closer to Nature and to the soil than is any modern tenant farmer.

The United Official Quarterly for May has resumed its former attractive appearance, and contains a very creditable assortment of literary matter. "Atmosphere", by Mrs. Shepphird, is a thoughtful and pleasing essay, whose second half well describes the individuality of the various amateur authors and editors. "The Kingly Power of Laughter", by Louena Van Norman, is no less just and graphic, illustrating the supreme force of humour and ridicule. Leo Fritter, in "Concerning Candidates", points out some important details for office-seekers, whilst Ira A. Cole, in "Five Sticks on Finance", gives some interesting suggestions for economy. "Opportunity", an essay by Mildred Blanchard, concludes the issue, and successfully disputes the noxious old platitude, that "Opportunity knocks but once at each man's door." With the Quarterly is bound The New Member, reviewed elsewhere, the two forming a tasteful and meritorious magazine.

The Woodbee for July is an issue of unusual interest, revealing the more serious and substantial activities of the prosperous Columbus club. The opening feature is a sonnet by Alma Sanger, "To Autumn Violets", which exhibits some poetical talent and a just sense of metrical values. We are sure that the defective second line is the fault of the printer rather than of the author. "The Blind Prince", by Henriette Ziegfeld, is an excellent juvenile tale involving a fairy story. The only serious objection is the undercurrent of adult comment which flows through the narrative. Particularly cynical is the closing sentence: "'And here's Mother,' finished poor Auntie with a sigh of relief." The ordinary fairy stories told to children are bits of actual Teutonic mythology, and should be related with a grave, absolute simplicity and naiveté. However, as a psychological study of the typical childish auditor, the sketch as a whole is highly meritorious. We are inclined to wonder at the possible meaning of the word "alright", which appears more than once in Miss Ziegfeld's tale. It is certainly no part of our language, and if it be a corruption of "all right", we must say that we fail to perceive why the correct expression could not have been used. "What's in a Name?", by Irene Metzger, is a clever sketch concerning the silly modern practice of giving fancy names to helpless infants. Glancing backward a little through history, Miss Metzger would probably sympathise with the innocent offspring of the old Puritans, who received such names as "Praise-God", and the like. Praise-God Barebones, a leading and fanatical member of Cromwell's rebel parliament, went a step further than his father, naming his own son "If-Jesus-Christ-had-not-died-for-thee-thou-hadst-been-Damned"! All this was actually the first name of young Barebones, but after he grew up and took a Doctor's degree, he was called by his associates, "Damned Dr. Barebones"! "Moonlight on the River", by Ida Cochran Haughton, is an exquisite sentimental poem, each stanza of which ends with the same expression. The atmosphere is well created, and the images dexterously introduced. The whole piece reminds the reader of one of Thomas Moore's beautiful old "Irish Melodies".[7] That Mrs. Haughton's talent has descended to the second generation is well proven by Edna M. Haughton's "Review of the Literary Work of the Quarter". Miss Haughton is a polished and scholarly reviewer, and her criticisms are in every instance just and helpful. The editorial on "Miss

United" is very well written, and should be carefully perused by those in danger of succumbing to the autumnal advances of that sour old maid, Miss National.

EDITOR'S NOTE FP: *United Amateur* 15, No. 2 (September 1915): 17–27 (signed "Howard P. Lovecraft, Chairman"). The longest single DPC written by HPL, amounting to 7,225 words. HPL comments briefly on the journals he himself edited or coedited, the *Conservative* and the *Providence Amateur*.

*Notes*

1. "Quinsnicket Park," l. 95 (AT 269).
2. The remark again suggests that HPL revised the poem.
3. See p. 45.
4. Munroe was a boyhood friend of HPL's. See "Introducing Mr. Chester Pierce Munroe" (p. 34).
5. HPL refers to "New Department Proposed: Instruction for the Recruit" (p. 47).
6. The reference is to a celebrated novel, *Robert Elsmere* (1888), by British novelist Mrs. Humphry (Mary Augusta) Ward (1851–1920).
7. Thomas Moore (1779–1852), *Irish Melodies* (1808–34). HPL owned an edition of Moore's *Poetical Works* (LL 618). Moore is quoted in "The Nameless City" (D 103) and "Under the Pyramids" (D 227).

# EDITORIAL

*(October 1915)*

Weak and pliant indeed is he who maketh no enemies. Ever since The Conservative commenced his series of frank criticisms and unvarnished comments, his heels have been annoyed by the vindictive snappings of a dozen or more vituperative little curs whose bristles he seems to have brushed the wrong way as he passed by them. Not all of these have yet expressed themselves in print, but from the gifted Charles D. Isaacson down to the wretched, sneaking mongrel "Bab Bell", they have each taken their "little fling" at the newcomer. Now The Conservative has no wish to trample the under dog, nor even to stifle the feeble yelps that assail this paper; wherefore he extends herewith an invitation for every hostile amateur journalist, human, Nationalite, or "Bab Bell", to submit for publication herein any and all sneers, attacks, or insults which he may have prepared against The Conservative. Reasonable brevity will ensure publication without deletion. The Conservative believes that no one possesses the right to attack him unless willing to have that attack printed with original spelling, style, and grammar in these pages, directly beside the articles whose tone he is denouncing. The public may then be able intelligently to compare the reasoning and attainments of The Conservative and his critics. It is to be hoped that these critical canines and insulting insects will by next issue have furnished The Conservative with sufficient venom to start a new column, to be entitled "From the Enemy's Camp".

It scarcely need be remarked that the above has no reference to those persons of intelligence and good manners who conscientiously disagree with The Conservative in gentlemanly fashion. These critics and dissenters are but to be praised for their sturdy independence of thought, and their admirable restraint of expression. For them is reserved the friendly answer, and, when possible, the apologetic recantation. It may be noticed that in this issue The Conservative has conceded practically all points to Mr. Kleiner in the discussion concerning allowable rhymes.[1]

EDITOR'S NOTE  FP: *Conservative* 1, No. 3 (October 1915): 6–7 (unsigned). HPL somewhat superciliously promises to respond to critics of his earlier issues, but in fact did not do so; nor did he fulfill his possibly joking vow of printing hostile comments in his own paper.

*Notes*

1. HPL alludes to his essay, "The Allowable Rhyme" (*Conservative*, October 1915; CE2).

---

# THE CONSERVATIVE AND HIS CRITICS
*(October 1915)*

"Melius non tangere, clamo!"[1]
—Horace.

It appears that The Conservative's review of Charles D. Isaacson's recent paper was not accepted in the honestly critical spirit intended, and that Mr. Isaacson is preparing to wreak summary verbal vengeance upon the crude barbarian who cannot appreciate the loathsome Walt Whitman, cannot lose his self-respect as a white man, and cannot endorse a treasonable propaganda designed to deliver these United States as easy victims to the first hostile power who cares to conquer them. In view of The Conservative's frank and explicit recognition of Mr. Isaacson's unusual talent, the predicted reprisal seems scarcely necessary; yet if it must come, it will find its object, as usual, not unwilling to deliver blow for blow. The Conservative possesses very definite opinions on the questions involved, and has by no means exhausted all his armoury of darts in their defence. Owing to the uncertainties of the press, Mr. Isaacson's contemplated screed may have appeared ere this; in any case The Conservative may with propriety announce his attitude in the words which Colley Cibber, reviser of Shakespeare, puts into the mouth of King Richard:

"Hark! the shrill trumpet sounds, to horse, away,
My soul's in arms, and eager for the fray!"[2]

EDITOR'S NOTE  FP: *Conservative* 1, No. 3 (October 1915): 7–8 (unsigned). HPL suggests that he will respond to Charles D. Isaacson's criticisms of him in *In a Minor Key*, but he in fact never did so in print; his long satirical poem, "The Isaacsonio-Mortoniad" (1915; AT 208–11), remained unpublished until long after his death.

*Notes*

1. "It is better not to touch [me], I cry!" Horace, *Satires* 2.1.45.
2. From Colley Cibber's adaptation of *The Tragical History of King Richard III* (1700), 5.5.86–87.

•

## THE YOUTH OF TODAY

The aggressive intellectual tone of the rising generation is indeed refreshing. With-out the encumbering polish of former ages, the schoolboys of today fear not to speak as they think, and to attack dissenting opinion whenever and wherever they en-counter it. Seldom has The Conservative enjoyed a livelier or more unexpected pleas-ure than that which followed the sending of his first issue to a youthful United recruit, Master David H. Whittier, who has just graduated from a prominent Boston high school. Master Whittier, like his famous poetical relative, pounces virtuously upon un-orthodox ideas wherever he may find them, hence he sent The Conservative a long, bitter, and unsolicited criticism of the (March) article on pan-Teutonism as soon as he had read it. Being not particularly designed for the Bostonian type of involved intellect, "The Crime of the Century" failed to appeal to Mr. Whittier's refined taste, wherefore the young man admitted frankly that he did not like it, stated that The Conservative is a superficial, unscientific, and prejudiced reasoner, and accounted for his own violent opposition on the grounds that The Conservative's point of view 'so revolted him!' Mr. Whittier has requested permission to use in print certain portions of The Conser-vative's letters to him.[1] This permission is hereby granted with extreme pleasure, since no pursuit is more gratifying than that of helping a worthy youth to shake off his natu-ral timidity, and to come forth fearlessly into the United's public eye as a controversial giant. So long as The Conservative shall exist, Mr. Whittier need never want a victim for his bold sallies. Edgar Ralph Cheyney, in the May *New Member*, calls upon adoles-cence to express itself. Let him look Bostonward, for in David H. Whittier he may be-hold such expression at most exquisitely developed pitch!

EDITOR'S NOTE  FP: *Conservative* 1, No. 3 (October 1915): 11–12 (unsigned). A brief com-ment on David H. Whittier, a young amateur who had strongly deprecated HPL's racist views as expressed in "The Crime of the Century" (*Conservative*, April 1915; CE5). Whit-tier did not become a close colleague of HPL, but HPL did publish Whittier's short story, "The Bond Invincible," in the *Conservative* 2, No. 3 (October 1916): [5–6].

*Notes*

1. It does not appear that Whittier in fact published any portions of HPL's letters in any amateur journal.

## AN IMPARTIAL SPECTATOR

Mr. John Russell, the United's clever satirist, has composed the following lines con-cerning the controversy over regular metre lately waged through the pages of *The Looking Glass, The Lake Breeze,* and *The Conservative.*

## METRICAL REGULARITY;
### OR, BROKEN METRE.

Dear Youth, if you would be a poet,
Pray study this, and see you know it:
With careful rhyme and one smooth metre,
Your poem can't be much neater.
Should you prefer to rhyme in anapaest,
Convinc'd that such conveys your fancy best,
Change not the form, nor try heroic lines,
Howe'er your fleeting mood your pen inclines.
Just see that you hold to the same old refrain,
For if you change once, sure you'll change it again.
And the critics (confound them) will haughtily say
'Tis the worst thing they've seen for full many a day.
And now, in conclusion, pray shun the illusion
That all you've to do is to write:
If you study your rhymes; feet, metre and times,
You'll a masterpiece some day indite!

J. R.

While Mr. Russell's words seem to constitute a very keen thrust at The Conservative, his cleverly varied metre satirises with equal keenness the other side of the discussion; wherefore he must be classified by means of that much abused hypothetical term, "neutral".

EDITOR'S NOTE  FP: *Conservative* 1, No. 3 (October 1915): 12 (unsigned). On a poem by John Russell.

---

# [UNTITLED NOTES ON AMATEUR JOURNALISM]

William J. Dowdell, in transforming his *Bearcat* into a 7 × 10 journal of high and conservative ideals, is demonstrating very forcibly the fine quality of truly ambitious youth. Let the National rail about our young members if it chooses; they are certainly doing better than most of the National's *old* members! Mr. Dowdell's new policy is one of sense and soundness, and his paper will soon attain an envied position through the dignified tone of its contents, both contributed and editorial. During the present year Mr. Dowdell has printed articles by some of our most gifted members. This condition will undoubtedly continue, and the improved aspect of the publication will attract even more amateurs of prominence to its pages.

---

The Conservative desires very sincerely to felicitate Mr. William T. Harrington on his latest *Coyote*. The transition from the March standard is almost startling, and the whole present atmosphere of the periodical prophesies future improvement at no tardy rate.

---

Having learned of the adoption of amateur journalism by an inmate of the Columbus penitentiary, The Conservative is impelled to reflect that a good many other amateurs, particularly in the National, ought to be in gaol as well.

---

The editor of *The Tryout*,[1] a National paper, takes issue with *The Lake Breeze* concerning the status of "the small boy with a printing-press" in amateur journalism. Mr. Smith declares that upon this same boy the whole past, present, and future of amateur journalism depends; but The Conservative is of a different opinion, being unable to see why the typesetter or pressman is so essentially affiliated with the art of literature. True, some of the best amateurs have also been printers, as attested by Messrs. Dowdell, Sandusky, Porter, Macauley,[2] and the formerly active genius Edward Cole; but these cases by no means prove that the pen and the type-stick are kindred implements. If the claim of Mr. Smith be true, why does not his beloved National choose eminent master printers for Laureate Judges in Poetry?

---

When Victor L. Basinet's new paper, *The Rebel*, shall appear, the amateur public will have an opportunity to behold the workings of a very extraordinary mind. Mr. Basinet is in some respects a true genius, blessed with an almost instinctive perception of the delicate and the artistic, and possessing a rhetorical style of remarkable vigour. But superadded to these qualities is such a strange point of view on social problems and systems, that the rational reader will stand aghast at the thoughts revealed. How Mr. Basinet became successively a socialist and a confessed anarchist is more than The Conservative can say, though he has met the gentleman personally. Utter disregard of the fundamental failings of humanity seems to be the keynote, however, since this dreamer refuses to believe that mankind cannot live forever in brotherhood under the Golden Rule, once that happy state of affairs is established. But his own arguments ought to correct his beliefs. He tells us that capitalists should be dethroned, since they abuse their privileges and oppress their brothers, etc. etc. But, he adds, all men are equal. Then how can he say that his proposed earth-wide brotherhood will not be marred with strife more hideous and universal than any yet known? It is all in the education, he says. But are not his hated capitalists taught the Golden Rule also? The world would like to live just as Mr. Basinet would have it, but fortunately most of us are conservative enough not to tear down our present system of society when we know of no better one to supersede it.

---

Another amateur whom The Conservative has met several times in person is Mr. John T. Dunn, the Irish Patriot. Mr. Dunn is a man of undoubted talent, being now editor of *The Providence Amateur*, yet his anti-English views are such that they call for correction. The Conservative has no particular antipathy toward the Green Isle and its people, yet he must protest at the rebellious, seditious, and treasonable attitude which some maintain toward that stronger race which governs them. England has admittedly been neglectful of Ireland's interests in the past, but that such old scores should be transmitted to the present well-treated generation of Irish and Irish-Americans is anomalous. Through Britannia will come Hibernia's greatest days of glory, yet an ungrateful, revengeful few will do their best to obstruct progress, bite the hand that feeds them, and calumniate the loyal Irish People who are faithful to England. Ireland is now an equal and integral part of the British Empire, and he who slanders that Empire indirectly slanders Ould Oireland herself.[3]

———

That metrical precision is still appreciated by the sounder school of critics is well shewn by the awarding of poetical honours in the United this year. Our new Laureate, justly enough, is Mr. Rheinhart Kleiner, a supreme master of perfect rhyme and metre, and the poem on which the award was based is "The Evening Prayer", a chastely lustrous gem of thought whose devout and delicate atmosphere is adorned with a technical finish beyond reproach. What radical is so extreme, that he would wish to see this faultless jewel marred by irregular cutting or splintered by the mallet of "liberalism"?

The inferior award, proudly flaunted by The Conservative, is certainly a triumph of technique, since his "poem" in the *Official Quarterly* contains little merit beyond having exactly ten syllables in each line.[4]

———

The August *United Amateur* is indeed a credit to our new Official Editor. The list of members shews considerable change, and reveals the regrettable fact that our two latest ex-Presidents have retired to honorary membership, leaving the Official Editor himself as our only active ex-President. If this is to happen in the future, and the Presidency is to be considered only as a step toward retirement, we shall be tempted to become a monarchy, with our present Executive as King Leo I.

EDITOR'S NOTE FP: *Conservative* 1, No. 3 (October 1915): 14–16 (unsigned). Miscellaneous notes on amateur journalism, including one on Victor L. Basinet, who in the first issue (June 1915) of the *Providence Amateur* was listed as President of the Providence Amateur Press Club. His name does not appear in the second and last issue (February 1916), suggesting that he had left the club shortly after publication of the first issue.

*Notes*

1. Charles W. Smith (1852–1948), longtime friend of HPL. See "The Haverhill Convention" (p. 289).
2. Albert A. Sandusky (d. 1934), who printed several issues of HPL's *Conservative* (July 1915, October 1915, January 1916, April 1916, and possibly July 1916); Wesley H. Porter, editor of *Toledo Amateur*; George W. Macauley, coeditor with HPL of the *New Member*.
3. HPL's letters to Dunn—many discussing the Irish question as well as amateur journalism matters—have now been published as "H. P. Lovecraft: Letters to John T. Dunn," ed. S. T. Joshi, David E. Schultz, and John H. Stanley, *Books at Brown* 38–39 (1991–92): 157–223.
4. HPL, "To the Rev. James Pyke" (*United Official Quarterly*, November 1914; AT 336).

## LITTLE JOURNEYS TO THE HOMES OF PROMINENT AMATEURS: II. ANDREW FRANCIS LOCKHART

The biographer of prominent amateur journalists, confronted as he is with an uniquely select type of intellectual humanity, is never at a loss for inspiring and interesting material. The same mental characteristics that mould the true amateur of high grade must inevitably discover themselves in his acts outside the press association, and remove his whole career from that monotonous mediocrity which forms the life of the dull "ordinary citizen".

In no case is this originality of thought and activity of temperament more marked than in that of the subject of this sketch, Mr. Andrew Francis Lockhart of Milbank, South Dakota: Scholar, Editor, Reformer, Poet, and Member of the United.

Andrew Francis Lockhart was born in the city of Milbank on April 5, 1890, and is in direct paternal line descended from an ancient and respected Scottish house. His great-grandfather was a sincere patron of letters, and a close friend of the poet Burns. From the maternal side Mr. Lockhart derives the virile, conquering blood of the Vikings, for his mother is a native of Norway, the cradle of that resistless Scandinavian force which has swayed nations from the Mediterranean to the Arctic, from the shores of Sicily to that vast unknown realm in the West whose discovery Columbus was later to claim.

Mr. Lockhart acquired his elementary education in the schools of his native city, graduating from the high school in 1909, but even before emerging from boyhood his active brain began to seek a wider expression than the commonplaces of conventional life can afford, hence we find him a United member and amateur editor at the age of fifteen. In his graduation year at Milbank High School Mr. Lockhart was made editor of *The White Rose*, the regular annual publication of the school.

His school days having been finished, Mr. Lockhart immediately entered the University of South Dakota as a student of law. The legal training there obtained was destined to aid him greatly in his future career, though he has no intention of ever becoming a practicing attorney. About the time of his transition from school to college Mr. Lockhart commenced his extensive series of contributions to the professional press, which has averaged about 2000 column inches per year. In 1912 he became city editor of *The Grant County News*, continuing in that position until last year, when his paper was forced by the detestable, all-engulfing liquor interests to suspend publication.

It was in 1910 that Mr. Lockhart first took up the moral reform work for which he is now famous. Within a year he was actively at war against the repulsive evils of the liquor traffic, and throughout his editorship of *The Grant County News* he was an outspoken and effective foe to rum. His efforts were from the first hampered by the "whiskey gang" of his city; his safety has been jeopardised, his life threatened, his person attacked, and his character misrepresented; but despite all obstacles, his path has been one of success. He weighs 124 pounds, and fears nothing on earth.

In January, 1915, after the failure of the *News*, Mr. Lockhart issued the first number of *Chain Lightning*, a monthly reform magazine which startled his entire state with its open and determined attitude against liquor. The contents, both prose and verse, were written in a vigorous colloquial style which took the public by storm and aroused shame in many a hardened breast which had never before felt the impulse of decency regarding rum and its dire effects. Three months later an election was held in Milbank, and for the first time in its history the city abolished its licenced dens of drunkenness! Since this signal victory *Chain Lightning* has prospered exceedingly, becoming nation-wide in its appeal, and fearlessly attacking the blackest vices of mankind. Last July Mr. Lockhart succeeded in closing one of the vilest resorts in all South Dakota, and in revenge was struck down from behind in his office by a dastardly, treacherous blow from one of the sottish beasts who had been connected with the evil place. But as ever, Mr. Lockhart rose, undaunted by the vicious attack, and though sorely racked with pain arising from dangerous later complications, he issued a number of his magazine which breathed forth only the more defiance to vice and its minions. Much of Mr. Lockhart's recent work has been dictated from the sick-bed to which his injuries have confined him.

Apart from his reform work and journalistic activity, Mr. Lockhart has a multitude of hobbies and diversions. He is an amateur actor of great merit, and though determined not to enter the theatrical profession, has received many offers from managers. As a director and playwright he is equally gifted. Before coming of age he wrote six plays, one of which, entitled "The One Lone Man of Elmwood", he produced in 1914. The number of plays which he has directed is about twenty, not to mention the more than six hundred amateur actors whose stage countenances he has so skilfully "made up". His own dramatic talent is versatile in the extreme, taking him all the way from farce to tragedy. He has played about thirty-five different parts.

Pictorial art has likewise claimed its share of Mr. Lockhart's attention, his oil paintings and sketches being of a very high order. But above all else, Mr. Lockhart is a collector. Stamps, coins, weapons, relics, specimens, gems, and the like crowd the shelves of his spacious cabinets, and he scarcely ever makes a journey without finding something to add to his curiosities.

In politics Mr. Lockhart has been active and enthusiastic as a Progressive Republican. He managed the successful campaign, in his home county, of U.S. Senator Thomas Sterling, being then hailed as South Dakota's youngest politician. In 1912 he campaigned with his friend Congressman Royal C. Johnson, during which campaign he encountered the eccentric old character who forms the subject of his recently published poem, "Now I'm Old".

Mr. Lockhart's travels through various parts of the country have been extensive, and his studies of moral conditions in different cities have helped him greatly in his campaign for reform. Not many men of his age know the world and the underworld so thoroughly, nor are consequently so well equipped for the effective suppression of vice.

The home life of Mr. Lockhart, spent with his parents, affords a brilliant and pleasing contrast to the dark scenes among which his duty calls him. Surrounded by his private library and encircled by his cabinets of curiosities, he leads an ideal retired existence, with old books for constant companions, and a few congenial literary men or lecturers as frequent visitors. In summer he inhabits a country house at Big Stone Lake, about which he indulges in the pleasures of hunting and fishing. Cameras and motorcars likewise add to his wholesome recreations.

The amateur career of Mr. Lockhart began in 1905, when he joined the United and became associate editor of *The Coyote*, then conducted by Mr. Louis J. Lockhart. This paper, which has no connexion with the present journal bearing its name, was later edited alone by the youthful recruit. Another early venture was *The American Eagle*, which was issued but once. In 1906 Mr. Lockhart founded *The Blots Magazine*, devoted to wit and humour, and in 1907 he issued an anthology of amateur verse entitled "Musings". He is now about to publish another such collection. His original poetry has frequently graced the columns of United papers, over thirty pieces having been published in the year 1908, and a volume de luxe containing eleven poems having appeared in 1915. Mr. Lockhart was Western Manuscript Manager in 1907, and Laureate Recorder in 1908. He is at present a member of the Recruiting Committee.

As a prose writer, Mr. Lockhart possesses immense force and convincingness. Especially is he a master of pathos. His best verse is all in the satirical strain, and few censors of contemporary manners and morals are keener or more discriminating than he.

The future which Mr. Lockhart has planned for himself is one of hard, unremitting reform work. He hopes to enter the field of lyceum lecturing, at the same time making of *Chain Lightning* an increasingly efficient force against evil. With talented tongue and powerful pen thus labouring toward a common end, who can say what successes in the battle for righteousness he may not achieve? Great indeed are the obstacles in his way—the sordid opposition of the vicious, and the supercilious sneers of the primly conventional; but despite it all, he will some day emerge triumphant from the fray. His whole life dedicated to the betterment of humanity, Andrew Francis Lockhart stands out amongst us as a man who inspires our fraternal affection, and compels our admiring respect. Of him may be uttered a praise which few other mortals could justly elicit.

EDITOR'S NOTE FP: *United Amateur* 15, No. 3 (October 1915): 39–41 (as by "El Imparcial"). The second in a series of articles; the first article was on HPL by Lockhart, the first biographical article on HPL ever written (see Peter Cannon, ed., *Lovecraft Remembered* (Sauk City, WI: Arkham House, 1998), pp. 79–81). HPL also wrote the fifth article in the series (see p. 165). The information on Lockhart was surely provided to HPL by correspondence. HPL was highly sympathetic to many of Lockhart's views, notably those on temperance; see further "More *Chain Lightning*" (*United Official Quarterly*, October 1915; CE5).

---

# REPORT OF FIRST VICE-PRESIDENT
*(November 1915)*

Fellow-Amateurs:

The Recruiting Committee, though somewhat hampered by the outside duties of many of its members and by the absence of suitable printed matter, continues to work with gratifying success. Mr. Albert A. Sandusky, of Cambridge, Mass., has been added to our personnel, and has proved a highly efficient factor in the maintenance of our activity.

The long-promised recruiting booklet is now in press at Columbus, O., having been financed jointly by President Fritter and the undersigned. It will contain twelve attractively printed pages, and will be of a smallness suitable for mailing in ordinary letter size envelopes. The text is of dignified nature, offering a sharp contrast to the sensational advertising of some of the inferior associations. When this booklet shall be in use, the labours of recruiting will be much less arduous and much more effective than at present.[1]

In January this Committee will coöperate with the Auxiliary Committee in publishing *The Looking Glass*, which will contain not only the work of the new members, but short biographical accounts of them as well, thus introducing them with due ceremony to the United.

The most prominent recruit so far secured by this Committee is Rev. James T. Pyke, of Riverside, R. I., a poet who probably stands unique amongst us in his excellence. His enrolment in the ranks is perhaps our most considerable achievement up to date.

A less spectacular but nevertheless considerable work is the gradual free distribution of files of *The Amateur Journalist*, Mr. James H. Chase's extremely valuable but now discontinued magazine, among the newer members of high grade. The complete file consists of five numbers, and will be sent on application to any person who has not already received it. The undersigned has at his disposal, through the generosity of Mr. Chase, the entire remaining stock of the magazine, approximately one hundred complete sets.

EDITOR'S NOTE FP: *United Amateur* 15, No. 4 (November 1915): 56 (signed "H. P. Lovecraft, First Vice-President"). The first of two such reports, the other appearing in the *United Amateur* for January 1916. This article is noteworthy for its discussion of one of the rarest of his early pamphlets.

*Notes*

1. HPL alludes to *United Amateur Press Association: Exponent of Amateur Journalism* (p. 91). His remarks here suggest that the booklet appeared in late 1915 and was printed by Leo Fritter (Columbus, OH).

# DEPARTMENT OF PUBLIC CRITICISM

*(December 1915)*

At *Face Value* for October is the first number of an individual publication by Miss Coralie Austin. Though known to the United chiefly as a poet, Miss Austin is here beheld as a writer of fiction, exhibiting considerable talent in the development of dialogue. Her short story, a tale of the *Youth's Companion* type entitled "Jane", is generally commendable in action and atmosphere, and open to criticism only in climax and conclusion. The latter features are not quite commensurate with the detailed and extended action. "My Wish", by Dora M. Hepner, is a tuneful poem of substantial merit, whose sentiments arouse a response from every breast. The metre is neither of rigid classicism nor of ultra-modern amorphousness, but pleasantly harmonious, and well adapted to the simple subject chosen.

Mrs. Renshaw, who superintended the issuing of the paper, is well represented therein. Her "Lyric of Life", a graphic depiction of the call of Nature to mankind, gains double effectiveness through its regular structure. "Night's Message" is another well-conceived and well-executed specimen of verse, whose only two technical flaws are the attempted rhyming of "twilight" and "midnight", and the use of "hours" as a dissyllabic word.

Rev. E. P. Parham presents an excellent prose essay entitled "Autumn Musings", wherein he exhibits and urges a greater appreciation of natural beauty than is common in this vulgar age. "The Lost Soul", by Mrs. Maude K. Barton, is a poem of much power, whose dark images are extremely vivid. Mrs. Barton's style is slightly deficient in polish, but will soon attain through practice the little it now lacks. As a first issue, *At Face Value* may be deemed wholly satisfactory, the paper forming a very welcome addition to the list of current amateur journals.

*The Boys' Herald* for November opens with a reprint of Miss Nita E. Gerner's prize-winning poem, "Autumn Evening", whose original parts are of striking merit, and whose Shakespearian lines are cleverly introduced and rhymed. Other pages of the issue contain the long letters of Mr. Truman J. Spencer, describing amateur conventions of 1891, 1892, and 1894. Historically, these epistles are of great value, and their publication very desirable. *The Boys' Herald* is performing an immense service for Amateur Journalism by thus reviving records and memories of the past, and we hope that its threatened discontinuance may not materialise.

*The Brooklynite* for October is notable for Mr. Rheinhart Kleiner's lucid reviews of current amateur journals. Our chief poet shines with equal brilliancy as a critic. "Just Gossip", by William B. Stoddard, is a news column of informing and attractive quality. "A British View of American Amateur Journalism", by Ernest A. Dench, is a well-written summary of amateur conditions on this side of the Atlantic. The author's opinions are for the most part just, and his style is commendably free from frivolity. Mr. Otto P. Knack's "Song on Preparation" shews considerable cleverness in rhyming, despite the "armor—on her" attempt. The "brighter" rhyme in the last stanza we judge to be the typographical perversion of a perfectly proper "brighter—lighter" rhyme. It is to the sentiment that we must object, for Mr. Knack boldly asks us if our national honour and territorial integrity be "worth the candle"! The tone betrays only too clearly the influence of the unpatriotic radicals that infest our cosmopolitan cities.

*The Capital City News* for October is the product of Mr. Raymond B. Nixon, aged fourteen years, and is issued at Tallahassee, Fla. In the editorial column, Mr. Nixon exhibits a praiseworthy sentiment in favour of Prohibition, and it is to be hoped that he may evolve with the years into a second Andrew Lockhart, wielding in the South that effective type of "Chain Lightning" with which our Dakota fellow-amateur so powerfully strikes at vice in the North.[1] The anonymous Prohibition Song in this issue shews much force, though it is not perfect technically. "Billy's Daring Rescue", a short and stirring story of love and adventure, is evidently juvenile work, but despite the considerable crudity of plot and melodramatic manner of development, it shews in its author an unmistakable fluency which promises better things.

*The Capital City News* is at present a highly creditable embodiment of the older Amateur Journalism—the art evolved by the "boy with a printing-press". It will undoubtedly grow up with Mr. Nixon, and shine eventually in the newer Amateur Journalism—the domain of culture and literature.

*The Coyote* for October opens with "Ideals", an excellent poem in the heroic couplet by McLandburg Wilson. The sentiment is true to life, and the construction faultless. We hope to see much more of Mr. Wilson's work in the amateur press, since he possesses a metrical facility too seldom encountered in this loose age. That king of all measures, the now neglected heroic couplet, should find in his capable hands a renewed popularity.

"Autocracy vs. Democracy", by William T. Harrington, is brief but well written, expressing the popular political sentiments of the masses. We are not inclined to agree with the rather superficial views expressed, for we believe that the evils of pure democracy would be infinitely more horrible than the worst faults of autocracy; but since Mr. Harrington believes as he does, we can but congratulate him on his ease of composition. "The Teacher's Philosophy", by Mabel Harrington, is a concise and thoughtful summary of the five ages of normal educational progress. The editorials in this number shew Mr. Harrington's continued interest in the cause of Amateur Journalism, and promise well for the future development of his attractive little paper.

*The Crazyquilt* for July is undoubtedly the most artistic specimen of magazine-making which has graced the amateur world since the passing of the *Olympian*.[2] Incomparably tasteful in typography, its contents are worthy of their attire, and the whole is a striking testimonial to the ability of its publishers. Mr. Melvin Ryder, from whose pleasing pen all the literary matter may be presumed to proceed, is a young man of vigorous originality and forceful though informal expression, as shewn by his able editorship of the *Ohio State Lantern* and his new-born fame as author of a professionally published book.[3] His easy and unusual style is here displayed at its best, and while it departs widely from that dignity so much to be desired in ordinary prose, it yet attracts us in spite of its levity. To treat separately the various "articles" in The *Crazyquilt* were to do them injustice. As Mr. Pope would express it, "All are but parts of one stupendous whole",[4] for through the entire thirteen pages runs a uniform and continuous system of sprightly undergraduate philosophy whose youthful optimism is as diverting as it is inspiring. The effervescent manner affected by Mr. Ryder as he dallies with the lighter beauties of expression has drawn down upon The *Crazyquilt* at least one unfavourable amateur review, but we believe that the very airiness of touch which now creates such unsubstantial and evanescent images will later prove the source from which a deeper and maturer style will derive a just ornament. The *Crazyquilt* is assuredly a literary achievement wherein both the editor and the Association have reason to take pride.

*Hit and Miss* for August is a neat and attractive little leaflet by Miss Rose Baker, which, though not new to Amateur Journalism, now makes its first appearance in the United. The general tone of this individual publication is Socialistic, though a generous space is allotted to the amateur world. Miss Baker's ideas on economics seem not unlike those of her fellow-amateurs, Messrs. Shufelt and Basinet,[5] though the methods she urges are probably less violent in the last analysis. The Exchange Column is very interesting, though the reviews are all rather brief. We shall officially bear in mind the anti-critic paragraph, and strive not to be quite so harsh as the type therein delineated.

Two pieces of Miss Baker's verse are also contained in *Hit and Miss*. While not of perfect taste or execution, they display a marked leaning toward metrical expression on the author's part, and impel us to advise both a further study of poetical art, and a careful perusal of the works of the best bards, with especial attention to regularity of lines, placing of accents, and selection of appropriate words or phrases. *Hit and Miss* improves with each issue, and from the conscientious ambition of its editor we may reasonably expect to behold its rapid approach to the front rank of informal amateur journals.

*Just a Few Verses* is the title of Mr. Andrew Francis Lockhart's latest volume of metrical matter. The general tone is perhaps a little lighter than that of Mr. Lockhart's previous work; but the same quaint touch prevails throughout, and the author's homely philosophy of the commonplace is here expounded as effectively and attractively as ever. "My First Cigar" is a clever piece well worthy of appearance in the professional press. "It Can't Be Done" is more serious, and very meritorious, the continuous development of the theme being a notable feature. The colourful rural dialect employed in this poem and in many others by Mr. Lockhart is deserving of particular mention on account of its universality of appeal. It is eminently expressive and characteristic of the shrewd Yankee rustic, yet is in no sense local, and may be understandingly appreciated throughout the United States. It is a symbolic breath of the old native American atmosphere which is too soon passing away. "The Age of Discretion" is another pleasing dialect piece, which reminds one of Mr. Lockhart's previous verse, "Now I'm Old". "According to Hoyle" well illustrates its author's practical knowledge of human nature, and exhibits vividly the waning power of the bucolic sage. "Have You Ever Felt That Way?" is cast in verse of more regular structure, and we cannot but wish that Mr. Lockhart would more frequently favour us with metre of this sort. The sentiment is commendably optimistic, and the whole very creditable. "At Galveston" is a keen bit of humour, whilst "In the Long, Long Ago" is a conventional but well-phrased "bachelor's reverie". "The Old Standby", which concludes the volume, is a clever satire on the inevitable inanities of common conversation. When we pause to sound the stream of "small talk", we must needs smile with Mr. Lockhart at the shallowness there revealed.

*The New Member* for October is, like the May number, bound with *The United Official Quarterly*. At the head of the contents stands "The Buttercup", a poem by Mrs. Maude K. Barton, whose merit is somewhat below that of its author's more recent work. There is an unmistakably pleasing atmosphere about the lines, yet vagueness and forced construction are not absent. Mrs. Barton's technique is rapidly increasing in polish, so that these light verses must not be taken as any criterion of ability. "Jack of Today", a versified composition by Inez Gray Hall, exhibits commendable ambition and capability of improvement. With unremitting study of the best poets, and incessant care in the avoidance of unpoetical constructions, Miss Hall may at no distant date acquire an attractive informal style.

"A Tale of the Sea" is a remarkably good short story by Miss Florence Brugger, aged fourteen years. While traces of juvenile technique are to be detected both in plot and diction, the whole is developed and written with a skill quite surprising in an author so youthful. The sea with its changing moods, and the sailor with his countless superstitions, are described with a vividness which many an older writer might well covet. Many amateur critics will doubtless cavil at the nature of the subject, and urge Miss Brugger to confine her pen to tamer themes; but we are inclined to distrust the precepts which thus limit the activities of the young. If a beginner be endowed with a fertile imagination and a reasonable amount of taste, restriction is as useless as it is annoying.

*The Piper* for September once more presents the pleasing mixture of verse and criticism for which Mr. Kleiner's journal has been famous since its first appearance last year. Mr. Kleiner opens the issue with an unusual array of verse, beginning with an intentionally mediocre poem, written in jest by another amateur, and continuing with a masterly series of his own imitations of the various styles which other bards might have employed in handling the same subject. Too much cannot be said of the skill with which Mr. Kleiner copies the literary idiosyncrasies of his fellow-amateurs. In no case does he sink to burlesque, but gives with full seriousness a set of poems which none of the authors imitated could justly wish to disclaim. We speak from experience, since we are one of the versifiers honoured with Mr. Kleiner's attention.[6] Most of the critical opinions expressed in this number are of satisfying soundness, encouraging the cultivation of regular metrical forms amongst amateur poets. To our careless or wantonly radical bards they may well be recommended. In reviewing a recent pastoral poem by Ira A. Cole, however, Mr. Kleiner seems a little stern with his condemnation of eighteenth-century style. Such a style may not coincide with the mass of modern opinion, but it is distinctly an artistic achievement, and thrice pleasing on account of its rarity. Would that we had more of these inspiring old pastorals to turn our minds from the sordid commonplaces of today! *The Piper* closes with an original poem by Mr. Kleiner, entitled "To Mary of the Movies", in whose tuneful lines the author shews all his accustomed sweetness of sentiment, grace of garb, and cleverness of comparison.[7]

*The Pippin* for July is made attractive by its numerous illustrations, which introduce to the United the newer members of the Appleton club, and increase our familiarity with those of former years who yet remain. "A Wild Night at Camp", by Alfred Pingel, is very acceptable as a narrative, detailing in smooth fashion the trials of a rowing party in a storm. However, so far as we can perceive, the "wild night" was not *at*, but *away from*, the camp. "*The Campers' Wild Night*" might be more apt as a title. Well-selected photographs enhance the value of this excellent sketch. "The Pippin Portrait Gallery" is from the pen of our old friend, "A. J. Bird", whose smooth heroic verse we had occasion to praise a year ago. This feathered warbler sings as sweetly in prose as in poetry, and comments in pleasingly colloquial diction on the various portraits displayed. As a whole, the current *Pippin* is of marked merit, and we are inclined to be impatient for another issue, even though none is promised until next year.

*Poesy* for September is published by Mr. Edward F. Herdman, a veteran amateur of Bishop-Auckland, England, as a semi-professional medium through which the youthful bard may bring before the public his first efforts. The present number contains fifteen versified pieces of varying merit, the most impressive of which is perhaps that on "Flamborough Rocks", by E. C. "Questionings", by J. H. Moyse Walker, contains noble conceptions, but is marred by grammatical and metrical errors. In line 2 the word "fashion'd" is so placed that the accent must fall wrongfully on the second syllable. Archaic verb-forms also seem to offer difficulties to Mr. Walker, as shewn in the last two lines of his poem. "Canst", in line 13, should be "can", for it is in the third person; whilst "needeth", in line 14, should be "needest", since it is in the second person. Though much of the contents of the September number shews lack of literary polish, the promised addition of a set of critics to the editorial staff will doubtless eliminate many roughnesses. Just now we may agree with Mr. Kleiner in comparing *Poesy* to Mr. Baxley's *Alabamian*.

*The Summer Girl*, and Ten Other Poems, is an exquisitely edited little brochure whose contents are wholly from the gifted pen of Mr. Andrew F. Lockhart. The outward form alone would be sufficient to prove the artistic tendencies of the author-publisher, while the verses within well shew by their fundamental keenness of thought, and aptness of expression, his substantial ability as a satirist. Perhaps Mr. Lockhart's weakest point is exhibited in the handling of metre. His lines are obviously designed to be recited rather than read, hence when scanned with an eye for technique occasionally defy exact classification. They possess, however, a certain rugged force which renders their homeliness not entirely out of place; and in every case where rural dialect is introduced, this homeliness becomes a positive asset. We should, on general principles, advise Mr. Lockhart to study as models the classic English satirists and satirical translators from Dryden to Gifford; yet we are forced to add that where certain odd characters and types are represented as speaking, he might well remember his present style. Though printed without especial prominence in the booklet, the poem "Now I'm Old" is undoubtedly the leading feature. Short as it is, it presents not only a biting attack on the essential emptiness and hypocrisy of blatant political methods, but a real pathos as well, as it exhibits the disillusioned old man, deluded for years by the specious orations of office-seekers, but now pitifully aware of the rottenness of factions and parties. This sketch was drawn from real life, which lends to its well-formed images an additional interest. "His Master's Voice" is one of the most powerful Temperance poems we have yet perused. Such a cleverly stinging blow to the noxious daemon of drink deserves painstaking metrical polish and subsequent republication as a syndicate feature throughout the country, to counteract the vile and shameless anti-Prohibition arguments with which the bloated beer-brewers are just now flooding the nation's press. Another splendid assault against Rum is "The Old Argument". The three morally stultified and indifferent old men, "Geek", "Brown", and "Bell", are realistic portraits of our typical bucolic advocates of "let well enough alone". It is through such agrestic callousness that the small towns which border on large, well-regulated cities become recognised centres of vice and intemperance. The politicians desire material prosperity and nothing more, hence, while possibly decent enough themselves, they harbour the filth which the cities are trying to cast out. "The Summer Girl", which heads the contents and gives its title to Mr. Lockhart's volume, is clever, but lacking in novelty. This is not the first time we have heard of strange transformations in social position caused by the close of the vacation season.

As a whole, Mr. Lockhart has by this book made a substantial contribution to amateur letters. The piercing shafts of sarcasm, swiftly penetrating the well-seeming garments which cover the less noble phases of human life, stamp the author as a man of wit and sense, while the quality of the taste exhibits an infinite capability of development. It is not without reason that we may call Mr. Lockhart an amateur Juvenal, just as we may designate Mr. Goodwin as an amateur Martial, and Mr. John Russell as an amateur Horace.

The Trail for Summer is of a quality equal to that of the Spring number, and forms the valedictory of the magazine in the United. Commencing with the November issue, it became a full-fledged professional publication, advocating a variety of social changes which Editor Huchinson favours. In the present number Rev. Graeme Davis reviews in interesting and scholarly fashion the editor's book, "The Limit of Wealth",[8] whose precepts Mr. Hutchinson is about to reiterate in the professionalised Trail. Mr. Davis possesses a prose style of unusual beauty and power, being a veritable connoisseur in his appreciation of the quality and harmony of words. "On a New-England Village Seen by Moonlight" is the name of an alleged poem by ourselves, whose merit is in no way enhanced by the misprint in the last line, where "drap'd" is shorn of its initial letter. "Dr. Frederick A. Cook: A Pen Picture" exhibits Mrs. E. L. Whitehead as a keen observer and an able essayist. While her faith in the explorer's glowing tale is not shared by many persons, her manner of narration and of drawing a moral is none the less highly commendable. Had Dr. Cook actually accomplished what he asserts, he would deserve just such a defence. However, it must be remembered that every circumstance in the Cook affair points to the falsity of the doctor's stories; that experts of every kind have agreed upon the absolute impossibility of his having reached either the Pole or the summit of Mount McKinley.[9] "Optimism", by Leo Fritter, confirms the wisdom of the Laureate Judges in proclaiming our President chief essayist of the United, for Mr. Fritter here continues to display his unusual power in the domain of poetical prose. There is one misprint in his essay, the word given on page 19 as "dodged" being properly "dogged". "The Tale of a Tramp", by Editor Hutchinson, is an account in heroic verse of last summer's Rocky Mount convention. The metre is well handled, moving along with the good old-fashioned swing which we, personally, admire. Were the language and treatment of the theme more closely adapted to the classical measure, the piece would have an additional value. The Trail concludes with a colloquial convention song, composed and published by Mr. Hutchinson during the course of a single morning. The piece is palpably not the fruit of long labour or painstaking polishing, yet is both clever and appropriate for its purpose.

The United Amateur for October is indeed a credit to our capable Official Editor,[10] for in literary quality it undoubtedly surpasses all previous efforts of like nature. The average official organ of an amateur press association is tediously political, and fails wholly to appeal to that higher grade of amateurs who care more for the beauties of letters than for the Saharan sands of administrative annals; but in his October number Mr. Daas has provided us with what is really a broadly constructed general magazine of unusual merit. After viewing excellent portraits of Messrs. Daas and Lockhart, and perusing a brief biography of the latter, the reader is attracted by Mr. J. W. Renshaw's well-worded epitome of a month's recruiting record in the United. The author, by introducing the latest recruits to the older members, here supplies a need of long standing in Amateur Journalism, for under ordinary circumstances many months are required for a newcomer to make himself known among us. Mr. Renshaw shews himself still further solicitous of the stranger's welfare by suggesting the organisation of a reception committee to adjust each recruit to his novel surroundings. This suggestion is one of great importance, and should be acted upon as soon as conditions permit. "The Dwarf", a tragical short story by Mrs. Ella Colby Eckert, shews decided ability in the construction and development of plot, and handling of dialogue. The descriptions are unusually realistic, and the local colour of the scenes well reproduced. "The Story of the Interview", by Melvin Ryder, is a lucid descriptive and historical article on one of the most important phases of modern professional journalism. Mr. Ryder follows his theme with commendable fluency, and displays a satisfactory familiarity with his subject. "A Best Book", by Mary Faye Durr, is a brief but delightful essay which reveals a just appreciation of the broader functions of literature. The remainder of the October issue is devoted entirely to verse. "Mater Dolorosa", by Jeanette Aylworth, is a piece of great attractiveness, whose metre and atmosphere have in them something of pleasing quaintness. "To Elbert and Alice Hubbard", by Olive G. Owen, is an elegy whose undoubtedly great beauty is marred by the astonishingly erroneous use of singular pronouns in connexion with plural subjects. "Thee", "thy", and "thine" cannot be used when *two* persons are addressed. "Jist Dae the Utmaist That Ye Can", by John Russell, is an attractive moral poem in Caledonian dialect, written around the motto of the Blue Stocking Club of Rocky Mount. The versification is correct, and the phraseology ingenious, the whole forming one of the best dialect pieces of the season. "The World War", by W. S. Harrison, is a stately poem on peace, clothed in skilfully wrought heroic blank verse. Mr. Harrison possesses the true technique of the polished poet, and so wholly escapes the jarring modern touch, that we pray he may become a very frequent contributor to the amateur press. "Sunsets of Yesterday", by Mrs. Renshaw, is an exquisite array of vivid and delicate imagery, cast in a tuneful dactylic measure. "Iconoclasts", by Kathleen Baldwin, is both ingenious in conception and harmonious in metre. We believe that Miss Baldwin is much above the amateur average as a poet. "A Vision", by Mary Evelyn Brown, is a short but intense lyric of undoubted art. "To Pavlowa", by Jean F. Barnum, is a very melodious bit of trochaic verse which contains some apt imagery. "The Fairy Stone", by James Riddick Laughton, is worthy of especial praise for its beauty of thought, though some of our readers may not be familiar with the object and legend which inspired it. The "fairy stone", or "staurolite", is a small, brownish, cruciform, crystalline geological formation peculiar to Virginia and North Carolina, and chemically composed of a silicate of iron and aluminum. Fairy stones are the subject not only of the legend used by Mr. Laughton, but of another which holds them to be the product of fairy artificers who dwelt in the mountain caves, and who carved the little crosses in remembrance of Christ when they heard of His crucifixion. The issue closes with "L'Envoi", a poem by George W. Stokes which possesses much beauty of sentiment and artistry of expression.

Viewed as a whole, the October Official Organ is an amateur paper as nearly ideal as any we have hitherto beheld. The tastefully selected and pleasingly varied nature of the contributions, the number and quality of the illustrations, and the general accuracy and neatness of form, all combine to place it in the very front rank of contemporary amateur journals.

The United Official Quarterly for October contains Leo Fritter's excellently written moral essay entitled "Personality". Mr. Fritter is unusually skilful in this department of literature, and we wish he might some time embody his sentiments in verse, producing a didactic poem of the type of Pope's Essay on Man. "Watered Stock", by William J. Dowdell, is a lucid and interesting account of the manufacture of paper. Mr. Dowdell's prose is steadily gaining in grace and dignity.

The Woodbee for October is edited by President Fritter, and contains his forceful editorial entitled "A Free Press", wherein he convincingly opposes the persistent fallacy that the columns of our journals should be devoted exclusively to amateur matters. Mr. Fritter well emphasises the fact that the press associations are not little worlds apart, but societies through which we should discuss general topics as in other educational bodies. We note with pleasure Mr. Fritter's stand for Temperance. "Search Me", the only story in the magazine, is a clever piece of humour by Florenz Ziegfeld. The development is easy and natural, whilst the climax is well calculated to surprise and delight the reader. The solitary poem in this issue is by Freda M. Sanger, and is entitled "Two Days". The rather uncommon metrical form and rhyming arrangements are not displeasing, and the images and general sentiment are alike deserving of commendation. Mr. Benjamin Repp offers an essay, "Girls among Girls", which deplores the tendency of the fair to condemn so utterly those of their number who have departed from absolute rectitude. The topic is not of great novelty, Dr. Johnson having dwelt upon it over a century ago, but its renewed presentation is by no means out of place. In the technique of the article, we lament evidences of haste and colloquialism. On page 4 it is stated that "a boy can go . . . almost every place". Since "go" is an intransitive verb, a preposition is here required, making the phrase read: "go to almost every place". The provincialism "onto" at the head of page 5 should be changed to "upon", whilst the expression "from where" should give place to "whence". Mr. Newton A. Thatcher's "Dissertation on the Needle" shews marks of immaturity, yet possesses much real humour. The use of "like" for "as" at the bottom of page 6 is not to be applauded.

As a whole, the October Woodbee is of encouraging excellence, and promises well for Mr. Fritter's term of editorship.

EDITOR'S NOTE FP: United Amateur 15, No. 5 (December 1915): 64–69 (signed "Howard P. Lovecraft, Chairman").

Notes

1. See "More Chain Lightning" (CE5), on Lockhart's temperance journal of that title.
2. The Olympian was an amateur journal published for the NAPA by Edward H. Cole, a colleague of HPL's. It appeared sporadically up to 1917, then ceased until Cole revived it in 1940 to publish an issue devoted to memoirs of HPL.
3. Melvin Ryder (1893–?), Rambles Round the Campus (Boston: Sherman, French & Co., 1915). Ryder later edited a journal, Civilian Front: National Weekly Newspaper for Civilian Defense (1933f.).
4. Alexander Pope, An Essay on Man (1733–34), 1.267.

5. HPL refers to Joseph E. Shufelt and Victor L. Basinet; the latter was president of the Providence Amateur Press Club. See "[Untitled Notes on Amateur Journalism]" (*Conservative*, October 1915) (p. 76).

6. See Rheinhart Kleiner, "Dream Days; or, Metrical Musings," *Piper* No. 3 (September 1915): 9–10. Section III of the poem (p. 9) is subtitled: "As Howard P. Lovecraft Might Have Given It Eighteenth Century Garb, in His Favorite Metre:"

> Descend soft-shaded night! Remove our cares,
> Soothe us with slumber, lull with Lydian airs!
> Banish the hurts that haress'd [*sic*] human kind,
> And may we now in thee sweet solace find!
> Bring to our senses, bound in Lethe's pow'r,
> Visions of childhood and a kinder hour,
> When we in busy street, or shady lane,
> Our simple sports prolong'd, a merry train!
> Where "London Bridge" might fall on lad and lass,
> And each must pay some penalty to pass;
> Where "Mulberry Bush," besides, and "Ding Dong Bell,"
> For childish mirth and laughter served as well.
> Ah, never have we join'd in sport as rare
> As innocence has frisk'd and gambol'd there!
> So, kindly sleep, come down—but stay! the blush
> Of dewy morn, wakes sparrow, now, and thrush;
> And though we fain in dreaming would engage,
> For bread we choose the turmoil of the age!

7. HPL's poem "To Charlie of the Comics" (1915; AT 93), about Charles Chaplin, was a response to this poem by Kleiner (about Mary Pickford).

8. Alfred L. Hutchinson (1859–?), *The Limit of Wealth* (New York: Macmillan; London: Macmillan, 1907). Hutchinson also published *Storm Bound: A Series of Character Sketches and Scenes from Life* (1909).

9. Frederick A. Cook (1865–1940), American physician and explorer, claimed to have reached the North Pole on 21 April 1908, nearly a year before Robrt E. Peary, but this appears to be a fabrication, as does his claim in his book, *To the Top of the Continent* (1908), that he was the first to have reached the top of Mt. McKinley in 1906.

10. Edward F. Daas, who recruited HPL into the UAPA.

## SYSTEMATIC INSTRUCTION IN THE UNITED

In the earlier days of our association, the two bureaus now called the Departments of Public and Private Criticism were grouped together under the collective name of "Department of Instruction and Criticism". Experience, however, well demonstrated the inability of such a bureau to furnish definite correspondence courses in literature, and the broadly educational function was eventually eliminated in the interests of a more thorough development of the purely critical features. But the perfection of improvement of the critical bureaus has in no way supplied the need of a real literary school, and we are today as far as ever from furnishing the unpolished novice with the easy elementary instruction he so sadly requires.

In the June *Lake Breeze* appeared the outline of a plan for establishing a systematic "Department of Instruction", separate from the critical boards, and conducted exclusively by professional teachers of English. During the ensuing months many teachers and professors of great culture and ability have become affiliated with us, wherefore it seems now feasible to commence actual work toward the formation of the desired department.

The exact scope of the innovation is first to be considered; that is, the nature of the proposed pupils and the amount of knowledge to be conferred upon them by the department. While both must necessarily vary, a fair estimate can be made by reflecting upon the prevailing type of young amateur. Ambition is never lacking in the United novice, since it is ambition which draws him into amateur journalism; but general education is often imperfect, and it is not too much to say that the new "school" must be prepared to deal with the very foundations of simple grammar. A specific case which has confronted the Department of Private Criticism during Mr. Moe's Chairmanship is that of a young man of the highest ambition and keenest energy, who has not the slightest comprehension of the proper meaning, use, and relations of English words, and who is therefore wholly beyond help unless a "primer course" be created to aid him. And this case is, though extreme, by no means unique as a type. Scores of our youthful members are stumbling along on cant phrases and popular idioms without the slightest idea of logical verbal construction. These folks have nothing on which to build a presentable style; they are blindly wandering, and must first of all be thoroughly drilled in plain, formal grammar.

Assuming that correct grammar may be easily taught by the Department of Instruction, we have next to deal with the first steps in literature. Here the problem is less simple, since a student's grasp of grammar or his ability to write properly is no fair index of his reading and taste; and again, his reading is not always a criterion of his original accomplishments. But certain generalities must needs assist us. A number of English classics are supposed to have been ready by everyone, and it is the duty of the department to see that every pupil has read them. A list of these necessary works, from whose styles an amateur may be expected to adapt or select his own, might well represent the standard college entrance requirements in English. This well-directed reading should do much toward counteracting the present tendency of certain classes of young members to copy inferior but popular models both in prose and in verse. Original exercises on subjects connected with the prescribed text, and the following up of all references and allusions therein, should be practiced as in regular high-school English courses. But as compared with the high-school, the United must ever suffer from one disadvantage; the absence of educational courses apart from English. Science, history, the languages, the fine arts, and a thousand other things must be acquired in order to produce real culture. These we cannot hope to impart. We cannot give to a recruit the erudition which shall impel him to become an author; it is enough that we give him means of expression, assuming that he has already something to express.

Besides the elementary course, a second and more advanced branch of the new department would undoubtedly supply a very real need. There are a numerous set of amateurs, who, though possessing a satisfactory knowledge of the essentials of literature, and a tolerable familiarity with all the best models, are yet lacking in that exquisite development of taste which is necessary for the perfection of their own prose or metrical styles. Such individuals often obtain the required aid from the Department of Private Criticism, but since their needs are so much alike, it would be advantageous if a regular course were offered them. This course would be mainly technical, and would present but little difficulty.

Of the general construction of the proposed department, enough has been previously said in *The Lake Breeze*. The use of a standard text-book on rhetoric, supplemented by notes fitting it for peculiarly amateur purposes; the modification of the courses of reading to suit particular cases; the closely individual instruction to accompany the formal precepts; and the sympathetic revision and publication of the pupils' original efforts; have all been recommended.

It remains, then, but to venture the opinion that the taking of these courses should be wholly optional with the possible pupils. If study were compulsory; that is, if it were made a condition of membership for persons unable to pass a stated entrance examination, much good material might be lost. The United must still be able to accommodate those who seek only the playful pastime of attempted authorship. There will, however, be no lack of willing pupils, and such is the sincere enthusiasm of most of our youth, that the instructors will probably find themselves busy from the first.

The time has now arrived for interested English teachers and professors to offer themselves to Pres. Fritter for service in the proposed department, and it is to be hoped that before many months have elapsed, an organising committee will have been formed, and the gravely needed literary course become an assured prospect.

EDITOR'S NOTE  FP: *Ole Miss'* No. 2 (December 1915): 4–5. HPL continues his plans (first propounded in "New Department Proposed," p. 47 above) for a Department of Instruction to assist literarily crude amateur writers to eliminate errors of style and taste.

---

# UNITED AMATEUR PRESS ASSOCIATION: EXPONENT OF AMATEUR JOURNALISM

## ITS OBJECT

The desire to write for publication is one which inheres strongly in every human breast. From the proficient college graduate, storming the gates of the high-grade literary magazines, to the raw schoolboy, vainly endeavouring to place his first crude compositions in the local newspapers, the whole intelligent public are today seeking expression through the printed page, and yearning to behold their thoughts and ideals permanently crystallised in the magic medium of type. But while a few persons of exceptional talent manage eventually to gain a foothold in the professional world of letters, rising to celebrity through the wide diffusion of their art, ideals, or opinions; the vast majority, unless aided in their education by certain especial advantages, are doomed to confine their expression to the necessarily restricted sphere of ordinary conversation. To supply those especial educational advantages which may enable the general public to achieve the distinction of print, and which may prevent the talented but unknown author from remaining forever in obscurity, has risen that largest and foremost of societies for literary education—*The United Amateur Press Association*.

# ITS ORIGIN

Amateur journalism, or the composition and circulation of small, privately printed magazines, is an instructive diversion which has existed in the United States for over half a century. In the decade of 1866–1876 this practice first became an organised institution; a short-lived society of amateur journalists, including the now famous publisher, Charles Scribner, having existed from 1869 to 1874. In 1876 a more lasting society was formed, which exists to this day as an exponent of light dilettantism.[1] Not until 1895, however, was amateur journalism established as a serious branch of educational endeavour. On September 2nd of that year, Mr. William H. Greenfield, a gifted professional author,[2] of Philadelphia, founded *The United Amateur Press Association*, which has grown to be the leader of its kind, and the representative of amateur journalism in its best phases throughout the English-speaking world.

# ITS NATURE

In many respects the word "amateur" fails to do full credit to amateur journalism and the association which bests represents it. To some minds the term conveys an idea of crudity and immaturity, yet the *United* can boast of members and publications whose polish and scholarship are well-nigh impeccable. In considering the adjective "amateur" as applied to the press association, we must adhere to the more basic interpretation, regarding the word as indicating the non-mercenary nature of the membership. Our amateurs write purely for love of their art, without the stultifying influence of commercialism. Many of them are prominent professional authors in the outside world, but their professionalism never creeps into their association work. The atmosphere is wholly fraternal, and courtesy takes the place of currency.

The real essential of amateur journalism and *The United Amateur Press Association* is the amateur paper or magazine, which somewhat resembles the average high-school or college publication. These journals, varying greatly in size and character, are issued by various members at their own expense, and contain, besides the literary work of their several editors or publishers, contributions from all the many members who do not publish papers of their own. Their columns are open to every person in the association, and it may be said with justice that no one will find it impossible to secure the publication of any literary composition of reasonable brevity. The papers thus published are sent free to all our many members, who constitute a select and highly appreciative reading public. Since each member receives the published work of every other member, many active and brilliant minds are brought into close contact, and questions of every sort, literary, historical, and scientific, are debated both in the press and in personal correspondence. The correspondence of members is one of the most valuable features of the *United*, for through this medium a great intellectual stimulus, friendly and informal in nature, is afforded. Congenial members are in this way brought together in a lettered companionship, which often grows into life-long friendship, while persons of opposed ideas may mutually gain much breadth of mind by hearing the other side of their respective opinions discussed in a genial manner. In short, the *United* offers an exceptionally well-proportioned mixture of instruction and fraternal cheer. There are no limits of age, sex, education, position, or locality in this most complete of democracies. Boys and girls of twelve and men and women of sixty, parents and their sons and daughters, college professors and grammar-school pupils, aristocrats and intelligent labourers, Easterners and Westerners, are here given equal advantages, those of greater education helping their cruder brethren until the common fund of culture is as nearly level as it can be in any human organisation. Members are classified according to age; "A" meaning under sixteen, "B" from 16 to 21, and "C" over 21. The advantages offered to those of limited acquirements are immense, many persons having gained practically all their literary polish through membership in the *United*. A much cherished goal is professional authorship or editorship, and numerous indeed are the *United* members who have now become recognised authors, poets, editors, and publishers. True, though trite, is the saying that amateur journalism is an actual training school for professional journalism.

## ITS PUBLISHING ACTIVITIES

Members of the *United* may or may not publish little papers of their own. This is a matter of choice, for there are always enough journals to print the work of the non-publishing members. Youths who possess printing-presses will find publishing an immense but inexpensive pleasure, whilst other publishers may have their printing done at very reasonable rates by those who do own presses. The favourite size for amateur papers is 5 × 7 inches, which can be printed at 55 or 60 cents per page, each page containing about 250 words. Thus a four-page issue containing 1000 words can be published for less than $2.50, if arrangements are made, as is often the case, for its free mailing with any other paper. Certain of the more pretentious journals affect the 7 × 10 size, which costs about $1.60 for each page of 700 words. These figures allow for 250 copies, the most usual number to be mailed. Mr. E. E. Ericson of Elroy, Wisconsin, is our Official Printer, and his work is all that the most fastidious could demand. Other printers may be found amongst the young men who print their own papers. In many cases they can quote very satisfactory prices. Two or more members may issue a paper coöperatively, the individual expense then being very slight.

## ITS CONTRIBUTED LITERATURE

The *United* welcomes all literary contributions; poems, stories, and essays, which the various members may submit. However, contribution is by no means compulsory, and in case a member finds himself too busy for activity, he may merely enjoy the free papers which reach him, without taxing himself with literary labour. For those anxious to contribute, every facility is provided. In some cases negotiations are made directly between publisher and contributor, but the majority are accommodated by the two Manuscript Bureaux, Eastern and Western, which receive contributions in any quantity from the non-publishing members, and are drawn upon for material by those who issue papers. These bureaux practically guarantee on the one hand to find a place for each member's manuscript, and on the other hand to keep each publisher well supplied with matter for his journal.

## ITS CRITICAL DEPARTMENTS

The two critical departments of the *United* are at present the most substantial of the various educational advantages. The Department of Private Criticism is composed exclusively of highly cultured members, usually professors or teachers of English, who practically mould the taste of the whole association, receiving and revising before publication the work of all who choose to submit it to them. The service furnished by this department is in every way equal to that for which professional critical bureaux charge about two dollars. Manuscripts are carefully corrected and criticised in every detail, and authors are given comprehensive advice designed to elevate their taste, style, and grammar. Many a crude but naturally gifted writer has been developed to polished fluency and set on the road to professional authorship through the United's Department of Private Criticism.

The Department of Public Criticism reviews thoroughly and impartially the various printed papers and their contents, offering precepts and suggestions for improvement. Its reports are printed in the official organ of the association, and serve as a record of our literary achievement.

## ITS LITERARY AWARDS

To encourage excellence amongst the members of the United, annual honours or "laureateships" are awarded the authors of the best poems, stories, essays, or editorials. Participation in these competitions is not compulsory, since they apply only to pieces which have been especially "entered for laureateship". The entries are judged not by the members of the association, but by highly distinguished litterateurs of the professional world, selected particularly for the occasion. Our latest innovation is a laureateship for the best home-printed paper, which will excite keen rivalry among our younger members, and bring out some careful specimens of the typographical art. Besides the laureateships there are other honours and prizes awarded by individual publishers within the United, many of the amateur journals offering excellent books for the best stories, reviews, or reports submitted to them.

## ITS OFFICIAL ORGAN

The association, as a whole, publishes a voluminous 7 × 10 monthly magazine called The United Amateur, which serves as the official organ. In this magazine may be found the complete revised list of members, the reports of officers and committees, the ample reviews issued by the Department of Public Criticism, a selection of the best contemporary amateur literature, together with the latest news of amateur journalists and their local clubs from all over the Anglo-Saxon world. The United Amateur is published by an annually elected Official Editor, and printed by the Official Publisher. It is sent free to all members of the association.

## ITS GOVERNMENT

The United Amateur Press Association is governed by a board of officers elected by popular vote. The elections take place at the annual conventions, where amateurs from all sections meet and fraternise. Those who attend vote in person, whilst all others send in proxy ballots. There is much friendly rivalry between cities concerning the selection of the convention seat each year. The principal elective officers of the United are the President, two Vice-Presidents, the Treasurer, the Official Editor, and the three members of the Board of Directors. There are also a Historian, a Laureate Recorder, and two Manu-script Managers. Appointed by the President are the members of the two Departments of Criticism, the Supervisor of Amendments, the Official Publisher, and the Secretary of the association. All save Secretary and Official Publisher serve without remuneration. The basic law of the *United* comprises an excellent Constitution and By-Laws.

## ITS LOCAL CLUBS

The *United* encourages the formation of local literary or press clubs in cities or towns containing several members. These clubs generally publish papers, and hold meetings wherein the pleasures of literature are enlivened by those of the society. The most desirable form of club activity is that in which a high-school instructor forms a literary society of the more enthusiastic members of his class.

## ITS PLACE IN EDUCATION

During the past two years, as it has approached and passed its twentieth birthday, the *United* has been endeavouring more strongly than ever to find and occupy its true place amongst the many and varied phases of education. That it discharges an unique function in literary culture is certain, and its members have of late been trying very ac-tively to establish and define its relation to the high-school and the university. Mr. Mau-rice W. Moe, Instructor of English at the Appleton High School, Appleton, Wisconsin, and one of our very ablest members, took the first decisive step by organising his pupils into an amateur press club, using the *United* to supplement his regular class-room work. The scholars were delighted, and many have acquired a love of good literature which will never leave them. Three or four, in particular, have become prominent in the affairs of the *United*. After demonstrating the success of his innovation, Mr. Moe described it in *The English Journal;*[3] his article arousing much interest in educational circles, and being widely reprinted by other papers. In November, 1914, Mr. Moe addressed an assemblage of English teachers in Chicago, and there created so much enthusiasm for the *United*, that scores of instructors have subsequently joined our ranks, many of them forming school clubs on the model of the original club at Appleton. Here, then, is one definite destiny for our association; to assist the teaching of advanced English in the high-school. We are especially eager for high-school material, teachers and pupils alike.

But there still remain a numerous class, who, though not connected with school or college, have none the less sincere literary aspirations. At present they are benefited im-mensely through mental contact with our more polished members, yet for the future we plan still greater aids for their development, by the creation of a systematic "Department of Instruction", which will, if successfully established, amount practically to a free corre-spondence school, and an "Authors' Placing Bureau", which will help amateurs in enter-ing the professional field.[4] Our prime endeavour is at present to secure members of high mental and scholastic quality, in order that the *United* may be strengthened for its in-creasing responsibility. Professors, teachers, clergymen, and authors have already re-sponded in gratifying numbers to our wholly altruistic plea for their presence among us. The reason for the *United's* success as an educational factor seems to lie principally in the splendid loyalty and enthusiasm which all the members somehow acquire upon joining. Every individual is alert for the welfare of the association, and its activities form the subject of many of the current essays and editorials. The ceaseless writing in which most of the members indulge, is in itself an aid to fluency, while the mutual examples and criticisms help on still further the pleasantly unconscious acquisition of a good literary style. When regular courses of instruction shall have been superimposed upon these things, the association can indeed afford to claim a place of honour in the world of education.

## ITS ENTRANCE CONDITIONS

The only requirement for admission to the *United* is earnest literary aspiration. Any member will furnish the candidate for admission with an application blank, signed in recommendation. This application, filled out and forwarded to the Secretary of the association with the sum of fifty cents as dues for the first year, and accompanied by a "credential", or sample of the candidate's original literary work, will be acted upon with due consideration by the proper official. No candidate of real sincerity will be denied admittance, and the applicant will generally be soon rewarded by his certificate of membership, signed by the President and Secretary. Papers, letters, and postal cards of welcome will almost immediately pour in upon him, and he will in due time behold his credential in print. (Unless it be something already printed.) Once a member, his dues will be one dollar yearly, and if he should ever leave the *United,* later desiring to join again, his reinstatement fee will be one dollar.

## ITS REPRESENTATIVES

*The United Amateur Press Association* is anything but local in its personnel. Its active American membership extends from Boston to Los Angeles, and from Milwaukee to Tampa, thus bringing all sections in contact, and representing every phase of American thought. Its English membership extends as far north as Newcastle-upon-Tyne. Typical papers are published in England, California, Kansas, Wisconsin, Ohio, Illinois, Alabama, Mississippi, North Carolina, District of Columbia, New York, and Rhode Island.

In writing for entrance blanks or for further information concerning the *United,* the applicant may address any one of the following officers, who will gladly give details, and samples of amateur papers: Leo Fritter, President, 503 Central National Bank Bldg., Columbus, Ohio; H. P. Lovecraft, Vice-President, 598 Angell St., Providence, R.I.; Mrs. J. W. Renshaw, Second Vice-President, Coffeeville, Miss.; William J. Dowdell, Secretary, 2428 East 66th St., Cleveland, Ohio; or Edward F. Daas, Official Editor, 1717 Cherry St., Milwaukee, Wis. Professional authors interested in our work are recommended to communicate with the Second Vice-President, while English teachers may derive expert information from Maurice W. Moe, 658 Atlantic St., Appleton, Wis. Youths who possess printing-presses are referred to the Secretary, who is himself a young typographer.

## ITS PROVINCE SUMMARISED

*If you are* a student of elementary English desirous of attaining literary polish in an enjoyable manner,
 *If you are* an ordinary citizen, burning with the ambition to become an author,
 *If you are* a solitary individual wishing for a better chance to express yourself,

*If you own* a printing-press and would like to learn how to issue a high-grade paper,

*If you are* a mature person eager to make up for a youthful lack of culture,

*If you are* a professor or teacher seeking a new method of interesting your English class, or

*If you are* an author or person of ripe scholarship, anxious to aid your cruder brothers on their way, then,

YOU ARE CORDIALLY INVITED TO BECOME A MEMBER OF THE UNITED AMATEUR PRESS ASSOCIATION.

EDITOR'S NOTE FP: Pamphlet ([Columbus, OH: Leo Fritter, 1915]). A recruiting brochure, signed "H. P. LOVECRAFT, Vice President," hence issued during HPL's term as First Vice-President (August 1915–July 1916). It was issued late in 1915, as indicated in "Report of First Vice-President" (November 1915). The brochure concisely embodies HPL's goals for the UAPA, particularly as an organisation of education and the development of literary expression in a non-remunerative context.

*Notes*

1. I.e., the NAPA.
2. Greenfield was in fact only fourteen years old when he founded the UAPA. He later published the novel *Ring and Diamond* (Athol, MA: Cook Publishing Co., 1921).
3. Maurice W. Moe, "Amateur Journalism and the English Teacher," *English Journal* 4, No. 2 (February 1915): 113–15. It was an address delivered at a meeting of the National Council of Teachers of English in Chicago, 27 November 1914.
4. No such bureau ever came into existence.

---

# INTRODUCING MR. JAMES PYKE

Of the many gifted poets entering The United Amateur Press Association during the present period of improved literary standards, few can bear comparison with the one who now makes his first appearance in these pages, Mr. James T. Pyke of Riverside, East Providence, R.I.

Mr. Pyke is a gentleman blessed equally with the advantages of highest culture and of highest intellectual endowments. He is a graduate both of Brown University and of Andover Theological Seminary, having been Class Poet at the latter institution. Upon his graduation from Andover, Mr. Pyke was ordained to the Congregational ministry, to which profession he lent all the remarkable genius with which favouring fortune has invested him; but the tremendous strain of pastoral activity on a delicate constitution at last proved excessive, and he has now retired to a quiet life of letters, cultivating the Muses in his cottage at Riverside, overlooking the sparkling reaches of Narragansett Bay.

The unusual modesty of Mr. Pyke has veiled a poetical genius which will now blaze out all the more resplendently because of its previous concealment. His first efforts were made in boyhood, and specimens written at the age of seventeen shew all the inspiration and polish to be expected from a man of mature years. But these were no more than the faint promise of future excellence. His poems of manhood are infinitely moving and beautiful. Nature, viewed through the medium of his sonnets, takes on new and lovelier aspects, whilst his longer poems cover every phase of human life and aspiration. The Conservative's lines in the United Official Quarterly for November, 1914, were an endeavour to convey some idea of their grace and loftiness.

Mr. Pyke's particular models in verse have ever been the New England poets, and to the classic coterie of the preceding century he may be justly deemed a legitimate successor.

It is not often that an organisation of amateurs can boast the membership of a genius of Mr. Pyke's type, and The Conservative has scant need to say that he is vastly proud to have been the means of bringing Mr. Pyke into his beloved United Amateur Press Association.

EDITOR'S NOTE  FP: Conservative 1, No. 4 (January 1916): 1–2 (unsigned). HPL introduces a recruit from East Providence, RI. In his autobiographical letter of 1 January 1915, HPL states that his move from 454 to 598 Angell Street in 1904 caused him to be "brought into closer contact with the Rev. James Pyke and his aged mother, both poets, whom we had always known, but who were now our next-door neighbours" (SL 1.9). No doubt Pyke moved to East Providence at some point after 1904. Appended to the poem "To the Rev. James Pyke" (United Official Quarterly, November 1914; AT 336), HPL has written the note "Rev. Mr. Pyke is an elderly retired Congregational minister who possesses poetical talent of the very highest order, but who, from native modesty, declines absolutely to have his works published. He has written verse since early boyhood, and has in manuscript enough lyrics, dramas, epics, sacred poems, and the like to fill about ten good-sized volumes." Two poems by Pyke, "Maia" (p. 3) and "The Poet" (p. 3), appeared in this issue of the Conservative, but no other work by Pyke appeared in the Conservative, and one can assume that Pyke either died or ceased to be a colleague of HPL.

# REPORT OF FIRST VICE-PRESIDENT

*(January 1916)*

Fellow Amateurs:—

The Recruiting Committee, since the last previous report of the undersigned, has been endeavouring to fulfil as best it may the promises made at the beginning of the present administrative year. The Looking Glass, financed in connexion with the other Committee and edited by the Second Vice-President, has been mailed; whilst the paper of credentials, announced last August, will later be published under the editorship of the Eastern Manuscript Manager. Contributions or pledges of small amounts are solicited for the financing of this very necessary paper. Mr. Lockhart now heads the list of donors, with a pledge of $10; or more, if necessary.

Mr. David H. Whittier, of this Committee, is planning a systematic handling of recruiting work which shall ensure a division of labour and concentration of energy far superior to that hitherto existing in this department.

Up to the present time our committeemen have received no monetary aid from the United at large, but have borne all postal expenses personally, besides contributing $13 in cash to the publication of The Looking Glass. This lack of support has proved a retarding influence, but has not prevented us from accomplishing a reasonably satisfactory amount of work.

In view of the heavy expenses of this Committee, requests for files of Chase's *Amateur Journalist* should henceforth be accompanied by 6 cents in stamps, as payment for postage.

EDITOR'S NOTE FP: *United Amateur* 15, No. 6 (January 1916): 72. The second of HPL's two reports as First Vice-President.

# EDITORIAL
*(February 1916)*

Among the correspondence of *The Providence Amateur* is a letter from a prominent United poet, containing a passage so significant that it deserves repetition. "Redoing prose work," writes this gifted versifier, "I simply can't. I have tried time and again, but it won't work." Now the significance of this statement lies in its universality of application; for whilst our association abounds with poets of satisfactory attainments, good prose is among us a thing of lamentable rarity. That a majority of members possess prose styles both fairly grammatical and reasonably perspicuous is indeed true; but that this prose is proportionately far less developed than the contemporary mass of verse, is equally true.

In glancing over the journals of the day, one is impressed with the various types of literary looseness encountered in the prose articles and stories. The crudities of youth or inexperience are to be expected, but that old and practiced amateurs should thus neglect precision and harmony is highly reprehensible.

The defects of amateur prose, as exhibited by our better grade of writers, may perhaps be grouped into three classes: (1) Intentional slang, (2) Grammatical weakness in otherwise flowing and harmonious work, and (3) Grammatically correct, but abrupt and repellent constructions. The first of these defects is more the result of bad taste than of bad scholarship, while the second may justly be attributed to carelessness. It is the third, or grammatical but harsh style, that demands severest censure, since in this cacophonous correctness we may most plainly trace the subtle undermining influence that is rapidly making good prose writing a lost art.

Briefly, the situation seems to be that in our desire for simplicity and clearness, we are forgetting that literary prose is an art at all; forgetting that it is not a mere succession of dissonant and dissociated sounds and statements, but a medium of expression whose verbal flow and harmony are governed by laws as immutable, if less exacting, than those of verse. Modern forms of instruction are possibly responsible for this indolent attitude. Tired of dwelling minutely on the construction of periodic sentences, or of exactly defining the use of synonyms, inversions, transpositions, periphrasis, amplification, variety, unity, strength, harmony, purity, propriety, alliteration, onomatopoeia, figurative language, antithesis, parallel, climax, allusion, and the like; our hurried preceptors are willing to accept any sort of prose which is at once clear, and conformable to general grammatical arrangements.

But whilst the non-literary public may well be satisfied with such unornamented diction, we feel that those who aspire to the crown of scholarship should inquire more deeply into the fundamentals of the art of prose, and observe those proprieties which lent grace to the sentences of other and happier days. Continued neglect of this important branch of letters will inevitably lead to a condition wherein everyone desirous of elegant non-metrical expression must needs find himself embarrassed, and will doubtless have to exclaim with our poetical friend, that prose "won't work"! Shall we not, then, seek rather to study the formal graces of artistic prose, than to rush blindly on toward an era of decadence when every polished author will perforce be a rhymester?

There is no advantage, however great, which entirely lacks its compensating touch of disadvantage. During the preceding year our United has risen to hitherto unknown heights through the influx of cultured members, yet we are now confronted by the problem of maintaining a sufficient number of journals to publish and diffuse the work of our gifted novices. The amateur world of the past contained a profusion of papers, but a scarcity of sense; the amateur world today has an abundance of high-grade literary matter, yet lacks facilities for its publication. The cause of the change is not difficult to discern. The "small boy with a printing-press", and his frequent but crude publications, is passing from our midst, and in his stead has arrived the true man of letters, desirous of writing, yet disdaining the apparently childish pastime of issuing an amateur journal. Now this condition requires remedy, for no elevation of our standards can prove effective unless made practical by the continuance of the amateur press.

Since the home-printed journal is so much a thing of the past, we must if possible arouse among the newcomers a contagious enthusiasm for the issuing of outside printed papers. We must seek to discourage the erroneous idea that there is anything of puerility in the general distribution of 5 × 7 or 7 × 10 leaflets. If we were to call our journals "tracts", "leaflets", "privately printed matter", or anything but "journals", this would be easy, but it is difficult to convince the cultured recruit that a tiny amateur sheet purporting to be a real "magazine" is anything but a juvenile sham.

The present writer would be wholly willing to witness the departure of the term "journal", "paper", or "magazine", and to behold the name of our society changed to "The United Association for the Cultivation of Letters". He would gladly efface the slight journalistic touch both from the present collection of literary matter and from his own *Conservative*, if such precedent would encourage the heretofore silent amateurs to issue similar "leaflets", or "privately printed articles and verses". But so strong is the sentiment of our veteran element, that such a deviation from custom would probably be impossible. Can we not all, then, try otherwise to disabuse our new and cultivated associates of the notion that we are "playing editor"? Can we not shun our more obvious limitations of professional methods, and seek to emphasise the literary side of our labours? Andrew Francis Lockhart has done this in both of the attractive booklets of verse which he issued last year.

An alternative means of ensuring the publication of amateur matter is the permanent enlargement of *The United Amateur*, as long ago proposed by Paul J. Campbell. This thick 7 × 10 magazine lacks the suggestion of immaturity offered by the smaller individual papers; and being truly a journal, may well assume the air of actual journalism. Editor Daas has done his best to carry out Mr. Campbell's idea, but financial aid from the members at large has been lacking. Why do we not respond more generally to Pres. Fritter's call for contributions to the official organ fund? With adequate monetary resources, *The United Amateur* can become the medium whereby all our literary efforts may reach the amateur public, while its dignified appearance under the skilled editorship of Mr. Daas will make every member eager to adorn its pages with his work.

But whether through a stimulated renaissance of the individual paper, or an enlargement of the official organ, it is plainly our duty to take steps toward increasing the publishing efficiency of the association. Our avowed purpose is to furnish a medium of expression for the literary aspirant, and until we shall have accomplished this, we cannot justly claim the supreme laurels of success.

EDITOR'S NOTE  FP: *Providence Amateur* 1, No. 2 (February 1916): 9–13. In this second and last issue of the *Providence Amateur*, HPL is listed as Official Editor; the Providence Amateur Press Club broke up shortly after its issuance. HPL here harps on a familiar subject— the poor quality of the prose written by many amateurs.

# DEPARTMENT OF PUBLIC CRITICISM

*(April 1916)*

*T*he *Brooklynite* for January contains one of Rheinhart Kleiner's characteristic poems, entitled "A Mother's Song". Mr. Kleiner's command of good taste, harmony, and correctness requires no further panegyric amongst those who know him; but to the more recent United members who have not yet read extensively in our journals, his work may well be recommended as undoubtedly the safest of all amateur poetical models for emulation. Mr. Kleiner has a sense of musical rhythm which few amateur bards have ever possessed, and his choice of words and phrases is the result of a taste both innate and cultivated, whose quality appears to rare advantage in the present degenerate age. This remarkable young poet has not yet fully displayed in verse the variety of thoughts and images of which his fertile brain and well-selected reading have made him master, but has preferred to concentrate most of his powers upon delicate amatory lyrics. While some of his readers may at times regret this limitation of endeavour, and wish he might practice to a greater extent that immense versatility which he permitted the amateur public to glimpse in the September *Piper*; it is perhaps not amiss that he should cultivate most diligently that type of composition most natural and easy to him, for he is obviously a successor of those polished and elegant poets of gallantry whose splendour adorned the reigns of Queen Elizabeth and King James the First.

The *Conservative* for January opens with Winifred Virginia Jordan's "Song of the North Wind", one of the most powerful poems lately seen in the amateur press. Mrs. Jordan is the newest addition to the United's constellation of genuine poetical luminaries; shining as an artist of lively imagination, faultless taste, and graphic expression, whose work possesses touches of genius and individualism that have already brought her renown in amateur circles. In the poem under consideration, Mrs. Jordan displays a phenomenal comprehension of the sterner aspects of Nature, producing a thoroughly virile effect. Words are chosen with care and placed with remarkable force, whilst both alliteration and onomatopoeia are employed with striking success. By the same author is the shorter poem entitled "Galileo and Swammerdam", which though vastly different in aspect and rhythm, yet retains that suggestion of mysticism so frequently encountered in Mrs. Jordan's work.

James Tobey Pyke, a lyrical and philosophical poet of high scholastic attainments, contributes two poems; "Maia" and "The Poet". The latter is a stately sonnet, rich in material for reflection. Such is the quality of Pyke's work, that his occasional contributions are ever to be acclaimed with the keenest interest and appreciation.

Rheinhart Kleiner, our Laureate, is another bard twice represented in the January *Conservative*. His two poems, "Consolation" and "To Celia", though widely different in structure, are yet not unrelated in sentiment, being both devoted to the changing heart. One amateur critic has seen fit to frown upon so skilled an apotheosis of inconsistency, but it seems almost captious thus to analyse an innocuous bit of art so daintily and tastefully arrayed. "To Celia" is perhaps slightly the better of the two, having a very commendable stateliness of cadence, and a gravity of thought greater than that of "Consolation".

"The Horizon of Dreams", by Mrs. Renshaw, is a graphic and enthralling venture into the realm of nocturnal unreality. The free play of active imagination, the distorted and transitory conceptions and apparitions, and the strangely elusive analogies, all lend charm and colour to this happy portrayal of the vague boundaries of Somnus' domain. Mrs. Renshaw's rank as a poet is a very high one, most of her productions involving a spiritual insight and metaphysical comprehension vastly beyond that of the common mind. But this very nobility of imagination, and superiority to the popular appeal, are only too likely to render her best work continually underestimated and unappreciated by the majority. She is not a "poet of the masses", and her graver efforts must needs reach audiences more notable for cultural than numerical magnitude. Of Mrs. Renshaw's liberal metrical theories, enough is said elsewhere. This Department can neither endorse principles so radical, nor refrain from remarking that want of proper rhyme and metre has relegated to obscurity many a rich and inspired poem.

"Departed", by Maude Kingsbury Barton, is a sentimental poem of undoubted grace and sweetness, happily cast in unbroken metre.

*The Coyote* for January is adorned by no less than three of Mrs. Winifred V. Jordan's exquisite short poems. "The Night-Wind" is a delicately beautiful fragment of dreamy metaphor. There is probably a slight misprint in the last line, since the construction there becomes somewhat obscure. "My Love's Eyes" has merit, but lacks polish. The word "azure", in the first stanza, need not be in the possessive case; whilst the use of a singular verb with a plural noun in the second stanza (smiles—beguiles) is a little less than grammatical. "Longing" exhibits the author at her best, the images and phraseology alike shewing the touch of genius.

Other poetry in this issue is by Adam Dickson, a bard of pleasing manner but doubtful correctness. "Smile" needs rigorous metrical and rhetorical revision to escape puerility. "Silver Bells of Memory" is better, though marred by the ungrammatical passage "thoughts doth linger". In this passage, either the noun must be made singular, or the verb form plural.

"Prohibition in Kansas" is a well-written prose article by Editor William T. Harrington, wherein he exhibits a commendably favourable attitude toward the eradication of the menace of strong drink. Mr. Harrington is an able and active amateur, and takes an intelligent interest in many public questions. His style and taste are steadily improving, so that *The Coyote* has already become a paper of importance among us.

*The Dixie Booster* for January is Mr. Raymond B. Nixon's *Capital City News*, transferred to the amateur world, and continued under the new name. With this number the editor's brother, Mr. Roy W. Nixon, assumes the position of Associate Editor. This neat little magazine is home printed throughout, and may well remind the old-time amateurs of those boyish "palmy days" whose passing they lament so frequently. By means of a cut on the third page, we are properly introduced to Editor Nixon, who at present boasts but thirteen years of existence. The gifted and versatile associate editor, Mr. Roy W. Nixon, shews marked talent in three distinct departments of literature; essay-writing, fiction, and verse. "Writing as a Means of Self-Improvement" is a pure, dignified, and graceful bit of prose whose thought is as commendable as its structure. "A Bottle of Carbolic Acid" is a gruesome but clever short story of the Poe type, exhibiting considerable comprehension of abnormal psychology as treated in literature. "My Valentine" is a poem of tuneful metre and well-expressed sentiment, though not completely polished throughout. The third stanza, especially, might be made less like prose in its images.

*Dowdell's Bearcat* for December is quaint and attractive in appearance. The youthful editor has provided himself with a series of cuts of the metaphorical "Bruin" in various attitudes and various employments, these clever little pictures lending a pleasing novelty to the cover and the margins. Judiciously distributed red ink, also, aids in producing a Christmas number of truly festive quality. Mr. Dowdell's "Growls from the Pit" is a series of editorials both timely and interesting, while his "Did You Hear That" is a lively page of fresh news. This issue is notable for Mrs. Winifred V. Jordan's poetical contributions, of which there are three. "Life's Sunshine and Shadows" is a tuneful moral poem whose rhythm and imagery are equally excellent. "Contentment" is brief but delightful. "When the Woods Call" is a virile, graphic piece; vibrant with the thrill of the chase, and crisp with the frosty air of the Northern Woods.

The present reviewer's lines "To Samuel Loveman"[1] contain five misprints, as follows:

| Line | 3 | for *are* ....read ....... *art* |
| --- | --- | --- |
| " | 5 | *Appollo* ....." ........... *Apollo* |
| " | 6 | *versus* ......." ........... *verses* |
| " | 15 | *eternal* ......" ........... *ethereal* |
| " | 18 | *the* ............" ........... *thee* |

"Beads from My Rosary", by Mary M. Sisson, is a collection of well-written and sensible paragraphs on amateur journalism, which ought to assist in arousing enthusiasm amongst many members hitherto dormant. Editor Dowdell's pithy little epigrams at the foot of each page form an entertaining feature, many of them being of considerable cleverness. *Dowdell's Bearcat* will soon revert to its original newspaper form, since Mr. Dowdell intends to make newspaper work his life profession.

*The Inspiration* for November is a decidedly informal though exceedingly clever personal paper issued by Miss Edna von der Heide as a reminiscence of the Rocky Mount convention. Prose and verse of whimsically humorous levity are employed with success in recording the social side of the amateur gathering.

*The Looking Glass* for January is composed wholly of biographical matter, introducing to the association the multitude of accomplished recruits obtained through Mrs. Renshaw and others. In these forty life stories, most of them autobiographical, the student of human nature may find material for profound reflection on the variety of mankind. The more recent members of the United, as here introduced, are in the aggregate a maturer, more serious, and more scholarly element than that which once dominated the amateur world; and if they can be properly welcomed and acclimated to the realm of amateur letters, they will be of great value indeed in building up the ideals and character of the association. For this influx of sedate, cultivated members, the United has Mrs. Renshaw to thank, since the present policy of recruiting was originated and is conducted largely by the Second Vice President.

*Ole Miss'* for December is the most important of all recent additions to amateur letters, and it is with regret that we learn of the magazine's prospective discontinuance. The issue under consideration is largely local, most of the contributions being by Mississippi talent, and it must be said that the contributors all reflect credit upon their native or adopted State.

Mr. J. W. Renshaw's page of editorials is distinguished equally by good sense and good English. His attitude of disapproval toward petty political activities and fruitless feuds in the United is one which every loyal member will endorse, for nearly all of the past disasters in amateur history have been caused not by serious literary differences, but by conflicting ambitions among those seeking no more than cheap notoriety.

Mrs. Renshaw is well represented both by prose and by verse, the most interesting of her pieces being possibly the essay entitled "Poetic Spontaneity", wherein more arguments are advanced in her effort to prove the inferior importance of form and metre in poesy. According to Mrs. Renshaw, the essence of all genuine poetry is a certain spontaneous and involuntary spiritual or psychological perception and expression; incapable of rendition in any prescribed structure, and utterly destroyed by subsequent correction or alteration of any kind. That is, the bard must respond unconsciously to the noble impulse furnished by a fluttering, bird, a dew-crowned flower, or a sun-blest forest glade; recording his thoughts exactly as evolved, and never revising the result, even though it be detestably cacophonous, or absolutely unintelligible to his less inspired circle of readers. To such a theory as this we must needs reply, that while compositions of the sort indicated may indeed represent poesy, they certainly represent art in its proper sense no more than do "futuristic" pictures and other modern monstrosities of a like nature. The only exact means whereby a poet may transmit his ideas to others is language, a thing both definite and intellectual. Granting that vague, chaotic, dissonant lines are the best form in which the tender suitor of the Muses may record his spiritual impressions for his own benefit and comprehension, it by no means follows that such lines are at all fitted to convey these impressions to minds other than his own. When language is used without appropriateness, harmony, or precision, it can mean but little save to the person who writes it. The soul of a poem lies not in words but in meaning; and if the author have any skill at all in recording thought through language, he will be able to refine the uncouth mass of spontaneous verbiage which first comes to him as representing his idea, but which in its original amorphous state may fail entirely to suggest the same idea to another brain. He will be able to preserve and perpetuate his idea in a style of language which the world may understand, and in a rhythm which may not offend the reader's sense of propriety with conspicuous harshness, breaks, or sudden transitions.[2]

"Flames of the Shadow", Mrs. Renshaw's longest poetical contribution to this issue, is a powerful piece which, despite the author's theory, seems in no way injured by its commendably regular structure. "Immortality of Love" is likewise rather regular, though the plan of rhyming breaks down in the last stanza. "For You" and "Sacrament of Spirit" are short pieces, the former containing an "allowable" rhyming of "tongue" and "long", which would not meet with the approval of the Kleiner type of critic, but upon which this Department forbears to frown.

James T. Pyke's two poems, "To a Butterfly" and "Life and Time", are gems of incomparable beauty. "Ole Gardens", by Winifred V. Jordan, is a haunting bit of semi-irregular verse which deserves warm applause for the cleverness of its imagery and the aptness of its phraseology. "The Reward of It All", by Emilie C. Holladay, is a potent but pathetic poem of sentiment, whose development is highly commendable, but whose metrical construction might be improved by judicious care. "A Mississippi Autumn" was written as prose by Mrs. Renshaw, and set in heroic verse without change of ideas by the present critic.[3] The metaphor is uniformly lofty and delicate, whilst the development of the sentiment is facile and pleasing. It is to be hoped that the original thoughts of the author are not impaired or obscured by the technical turns of the less inspired versifier. "My Dear, Sweet, Southern Blossom", dedicated to Mr. and Mrs. Renshaw with Compliments of the Author, James Laurence Crowley, is a saccharine and sentimental piece of verse reminiscent of the popular ballads which flourished ten or more years ago. Triteness is the cardinal defect, for each gentle image is what our discerning private critic Mr. Moe would call a "rubber-stamp" phrase. Mr. Crowley requires a rigorous course of reading among the classic poets of our language, and a careful study of their art as a guide to the development of his taste. At present his work has about it a softness bordering on effeminacy, which leads us to believe that his conception of the poet's art is rather imperfect. It is only in caricature that we discover the poet as a sighing, long-haired scribbler of gushing flights of infantile awe or immature adoration. Earnestness, dignity, and, at times, sonorous stateliness, become a good poet; and such thoughts as are generally suggested by the confirmed use of "Oh", "Ah", "dear", "little", "pretty", "darling", "sweetest flow'ret of all", "where the morning-glory twineth", and so on, belong less to literary poetry than to the Irving Berlin song-writing industry of "Tin Pan Alley" in the Yiddish wilds of New York City. Mr. Crowley has energy of no mean sort, and if he will apply himself assiduously to the cultivation of masculine taste and technique, he can achieve a place of prominence among United bards.

W. S. Harrison deserves a word of praise for his poem of Nature, entitled "Our Milder Clime", wherein he celebrates the charms of Mississippi, his native state. The lines contain an old-fashioned grace too often wanting in contemporary verse. Other contributions to *Ole Miss'* are Mrs. Maude K. Barton's "Something of Natchez", a very interesting descriptive sketch in prose, and Mr. Rolfe Hunt's two negro dialect pieces, both of which are of inimitable wit and cleverness.

*The Pippin* for February is the first number of this important high-school journal to be issued without the supervision of Mr. Moe, and its existence well attests the substantial independent merit of the Appleton club. The city of Appleton forms the dominant theme in this number, and with the assistance of seven attractive half-tone illustrations, the publication well displays the beauty and advantages of the pleasant Wisconsin town. Miss Eleanor Halls cleverly weaves into conversational form much information concerning the remote history of Appleton, emphasising the superior character resulting from the select quality of the settlers, and the early introduction of learning. Mr. Alfred Galpin surprises many readers when he reveals the fact that Appleton possessed the first of all telephone systems, a surprise quickly followed by Mr. Joseph Harriman's illustrated paragraph telling of the first street car, also an Appleton innovation. Among other articles, that by Miss Torrey on Lawrence College is of unusual interest. "The Immortalization of the Princess", by Miss Fern Sherman, is an excellent Indian tale, whose structure and atmosphere well suggest not only the characteristic tribal legends of the red folk, but other and more classical myths as well. Though Miss Sherman is not yet a member of the United, one of such gifts would be heartily welcomed in the ranks.

*The Plainsman* for December is the most substantial number of his journal which Mr. Ira Cole has yet issued. First in order of importance among the contents is perhaps the editor's own prose sketch entitled "Monuments", wherein Mr. Cole reveals to particular advantage his exceptional skill in depicting and philosophising upon the various aspects and phenomena of Nature. Mr. Cole's style is constantly improving, and though not now of perfect polish, it is none the less remarkable for its grace and fluency. "To Florence Shepphird", also by Mr. Cole, is a rather long piece of blank verse, containing many beautiful passages. The author's skill in stately and sonorous poetry is far above the common level, and his work has about it an atmosphere of the polished past which that of most amateur bards lacks; yet the present poem is not without errors. The passage (lines 10–11) reading: "calm *days* that *knoweth* not dread Boreas' chilling breath" must be changed so that either the noun shall be singular or the verb plural. The double negative in line 23 might well be eliminated. Two lines whose metre could be improved are the 13th and 50th. The final quatrain is pleasing to the average ear, including that of the present critic; though the very exact taste of today, as represented by Mr. Kleiner, frowns upon such deviation from the dominant blank verse arrangement. "On the Cowboys of the West" is a brief bit of verse by this reviewer,[4] accompanied by a note from the pen of Mr. Cole. The note is better than the verse, and exhibits Mr. Cole's vivid and imaginative prose at its best. "The Sunflower", a versified composition by James Laurence Crowley, concludes the issue. There is much attractiveness in the lines; though we may discover, particularly in the second stanza, that touch of excessive softness which occasionally mars Mr. Crowley's work. No one can fail to discern the weakness of such a line as "You big giant of all the flowers".

*The Providence Amateur* for February is worthy of particular attention on account of Peter J. MacManus' absorbing article on "The Irish and the Fairies". Mr. MacManus firmly believes not only that fairies exist in his native Ireland, but that he has actually beheld a troop of them; facts which impart to this article a psychological as well as a literary interest. The prose style of Mr. MacManus is very good, being notable alike for fluency and freedom from slang, whilst his taste is of the best. His future work will be eagerly awaited by the amateur public. Edmund L. Shehan contributes both verse and prose to this issue. "Death" is a stately poem on a grave subject, whose sentiments are all of suitable humility and dignity. The apparently anomalous pronoun "her", in the tenth line, is a misprint for "he". The piece ends with a rhyming couplet, to which Mr. Kleiner, representing correct modern taste, takes marked exception. The present reviewer, however, finds no reason to object to any part of Mr. Shehan's poem, and attributes this concluding couplet to the influence of similar Shakespearian terminations. The prose piece by Mr. Shehan well describes a visit to a cinematograph studio, and is entitled "The Making of a Motion Picture". In the verses entitled "A Post-Christmas Lament", Mr. John T. Dunn combines much keenness of wit with commendable regularity of metre. Mr. Dunn is among the cleverest of the United's humorous writers. "To Charlie of the Comics"[5] is a harmless parody on our Laureate's excellent poem "To Mary of the Movies", which appeared some time ago in *The Piper*. In "The Bride of the Sea", Mr. Lewis Theobald, Jr., presents a rather weird piece of romantic sentimentality of the sort afforded by bards of the early nineteenth century.[6] The metre is regular, and no flagrant violations of grammatical or rhetorical precepts are to be discerned, yet the whole effort lacks clearness, dignity, inspiration, and poetic spontaneity. The word printed "enhanc'd" in the sixth stanza is properly "entranc'd".

*Tom Fool, Le Roi* bears no definite date, but is a sort of pensive autumn reverie following the Rocky Mount convention of last summer. This grave and dignified journal is credited to the House of Tillery, and if typographical evidence may be accepted, it belongs most particularly to that branch now bearing the name of Renshaw and having its domain in Coffeeville, Mississippi. "Mother Gooseries from the Convention", by Emilie C. Holladay, is a long stanzaic and Pindaric ode, whose taste and technique are alike impeccable. The exalted images are sketched with artistic touch, whilst the deep underlying philosophy, skilfully clothed in well-balanced lines, arouses a sympathetic reaction from every cultured intellect. "The Carnival", by Mrs. E. L. Whitehead, is an admirable example of stately descriptive prose mixed with aesthetic verse. The long and euphonious periodic sentences suggest the style of Gibbon or of Dr. Johnson, whilst the occasional metrical lines remind the reviewer of Dr. Young's solemn "Night Thoughts".[7] "Dummheit", by Dora M. Hepner, is a grave discourse on Original Sin, describing the planning of *Tom Fool, Le Roi*. Elizabeth M. Ballou's article entitled "Our Absent Friend" forms a notable contribution to amateur historical annals, and displays Miss Ballou as the possessor of a keen faculty for observation, and a phenomenally analytical intellect. "Banqueters from the Styx", Mrs. Renshaw's masterly description of the convention dinner and its honoured guests from the regions of Elysium and elsewhere, reminds the reviewer of the 11th book of the Odyssey and the 6th book of the Aeneid, wherein the fraternising of men with the shades of men is classically delineated.

*Tom Fool* is a memorable publication, suggesting the old "fraternal" papers, whose passing so many amateurs regret.

*The United Amateur* for November contains besides the official matter a small but select assortment of poems, prominent among which is "The Meadow Cricket", by Jas. T. Pyke. It is impossible to overestimate the beauty of thought and expression which Mr. Pyke shews in all his verses, and the United is fortunate in being able to secure specimens of his work.

"Remorse", by James Laurence Crowley, is one of the best samples of this gentleman's poesy which we have yet seen, though Mr. Crowley insists that one of the punctuation marks has been wrongfully located by the reviser. Since the present critic prepared the manuscript for publication, he is willing to assume full culpability for this crime. There is genuine poetic feeling in this short piece; and it seems an undoubted fact that Mr. Crowley, with a little added restraint and dignity of expression, is capable of producing excellent work. "List to the Sea", by Winifred V. Jordan, is a delightfully musical lyric, whose dancing dactyls and facile triple rhymes captivate alike the fancy and the ear. "The Wind and the Beggar", by Maude K. Barton, is sombre and powerful. "Ambition", by William De Ryee, is regular in metre and commendable in sentiment, yet not exactly novel or striking in inspiration. "Choose ye", by Ella C. Eckert, is a moral poem of clever conception and correct construction.

*The United Official Quarterly* for January opens with "A Prayer for the New Year", by Frederick R. Chenault. Mr. Chenault is a poet of the first order so far as inspiration is concerned, but his work is frequently marred by irregularity of metre, and the use of assonance in place of rhyme. The metre of this poem is correct, but the two attempted rhymes "deeper-meeker" and "supremely-sincerely" are technically no more than assonant sounds. Pres. Fritter writes very powerfully on our publishing situation in this number; and his article should not only be perused with attention, but heeded with sincerity and industriousness.

"Behind the Canvass Wall", by William J. Dowdell, is one of the cleverest and most ingenious bits of fiction which the amateur press has contained for some time. That it is of a nature not exactly novel is but a trivial objection. The homely, appealing plot, and the simple, sympathetic treatment, both point to Mr. Dowdell as a possible success in the realm of short story writing, should he ever care to enter it seriously. Another excellent tale is "The Good Will of a Dog", by P. J. Campbell. The plot is of a well-defined type which always pleases, whilst the incidents are graphically delineated. "The Bookstall" is a metrical monstrosity by the present reviewer.[8] Mr. Maurice W. Moe, the distinguished Private Critic, lately gave us the following opinion of our verse. "You are," he writes, "steeped in the poetry of a certain age; an age, by the way, which cut and fit its thought with greater attention to one model than any other age before or since; and the result is that when you turn to verse as a medium of expression, it is just as if you were pressing a button liberating a perfect flood of these perfectly good but stereotyped formulae of expression. The result is very ingenious, but just because it is such a skillful mosaic of Georgian 'rubber-stamp' phrases, it must ever fall short of true art." Mr. Moe is correct. We have, in fact, heard this very criticism reiterated by various authorities ever since those prehistoric days when we began to lisp in numbers. Yet somehow we perversely continue to "mosaic" along in the same old way! But then, we have never claimed to possess "true art"; we are merely a metrical mechanic. "A New Point of View in Home Economics", a clever article by Miss Eleanor Barnhart, concludes the *Official Quarterly* proper.

But the *New Member* supplement, with its profusion of brilliant credentials, yet remains to be considered. "Dutch Courage", by Louis E. Boutwell, is a liquorish sketch whose scene is laid in a New Jersey temple of Bacchus. Being totally unacquainted with the true saloon atmosphere, we find ourself a little embarrassed as to critical procedure, yet we may justly say that the characters are all well drawn, every man in his humour. "Ol' Man Murdock" is a quaint, and in two senses an *absorbing*, figure. The rest of the issue is given over to the Muses of poesy. "The Saturday Fray" is a clever piece by Daisy Vandenbank. The rhyming is a little uneven, and in one case assonance is made to answer for true rhyme. "Cream" and "mean" cannot make an artistic couplet. "The Common Soldiers", by John W. Frazer, is a poem of real merit; whilst "Little Boy Blue", by W. Hume, is likewise effective. Mr. Hume's pathetic touch is fervent and in no manner betrays that weakness bordering on the ridiculous, to which less skilful flights of pathos are prone. "The Two Springs" is a pleasant moral sermon in verse by Margaret Ellen Cooper. Concluding the issue is "The Under Dog in the Fight", a vigorous philosophical poem by Andrew Stevenson.

*The Woodbee* for January is distinguished Mrs. Winifred V. Jordan's brilliant short poem entitled "Oh, Where Is Springtime?" The sentiment of the piece is an universal one, and the pleasing lines will appeal to all. "Retribution", by Mrs. Ida C. Haughton, is a clever story, but the present critic's extreme fondness for cats makes it difficult to review after reading the first sentence. However, the well-approached conclusion is indeed just. The "moral" is a pathetic example of unregeneracy! Miss Edna M. Haughton's critical article is direct and discerning; the Woodbee Club is fortunate in having among its members so capable a reviewer. Editor Fritter likewise mounts the reviewer's throne in this issue, proceeding first of all to demolish our own fond dream of yesterday; *The Conservative*. Looking backward adown the dim vista of those bygone but memory-haunted days of October, 1915, when we perpetrated the horribly plain-spoken and frightfully ungentle number whereof Mr. Fritter treats, we are conscious of our manifold sins, and must beg the pardon of the liquor interests for shouting so rudely in the cause of total abstinence. Pres. Fritter's critical style is a good one, and is developing from month to month. His advocacy of lukewarmness in writing is perhaps not so complete as one might judge from this article; though his use of the cautious phrase "it is rumored" in connexion with a well-known statement seems hardly necessary. Rigid impartiality, the critic's greatest asset, is manifest throughout the review, and we thoroughly appreciate the favourable mention not infrequently accorded us. In passing upon the merits of *Dowdell's Bearcat,* Mr. Fritter shews equal penetration and perspicuity, and we are convinced that his rank amongst amateur reviewers is very high.

EDITOR'S NOTE  FP: *United Amateur* 15, No. 9 (April 1916): 111–17 (signed "H. P. LOVE-CRAFT, Chairman"). HPL devotes considerable attention to his own January issue of the *Conservative,* although focusing chiefly on contributions by others; in fact, HPL had only two small items in the issue. He discusses the poetic contributions of a new member, Winifred V. Jordan (later Winifred V. Jackson), a matter of some consequence as conjectures have been made regarding a "romance" between her and HPL in the period 1918–21 (see Joshi, *Life* 199–201). HPL also examines the February *Providence Amateur.*

*Notes*

1. See AT 94–95.
2. For HPL's further thoughts on this subject, also directed in part at Anne Tillery Renshaw, see "Metrical Regularity" (*Conservative,* July 1915; CE2).
3. See AT 271–72.
4. See AT 94.
5. See AT 93.
6. More properly, "Unda; or, The Bride of the Sea." See AT 211–13.
7. Edward Young (1683–1765), *Night Thoughts on Life, Death and Immortality* (1742–45), a celebrated poem by one of the eighteenth-century "graveyard poets." HPL had an edition of *The Poetical Works of Milton, Young, Gray, Beattie, and Collins* (1841; LL 704).
8. See AT 95–97.

# AMONG THE NEW-COMERS

## Jonathan E. Hoag

Jonathan E. Hoag, poet, dreamer, lover of Nature, essayist, traveller, newspaper correspondent, and scientific enthusiast, was born on a farm in New York State in the year 1831. His ancestry is of enviable distinction, including the first Earl of Buckingham, standard bearer to William the Conqueror, and Ethan Allen, the American revolutionist.

As a youth, Mr. Hoag knew the idyllic life and inspiring atmosphere of the primitive countryside, obtaining his education at the "little red schoolhouse" and at the neighbouring academy, both of which he has since described so attractively in his essays. Ever responsive to the appeal of natural grandeur and beauty, and keenly appreciative of the wealth of historical tradition in the woods, hills, streams, and waterfalls of his native locality, Mr. Hoag early developed a poetical temperament which not only inspires his versified compositions, but which lends to his prose work a facile grace of imagination. His intellectual zeal, fostered by his wholesome rural environment and happily vigorous health, manifested itself in a lifelong devotion to the pleasures of books, and made of him an extensive and omnivorous reader; while as a natural consequence he turned to the pen to express those thoughts which his learning, so eagerly acquired and so thoroughly assimilated, had aroused in him. Under the pseudonym of

"Scriba" Mr. Hoag became a regular contributor to his local paper, *The Greenwich (N.Y.) Journal,* and has never ceased to enliven its columns with tastefully written matter whose interest is equalled only by its variety.

Over a decade ago Mr. Hoag made an extended tour of the United States, beholding the scenic wonders of the West, and philosophically observing the condition of mankind all over the broad expanse of our nation. He saw a sunset from Pike's Peak; talked with old Geronimo, that last relic of aboriginal savagery; and accumulated that fund of travel lore which so powerfully inspires and so gracefully adorns many of his recent essays.

Mr. Hoag's scientific activity is well exhibited by his accurate observation of a peculiar atmospherical appearance which manifested itself at sunset one day early last December. His newspaper article on this phenomenon aroused much interest, and his explanatory theory is very soundly constructed.

In person, Mr. Hoag presents a vigorous and commanding figure. He is well above the middle stature, boasting six feet of altitude without his shoes; and his weight, 200 solid pounds, well corresponds. At the age of eighty-five his hair is pure silver, and he seems to fit very naturally into his new place as dean of amateur letters. In buoyant health and enduring physique he flourishes to an extent which many men twenty or thirty years his junior might well envy. His children and grand-children form a family of which he is justly proud.

Mr. Hoag's introduction to the United Amateur Press Association came through his gifted friend and fellow-resident of Greenwich, Miss Verna McGeoch, and through our indefatigable Second Vice-President, Mrs. Renshaw. Though at first reluctant to enter a new field, he at length fell a victim to the efforts and machinations of the recruiters, and is now duly enrolled among us as a member. Several of his beautiful imaginative poems, including "The Falls of Dionondawa" and "Mother and Child", will soon appear in the amateur press, as will also some of his pleasant descriptive prose. His latest piece follows:

## THE SHIP THAT SAILS AWAY

In early morn, when stars are watching still,
And balmy winds touch rose and daffodil,
And tender leaves on woodland hills afar
Bid welcome to yon flaming morning star;
When birdlings, by their mother's carol blest,
Attend her song in bough-hung, downy nest,
Where she her charge protects with loving care,
Glad as the swaying vine and fragrant air;
Our thoughts on Life's experience we bestow,
And Disappointment, all too bitter, know:
When lips would touch Elysian waters sweet,
The cup was dash'd untasted at our feet!
Though earthly pleasures serve not to restrain,
For those we love we longer would remain;
But unseen hands one day our anchor lifts:
We sail away—into the silence drift!
With shaded eyes fix'd on the distant shore,
What forms are those we see in realms before?

In waving plumes array'd, they seem to ask:
"Why tarry ye behind on earthly task?"
The rising anchor grants no more delay;
And last we sail away—we sail away!

The interests of "Scriba" are many and varied. With our astronomical members he discusses astronomy; with our purely literary members he analyses literature; and with our philosophical members he dwells brilliantly on philosophy and metaphysics. His is a many-sided and well-rounded character, and in securing so congenial a member as he, our society may well congratulate itself.

## Henry Cleveland Wood

Of the numerous writers of note composing the United's membership, few are more gifted, versatile, and interesting than Henry Cleveland Wood of Harrodsburg, Kentucky, who has but recently entered our ranks. Mr. Wood is equally distinguished in the realms of poetry and of fiction; and is a novelist of no small reputation, having been the author of serial tales in many well-known magazines, and a successful book, "The Night Riders", based on rustic life in Kentucky.[1]

As a winner of prizes in literary contests, Mr. Wood has a highly enviable record. Prior to the St. Louis fair of 1904 he captured first honours in a competition for the best poem describing the "Skinner Road", a model rural highway which formed the main avenue of approach to the exposition grounds. At another time both Mr. Wood and his late mother obtained heavy cash prizes for their verses in a competition held by the famous commercial house of Proctor and Gamble.

Mr. Wood's short stories are in great demand among magazine editors, *Harper's Weekly*, *The Youth's Companion*, *Woman's Home Companion*, and *Ainslee's Magazine* being but a few of the periodicals in which his stirring tales appear. His serials are as follows: "Seal and Clay" (collaborated), "The Mountain Outlaw", and "The Love That Endured", in *The New York Ledger*; "Faint Heart and Fair Lady" in *The Designer*; "The Night Riders" in *Taylor-Trotwood*; and "Weed and War" in *Farm and Home*.

As a poet, Mr. Wood possesses talent of no common order; his verses having a loftiness of inspiration, grace of imagery, harmony of cadence, and correctness of technique which places him amongst [the best of] his contemporaries. The following specimen, taken from *Ainslee's Magazine*, may serve to illustrate his pure and delicate style:

## NATURE'S BENEDICTION

A stretch of fields where evening shadows lie;
   Rich purplish lights—night creeping on apace;
   A tall swart line of distant trees that trace
Fantastic forms against the sunset sky.
A moon half crescent hangs her lamp on high,
   Attended by the peaceful evening star,
   And on the tranquil scene, anear and far,
A silence falls as a holy Grace.

The home in whose cheerful atmosphere Mr. Wood leads his ideal bachelor existence is one whose beauty attracts admiring attention throughout Kentucky. Like our South Dakota member, Mr. Lockhart, Mr. Wood is an ardent and discriminating collector of relics, and has adorned his hall with valuable memories of Indian and pioneer life. Cherished above all the rest is a bit of oak tree bark, wherein are carven the initials "D. B." These letters were traced by the knife of no less a character than Daniel Boone, the pioneer, who spent the winter of 1769 in a cave, above which stood the tree thus immortalised. Mr. Wood's conservatory is a truly poetic nook where reigns perpetual summer, and his dining room is notable for the delightful mural decorations which are tokens of his own skill with the brush. Further evidence of our author's versatility in the arts is afforded by his picturesque parlour, whose exquisite furniture is almost without exception the product of his own hands.

Mr. Wood's autograph album is embellished with the signatures and impromptu effusions of some of the most eminent persons of the age, representing every branch of intellectual endeavour, and it forms a human document of which the possessor may well be proud.

The United takes much pleasure in welcoming to its midst a recruit of Mr. Wood's quality, and it is to be hoped that this gifted author's affiliation with us may prove a permanent one.

EDITOR'S NOTE FP: *United Amateur* 15, No. 10 (May 1916): 134–36 (as by "El Imparcial"). HPL discusses two new members of the UAPA, the elderly poet Jonathan E. Hoag and the poet and fiction writer Henry Cleveland Wood. HPL would later write ten birthday tributes to Hoag for the period 1918–27, and an elegy, "Ave atque Vale" (*AT* 382–83), when Hoag died at the age of ninety-six. HPL does not appear to have developed close ties to Wood.

*Notes*

1. Henry Cleveland Wood (1855–?), *The Night Riders: A Story of Love, Hate and Adventure* (Chicago: Laird & Lee, 1908).

# DEPARTMENT OF PUBLIC CRITICISM

(June 1916)

The *Coyote* for July opens with Harry E. Rieseberg's verses entitled "The Sum of Life", whose structure is excellent as a whole, though defective in certain places. The word "mirage" is properly accented on the second syllable, hence is erroneously situated in the first stanza. "A mirage forever seeming" is a possible substitute line. Other defects are the attempted rhymes of "decay" with "constancy", "carried" with "hurried", and "appalled" with "all". The metre is without exception correct, and the thoughts and images in general well presented, wherefore we believe that with a little more care Mr. Rieseberg can become a very pleasing poet indeed. "The Philippine Question", by Earl Samuel Harrington, aged 15, is an excellent juvenile essay, and expresses a very sound opinion concerning our Asiatic colonies. It is difficult to be patient with the political idiots who advocate the relinquishment of the archipelago by the United States, either now or at any future time. The mongrel natives, in whose blood the Malay strain predominates, are not and never will be racially capable of maintaining a civilised condition by themselves. "How Fares the Garden Rose?" is a poem bearing the signature of Winifred Virginia Jordan, which is a sufficient guarantee of its thorough excellence. "To a Breeze", also by Mrs. Jordan, is distinguished by striking imagery, and displays in the epithet "moon-moored", that highly individualistic touch which is characteristic of its author. "Peace", by Andrew Francis Lockhart, is a poem of excellent construction, though marred by two serious misprints which destroy the harmony of the first and third lines.

The Dixie Booster for March–April is an exceedingly neat and clever paper from the House of Nixon. "Spring in the South", a poem by Maude K. Barton, opens the issue in pleasant fashion, the attractive images well atoning for certain slight mechanical deficiencies. "Dick's Success", by Gladys L. Bagg, is a short story whose phraseology exhibits considerable talent and polish. The didactic element is possibly more emphasised than the plot, though not to a tedious extent. Whether or not a rough draught of a novel may be completed in the course of a single afternoon, a feat described in this tale, we leave for the fiction-writing members of the United to decide! Of the question raised regarding the treatment of the Indian by the white man in America it is best to admit in the words of Sir Roger de Coverly, 'that much might be said on both sides'.[1] Whilst the driving back of the aborigines has indeed been ruthless and high-handed, it seems the destiny of the Anglo-Saxon to sweep inferior races from his path wherever he goes. There are few who love the Indian so deeply that they would wish this continent restored to its original condition, peopled by savage nomads instead of civilised colonists. "The Deuce and Your Add", by Melvin Ryder, is a bit of light philosophy whose allegorical case is well maintained. "To a Warbler", by Roy W. Nixon, is a meritorious piece of verse whose rhythm moves with commendable sprightliness, though the first line of the first stanza might be made to correspond better with the first line of the second stanza. The word "apparent" in the last line seems a little unsuited to the general style of the poem, being more suggestive of the formal type of composition. "Grandma", also by Mr. Roy Nixon, in a noble sonnet whose quality foreshadows real poetical distinction for its author. "You", by Dora M. Hepner, contains sublime images, but possesses metrical imperfections. The general anapaestic or dactylic rhythm is much disturbed by the iambic fourth line of the first stanza. The editorials, jokes, and jingles in this issue are all clever, and proclaim Mr. Raymond Nixon as a capable and discriminating editor.

Literary Buds for February exhibits the amateurs of Harvey, Illinois, after a long absence from the publishing arena. The present issue, edited by Mr. Caryl Wilson Dempsey, contains matter of merit and interest. "The Dells of the Wisconsin", by A. Myron Lambert, is an interesting account of an outing spent amidst scenes of natural grandeur and beauty. The author's style is fluent and pleasing, though a few slight crudities are to be discerned. On page 1, where the height of a large dam in mentioned, it is stated "that the water must raise that distance before it can fall". Of course, "rise" is the verb which should have been used. Another erroneous phrase is "nature tract". "Nature" is not an adjective, but a noun; "natural" is the correct word. However, this anomalous use of nouns for adjectives has only too much prevalence amongst all grades of writers today, and must not be too harshly censured in this case. On page 4 the word "onto" should be supplanted by "upon", and the awkward phrase: "to be convinced that we had ventured to a place that we did not know any dangers were connected with", should be changed to something like this: "to convince us that we had ventured to a seemingly dangerous place whose apparent dangers we had not then noticed". "A Song of Love", by Editor Dempsey, is cast in uniformly flowing and regular metre, but some of the words require comment. *"Lover"* is not generally applied by bards to adored members of the gentler sex, *"love"* being the conventional term. Likewise the phrase "heart which always softly does its beating" might well be revised with greater attention to poetical precedent. Yet the whole is of really promising quality, and exhibits a metrical correctness much above the average. "The Operation" in a very witty sketch by Miss Clara I. Stalker, with a sudden turn toward the end which arouses the complete surprise and unexpected mirth of the reader. "The High Cost of Flivving", by Albert Thompson, is a bright bit of versified humour involving novel interpretations of certain technical terms of literature. The swinging dactylic rhythm is well managed except where the words "descending" and "ascending" occur, and where, in line 24, the metre becomes momentarily anapaestic.

*The Looking Glass* for May is the final number of Mrs. Renshaw's journal of introductions, and makes known to the association a group of 27 new members. One of the most interesting autobiographies is that of Mr. J. E. Hoag of Greenwich, New York, whose friendly sentences, written from the cumulative experience of 85 years of life, possess an elusively captivating quality. Of the non-biographical matter in this issue, Mrs. Renshaw's compilation entitled "Writing for Profit" deserves particular perusal. This is well set off by the same author's colloquial lines, "Pride o' the Pen", wherein the lethal taint of trade in literature in effectively deplored. "Something", by David H. Whittier, is a thoughtful analysis of conditions in the United, with suggestions for improvement. "One Bright Star Enough for Me", by Mr. John Hartman Oswald of Texas, is a pious poem reminding one of Mr. Addison's well-known effort which begins: "The spacious firmament on high".[2] We doubt, however, if Mr. Addison has been much improved upon, since several instances of imperfect poetical taste are to be found in Mr. Oswald's lines. But there are evidences of a great soul throughout the ten stanzas, and the metre is in the main correct. What Mr. Oswald appears to require is a thorough reading of the English classics, with minute attention to their phraseology and images. With such study we believe him capable of development into a poet of enviable force and sincerity.

*Toledo Amateur* for April marks the welcome reappearance of Mr. Wesley H. Porter's neat little journal after a year's absence. "A Story", by David H. Whittier, possesses a tragical plot whose interest is slightly marred by triteness and improbable situations. Of the latter we must point out the strained coincidence whereby four distinct things, proceeding from entirely unrelated causes, give rise to the final denouement. The culmination of the aged father's resolve to kill his enemy, the conditions which make possible the return of the son, the presence of the enemy's hat and coat under the wayside tree, and the storm which prompts the son to don these garments, are all independent circumstances, whose simultaneous occurrence, each at exactly the proper time to cause the catastrophe, may justly be deemed a coincidence too great for the purpose of good literature. In an artistically constructed tale, the various situations all develop naturally out of that original cause which in the end brings about the climax; a principle which, if applied to the story in question, would limit the events and their sequences to those arising either directly or indirectly from the wrong committed by the father's enemy. Since there is no causative connexion between the immediate decision of the father to kill his foe, and the developments or discoveries which enable the son to return, the simultaneous occurrence of these unusual things is scarcely natural. Superadded to this coincidence are two more extraneous events; the rather strange presence of the hat and coat near the road, and the timely or untimely breaking of the storm; the improbability indeed increasing in geometrical progression with each separate circumstance. It must, however, be admitted that such quadruple coincidences in stories are by no means uncommon among even the most prominent and widely advertised professional fiction-blacksmiths of the day. Mr. Whittier's style is that of a careful and sincere scholar, and we believe that his work will become notable in this and the succeeding amateur journalistic generation. The minuteness of the preceding criticism has been prompted not by a depreciatory estimate of his powers, but rather by an appreciative survey of his possibilities. "Say, Brother", by Mrs. Renshaw, is a poem describing life in the trenches of the Huns. The metre is quite regular, and the plan of rhyming but once broken. Mr. Porter's prose work; editorial, introductory, and narrative, is all pleasing, though not wholly free from a certain slight looseness of scholarship. We should advise rigorous exercise in parsing and rhetoric. "Respite", by Edgar Ralph Cheyney, shews real poetical genius, and the iambic heptameters are very well handled, save where one redundant syllable breaks the flow of the last line. Even that would be perfect if the tongue could condense the noun and article *"the music"* into *"th' music"*.

The *Tornado* for April constitutes the publishing debut of Mrs. Addie L. Porter, mother of *Toledo Amateur's* gifted young editor. Mrs. Porter's "Recollections from Childhood" are pleasant and well phrased, bringing to mind very vividly the unrivalled joys of Christmas as experienced by the young. Wesley H. Porter, in "My Vacation", tells entertainingly of his visit to the hive of the Woodbees last September. The editorial and news paragraphs are all of attractive aspect, completing a bright paper whose four pages teem with enthusiasm and personality. It is to be hoped that other comparatively new United members may follow Mr. Porter's example in entering the publishing field; for individual journals, though of no greater size than this, are ever welcome, and do more than anything else to maintain interest and promote progress in the association.

The *Trail* for April must by no means be confused with Alfred L. Hutchinson's professionalised magazine of identical title, for this *Trail* is an older and emphatically non-professional publication issued coöperatively by Dora M. Hepner and George W. Macauley. Non-professionalism, indeed, seems to dominate the entire issue to a degree unusual in the broadened and developed United. With the exception of one poem and one short story or sketch, the contents are wholly personal and social. "He Reached My Hand", by Dora M. Hepner, is an excellent piece of verse, though perhaps not of that extreme polish which is observed in the productions of very careful bards. Miss Hepner has great refinement of fancy and vigour of expression, but evidently neglects to cultivate that beautiful rhetoric and exquisite rhythmic harmony which impress us so forcibly in the work of scholars and bookmen like Rheinhart Kleiner. "A Girl of the U. S.", by George W. Macauley, is a prose piece whose nature seems to waver between that of a story and a descriptive sketch. Though description apparently preponderates, the narrative turn toward the conclusion may sanction classification as fiction. The faults are all faults of imperfect technique rather than of barren imagination, for Mr. Macauley wields a graphic pen, and adorns every subject he approaches. In considering minor points, we must remark the badly fractured infinitive "to no longer walk", and the unusual word "reliefful". We have never seen the latter expression before, and though it may possibly be a modernism in good usage, it was certainly unknown in the days when we attempted to acquire our education. Mr. Macauley, with his marked descriptive ability, is less at ease in stories of contemporary life than in historical fiction, particularly mediaeval and Oriental tales. His genius is not unlike that of Sir Walter Scott, and shews to special advantage in annals of knights and chivalry. "Scratchings" are by the pen of Miss Hepner, and display an active wit despite the profusion of slang.

It would seem, however, that so brilliant a writer could preserve the desired air of vivacity without quite so many departures from the standard idioms of our language.

Miss Hepner's remarks on the assimilation of new United members are worthy of note. The cruder amateurs should not feel discouraged by the extraordinary average scholarship of the recent element, but should rather use it as a model for improvement. They should establish correspondence with the cultivated recruits, thereby not only benefiting themselves, but helping each gifted newcomer to find a useful and congenial place amongst us. The present situation is pitifully ludicrous, for practically all young aspirants call upon only one or two sadly overburdened older members for literary aid, forgetting that there are scores of brilliant writers, teachers, and professors waiting anxiously but vainly to be of real service to their fellow-amateurs. Several of the scholarly new members have particularly inquired how they can best assist the association; yet the association, as represented by its literary novices, has failed to take advantage of most of these offers of instruction and coöperation. We are impelled here to reiterate the slogan which Mr. Daas has so frequently printed in his various journals: *"Welcome the Recruits!"* Such a welcome is certain to react with double felicity upon the giver.

"From the Michigan Trail" is Mr. Macauley's personal column, and contains so bitter an attack on some of the United's policies of improvement, that we are tempted to remonstrate quite loudly. The captious criticism of the Second Vice-President's invaluable activities, constructive labours which have practically regenerated the association and raised it to a higher plane in the world of educational endeavour, is positively ungenerous. To speak of the article in *Ole Miss'* entitled "Manuscripts and Silver" as "mercenary", is the summit of injustice, for it was nothing more or less than the absolutely gratuitous offer to the United of what is now the Symphony Literary Service.[3] We are rather at a loss to divine Mr. Macauley's precise notion of amateur journalism. He speaks of it as a "tarn", but we cannot believe he would have it so stagnant a thing as that name implies. Surely, the United is something greater than a superficial fraternal order composed of mediocre and unambitious dabblers. Progress leads toward the outside world of letters, and to cavil at work such as Mrs. Renshaw's is to set obstacles in the path of progress. Professional literary success on the part of amateur journalists can never react unfavourably on the United, and it seems far from kind and proper to impede the development of members. Why is a professional author necessarily less desirable as an amateur journalist than a professional plumber or boiler-maker? But there is one sound principle at the base of Mr. Macauley's argument, which deserves more emphasis than the points he elaborates. Professionalism must not enter into the workings of the association, nor should the professionalised amateur take advantage of amateur connexions to create a market for writings otherwise unsalable. This applies to the now happily extinct tribe of "ten-cents-a-year" publishers, who coolly expected all amateur journalists to subscribe to their worthless misprints as a matter of fraternal obligation. Mr. Macauley is an extremist on the subject of amateur rating, a fact which explains many otherwise puzzling allusions in his current editorials.

*The United Amateur* for February is the final number of the Daas regime, and constitutes a noble valedictory indeed. We find it impossible to express with sufficient force our regret at the withdrawal of Mr. Daas from the United, and we can but hope that the retirement may prove merely temporary. The February official organ is wholly literary in contents, and in quality sustains the best traditions of amateur journalism. Miss Olive G. Owen's poem, "Give Us Peace!", which opens the issue, is tasteful in imagery and phraseology, and correct in rhyme and metre, but contains the customary unrealities and substitutions of emotion for reasoning which are common to all pacific propaganda. "The Little Old Lady's Dream", by M. Almedia Bretholl, is a short story of the almost unpleasantly "realistic" type, whose development and atmosphere exhibit much narrative talent and literary skill. "The Teuton's Battle-Song" is an attempt of the present critic to view the principles of human warfare without the hypocritical spectacles of sentimentality.[4] "Nature in Literature", by Arthur W. Ashby, is an essay of unusual quality, revealing a depth of well-assimilated scholarship and a faculty for acute observation and impartial analysis, of which few amateur writers may justly boast. "His All" is an excellent poem by Mrs. Elia Colby Eckert, distinguished equally for its noble thought and facile rhythm. "'Twixt the Red and the White", a short story by Miss Coralie Austin, displays marked skill in construction and phraseology, though its development is not without a few of the typical crudities of youthful work. There is a trifling suspicion of triteness and banality in plot and dialogue; which is, however, compensated for in the artistic passages so frequently encountered. "Romance, Mystery, and Art", an essay by Edgar Ralph Cheyney, reflects the learning and thoughtfulness of its author. The poetical fragments entitled "Songs from Walpi", by Mrs. Winifred V. Jordan, describe the hopeless affection of a Southwestern Indian prince for a maiden of the conquering white race. The atmosphere and images are cleverly wrought, whilst the rhythm is in every detail satisfactory. "Nescio Quo", by Kathleen Baldwin, is a poem of great attractiveness in structure and sentiment. "A Crisis", by Eleanor J. Barnhart, is a short story of distinctly modern type, whose substance and development compare well with professional work. "My Heart and I", a sonnet by James T. Pyke, exhibits the skill and philosophical profundity characteristic of its author. "My Native Land", a poem by Adam Dickson, describes the Scottish Border with pleasing imagery and bounding anapaestic metre. Mr. Dickson is a poet whose progress should be carefully watched. His improvement is steady, the present piece being easily the best specimen of his work to appear in the amateur press. "Poetry and Its Power", by Helen M. Woodruff, is a delightful essay containing liberal quotations from various classic bards. "A Resolution", by Harry Z. Moore, seems to be modelled after Mrs. Renshaw's well-known poem, "A Symphony". The various precepts are without exception sound and commendable. Helene E. Hoffman presents a brief but pleasing critique of Sir Thomas Browne's "Hydriotaphia, Urn-Burial; or a Discourse of the Sepulchral Urns lately found in Norfolk". It in refreshing to discover a modern reader who can still appreciate the quaint literature of the seventeenth century, and Miss Hoffman is to be thanked for her sympathetic review of the pompous, Latinised phrases of the old physician. "He and She", by Margaret A. Richard, is a thoroughly meritorious poem whose two "allowable rhymes", "fair-dear", and "head-prayed", would be censured only by a critic of punctilious exactitude. "At Sea", a witty bit of *vers de société* by Henry Cleveland Wood, forms an appropriately graceful conclusion to a richly enjoyable issue of the magazine.

The United Amateur for March brings to the fore Mr. George S. Schilling's unusual editorial talent, and makes manifest the bright future of the official organ for the balance of the present administrative year. The chief literary contribution is "Hail, Autumn!", one of Mr. Arthur Ashby's brilliant and scholarly essays on Nature. The quality of Mr. Ashby's work deserves particular attention for its reflective depth of thought, and glowing profusion of imagery. His style is remarkably mature, and escapes completely that subtle suggestion of the schoolboy's composition which seems inseparable from the average amateur's attempts at natural description and philosophising. Mr. Schilling's editorials are forcible and straightforward, vibrant with enthusiasm for the welfare of the association. "A Representative Official Organ", by Paul J. Campbell, serves to explain the author's highly desirable constitutional amendment proposed for consideration at the coming election, which will open the columns of *The United Amateur* to the general membership at a very reasonable expense. The News Notes in the present issue are sprightly and interesting.

*The United Amateur* for April is made brilliant by the presence of Henry Clapham McGavack's terse and lucid exposure of hyphenated hypocrisy, entitled "Dr. Burgess, Propagandist". Mr. McGavack's phenomenally virile and convincing style is supported by a remarkable fund of historical and diplomatic knowledge, and the feeble fallacies of the pro-German embargo advocates collapse in speedy fashion before the polished but vigorous onslaughts of his animated pen. Another essay inspired by no superficial thinking is Edgar Ralph Cheyney's "Nietzschean Philosophy", wherein some of the basic precepts of the celebrated iconoclast are set forth in comprehensive array. "The Master Voice of Ages Calls for Peace", a poem by Mrs. Frona Scott, has fairly regular metre, though its sentiment is one of conventional and purely emotional pacifism. "A Gentle Satire on Friendship", by Freda de Larot, is a very clever piece of light prose; which could, however, be improved by the deletion of much slang, and the rectification of many loose constructions. "A Wonderful Play" is Mrs. Eloise N. Griffith's well-worded review of Jerome K. Jerome's "The Passing of the Third Floor Back", as enacted by Forbes-Robertson.[5] Mrs. Griffith has here, as in all her essays, achieved a quietly pleasing effect, and pointed a just moral. "Fire Dreams" is a graphic and commendably regular poem by Mrs. Renshaw. "The Beach", a poem by O. M. Blood, requires grammatical emendation. "How better could the hours been spent" and "When life and love true pleasure brings", cannot be excused even by the exigencies of rhyme and metre. After the second stanza, the couplet form shifts in an unwarranted manner to the quatrain arrangement. The phraseology of the entire piece displays poetical tendencies yet reveals a need for their assiduous cultivation through reading and further practice. "My Shrine", by James Laurence Crowley, exhibits real merit both in wording and metre, yet has a rather weak third stanza. The lines:

> "One day I crossed the desert sands;
> One day I ride my train";

are obviously anticlimactic. To say that the subject is trite would be a little unjust to Mr. Crowley's Muse, for all amatory themes, having been worked over since the very dawn of poesy, are necessarily barren of possibilities save to the extremely skilled metrist. Contemporary love-lyrics can scarcely hope to shine except through brilliant and unexpected turns of wit, or extraordinarily tuneful numbers. The following lines by Margaret, Duchess of Newcastle, who died in 1673, well express the situation despite their crudeness:

> "O Love, how thou art tired out with rhyme!
> Thou art a tree whereon all poets climb;
> And from thy branches every one takes some
> Of the sweet fruit, which Fancy feeds upon.
> But now thy tree is left so bare and poor,
> That they can hardly gather one plum more!"[6]

"Indicatory", a brilliant short sketch by Ethel Halsey, well illustrates the vanity of the fair, and completes in pleasing fashion a very creditable number of our official magazine.

The United Amateur for May forms still another monument to the taste and energy of our official editor, Mr. Schilling. Biography is the keynote of the current issue, Mrs. Renshaw, Mr. J. E. Hoag, and Mr. Henry Cleveland Wood each receiving mention. Miss Emilie C. Holladay displays a pleasing prose style in her account of our Second Vice-President, and arouses interest with double force through the introduction of juvenile incidents.

"Happiness Defined" is a delightful little sketch by Ida C. Haughton, whose philosophy will awake an universal response from the breasts of the majority. "The Wind Fairies", by Jean F. Barnum, is a poem in prose which contains more of the genuine poetic essence than does the average contemporary versified effort. The grace and grandeur of the clouds and the atmosphere have in all ages been admired, and it is but natural that they figure to a great extent in the beautiful legends of primitive mythology. "The Ship That Sails Away", by J. E. Hoag, in a delicate and attractive poem whose images and phraseology are equally meritorious. Mr. Hoag's poetical attainments are such that we await with eagerness the appearance of the pieces predicted in his biography. "To Flavia", by Chester Pierce Munroe, is a sweet lyric addressed to a young child and pervaded throughout with a quaintly whimsical, almost Georgian, semblance of stately gallantry. The first word of the seventeenth line should read "small" instead of "swell". As misprinted, this line conveys a rather incongruous impression. "Mountains in Purple Robes of Mist", a vivid and powerful poem of Nature by Rev. Eugene B. Kuntz, is cast in Alexandrine quatrains, a rather uncommon measure. The only possible defect is in line thirteen, where the accent of the word "sublime" seems to impede the flow of the metre. Line nineteen apparently lacks two syllables, but the deficiency is probably secretarial or typographical rather than literary. "Man as Cook", also by Dr. Kuntz, is a clever bit of humorous verse in octosyllabic couplets. "Consolation" well exhibits Andrew Francis Lockhart's remarkable progress as a poet. His verse is increasing every day in polish, and is fast becoming one of the most pleasing and eagerly awaited features of amateur letters. "At the End of the Road", by Mary Faye Durr, is graphic and touching description of a deserted schoolhouse. The atmosphere of pensive reminiscence is well sustained by the judiciously selected variety of images and allusions. "There's None Like Mine at Home", by James Laurence Crowley, is a characteristic bit of Crowleian sentimentality which requires revision and condensation. There is not enough thought to last out three stanzas of eight lines each. Technically we must needs shudder at the apparently incurable use of "m-n" assonance. "Own" and "known" are brazenly and repeatedly flaunted with "roam" and "home" in attempted rhyme. But the crowning splendour of impossible assonance is attained in the "Worlds-girls" atrocity. Mr. Crowley needs a long session with the late Mr. Walker's well-known Rhyming Dictionary![7] Metrically, Mr. Crowley is shewing a decided improvement of late. The only censurable points in the measure of this piece are the redundant syllables in lines 1 and 3, which might in each case be obviated by the substitution of "I've" for "I have", and the change of form in the first half of the concluding stanza. Of the general phraseology and imagery we may only remark that Mr. Crowley has much to forget as well as to learn, before he can compete with Mr. Kleiner or other high-grade amatory poets in the United. Such expressions as "my guiding star", "my own dear darling Kate", or "she's the sweetest girl—that e'er on earth did roam", tell the whole sad story to the critical eye and ears. If Mr. Crowley would religiously eschew the popular songs and magazine "poetry" of the day, and give over all his time to a perusal of the recognized classics of

English verse, the result would immediately be reflected in his own compositions. As yet, he claims to be independent of scholarly tradition, but we must remind him of the Latin epigram of Mr. Owen, which Mr. Cowper thus translated under the title of "Retaliation":

> "The works of ancient bards divine,
>    Aulus, thou scorn'st to read;
> And should posterity read thine,
>    It would be strange indeed!"[8]

So energetic and prolific a writer as Mr. Crowley owes it alike to himself and to his readers to develop as best he can the talent which rests latent within him.

The Woodbee for April opens with a melodious poem by Adam Dickson, entitled "Love". While the metre might well be changed in the interests of uniformity, the general effect is not at all harsh, and the author is entitled to no small credit for his production. The only other poem in the magazine is "Alone with Him", by Mrs. Ida C. Haughton. This piece is remarkable for its rhyming arrangement, each rhyme being carried through four lines instead of the usual couplet. The sentiments are just, the images well drawn, and the technique correct; the whole forming a highly commendable addition to amateur literature. "The Melody and Colour of 'The Lady of Shalott'", by Mary Faye Durr, is a striking Tennysonian critique, whose psychological features, involving a comparison of chromatic and poetic elements, are ingenious and unusual. Miss Durr in obviously no careless student of poesy, for the minute analyses of various passages give evidence of thorough assimilation and intelligent comprehension. "On Being Good", by Newton A. Thatcher, contains sound sense and real humour, whilst its pleasingly familiar style augurs well for Mr. Thatcher's progress in this species of composition. "War Reflections", by Herbert Albing, is an apt and thoughtful epitome of the compensating benefits given to mankind by the present belligerent condition of the world. The cogent and comprehensive series of reviews by Miss Edna M. Haughton, and the crisp and pertinent paragraphs by Editor Fritter, combine with the rest of The Woodbee's contents to produce an issue uniformly meritorious.

EDITOR'S NOTE  FP: *United Amateur* 15, No. 11 (June 1916): 143–49 (signed "H. P. LOVECRAFT, Chairman"). HPL devotes a majority of space in this column to the monthly issues of the *United Amateur*. His comments on "A Story" by David H. Whittier (in *Toledo Amateur*) suggest that he had already grasped the principles of fiction writing and perhaps indicate a wish to resume the writing of fiction, which he had abandoned in 1908; HPL would do so in the summer of 1917 with "The Tomb" and "Dagon."

*Notes*

1. Roger de Coverley [sic] is a character found in various contributions by Joseph Addison and Richard Steele in *The Spectator* (1711–14; LL 7, 9, 10). The phrase cited by HPL is not an exact quotation of any remark spoken by Coverley, but a paraphrase of his comments in *The Spectator* (14 July 1711; written by Addison) in which he debates the reality of witchcraft: "There are some opinions in which a man should stand neuter, without engaging his assent to one side or the other."

2. Joseph Addison (1672–1719), "An Ode," l. 1.

3. Evidently a revisory service founded by Anne Tillery Renshaw (editor of the amateur journal, the *Symphony*). Either at this time or somewhat later, HPL himself joined the service. See Joshi, *Life* 189.

4. See *AT* 395–96.

5. Jerome K. Jerome (1859–1927), *The Passing of the Third Floor Back* (1908), a celebrated social drama by a popular British dramatist of the period. Johnston Forbes-Robertson (1852–1937), a well-known British actor and manager, played The Stranger in the London premiere of the play (St. James's Theatre, 1 September 1908) and in several subsequent revivals.

6. Margaret Cavendish, Duchess of Newcastle (1624–1674), "Of the Theam of Love," *Poems and Fancies* (London: Printed by T. R. for J. Martin and J. Allestrye, 1653), p. 141.

7. John Walker (1732–1807), A *Dictionary of the English Language, Answering at Once the Purposes of Rhyming, Spelling, and Pronouncing* (1775); later editions use the title *The Rhyming Dictionary of the English Language*. HPL did not own this work, but did own two other reference works by Walker (*LL* 914–15).

8. William Cowper (1731–1800), "Retaliation" (1799), translated from the Latin of John Owen (1563?–1622).

# DEPARTMENT OF PUBLIC CRITICISM

*(August 1916)*

## First Annual Report 1915–1916

Following a novel idea originated by the present Columbus administration, the Department of Public Criticism will herewith submit for the first time in its history an annual report, or summary of the preceding year's literary events within the United Amateur Press Association.

The programme of improvement informally decided upon in the official year of 1913–1914 received its definite ratification at the Rocky Mount Convention, when the assembled representatives of the United pledged "individual and collective support" to Mr. Fritter, the new President, in his endeavours to raise the literary standard of our society, and when an absolutely unanimous vote invested Mrs. J. W. Renshaw, the leading spirit of progress, with the important office of Second Vice-President. Pres. Fritter has since discharged his obligations and sustained his responsibilities in a thoroughly satisfactory manner despite many trying difficulties, whilst Mrs. Renshaw, as a recruiter, has succeeded in laying the foundations of a completely broadened, elevated, and rejuvenated association. Yet all that has been accomplished is merely the prologue of that greater period of change which must bring about the final assimilation of Mrs. Renshaw's phenomenally gifted recruits, and the materialisation of the still nebulous plans evolved during the past twelvemonth.

The undersigned has on several occasions advocated the formation of a regular "Department of Instruction" in the United, to be conducted by professional teachers and college instructors for the purpose of guiding the more or less inexperienced members. He has communicated his idea to several high-school preceptors of great ability, and has learned that under present conditions such a department is not perfectly feasible. It has been suggested that if each experienced and educated amateur would assume a personal and sympathetic advisory position toward some one of the younger or cruder members, much actual good might result. As our list now stands, the crude and the cultured are perhaps evenly balanced, yet instant success even in this modified course can scarcely be expected. At least another year seems to be required, in which the various members may gain a closer knowledge of each other through the wider diffusion of their printed efforts. However, the need for a more uniformly educated membership is pressing, and the undersigned will welcome aid or advice of any kind from those willing to assist him in establishing some sort of scholastic Department.

Another idea which has received undeserved neglect and discouraging opposition is the Authors' Placing Bureau or "United Literary Service", as outlined by the Second Vice-President. The normal goal of the amateur writer is the outside world of letters, and the United should certainly be able to provide improved facilities for the progress of its members into the professional field. The objections offered to this plan are apparently less vital than those affecting the Department of Instruction, and it is to be hoped that the mistaken zeal of our non-professional sticklers may not serve to prevent a step so sorely needed.

Passing on to the details of Departmental work, the undersigned is pleased to report a remarkable increase in the literary value of the compositions brought forth in the United this year; an increase which may be fairly declared to constitute a true elevation of our intellectual standard, and which undoubtedly compensates for the present regrettable paucity of amateur publishing media. In verse, particularly, is the advance notable. Some of our poets are securing recognition in the outside world of letters, whilst many lesser bards shew a steady upward trend in their amateur efforts. Prose continues to suffer because of the seemingly unavoidable brevity of the average amateur journal. It in impossible to crowd any really well-developed piece of prose within the limits generally assigned, hence our best authors seem almost to be driven into verse as a medium of expression. Financial prosperity of sufficient extent to ensure the publication of larger papers is obviously the only remedy for this deplorable condition.

Of our poets, the Laureate Rheinhart Kleiner (also Laureate of the National for 1916–1917) continues as the foremost technician and harmonist. His accurate and tasteful lines satisfy the ear and the understanding with equal completeness, and he shews no sign of yielding to the corrupting influences of decadent modern standards. In his own journal, *The Piper,* he reveals a versatile and phenomenally well-stocked mind. The September number, containing imitations of the work of other amateur poets, will long be remembered. Mrs. Renshaw maintains her high place as a philosophical and expressionistic bard, though hampered by unusual theories of spontaneous versification. A greater deference to the human ear and metrical sense would render her already lofty poetry as attractive as it is exalted. Miss Olive G. Owen, former Laureate, has lately returned to activity, and may well be expected to duplicate her former successes in the domain of the Muses. The poetical progress of Andrew Francis Lockhart is a notable feature of amateur letters this year. Mr. Lockhart has always possessed the true genius of the bard, writing ably and voluminously; but his recent technical care is bringing out hitherto undiscovered beauties in his verse, and placing him in the very front rank of United poets. "Benediction" and "Consolation" are vastly above the average.

Of the new poets of prime magnitude who have risen above our horizon during the past year, Mrs. Winifred Virginia Jordan of Newton-Center, Mass., deserves especial mention both for high quality and great volume of work. Mrs. Jordan's poetry is of a tunefully delicate and highly individualistic sort which has placed it in great demand amongst amateur editors, and it is not unlikely that the author may be rewarded with a Laureateship at no distant date. The work is invariably of spontaneously graceful rhythm and universally pleasing in sentiment, having frequently an elusive suggestion of the unreal. A few of Mrs. Jordan's poems are of the grimly weird and powerful variety. "The Song of the North Wind" is a remarkable contribution to amateur letters, and has won the enthusiastic admiration of the United's poetical element. Professional success has recently crowned the efforts of Mrs. Jordan. *Weekly Unity* for June 17 contains her lines on "The Singing Heart", whilst several other poems from her pen have been accepted by *The National Magazine*. Rev. James Tobey Pyke is another poet of the first order whose writings have lately enriched the literature of the United. His style is correct, and his thought deep and philosophical. "The Meadow Cricket" is a poem which deserves more than a superficial perusal. John Russell, formerly of Scotland but now of Florida, is a satirist and dialect writer of enviable talent. His favourite measure is the octosyllabic couplet, and in his skilled hands this simple metre assumes a new and sparkling lustre. Rev. Frederick Chenault is a prolific lyrical poet whose sentiments are of uniform loftiness. The substitution of exact rhyme for assonance in his lines would double the already immense merit of his work. Other new bards of established ability are W. S. Harrison, Kathleen Baldwin, Eugene B. Kuntz, Mary Evelyn Brown, Henry Cleveland Wood, John W. Frazier, William Hume, Ella Colby Eckert, J. E. Hoag, Edgar Ralph Cheyney, Margaret A. Richard, William de Ryee, Helen H. Salls, and Jeanette Aylworth.

Of the poets whom we may term "rising", none presents a more striking figure than Ira A. Cole of Bazine, Kansas. Previously, well known as a prose writer and publisher, he made his debut as a metrist just a year ago, through a very beautiful piece in the heroic couplet entitled "A Dream of the Golden Age". Mr. Cole is one of the few survivors of the genuine classic school, and constitutes a legitimate successor to the late Georgian poets. His development has been of extraordinary rapidity, and he will shortly surprise the amateur public both by a poetic drama called "The Pauper and the Prince", and by a long mythological poem not unlike Moore's "Lalla Rookh".[1] The natural and pantheistic character of Mr. Cole's philosophy adapts him with phenomenal grace to his position as a mirror of classical antiquity. Another developing poet is Mr. Roy Wesley Nixon of Florida. "Grandma", his latest published composition, is a sonnet of real merit. Adam Dickson, a Scotsman by birth, but now a resident of Los Angeles, writes tunefully and pleasantly. His pieces are not yet of perfect polish, but each exhibits improvement over the preceding. He tends to favour the anapaest and the iambic tetrameter. Mrs. Ida Cochran Haughton of Columbus in scarcely a novice, but her latest pieces are undeniably shewing a great increase of technical grace. Chester Pierce Munroe of North Carolina is a delicate amatory lyrist of the Kleiner type. He has the quaint and attractive Georgian touch, particularly evident in "To Flavia" and "To Chloris". Miss M. Estella Shufelt is absolutely new to the kingdom of poesy, yet has already produced work of phenomenal sweetness and piety. Mrs. E. L. Whitehead, though formerly confined wholly to prose, has entered the poetical field with intelligent and discriminating care. Her words are thoughtfully weighed and selected, whilst her technique has rapidly assumed a scholarly exactitude. Two new poets whose work requires much technical improvement are Mrs. Agnes R. Arnold and Mr. George M. Whiteside. Mr. Whiteside has indications of qualities not far remote from genius, and would be well repaid by a rigorous course of study. Messrs. John Hartman Oswald and James Laurence Crowley are both gifted with a fluency and self-sufficiency which might prove valuable assets in a study of poesy. W. F. Booker of North Carolina possesses phenomenal grace, which greater technical care would develop into unusual power. Rev. Robert L. Selle, D. D., of Little Rock, Arkansas, is inspired by sincerest religious fervour, and has produced a voluminous quantity of verse whose orthodoxy is above dispute. Mrs. Maude K. Barton writes frequently and well, though her technical polish has not yet attained its maximum. John Osman Baldwin of Ohio is a natural poet of spontaneous grace, though requiring cultivation in correct style.

From the foregoing estimate it may easily be gathered that imperfect technique is the cardinal sin of the average amateur poet. We have among us scores of writers blest with beautiful thoughts and attractive fluency, yet the number of precise versifiers may be counted on one's fingers. Our association needs increased requirements in classic scholarship and literary exactitude. At present, it is impossible for an impartial critic to give unstinted approval to the technique of any well-known United poet save Rheinhart Kleiner.

Turning to the consideration of our prose writers, the undersigned finds it difficult to render a true judgment, owing to the adverse conditions mentioned earlier in this report. Many fluent pens are doubtless cramped into feebleness through want of space.

Fiction is among us the least developed of all the branches of literature. Really good stories are rare phenomena, whilst even mediocrity is none too common. The best short stories of the year are probably those by M. Almedia Bretholl and Eleanor Barnhart; the others are mainly juvenile work. Roy W. Nixon and Miss Coralie Austin represent the extremes of excitement and tameness, with "A Bottle of Carbolic Acid" on the one hand, and with "Jane" and "'Twixt the Red and the White" on the other. Both of these authors possess substantial ability. David H. Whittier is developing along classic lines, and will be a prominent figure in the next generation of amateur journalists. Mr. Moe's pupils are all good story-tellers, the work of Miss Gladys L. Bagg standing forth quite prominently this year. Florence Brugger's "Tale of the Sea" is a graphic narrative from a youthful pen, as is William Dowdell's "Behind the Canvas Wall", in a somewhat different way. Henriette and Florenz Ziegfeld have each contributed excellent work, nor must Mary M. Sisson's "Tempora Mutantur" be forgotten.

The rather loosely defined domain of the "sketch" has thriven this year, since it elicits fluent expression from those less prolific in other branches of literature. Mr. Melvin Ryder has entertained us with an entire magazine of this sort of material, whilst Mrs. Ida C. Haughton, Irene Metzger, Benjamin Repp, Mary Faye Durr, Ethel Halsey, Clara Inglis Stalker, Freda de Larot, Helene E. Hoffman-Cole, Helen M. Woodruff, Ira A. Cole, and Eloise N. Griffith prove no less entertaining with shorter sketches.

Criticism is well represented by Leo Fritter, Edna M. Haughton, Mrs. J. W. Renshaw, and Rheinhart Kleiner. The latter is no less gifted a critic than a poet, and gives out very acute judgments in his journal, *The Piper*.

In viewing the formal essays of the year, one is impressed with the profusion of mere schoolboy compositions. Masters of the Addisonian art are few, but those few almost atone for the general lack of polish. Henry Clapham McGavack leads the list with a clarity of style and keenness of reasoning unsurpassed in the association. His "Dr. Burgess, Propagandist", is an amateur classic. Edgar Ralph Cheyney is an extreme radical, but is none the less a masterful essayist. His articles take a very high rank both for thoughtfulness and for diction. A third writer of unusual power and analytical depth is Arthur W. Ashby, whose essays on the varied aspects of Nature command our serious attention. The two Schillings, George and Samuel, deserve more than a passing mention, whilst Pres. Fritter's Laureateship well attest his merit. Rev. E. P. Parham has produced work of attractive quality. Joseph W. Renshaw's essays and editorials command notice whenever beheld; whilst Ira A. Cole, ever versatile, will shortly display his epistolary skill in the now unpublished series of "Churchill-Tutcomble Letters". William T. Harrington has progressed by leaps and bounds to a prominent place amongst our essay-writers, his able encomiums of Old England being a delightful feature of the year. It would be gratifying to speak of Maurice W. Moe's splendid style and terse English at this point, for he is one of our very foremost essayists; but his enforced inactivity in amateur journalism this year has deprived us of any current specimens save the brief editorial in the February *Pippin*.

The general quality of our prose is by no means satisfactory. Too many of our authors are contaminated with modern theories which cause them to abandon grace, dignity, and precision, and to cultivate the lowest forms of slang.

Papers and magazines have been neither ample nor numerous this year; in fact, the tendency of the times appears to be a centralisation of effort in *The United Amateur*; something which is for many reasons to be applauded, and for a few reasons to be deplored. Those members who feel capable of issuing individual papers should be encouraged to do so; whilst those who are ordinarily silent, should be encouraged to join the contributing staff of *The United Amateur* as provided by the Campbell amendment.

The best individual journal of the year is *Ole Miss'*. For frequency and regularity, *The Scot*, *The Woodbee*, *The Dixie Booster*, and *The Coyote* are to be commended. *The United Amateur* has prospered as a monthly despite adverse conditions. The elaborate September, October, and February numbers put us in deep debt to Mr. Edward F. Daas, while subsequent examples of good editorship must be accredited to Mr. George Schilling. It is gratifying to note the increasing literary character of the Official Organ; purely official numbers are invariably tedious, many of the long, detailed reports being quite superfluous. It is a strong and sincere hope of the undersigned, that Mr. Daas may rejoin us at and after the present convention. The resumption of *The Lake Breeze* would supply a pressing need. Mr. Moitoret's *Cleveland Sun*, which promises to be a frequently issued paper, made its first appearance lately, and will, after much of its "loudness" has been removed, be of substantial benefit to new members. The "sporting" features should be eliminated at once, as not only being in bad taste, but exerting a noxious influence over the literary development of the younger members.

While upon the subject of papers, the undersigned would like to enter a renewed protest against the persistent use of certain distorted forms of spelling commonly called "simplified". These wretched innovations, popular amongst the less educated element during the past decade, are now becoming offensively prominent in certain periodicals of supposedly better grade, and require concerted opposition on the part of all friends of our language. The advantages claimed for the changes are almost wholly unsubstantial, whilst the inevitable disadvantages are immense. Let us see fewer "thrus" and "thoros" in the amateur press!

What the association needs above all things is a return to earlier forms in prose and verse alike; to poetry that does not pain the ear, and paragraphs that do not affront the aesthetic sense of the reader. If our writers would pay more attention to the tasteful Georgian models, they would produce work of infinitely less cacophonous quality. Almost every one of our authors who is familiar with the literature of the past, is distinguished by exceptional grace and fluency of expression.

As this report draws toward its conclusion, a few minor aims of the Department of Public Criticism are to be noted. It is now the desire of the undersigned to aid authors in rectifying the injustices to which they are subjected by the wretched typography of most amateur journals. Writers are hereby encouraged to transmit to this Department corrected copies of all misprinted work, the corrections to be made public in *The United Amateur*. By this method it is hoped that no amateur journalist will again be forced to suffer for faults not his own, as so many have suffered in the past. Of course, the critical reports themselves are frequently misprinted, but the vast majority of mistakes may with care be eliminated.

Concerning the name of this association, which a number wish changed in a manner that will eliminate the word "amateur", the undersigned feels that the sentiment of the veteran element is too strongly against such a move to warrant its immediate adoption. The primary object is the training of young writers before they have attained the professional grade, wherefore the present title is by no means such a misnomer as might be inferred from the talents of the more cultivated members. However, the proposed alteration is certainly justified in many ways, hence the idea should be deferred rather than abandoned altogether.

The wane of interest in amateur political affairs is to be commended as a recognition of the superior importance of literary matters. Amateur journalism is rapidly progressing nearer and nearer its ideal; a device for the instruction of the young and crude, and an aid for the obscure author of any sort rather than a playground for the aimless and the frivolous.

Last of all, the undersigned wishes to thank the membership for its kind reception of the Department's reports. It is ever the Chairman's design to render impartial judgment, and if harshness or captiousness may at any time have been noticed in the reports, it has in each case been unintentional. An ideal of sound conservatism has been followed, but in no instance has the critic sought to enforce upon others that peculiarly archaic style of which he is personally fond, and which he is accustomed to employ in his own compositions. The Department of Public Criticism aspires to be of substantial assistance to the members of the United, and hopes next year to coöperate with Mr. Lockhart in presenting reviews of truly constructive quality.

Solicitous for the approval, and confident of the indulgence of the association, the Department herewith has the honour to conclude its first annual report; in the hope that such a summary of events and estimate of conditions may be of use to the incoming administration.

EDITOR'S NOTE   FP: *United Amateur* 16, No. 1 (August 1916): 6–10 (signed "H. P. LOVECRAFT, Chairman"). HPL's first column of the 1916–17 term, in which he was reappointed Chairman of the Department of Public Criticism by President Paul J. Campbell. He presents an overview of amateur writing for the previous year. No such column was ever published in the UAPA in subsequent years, but HPL feels the need to sum up the amateur accomplishments of the year as a harbinger of progress to come. HPL typically minimizes his own amateur work, saying nothing of the four issues of the *Conservative* issued during the period under review nor of his other bountiful contributions to other amateur papers.

*Notes*

1. Thomas Moore, *Lalla Rookh* (1817). See n. 7 to DPC (September 1915).

---

# DEPARTMENT OF PUBLIC CRITICISM

*(September 1916)*

*The Amateur Special* for July is a voluminous magazine of credentials and other work of new members, edited by Mrs. E. L. Whitehead, retiring Eastern Manuscript Manager, with the assistance of the Recruiting Committee. Of all papers lately issued in the

United, this is without doubt among the most valuable and most significant; since it is the pioneer of the new regime, whereby the talent of all our membership is to be brought out by better publishing facilities. Mrs. Whitehead, with notable generosity, has reserved for herself but one page, on which we find a clever and correct bit of verse, and a number of graceful acknowledgments and useful suggestions. The contents in general are well calculated to display the thorough literary excellence and supremacy of the United in its present condition; for in this collection of stories, poems, and articles, taken practically at random from the manuscript bureaus, there is scarce a line unworthy of commendation.

"Tatting", by Julian J. Crump, is a fluent and graceful colloquial sketch. "Mother and Child", by J. E. Hoag, is a sombre and thoughtful poem having a certain atmosphere of mysticism. The metre, which is well handled, consists of regular iambic pentameter quatrains with a couplet at the conclusion. An annoying misprint mars the first stanza, where "*sigh*" is erroneously rendered as "*sight*". "Homesick for the Spring", a poem by Bessie Estelle Harvey, displays real merit in thought and construction alike. "Mother Earth", by Rev. E. P. Parham, is a well-adorned little essay in justification of the traditional saying that "the earth is mother of us all". George M. Whiteside, a new member of the United, makes his first appearance before us as a poet in "The Little Freckled Face Kid". Mr. Whiteside's general style is not unlike that of the late James Whitcomb Riley,[1] and its prevailing air of homely yet pleasing simplicity is well maintained. "To Chloris", by Chester Pierce Munroe, is a smooth and melodious amatory poem of the Kleiner school. The imagery is refined, and the polish of the whole amply justifies the inevitable triteness of the theme. The word "*adorns*", in next the last line, should read "*adorn*". "A Dream", by Helen Harriet Salls, is a hauntingly mystical succession of poetic images cast in appropriate metre. The natural phenomena of the morning are vividly depicted in a fashion possible only to the true poet. The printer has done injustice to this exquisite phantasy in three places. In the first stanza "*wonderous*" should read "*wondrous*", while in the seventh stanza "*arient*" should be "*orient*". "*Thou'st*", in the eleventh stanza, should be "*Thou'rt*". "Prayers", a religious poem by Rev. Robert L. Selle, D. D., displays the classic touch of the eighteenth century in its regular octosyllabic couplets, having some resemblance to the work of the celebrated Dr. Watts. "Snow of the Northland", by M. Estella Shufelt, is a religious poem of different sort, whose tuneful dactylic quatrains contain much noble and appropriate metaphor. In the final line the word "*re-cleaned*" should read "*re-cleansed*". "In Passing By", by Sophie Lea Fox, is a meritorious poem of the thoughtful, introspective type, which has been previously honoured with professional publication. "A Time to Sing", by M. B. Andrews, introduces to the United another genuine poet of worth. The lines are happy in inspiration and finished in form, having only one possible defect, the use of "*heralding*" as a dissyllable. "The Stately Mountains", by Rev. Eugene B. Kuntz, D. D., is a notable contribution to amateur poetic literature. Dr. Kuntz chooses as his favourite metre the stately Alexandrine; and using it in a far more flexible and ingenious manner than that of Drayton, he manages to achieve a dignified and exalted atmosphere virtually impossible in any other measure. The even caesural break so common to Alexandrines, and so often urged by critics as an objection against them, is here avoided with great ingenuity and good taste. Dr. Kuntz's sentiments and phrases are as swelling and sublime as one might expect from his metre. His conception of Nature is a broad and noble one, and his appreciation of her beauties is that of the innate poet. "An April Memory" acquaints us with W. Frank Booker, a gifted lyrist whose lines possess all the warmth, witchery, and grace of his native Southland. James J. Hennessey, in his essay on "The Army in Times of Peace", exhibits very forcibly the various indispensable services so quietly and efficiently performed by the United States Army in every-day life. Mr. Hennessey makes plain the great value of having among us a body of keen, versatile, and well-trained men ready for duty of any sort, and ever alert for their country's welfare in peace or in war. The American Soldier well deserves Mr. Hennessey's tribute, and the present essay adds one more to the already incontrovertible array of arguments in favour of an adequate military system. As printed, the article is marred by a superfluous letter "s" on the very last word, which should read "*citizen*". "Sowing the Good", a brief bit of moralising by Horace Fowler Goodwin, contains a serious misprint, for the final word of line 1, stanza 2, should be "*say*". "Bobby's Literary Lesson", by Gladys L. Bagg, is a delightful specimen of domestic satire in prose. The handling of the conversation exhibits Miss Bagg as a writer of considerable skill and promise. "The Leaf", a clever poem of Nature by Emily Barksdale, contains some gruesome atrocities by the printer. In the second stanza "*it's*" should be "*it*", and "*wonderous*" should be "*wondrous*". In the third stanza the typographical artist has killed a pretty woodland "*copse*" with the letter "r", so that it reads "*corpse*"! In the fourth stanza "*head*" should read "*heard*". Perhaps the "r" which murdered the "*copse*" escaped from this sadly mutilated word! In stanza five, "*chaots*" should be "*chants*". But why continue the painful chronicle? Mr. Kleiner said just what we would like to say about misprints over a year ago, when he wrote "The Rhyme of the Hapless Poet"! "Submission", by Eugene B. Kuntz, is a delightful bit of light prose, forming the autobiography of a much-rejected manuscript. This piece well exhibits Dr. Kuntz's remarkable versatility. The humour is keen, and nowhere overstrained. "Number 1287", a short story by Gracia Isola Yarbrough, exhibits many of the flaws of immature work, yet contains graphic touches that promise well for the author. The lack of unity in plot and development detracts somewhat from the general effect, while the unusual lapses of time and artificial working up of the later situations are also antagonistic to technical polish. Triteness is present, but that is to be expected in all amateur fiction. "A Drama of Business", by Edgar Ralph Cheyney, is a terse bit of prose which might well serve as an editorial in a liberal literary magazine. "The Schools of Yesterday and Today", a sketch by Selma Guilford, presents in pleasing fashion an interesting and optimistic contrast. In "Mother", George M. Whiteside treats a noble theme in rather skilful fashion, though the rhyming of "*breezes*" and "*trees is*" can hardly be deemed suitable in a serious poem. "When the Sea Calls", a poem by Winifred Virginia Jordan, is possibly the most striking feature of the magazine. Mrs. Jordan's style in dealing with the wilder aspects of Nature has a grim potency all its own, and we can endorse without qualification the judgment of Mr. Moe when he calls this poem "positively magnificent in dynamic effect". To Mrs. Jordan is granted a natural poetic genius which few other amateurs can hope to parallel. Not many of our literary artists can so aptly fit words to weird or unusual passages, or so happily command all the advantages of alliteration and onomatopoeia. We believe that Mrs. Jordan's amateur eminence will eventually ripen into professional recognition. "Preachers in Politics", by Rev. James Thomas Self, is a long, thoughtful, and extremely well-phrased essay against the descent of the ministry to the uncertain affairs of practical legislation. Dr. Self has a just idea of the dignity of the cloth; an idea which some clergymen of less conservative habits would do well to acquire. Very painful is the sight of the slang-mouthing "evangelist" who deserts his pulpit for the stump or the circus-tent.[2] "Peace, Germany!", a poem by Maude Kingsbury Barton, constitutes an appeal to the present outlaw among nations. We feel, however, that it is only from London that Germany will eventually be convinced of the futility of her pseudo-Napoleonic enterprise. And when peace does come to Germany, it will be British-made peace! The structure of Mrs. Barton's poem is regular, and many of the images are very well selected. The worst misprints are those in the sixth stanza, where *"in"* is omitted before the word *"pomp"*, and in the seventh stanza where *"come"* is printed as *"came"*. In the biographical sketch entitled "Two Lives", Helen Hamilton draws a powerful moral from the contrasted but contemporaneous careers of Florence Nightingale and the ex-Empress Eugenie. "Class-Room Spirits I Have Known", an essay by Bessie Estelle Harvey, displays a sound comprehension of pedagogical principles. Two more poems by Mrs. Jordan conclude the issue, "The Time of Peach Tree Bloom" is the fourth of the "Songs from Walpi", three of which appeared in *The United Amateur*. "In a Garden" is a gem of delightful delicacy and ethereal elegance. It is indeed not without just cause that the author has, from the very first, held the distinction of being the most frequent poetical contributor in all amateur journalism.

The *Cleveland Sun* for June is the first number of an amateur newspaper edited by Anthony F. Moitoret, Edwin D. Harkins, and William J. Dowdell; and remarkable for an excellent heading, drawn by a staff artist of the *Cleveland Leader*. The present issue is printed in close imitation of the modern professional daily, and displays some interesting examples of "newspaper English". Mr. Moitoret is an old-time United man, now reëntering the sphere of activity, and he is to be commended warmly both for his generous attitude toward the new members, and for his really magnanimous offer of aid to those desirous of issuing individual papers. His editorial hostility toward the Campbell amendment is, we believe, mistaken; yet is none the less founded on a praiseworthy desire to serve what he deems the best interests of the Association. Were Mr. Moitoret more in touch with the rising ideals of the newer United, he would realise the essential childishness of our "official business" as contrasted with the substantial solidity of our developing literature. Possibly the plan of Mr. Campbell, as experimentally tried during the present year, will alter Mr. Moitoret's present opinion. Taken altogether, we are not sure whether the *Sun* will prove beneficial or harmful to the United. We most assuredly need some sort of stimulus to activity, yet the comparatively crude atmosphere of newspaperdom is anything but inspiring in a literary society. We cannot descend from the ideals of Homer to those of Hearst without a distinct loss of quality, for which no possible gain in mere enthusiasm can compensate. Headlines such as "Columbus Bunch Boosting Paul" or "Hep Still Shows Pep", are positive affronts to the dignity of amateur journalism. There is room for an alert and informing news sheet in the United, yet we feel certain that the *Sun* must become a far more sedate and scholarly publication before it can adequately supply the need. At present, its garish rays dazzle and blind more than they illuminate; in a perusal of its pages we experience more of *sunstroke* than of *sunshine*. Of "The Best Sport Page in Amateurdom" we find it difficult to speak or write. Not since perusing the delectable lines of "Tom Crib's Memorial to Congress", by jovial old "Anacreon Moore", have we beheld such an invasion of prizefight philosophy and race-track rhetoric.[3] We learn with interest that a former United member named "Handsome Harry" has now graduated from literature to *left field,* and has, through sheer genius, risen from the lowly level of the ambitious author, to the exalted eminence of the *classy slugger*. Too proud to *push the pen,* he now *swats the pill.* Of such doth the dizzy quality of sempiternal Fame consist! Speaking without levity, we cannot but censure Mr. Dowdell's introduction of the ringside or ballfield spirit into an Association purporting to promote culture and lettered skill. Our members can scarcely be expected to place the Stygian-hued John Arthur Johnson, Esq.,[4] on a pedestal beside his well-known namesake Samuel; or calmly to compare the stinging wit of a Sidney Smith with the stinging fist-cuffs of a "Gunboat" Smith.[5] In a word, what is suited to the street-corner is not always suited to the library, and the taste of the United is as yet but imperfectly attuned to the lyrical liltings of the pool-room Muse. It is both hard and unwise to take the "Best Sport Page" seriously. As a copy of "yellow" models it is a work of artistic verisimilitude; indeed, were Mr. Dowdell a somewhat older man, we might justly suspect a satirical intention on his part.

We trust that *The Cleveland Sun* may shine on without cloud or setting, though we must needs hope that the United's atmosphere of academic refinement will temper somewhat the scorching glare with which the bright orb has risen.

*The Conservative* for April opens with Andrew Francis Lockhart's melodious and attractive poem entitled "Benediction". As a whole, this is possibly the best piece of verse which Mr. Lockhart has yet written; the sentiment is apt, if not entirely novel, whilst the technical construction is well-nigh faultless. Such expressions as "pearl-scarr'd" serve to exhibit the active and original quality of Mr. Lockhart's genius. "Another Endless Day", by Rheinhart Kleiner, is a beautiful and harmonious poetical protest against monotony.[6] Much to be regretted is the misprint in line 3 of the third stanza, where the text should read:

"A love to thrill with new delight."

"April", by Winifred Virginia Jordan, is a seasonable and extremely tuneful poem whose imagery is of that dainty, sprightly sort which only Mrs. Jordan can create. "In Morven's Mead", also by Mrs. Jordan, contains an elusive and haunting suggestion of the unreal, in the author's characteristic style. "The Night Wind Bared My Heart" completes a highly meritorious trilogy. In justice to the author, it should be stated that the last of these three poems is, as here presented, merely a rough draught. Through our own reprehensible editorial oversight, the printer received this unpolished copy instead of the finished poem. The following emendations should be observed:

Stanza I, line 4, to read: "Awak'd my anguish'd sighs."
Stanza II, line 3, to read: "But Oh, from grief *were* prest."

"The Best Wine", by William De Ryee, is an earnestly introspective poem, well cast in iambic pentameter quatrains. "Ye Ballade of Patrick von Flynn"[7] is a comic delineation of the cheap pseudo-Irish, England-hating agitators who have been so offensively noisy on this side of the Atlantic ever since the European war began, and particularly since the late riots in Dublin. This class, which so sadly misinterprets the loyal Irish people, deserves but little patience from Americans. Its members stutter childishly about "breaches of neutrality" every time a real American dares speak a word in favour of the Mother Country; yet they constantly violate neutrality themselves in their clumsy attempts to use the United States as a catspaw against England. The actual German propagandists have the excuse of patriotism for their race and Vaterland, but these Hibernian hybrids, neither good Irishmen nor good Americans, have no excuse whatever when they try to subvert the functions of the country which is giving them protection and livelihood.[8]

*The Conservative* for July pays a deserved tribute to one of the most lucid and acute of our amateur essayists, by devoting the entire issue to his work. Henry Clapham McGavack, in "The American Proletariat versus England", exposes with admirable fearlessness the silly Anglophobic notions which a mistaken conception of the Revolution, and an ignorant Irish population, have diffused among our lower classes. It is seldom that an author ventures to speak so frankly on this subject, for the servile tendency of the times impels most writers and publishers to play the demagogue by essaying to feed the Irish masses with the anti-English swill they desire; but Mr. McGavack wields an independent pen, and records the truth without fear of the *mobile vulgus* and its shallow views. In power, directness, urbanity, and impartiality, Mr. McGavack cannot be excelled. He marshals his arguments without passion, bias, or circumlocution, piling proof upon proof until none but the most stubborn England-hater can fail to blush at the equal injustice and stupidity of those who malign that mighty empire to whose earth-wide circle of civilisation we all belong.

*The Coyote* for April is a Special English Number, dedicated to our soldier-member, George William Stokes of Newcastle-on-Tyne. The opening poem, "To England", well exhibits the versatility of Mrs. Winifred V. Jordan, who here appears as a national panegyrist of commendable dignity and unexceptionable taste. The word at the beginning of the fourth line should read *"Is"* instead of *"To"*. The short yet stirring metre is particularly well selected. "Active English Amateurs I Have Met", by Ernest A. Dench, is a rather good prose piece, though not without marks of careless composition. "The Vultur", by Henry J. Winterbone of the B. A. P. A., is a remarkably good story whose development and conclusion would do credit to a professional pen. We hope Mr. Winterbone may join the United, thereby giving American readers a more ample opportunity to enjoy his work. Editor William T. Harrington, whose prose is so rapidly acquiring polish and fluency, contributes two brief but able essays: "History Repeats", and "How Great Britain Keeps Her Empire". In "History Repeats", certain parts of the second sentence might well be amended a trifle in structure, to read thus: "It must be remembered that the first half was a series of victories for the South, and *that* only after the Battle of Gettysburg did the strength of the North begin to assert itself." This number of *The Coyote* is an exceedingly timely and tasteful tribute to our Mother Country, appearing at an hour when the air of America reeks with the illiterate anti-British trash of the "Sinn Fein" simpletons and Prussian propagandists.

*Invictus* for July is the second number of Mr. Paul J. Campbell's personal organ, and represents the strictly individual magazine in its most tasteful and elaborate form. Unimpeachably artistic in appearance, its contents justify the exterior; the whole constituting a publication of the first rank, wherein are joined the virtues both of the old and the new schools of amateur journalism. Since Mr. Campbell is preëminently an essayist, it is to his dissertations on "The Pursuit of Happiness" and "The Age of Accuracy" which we turn most eagerly; and which in no way disappoint our high expectations. The first of these essays is a dispassionate survey of mankind in its futile but frantic scramble after that elusive but unreal sunbeam called "happiness". The author views the grimly amusing procession of human life with the genuine objective of an impartial spectator, and with commendable freedom from the hypocritical colouring of those who permit commonplace emotions and tenuous idealisings to obscure the less roseate but more substantial vision of their intellects. "The Age of Accuracy" presents an inspiring panorama of the evolution of Intellect, and of its increasing domination over the more elemental faculties of instinct and emotion. At the same time, much material for reflection is furnished, since it is obvious that the advance is necessarily confined to a comparatively small and select part of humanity. Instinct and emotion are still forces of tremendous magnitude, against which Reason wages an upward struggle of incredible bravery. Only the strong can escape the clutch of the primitive, wherefore there can be no successful social order which does not conform in its essentials to the blind impulses of the natural man or man-ape. We are in danger of overestimating the ascendancy and stability of Reason, for it is in reality the most fragile and rudimentary element in our mortal fabric. A heavy blow on certain parts of the skull, or a bullet in certain parts of the brain, can destroy in an instant all the accumulated intellect which aeons of heredity have bestowed, depressing the victim from the zenith of culture and refinement to a condition separated only by colour and contour from that of the negro or the gorilla; yet not all the edicts of the lawgiver, devices of the educator, measures of the reformer, or skill of the surgeon, can extirpate the ingrained instincts and seated superstitions of the average human animal.

The poetry of Mr. Campbell is represented in *Invictus* by three specimens, whose merit speaks well for the author's progress in the art. "The Sunshine Girl" is an amatory panegyric of no small skill and polish, though not strikingly novel in sentiment or expression. "German Kultur" is a scathing and virile indictment of the present enemies of humanity. The versification is bold, and in places rugged, whilst the imagery is appropriately grim and sardonic. Points which we might criticise are the repeated use of *"civilization"* as a word of only four syllables, and the archaic pronunciation of *"drowned"* as a dissyllable. This latter usage would not be objectionable in verse of stately or conservative cast, but here grates upon the ear as an anachronism. The trenchant wit of the piece is well sustained, and brought out with particular force in the second and fourth stanzas. "The Major Strain" is without doubt the foremost verse of the issue. This is real poetry. The sustained rhyming, whereby each stanza contains only one rhyming sound, is pleasing and unusual. Mr. Campbell's comment on "Amateur Affairs" really deserves to be classed as an essay, for its thoughtful conclusions and intelligent analyses of human nature certainly draw it within the pale of true literature. The broad comprehension and continued love of amateur journalism here exhibited, are potent justifications of the author's practically unanimous election to the Presidency of the United. *Invictus* is one of the very foremost journals of the amateur world, and the only possible objection which can be raised against it, is its infrequency of appearance. It is the voice of a virile and vibrant personality who unites vigour of thought with urbanity of expression.

*The Scot* for May marks the advent of this highly entertaining and well-conducted magazine to the United, and extends the northern frontier of amateur journalism to Bonnie Dundee, in Auld Scotland, the Land of Mountain and Flood. "Hidden Beauty", a poem in blank verse by R. M. Ingersley, opens the issue with a combination of lofty conceptions, vivid imagery, and regular structure. "England's Glory", by Clyde Dane, is a stirring tale of that fearless and self-sacrificing honour which has given to the Anglo-Saxon the supremacy of the world. It would be in bad taste to cavil at slight technical imperfections or instances of triteness when considering so earnest and glowing a delineation of the British character; the noblest human type ever moulded by the Creator. "Oh Rose, Red Rose!" is a tuneful little lyric by Winifred V. Jordan, whose work is never too brief to be pleasing, or too long to be absorbing. "Clemency versus Frightfulness", by William T. Harrington, is a thoughtful and lucid exposition of the British governmental ideal of lenient justice; an ideal whose practical success has vividly demonstrated its thorough soundness. "At Last", by Muriel Wilson, is a blank verse poem of much merit. "Do You Remember?", by the late Lieut. Roy Arthur Thackara, R. N., is a delicate sketch possessing the additional interest of coming from the pen of one who has now given his life for King and Country; the author having gone down with H. M. S. *India*. "A Battle with the Sea", a sketch by Midshipman Ernest L. McKeag, exhibits descriptive power of no common order, yet might well have a less abrupt conclusion. "To Some One", by Margaret Trafford, is a poem in dactylic measure, dedicated to the women of Britain. The sentiment is noble, and the encomium well bestowed, though the metre could be improved in polish. "Gum", by Henry J. Winterbone, is a delightfully humorous sketch. It is evident that those who depreciate British humour must have taken pains to avoid its perusal, since it has a quietly pungent quality seldom found save among Anglo-Saxons. Personally, we believe that the summit of clumsy pseudo-jocoseness is attained by the average "comic" supplement of the Hearst Sunday papers. These, and not the British press, present the pathetic spectacle of utter inanity and repulsive grotesqueness without the faintest redeeming touch of genuine comedy, legitimate satire, or refined humour. "Life's Voyage", by Matthew Hilson, is a poem of great attractiveness, though of scarcely impeccable construction. Concerning the expression "tempests wild *do* roar", we must reiterate the advice of Mr. Pope, who condemned the expletive "do", "doth", or "did" as a "feeble aid".[9] Such usage has, in fact, been in bad taste ever since the reign of Queen Anne; Dryden being the last bard in whom we need not censure the practice. Mr. McColl's editorials are brief but informing. He may well be congratulated on his work as a publisher, and he certainly deserves as hearty a welcome as the United can give.

The *Scot* for June is a "British Old-Timers' Number", confined wholly to the work of the senior amateur journalists of the Mother Country. Edward F. Herdman, to whom this number is dedicated, opens the issue with a religious poem entitled "Life", which compares well with the bulk of current religious verse. Mr. Herdman also contributes one of several prose essays on amateur journalism, in which the various authors view our field of endeavour from similar angles. "A Song of a Sailor", by R. D. Roosma-Le Cocq, exhibits buoyant animation, and considerable ease in the handling of a rollicking measure. The internal rhymes are for the most part well introduced, though greater uniformity might have been used in their distribution. The first two lines have none. In the last stanza there are two lines whose metre seems deficient, but being conscious of the uncertainties of the secretarial and typographical arts, we suspend judgment on the author. "A Song of Cheer", by Alfred H. Pearce, is an optimistic ode of real merit. The last line furnishes a particularly pleasing example of sprightly wit. Mr. Gavin T. McColl is sensible and perspicuous in all his editorial utterances. His work in issuing one of the only two regular monthly magazines in amateurdom has already brought him to prominence, though his connexion with the press associations is still new.

The *United Amateur* for June is given over largely to critical and official matter, though two pieces of verse serve to vary the monotony. "Content", from our own pen,[10] is an answer to Mr. Rheinhart Kleiner's delightful poem in the April *Conservative*, entitled "Another Endless Day". The lines are notable chiefly on account of some fearful and wonderful typographical errors. In the fourth line *"sublime"* should read *"sublimer"*. In the eighth line there should be no apostrophe in the word *"stars"*. In the second column, eleventh line from the end, "there should be no apostrophe in the word *"fathers"*, and finally, in the ninth line from the end, *"hollow'd"* should read *"hallow'd"*. "The Swing in the Great Oak Tree", by Mrs. Agnes Richmond Arnold,[11] is a reminiscent poem whose measure is as swinging as its subjects and whose atmosphere is pleasantly rural. There are flaws in the metre, and irregularities in the rhyming arrangements, but the spirit of the whole rises blithesomely above such slight technical matters. Editor Schilling's column is to be praised for its dignified style, and endorsed for its sound opinions.

The Woodbee for July is an attractive and important contribution to the history of amateur journalism; since it is entirely devoted to the biographies of the gifted Columbus amateurs, and to the annals of their brilliant local organisation. The Woodbees undoubtedly form the most active and representative adult club in the United; to which only the Appleton club, representing the juvenile Muse, may justly be compared. The Woodbees are typical, in a sense, of all that is best in the entire association. They are pursuing courses of serious literary study, producing a regularly issued magazine of unfailing merit and good taste, working enthusiastically for the welfare and expansion of the United, and leading or following every worthy or progressive movement in amateur politics. They reflect credit upon themselves, their society, the Association, and amateur journalism as a whole. The delightful biographical article which occupies the major portion of the current Woodbee is unsigned; but deserves particular praise, whoever the author may be. The various characters are well displayed, and their pleasing qualities and manifold activities well exhibited.

Mr. Fritter's editorials are as usual timely, lucid, and sensible. His advocacy of the Campbell Amendment is to be applauded; and will, we trust, be justified by the year's trial which that measure is now undergoing. The present issue marks the conclusion of Mr. Fritter's term as editor. He has given the amateur public a creditable volume, and is entitled to the gratitude of every member of our Association. A final word of praise is due the excellent group photograph of the Woodbees which forms the frontispiece of the magazine. Added to the biographical matter, it completes a thoroughly commendable introduction to a thoroughly commendable body of literary workers.

EDITOR'S NOTE   FP: United Amateur 16, No. 2 (September 1916): 25–31 (signed "H. P. LOVECRAFT, Chairman"). HPL discusses two issues of his own Conservative (April and July 1917), along with other journals of the preceding months.

*Notes*

1. The immensely popular dialect poet James Whitcomb Riley (1849–1916) died on 22 July 1916.

2. HPL refers to Billy Sunday (1862–1935), the histrionic evangelist who began touring the country, holding outdoor revival meetings, in 1896. In 1916 he was conducting a particularly popular series of meetings on the East Coast.

3. Thomas Moore, *Tom Crib's Memorial to Congress* (1819), a mock-heroic poem about a boxing match.

4. Jack Johnson (1878–1946), African American boxer who held the world heavyweight crown from 1908 to 1915.

5. Sydney Smith (1771–1845), British man of letters and cofounder of the *Edinburgh Review*. "Gunboat" Smith was an American boxer of the period.

6. HPL's poem "Content" (*United Amateur*, June 1916; AT 97–99) is subtitled: "An Epistle to RHEINHART KLEINER, Esq., Poet-Laureate and Author of 'Another Endless Day'." See p. 133.

7. See AT 206–7.

8. For further discussion of this subject, see the section "The Loyal Coalition" in the essay "Lucubrations Lovecraftian" (1921; p. 277).

9. See n. 3 to DPC (March 1915).

10. See AT 97–99.

11. See HPL to Alfred Galpin, 21 August 1918: "I am corresponding lately with a lady friend of yours—or your mother's—the would-be poetess Mrs. Agnes Richmond Arnold, who thinks you are a very bright child indeed. She seems to be a nice old lady, though she uses simplified spelling. She is very much interested in the Association, and if you can secure her aid you may be able to capture some adult recruits. Also—for Heaven's sake teach her how to use metre. She wants to be a poet very much, but must master many a technical rule first. I have amended one of her effusions and have offered to do more, for I have a very keen sympathy for the old folks who develop their ambitions too late in life to improve them. I judge Mrs. Arnold (though not from any real evidence) to be about 70—and if Mr. Hoag can succeed (with aid) at 87, there ought to be hope for her. I think she would appreciate your help, and in return might help your recruiting, as I said before." *Letters to Alfred Galpin* (New York: Hippocampus Press, 2003), p. 32.

## AMONG THE AMATEURS

Mr. John Russell of Florida, whose satirical and other verses have formed such a piquant feature of amateur letters, has recently accepted a position with the *Tampa Breeze*. He will be in complete charge of the advertising department, besides having duties of an editorial nature. Mr. Russell will be pleased to receive literary contributions from the more experienced amateurs, which he will accept for publication in his paper.

------

The Conservative has not infrequently pondered in perplexity over the persistent use of the expletive "do", "does", or "did" by various amateur bards. Were these versifiers professed disciples of Dryden and his predecessors, there would be less cause for wonderment, but in view of their largely modern tendencies it appears highly peculiar that they should employ an archaic device censured and ridiculed ever since the reign of Queen Anne. No stigma of poetical puerility or lax scholarship is so patent as a line wherein we are informed that the poet "does sigh" because his Phillis or Chloe "did cast" him aside. Exceptions to this rule of abstinence may be made in certain cases of imitative archaism, but for the average amateur writer, total abstinence is the safer course.

------

The attitude toward our Association recently expressed by members of the Pedroni "United" is very regrettable.[1] These worthy amateurs see fit threateningly to demand that we abandon our name in favour of their society, which they arbitrarily assume to be legally entitled to the designation "United". Whatever may be the advantages offered us by a more comprehensive title, we are certainly not to be frightened into a change by those who have at least no more right to the name than we.

------

In the Appleton, Wis., *Evening Crescent* for October 13 appears a highly interesting account of Maurice W. Moe's speech before the Northeastern Teachers' Convention, wherein our noted Private Critic treats of the uses of the phonograph in the teaching of English. Mr. Moe has opened up a wonderful field by his adaptation of the classics, beautifully rendered by the highest talent, to the daily routine of the classroom. Incidentally, it will prove a surprise to many persons to learn that such classics as Milton's "Comus", passages from Shakespeare, and snatches from the later poets, have been made available to the public in the most artistic oral form through the refinement of mechanical science.

———

Though dread of triteness usually deters The Conservative from conventional comment on "exchanges", he cannot but remark the great and sustained merit of Mr. W. Paul Cook's new publication, *The Vagrant,* whose September issue has just reached this office. Mr. Cook's editorials are of a closely personal character, and may recall many incidents of interest to members of the preceding amateur journalistic generation. Though *The Vagrant* bears no official connexion with this Association, we may hope that it may reach most of our members; since it contains a phenomenally picturesque and searching sketch of a certain aspect of rural society from the pen of no less a philosopher than Pres. Paul J. Campbell.

———

The *Schuylerville (N.Y.) Standard* for October 12 contains an admirably interesting essay on the Mohawk Trail by our gifted and venerable poet and essayist, Mr. J. E. Hoag of Greenwich. More of Mr. Hoag's work may shortly be expected in *The United Amateur* in the form of a poem treating of several natural and historical aspects of his native state.

———

The United's 1916–1917 Year Book, to be issued by a committee of which The Conservative is chairman, will contain a rather unusual feature, in the form of a biographical dictionary or "Who's Who" of the more prominent members of the Association. The idea is due to the fertile brain of Pres. Campbell, and will, it is hoped, serve as a means of creating a closer tie amongst our gifted litterateurs. Members are hereby invited to send biographical notes to this office, for inclusion in the forthcoming annual.[2]

EDITOR'S NOTE  FP: *Conservative* 2, No. 3 (October 1916): [11] (unsigned). Miscellaneous comments on amateur papers. HPL takes note of W. Paul Cook's new journal, the *Vagrant* (a NAPA paper), to which he would contribute many poems and stories in subsequent years.

*Notes*

1. HPL refers to Victor A. Pedroni, President of the United Amateur Press Association of America for 1916–17. See the Editor's Note to "The Morris Faction" (p. 33).

2. No such yearbook was ever issued. See further "A Request" (p. 138).

# CONCERNING "PERSIA—IN EUROPE"

> "Indignor quandoque bonus dormitat Homerus:
> Verum operi longo fas est obrepere somnum."
> —Horace, *Ars Poetica*.[1]

Editor Tryout:—

Since Mr. James F. Morton, Jr., so conclusively demonstrated his scholastic infallibility over a year ago, in his lofty essay on "Conservative Run Mad", the undersigned would like to inquire about a remarkable geographical statement contained in his clever article in your September number.

In suggesting the birthplace of an historical character whom he later shews to be a PERSIAN, the Great Radical describes the land as "one of the most backward countries of modern EUROPE". The undersigned, when seeking to guess who the unnamed individual might be, exhausted the previously recognised area of the European continent without avail; never dreaming that Persia had moved out of Asia into the more western grand division of the earth's surface. Is it a result of the war, or merely an incident in the progress of that Radicalism which heeds no boundary lines, either of reason or of territory?

Amateurdom would doubtless appreciate a more detailed knowledge of this unexpected change of continental allegiance on the part of an ancient state whose history is symbolical of the Orient and its spirit. Lacking this knowledge, our members are scarcely to be blamed for their failure to identify the heroine of Mr. Morton's sketch; in fact, it would be impossible for anyone to select the proper personage, with the search so plainly confined to Europe as we have hitherto known it.

It is only fair to add that the undersigned would have failed in any case; being unfamiliar with the minor theological vagaries of the modern Orientals, or with the fugitive freaks and fallacies of Eastern superstition which occasionally filter into this country to prey upon the minds and purses of the credulous.

EDITOR'S NOTE FP: *Tryout* 3, No. 2 (January 1917): [7–8]. HPL seizes upon a trivial slip of the pen by James F. Morton in a feeble attempt to get even with Morton for his devastating critique of HPL, "'Conservatism' Gone Mad," *In a Minor Key* No. 2 [1915]: [15–16] (see "In a Major Key," p. 56 above). HPL was not at this time personally acquainted with Morton; but when he and HPL finally did come into contact in 1920, they became close friends and colleagues.

*Notes*

1. "I am outraged when good Homer nods; but it is allowable for sleep to creep upon [the poet] in a long work." Horace, *Ars Poetica* 359–60.

## AMATEUR STANDARDS

Amateur journalism has always been a battle-ground betwixt those who, cognisant of its better possibilities, wish to improve their literary skill; and those who, viewing it merely as a field of amusement to which they can obtain easy access, wish to indulge in mock-politics, pseudo-feuds, and cheap social frivolities. In 1886 this disparity of aims was sufficient to cause the better element to withdraw for a time, forming a short-lived "Literary Lyceum of America", but experience proved that the cause of unprofessional letters can best be furthered by combating its evils within the confines of the regularly organised press associations. Since 1914 the United has striven with varying success to occupy a materially higher plane in the world of culture and education; the campaign for betterment being led at different times by Mr. Moe and Mrs. Renshaw, and now by Pres. Paul J. Campbell. But there has arisen in opposition to the progressive policies of these leaders a reactionary movement of such blatant vulgarity and puerile crudeness, that The Conservative feels impelled to protest at the display of impotent malice and infantile bitterness shewn by some of the treacherous anti-administration elements. Yellow journals have spread broadcast a silly series of attacks and aspersions on our best officials, setting by their glaringly plebeian atmosphere a dangerously bad example for the many youths whose cultural and literary improvement is the prime object of the Association. One of these peace-disturbers has wailed against the improvement of *The United Amateur*, declaring (despite the fact that it contained all but one of this year's laureate-winning pieces) that it has become a mere purveyor of "literary twaddle"; whilst another congenital "heckler" has recently launched a tirade of inexcusable commonness against President Campbell as a result of some disclosures in the news notes of the official organ. What President Campbell did was to expose some detestable trickery in the handling of proxy ballots last summer, and nothing save guilty resentment at this exposure could prompt this "heckler" to raise a veritable teapot tempest at Mr. Campbell's pleasantry regarding a former amateur; a pleasantry against which he rants with Pharisaical fervour. It is not the desire of The Conservative to enter the field of adolescent bickering, but he does deem it necessary and proper to warn the membership of the United against the sly malevolence, ambiguous statements, and apocryphal anecdotes whereby a fraction of malcontents is seeking to undermine confidence in the present administration; an administration whose leader has a longer and more brilliant record of amateur achievement than any other active member of the United Amateur Press Association.

EDITOR'S NOTE FP: *Conservative* 2, No. 4 (January 1917): [3–4] (unsigned). Part of a regular column (begun in the October 1916 *Conservative*) entitled "In the Editor's Study." HPL presents a vigorous defense of the new literary trend of the UAPA against unnamed dissenters (HPL probably had in mind such nemeses as William J. Dowdell and Anthony F. Moitoret).

## A REQUEST

The Conservative, as Chairman of the United's Year-Book Committee, will deem it a favour of great magnitude if every recipient of this paper will send him, as soon as possible, a set of autobiographical notes for use in the forthcoming annual. A complete biographical dictionary of amateurs is planned as a feature of that publication. The following specimen may serve as a guide to what is desired:

> 647c CAMPBELL, PAUL J., Farmer, Printer, Journalist. Born Georgetown, Ill., Nov. 8, 1884. Public School Education. Joined June, 1902, recommended by Ira E. Seymour. Published Ideal Politician, Scottish Highlander, Prairie State Journal, Illinoian, Scotchman, and Invictus. Contributed 59 articles to the amateur press in 1906, his most active year. Elected Director in 1908, Treasurer in 1915, President in 1916. Interested in Literature, Religion, History, Philosophy, and Free Thought.

It is particularly desirable that each member convey some idea of his literary tastes. Those who have already sent biographical matter, either to The Conservative or to *The Looking Glass,* need not send further matter unless they wish to do so in order to include points previously omitted. The granting of this request by every reader will help to make the Year-Book the most interesting and valuable number yet issued by the United. The Conservative thanks the membership in advance.

EDITOR'S NOTE  FP: *Conservative* 2, No. 4 (January 1917): [4] (unsigned). HPL continues to request information for the UAPA Year Book for 1916–17, a volume that was never published, although the ms. was apparently completed (see "President's Message" [November 1917], p. 173).

---

# DEPARTMENT OF PUBLIC CRITICISM
## (March 1917)

*T*he Conservative for October opens with Miss Olive G. Owen's tuneful lines on "The Mocking Bird". Of the quality of Miss Owen's poetry it is scarce necessary to speak; be it sufficient to say that the present piece ranks among her best. In the intense fervour of the sentiment, and the felicitous choice of the imagery, the touch of the born poet is alike shewn. Through an almost inexcusable editorial mistake of our own, the first word of this poem is erroneously rendered. Line 1 should read:

"*Where* Southern moonlight softly falls."

"Old England and the Hyphen" is an attempt of the present critic to demonstrate why relations between the United States and Mother England must necessarily be closer than those between the States and any of the really foreign powers. So patent and so inevitable is the essential unity of the Anglo-Saxon world that such an essay as this ought really to be superfluous; but its practical justification is found in the silly clamour of those Anglophobes who are unfortunately permitted to reside within our borders. "Insomnia", by Winifred Virginia Jordan, is a remarkable piece of verse whose dark turns of fancy are almost worthy of a Poe.[1] The grotesque tropes, the cleverly distorted images, the bizarre atmosphere, and ingeniously sinister repetitions all unite to produce one of the season's most notable poems. Each of the stanzas is vibrant with the hideous, racking turmoil of the insomnious mind. "Prussianism", by William Thomas Harrington, is a concise and lucid essay on a timely subject, reviewing ably the cause and responsibility of the present war. It is especially valuable at this season of incoherent peace discussion, for it explodes very effectively that vague, brainless "neutrality" which prompts certain pro-German pacifists to cry for peace before the normal and final settlement of Europe's troubles shall have been attained by the permanent annihilation of the Prussian military machine. "Twilight", by Chester Pierce Munroe, is a beautiful bit of poetic fancy and stately phraseology. Mr. Munroe, a Rhode Islander transplanted to the mountains of North Carolina, is acquiring all the grace and delicacy of the native Southern bard, while retaining that happy conservatism of expression which distinguishes his work from that of most contemporary poets. Callously modern indeed must be he who would wish Mr. Munroe's quaintly euphonious lines transmuted into the irritatingly abrupt and barren phraseology of the day. "The Bond Invincible", by David H. Whittier, is a short story of great power and skilful construction, suggesting Poe's "Ligeia" in its central theme. The plot is developed with much dexterity, and the climax comes so forcibly and unexpectedly upon the reader, that one cannot but admire Mr. Whittier's mastery of technique. Certain overnice critics may possibly object to the tale, as constituting incidents which no one survives to relate; but when we reflect that Poe has similarly written a story without survivors ("The Masque of the Red Death") we can afford to applaud without reservation. The complete absence of slang and of doubtful grammar recommends this tale as a model to other amateur fiction-writers. "Respite" is a lachrymose lament in five stanzas by the present critic.[2] The metre is regular, which is perhaps some excuse for its creation and publication. "By the Waters of the Brook", by Rev. Eugene B. Kuntz, D. D., is one of the noblest amateur poems of the year. While the casual reader may find in the long heptameter lines a want of sing-song facility; the true lover of the Nine pauses in admiration at the deep flowing nobility of the rhyme. The quick rippling of the brook is duplicated within each line, rather than from line to line. The imagery and phraseology are of the sort which only Dr. Kuntz can fashion, and are rich in that exalted pantheism of fancy which comes to him who knows Nature in her wilder and more rugged moods and aspects. "The Pool", by Winifred Virginia Jordan, contains an elusive hint of the terrible and the supernatural which gives it high rank as poetry. Jordan has two distinct, yet related, styles in verse. One of these mirrors all the joy and buoyant happiness of life whilst the other reflects that undertone of grimness which is sometimes felt through the exterior of things. The kinship betwixt these styles lies in their essentially fanciful character, as distinguished from the tiresomely commonplace realism of the average modern rhymester. Another bit of sinister psychology in verse is "The Unknown", by Elizabeth Berkeley.[3] Mrs. Berkeley's style is less restrained than that of Mrs. Jordan, and presents a picture of stark, meaningless horror, the like of which is not often seen in the amateur press. It is difficult to pass upon the actual merit of so peculiar a production, but we will venture the opinion that the use of italics, or heavy-faced type, is not desirable. The author should be able to bring out all needed emphasis by words, not printer's devices. The issue concludes with "Inspiration", a poem by Lewis Theobald, Jun.[4] The form and rhythm of this piece are quite satisfactory, but the insipidity of the sentiment leaves much to be desired. The whole poem savours too much of the current magazine style.

The *Coyote* for October is made notable by Editor Harrington's thoughtful and well-compiled article on "Worldwide Prohibition", wherein an extremely important step in the world's progress is truthfully chronicled. That legislation against alcohol is spreading rapidly through civilisation, is something which not even the densest champions of "personal liberty" can deny. The utter emptiness of all arguments in behalf of strong drink is made doubly apparent by the swift prohibitory enactments of the European nations when confronted by the emergencies of war, and by the abolition of liquor in a large number of American states for purely practical reasons. All these things point to a general recognition of liquor as a foe to governmental and industrial welfare. Mr. Harrington's style in this essay is clear and in most respects commendable; though certain passages might gain force and dignity through a less colloquial manner. In particular, we must protest against the repeated use of the vulgarism *booze*, a word probably brought into public favour by the new school of gutter evangelism, whose chief exponent is the Reverend William Sunday.[5] The verb *to booze, boose,* or *bouse,* meaning "to drink immoderately", and the adjective *boozy, boosy,* or *bousy,* moaning "drunken", are by no means new to our language, Dryden having written the form *bousy* in some of his verses; but *booze* as a noun signifying "liquor" is certainly too vulgar a word for constant employment in any formal literary composition. Another essay of Mr. Harrington's is "The Divine Book", a plea for the restoration of the Bible as a source of popular reading and arbiter of moral conduct. Whatever may be the opinion of the searching critic regarding the place of the Scriptures in the world of fact; it is undeniably true that a closer study of the revered volume, and a stricture adherence to its best precepts, would do much toward mending the faults of a loose age. We have yet to find a more efficacious means of imparting virtue and contentment of heart to the masses of mankind. "Pioneers of New England", an article by Alice M. Hamlet, gives much interesting information concerning the sturdy settlers of New Hampshire and Vermont. In the unyielding struggles of these unsung heroes against the sting of hardship and the asperity of primeval Nature, we may discern more than a trace of that divine fire of conquest which has made the Anglo-Saxon the empire builder of all the ages. In Mr. Harrington's editorial column there is much discussion of a proposed "International Amateur Press Association", but we fail to perceive why such an innovation is needed, now that the United has opened itself unreservedly to residents of all the countries of the globe.

*Merry Minutes* for November is a clever publication of semi-professional character, edited by Miss Margaret Trafford of London, and containing a pleasant variety of prose, verses, and puzzles. "King of the Nursery Realm", by Margaret Mahon, is a smooth and musical piece of juvenile verse which excels in correctness of form rather than in novelty of thought. "Bards and Minstrels, and The Augustan Age", by Beryl Mappin, is the second of a series of articles on English literature and its classical foundations. The erudition and enthusiasm displayed in this essay speak well for the future of the authoress, though certain faults of style and construction demand correction. Careful grammatical study would eliminate from Miss Mappin's style such solecisms as the use of *like* for *as*, whilst greater attention to the precepts of rhetoric would prevent the construction of such awkward sentences as the following: "The same if one is reading an interesting book, can one not see all that is happening there as clearly with one's inner eyes as if it was all taking place before one, and viewed with one's outer ones?" This passage is not only wanting in coherence and correctness of syntax, but is exceedingly clumsy through redundancy of statement, and repetition of the word *one*. This word, though essential to colloquial diction, becomes very tiresome when used to excess; and should be avoided in many cases through judicious transpositions of the text. The following is a revised version of the sentence quoted above: "Thus, in reading an interesting book, can one not see with the inner eyes all that is happening there, as clearly as if it were taking place in reality before the outer eyes?" Other parts of the essay require similar revision. Concerning the development of the whole, we must needs question the unity of the topics. Whilst the connecting thread is rather evident after a second or third perusal, the cursory reader is apt to become puzzled over the skips from the Graeco-Roman world to the early Saxon kingdoms, and thence to the dawn of our language amongst the Anglo-Normans. What Miss Mappin evidently wishes to bring out, is that the sources of English literature are twofold; being on the one hand the polished classics of antiquity, inspired by Greece, amplified and diffused by Rome, preserved by France, and brought to England by the Normans; and on the other hand the crude but virile products of our Saxon ancestors, brought from the uncivilised forests of the continent or written after the settlement in Britain. From this union of Graeco-Roman classicism with native Anglo-Saxon vitality springs the unquestioned supremacy of English literature. Assiduous devotion to the mastery of rhetoric, and the habit of constructing logical synopses before writing the text of articles would enable Miss Mappin to utilise her knowledge of literary history in a manner truly worthy of its depth. "Trinidad and Its People", by "F. E. M. Hercules", exhibits a somewhat maturer style, and forms a very interesting piece of geographical description. "The Pursuit of the Innocent" is a serial story by Miss Trafford, and though only a small part of it is printed in the current issue, we judged that it derives its general atmosphere from the popular "thrillers" of the day. The dialogue is not wholly awkward, but there is a noticeable want of proportion in the development of the narrative. Miss Trafford would probably profit by a more faithful study of the standard novelists, and a more complete avoidance of the type of fiction found in modern weekly periodicals such as *Answers* or *Tit-Bits*. Those who feel impelled to introduce stirring adventure into their tales, can do so without sacrifice of excitement and interest by following really classic writers like Poe and Stevenson; or semi-standard authors like Sir A. Conan Doyle. The puzzles propounded by Miss Hillman are quite interesting, though matter of this sort is scarcely to be included within the domain of pure literature. We guess *airship* as the answer to the first one, but have not space to record our speculations concerning the second. *Merry Minutes* closes with the following poem by Master Randolph Trafford, a very young author:

> "Once upon a time, there was a little boy,
>     And, if you please, he went to school;
> That little boy, he always would annoy,
>     And found at school a very nasty rule."

Without undue flattery to Master Trafford, we may conclusively state that we deem his poem a great deal better than most of the *vers libre* effusions which so many of his elders are perpetrating nowadays!

*The Scot* for July is devoted completely to the work of the feminine amateurs of the United States, and is announced by its editor as an "American 'Petticoat' Number"; a title which might possibly bear replacement by something rather less colloquial. "Over the Edge of the World", a poem by Olive G. Owen, is correct in construction and appropriate in sentiment, deriving much force from the continued repetition of the first line. "In Morven's Mead", by Winifred V. Jordan, is one of a series of fanciful poems all bearing the same title. The present verses shew all the charm and delicacy which characterise the whole. "Patience—A Woman's Virtue", is one of Mrs. Eloise N. Griffith's thoughtful moral essays, and is as commendable for its precepts as for its pure style. "His Flapper", by Edna von der Heide, is a clever piece of trochaic verse in Cockney dialect, which seems, so far as an American critic can judge, to possess a very vivid touch of local colour. "An Eye for an Eye", by the same authoress, seems vaguely familiar, having possibly been published in the amateur press before. If so, it is well worthy of republication. "Women and

Snakes", a sketch by Eleanor J. Barnhart, is not a misogynistical attempt at comparison, but a theory regarding the particular fear with which the former are popularly supposed to regard the latter. Whilst Miss Barnhart writes with the bravery of the true scientist, we are constrained to remark that a certain dislike of snakes, mice, and insects is a very real thing; not only amongst the fair, but equally amongst those sterner masculine souls who would stoutly deny it if questioned. It is an atavistical fear, surviving from primitive ages when the venomous qualities of reptiles, insects, and the like made their quick avoidance necessary to uninstructed man. "Be Tolerant", by Winifred V. Jordan, is a didactic poem of the sort formerly published in *The Symphony*. While it does not possess in fullest measure the grace and facility observed in Mrs. Jordan's more characteristic work; it is nevertheless correct and melodious, easily equalling most poetry of its kind. Mr. McColl's editorial column, the only masculine feature of the issue, contains a very noble tribute to the two soldier cousins of Miss von der Heide, who have laid down their lives for the cause of England and the right. From such men springs the glory of Britannia.

The Scot for August opens with Winifred V. Jordan's tuneful lines, "If You but Smile", whose inspiration and construction are alike of no mean order. "Hoary Kent", by Benjamin Winskill, is an exquisite sketch of a region where the past still lives. In an age of turmoil and unrest, it is a comfort to think that in one spot, at least, the destroying claws of Time have left no scars. There lie the scenes dear to every son and grandson of Britain; there are bodied forth the eternal and unchanging traditions that place it above the rest of the world.

> "This precious stone set in the silver sea—
> This blessed plot, this earth, this realm, this England."[6]

"Meditation of a Scottish Queen on Imprisonment", a poem by Margaret Trafford, contains noble passages, but is marred by defective technique. Passing over the use of the expletives *do* and *doth* as legitimate archaisms in this case, we must call attention to some awkward phraseology, and to the roughness of certain lines, which have either too few or too many syllables. The very first line of the poem requires contraction, which might be accomplished by substituting *hapless* for *unhappy*. Line 8 would read better if thus amended:

> "I would that death might come and me release."

The final line of the first stanza lacks a syllable, which might be supplied by replacing *vile* with *hateful*. The second stanza will pass as it is, but the entire remainder of the poem requires alteration, since but two of the lines are of normal decasyllabic length. The following is rough revision, though we have not attempted to build the poetry anew:

> Oh! could I breathe again dear Scotland's air;
> Behold once more her stately mountains high,
> Thence view the wide expanse of azure sky,
> Instead of these perpetual walls so bare!
>
> Could I but see the grouse upon the moor,
> Or pluck again the beauteous heather bell!
> Freedom I know not in this dismall cell,
> As I my anguish from my heart outpour.

> My Scotland! know'st thou thy poor Queen's distress,
> And canst thou hear my wailing and my woe?
> May the soft wind that o'er thy hills doth blow
> Waft thee these thoughts, that I cannot suppress!

"Six Cylinder Happiness", a brief essay by William J. Dowdell, presents in ingeniously pleasing style a precept not entirely new amongst philosophers. Mr. Dowdell's skill with the pen is very considerable, particularly when he ventures outside the domain of slang. We should like to suggest a slightly less colloquial title for this piece, such as "Real Happiness". "For Right and Liberty", a poem by Matthew Hilson, is commendable in sentiment and clever in construction, but lacks perfection in several details of phraseology. In the third line of the third stanza the word *ruinous* must be replaced by a true dissyllable, preferably *ruin'd*. "For Their Country", a short story by Margaret Trafford, is vivid in plot and truly heroic in moral, but somewhat deficient in technique, particularly at the beginning. Miss Trafford should use care in moulding long sentences, and should avoid the employment of abbreviations like *etc.* in the midst of narrative text. "That Sunny Smile", by John Russell, is a cleverly optimistic bit of verse whose rhythm is very facile, but which would be improved by the addition of two syllables to the third and sixth lines of each stanza. The rhyme of *round you* and *found true* is incorrect, since the second syllables of double rhymes must be identical. "The Evil One", by Narcissus Blanchfield, is announced as "A Prose-poem, after Oscar Wilde—a long way after". As an allegory it is true to the facts of the case; though one cannot but feel that there is room for a freer play of the poetic imagination in so great a subject.

Toledo Amateur for October is a literary publication which reflects much credit upon its young editor, Mr. Wesley Hilon Porter, and upon the several contributors. "Twilight", a correct and graceful poem by Miss van der Heide, opens the issue. "A Sabbath", by Mary Margaret Sisson, is a sketch of great merit, though not wholly novel in subject. The hypocrisy of many self-satisfied "pillars of the church" is only too well known both in life and in literature. At the very close of the piece, the word *epithet* is used in a slightly incorrect sense, meaning "motto". *Epithet*, as its Greek derivation shews, signifies an *adjective* or descriptive expression. "The Workers of the World", by Dora M. Hepner, is another sociological sketch of no small merit, pleasantly distinguished by the absence of slang. "Not All", by Olive G. Owen, is a poem of much fervour, albeit having a somewhat too free use of italics. The words and rhythm of a poet should be able to convey his images without the more artificial devices of typographical variation. Another questionable point is the manner of using archaic pronouns and verb forms. Miss Owen seems to use both ancient and modern conjugations of the verb indifferently with such subjects as *thou*. "A Day at Our Summer Home", by Emma Marie Voigt, is a descriptive sketch of considerable promise, and "My First Amateur Convention", by Mrs. Addie L. Porter, is a well-written chronicle of events. "The Wild Rose", by Marguerite Allen, is a poem of no little grace, though beset with many of the usual crudities of youthful work. In the first place, the quatrains should have their rhymes regularly recurring; either both first and third, and second and fourth lines; or only in second and fourth. A rhyme occurring only in first and third lines gives an unmusical cast, since it causes the stanza to end unrhymed. Secondly, the words *fence* and *scent* do not form a legitimate rhyme. The easy correctness of the metre is an encouraging sign, and indicates a poetic talent which Miss Allen would do well to cultivate. Mr. Porter's article on amateur journalism is interesting and quite just, though we hope that the United has not quite so "little to offer" the devotee of "so-called high-class literature" as the author believes. If we are to retain our cultivated members, or our younger members after they acquire cultivation, we must necessarily cater to the better grade of taste; though of course without neglecting the succeeding generation of novices. The editorial column of this issue is bright and fluent, concluding one of the best amateur journals of the season.

The United Amateur for September contains something only too seldom found in the amateur press; a really meritorious short story. "The Shadow on the Trail", by Eleanor J. Barnhart, possesses every element of good fiction; a substantial and really interesting plot, a logical development from beginning to conclusion, an adequate amount of suspense, a climax which does not disappoint, and a praiseworthy degree of local colour. Besides all of which it is fluent in language and correct in syntax. The rest of the literary department in this issue is devoted to verse. "To a Friend", by Alice M. Hamlet, is particularly pleasing through the hint of the old school technique which its well-ordered phrases convey. The one weak point is the employment of *thy*, a singular expression, in connexion with several objects; namely, "paper, pen, and ready hand". *Your* should have been used. The metre is excellent throughout, and the whole piece displays a gratifying skill on its author's part. "The Path along the Sea", by Rev. Eugene B. Kuntz, is a flawless and beautiful bit of sentimental poetry, cast in fluent and felicitous heptameter. "Dad", by Horace Fowler Goodwin, is decidedly the best of this writer's pieces yet to appear in the amateur press. The defects are mostly technical, including the bad rhyme of *engaged* and *dismayed*, and the overweighted seventh line of the final stanza. The latter might be rectified by substituting *blest*, or some other monosyllable, for *lucky*. "Li'l Baby Mine", by W. Frank Booker, is a quaint and captivating darky lullaby, whose accuracy of dialect and atmosphere comes from that first-hand knowledge of the negroes which only a Southern writer can possess. Mr. Booker is one of our most promising bards, and will be doubly notable when his style shall have received its final polish. "When I Gaze on Thee", by Kathleen Foster Smith, is an amatory poem of much grace and fluency.

The United Amateur for October furnishes us with a species of composition not frequently encountered in amateurdom; an official report which is also a literary classic. Pres. Campbell's message is really an essay on contemporary amateur journalism, and contains a multitude of well-stated truths which every member of the fraternity would do well to peruse. "The Wanderer's Return", by Andrew Francis Lockhart, is a beautiful piece of anapaestic verse whose flow is as pleasing as its sentiment.

The Woodbee for October is edited by Mrs. Ida C. Haughton, and though not of large size, does credit both to her and to the Columbus club. "To the Woodbees", a witty parody of Poe's "Annabel Lee", exhibits Miss Irene Metzger as the possessor of no little skill in numbers; and incidentally suggests that other young bards might well improve their styles by judicious exercises of this sort. Much of the spirit of metre may be absorbed through copying the works of the standard poets. "Louise's Letter", a short story by Norma Sanger, contains some of the defects of early composition, notably an undue hastening of the action immediately after the letter quoted in the text. The plot involves a rather unusual coincidence, yet is probably no more overstrained than that of the average piece of light fiction. "The Ruling Passion", by Edna M. Haughton, is a story of phenomenal power and interest, forming a psychological study worthy of more than one perusal. All the requirements of good fiction, both inspirational and technical, are complied with to the satisfaction of even the most exacting critic. Miss Haughton's work is of a very high grade, and would be welcomed in larger quantities by the amateur world. Miss Harwood's interesting News Notes and Mrs. Haughton's thoughtful editorial conclude an issue whose every feature deserves commendation.

EDITOR'S NOTE   FP: *United Amateur* 16, No. 7 (March 1917): 85–91 (signed "H. P. LOVECRAFT, Chairman"). HPL has allowed six months to pass since his previous column of September 1916, although the quantitative decline in UAPA papers—a subject of much discussion by HPL in future years—is already evident in the relative paucity of papers covered here. HPL writes at surprising length about his own *Conservative* (October 1916), but curiously does not discuss the issue of January 1917. Indeed, since no paper issued later than November 1916 is treated here, one is led to believe that the column was written several months prior to publication.

*Notes*

1. Portions of this poem appear to have influenced the opening of HPL's "Psychopompos" (1917–18).
2. See AT 103.
3. The poem is by HPL (see AT 18). HPL published the poem under Winifred Jackson's pseudonym "to mystify the [amateur] public by having widely dissimilar work from the same nominal hand" (HPL to the Gallomo, 31 August–12 September 1923; *Letters to Alfred Galpin*, p. 108).
4. By HPL. See AT 102–3.
5. See n. 2 to DPC (September 1916).
6. Shakespeare, *Richard II* 2.1.46, 50.

---

# DEPARTMENT OF PUBLIC CRITICISM

(*May 1917*)

*T*he *Conservative* for January deserves distinction for its opening poem, "The Vagrant", which proceeds from the thrice-gifted pen of Mrs. W. V. Jordan. The piece is one well worthy of close attention, since it contains to a marked degree those elements of charm which render its author so prominent among amateur bards. Bold and discriminating choice of words and phrases, apt and unique images and personifications, and a carefully sustained atmosphere of delicate unreality, all unite to impart a characteristic beauty to the lines. This beauty, searchingly analysed, reveals itself as something more sylvan and spontaneous than studied and bookish; indeed, all of Mrs. Jordan's verse is born rather than built.

"The Unbreakable Link", a prose sketch by Arthur W. Ashby, is smooth and graphic in its delineation of a dream or vision of the past. The ancient heritage of Old England and its hoary edifices is here vividly set forth. Mr. Ashby's work, always notable for its command and intelligent interpretation of detail, is welcome wherever encountered.

"When New-Year Comes", a poem by Rev. Eugene B. Kuntz, exhibits its brilliant author in a most felicitous though decidedly novel vein. Turning from his usual Alexandrines and heptameters, and laying aside his characteristically stately and sonorous vocabulary, Dr. Kuntz has produced a gem of brevity and simplicity in octosyllabic couplets. The ease and naturalness of the language are so great that the reader feels no other words or constructions could have been used with equal effect. The remainder of *The Conservative*, being the work of the present critic, deserves no particular mention.

*The Coyote* for January bears an attractive cover design illustrating the gentle beast after which the publication is named. The opening piece, an alleged poem by the present critic, contains an humiliating error for which none but the author is responsible. The impossible word *supremest* in line 16, should read *sublimest*. The author is likewise responsible for the omission of the following couplet after line 26:

> "Around his greatness pour disheart'ning woes,
> But still he tow'rs above his conquering foes."

The rest of the magazine is devoted to prose of practical nature, containing suggestions by Editor Hartington and Rev. Graeme Davis for the resuscitation of one of the dormant press associations.

*The Coyote* for April, home-printed and reduced to the conventional 5 × 7 page, opens with Mrs. Jordan's pleasant lines on "The Duty". While the general sentiment of this piece is by no means novel, the powerful and distinctive touch of the authoress is revealed by such highly original passages as the following:

> "And black-wing'd, clucking shadows
> Brought out their broods of fears."

A poet of rather different type is displayed in "The Five-Minute School", by Lovell Leland Massie. Mr. Massie is said to have "an unlimited supply of poems on hand which he desires to publish", but it is evident that some preliminary alterations would not be undesirable. In the first place, the metre requires correction; though it is remarkably good for beginner's work. Particularly weak lines are the second in stanza four, and the second in stanza six. The phraseology is stiff but by no means hopeless, and proclaims nothing more. serious than the need of greater poetic familiarity on the author's port. The rhymes are good with two exceptions; *past* and *class*, and *jewel* and *school*. Mr. Massie, however, is not the first bard to reduce *jew-el* to "*jool*"! "The Coyote", by Obert O. Bakken, is a worthy and interesting composition upon a well-known animal. "A Soul", by Olive G. Owen, is reprinted from the professional press, and amply merits the honour. The poem is of unexceptionable technique and adequate sentiment. Miss Owen's brilliant, fruitful, and long-continued poetical career has few parallels in the amateur world. "The Amateur Christian", a brief prose essay by Benjamin Winskill, presents more than one valuable truth; though we wish the word "*par*", near the close, might be extended to proper fulness. We presume that it is intended to stand for *paragraph*.

*The Crazyquilt* for December is a highly entertaining illustrated publication whose exact classification is a matter of some difficulty. We might perhaps best describe it as a bubbling over of youthful spirits, with here and there a touch of unobtrusive seriousness. The editor, Mr. Melvin Ryder, is to be commended upon his enterprise; which consists in approximately equal parts of prose, verse, and whimsical *vers libre*. It is the last named product which most absorbs our attention, since the given specimens afford a very brilliant satire on the absurd medium in which they are set. The choicest selections are due to the fertile pen of Mr. William S. Wabnitz, assisted by that not unknown classic called "Mother Goose", whose ideas accord well with the thought of the new "poetry". "A Futuresk Romance", by Mr. Wabnitz alone, is of exceeding cleverness. Among the genuine poems, we may give particular commendation to "Bluebirds Are Flying Over", by Mrs. Dora Hepner Moitoret; "Longin' and Yearnin'", "Spring", "Verses", and "Dreaming", by J. H. Gavin; and "Stars after Rain", by William S. Wabnitz. Mr. Gavin's "Dreaming" is a hauntingly pretty piece, though marred by an imperfect line (the twelfth) and by an incorrect accentuation of the word *romance*. This word should be accented on the final syllable. "Odd Patches and Even" is the title of the editorial column, which contains many words of wisdom (though not too grave) by Mr. Ryder. We hope to behold future issues of *The Crazyquilt*.

*Dowdell's Bearcat* for October, partly compiled and financed by the United's official board in lieu of the missing *Official Quarterly*, comes to us unbound and without a cover; yet contains, aside from the inexcusable editorials, a rich array of meritorious material. Mr. Dowdell's comment on radical eccentrics and malcontents is apt and clever, shewing how bright this young writer can be when he avoids bad taste and personalities.

"A Little Lovely Lyric", by Mrs. Dora H. Moitoret, is one of the choicest of this author's poems, having a spirit and cadence of rare quality. In "The Real Amateur Spirit", Pres. Campbell presents in vigorous prose many important truths and principles of amateur journalism. The concluding sentence forms a definition of our animating impulse which deserves repeated publication as a motto and inspiration. "An American to Mother England", by the present critic, is an expression of cultural and ancestral ties which have now, through the fortunes of war, grown doubly strong. The word *Saxon*, in the last line, should begin with a capital. "Dream Life" is a vivid piece of prose mysticism by our versatile and gifted Vice-President, Mr. Ira A. Cole. Defying precise grouping either as a sketch or a story, this enigmatical bit of fancy deserves highest praise for its fluent diction, rich imagination, potent atmosphere, and graphic colouring. Mr. Cole has a bright future in prose as well as in verse, for in both of these media he is a genuine and spontaneous poet. "United Impressions", by Mrs. E. L. Whitehead, is clear, interesting, and well-written, as is also the sketch by Mary M. Sisson entitled "Passion versus Calm". "The Elm Tree", by James Tobey Pyke, is a poem of remarkable sweetness and nobility, through whose lofty sentiment shines the true splendour of the inspired bard. There is a master touch in the passage referring to

"——————a sweet heaven
Of digging birds and whispering leaves."

Mrs. Winifred Virginia Jordan, without one of whose delightful verses no amateur publication can really compete, contributes a sparkling succession of amatory anapaests entitled "Dear". The middle stanza rises to great lyric heights, and should prove especially captivating to such discriminating critics of lyricism as our colleague Mr. Kleiner.

*The Enthusiast* for February is a hectographed publication issued by our latest young recruit, Mr. James Mather Mosely of Westfield, Mass. Mr. Mosely is a youth of sterling ability and great promise, whose work is already worthy of notice and encouragement. The editor's leading article, "The Secret Inspiration of a Man Who Made Good", shews unusual fluency and literary assurance, though we might wish for a more dignified title. The expression *to make good* is pure slang, and should be supplanted by one of the many legitimate English words and phrases which convey the same meaning. Mr. Mosely's editorials are likewise open to criticism on the ground of colloquialism, though the natural exuberance of youth excuses much. "The Birds", by Harold Gordon Hawkins, is a truly excellent specimen of juvenile verse, which contains much promise for the author's efforts. Increased familiarity with standard literary models will remove all evidences of stiffness now perceptible. "How Men Go Wrong", a conventional moral homily by Edgar Holmes Plummer, shews a slight want of original ideas and a tendency to commonplaces; though having much merit in construction. Another subject might display Mr. Plummer's talent to better advantage. The use of the word *habitat* for *inhabitant* or *denizen* is incorrect, for its true meaning is a natural locality or *place of habitation*. "Blueberry Time", by Ruth Foster, is obviously a schoolgirl composition, albeit a pleasing one.

F. R. Starr's cartoon scarcely comes within the province of a literary critic, but is doubtless an excellent example of elementary art. We question, however, the place of popular cartoons in serious papers; the "funny picture" habit is essentially a plebeian one, and alien to journalism of the highest grade. All things considered, *The Enthusiast* is a creditable exponent of junior letters, which deserves the encouragement and support of the United.

*Excelsior* for March is in many respects the most notable of the season's amateur magazines. Edited by our brilliant Laureate Recorder, Miss Verna McGeoch, it contains a surprisingly ample and impressive collection of prose and verse by our best writers; including the delectable lyricist Perrin Holmes Lowrey, whose work has hitherto been unrepresented in the press of the United. The issue opens with Mr. Jonathan E. Hoag's stately "Ode to Old Ocean", whose appropriate imagery and smooth couplets are exceedingly pleasant to the mind and ear alike. Mr. Hoag's unique charm is no less apparent in the longer reminiscent piece entitled "The Old Farm Home", which describes the author's boyhood scenes at Valley Falls, New York, where he was born more than eighty-six years ago. This piece has attracted much favourable notice in the professional world, having been reprinted in *The Troy Times*. Perrin Holmes Lowrey contributes a cycle of three poems touching on the beauties of the month of April; one of which, "April in Killarney", will this summer be set to music by Leopold Godowsky. The style of Mr. Lowrey possesses an attractive individuality and delicacy which is already bringing him celebrity in the larger literary sphere. What could be more thoroughly enchanting than such a stanza as the following?

> "Oh, it's April in Killarney,
> Early April in Killarney,
> Where the Irish lanes are merry
> And the lyric breeze blows
> And the scented snows of cherry
> Drift across the fields of Kerry—
> Oh, it's April in Killarney
> And she loves the April so."

"Treasure Trove", by Henry Cleveland Wood, is a pleasing and urbane bit of light verse; whilst "Percival Lowell", by Howard Phillips Lovecraft, is an abominably dull elegiac piece of heavy verse.[1] Edwin Gibson's "Sonnet to Acyion" deserves keen attention as the work of a capable and rapidly developing young bard. "Real versus Ideal" is a bright metrical divertissement by John Russell, which suffers through the omission of the opening line by the printer. This line is:

> "For sale—a cottage by the sea."

We recommend the final line to the attention of those careless bards who pronounce *real* as *reel*, and *ideal* as *ideel*. The correct quantities, as there given, will serve as examples. Verse of deeper quality is furnished by amateurdom's foremost expressionist, Anne Tillery Renshaw, two of whose poems appear. "The Singing Sea" contains an error of technique, *hope* and *note* being placed in attempted rhyme; but the structure is in general very regular, considering the author's radical theories. Of the merit of the sentiment it is unnecessary to speak. "A Wish" is cast in less fluent metre, but is so replete with aptness, grandeur, and refinement of ideas, that the sternest critic must needs view its form with lenient glance. The prose contents of *Excelsior* is worthy company for the verse. Paul J. Campbell is represented by a very brief though characteristic essay entitled "The Price of Freedom", wherein appears the sound reasoning and courageous philosophy for which Mr. Campbell has always been distinguished. Another notable essay or review is "English History", by Henry Clapham McGavack. Mr. McGavack here ably employs his keen analysis and lucid style in dissecting Prof. Meyer's absurdly biased but diabolically clever pro-German History of England.[2]

"The Association", by David H. Whittier, teems with good advice concerning the proper management of the United. Mr. Whittier's style is smooth and dignified, exhibiting a sober maturity unusual for a young author. "'Tonio's Salvation", a short story by Edna von der Heide, is the only bit of fiction in the magazine. This brief glimpse of the cosmopolitan child life of a modern city is marked equally by naturalness of plot and facility of technique, forming a piece quite professional in quality and atmosphere. *Excelsior* has done much to sustain the best traditions of the United, and we hope its future appearance will be frequent and regular. The editorial column reveals the genius and exquisite taste of its gifted publisher.

*Merry Minutes* for December–January is an interesting number of an interesting publication, opening with some extremely clever cartoons by the United's soldier-member, George William Stokes. "Merry Minutes", a poem in trochaic measure by Olive G. Owen, is distinguished by the touch of beauty characteristic of all its author's work; but has a singular sort of rhyming in the first and third of the stanzas. The cadence seems to call for double rhymes, yet only the final syllables agree. The last word of the first stanza is unfortunately shorn by the printer of its final *s*. "The Dancing Tiger" is an excellent short story by Raymond Blathwayt, which might, however, be improved in style by a slightly closer attention to punctuation and structure of sentences. "Home", by Margaret Mahon, is a poem in that rather popular modern measure which seems to waver betwixt the iambus and anapaest. The imagery is pleasing, and the sentiment, though not novel, is acceptable. "The Choice", a serial story by Beryl Mappin, exhibits the same immaturities of style which mark the didactic articles of this author; yet so active is the imagination shewn in some of the passages, that we believe Miss Mappin requires only time and harder study in order to become a very meritorious writer. The syntactical structure of this story is, on the average, smoother than that of Miss Mappin's essays; indeed, there is reason to believe that fiction is the better suited to her pen. "Absence", by Winifred Virginia Jordan, is a brief poem of faultless harmony whose quaintly sparkling imagery gives to an old theme a new lustre. "Education in Trinidad" is another of F. E. M. Hercules' terse and informing descriptive sketches. "Alley", by Mrs. Jordan, is a light pulsing lyric of almost Elizabethan quality, one of whose rhymes is of a type which has caused much discussion in the United's critical circles. The native pronunciation of New-England makes of *scarf* and *laugh* an absolutely perfect rhyme; this perfection depending upon the curtailed phonetic value of the letter *r*; which in a place such as this is silent, save as it modifies the quality of the preceding vowel. In the London of Walker's day the same condition existed. But the tongue and ear of the American West have become accustomed to a certain roll which causes *scarf* to be enunciated as *scarrrf*, thus throwing it out of rhyme with words of similar sound which lack the *r*. The Westerner would have to write *scahf* in order to express to his own mind the New-England sound of *scarf*. Hitherto, the present critic has called no notice to rhymes of this type, and has, indeed, frequently employed them himself; but recognition of etymological principles involved will hereafter impel him to abandon and discourage the practice, which was not followed by the older classicists. To the New-England author this renunciation means relinquishment of many rhymes which are to his ear perfect, yet in the interests of tradition and universality it seems desirable that the sacrifice be made. "Why Mourn Thy Soldier Dead" is a poem of brave sorrow by Olive G. Owen. The fervour of the lines is deep, and the sentiments are of great nobility. Structurally the piece is flawless. "Chaucer, the Father of English Poetry", is the third of Miss Mappin's series of articles on literary history. An unfortunate misprint relegates to the bottom of the footnote a line which should immediately follow the specimen verse. The style is decidedly clearer and better than that of the preceding instalment of the series. "When You Went", by Mrs. Jordan, is an engagingly pathetic poem; with just that touch of the unseen which lends so particular a charm to Jordanian verse. Miss Trafford's appealing lines on "A Girl to Her Dead Lover" form a vividly pathetic glimpse into low life. The poetic form is quite satisfactory. As a whole, *Merry Minutes* constitutes a rather remarkable enterprise, sustaining through troubled times the spark of activity which will kindle anew the fires of British amateur journalism after the victorious close of the war. May America, in her new crisis, do as well!

*Merry Minutes* for February opens with Margaret Mahon's poem "God's Solace", a smooth and restful bit of versification. "Spencer and the Beginning of the Elizabethan Era" is the current article of Beryl Mappin's series on English Literature, and contains some very promising passages, especially the almost poetic introduction. Miss Mappin has an unusual fund of knowledge, and a pleasing gift of expression; but these advantages are not yet fully systematised or marshalled to best effect. Miss Trafford's serial, "The Pursuit of the Innocent", concludes in this number. This story bears many of the signs of juvenile workmanship, the present instalment being so hurried in action that it almost attains the brevity of a synopsis. Careful and analytical perusal of standard fiction would assist greatly in maturing and perfecting the author's style. "Religion and Superstition" is the current article in F. E. M. Hercules' interesting series on Trinidad; and exhibits all the polish, lucidity, and conciseness of its predecessors. "His Photo", by Master Randolph Trafford, is a very promising poem by a youthful bard. Every rhyme is correct, which is more than can be claimed for a great deal of the poesy perpetrated by older and more pretentious versifiers on this side of the Atlantic. The present instalment of "The Choice", by Beryl Mappin, is marked by considerable fluency and animation, though possessed of certain limitations previously mentioned.

*Merry Minutes* for March commences with the present critic's dull lines "On Receiving a Picture of the Marshes at Ipswich".[3] Passing to more meritorious matter, we encounter Miss Mappin's latest literary article, "Shakespeare", which interests even whilst it reveals deficiencies of prose technique. "Jimmy's Little Girl", by Joseph Parks, is a vivid transcript of military life by a military author. While the tale is not one of vast originality, it nevertheless recommends itself through simplicity and verisimilitude. Miss Mappin's serial, "The Choice", concludes in this issue. It is very praiseworthy for its many colourful passages, but mildly censurable for its melodramatic atmosphere and rhetorical lapses. The opening sentence of this instalment contains instances of both of these faults: "A terrible foreboding gripped Christabel's heart in bands of steel, as if for a moment to cleave her tongue to the roof of her mouth." This is the last number of the publication to appear under the present name. Beginning with the April issue it will be known as *The Little Budget*; and will contain, on the average, a rather higher grade of reading matter than heretofore. But in forming a judgment of any kind, it is well to recognise that the magazine's appeal is frankly popular.

*Pep* for February is the first number of a somewhat extraordinary enterprise conducted by George W. Macauley with the laudable object of waking up a sleeping amateurdom. The editor very justly takes the press associations to task for their manifold sins, particularly the dubious circumstances surrounding a recent convention, in which it is needless to say the United had no part. Mr. Macauley's literary attainments are very considerable, but as yet unperfected. Possessed of rare charm in descriptive prose, he needs to exercise a greater nicety of construction in order to develop fully the riches which are his. Gifted with a large, facile, and ingenious vocabulary, he is not sufficiently precise and discriminating in his employment of words according to their finer shades of meaning. This carelessness makes faults of his very virtues; for his vigour of expression tends to take the form of *outré* and inadmissible rhetoric, whilst his talent for the form of word-painting tends to degenerate into word-coining. It would be quite possible for an acute critic to compile a dictionary of peculiarly Macaulian words and phrases, to which the current *Pep* might contribute such terms as *probverb* (proverb?). Spelling and punctuation also should claim more of Mr. Macauley's time and attention; for he might easily avoid such slips as *believeing*, *it's* (for *its*), *thots*, and the like. In short, Mr. Macauley is at present a gifted writer and brilliant editor labouring under the disadvantages of haste, carelessness, and perhaps a dash of radicalism.

*The Phoenician* for Spring is the first number of an enthusiastically conducted semi-professional venture of juvenile nature, whose connexion with the United hinges on the associate editorship of our clever recruit, Mr. James Mather Mosely. Like *Merry Minutes*, this publication is of the popular rather than conservative sort; being obviously designed primarily to please, secondarily to instruct. We deplore the use of commonplace and sensational topics, colloquial expressions, and malformed spelling; but make due concessions to the youth of the editorial staff and the nascent state of the periodical. So promising are the young publishers, that time cannot fail to refine and mature their efforts. "An Hour with a Lunatic", by Harry B. Sadik, is a very short and very thrilling tale of the "dime novel" variety. Mr. Sadik has a commendable sense of the dramatic, which would serve him well should he choose a less sensational field of endeavour. "Our Soldiers", a Canadian mother's war song by Mrs. Minnie B. Taylor, exhibits merit, though having many signs of imperfect technique. In line 2 of the first stanza *bid* should be replaced by *bade*. The final rhyme of the poem, that of *gain* and *name*, is false and inadmissible. Metrically there is much roughness, which careful study and diligent reading of good verse can in time correct. "Candy and Health", and "If You Were Down and Out", by James Mather Mosely, are two typical newspaper interviews with representative men. Mr. Mosely shews much aptitude as a reporter, having an almost professional ease and fluency. This is not literature, but it is good journalism. "The Dinner Never Paid For", by Viola Jameson, is a piece of characteristic light fiction; commendably innocuous, and not at all overburdened with philosophical complexity. "The Secret of Success", by Edith L. Clark, is a promising bit of didactic prose. "The End of the Road", by Pearl K. Merritt, is a brief essay of substantial worth. "The Toll of the Sea", a poem by Harold Gordon Hawkins, shews considerable merit despite irregularities. "Memories", by Arthur Goodenough, well sustains the high poetical reputation of its author, though it is cruelly marred by the illogical and censurable "simplified" spelling which the young editors see fit to employ. One line affords a silent but striking instance of the utter senselessness and confusion of the new orthographical fad. This line reads:

"Of human *thot* might well be *wrought*"

Now in the first place, *thot* does not express the true pronunciation of *thought*. The word, thus written, tends to acquire the vocal quality of *shot* and *blot*, as distinguished from *taught* or *brought*. Secondly, in this place it is out of accord with *wrought*, which is correctly spelled. If Messrs. Plummer and Mosely would be logical, let them write *wrought* as *wrot*—or perhaps plain *rot* would be still more correct and phonetic, besides furnishing a laconic punning commentary on simple spelling in general. *The Phoenician's* editorial column is conducted with laudable seriousness, the item of "The Power of Books" being well worthy of perusal. What could best be spared from the magazine are the vague jokes and cartoons, purposeless "fillers" of miscellaneous nature, and columns of idle gossip about things in general. Some of the moving picture items are greatly suggestive of what a newspaper man would dub "press agent stuff". The magazine represents a degree of purpose and energy quite rare amongst the anaemic youth of today, and should receive corresponding encouragement from the members of the United. Those who are inclined to censure its professional aspect would do well to remember the much-vaunted beginnings of amateur journalism, when the most highly respected sheets were of this selfsame variety.

*The United Amateur* for November is heavily burdened with a sombre and sinister short story from our own pen, entitled "The Alchemist". This is our long unpublished credential to the United, and constitutes the first and only piece of fiction we have ever laid before a critical and discerning public; wherefore we must needs beg all the charitable indulgence the Association can extend to an humble though ambitious tyro. A more interesting feature of the magazine is the biography of Mr. Fritter, written by our brilliant Official Editor, Andrew Francis Lockhart. Mr. Lockhart's quaint and friendly prose style is here displayed at its best, giving a vivid and sympathetic portrayal of his prominent subject. "Beyond the Law", by Mary Faye Durr, is a light short story of excellent idea and construction, whose only censurable point is the use of "simplified" spelling. We believe that some procedure of quite drastic nature should be taken against the spread of his empty innovation before our settled orthography shall have become completely disorganised. Even in the United we can "do our bit". Our editors should band together in an effort to exclude the new forms from their publications, and our manuscript managers should see that every piece passing through their hands is duly purged of these radical distortions. At the same time, a series of articles explaining and analysing the spelling problem should be given wide publicity. The poetry in this issue is of encouraging quality. George M. Whiteside, in "Dream of the Ideal", gives indications of real genius; at the same time displaying a little of the technical infelicity which has marked his earlier verse. Mr. Whiteside's greatest weakness is in the domain of rhyme, a noticeable error in the present poem being the attempted rhyming of *hours* with *bars* and *stars*. "I Know a Garden", by Agnes Richmond Arnold, is a tuneful and beautiful lyric of a somewhat Elizabethan type. The metre, as the lines are rendered, appears to be quite unusual; but scansion reveals the fact that it is none other than the octosyllabic couplet, disguised by the printer's art.

*The United Amateur* for December begins with "A Girl's Ambition", a poem by Margaret Trafford. The general idea of the piece is both ingenious and appropriate, but the language and technical development leave considerable to be desired. In the first place, the rhyming plan is unfortunate; the opening and concluding couplets of each stanza being unrhymed. In the second place, the metre is irregular; departing very widely in places from the iambic heptameter which appears to be the dominant measure. Miss Trafford should cultivate an ear for rhythm, at the same time counting very carefully the syllables in each line she composes. A third point requiring mention is the occasional awkwardness of expression, a juvenile fault which will doubtless amend itself in time. Just now we will call attention to only one defect—the exceedingly forced abbreviation "*dresses'd*" for *dresses would*. "To My Physician", by M. Estella Shufelt, is a smooth, graceful, and serious poem whose only possible fault is the infrequency of rhyme. This is not a technical defect, since the plan of construction is well maintained throughout; but we believe a poem of this type requires more than one rhyme to each stanza of eight lines. "The Old Inn", a stirring short story by Gertrude L. Merkle, is a very promising piece of work, albeit somewhat conventional and melodramatic. The alliterative romance of Harry Henders and Hazel Hansen has a genuinely mid-Victorian flavour. "Dead Men Tell No Tales", a short story by Ida Cochran Haughton, is a ghastly and gruesome anecdote of the untenanted clay; related by a village dressmaker. The author reveals much comprehension of rural psychology in her handling of the theme; an incident which might easily shake the reason of a sensitive and imaginative person, merely "unnerves" the two quaint and prim maiden ladies. Poe would have made of this tale a thing to gasp and tremble at; Mrs. Haughton, with the same material, constructs genuine though grim comedy!

The *United Amateur* for January contains Editor Lockhart's captivatingly graceful retrospect of the older amateur journalism, concluding with a just and eloquent appeal for the revival of our ancient enthusiasm. "Who Pays", by Helene H. Cole, is a brief and tragic story of considerable sociological significance. We deplore the use of the false verbal form *alright;* for while the expression *all right* may well occur in conversation of the character uttering it, the two words should be written out in full. "To a Babe", by Olive G. Owen, embodies in impeccable verse a highly clever and pleasing array of poetical conceits; and deserves to be ranked amongst the choicest of recent amateur offerings. "Girls Are Like Gold", by Paul J. Campbell, is a striking and witty adaptation of Thomas Hood's celebrated lines on

> "Gold! Gold! Gold! Gold!
> Bright and yellow, hard and cold."[4]

Mr. Campbell exhibits both ingenuity and metrical ability in this facile *jeu d'esprit.*

The *United Amateur* for March contains "Love's Scarlet Roses", an exquisite piece of lyric verse by Mary Henrietta Lehr of California. Miss Lehr, a scholar and poetic genius of high order, is a prominent amateur of a few years ago, lately returned to activity after a period of endeavour in other fields. Her verse is uniformly distinguished by depth of inspiration, delicacy of sentiment, and grace of structure; occupying a place amongst the rarest products of amateurdom. Another poem of remarkable merit in this issue is "The Gods' Return", by Olive G. Owen. Inspired by a recent article from the pen of Richard Le Gallienne, these well-wrought lines interpret one of the subtlest yet most potent of the varied moods created in the human breast by the momentous occurrences of the age. Looking over the file of The *United Amateur* for the present administrative year, one may discover a diverse and meritorious array of poetry and prose, which amply proves the contention of Pres. Campbell that a literary official organ is not only feasible but eminently desirable.

The *Woodbee* for January introduces to amateurdom a new bard, Mr. J. Morris Widdows, Hoosier exponent of rural simplicity.[5] Mr. Widdows has enjoyed considerable success in the professional world as a poet, song-writer, and musical composer; hence it is no untried or faltering quill which he brings within our midst. "Stringtown on the Pike", which adorns the first page of the magazine, is a very pleasing bit of dialect verse whose accent and cadences suggest the work of the late James Whitcomb Riley. The metre is gratifyingly correct, and the rusticisms exceedingly colourful; though the average reader might find it somewhat difficult to associate the name *Mike* with Yankee countryside. Such a praenomen carries with it suggestions of a rich brogue rather than a nasal drawl. "Personal Liberty", a brilliant short essay by Leo Fritter, ably and sensibly explodes one of the characteristically specious arguments of the liquor advocates. Mr. Fritter's legal training aids him in presenting a clear, polished, and logical arraignment of anti-prohibition hypocrisy. "Just a Little Love Tale", by Elizabeth M. Ballou, is a smoothly constructed bit of very light fiction. Mrs. Haughton's editorial, "A Review of Reviews", is concise and sensible; giving a merited rebuke to those who seek to create unrest and dissatisfaction in amateur journalism.

*The Woodbee* for April is an ample and attractive number, opening with Dora H. Moitoret's excellent poem in the heroic couplet, "The April Maiden". The metre of this piece follows the fashion of the nineteenth rather than of the eighteenth century, having very few "end-stopt" lines or sense-limiting couplets. The final rhyme of *caprice* and *these* is somewhat imperfect, the effect being that of an attempted rhyme of *s* and *z*. "Her Fateful Day", a short story by Maude Dolby, is pleasing and ingenious despite certain improbabilities. "Ashes of Roses", by Freda M. Sanger, belongs to that abnormal and lamentable type of pseudo-literature known as *vers libre,* and is the first serious specimen of its kind ever inflicted upon the United.[6] We are sincerely sorry that one so gifted as Miss Sanger should descend to this hybrid, makeshift medium, when she could so well express her thoughts either in legitimate prose or legitimate verse. "Free Verse" has neither the flow of real verse nor the dignity of real prose. It tends to develop obnoxious eccentricities of expression, and is closely associated with bizarre and radical vagaries of thought. It is in nine cases out of ten a mere refuge of the obtuse, hurried, indolent, ignorant, or negligent bard who cannot or will not take the time and pains to compose genuine poetry or even passable verse. It has absolutely no justification for existence, and should be shunned by every real aspirant to literary excellence, no matter how many glittering inducements it seems to hold out. True, a person of very little knowledge or ability can make himself appear extremely cultured, aesthetic, and aristocratic by juggling a few empty words in the current fashion; scribbling several lines of unequal length, each beginning with a capital letter. It is an admirably easy way to acquire a literary reputation without much effort. As the late W. S. Gilbert once wrote of a kindred fad:

> "The meaning doesn't matter
> If it's only idle chatter
> Of a transcendental kind."[7]

But we believe that the members of the United are more earnest and solid in their ambition, hence we advise Miss Sanger to turn her undoubted talent into more substantial channels. That she possesses genuine poetic genius is amply evident, even from the specimen of *vers libre* before us. The labour of real versification will be more arduous, but the fruits will prove richer in proportion. It is better to glean a little gold than much fools' gold. Miss Sanger's nephew, Mr. Norman Sanger, is more conservative in his tastes, and is creditably represented by his lines on "The Ol' Fishin' Hole". This piece contains many of the rhythmical defects common to juvenile composition, but is pervaded by a naturalness and pastoral simplicity which promise well for its young author. Wider reading and closer rhetorical study will supply all that Mr. Sanger now lacks. At present we should advise him to seek metrical regularity by taking some one well-defined line as a model, and moulding all the others to it by counting the syllables and intoning the accents in each. In the case of the present poem, the very first line will serve as a perfect guide; its conformity to the iambic heptameter plan being absolute. The alternating stresses of the fourteen syllables should be noted and copied:

"The *days* are *get*-tin' *balm*-y now, and *first*-est *thing* you *know*."

Two defects of rhyme are to be noted. By and *lullaby* cannot properly be rhymed, since the rhyming syllables are *identical,* instead of merely *similar*. *"Rapcher"* and *laughter* do not rhyme at all. Miss Haughton's essay "Is a Lie Ever Justifiable?" forms a prominent feature of the magazine, and presents some very ingenious though dogmatic reasoning. Miss Haughton's editorial, "United We Stand", is an exceedingly timely appeal for genuine amateur activity, and should be of much value in stimulating a renaissance of the Association. The passage reading "Who has been the latest victim of Cupid? *Whom* of Hymen?" arouses a query as to the grammatical status of *whom*. We fear this is what Franklin P. Adams of the *New York Tribune* playfully calls a *"Cyrilisation"*.[8] It is, as all readers of "The Conning Tower" can testify, a remarkably common error; and one into which many of the leading authors of the age frequently fall. The jingle "A Soldier's Delight", by George William Stokes, concludes the current issue in tuneful manner.

Amidst the present dearth of amateur magazines it is ever a delight to behold *The Woodbee;* meritorious in contents and regular in issuance. The debt of the United to the Columbus club is indeed a heavy one.

EDITOR'S NOTE   FP: *United Amateur* 16, No. 8 (May 1917): 106–14 (signed "H. P. LOVECRAFT, Chairman"). HPL attempts to catch up on his coverage of UAPA papers, a matter of particular urgency as the *United Amateur* was compelled to abandon monthly publication (carried on from August 1915) and resume its customary bimonthly issuance. HPL covers papers published from October 1916 to April 1917, including brief notes on the January 1917 *Conservative* and the first publication of a horror tale by HPL, "The Alchemist," in the *United Amateur* for November 1916. "The Alchemist" was HPL's "credential" (i.e., proof of literary ability that all prospective amateurs are obliged to submit as part of the membership requirements), although it is anomalous that it was published so long after HPL's entry into amateur journalism in April 1914.

*Notes*

1. See *AT* 107.
2. The reference is to *England: Its Political Organization and Development and the War against Germany* (1916) by Eduard Meyer (1855–1930), a translation of *England: seine staatliche und politische entwicklung und der krieg gegen Deutschland* (1915).
3. See *AT* 275.
4. Thomas Hood the Elder (1799–1845), *Miss Kilmansegg and Her Precious Leg* (1840), last stanza.
5. J[oseph] Morris Widdows (1861–?) published *Rainy Day Poems from the Farm* (1902) and other poems and songs. HPL ridiculed him in two undated epigrams, "On a Poem for Children, Writ by J. M. W." and "On a Poetic Poem, by J. M. W." (*AT* 259–60).

6. See further HPL's essay "The Vers Libre Epidemic" (1917; CE2).

7. Gilbert and Sullivan, *Patience* (1881), Act I.

8. Franklin P. Adams (1881–1960), widely published American journalist. His column, "The Conning Tower," ran in the *New York Tribune* (1914–22), the *New York World* (1922–31), the *New York Herald-Tribune* (1931–37), and the *New York Post* (1938–41).

## A REPLY TO *THE LINGERER*

Editor Tryout:—

It was with no little interest that I perused the recent attack on the United Amateur Press Association made by the Rev. Graeme Davis in his excellent publication *The Lingerer*. Since the culture and intellectual quality of Mr. Davis forbid one to charge him with the trivial and illiberal prejudices of association politics, it is an inevitable deduction that his anti-United attitude arises from lack of recent information concerning the two major societies and their places in the amateur world today.

It is entirely true that much puerility and much immaturity does exist within the United. The discovery of this condition requires no considerable acumen, nor does its mention in an United paper constitute either a treasonable revelation or a naive admission. The *Conservative* editorial[1] from which Mr. Davis derives such unholy glee was a frank criticism of a remediable fault; and was directed against a small clique, also active in the National, whose maleficent energy seems now quite spent. For evidence of a puerility that is permanent and an immaturity that is immutable, our critic should look elsewhere; nor should he close his eyes to his own association whilst sifting out the flaws of another.

To speak brutally and impartially, all amateurdom is more or less homogeneously tinctured with a certain delicious callowness. To confound this callowness with downright density would be most unjust, for it is merely a healthy adolescence which results from the continual infusion of young blood. But why exclude the United from this charitable interpretation? Is the ancient and honourable lineage of the National a fetish so potent that what passes for budding genius within its own fold, must in the United be branded with alliterative ingenuity as "permanent puerility and immutable immaturity"? I would admonish Mr. Davis that it ill becomes the pot to call the kettle black.

When Mr. Davis essays a direct comparison between the United and National, he exhibits most clearly the effects of his long absence from amateurdom. Proud of the justly famous personages in the old association, he is entirely ignorant of the new and commanding figures in the literary life of the United; men and women of ideals and scholarship who have appeared above the horizon during his seven years of retirement.

Perhaps it is the dormant state of the amateur press which has kept many of these gifted recruits from his notice, but he at least owes it to the United to withhold invidious comparisons before acquainting himself with our present personnel.

To refute Mr. Davis' none too generous suggestion that my own loyalty to the United is caused by a conceited desire to stand out against a background even more mediocre than myself, I need only mention the names of a score of fellow members, to each of whom I can justly and gladly concede the palm of vastly superior genius, scholarship, and expression. Were I desirous of shining at the expense of youth and crudity,

I am sure that my search for suitable "foils" would lead me through pastures much closer to Mr. Davis than the United.

If in the preceding paragraphs I have seemed to bear criticism with less than Christian meekness and acquiescence, it is because of the peculiarly unprovoked and uncalled-for nature of Mr. Davis' attack on the United. It would perhaps have been more seemly and logical to explain to *The Lingerer* some of the ceaseless and laborious enterprises undertaken by the United in the ill-rewarded cause of serious educational service; enterprises whose very spirit and essence are unknown to the basically dilettante mind of the typical Nationalite; but I feel that he should have known of these before seizing upon an exceptional case of criticism as grounds for a polite sneer. The standards of a decade ago are no longer to be applied to amateurdom, for the United has left the beaten path and is pioneering in fields to which the National does not aspire. Each association has now its separate niche, and the need for mutual rivalry, jealousy, and hostility is past.

Rev. Graeme Davis is deservedly classed as one of the elect in our miniature world. His *Lingerer* is one of the few papers of which no recipient will ever throw away a copy. Must he not, considering the intellectual height from which he views the panorama of amateurdom, soon grasp the scene as a whole, without the prejudices common to less disciplined mentalities?

EDITOR'S NOTE  FP: *Tryout* 3, No. 7 (June 1917): [9–12]. HPL rebuts Graeme Davis (who would become Official Editor of the NAPA for 1917–18), who in an unlocated issue of his amateur journal, the *Lingerer*, attacked the UAPA, in which HPL himself was apparently mentioned.

*Notes*

1. Evidently a reference to "Amateur Standards" (p. 137).

# THE UNITED'S PROBLEM

In the April issue of *The Woodbee*, Mrs. Ida C. Haughton makes a much needed appeal to the members of our Association to preserve the amateur literary world from unmerited extinction. It may be that for some reason amateur journalism has lost its charm; and that our members, impressed with the difficulties of literary perfection, are turning to less exacting sources of diversion; but this The Conservative is loath to believe. Surely the benefits of amateurdom are as substantial as ever, and as worthy of enthusiastic support as they were in the proudest of the old Halcyon Days. A large number of amateurs will be unable to serve their country in active fashion during the coming period of trial, and how may they better spend the dark days of war than in the maintenance of an institution which cannot but alleviate in wholesome fashion the prevailing sombreness of the period? Let us write, and above all, PUBLISH. Publications alone can furnish the common bond of interest for our numerous and intellectually heterogeneous organisation.

EDITOR'S NOTE  FP: *Conservative* 3, No. 1 (July 1917): [4] (unsigned). A brief discussion of declining enthusiasm in the UAPA, perhaps as a result of the war.

## EDITORIALLY

As the United Amateur Press Association concludes its twenty-second year of existence, its members may well pause to consider the commanding position it now
occupies in the world of amateur letters. Beginning as an obscure competitor to an association big with pride of achievement and hoary with years and traditions, our
United has forged to the front rank with a steady certainty which speaks well for its
equal loftiness and liberality of ideals.

This position of preëminence was lately emphasised in no doubtful manner by the
thoughtless attack made upon us by the Rev. Graeme Davis, an exponent of the dying
dilettantism of the past.[1] In comparing the United to the National Amateur Press Association, to which he owes allegiance, Mr. Davis unconsciously paved the way for a
parallel which cannot but be deadly so far as the older body is concerned. One of our
correspondents, perhaps the most gifted man in amateurdom today, has favoured us
with a copy of a letter to Mr. Davis which strikingly shews the supremacy of the
United, and which deserves publication in these columns if for no other purpose than
to demonstrate our gratifying progress. The following is an extract:

"It seems to me that this year is a particularly inauspicious time to put the National on exhibition against the United; for never has the latter been better able to
stand the deadly parallel. In the mail yesterday I received two official organs, and they
afford a good place to start our comparisons. The National's is an eight-pager, the
United's a twenty-pager, and the larger size of the National Amateur's page doesn't
even begin to make up the difference. The United reports four new members, the National three; the United three reinstatements, the National one. The National reports
twelve entries for laureate award in all departments, and from the language of the report I should judge that this is to be the total for the year; the United reports twenty-
three entries in all departments, and the serial numbers which the businesslike recorder has put on each entry indicate that the total entries for the year amount to
forty-six. I have read nearly all the entries noted in both reports, and from my memory
of them, I am sure that the United group could enter in competition with the National
group and take the title in every department. The United department of criticism is
over eight pages long; the National bureau of critics merely reports: 'the chairman . . .
has very little of personal effort to record. . . .' In addition to that the United brings out
its official organ every month. The main activity of the National this year seems to me
to have been the alternate satire and supplication emanating from New York and Boston, castigating the dormant members and trying to 'whoop up things' a bit.

"So much for the present. And that is all we need to appeal to, for the association
is in a bad way that has to rest solely on its golden past. It has been a favourite witti-
cism among National members to poke fun at the name of the United on account of
the splits that have occurred within it. It is more the fortunes of war than anything else
that gives the National a clean slate in that regard. Certainly the inherent dignity and
traditions of the National have not prevented disruption, for the people who secede
are not the kind to be deterred by any such consideration. As for political chicanery,
manipulation of elections, stealing of proxies, minor dissensions, and general acrimony,
the National has to admit a great deal more of than the United—simply because her
history extends farther into the past. If we are going to joke about names, the present

National should tread lightly, for while it has two members in Oregon and three in California, only about thirty are recorded west of the Atlantic coast states, and the great bulk of the membership is congested in three states.

"The one thing that the National has and the United can't get is that past so halcyon in perspective. The great papers of a twenty-year period, when mentioned in a breath, make an imposing showing, and we may well despair of equalling some of them. But the contributions I have received from your collection and others show me that the mediocre papers were just as atrocious as today. And oh, the irony of it! That golden past in the shape of the Fossils in convention assembled has now risen up and excommunicated us, thrown us out into the cold, said that amateur journalism is dead and they will none of us. With its grand old past cut off, the poor National seems to me to be in a bad way. I like both associations and intend to stand by them, but I don't think they can afford to take flings at each other."

EDITOR'S NOTE FP: *United Amateur* 16, No. 9 (July 1917): 130–31 (unsigned). The first of six separate contributions by HPL to this issue of the *United Amateur*, the others being "The 'Other United'" (p. 160), "Department of Public Criticism" (p. 161), "Little Journeys to the Homes of Prominent Amateurs" (p. 165), "News Notes" (p. 169), and the poem "Ode for July Fourth, 1917" (*AT* 411). HPL was obliged to assume editorship of this issue of the *United Amateur* because the current Official Editor, Andrew F. Lockhart, resigned. See HPL to John T. Dunn, 6 July 1917; *Books at Brown* 38–39 (1991–92): 217. The bulk of the present article is a quotation of a letter received by HPL from a correspondent—possibly Maurice W. Moe.

*Notes*

1. See "A Reply to *The Lingerer*" (p. 157).

# THE "OTHER UNITED"

It is a source of continued distress to us, that many old members of our Association persist in remaining aloof from the fold on account of the juvenile dissensions of five years ago, when the action of the La Grande Convention caused a division in the ranks. For several years a second "United" managed to maintain its existence in spite of many difficulties, commanding the allegiance of such able figures as W. Paul Cook, J. F. Roy Erford, and the Rowells of Seattle. Now, however, the "pseudo-United" seems to have disappeared beneath the horizon of adversity, leaving these and other persons of talent without associational affiliations. If these gifted writers and publishers are truly desirous of aiding the cause of the United against her rivals, they will forget their differences and affiliate with the Association which most certainly deserves by virtue of achievement to be recognised as the real United. It may be that their convictions against our society are both deep and sincere; but we believe political quarrels to be beneath the notice of genuine literary workers, and unworthy of consideration when the furtherance of the amateur cause is concerned. Whatever may have occurred in the remote past, the fact remains that our Association is the only United visible to the naked eye. The liberal traditions of the old United are ours, and a large percentage of our present gifted membership have no interest in or knowledge of the "split" which seems so all-important to the few who happened to be members at the time of its occurrence.

We are willing to recognise the sterling labours for the cause accomplished by our "rivals," and they in turn should recognise what we have done toward maintaining the United's fame in the amateur world. The United should be and is more than a formally organised band of hide-bound partisan politicians. It represents an idea and an ideal— a type of scholastic endeavour and literary democracy which can be found only amongst its adherents. The line separating the "Campbell United" and the "Pedroni United" is purely arbitrary, and would be immediately eradicated if both sides would devote a little more dispassionate thought to the problem of union or disunion.

The reaffiliation of the "Pedroni" amateurs is by no means a necessity to this association. Surely we need complain of no lack of brilliant members. But we wish all former United supporters could enjoy the benefits of the associational life, and that such splendid publications as Mr. Cook's *Vagrant* might no longer have to wander about in a quasi-homeless isolation. If the participants in the La Grande unpleasantness could but realise how small their grievances appear in perspective to the newer amateurs, we are sure that they would give their sense of humour full play, clasp hands with a smile, and begin a new coöperation for the progress and expansion of the United Amateur Press Association.

EDITOR'S NOTE   FP: *United Amateur* 16, No. 9 (July 1917): 131 (unsigned). One more screed against the UAPA of America, led by J. F. Roy Erford (see "The Morris Faction" [p. 33] and the articles cited in the Editor's Note there).

# DEPARTMENT OF PUBLIC CRITICISM

*(July 1917)*

*The Conservative* for July opens with Ira A. Cole's delightful and melodious lines "In Vita Elysium" (Heaven in Life), which present a strong arraignment of those conventional theologians who deem all things beautiful reserved for a vague existence after death. While the orthodox reader may deem the flight of the imagination too free, the rational and appreciative litterateur will delight in the vigour of imagination and delicacy of fancy displayed. The metrical structure is beyond reproach in taste and fluency, the regular and spirited heroic couplets affording a refreshing contrast to the harsh and languid measures of the day. Mr. Cole's poetical future is bright indeed, for he possesses an innate conception of fitness and poetic values which too few of his contemporaries can boast. We wish to emphasise to those readers who are familiar with *The Conservative's* editorial policy, that the lines appear practically without revision; every bold conception and stroke of genius being Mr. Cole's own. Two couplets in particular delight the ear and the imagination, proving the author's claim to distinction as a poet of the purest classical type:

> "Go! Go! vain man, to those unbounded fanes
> Where God's one proven priest—fair Nature—reigns."

> "Uplifted, glad, thy spirit then shall know
> That life is light, and heaven's here below!"

"The Genesis of the Revolutionary War", by Henry Clapham McGavack, is one of those searchingly keen bits of iconoclastic analysis which have made Mr. McGavack so famous as an essayist since his advent to the United. Our author here explodes conclusively a large body of bombastic legend which false textbooks have inflicted upon successive generations of innocent American youth. We are shewn beyond a doubt that the Revolution of 1776 was no such one-sided affair as the petty political "historians" would have us believe, and that our Mother Country indeed had a strong case before the bar of international justice. It is an article which makes us doubly proud of our racial and cultural affiliations.

"Sweet Frailty", a poem by Mary Henrietta Lehr, contains all those elements of charm, delicacy, and ingenuity which mark its author as one of amateurdom's most cultivated and gifted members.

Of the editorial column modesty forbids us to speak, but we hope the amateur public may be duly charitable with our shortcomings as therein displayed.

The Inspiration for April is a "Tribute Number", dedicated to the amateur journalists of Great Britain and Canada who have devoted their lives and fortunes to the cause of civilisation and the Empire. With so wonderfully inspiring a subject, it is small wonder that the magazine lives gloriously up to its name. Miss von der Heide shews extreme skill and sympathy in the editorship of the publication, and in the verses which she contributes; proving herself worthy indeed of the high place she has occupied in amateurdom for so many years.

"The Lion's Brood", by Henry Clapham McGavack, exhibits the versatility of this brilliant writer; for though he is by preference a concise essayist, he here rises to great heights in the domain of rhetorical panegyric. His stirring encomium is ingeniously continued by Mr. William T. Harrington, who adds many merited words of praise for our kindred across the seas. The present critic's lines are as full of heartfelt love of England as they are wanting in merit;[1] while the lines of Olive G. Owen possess both deep fervour and conspicuous merit. Mrs. Griffith's tribute, "He Conquers Who Endures", breathes out the true spirit of the American nation today, anticipating the official action of a cautious and slow-moving government. The "Open Letters" of Messrs. Macauley, Stokes, and Martin speak the brave spirit of the age, and make us the more sharply regretful of our own rejection for military service. "Treasure", by Miss von der Heide, is an appealing bit of sentiment, whose interest is timely indeed.

Viewed as a whole, The Inspiration takes first rank amongst the amateur papers published since March.

The Little Budget for May opens with Paul J. Campbell's meritorious poem entitled "Signals". Mr. Campbell, always facile in metre, exhibits increasing power in the realm of poetical imagination, and is entitled to a substantial place on the slopes of Parnassus. A misprint in the present version of "Signals" gives look where looked should appear.

"The Adventures of 'Dido' Plum", by Joseph Parks, is a pleasing story of military life by one who is himself a soldier. Mr. Parks's brief sketches form a pleasing feature of the contemporary amateur press, being distinguished by a naturalness which intensifies their interest as literal transcripts of the army atmosphere. "Road Song", a tuneful lyric by Eleanor J. Barnhart, marks the first appearance of that brilliant author as a poet. Her inexperience in this art, however, is not at all to be suspected from this fervent and finished composition; which might well do credit to some of our veteran bards. "Impulse", by Norah Sloane Stanley, is described as "A Parisian Fragment", and exhibits much ingenuity in spirit and atmosphere. "Keep a Cheerful Countenance", by

Eugene B. Kuntz, is a poem of great merit despite the doubtful rhyme of *way* and *quality* in the last stanza. Miss Mappin, in her article in Milton, displays her ample knowledge of literary history, and even more than her customary fluency. "The Contented Robin", a poem by Margaret Mahon, is apt, pleasing, and harmonious; whilst Miss Trafford's brief jingle is quaint and clever. "Spring", by Randolph Trafford (aetat 10), is full of the exuberant vigour of youth, and speaks well for the future of this bright young bard.

The *Little Budget* for June gains distinction from Henry Clapham McGavack's brilliant essay on American Anglophobia, entitled "Blood Is Not Thicker Than Water". This acute analysis of anti-British sentiment among certain classes in the States reveals a lamentable result of bigotry and historical ignorance; which may, we hope, be cured by the new bonds of alliance betwixt the Old and the New Englands. As Mr. McGavack well demonstrates, most of our Anglophobia is manufactured by the alleged "historians" who poison the minds of the young through mendacious textbooks. This species of false teaching, an evil potently fostered by the Fenians and Sinn Feiners who lurk serpent-like in our midst, is one which cannot too soon be eradicated; for the cultural identity and moral unity of the States and the Empire make such sources of unintelligent prejudice increasingly nauseous and detrimental. We may add that the textbook treatment of our War between the States is almost equally unfair, the Northern cause being ridiculously exalted above the brave and incredibly high-minded attitude of the Confederacy.

Another delightful prose contribution is "Back to Blighty", by Joseph Parks, a vivid vignette of one phase of military life. "Trinidad and Its Forests", by F. E. M. Hercules, is marked by its author's customary ease of expression and felicity of diction; presenting many facts of general interest. The poetry in this issue includes work from the pens of J. E. Hoag, H. P. Lovecraft,[2] Rev. Eugene B. Kuntz, Beryl Mappin, and the Editor. Dr. Kuntz's lines to the memory of Phillips Gamwell[3] are animated with a nobility which well befits their subject, though the rhyme of *day* and *melody* is not strictly correct. Few amateur poets are able to achieve the sonorous dignity which Dr. Kuntz imparts to his flowing Alexandrines, or to select with equal appropriateness the vivid and musical words that so irresistibly delight the ear and impress the imagination. Miss Mappin's metrical effort, entitled "Only a Thought", betrays some of the crudities of youth; including the attempted rhyme of *alone* and *home*. The metre, phraseology, and plan of rhyming demand extensive revision, the following being a possible amended version of the piece:

> As sad and alone in a distant land
>     I sat by the dismal shore,
> My chin laid pensively in my hand,
>     And my dreams all of home once more;
> I watch'd and mus'd o'er the sunless sea,
>     And study'd the cruel foam;
> For the waves bore an exile's woe to me,
>     From my kindred forc'd to roam.
>
> But lo! floating light upon the wind
>     And murm'ring o'er ocean crest,
> Come the thoughts of those I left behind,
>     Bringing comfort and love and rest.
> Only a word—aye, only a thought!
>     Each speeds like a heav'n-sent dart;

> Who can measure the gladness and aid they've brought—
> These thoughts—to the breaking heart?

The first line of the original, "*Far away* in a *distant* land", is lamentably pleonastic; whilst the identity or intended identity of the second and fourth rhymes is undesirable. In a verse of this type, it is not well to repeat a rhyme immediately. In the second stanza the first and third lines and the fifth and seventh are unrhymed, a variation from the original design which is not sanctioned by custom. Once a poet decides on his metre and plan of rhyme, he should maintain them unchanged throughout the poem. In the foregoing revised version, all these defects have been remedied. Miss Trafford's poem, "After a Dream", shews much promise both technically and in the thought. The final line of the first stanza, "And the joy it contains is much", is very weak; and should be changed to read: "And of joy it contains so much." In writing the definite article, Miss Trafford mistakenly uses the contracted form *th'* when full syllabic value is to be given. This contraction is employed only when the article is metrically placed as a proclitic before another word, and is thereby shorn of its separate pronunciation as follows:

> *Th' ambitious* bard a nobler theme essays

The illustrated bit of humour by George William Stokes deserves mention as presenting one of the cleverest drawings to appear lately in the amateur press. It is difficult to decide in which domain Mr. Stokes shines the more brightly, literature or pictorial art. His heading for *The Little Budget* is a masterpiece of its kind.

*The Pippin* for May brings once more to our notice amateurdom's foremost high-school club, the Appleton aggregation whose existence is due to Mr. Maurice W. Moe's untiring efforts. "Doings of the Pippins", by Joseph Harriman, is a terse and informing chronicle of recent activity. "Once Upon a Time", by Florence A. Miller, is a bit of humorous verse whose metre might be improved by the use of greater care. "Some Cloth!", by John Ingold, is an exceedingly clever piece of wit; which, though avowedly Irish, bears the characteristic hall-mark of native American humour. The delightful exaggerations recall some of the brightest spots in American light literature. "Speed", by Matilda Harriman, is an interesting sketch recalling Poe's "Mellonta Tauta" in its imaginative flights. "From over the Threshold", by Ruth Ryan, shews much promise in the realm of fiction. "Once an Amateur, Always an Amateur" is one of those rare bits of prose with which our distinguished Critical member, Mr. Moe, favours us. We are proud of the unshaken amateur allegiance of so brilliant a personality, and trust that some day he may realise his dream of "an attic or basement printshop". "The Press Club", by Ruth Schumaker, is a pleasing sketch, as is also Miss Kelly's "Our Club and the United". We trust that the Appleton Club may safely weather the hard times of which Miss Kelly complains.

*The United Amateur* for May contains a captivating and graceful sketch by W. Edwin Gibson, entitled "Beauty". Mr. Gibson is one of our younger members who bids fair to become prominent in the coming amateur generation. Of the month's poetry, we may mention with particular commendation Miss von der Heide's "Worship", though through some error, possibly typographical, the final line of the second stanza seems to lack two syllables. "When Dreams Come True", by Kathleen Foster Smith, is likewise of more than common merit, though the word *hear* in the second line of the second stanza is probably a misprint for *heard*. "Smile", by O. M. Blood, is ingenious though scarcely novel. Its chief defects are inequalities in the lines, which care should be able to correct. The first line contains two superfluous syllables, while the fourth line contains one too many. The ninth line of the final section contains two syllables too many, as do the tenth and eleventh lines as well. The rhyme of *appear* and *disappear* is incorrect, since syllables in rhyme should be merely similar—not the same. Mr. Blood requires much practice in poetry, but undoubtedly possesses the germ of success. "To the U. A. P. A.", by Matthew Hilson, is acceptable in construction and delightful in sentiment, laying stress on the new Anglo-American unity—the one redeeming feature of the present international crisis. *The United Amateur* closes with a quotation from Euripides, which we will not attempt to review here, since the author has been receiving critical attention from far abler men for many centuries!

EDITOR'S NOTE  FP: *United Amateur* 16, No. 9 (July 1917): 122–24 (signed "H. P. LOVECRAFT, Chairman"). HPL discusses his own *Conservative* (July 1917) and other journals of the period.

*Notes*

1. HPL, "Britannia Victura" (*AT* 405–6).
2. "To Mr. Lockhart of Milbank, South Dakota, U.S.A., on His Poetry," a reprint of "To Mr. Lockhart, on His Poetry" (*Tryout*, March 1917; *AT* 341–42).
3. HPL's cousin, who died on 31 December 1916. See HPL's poem "An Elegy to Phillips Gamwell, Esq." ([Providence] *Evening News*, 5 January 1917; *AT* 434–35).

## LITTLE JOURNEYS TO THE HOMES OF PROMINENT AMATEURS: V. ELEANOR J. BARNHART

In forming the acquaintance of a leading amateur journalist, it is natural to expect a character at once brilliant and unusual. Seldom, however, may one discover a personality more distinguished for striking mentality, unquenchable intellectual enthusiasm, and untiring educational endeavour than that of the United's present Secretary, Miss Eleanor Barnhart of Alden, Minnesota.

Eleanor J. Barnhart, Scientist, Philosopher, Poet, Essayist, and Fiction Writer, was (to quote from her autobiography) "born in Minneapolis at a very early age". Her parents having both died before she was four, she was adopted by her father's closest friend; who had entered into a mutual agreement with Mr. Barnhart that if one of the two should die, the other would care for the fatherless family.

It is a singular circumstance that Miss Barnhart's new parents were both deaf mutes, giving to her childhood an atmosphere of silence and uncommunicativeness which doubtless had no little share in directing her mind into studious channels. Forbidden the society of childish playmates, she perforce turned bookworm. Up to the age of six she would seldom consent to use speech, though abundantly able to do so when disposed to break her voluntary silence. Her early reading was in more than one respect unusual; all the ordinary literature of infancy, including "Mother Goose", having been religiously withheld from her eyes. Strange indeed is the triad of books which composed her first mental diet; an illustrated Bible, Hawthorne's "Tanglewood Tales", and Holmes' "Elsie Venner". The last named, she admits, was probably perused surreptitiously and comprehended imperfectly.

Thus segregated from other children in a little world of paper and print, the future authoress soon became proficient in everything save pronunciation. Lacking oral discourse, it is small wonder that typographical symbols failed to identify themselves with spoken words in her mind. When, in later childhood, she began to correlate vocal and written language, she discovered that many of her instinctive pronunciations differed widely from the true sounds. She had, for example, thought of *occupy* as *"oseeseeupi"*!

Miss Barnhart's entrance into school abruptly broke the self-imposed dumbness of previous years, and from a virtual mute she became a veritable chatterbox; plying all her associates with endless and curious questions of unconsciously philosophical tenor. A spell had been broken, and one chapter of life closed. Hitherto reared according to the formal precepts of a book, our authoress was now subject to the broader influences necessary to normal intellectual development.

At school Mss Barnhart displayed marked aptitude, frequently skipping a half-grade in her upward progress; yet she entertained no great regard for her studies. Equally lukewarm was her interest in other children and their more or less inane pastimes. Dolls, however, continued to hold her fancy, and she is credited with never having broken a single member of her wax and china family. Sewing for her brood of over twenty dolls was the only diversion which seriously rivalled reading as a claimant for her attention. Her reading was omnivorous, and was conducted with a serious perseverance which clearly showed the fine mental fibre of the born student. She never failed to finish a book once commenced, no matter how dull or dry it might prove. Foremost in her regard came historical fiction, especially the romantic novels of Scott, Ebers,[1] and Dumas.

Though inevitably impelled toward authorship by mental calibre and experiences of early childhood, it was at school that Miss Barnhart first exhibited the impulse of literary expression. At the suggestion of a kindly seventh-grade teacher she began contributing to the *Journal Junior*, the children's page of the *Minneapolis Sunday Journal*, where her very first effort gained a prize. She was thereafter a regular contributor to the *Journal* till the termination of her high-school studies in 1910.

But in the meantime many important events in Miss Barnhart's career had taken place. At about the time of her tenth year the family migrated to southern California for the sake of her foster-father's health; there leading a quiet and pleasant life in a somnolent half-Spanish town. The coming writer, having defective eyesight, was exempted from attendance at school, and spent her time in the congenial society of her invalid foster-parent. Two years later the kind friend and second father found rest; and the adopted daughter, having the sensations of an outsider in the household of the bereaved wife and young children, took the first radical and independent step of her eventful career. Conscious of the affectionless and perfunctory (though dutiful) nature of her foster-mother's care, she withdrew from the household and at the age of twelve commenced the battle of life absolutely alone.

Miss Barnhart's first position in the outside world was in a crowded Minneapolis box factory which she laconically describes as "wretched". It was her sanguine design to save enough money to support herself through a high-school course, for she little realised the meagreness of her tiny salary. This factory experience, though marked by no particular disaster or unhappiness, proved far from beneficial; since it not only had a physically deleterious effect, but placed the youthful aspirant in exceedingly uncongenial surroundings. Unable to raise her commonplace associates to her own intellectual level, she became reserved and solitary; living in an imaginary world of her own.

A year later the acquaintanceship of an intelligent young Jewess, formed at the Public Library, brought about another turning point in Miss Barnhart's life. Stimulated by her new friend's Semitic spirit of practical enterprise, she obtained through advertising a situation as assistant in an excellent family; an arrangement which permitted her to realise her ambition of attending high-school. At school she was immediately distinguished for brilliancy and earnestness, and was soon surrounded by an almost bewildering host of sincere friends and advisers. Completing a four-year course in three years, she was prominent in literary and debating circles, and graduated in 1910 as an honour student.

During this period Miss Barnhart had lived with several families, finally finding a congenial atmosphere in the well-ordered home of the assistant principal of her school. It is there that she gained much of that experience with children which so well fitted her for pedagogical pursuits.

About this time there fell to her lot the singular circumstance of making her own sister's acquaintance. When the death of Mr. Barnhart had placed Eleanor in the care of his friend, her younger and only sister had gone with a grandmother. That lady having died, the sister had fallen into the charge of a woman of very unkind tendencies when our authoress finally obtained track of her and brought her to Minneapolis.

As the high-school career of Miss Barnhart drew to its close, she was besieged with well-meant advice for the future; and as quite at a loss whether to be an English teacher, a Latin teacher, domestic science teacher, country school teacher, normal school pupil, newspaper woman, or nurse. She herself favoured the last named vocation, but was debarred through lack of bodily strength. Eventually she decided to become a collegian, and with admirable perseverance worked her way through Minnesota University; remaining out a year in the middle of the course to teach in a rural school. Graduating from college in 1915, Miss Barnhart accepted a position as instructor of Home Economics in the high-school at Alden, Minnesota; which position she still holds with credit and distinction.

Miss Barnhart's connexion with the United began in 1908, when some of her fiction in the *Journal Junior* was seen by our discerning recruiter and ex-President, Mr. J. F. Roy Erford. Joining upon Mr. Erford's recommendation, she was assigned to the recruit committee, where she made an enviable record in securing new members for the Association. Her first offerings to the amateur press appeared in Mr. George Conger's journal *The Bobbin*, afterward called *The Trumpeter*. The May, 1912, number of that paper, dedicated to Miss Barnhart and composed entirely of her contributions, well expresses the appreciation felt by the United for so gifted an authoress. In 1910 Miss Barnhart issued *Polaris* in partnership with Mr. Russel Rex Strom. Other papers to which she has contributed are *Idle Hours, The Lone Star, Our Girls, The By-Path, The Courier, Unter den Linden, The Emissary, The Official Feminine, The United Official Quarterly, The Scot,* and *The United Amateur*. Two story Laureateships and one essay Laureateship have rewarded her efforts. Miss Barnhart was elected Second Vice-President in 1910, but on account of illness was unable to serve. She has since been elected Historian and appointed Supervisor of Amendments. At the beginning of the present administrative year she was elected Laureate Recorder, but circumstances led to her almost immediate elevation to the more responsible appointive office of Secretary. Here she has distinguished herself as one of the most active, dependable, and conscientious officers of the Association.

Of her literary work Miss Barnhart has said: "Writing is more than a mere hobby with me; it is a necessity in the way of self-expression. I am by nature, or more possibly by circumstances, painfully inarticulate in the ordinary forms of discourse; so that literary composition has afforded me considerable relief from self-expression, as well as conscious pleasure in attempting artistic creation." Could a more accurate description be given of the animating motives of the genuine author as distinguished from the mere seeker after fame or reward? Evident indeed is the fact that Miss Barnhart is no commercialised hack-writer or affected dabbler in things literary.

Whilst the comparative scarcity of good stories in amateurdom has caused her own well-written tales to stand out in sharp relief, leading the members to regard her primarily as an author of fiction; it is in the domain of the essay that Miss Barnhart's genius is most thoroughly displayed. Her sketches, generally dealing with human nature and based for the most part on her own experiences and observations, are marked by an intellectual power, philosophical insight, and interpretation of detail which leave little to be desired and which entitle their author to a place amongst the genuine literati of the United. Her autobiography, published serially a few years ago in *Our Girls*, is in many ways a remarkable document; which may likewise be said of such pieces as "The Guest of God" in *The Official Feminine*, "The Fear of the Lord" in *Unter den Linden*, or "Concerning Geese, with Some Thoughts on the Preparation of Lessons" in *The Trumpeter*.

Miss Barnhart's fiction partakes of the intelligent qualities which distinguish her essays. "The Desertion of Mrs. Heaggy" in *The Trumpeter*, and "The Ghost of Lone Hill", "A Crisis", and "The Shadow on the Trail" in *The United Amateur*, are as notable for their acute analyses of character as for their intrinsic interest.

Though hitherto appearing only as a writer of prose, Miss Barnhart is by no means unfamiliar with the art of versification. Several unpublished lyric pieces which the present biographer has been permitted to see exhibit a poetic talent of no common order, and herald the advent of a new bard to the Heliconian heights of amateurdom.

In composition Miss Barnhart is deliberate and painstaking; writing slowly and thoughtfully, and revising with extreme care. She is seldom satisfied with her finished work, finding more joy in actual creation than in the contemplation of the result. Her general literary trend may be said to be realistic rather than romantic; a characteristic reflected from her dominant taste in reading, though she confesses to an apparently inconsistent predilection for romantic verse. Her favourite author of fiction is Arnold Bennett, after whom come Joseph Conrad and Edith Wharton. Older favourites are George Eliot and Thackeray. Apart from fiction, Miss Barnhart is fond of books on travel and of light essays such as those of Mark Twain, Stevenson, and Arthur Benson.

The personality of Miss Barnhart is quiet, reserved, and unassuming; far more so than one might judge from her keenly scientific attitude as an author. Usually rather reticent, she can on occasion become as eloquent as the situation may demand. Of herself she has said: "It is quite true that I tend too much to find life more interesting as an observer than as a participant."

That one of her objective and analytical mind and searching philosophical comprehension will become a potent factor in the intellectual world, seems assured beyond a doubt. Her literary and scientific traits are coöperative; science lending precise intelligence to her compositions, whilst literature imparts its romantic spirit and infectious interest to the facts and principles of her scientific pursuits. As a science teacher she has achieved marked success, and as an author no less a triumph may be expected. One of her ambitions for the remote future is to issue, when "fat and forty", a "thin, aristocratic volume of essays which might be read and enjoyed by discriminating people".

The career of Miss Barnhart exemplifies in almost wonderful fashion the victory of a brilliant mentality over obstacles which would deter and stifle the more ordinary mind. With phenomenal ambition and independence she has defeated the retarding influences of an unsettled and eventful childhood and youth; standing today as an inspiration and example to the struggler, and reflecting credit of the brightest sort upon the Association of which she is so useful and so earnest a member.

EDITOR'S NOTE FP: *United Amateur* 16, No. 9 (July 1917): 125–28 (as by "El Imparcial"). The second of HPL's contributions to this series (for the first, see p. 78). The information on Eleanor J. Barnhart (who later married Paul J. Campbell; see "President's Message" [January 1918]) was surely supplied by correspondence with Barnhart. She does not otherwise seem to have become a close colleague of HPL.

*Notes*

1. Georg Ebers (1837–1898), German author of historical romances.

---

# NEWS NOTES

*(July 1917)*

Mr. Frank G. Morris of Armour, S. D., one of our newer recruits, is Recorder of Deeds for Douglas County, and a successful office-holder in spite of physical handicaps. He aspires to become proficient in the domain of song-writing, and has been placed in correspondence with our successful composer, J. Morris Widdows.

J. Morris Widdows, one of our Hoosier poets, has an excellent piece of verse in the current issue of *The National Magazine*, entitled "A Rainy Day". An account of Mr. Widdows and a picture of his beautiful country home also appear in this number. *The National* has more than once contained the work of United members, Mrs. W. V. Jordan and H. P. Lovecraft being regular contributors.[1]

Prof. P. B. McDonald, late Literary Director of the Thesis Club of Toledo, is attending summer school at the University of Chicago. He has accepted a chair as Instructor of English at the University of Colorado beginning September 1st.

E. Edward Ericson, the well-known amateur printer and former editor of *Quillings*, is spending his vacation at Garrison, North Dakota.

Eleanor J. Barnhart was the guest of Beulah Amidon of Fargo, N. D., for a few weeks in June.

Mr. Edward F. Daas entertained at dinner at the Hotel Maryland, May 30th, the occasion being his ——-th birthday. His guests were Mr. and Mrs. Fred Nieman, Mr. and Mrs. Arthur C. Peterson, the Misses Irene and Crescens Wamser, Eleanor Gutman, Carrie Brandt, and the Messrs. Walter F. and Herbert G. Zahn and Alfred Kohler.

Rev. David V. Bush of St. Louis, erstwhile "Peace Poet", is responding to the emergencies of the hour and delivering a series of patriotic services in his church. He expects to revive his monthly magazine of humorous verse on current topics within a short time.[2]

George W. Macauley, whose mediaeval tales have attracted such favourable notice, is planning to attend the Chicago Convention. His brother Glenn is now a soldier at Fort Sheridan.

Andrew Francis Lockhart, victim of political persecution, has returned to his home after a trying experience at the hands of unjust lawmakers. He will undergo a period of rest before entering upon the second trial of his case, in which he hopes to secure justice at last.

Rev. Eugene B. Kuntz, D.D., who has recently completed a stirring and magnificent array of patriotic poetry, is about to take a trip into the Rocky Mountains with his brother. He writes us that he is going to a place "whose medicine is fresh mountain air, the songs and laughter of brooks, the whispering symphonies of the pine and spruce forests, and the lullabies of the aspen". We anticipate some noble poetical results of his coming communion with Nature.

H. P. Lovecraft, the original "Pooh-Bah" of amateurdom, is now serving as Official Editor, Chairman of the Department of Public Criticism, and Chairman of the Year-Book Committee. He deserves to be expelled from the United for his inexcusable delay in issuing the Year-Book, but vows that he will eventually complete the labour or perish in the attempt.

W. Paul Cook, sterling Old-Timer in amateurdom and editor of *The Vagrant*, will attend the Grand Army encampment at Boston next August with the Sons of Veterans; following which he will make a tour of Southern New England, dropping in at the *Conservative* office, where he will receive a hearty welcome.[3]

William B. Stoddard, author of "A Lovable Degenerate", is returning to the East after a season at the Pacific Coast. His engagement to a fair maiden of the West has been announced, and the culminating event set for next Easter.

Maurice W. Moe, Chief of our Department of Private Criticism, is trying a novel experiment this summer for the sake of his health. He has undertaken a labourer's work on one of the new buildings at Lawrence College, lifting planks, shovelling mud, and wheeling bags of cement like a seasoned workingman. While painful at first, the regimen is proving actually beneficial, and Mr. Moe is proud of the physical prowess he is beginning to exhibit. One of our amateur poetasters recently perpetrated the following four lines on the unusual occurrence of a learned instructor working manually upon a college building:[4]

### To M. W. M.

> Behold the labourer, who builds the walls
> That soon shall shine as Learning's sacred halls;
> A man so apt at ev'ry art and trade,
> He well might govern what his hands have made!

Jonathan E. Hoag, venerable bard of Greenwich, New York, is one of the most active of workers in the Prohibition Party. His efforts against the drink demon cover an extensive span of time, and he is happy in living to see the wane of the liquor evil on sound practical grounds. Many of his poems which have appeared in the amateur press are exciting favourable notice in the professional press of his native state, some being reprinted in *The Troy Times* with marks of great distinction.[5]

One of the latest acquisitions to Amateurdom is Hon. Elias H. Cheyney, of Lebanon, New Hampshire, proposed by his son, the Official Publisher of *The United Amateur*. The new member is unquestionably qualified by age for association with us, being on the 28th of this month only six months past his eighty-fifth milestone. Mr. Cheyney was for about thirty years in the United States consular service, in Cuba prior to the insurrection and after that in the Dutch West Indies. He is still editing the paper which he bought in 1861. His "credential" is a poem written while in the West Indies and polished off since his return to his home. He has been an occasional writer of verse. Some of his hymns are sung in his home church, Baptist, and he has himself translated some of his verse into Spanish.

Through the good offices of Dr. O. M. Blood, Chairman of the Convention Reception Committee, the services of his sister, Miss Blanche Blood of the Auditorium Lyceum School, have been secured in arranging a musical programme for the entertainment of Convention visitors, in the parlours of Hotel Atlantic on Friday evening, July 27. Our talented new member, Miss Mary R. Hulsman, will sing several songs of her own composition on this occasion. Miss Hulsman enjoys the unique distinction of having written 150 musical compositions, songs, piano solos, violin and piano numbers, at the age of 22. She is a member of the Ben Hur Players, who have just completed a very successful Chautauqua tour.

The Thesis Club of Toledo held its last meeting at Perrysburg, O., the home of one of the members.

Chester Pierce Munroe, poet of the Southland and member of the Year-Book Committee, was on June 5th united in matrimony to Miss Mary Doris Davenport of Asheville, N. C. The couple will be at home after July 1st.

EDITOR'S NOTE FP: *United Amateur* 16, No. 9 (July 1917): 128, 131, 134, 137 (unsigned). News items on the doings and accomplishments of various amateurs; a regular feature in the *United Amateur*, and customarily written by the Official Editor. HPL wrote a great proportion of the "News Notes" in the *United Amateur* for the period 1920–25, when he served almost continuously as Official Editor (except for the period 1922–23). HPL's comments on David Van Bush, W. Paul Cook, Maurice W. Moe, and other colleagues are to be noted.

*Notes*

1. HPL had seven poems in the professional *National Magazine* of Boston, all reprints from amateur journals.
2. HPL later revised many books of verse and popular psychology for Bush, who became HPL's most reliable revision client until about 1925.
3. For Cook's first meeting with HPL, see his *In Memoriam: Howard Phillips Lovecraft* (1941; rpt. West Warwick, RI: Necronomicon Press, 1991), pp. 7–8.
4. The poem is by HPL himself.
5. Several of HPL's birthday tributes to Hoag were reprinted in the *Troy* (N.Y.) *Times*.

# PRESIDENT'S MESSAGE

(*September 1917*)

Fellow Amateurs:—

The present administrative year, despite the financial and other disadvantages incident to a time of war, promises to develop a considerable amount of renewed activity in the United. The new official board is one of remarkable quality and capability, and individual enthusiasm seems at a high tide. Many new papers are expected in the near future, whilst a large number of the older members have signified an intention of resuming their publications.

The most important innovations are those created by the passage of the amendments relating to laureateships and recruiting work. Members should note that in order to ensure the usual awards in all laureate classes, ten entries must be made in each; wherefore we must not be backward in entering our various compositions, even though some of us may not have been eager to compete in the past.

The amendments creating third and fourth Vice-Presidencies are well calculated to improve recruiting in colleges and high schools, respectively. Miss Mary Henrietta Lehr, originator of the plan, has been appointed Third Vice-President, and is preparing for a vigorous and systematic campaign amongst collegians. A Fourth Vice-President will soon be appointed, and high school recruiting may be expected to reach satisfactory proportions. Recruiting Committees will be announced as soon as formed.

Miss Mary Faye Durr of Mount Sterling, Ohio, has accepted appointment as Secretary, her occupancy of that important office ensuring an efficient and business-like handling of the records.

The election of Miss Verna McGeoch to the Official Editorship, perhaps the most important of our offices, forecasts the publication of *The United Amateur* on a very high plane; qualitatively if not quantitatively. Outlines of reading courses, and other educational features, will tend to open a new era in the conduct of the official organ. The appointment of a permanent Official Publisher will be announced in the next report. Present high prices make the financing of *The United Amateur* extremely difficult, and contributions to the Official Organ Fund (care of Miss McGeoch) will much facilitate the work of the Association.

The Department of Public Criticism has been completely reorganised, and now represents the best critical talent of the Association. We are extremely fortunate in securing as its Chairman Mr. Rheinhart Kleiner, noted alike as a reviewer and as a creative artist, who can thoroughly fulfil the precept of Mr. Pope:

"Let such teach others who themselves excel,
And censure freely who have written well."[1]

Associated with Mr. Kleiner is Mr. Maurice Winter Moe, who represents the deepest scholarship in amateurdom, and who has served ably in this capacity in the past. Reviews will until further notice be composite and anonymous, in order to avoid a repetition of the unjust accusations of personal harshness and prejudice lately made against the Department.

Prof. P. B. McDonald of the University of Colorado has accepted the Chairmanship of the Department of Private Criticism, and is prepared to furnish advice and revision of sound constructive value to interested applicants. Writers of prose are urged to submit their manuscripts to him before publication. Mr. Kleiner, in addition to his new duties in the other Department, will continue to act as private critic of verse manuscripts; his thorough knowledge of poetical technique rendering him a highly effective tutor to those who seek his advice. Members in general are urged to make a more extensive use of this Department than they have made during the past year.

Mr. Edward F. Daas, a veteran whose name guarantees the success of any enterprise with which it is connected, has been appointed Chairman of the Reception Committee for the 1918 Convention, to be held at the beautiful Dells of the Wisconsin

River. This will be the United's first assemblage at a rural spot, and those who attend will be amply repaid by the rugged and singular nature of the scenery. Mr. Daas will also be active as a local club organiser in Milwaukee, and to some extent as a publisher.

The delayed report of Clarence S. Darrow, Judge of Essays, has been received. He assigns the highest award to Paul J. Campbell for "The Age of Accuracy" and Honourable Mention to Helene Hoffman Cole for "The Epic of the Poor".

In concluding, the undersigned desires to express his appreciation of the honour bestowed upon him by the membership, and particularly to acknowledge his indebtedness to his energetic, enthusiastic, and illustrious predecessor, Mr. Paul J. Campbell, whose wise advice and unselfish coöperation will prove, as in the past, an inspiration and source of reliance to the Association.

EDITOR'S NOTE  FP: *United Amateur* 17, No. 1 (September 1917): 12–13 (signed "H. P. LOVECRAFT, President," and dated September 11, 1917). The first of HPL's messages after his election as President of the UAPA for the 1917–18 term.

*Notes*

1. Pope, *An Essay on Criticism* (1711), ll. 15–16.

---

# PRESIDENT'S MESSAGE

*(November 1917)*

Fellow-Amateurs:—

The fourth month of the United's official year opens with the organisation still nearer completion; Mrs. Helene Hoffman Cole, former President and thoroughly active and capable amateur, having accepted appointment as Supervisor of Amendments.  The Fourth Vice-Presidency has been accepted by Alfred Galpin, Jr., 779 Kimball St., Appleton, Wisconsin.

The Official Editor is to be commended for the excellence of the September *United Amateur*, as is also the printer, Mr. W. Paul Cook. The Association will be gratified to hear that Mr. Cook has accepted the position of Official Publisher for the year; but the members must remember that only by their liberality in replenishing the Official Organ Fund can regular issuance be ensured.

The 1916–1917 Year Book of the Association, having been completed by the Committee, is now undergoing critical inspection and condensation by the expert judgment of Messrs. Paul J. Campbell and Edward F. Daas.  Here again we appeal to the generosity of the members, especially the veteran members, to make possible the publication in full of this epitome of amateur history.  Unless the Year Book Fund is materially swelled, the volume cannot possibly be printed in its unabridged form of sixty-three closely typed manuscript pages.

The amateur press is now shewing signs of a gradual recovery from the late period of minimum activity.  Mr. Martin's remarkable production, *The Sprite*, Mr. Lindquist's two numbers of *The Dabbler*, Mr. and Mrs. Cole's welcome *Olympian*, Mr. Cook's wonderfully ample *Vagrant*, and Mr. John H. D. Smith's small but enterprising *Yerma*, all attest the reality of this awakening.  Within the next few months many more papers are to be expected; including an excellent one from Miss Lehr, a scholarly *Piper* from Mr. Kleiner, a brilliant first venture, *The Arcadian,* from Mrs. Jordan, and both a *Vagrant* and a *Monadnock* from Mr. Cook. Mr. Cook makes a truly philanthropic offer to print small papers at reasonable rates, and it is to be hoped that a large number of members will avail themselves of it, communicating with Mr. Cook regarding particulars.[1] His address is 451 Main St., Athol, Mass.

Recruiting proceeds steadily if not with meteoric rapidity, some excellent material having been obtained since the beginning of the year's campaign. The most serious defect in our system is the lack of a general welcome shewn the new members, particularly as regards the distribution of papers. One of our most important recruits of last July, now a responsible officer, declares he has seen but a fraction of the papers issued since his entrance; a fact indicating a censurable but easily remediable condition. Let us impress it upon ourselves, that if we would do our full share toward maintaining the Association and its literary life, we must see that all our respective publications reach *every* member new or old. A considerable part of our yearly losses in membership are undoubtedly due to the indifferent reception which so many gifted newcomers receive.

The general signs of the times are bright and encouraging. A renascent amateur press, a closer coöperation between members, an influx of interested recruits, and an improved state of relations with our contemporaries, are but a few of the good omens which promise to make the coming year a pleasing and profitable one.

EDITOR'S NOTE FP: *United Amateur* 17, No. 2 (November 1917): 29–30 (signed "H. P. LOVECRAFT, President," and dated October 28, 1917). The second of HPL's reports. He continues to discuss the 1916–17 Year Book (never published, although by its description here it contained invaluable information on the amateurs of the period) and praises renewed publishing activity by the members.

*Notes*

1. See further *SL* 1.49–50.

# PRESIDENT'S MESSAGE

*(January 1918)*

Fellow-Amateurs:—

The dawn of the new year discovers the United in what may, considering the general condition of the times, be called a very enviable position. With a full complement of officers, and with the recruiting machinery fairly under way, our course seems clear and our voyage propitious.

The November Official Organ deserves praise of the highest sort; and will remain as a lasting monument to the editorial ability of Miss McGeoch and the mechanical good taste of Mr. Cook. It has set a standard beneath which it should not fall, but to maintain which a well-supplied Official Organ Fund is absolutely necessary. If each member of the Association would send a dollar, or even less, to Custodian McGeoch, this Fund might be certain of continuance at a level which would ensure a large and regularly published *United Amateur*.

The publication of lists by new and prospective members should arouse every amateur to recruiting activity, and cause each newcomer to receive a goodly number of letters, papers, and postcards. It would be well if the line of demarcation between Recruiting Committees and the general amateur public were not so sharply drawn; for whilst it is the duty of the official recruiter to approach these new names, any other members confer no less a favour on the United by doing so unofficially. We must remedy the condition which permits able writers to join and pass out of the Association almost without a realisation of the fact of their membership. How few of those gifted amateurs who entered in 1915–1916 are now with us!

Publishing activity is strikingly exemplified by the appearance of *Spindrift,* a regularly issued monthly from the able pen of Sub.-Lieut. Ernest Lionel McKeag of the Royal Navy. When a busy naval officer in active service can edit so excellent a magazine as this, no civilian should complain that the present war has made amateur journalism an impossibility! The number of papers expected in the near future has been increased by a plan of the Second Vice-President to unite the members of the Recruiting Committee in a coöperative editorial venture. It is to be hoped that this enterprise may succeed as well as similar papers conducted during former administrations. Of great interest to the literary element will be Mr. Cook's contemplated volume of laureate poetry, containing the winning pieces of all our competitions from the establishment of Laureateships to the present time.

The Association extends its heartiest congratulations, individually and collectively, to ex-Pres. Campbell and Treasurer Barnhart, who were most auspiciously joined in wedlock on Thanksgiving Day. Its heartfelt sympathy is transmitted to relatives of the late Rev. W. S. Harrison, whose death on December 3d left a vacancy in the ranks of stately and spiritual poets which cannot be filled.

A final word of commendation should be given to those more than generous teachers, professors, and scholars who are making "The Reading Table" so pleasing and successful a feature of the United's literary life. The idea, originated by Miss McGeoch, has been ably developed by Messrs. Moe and Lowrey, and is likely to redeem many of the promises of real progress which have pervaded the Association during the past few years.

EDITOR'S NOTE    FP: *United Amateur* 17, No. 3 (January 1918): 48–49 (signed "H. P. LOVECRAFT, President," and dated January 2, 1918). The third of HPL's reports.

# DEPARTMENT OF PUBLIC CRITICISM

*(January 1918)*

*The Bema* for January marks the revival of Mr. Edward H. Cole's able editorial sheet, devoted to amateur administrative matters not exactly appropriate for the more formal and classical *Olympian.* We believe this revival to be a very wise step on Mr. Cole's part, since it will permit him to present his views at times when the issuance of an *Olympian* would be impossible. The high standard of the latter may be preserved untainted, yet the editor need not always remain silent till he is able to publish a magazine of that size and grade. The current issue reveals Mrs. Cole as a co-editor, and in a sense a representative of the United as Mr. Cole is of the National.

"Give", the opening article, is by Mr. Cole, and though applied to National affairs will serve equally well as a homily for United members. A further editorial by Mr. Cole is "The Current Year", which covers both associations in an intelligent résumé of conditions, and concludes with some pointed and valuable remarks on the status of amateur journalism as a whole in war time. The views there expressed are based on very sound sense; for no judicious amateur could wish to see his hobby crushed out completely by the stress of the period. Amateurdom indeed has its legitimate place amongst the necessary recreations, and will doubtless serve to stimulate many a war worker to greater and better effort through the mild and pleasing relaxation it affords. Its enthusiastic support by members actually in military and naval service, is enough to demonstrate its propriety and beneficent effects at this time. Mr. Cole is to be thanked for his clear statement and sound opinion.

Mrs. Cole's leading contribution is entitled "The United's Constitution", and displays her in her official capacity as Supervisor of Amendments. It is her desire to reconcile our constitution to actual needs and practice as far as possible, without removing all activity obligations on the part of officers; and in this desire she will doubtless be followed by a large number of members. Though enforcement of the activity clause is just now obviously impossible, it may be well not to remove it altogether; but to continue in our present mode of allowing it to lie dormant on the statute book until some happier day shall restore normal conditions in amateurdom. Debate on the proposed amendment, which will doubtless follow its publication in the current *United Amateur,* will elicit many views and help clear the situation.

"Hooverizing Amateur Journalism", by Mrs. Cole, is a wily and ingenious scheme for replenishing our depleted treasuries through a strict programme of domestic economy.

The current *Bema,* as welcome as it was unexpected, may well be taken as a suggestion for our publishers in general. Brief and unostentatious sheets of this sort would be very acceptable from the many members who are unable to issue more elaborate publications.

The *Brooklynite* for November is not a large paper, but its quality more than atones for its quantitative slenderness. The opening and closing features are two poems of exquisite workmanship; "Raymond Pratt Adams", a tribute to one of amateurdom's youngest generation, and "What It Means", an amatory lyric of phenomenal grace and delicacy. Since these pleasing contributions are unsigned, they may safely be attributed to the editor, Mrs. Alice L. Lewis, who is known to be a bard of the highest order.

"Personal Work in Amateur Journalism", by Helene Hoffman Cole, is a well-phrased presentation of some sensible and opportune truths and hints for active amateurs. The author's success in literary and administrative efforts lends weight to her remarks, and renders her precepts worthy of close following.

"Life's Mysteries", a piece of metrically correct verse by Emolyn G. S. Isaacson, reflects with somewhat grim humour the superficial and none too patriotic feelings of the masses regarding the war and its effects. The attempt to group the status of the Huns with that of the Allied powers in the struggle strikes one a little unpleasantly. The present war is anything but an attempt to "settle selfish squabbles"; never since the barbarism attacks on Rome has there been a more clearly defined defensive effort to ensure the existence of liberal civilization against the ravages of powerful and ruthless adversaries.

"Intensive Gardening", an oddly whimsical sketch by Katherine B. Collier, furnishes a delightful burlesque on the various elaborate and unpractical hints for agricultural success which appear with such minute precision in various papers and magazines. Its unsmiling gravity of style suggests the gentle humour of Mr. Addison, who scorned to raise a laugh by means of ostentatious verbal hilarity.

The editorial column and news notes of the current issue all redound to the credit of the editor, and stamp *The Brooklynite* as one of the most delightful of amateurdom's permanent institutions.

*The Coyote* for October is announced as possibly the final number, since the editor has well-defined military intentions, and may choose the camp in preference to the sanctum before many weeks have passed. We trust, however, that he will reconsider his farewell, nor allow his soldierly duties to crush his journalistic efforts *in toto*. As precedents for soldier and sailor editors he need look no farther than Messrs. McKeag and Yaldren of our own Association, who are issuing excellent publications despite their engagement in the noblest and manliest of callings. We may here remark in passing, that Mr. Harrington's description of himself as a "Wilson conscript" is a trifle erroneous. His registration for the draft is but the preliminary of actual conscription, and if his present plans mature, it is more than likely that he will enjoy the more notable distinction of being a volunteer. The United extends to Mr. Harrington its proudest felicitations on his coming adventure.

The current *Coyote* opens with "Lights Out", a meritorious and intensely emotional poem by Olive G. Owen. Miss Owen's position as the Sappho of Amateurdom seems well assured, her lines all reflecting the passion and polish proper to a cultivated lyricist. If any objection might be offered, it is to her frequent employment of typographical devices in conveying strong emotion. The natural glow of the heart should, it seems to us, be able to blaze forth without the aid of italics, parentheses, and dotted lines. However, since critics have no hearts, we cannot speak with complete authority on such a nice question.

In his article on "Publishing an Amateur Paper", Editor Harrington initiates us into the mysteries of his craft with considerable skill and smoothness. His right to define the true amateur spirit is well proven by his own evolution since joining the United.

"A New Era" displays Mr. Harrington as a religious enthusiast; and while his conclusions are scarcely in accord with the enlightened mind, none may gainsay the soundless of the virtues he prescribes. We do not quite agree with the author that Germany's materialism caused the war. We believe that German theological conceptions are equally responsible. Religion is a thing of many aspects and interpretations, and according to the sanguinary precepts of the Old Testament, not even the worst of the Hun's atrocities are necessarily irreligious. Indeed, in the martial madness of the Kaiser and his minions we may discern more than a trace of the blind religious mania which covered the Middle Ages with the blood of unnumbered martyrs. Sound reason and good sense outvie the church in proclaiming the equal folly and criminality of the Prussian course.

"China, Japan, and Corea" is a terse essay which reveals Mr. Harrington's command of political and economic truths. Whether or not he is unjust to the rising Japanese nation is something which only subsequent history will prove.

"The Oncoming Autumn", by W. Alvin Cook, is a very poetical piece of prose, whose images and sentiments are not altogether unfamiliar. If we lived as far South as Mr. Cook, we should share his emotions, but Autumn in the North is no occasion for rejoicing.

Mildred LaVoie, in "The Song of a Poet", likewise presents poetical ideas of not unaccustomed tone in the medium of graceful prose. It is indeed true that the poet can extract rare beauty from the commonplace, yet we wish the progressive bards of this generation were not so exclusively confined to that unaspiring realm.

"The Narrow Street", by Winifred Virginia Jordan, mirrors the regret of the urban denizen at the passing of that untrammelled Nature which once reigned supreme "where the crooked narrow street winds and twists and turns". The sentiment is a universal one, except in those confirmed Cockneys to whom bustle and artificiality have become idols. The technique of the present piece shows no deficiency, and the images are without exception tasteful and appealing.

Altogether, the October *Coyote* is a typical amateur paper of sterling merit. Ably edited, home printed, and filled with an abundance of acceptable literature, it combines the virtues of the old and new schools of amateurdom.

Down in the fair municipality of Tampa, just across the bay from our St. Petersburg editorial offices, there dwells a youth yclept Raymond B. Nixon, who was introduced to the pleasures of amateur journalism some two or three years ago. As editor of *The Dixie Booster* he deserved and received a considerable amount of praise, and bore a high rating amongst the active amateurs of the day. What, then, can prompt the savage attack which he makes upon the personnel of amateurdom in his November issue? Master Nixon is dissatisfied. This he makes quite clear. But in complaining of the inactivity of the present press associations it was by no means necessary for him to abandon politeness and good taste as he has done, and to forget the traditions of Southern courtesy in a brutal attack upon his elders.

Master Nixon maintains that amateur journalism should be confined to small boys who print little papers on little printing presses, and declares with fine contempt that contemporary amateurs are "unsuccessful adult writers who join for the purpose of inflicting their worthless junk upon the editors". Would he deny the privilege of expression to all who have not those peculiar gifts which enable them to reach the general public professionally? Obviously, he would; and in this denial reveals his ignorance of the impulse of artistic creation; an impulse keen and potent, though not always supported by the attributes essential to professional success. Very few of our writers are classifiable as "unsuccessful". The majority have not attempted professional careers, while a number have attempted them and succeeded in them. When Raymond is older, he will come to understand the singular value of amateur journalism to the persons now affiliated with the movement, for he is too bright a boy to cling to his present fallacy. In the meantime it would be well for him to remember his slender years, and to study the modes of restrained utterance observed amongst gentlemen.

Aside from the editorial column, the current *Booster* contains matter of considerable merit. Roy Welsey Nixon has substantial gifts in prose and verse alike, and with a little more technical polish would be able to assume among our leading writers. We welcome the *Booster,* and do not wish to be too harsh in dealing with its young editor; but his present course seems quite like a violation of hospitality. We trust that succeeding issues may display a more fraternal amenity.

The Autumn *Phoenician* has so thoroughly professional an aspect, that we almost hesitate to classify it as an amateur publication; but remembering the affiliations of its bustling young editor, James Mather Mosely, we acknowledge kinship. Without any pretence to the quality of literature, the briskly written contents reflect the crisp spirit of successful popular reading matter—the sort one buys in waiting rooms and reads on the train. In grasp of contemporary journalistic methods, Mr. Mosely is equalled only by Mr. Moitoret of the *Cleveland Sun* and navy fame. It is with a half sigh that we wish he might turn to the deeper, quieter ways of real literary art and craftsmanship.

*Spindrift* for September is the answer of invincible amateurdom to those pessimists who predict the downfall of the institution through the ravages of war. While our civilian members, enjoying the comparative ease of their homes, complain of the difficulty of these times; Sub-Lieutenant Ernest Lionel McKeag of the Royal Navy finds an opportunity to become a frequent publisher amidst the hardships of active service, and founds a magazine whose merit and regularity of appearance might well be emulated by any of us in the armchair brigade of civilisation's defence.

The principal feature of the September issue is the first instalment of a very interesting serial by the editor, entitled "A Mid-winter Night's Dream". This story, aside from its intrinsic interest and clever development, points a vivid and much needed moral to the various would-be Northcliffes and fireside strategists who sagely map out the conduct of the war and the condemn the errors of the naval and military forces from the snug security of their homes. It is an undeniable truth that the average citizen underestimates the enormous sacrifice made by the sailor or soldier, and the purely practical problems which prevent our armies and navies from achieving that instant victory which the theorist can plan with such ready facility. A notable feature of Lt. McKeag's story is a graphic and accurate description of life on a destroyer, a description drawn from actual experience. The stern reality contrasts sharply with the conceptions of those who have studied naval affairs only from attending performances of "H. M. S. 'Pinafore'".

Another story in this issue is "P. C. Jerikims' Cop", by R. H. Cragg. At this smoothly written piece must be directed the charge of triteness, for the situation is undeniably a very old one, which has served many a comic author in some form or other. Mr. Cragg possesses an excellent style, which will no doubt lend its animation to other and more original themes in the course of time.

"An Amateur's Recollections", by Pte. Joseph Parks, is one of those bits of history which delight the heart of the typical "old-timer". It would be interesting if other well-known amateurs were to narrate in similar style their childish literary and editorial attempts. Pte. Parks' present prominence amongst our fiction writers lends unusual interest to his reminiscences.

The only poem in the magazine is "Roll On", by Margaret Trafford. In spite of several obvious defects of metre, this little lyric possesses a deep and genuine poetic fervour which deserves no common praise. Miss Trafford, still a juvenile bard in point of years, may be expected to take high rank in the Heliconian galaxy of the next amateur generation. Her prime need at present is thorough drilling in the mechanical forms of versification, and it is to be hoped that she will spare no pains in developing the talent which she so abundantly exhibits.

*Spindrift* for October opens with an excellent poem by Vere M. Murphy, entitled "Yesterday". Its form is unusual, but two rhyming sounds extending through twelve lines, or three stanzas. The omission of a syllable from the first lines of the stanza, apparently intentional, also gives a singular effect of variety. The languid motion of the metre is well adapted to the gentle melancholy of the theme, though one line, which we will here append, seems less fluent than might be desired.

"The snow lies still pearling the grey twilight"

"The Tale of Books", by Benjamin Winskill, is just such a delightful essay as we might expect from its author's gifted pen. Mr. Winskill is very proficient in reflective themes of this nature, and possesses a style others might copy to advantage, except as regards long sentences such as that which comprises the entire third paragraph of the present essay.

*Spindrift* for November contains a very vivid prose sketch by Jean Birkmyre, entitled "In the Twilight". This "memory of the Highlands", as it is described, contains a multitude of appealing images presented in judiciously chosen language; and for all its prose form is more nearly a poem than many metrical or semi-metrical attempts of the present age.

"Children at Sea", a brief poem of heroic couplets by Vere M. Murphy, depicts strikingly one aspect of the present earth-wide calamity; and views the Hun-infested ocean from the standpoint of happy, careless childhood. The form and phraseology are handled with that good taste characteristic of the author, though certain lines will bear inspection metrically. Line 4, for instance, reads

"Blessed baby hearts, unshadowed by fear!"

Owing to the senseless modern practice in poetry of writing out pasts and praeterites in full, as in *"blessed"* instead of *"bless'd"*, and *"unshadowed"* instead of *"unshadow'd"*, when the elision is observed, we are unable to tell just how the author intends the syllables to be disposed. Probably the following is meant:

*"Bless'd* baby hearts, *unshadow-ed* by fear!"

If our contemporary writers insist on giving *"blessed"* when they mean *"bless'd"*, they should at least be consistent enough to place a diacritical mark over the *"e"* in verbs where they do desire the archaic syllable to be retained. Poetry, which so frequently resorts to archaisms, should in the interests of common sense be written with the marks of elision where elision is intended; but since fashion has weaned most authors away from the old custom, perhaps it is a waste of ink or breath to protest. In line 6,

"There's chatter of 'jumping in', 'tin-fish,' and 'fight'"—

Miss Murphy probably intends the phrase *"chatter of"* to be run into two syllables: *"chatt'r of"*, after the manner of many bards of the nineteenth and twentieth centuries.

This issue closes with the first instalment of a "follow-my-leader" serial, "The Mystery of Murdon Grange", contributed by Joseph Parks. Naturally this type of tale is more liable to develop interest than literary finesse, but Mr. Parks acquits himself very creditably in the opening. The United will watch with interest the progress of this fictional mosaic, and will be anxious to see what the various storytellers of amateurdom will make of the fertile theme presented them.[1]

*Spindrift* for December contains a very clever bit by B. C. Lewis, entitled "The Broken Reverie". Whilst the humour is not precisely new, it is nevertheless handled ingeniously and competently.

"The Mystery of the Murdon Grange" receives its second instalment from the not unpracticed hand of Miss Beryl Mappin, and continues in the pleasantly conventional channel mapped out by Mr. Parks in the preceding chapter. The plot thickens!

"Evening in the Himalayas", a poem by Vere M. Murphy, merits high praise; though a strict technician would frown upon the rhyme of *"harmonious"* and *"Angelus"*, which is made of syllables having only a secondary accent. Whilst one syllable of a rhyme may legitimately be one of secondary accent, both should not be.

Another poem of merit is "Dawn", by S. L. The present critic does not know the identity behind the initials, but will hazard a guess that it is *not* Mr. Samuel Loveman. Line 4 is marred by an extra syllable, and lines 8 and 9 each lack one.

Lieut. McKeag's editorial remarks are brief and to the point, rounding out a thoroughly commendable issue.

*The United Amateur* for November is the first literary number to be issued under the present regime, and it is not too much to say that the publication reflects credit of the brightest sort upon both editor and publisher. The cover is neat and tasteful; whilst throughout the magazine there is a harmony and good taste obtainable only by the judicious coöperation of an able editor and skilful printer.

The opening feature is "November", an exquisite poem in two stanzas from the cultivated pen of Perrin Holmes Lowrey. Work from such a source needs neither introduction nor comment, though we cannot help remarking the pure melody of the liquid lines, with their facile flow and carefully selected words. Mr. Lowrey is one whom no mere correctness satisfies. Besides a perfect command of metre, he demands a smoothness of sound which can be achieved only by virtue of a large vocabulary, and a tasteful ability to select words both for their sense and their phonetic value. His poetry is worthy of close study on the part of his fellow-members.

"A Reminiscence of Dr. Samuel Johnson" is an attempt at reproducing the style and atmosphere of a century and a half ago. The author, who wisely masks his identity under a *nom de plume*, seems to have a fair knowledge of archaic diction and Georgian literary history; yet never escapes from a certain stiffness and suggestion of forced composition. Incidentally, we may remark that the general style and spelling are rather pre-Johnsonian that Johnsonian.[2]

"The Celtic's Dream of His Erin Home" is a delightful bit of Irish dialect verse from the gifted pen of Jonathan E. Hoag. It has a homely verisimilitude which goes straight to the heart of the not too sophisticated reader, and we have been told that a discriminating Hibernian recently pronounced it to be a remarkably natural and appealing breath from Ould Sod. Mr. Hoag, it may be added, is a skilful reciter in brogue, so that his phonetic renderings are more accurate than those we frequently see in newspapers and magazines.

"Our Natupski Neighbors", by Helene H. Cole, is a graceful review of the well-known novel of Mrs. Edith Miniter.[3] Mrs. Cole has mastered the art of book reviewing to a phenomenal degree, and is expert in selecting the right extracts and making the most essential and pertinent comments.

"Yesterday", by Andrew Francis Lockhart, is a poem of appealing sweetness with a touch of sorrow. Mr. Lockhart is making rapid strides as a technician, and his simple lyrics should soon command respect not only in the amateur but in the professional world.

"The Reading Table", an educational course introduced by Official Editor McGeoch, is this month graced by a valuable contribution from Maurice Winter Moe. The same fine touch and insight which make Mr. Moe so successful a classroom instructor, appear very pleasantly in the article, and should serve to popularize literary research amongst our younger members.

Miss McGeoch's editorial is the most sensible summary yet made of the relations between the United and the National Associations. We believe, with her, that each has its own peculiar place, and that neither need attack or encroach upon the other. In the interests of harmony, belligerents on either side should be promptly silenced.

If the present standard of publication is maintained throughout the year, and it can be maintained if sufficient financial support is forthcoming, we believe that an unexcelled volume of *The United Amateur* will result. Never before have the qualitative regulations been so strict, nor has anything like "The Reading Table" been attempted in the past. Perusal of the November issue places us in a very optimistic mood.

In the case of so elaborate a publication as W. Paul Cook's *Vagrant* for November 1917, it is somewhat difficult to decide which feature first attracts attention and is most deserving of remark. The 92 pages of the present issue contain so many things in the way of verse, story, essay, and editorial, which hold the interest and awaken the admiration of the reader, that it is quite impossible even to enumerate them all. There is a particular abundance of verse, and when those verses are signed by names so familiar as Harriet L. Trieloff, Edna von der Heide, Olive G. Owen, Howard P. Lovecraft,[4] Rheinhart Kleiner, Arthur H. Goodenough, Ethelwyn Dithridge, Winifred Virginia Jordan, and others, we may at least be sure of the quality of such contributions. One or two of the bards represented are open to criticism because of certain evidences of haste to be found in their efforts, which are hardly to be forgiven when the experience or reputation of the writer is considered. John Osman Baldwin, for instance, mistakes assonance for rhyme when joins "*alone*" and "*home*"; to say nothing of more serious errors in the "*humanity*", *serenity*", and "*loyalty*" rhymes which occur in every fourth line throughout his poem.

O. Byron Copper, in "Susan Spreckles' Foxy Lover", makes practically the same mistakes. "*Too*" and "*two*" are no more correct, as rhymes, than "*hand*" and "*damned*". Mr. Copper, however has an undoubted command of metre, and his lines run trippingly from beginning to end.

Among the prose contributions, "People As They Seem and Are", by Pearl K. Merritt, leaves a distinct impression with the reader. In fact, this may be said of all Miss Merritt's essays which have appeared from time to time in various amateur papers. As an essayist Miss Merritt reveals her possession of humour, charm, and an unmistakable individuality. Her mastery of the intensely subjective essay is almost Elia-like, and certainly not equalled by any other amateur writer now in the field.

If Mr. Cook has shown discrimination in his choice of contributions to the *Vagrant*, he is even more successful as a writer of paragraphs in connexion with the amateur careers and events of other days, and as a judge of what is worthy of re-publication among his apparently inexhaustible files of letters and papers. Mr. Cook's precision in the matter of dates and names, and his passion for ascertaining all facts bearing on past literary or political history, mark him as a born archaeologist. The results of his various investigations are of genuine interest, and every amateur journalist much feel grateful to him for the patience and zeal he displays in his self-imposed task.

No attempt has been made here to do full justice to Mr. Cook's achievement in publishing the November *Vagrant*. Such an attempt would require more space than could be spared, but scarcely more than he deserved. Not only does the *Vagrant* take a very high place among the very best publications that have appeared since the last convention, but in more than one respect it surpasses them so easily that comparison is quite out of the question.

The *Woodbee* for October is a magazine of wonderful merit, reflecting the sound scholarship of its gifted editor, Mrs. Ida Cochran Haughton. Mrs. Haughton feels constrained to apologise because of the prevalence of material from the pens of members of her family, but she has no reason to do so, since it would be difficult to find better literature than that which she has used. "The Village", a delightful study by our Secretary, Miss Durr, is replete with vividness of atmosphere and delicacy of touch; though it is closely rivalled by the masterly bit of psychology from the hand of the editor, entitled "An Interpretation". Mrs. Haughton, in this production, displays a most sympathetic comprehension of the relation between the arts.

"The Spirit of Adventure", by Edna Mitchell Haughton, is vibrant with philosophic insight and alive with felicity of diction. In some respects it is quite Campbellian in its grasp of verities. It is to be regretted that Miss Haughton's reviews and essays do not appear with greater frequency.

The editorial comment, news notes, and other miscellaneous matter are of that high standard which one naturally expects from a writer of Mrs. Haughton's culture and attainments; and it is not too much for the impartial critic to say that her management of the *Woodbee* has set a new standard in correct and graceful editorship. The October number is an issue to which amateurdom may well point with pride as one of the most substantial achievements of the year.

EDITOR'S NOTE   FP: *United Amateur* 17, No. 3 (January 1918): 42–48 (unsigned). HPL notes (letter to Arthur Harris, 12 January 1918; ms., JHL) that Rheinhart Kleiner, whom HPL had appointed Chairman of the Department of Public Criticism for 1917–18, found that he was unable to serve, so that HPL wrote the articles for January, March, and May. Of particular interest is HPL's discussion of the round-robin story "The Mystery of Murdon Grange" (in *Spindrift*), which has long been believed to be a "lost" work by HPL (see further n. 1). HPL also praises Cook's *Vagrant* for November 1917.

*Notes*

1. HPL himself contributed at least one segment to this round-robin serial, although in his few mentions of it in his correspondence he seems to suggest that he wrote the whole of it under various pseudonyms, publishing it in his manuscript magazine, *Hesperia* (see SL 1.68).
2. The story is by HPL, published under his pseudonym "Humphry Littlewit, Esq."
3. Edith Miniter, *Our Natupski Neighbors* (New York: Henry Holt & Co., 1916).
4. HPL contributed the poem "To Greece, 1917" (AT 409–10) to the issue.

# PRESIDENT'S MESSAGE

*(March 1918)*

Fellow-Amateurs:—

As the second half of the official year progresses, we behold the United in excellent condition, though not marked by as great a degree of activity as might be desired. The official organ faithfully maintains its phenomenally high standard, the January issue indeed eclipsing all precedents; but a larger number of other papers must be published, if we are to make the present term as memorable quantitatively as it is qualitatively. An excellent example is set by Mrs. Jordan, whose newly established *Eurus* comes so opportunely. May this publication prove permanent, and of frequent appearance! Besides this, we are indebted to Miss Trafford, Lieut. McKeag, and Mr. Martin for a *Little Budget*, *Spindrift*, and *Sprite*, respectively. Several other papers are reported in press, including what promises to be a very remarkable *Vagrant*.

In order to increase the publishing activity of the Association, the administration will endeavour to arrange for the publication of one or more coöperative papers. Any United member able to contribute $1.50 or more to such an enterprise should communicate with the undersigned, who will attend to the details of issuance if a sufficient number of contributing editors can be obtained. $1.50 will pay for one page, 7 × 10, and each contributor is at liberty to take as many pages as he desires at that rate. Contributors may utilise their space according to their own wishes, and all will be equally credited with editorship. This plan, successfully practiced four years ago, should enable many hitherto silent members to appear in the editorial field to great advantage, in a journal whose contents and appearance will alike be creditable.[1]

The comparative scarcity of entries makes imperative a second warning regarding the new conditions in the Laureateship department. Ten persons must compete in any class before an award in that particular division can be granted, and at present no class contains an adequate variety of entries. Again it is urged that the members lose no time in submitting their printed literary productions to Mr. Hoag for entry.

A careful study of the four proposed constitutional amendments is necessary to ensure intelligent voting next July. The undersigned, as their author, naturally favours their passage; but the one providing for an abolition of the officers' activity requirements should not be adopted without ample opportunity for debate and interchange of views.

The congratulations of the Association are extended to Mr. and Mrs. Edward H. Cole upon the advent of a son, Edward Sherman Cole, on February 14. With equal sincerity the United felicitates ex-President Leo Fritter on his marriage to Miss Frances P. Hepner, March 6.

The United's 22nd annual convention will be held on July 22nd, 23d, and 24th, at the Dells of the Wisconsin River. Under the direction of Mr. Daas this event cannot fail to be of interest and pleasure to all delegates, and every member who finds attendance possible is urged to be present.

To commend the official board for its generous, harmonious, and industrious coöperation this year seems but a reiteration of a needless panegyric; yet it would not be just to conclude this message without some such expression of grateful appreciation. The enthusiastic and unswerving loyalty of all our leaders has been a constant shield against the adversity of these gloomy times, and has been wonderfully successful in maintaining the United at a high cultural level.

EDITOR'S NOTE   FP: *United Amateur* 17, No. 4 (March 1918): 70 (signed "H. P. LOVECRAFT, President," and dated March 8, 1918). The fourth of HPL's reports, in which HPL recommends the establishment of cooperative papers as a means of increasing publishing output among the members.

*Notes*

1. Under this plan, three issues of the *United Co-operative* (December 1918, June 1919, and April 1921), all with contributions by HPL, were published.

# Department of Public Criticism

*(March 1918)*

*The Little Budget* for October well sustains the worthy traditions of this ample, pleasing, and regularly issued monthly. Mr. Hilson's lines on "The Sabbath Day" exhibit a very commendable piety, and are in general smooth and acceptable. A few metrical irregularities, however, have crept in. Line 7 of the first stanza should have another syllable, whilst line 4 of the second stanza should have one less. Line 7 of the third stanza has a missing syllable, whilst 5 of the final stanza also lacks one. Certain members of our board of criticism would cavil at the use of the contraction *o'er*, in the fourth stanza; but the present reviewer does not believe so common and unobtrusive an expression can possibly be deemed offensively archaic or even excessively conventional. Certain masterpieces of literature, produced by all the ages, form an immutable standard of good rhetoric and classical diction which no evanescent fashions or changing customs of the moment can overthrow. *O'er* and kindred poetical forms are so firmly entrenched in the language of versification by long and illustrious usage, that any attempt at discrediting them must be taken as savouring a trifle of radicalism.

"The Man Who Didn't", by Fenella, is a serial story running through several numbers, and while not of striking force or originality, is nevertheless marked by a certain fluency and assurance which speak well for the author's future development.

Miss Ruth Blackwell's "Ode to Death" is a poem of marked power and excellent technique, exhibiting a complacent aspect of Epicurean philosophy.

"Le Manuel", by F. G., is undoubtedly the best short story which has hitherto appeared in the *Budget*, being marked by an appealing simplicity and unaffected pathos which closely approach the borders of genuine literature. In plot, development, and local colour, the tale is of truly professional quality and polish.

"The Victorious Knight", a piece of versification by Master John Drury-Lowe, is obviously juvenile work; yet exhibits poetical tendencies which may some day be successfully matured. At present we should advise Master Drury-Lowe to peruse and emulate the masters of literature with greater assiduity. In the first place, he has not given any very well-defined thought in all the sixteen lines of his piece. He states something, but not with any of the pointedness or colouring which alone form true poetry. In the second place, he is trite in expression, abounding in stock phrases. We have actually seen the precise line, "As the golden sun was sinking in the west", in other versified effusions. Not that the author copied it consciously, but that is a phrase so common as to be a time-honoured auxiliary of all writers who seek a maximum of rhetorical effect with a minimum of labour after originality. The diction is likewise artificial in the extreme, especially as regards the expletive *did*, in such expressions as "*did* stand", "*did* hold", "*did* rest", and so forth. Study of the easy classic writers would eliminate this tendency in Master Drury-Lowe. The metre of the composition is so irregular as to approach amorphousness; revealing a want of systematic prosody and syllable-counting, whilst the *morn-renown* rhyme is false. We do not desire to discourage Master Drury-Lowe, but merely offer these remarks in a constructive spirit. His later work will doubtless be free from those asperities which youth and inexperience now create.

"A Bit from Russia", by Goolia Lepeshkene, is an interesting and well-written glimpse into the social customs of an unfortunate ex-nation. Perhaps the childishness and superstitiousness of the Slavic character, as here described, have been leading factors in the rise of the hare-brained and visionary Bolsheviki, and the piteous collapse of civilisation in our former Ally.

"The Song of the Sea", by Margaret Mahon, is clever and forceful, though the metre might well be somewhat smoother, and the diction slightly more felicitous. The sentiment is to be applauded.

"The Pond", a fragment by Jean Birkmyre, has genuine tragic worth and vivid colouring, concluding the October *Budget* in very able fashion.

*The Little Budget* for November opens with Nell Hilliard's lines on "The Moon"; very smooth and meritorious in metre, though not exactly novel in theme of sentiments. The principal defect is the pleonastic line:

"But *yet* her light doth *still* entrance,"

which also contains an expletive, *doth,* whose use is scarcely to be encouraged. Miss Hilliard seems to possess a metrical ear much more correct than that of other young poets, her verse being almost a model for her fellow-aspirants so far as cadence is concerned. Such a gift should be supplemental by careful study of the best authors, and diligent cultivation of taste.

Miss Mappin's current article on Modern English Literature treats of Robert Burns, whose erratic and unfortunate career is sketched with considerable fluency and felicity. Two errors that demand notice are the use of *which* for *whom* in the 24th line on page 95, and the use of the impossible word *"enrichened"* for *enriched* on page 96.

"Sing Me a Song", a poem my Matthew Hilson, shows true poetic quality despite a certain all-pervading laxity of metre. We wish Mr. Hilson would cultivate that strict ear for versification which we noted above in connexion with Miss Hilliard's poem. His lines want definiteness and balance; the reader is not borne along readily on the current, but is conscious of a retarding roughness or deficiency in accentual stress. A greater evenness of syllabification, however, would remove many of the more obvious flaws in the present piece.

"The Stately Mountains", a remarkable poem by Rev. Eugene B. Kuntz, which first appeared *The Amateur Special,* was reviewed in these columns some time ago; hence we may now but reiterate the praise then accorded it. Dr. Kuntz's unique merit in the field of Nature poetry deserves a wider recognition in amateur journalism that it has yet obtained.

"The Little Book", a poem by Ruth Blackwell, is quite unusual in metre, containing some clever triple rhymes. The theme is a lyrical one, and is developed with a reasonable amount of skill, though a connoisseur of words and phrases would detect several inharmonious elements such as the more or less commonplace expression "visions grand".

"Padcroft", by the editor, is an interesting and well-written account of a Police Court Mission's home for boys; a charity in which the *Budget* is deeply and benevolently interested. One of the inmates, a lad named "Ginger" on account of his crowning glory, is very attractively and sympathetically described.

"Why the Willows Weep", by Jean Birkmyre, is a fairy tale of no little charm and merit; marked by that delicacy of style which is characteristic of its author.

"Snowball", by Mistress Molly Corcoran (aetat 9), is a very short and meritorious tale of a race horse. The youthful authoress shows a directness of style, and perception of dramatic values, which will serve her well in years to come.

*The Little Budget* for December is a generous Christmas number, opening with Mr. Matthew Hilson's poem on "Christmas Day Memories". The sentiment is meritorious and appropriate, though the metre could be improved by stricter attention to the details of syllabification.

"Appreciation", by W. Townsend Ericson, is a terse and acceptable moral essay, aptly embellished by a pleasing quotation.

"An American to the British Flag", by H. P. Lovecraft,[1] is the spontaneous sigh of a Rhode Island Anglo-Saxon as he reflects on the cosmopolitan decadence which has affected the scenes about him, and depressed New England beneath her ancient British standard of excellence. It is said to have been composed last year, as the author beheld the Old Flag flung to the breeze as a symbol of war-time alliance. The metre is regular and the rhymes correct, though there is no very distinguished merit in the effusion. In the last stanza a rather ludicrous impression is created by the misprinting of line 3, in which the word *thy* is given instead of *with*. According to the erroneous version, the face of the flag, not of the spectator, is wistful!

"Ye Christmas Bells", a poem by the editor, is marked by merit and smoothness.

"After the War", a thoughtful essay by Benjamin Winskill, contains much good sense, yet is not altogether without rhetorical awkwardnesses, such as "a nobility which, in their comfortable ease, they had not suspected the existence of". This phrase should thus be rectified: "a nobility whose existence they had not, in their comfortable ease, ever suspected".

*The Little Budget* for January is enlivened by Mr. Alfred H. Pearce's buoyant and delightful "Song of Cheer", whose rollicking metre is admirably well fitted to its subject. Mr. Pearce is to be commended upon his work, whose technique shows the hand of a clever and practiced writer.

"The Essays of a Dreamer", by W. Townsend Ericson, are virtuously didactic, and grammatically satisfactory except in one or two such instances as the following: "To be able to speak our thoughts was the reason for giving us tongues." Here is naught but confusion of parts; the sentence should be made coherent somewhat as follows: "The reason for giving us tongues, was that we might be able to speak our thoughts."

"To My Mother", by Nell Hilliard, exhibits that clear-cut metre which its author never fails to achieve, yet is not entirely flawless in its details. Owing to the archaism of the pronouns, the verbs should be archaic; hence *show*, in line 2 stanza 2 should be *show'st*, and so forth. Such trite phrases as "livelong day" are not to be recommended. The sentiment of the poem is just and acceptable.

"The Little Brother", by Norah Sloane Stanley, is a short story of remarkably polished development, with an almost professional atmosphere about it. Among the minor defects may be noticed the false verb-form *awoken*, which should be *awaked* or *awakened*, and the impossible description of a *crescent* moon rising in the *evening*. It is needless to say that when the moon is a crescent in the evening sky, it is always in the west, about to set; having risen during the preceding daylight hours. Conversely, the only time we may see the crescent rise, is during the moon's wane, in the early morning hours. Astronomical errors, however, are no unusual faults amongst fiction-writers; some very prominent authors having come to grief concerning the details of celestial mechanism.

"Crossing the Bay", by Joseph Parks, is a singularly vivid description of a stormy voyage, whose minute details and graphic colouring leave little doubt but that Mr. Parks has at some time actually participated in such a thrilling experience. The style shows much power, Nature's wilder moods being very realistically reflected in the words and paragraphs.

"The Night Is Wild", by Olive G. Owen, is a poem whose excellence would be manifest even if we did not know the author's name. Miss Owen, it may be remarked, is one of the only two poetical "Literati" in the United, according to the recent amendment giving this title to the winners of three laureateships in the same department. The co-recipient of this honour is Mr. Arthur Goodenough.

"The Critical Moment", by Henry Davison, Jun., is a story of great cleverness and humour, whose plot and situations are genuinely and unforcedly comic. The writer is to be congratulated. However, we must needs deplore the lamentably faulty grammar which permeates the entire composition, standing out in sharp contrast to the unusual merit of the theme and treatment. It behooves Mr. Davison, considering his gifts as an author, to acquire a correctness of syntax which may correspond with the excellence of his work.

*The Spectator* for September is not the original venture established in 1711 by Messrs. Steele and Addison, but one of the most pleasing and creditable of its numerous successors. Established in 1893, it has undergone a dormant period of considerable duration, now emerging once more under auspicious conditions. Its editor, Rev. W. W. Burton, is a writer of warmth and sincerity, with a philanthropic desire to inculcate virtue in a degenerate race of men. His precepts are deserving of wide attention and close obedience, and we trust that his influence will have a wide effect. "Of What Use Are Flowers" is a delightful sketch which displays Mr. Burton's aesthetic perception and refinement of fancy. "Change the Classification" and "Where Are We Drifting" lament with justice the degeneracy of the magazine press. Whether any direct remedy for decadent literature be possible, however, is a deeper question. The vices of the press are but those of mankind transferred to paper. Purify society, and literature will purify itself! Probably the best remedy for the times would be a witty and urbane satirist, like the founders of the very journal from which Mr. Burton's paper is named. The bulk of mankind are quickly bored by a sober-faced preacher or preceptor, but will listen to a cultivated jester. Let vice and folly be made ridiculous, as they were by Addison and Steele two centuries ago, and they will be laughed off the stage! Sundry other notes by Mr. Burton prove his qualifications for editorship, and make us hope that his paper will be a frequent visitor.

*Spindrift* for Christmas is both a surprise and a delight. Having seen the regular December number, we scarce hoped to be favoured again till January; but with characteristic energy and enthusiasm Lieut. McKeag has treated us to a mid-month number, thus establishing something of a record for frequency of publication!

"Mountain Mist", by Vere M. Murphy, is a delightful short poem whose sentiment and construction leave little to be desired. Miss Murphy easily claims a place amongst the leading bards of amateurdom, and we trust her contributions will appear with greater frequency not only in British but in American journals.

Mr. Benjamin Winskill continues "The Mystery of Murdon Grange" with much cleverness, carrying us back into the past for the source of a strange curse.

"A Christmas Fantasy", by Jean Birkmyre, is a sketch containing a multiplicity of beautiful thoughts and images, set forth with inimitable cleverness. The only point open to criticism is the introduction of *minarets* into a vision of the palace of St. Nicholas. These architectural features are so intimately characteristic of Mohammedanism and the Orient, that they must needs strike the reader strangely when connected with the presumably Northern and Gothic realms wherein our best beloved saint holds his abode.

"Snowflakes", by Joseph Parks, is a beautiful sketch of winter scenery which almost deserves a metrical setting. Mr. Parks has a rare sense of literary values which lends charm to his work both in fiction and in other forms of prose.

Editor McKeag furnishes an interesting editorial column this month, besides being (in all probability) responsible for the interesting and informative article on "Christmas at Sea". The signature of said article, "Sub-Loot", has a suspicious resemblance to Mr. McKeag's naval rank! We cannot cease without adding a tribute to the editor's cleverness in finding apt quotations to embellish his periodical. The brief extracts from Goethe and Shakespeare are both of singular appropriateness.

*The Sprite* for January is less ambitious in magnitude than the August number, but is distinguished by a merit truly Martinique. The admission of verse with dubious technique renders the average quality slightly lower than we are accustomed to expect from Mr. Martin, but for this ample atonement is made by the editor's impeccable prose article on "Shakespeare and Religion". The point which Mr. Martin makes in this polished "fragment" is one which should be appreciated by all students of the drama, especially those who are carried away with evangelical and other propagandist notions. The supreme master of the stage owes no small part of his universal appeal to his wise avoidance of extravagant doctrines and unsubstantial speculations. He transcribed Life as it is, with all its elements in due proportion, and in so doing achieved a fame which none can approach.

In "Ripples", a poem, Mr. John Osman Baldwin reserves the right to perpetuate an attempted rhyme of *rode* and *road*—an attempt which is impossible of success, since identical syllables cannot rhyme. Aside from poor technique, Mr. Baldwin is a bard of undoubted merit; some of his lines being distinguished by phenomenal grace and beauty. The present effort, indeed, flows with a truly Aonian felicity of fancies and images. Mr. Baldwin is a natural poet who should make every possible effort to improve and refine his art. It is almost provoking that one so gifted should reject so curtly every offer of assistance in technical training. However, the assiduity with which Mr. Baldwin 'reserves all rights' leads us to believe that he contemplates more ambitious ventures, wherein he must of necessity discard the crudity to which he now jealously clings.

The lines of J. Clinton Pryor are commendable in sentiment and fairly smooth in construction, though they lack a certain ethereal grace which may come with further practice. In the specimens here given we note one false rhyme, the attempt to couple *atones* with *homes*. Such lines as the following are hopelessly unpoetical, at least, so far as serious verse is concerned: "If I cheat myself, I'd like to know who wins."

In "Views Martinique", the editor regales us with that sensible comment on amateur affairs for which he is so justly celebrated, ably concluding one of the most pleasing and interesting amateur journals of the season.

EDITOR'S NOTE  FP: *United Amateur* 17, No. 4 (March 1918): 66–70 (unsigned). HPL devotes a large part of the column to a discussion of several issues of the British amateur journal, the *Little Budget of Knowledge and Nonsense.*

*Notes*

1. The text of this poem has not been located, as no copies of this issue of the *Little Budget* are known to exist.

---

# PRESIDENT'S MESSAGE

(*May 1918*)

Fellow-Amateurs:—

According to indications, the last few weeks of the United's administrative year will exceed their predecessors in general activity and work accomplished. The college recruiting campaign, delayed through an unavoidable combination of circumstances, is now taking definite form; and may be expected to shew some actual results even before the close of the present term, though its greatest fruits must necessarily be reaped by the next administration. General recruiting is on the increase, and a more satisfactory number of renewals and reinstatements is noted.

One of the greatest obstacles to be combated during this unsettled era is the mistaken notion that amateur journalism is a non-essential and a luxury, unworthy of attention or support amidst the national stress. The prevalence of this opinion is difficult to account for, since its logic is so feeble. It is universally recognised that in times like these, some form of relaxation is absolutely indispensable if the poise and sanity of the people are to be preserved. Amusements of a lighter sort are patronised with increased frequency, and have risen to the dignity of essentials in the maintenance of the national morale. If, then, the flimsiest of pleasures be accorded the respect and favour of the public, what may we not say for amateur journalism, whose function is not only to entertain and relieve the mind, but to uplift and instruct as well? Mr. Edward H. Cole has ably treated this matter in his recent *Bema*, and no one who thoughtfully reviews the situation can dispute the force and verity of his conclusions. As Mr. Cole points out in a later communication, war-time amateur effort must of course be less elaborate than in pre-war days; but amateurdom itself is now worthy of double encouragement, rather than discouragement, since by its soothing and steadying influence it becomes a source of calm and strength, and therefore an active factor in the winning of the war. Let us on this side of the Atlantic view the rejuvenescence of British amateurdom after four years of warfare, as exhibited in the formation of the prosperous Amateur Press Club by Messrs. Winskill and Parks. The moral is not hard to deduce.

Of the new publications of the season it is hard to speak without using superlatives, since Mr. Cook's epoch-making June *Vagrant* is among their number. This veritable book of 148 pages and cover constitutes the greatest achievement of contemporary amateurdom, and may legitimately be considered as one of the outstanding features in the recent history of the institution. It is the one product of our day which will bear actual comparison with the publications of the departed "Halcyon" period. A July *Vagrant*, of equal quality though lesser size, may be expected in the near future. A newcomer to our list of journals is *The Silver Clarion*, issued by Mr. John Milton Samples of Macon, Ga., a promising poet, essayist, and editor, who has just entered the Association. The *Clarion*, whose contents are distinguished for their wholesome tone and pleasing literary quality, is a regularly issued monthly, and forms a substantial addition to the literature of the United. Another welcome paper is *The Roamer*, published by Mr. Louis H. Kerber, Jr., of Chicago. This journal, devoted exclusively to travel articles, will occupy an unique place in the United. Among the papers to be expected before the close of the official year are a *Dabbler* from Mr. Lindquist and a *Yerma* from Mr. J. H. D. Smith, now a soldier in the service of his country at Camp Laurel, Md.

Responses to the proposal for a coöperative paper have been slow in coming in. Let the members once more reflect upon the advantages of the plan, and unite in an effort to increase the literary output of the Association.

The annual convention, to be held on the 22nd, 23d, and 24th of next July at the Dells of the Wisconsin River, may well be expected to stimulate interest to an unusually high pitch. A large attendance is urged, and since Mr. Daas is in charge of arrangements, the gathering will undoubtedly prove a bright spot in the year's programme.

EDITOR'S NOTE   FP: *United Amateur* 17, No. 5 (May 1918): 96–97 (signed "H. P. LOVECRAFT, President," and dated May 6, 1918). HPL attempts to combat the notion that amateur journalism is a luxury during the stressful period of the war.

# DEPARTMENT OF PUBLIC CRITICISM

*(May 1918)*

*Eurus* for February serves a double purpose; to introduce to the United in an editorial capacity the gifted poetess, Mrs. W. V. Jordan, and to commemorate the 87th natal anniversary of amateurdom's best beloved bard, Jonathan E. Hoag. The dedication to Mr. Hoag is both worthy and well merited. There are few whose qualities could evoke so sincere an encomium, and few encomiasts who could render so felicitous an expression of esteem. The entire production sustains the best traditions of Mrs. Jordan's work, and forms the most creditable individual paper to appear in the United since the dawn of the new year.

The issue opens with Mr. Hoag's stately and beautiful poem, "To the Falls of Dionondawa", which describes in an exquisite way the supposed history of a delightful cascade in Greenwich, New York. The lines, which are cast in the heroic couplet, have all the pleasing pomp and fire of the Augustan age of English verse; and form a refreshing contrast to the harsh or languid measures characteristic of the present day. Mr. Hoag beings down to our time the urbane arts of a better literary period.

"An Appreciation", by Verna McGeoch, is a prose-poetical tribute to Mr. Hoag, whose literary merit is of such a quality that we must needs lament the infrequency with this the author contributes to the amateur press. Of this piece a reader of broad culture lately said: "I have never read a production of this kind, more finely phrased, more comprehensive, more effective, and withal, so terse, and throughout, in such excellent taste." *Eurus* has good reason for self-congratulation on carrying this remarkable bit of composition.

"Chores", by Winifred Virginia Jordan, displays this versatile writer in a very singular vein; that of sombre, repellent, rustic tragedy. It has all the compelling power which marks Mrs. Jordan's darker productions, and is conveyed in an arresting, staccato measure which emphasises the homely horror of the theme. The phraseology, with its large proportion of rural and archaic words and constructions, adds vastly to the general effect and atmosphere. We believe that Mrs. Jordan analyses the New England rustic mind more keenly and accurately than any other amateur writer; interpreting rural moods and sentiments, be they bright or dark, with unvarnished simplicity and absolute verisimilitude, notwithstanding the fact that most of her verse is of a much more polished and classical character. In "Chores" we are brought vividly face to face with the bleakest aspect of rusticity; the dull, commonplace couple, dwelling so far from the rest of mankind that they have become almost primitive in thought and feelings, losing all the complex refinements and humanities of social existence. The poem intensifies that feeling of hidden terror and tragedy which sometimes strikes us on beholding a lonely farmer, enigmatical of face and sparing of words, or on spying, through the twilight, some grey, unpainted, ramshackle cottage, perched upon a wind-swept hill or propped up against the jutting boulders of some deserted slope, miles from the town and remote from the nearest neighbour.

"Young Clare", by Edith Miniter, is a narrative poem of that power and polish which might be expected of its celebrated author. The only considerable objection which could possibly be brought against it is a technical one, applying to the fourth line of the opening stanza:

> "To work a cabaret show"

Here we must needs wonder at the use of *work* as a transitive verb when the intransitive sense is so clearly demanded, and at the evident accentuation of *cabaret*. We believe that the correct pronunciation of *cabaret* is trisyllabic, with the accent on the final syllable, thus: "cab-a-ray". We will not be quite so dogmatic about *artiste* in line 2 of the last stanza, though we think the best usage would demand the accent on the final syllable.

"Gentle Gusts", the quaintly named editorial section, contains much matter of merit, clothed in a pleasantly smooth style. The classical name of the publication is here ingeniously explained, and its dedication formally made. The tribute to Mr. Hoag is as well rendered as it is merited. The editorial note on amateur criticism is sound and kindly; the author voicing her protests in a manner which disarms them of malice, and putting us in a receptive attitude. Personally, the present critic is in complete agreement with the remarks on poetical elision and inversions; but we are confident that those of our board who hold different views, will accept the dicta in the friendly spirit intended.

"Someone—Somewhere", by Jennie E. T. Dowe, is a delightful lyric by an authoress too well known in amateurdom to need an introduction. Mrs. Dowe writes with the polish of long experience and genuine culture, displaying an enviable poetic genius.

*Eurus* closes with some commendatory lines to Mr. Hoag from the pen of H. P. Lovecraft.[1] They are in heroics, and redolent of the spirit of two centuries ago. We discern no striking violations of good taste or metre, nor do we find any remarkable poetic power or elevation of thought.

The *Little Budget* for February and March is a double number, whose size and quality are alike encouraging. The issue opens with an ornate and felicitous Nature-poem by Rev. Eugene B. Kuntz, entitled "Above the Clouds", in which the author for once breaks away from his favourite Alexandrines and heptameters, presenting us with an equally beautiful specimen of the heroic quatrain. Despite the strong reasons which impel Dr. Kuntz to adhere to long measures, we believe he should compose more in pentameter. That his chosen metres have peculiar advantages, none will deny; but it seems plain that the standard shorter line has other advantages which amply outweigh them. It was not by chance that the line of five iambuses became the dominant metre of our language. In the present poem we discern a grace and flow far greater than any which could pervade an Alexandrine piece; a condition well shewn by parallel perusal of this and one of the same author's more characteristic efforts. As a creator of graphic, lofty, and majestic images, Dr. Kuntz has no peer in amateurdom. His sense of colour and of music weaves a rich and gorgeous element into the fabric of his work, and his sensitive literary faculty gives birth to happy combinations of words and phrases which not only please the imagination with their aptness, but delight the ear with their intrinsic euphony.

"The Drama as a Medium of Education", by Lieut. Ernest L. McKeag, is a short but terse essay on a neglected factor in liberal culture. It is true that our ordinary curricula lay all too little stress on dramatic art; and that as a result, this branch of aesthetic expression is grossly and consistently undervalued. The low estimate of the dramatic profession entertained by Dr. Johnson is a sad illustration of the one-sided state of mind prevailing even amongst scholars, concerning an art which is certainly not inferior to painting and sculpture, and probably much superior to music, in the aesthetic and intellectual scale.

"The Wizard of the North", an essay on Sir Walter Scott, is the current instalment of Miss Mappin's Modern Literature Series. It is marred by a seeming hiatus, discernible not so much in the flow of words as in the flow of the narrative, which leads us to believe that a considerable portion has been left out, either through accident, or through an attempt at abridgement.

"My Books", by Alfred H. Pearce, is a sonnet of apt idea and perfect construction.

"On Self-Sacrifice", by W. Townsend Ericson, is one of the "Essays of a Dreamer" which are regularly appearing in the *Budget*. The effort is marked by much sincerity and idealism, though in grammar and practicability it is less distinguished. We might mention the erroneous use of *whom* for *who* (a not uncommon defect amongst amateur writers), the faulty use of the word *usurping* where *depriving* is meant, and the split infinitive "to at least make"; all three of which mistakes occur on page 138. Mr. Ericson should drill himself more thoroughly in the principles of syntax. Other essays of this series are included in the present issue. "On Contentment" gives an illustration which we fear will injure Mr. Ericson's contention more than it will aid it. It is the *reductio ad absurdum* of the typical "Pollyanna" school of philosophy.

"Down an' Out", by Ernest L. McKeag, is a very clever ballad of the "rough and ready" school; picturesque in atmosphere, but somewhat defective in technique. Lieut. McKeag should pay a trifle more attention to his rhymes; which are not, however, worse than many of the rhymes in "Hudibras" and other comic pieces.[2]

"Why Roses Are White," a children's story by Margaret Mahon, is marked by much grace and ingenuity; the central idea being quite original so far as we know. Further contributions to the children's department are made by Miss Birkmyre, whose woodland sketches will be appreciated by older readers as well.

"Selfish Ambition", a poem by Nell Hilliard, is as correct and fluent in metre as we might expect from the author, though the expletive *does* in the final line of the first stanza is not to be commended. The sentiment is not precisely novel, but is well presented.

"The Flying Dutchman", a Romance of the Sea, by Joseph Parks, is more replete with nautical verisimilitude than with literary force. As compared with many of Mr. Parks' other tales, its plot is distinctly weak and lacking in symmetry. We must, however, praise the generally salty atmosphere. The picture of seafaring life is vivid and realistic.

The current *Budget* concludes with a summary of the year just closed, displaying a record of achievement of which the editors may well be proud.

*The Silver Clarion* for March is the publication of John Milton Samples, of Macon, Ga., a new member of the United. In tone the paper is quite serious and strongly inclined toward the religious; but so able are the majority of its contributions, that it lacks nothing in interest.

"Singing on the Way", a poem by James Larkin Pearson, opens the issue in attractive fashion. The lines are tuneful and felicitous, the triple rhymes giving an especially pleasing effect; though we must criticise the line

"Will certainly provide for us"

as being a trifle prosaic. We should recommend "plenteously provide", or something of that nature, as more poetic. Mr. Pearson is a poet of ability and experience, with a volume of published verse to his credit, whose work never falls below a high standard of merit.

"Just Icicles", by Sarah Story Duffee, is a sort of fairy tale with a juvenile exterior; which contains, however, more than a slight hint of the vanity of human wishes and fruitlessness of human endeavour. Whilst it exhibits no little cleverness in construction, we must own that it possesses a certain looseness, insipidity, and almost rambling quality, which detracts from its merit as a piece of literature. Mrs. Duffee would profit from a closer study of classical models, and a slighter attention to the more ordinary folk tales.

"The Blessings of Thorns", by Sallie M. Adams, is a religious poem of considerable excellence, containing a pious and worthy sentiment well expressed. The chief defects are technical. In the first stanza, line 3 lacks a syllable, whilst line 4 has one too many. Also, the *day-way* rhyme is repeated too closely. To have but one rhyming sound through two rhymes is a fault hard to excuse. All the defects above enumerated might be removed with ease, as the following revised version of the opening lines illustrates:

> When we thank our Heav'nly Father
>    For the boons each day bestow'd;
> For the flowers that are scatter'd
>    O'er the roughness of the road.

In the third stanza we find the *day-way* rhyme again repeated, also a superfluity of syllables in the sixth line. The latter might be cut down by the omission of the second *the.*

"Springtime in Dixieland", by John Milton Samples, is a tuneful pastoral which justifies the author's right to his first two names. But one or two defects mar the general delightful effect. The phrase "zephyr breeze", in the opening stanza, strikes us as a trifle pleonastic; since a *zephyr* is itself a *breeze;* not a quality of a breeze. The syntax of the latter part of this stanza is somewhat obscure, but might be cleared up if the seventh line were thus amended:

"And save when cloud-ships cross their track."

The sixth and seventh lines of the last stanza each have a syllable too many, and in line 6 the word *raise* is used incorrectly; *rise* being the word needed. This, of course, would necessitate a change of rhyme.

"One Face Is Passing", by Mamie Knight Samples, is a timely and excellent sketch concerning soldiers.

"Co-ee", a poem by Harry E. Reiseberg, contains much genuine pathos, and is generally smooth and commendable in technique.

"The Likeness of the Deity", by Arthur H. Goodenough, is one of the characteristically excellent products of its author, who holds the proud rank of "Literatus" in the United. The amount and quality of Mr. Goodenough's work is very unusual; few other amateurs producing so much verse of the first order. As a religious poet, he stands alone; resembling the celebrated Dr. Watts. He invests every theme he touches with an atmosphere truly and richly poetic.

"Astral Nights", by John Milton Samples, is a genuinely poetic piece of prose arranged in lines resembling those of verse. We believe that the loftiness and excellence of this composition would justify its metamorphosis into real verse.

Also by Editor Samples is the prose sketch entitled "The Present War a Blessing in Disguise". From the title, one would expect Mr. Samples' point of view to be akin to that of the esteemed Gen. von Bernhardi;[3] but such is not the case, since Mr. Samples means to say that he considers the conflict a just Divine Punishment for a sinful world—a punishment which will bring about a sinless and exemplary future. We wish it were so.

"Lord, Keep My Spirit Sweet", by Mr. Samples, is a religious lyric of substantial charm and grace.

The Editorials in this issue consist mainly of critical notes on previous numbers, and in general show a gratifying soundness of opinion.

*Spindrift* for January opens with "Mater Dolorosa", a poem by Vere M. Murphy, whose sentiment and technique are alike deserving of praise.

"The Spirit of January", a sketch by Jean Birkmyre, runs into the February issue, and is quite acceptable from every point of view, though not distinguished by that highly imaginative colouring which we find in many of Miss Birkmyre's similar pieces.

"The Mystery of Murdon Grange" this month falls into the hands of Editor McKeag, who furnishes one of the best chapters we have so far perused; possibly the very best. It is exasperating to be cut off abruptly in the midst of the exciting narrative, with the admonition to wait for page 47!

*Spindrift* for February has as its leading feature an essay on "Heredity or Environment", by the Editor. In this brief article many truths are stated, though we fear Lieut. McKeag slightly underestimates the force of heredity. We might remind him of the Darwin family, beginning with the poet and physician, Erasmus Darwin. The grandson of this celebrated man was the immortal Charles Darwin, whilst the sons of Charles have all occupied places of eminence in the world of intellect.

"To the Enlisted Men of the United States", by Edna Hyde,[4] is an ode of admirable spirit and faultless construction.

"A Fragment", by S. L. (whose identity is now known to us!), shews much poetical ability, though the metre would move much more smoothly if judiciously touched up here and there. The description of the crescent moon *sinking* in the morning, is astronomically erroneous.

"The Estates of Authors", by Albert E. Bramwell, is a brief but informative article. As the late Dr. Johnson said of the Ordinary of Newgate's account, 'it contains strong facts'.

*Spindrift* for March very appropriately commences with a poem on that blustering month, from the pen of Annie Pearce. Apparently the piece is a juvenile effort, since despite a commendably poetic atmosphere there are some striking errors of construction. In the third line of the first stanza there is a very awkward use of the impersonal pronoun *one.* This pronoun has no place in good poetry, and should always be avoided by means of some equivalent arrangement. In the second stanza it appears that the authoress, through the exigencies of versification, has fallen into the paradox of calling the "fair green shoots" "roots"! Perhaps we are mistaken, but our confusion is evidence of the lack of perspicuity in this passage. A rather more obvious error is the evidently transitive use of the verb *abound* in the last line of this stanza. Be it known, that *abound* is strictly an intransitive verb!

"The Soul of Newcastle", an historical article by John M'Quillen, begins in this number; and describes the Roman period. We regret the misprint whereby the name *Aelii* becomes *Aelu.* The presence of a Hunnish *umlaut* over the *u* adds insult to injury! Mr. M'Quillen writes in an attractive style, and we shall look forward to the remainder of the present article.

"Heart Thirst", by Vere M. Murphy, is a very meritorious lyric, containing an ingenious conceit worthy of a more classical age.

As the literary contributions to the *United Amateur* for January are mainly in the form of verse, I shall devote most of my attention to them. Poetry, like the poor, we have always with us; but the critic is moved to remark, as he casts his mind over the last twenty years of amateur publishing activity, that on the whole the tone of amateur poetry is distinctly higher than it used to be. Banal verse we still have in larger amounts than we should; but the amateur journals of a decade or two ago had reams of it. On the other hand, they contained not a few poems with more than a passing spark of the divine fire. The promising fact is that in the poetry of today's journals we get much more frequent glimpses of this true inspiration. In passing, the critic cannot forbear calling attention to Mr. Kleiner's "Ruth" in the February *Brooklynite,* which attains the highest levels of lyric expression, although only the simplest of figure and diction are employed.[5] It is not often that one runs across a poem so simple and yet so pregnant with sincere emotion.

The first poem in the *United Amateur* arouses mixed feelings. "Give Aid", by Julia R. Johnson, presents a thought that cannot be too often or too strongly stressed in this gloomy old world. Mrs. Johnson, furthermore, has carved out her own poetic medium, alternating two tetrameter lines with a single heptameter, a most unusual combination. It is always a promising sign to find a new poet experimenting with unhackneyed verse forms, although the experiments may not always be happy ones. But a word about the thought of the poem. It is one of those "recipe" poems, so-called because it can be produced in almost unlimited quantities by any writer clever enough to follow the formula. Some day the critic is going to take enough time off to write a book of poetic recipes, and already he has his subject so well blocked out that he is sure his book will contain the fundamental ingredients of a great majority of the amateur poems now appearing. The poem under consideration belongs to the "glad" recipe, an off-shoot of the Pollyanna school of fiction, and true to type it contains its quota of "glad" ingredients, such as "cheer", "merry song", "troubles", and "sorrows", the last two, of course, for the sake of contrast.

"Astrophobos", by Ward Phillips,[6] is another recipe poem; although his recipe is so much more intricate that it is not to be recommended for the Freshman. The critic would denominate a poem composed according to this recipe, a ulalumish poem, as it has so many earmarks of Poe. True to type, it is ulaluminated with gorgeous reds and crimsons, vistas of stupendous distances, coined phrases, unusual words, and general touches of either mysticism or purposeless obscurity. Such a poem is a feast for epicures who delight in intellectual caviar, but is not half so satisfying to the average poetic taste as Mr. Kleiner's "Ruth".

Theodore Gottlieb's "Contentment" is a clever and readable working out in verse of Mr. Ruskin's theme in his "King's Treasures"; namely, the satisfying companionship of great books. My Gottlieb shows commendable control of the felicitous phrase, while the literary allusions with which his lines bristle mark a catholicity of taste entirely beyond the ordinary.

Metrical versions of the Psalms are not at all new; they are used, in fact, in Scotch Presbyterian churches in place of regular hymns. The poetic paraphrase of the first Psalm by Wilson Tyler is well done, and only in a few such phrases as "winds that blow" and "perish and shall not be blest", does he get dangerously near redundancy for the sake of rhyme and metre.

"A Thought", by Dorothy Downs, is a pretty little thought indeed, and prettily expressed, although the term "holiness divine" is strained when applied to a rose, and "we will be surprised" is frankly ungrammatical as a simple future in the first person. The *sine qua non* of all poetry is absolutely correct grammar and freedom from redundancy.

The bit of verse heading the War Items written by F. G. Morris, is quite adequate except for a lack of rhyme is the last line, where the form of the stanza leads the reader to expect a rhyme for "part".

Matthew Hilson's rhymed greeting to the United from across the water, is on the whole graceful and well done, and the United acknowledges its receipt with thanks.

One other piece of work in this number deserves especial mention. Alfred Galpin's "Mystery" introduces to the association a thinker more gifted for his years than probably any other recruit within recent years. This judgment is not based alone on the short article under consideration, but even this little piece of thought, if carefully analysed, is enough to stamp him as one who thinks with extreme facility in the deepest of abstractions, and who for expression of that thought commands a vocabulary of remarkable range. Mr. Galpin is going far in this world, and we hope that he will sojourn long enough with us so that we can feel that whatever glory he may attain will cast some of its rays upon the Association.

The editorial remarks in this issue of the United Amateur are worthy of close perusal on account of their graceful literary quality. Seldom has the critic seen the subject of the New Year so felicitously treated as in this brief study by Miss McGeoch. The author's mastery of appropriate words, phrases, and images, and her intuitive perception of the most delicate elements of literary harmony, combine to make the reader wish she were more frequently before the Association as a writer, as well as in an editorial capacity.

EDITOR'S NOTE  FP: *United Amateur* 17, No. 5 (May 1918): 91–96 (unsigned). In this report, HPL discusses such new amateur journals as the first (and, as it turned out, the last) issue of Winifred Virginia Jordan's *Eurus* and John Milton Samples' *Silver Clarion*.

*Notes*

1. "To Jonathan E. Hoag, Esq.: On His Eighty-seventh Birthday, February 10, 1918" (AT 342–44).

2. Samuel Butler (1613–1680), *Hudibras* (1663), a lengthy satiric poem in octosyllabic meter. HPL comments on Butler's occasionally bizarre rhymes in the essay "The Allowable Rhyme" (*Conservative*, October 1915; CE2).

3. Friedrich von Bernhardi (1849–1930), a retired German general, published a widely translated book, *Deutschland und der nächste krieg* (1912; Eng. tr. as *Germany and the Next War*, 1912), in which he argued that Germany had a "duty" to make war to rid the world of inferior races.

4. Edna Hyde was formerly Edna von der Heide. Evidently she found it prudent to change her name to something less German-sounding.

5. HPL responded to the poem with "Grace" (*Conservative*, July 1918; AT 231).

6. The poem is by HPL. See AT 29–30.

---

# COMMENT

One of the rarest things in all the field of contemporary amateur journalism is the paper with a policy. Of publications, and of excellent publications, there are a great number; but latterly the universal desire to give as many authors as possible a hearing, has caused editors to throw open their columns indiscriminately, so that the papers of the day, wherever and whomever issued, present but little variety. In fact, the different journals might well be thought issues of the same journal, so far as the identity of the contributors and the general tone are concerned. Individuality is at a premium. Exceptions to this rule have hitherto occurred mostly amongst the smaller individual publications, but at last we behold an ample and regularly issued amateur monthly which bears the most undeniable stamp of fixed policy and original ideas. In *The Silver Clarion*, edited and published by Mr. John Milton Samples of Macon, Ga., amateurdom possesses an able and consistent exponent of that literary mildness and wholesomeness which in the professional world are exemplified by *The Youth's Companion* and the better grade of religious publications. Rigorously excluding every trace of levity, sensationalism, or worldly sophistication, Mr. Samples presents us with a monthly treat of refreshing simplicity, prepared by a specially selected staff of writers, many of whom are new to the associational world. Prominent among these writers is Mr. Samples himself, who possesses more than common genius in prose and verse alike.

In the April *Clarion* we discover, besides a generous assortment of portraits of editors and contributors, a large quantity of meritorious literary matter. Considering the season, it is natural that a majority of the poets should choose gentle spring's ethereal mildness for their theme. Kate Fort Codington presents a delightful little word picture whose only possible defect is a paucity of rhyme. In brief snatches of song like this, it is very desirable to give the verbal structure as perfect and as polished an artistry as the thought; and to this end a musical frequency of rhyme is very valuable. The writer believes it is not too much to say that no line of such a piece should be left unrhymed; though this statement will doubtless excite dispute. Editor Samples' two spring poems are of very pleasing quality. In "The Birth of Spring" a greater variety of rhymes would be a decided improvement, the -*inging* sound being repeated too soon. This difficulty could be overcome by substituting a *flowing-throwing* rhyme in lines 4 and 5. "April Showers" is a thoroughly excellent succession of apt metaphors. Still another spring poet is Mrs. Julia C. B. Webb, whose piece entitled "With Honeysuckle Growing" is the longest poem in the magazine. This captivating pastoral is marred by but one technical error, the rhyming of a syllable with itself in stanza 3. Poetical novices must always remember that just as the final consonants of a rhyme must be *alike*, so must the initial consonants be *different*. "Easter Thoughts", by Sarah Story Duffee, is a religious poem of acceptable sentiment and correct metre, reminiscent of the celebrated Dr. Watts. "Longing", by Mamie Knight Samples, presents many irregularities of metre, though the rhymes are without exception perfect. The thought is scarcely novel, but is very felicitously presented. If Mrs. Samples would select one unvarying metrical plan, then count her syllables very carefully in order to conform to it, the present asperities would undoubtedly be avoided. Arthur H. Goodenough, veteran amateur poet and honoured Literatus in the United, pays Editor Samples a highly artistic and fervent tribute in his lines entitled "Singer of the Silver Lyre". To comment on the excellence of Mr. Goodenough's verse is almost unnecessary, for few amateurs have equalled him in natural grace and sustained inspiration.

Of the prose contents of the April *Clarion*, the most notable piece is Editor Samples' reverie on the present world-wide war. The eloquence and fluency of this sketch deserve especial praise, being excellent material for oratory if recited aloud. One flaw to be noted is the slightly erroneous rendering of the quotation "The time is out of joint", from *Hamlet*.[1] Mr. Samples' omission of the article gives the extract a somewhat different apparent significance. Another defect is the use of the world *convulsive*, instead of *convulsed*, in the description of the human heart caused by the war.

Fiction is represented by one short story and the first instalment of a serial. "Her Ain Countree", by Loyce Weed Clay, is a smoothly written war tale of fairly familiar type. Much skill is observable in the technique, though the machinery creaks a little at the point where the shelling of the hospital forms a break in the narrative. The continuity should be interrupted a little more decidedly, possibly by a spacing or a division of the story into Parts I and II. "Tying Her Noose", by Sarah Story Duffee, begins most promisingly, having an informality of style very appealing to the average modern reader. In local colour and attention to detail, it reveals considerable story-telling genius.

As a whole, *The Silver Clarion* forms a valued and distinctive addition to amateur letters. High in ideals, increasingly urbane in atmosphere, and neat in appearance, it is a paper of which the press associations may well be proud. To its gifted editor, we may with justice repeat the couplet of Mr. Goodenough:

> "Yours is an ascending star,
> Whoso follows shall go far!"

EDITOR'S NOTE FP: *Silver Clarion* 2, No. 3 (June 1918): 6–8. A flattering survey of the early issues of the *Silver Clarion*, which HPL found distinctive in its conscious editorial policy emphasizing wholesomeness and piety. HPL would later contribute his first autobiographical statement to the magazine ("The Brief Autobiography of an Inconsequential Scribbler" [April 1919]), along with numerous poems, among which is the otherwise anomalous "Wisdom" (November 1919), a paraphrase of a chapter from the Book of Job.

*Notes*

1. Shakespeare, *Hamlet* 1.5.188.

# PRESIDENT'S MESSAGE

*(July 1918)*

Fellow-Amateurs:—

The conclusion of an administrative year is naturally a time for retrospection rather than for announcement and planning, and seldom may we derive more satisfaction from such a backward glance than at the present period.

The United has just completed a twelvemonth which, though not notable for numerousness of publications or expansion of the membership list, will nevertheless be long remembered for the tone and quality of its literature, and the uniformly smooth maintenance of its executive programme. The virtual extirpation of petty politics, and the elimination of all considerations save development of literary taste and encouragement of literary talent, have raised our Association to a new level of poise, harmony, dignity, and usefulness to the serious aspirant.

Prime honours must be awarded to our Official Editor and Official Publisher, who have given us an official organ unequalled and unapproached in the history of amateur journalism. The somewhat altered nature of contents, and radically elevated standard of editorship, mark an era in the progress of the Association; since *The United Amateur* is really the nucleus of our activity and a reflection of the best in our current thought and ideals. We have this year helped to shatter the foolish fetichism which restricts the average official organ to a boresome and needless display of facts and figures relating to the political mechanism of amateurdom. The organ has been a literary one, as befits a literary association; and has been conducted with a sounder sense of relative values than in times when amateurs seemed to place elections and annual banquets above art, taste, and rhetoric.

The publications of the year have been distinguished for their merit, general polish, and scholarly editorship. The percentage of crude matter appearing in print has been reduced to a minimum through the careful and conscientious critical service rendered both by the official bureau and by private individuals. The artistic standard of the United has evolved to a point where no aims short of excellence can win unqualified approval. The classics have become our sole models, and whilst even the most glaring faults of the sincere beginner receive liberal consideration and sympathetically constructive attention, there is no longer a seat of honour for complacent crudity. Genuine aspiration is our criterion of worth. The spirit of this newer amateur journalism is splendidly shewn by such magazines of the year as *Eurus, Spindrift, The Vagrant,* and the official organ.

Just before the close of the present term several new publications have appeared, amongst them a *Vagrant,* a *Conservative,* and Mr. Moloney's splendid first venture, *The Voice from the Mountains.* Early in the next fiscal year will appear *The United Cooperative,* the fruit of this year's planning, edited by Mrs. Jordan, Miss Lehr, Mr. J. Clinton Pryor, and the undersigned. A revival of manuscript magazines, inaugurated by the appearance of Sub.-Lieut. McKeag's *Northumbrian,* is in a measure solving the problems created by the high price of printing. Next month the undersigned will put into circulation *Hesperia,* a typewritten magazine designed to foster a closer relationship between British and American amateurdom.[1]

Judges of Award for the Laureateship contests have been appointed as follows. Poetry, Mr. Nixon Waterman, a New England bard who needs no introduction to the lover of lofty and graceful expression. Verse, Dr. Henry T. Schnittkind of the Stratford

Publishing Co. Essay, Prof. Lewis P. Shanks of the University of Pennsylvania. Study, Mr. J. Lee Robinson, Editor of the *Cambridge Tribune*. Story, Mr. William R. Murphy of the Philadelphia *Evening Ledger*, a former United man of the highest attainments. Editorial, Hon. Oliver Wayne Stewart, Associate Editor of *The National Enquirer*.

In doffing the official mantle after a year of executive endeavour, the undersigned must express regret at his inability to serve in as vigorous a manner as would the ideal President. He is acutely conscious of his shortcomings in a position which demands constant care and exertion, and which imposes a strain that only the robust are perfectly qualified to bear. It would be impossible for him fully to express his gratitude to his faithful and capable colleagues, to whose unremitting and faultlessly coördinated efforts all the successes of the present year must in justice be attributed. Valete!

EDITOR'S NOTE   FP: *United Amateur* 17, No. 6 (July 1918): 127–28 (signed "H. P. LOVECRAFT, President," and dated June 26, 1918). In this sixth and final report, HPL sums up the achievements of the previous year, bestowing greatest praise upon the Official Editor, Verna McGeoch, and Official Publisher, W. Paul Cook.

*Notes*

1. See n. 1 to "President's Message" (November 1917).

---

# AMATEUR CRITICISM

The somewhat remarkable attack of an amateur editor upon the United's critical bureau, made just a year ago, has apparently inaugurated a long period of debate regarding this phase of our literary activity. Exponents of mildness and severity, vagueness and frankness, personality and generality, archaism and modernism, each have had their say; without arriving at any very perfect community of ideas or consensus of opinion.

The Conservative in this issue publishes a brief contribution to the fray, from the pen of Prof. Philip B. McDonald, Chairman of the Department of Private Criticism.[1] Prof. McDonald is a modernist and liberalist; and while his remarks are undeniably the fruit of much erudition, mature reflection, and sincere conviction, it is hard to let them pass unchallenged. As former Public Critic, The Conservative feels impelled to defend the policy whereby he was always a strict upholder of classical standards and impeccable technique.

Prof. McDonald affirms, 'that it is more important to be interesting than to be correct', and in enunciating this dictum he is indeed speaking truly. All things, however, have their limits; and there are certain standards of technique below which no author may fall without impairing his literary strength, and distracting the attention of his readers by the grossness and numerousness of his faults. Style should be imperceptible; the crystal medium through which the theme is viewed. Laxity of technique is the least excusable of literary deficiencies; since it depends not on a want of natural parts, but on pure haste and indolence. We may pardon a *dull* writer, since his Boeotian offences arise from the incurable mediocrity of his genius; but can we thus excuse the *careless* scribbler whose worst blunders could be corrected by an extra hour of attention or research? The contemporary tendency to condone carelessness for the sake of brilliancy is as illogical as it is pernicious. No man ever wrote the duller for being correct, whilst many have transformed commonplaceness to pleasing urbanity by means of a graceful mode of expression.

Among amateur journalists, technique is the most neglected branch of literary art. We have scores of brilliant writers whose productions lose a considerable percentage of their possible force through lack of polish. Concretely, it may be pointed out that of our well-known poets only Messrs. Kleiner, Lowrey, and Loveman have an absolutely comprehensive and unfailing mastery of their medium, whilst the writers of elegant and musical prose are scarcely greater in number. It is in no spirit of cavilling or assumed superiority that The Conservative and other official critics have consistently laboured on the side of correctness. Any other course would have seemed, in their eyes, a flagrant dereliction of duty.

Regarding the element of individual taste and personal preferences in official criticism, it would be foolish to insist that the reviewer suppress all honest convictions of his own; foolish because such suppression is an impossibility. It is, however, to be expected that such an one will differentiate between personal and general dicta, nor fail to state all sides of any matter involving more than one point of view. This course The Conservative sought to follow during his tenure of the critical chairmanship, with the matter of *vers libre* as a single possible exception. That abominable species of artistic Bolshevism, condemned with equal vigour by every person who has ever been connected with the United's critical bureau, has no more right to a defence than political Bolshevism or any other sort of anarchy. Fortunately but few specimens have been inflicted upon our Association.

Within the last few weeks one of amateurdom's most prominent critics, a man who has served for more than a decade on either the public or private board, expressed in a personal letter the belief that all amateur criticism is futile; that if honest it offends too deeply to instruct, and that if "sugar-coated" it has no power to inculcate ideas. The Conservative does not entirely coincide with this view, but experience and observation have done much to remove from his mind the opposite opinion.

EDITOR'S NOTE FP: *Conservative* 4, No. 1 (July 1918): 5–6 (unsigned). Part of the column "In the Editor's Study," this article takes to task an article in the same issue of the *Conservative* by Prof. Philip B. McDonald. HPL later criticized McDonald again in "The Case for Classicism" (*United Co-operative*, June 1919; CE2).

*Notes*

1. Philip B. McDonald, "Criticism of Amateur Journals," *Conservative* 4, No. 1 (July 1918): 2–3.

---

# THE UNITED 1917–1918

The Conservative views with profound gratification the official year just completed by the United Amateur Press Association, proud to have borne the honour of the presidency through this period of cultural excellence and intensive development. Too much cannot be said in grateful praise of the perfect harmony and complete fidelity of the official board, and of the tireless effort and brilliant work of the critical bureaux. *The United Amateur* has surpassed all standards hitherto known to amateur journalism, writing the names of Miss McGeoch and Mr. Cook imperishably into the pages of our history. The lack of numerous publications has been more than atoned for by the quality of those which have appeared. *The Vagrant* is a magazine worthy to be compared with anything the amateur world has produced since the beginning, and the smaller publications have been close rivals in quality, however much exceeded in bulk.

For the new year the prospect is encouraging. The war will naturally curtail the production of papers to a greater or less extent, but that our present high ideals will be sustained and amplified, there is no reason to doubt. Free from friction with contemporaries, whose correct and liberal attitude is most heartening to observe, the United moves prosperously in its chosen sphere.

EDITOR'S NOTE FP: *Conservative* 4, No. 1 (July 1918): 6 (unsigned). Part of the column "In the Editor's Study." HPL again praises McGeoch and Cook for the success of the preceding amateur year, during which HPL was president.

# THE AMATEUR PRESS CLUB

Attention is directed to the new international organisation of amateur journalists founded in the Mother Country by Messrs. Benjamin Winskill and Joseph Parks, and denominated "The Amateur Press Club". This society, which now possesses nearly an hundred members both in England and the States, is designed for the diffusion of higher literary standards amongst amateurs, and commands the services of such earnestly progressive writers and critics as Sub-Lieut. Ernest Lionel McKeag and Miss Vere M. Murphy. The Conservative not long ago joined the Amateur Press Club, and believes it would be to the advantage of amateurdom if his readers were to do likewise; for the drawing together of amateur interests on both sides of the sea is something much to be desired in this period of decreased general activity. Detailed information may be obtained from the Secretary, Joseph Parks, Esq., 38, Garnet St., Saltburn-by-the-Sea, Yorkshire, England.

EDITOR'S NOTE FP: *Conservative* 4, No. 1 (July 1918): 6–7 (unsigned). Part of the column "In the Editor's Study." HPL points out a press club in England, although it does not appear as if he himself ever had much contact with it.

# *LES MOUCHES FANTASTIQUES*

Extreme literary radicalism is always a rather amusing thing, involving as it does a grotesque display of egotism and affectation. Added to this comic quality, however, there is a distinct pathos which arises from reflection on the amount of real suffering which the radical must, if serious, endure through his alienation from the majority.

Both of these aspects lately impressed The Conservative with much force, as he glanced over a new and most extraordinary amateur publication entitled *Les Mouches Fantastiques*, published by Miss Elsie Alice Gidlow and Mr. Roswell George Mills of Montreal. Miss Gidlow and Mr. Mills are sincere and solemn super-aesthetes, fired with the worthy ambition of elevating dense and callous mankind to their own exalted spiritual plane, and as such present vast possibilities to the humourist; but it is also possible to view their efforts in another light, and to lament the imperfect artistic vision which imparts to their utterances so *outré* an atmosphere.

The Gidlow-Mills creed, so far as may be discovered from their writings, is that Life is a compulsory quest of beauty and emotional excitement; these goals being so important that man must discard everything else in pursuing them. Particularly, we fancy, must he discard his sense of humour and proportion. The sceptical bulk of humanity, who cannot or do not enter upon this feverish quest, are (as Miss Gidlow tactfully tells us) "unnecessary".

And of what do these great objects of Life, as revealed in the pages of Les Mouches, consist? The reader may, up to date, unearth nothing save a concentrated series of more or less primitive and wholly unintellectual sense-impressions; instinct, form, colour, odour, and the like, grouped in all the artistic chaos characteristic of the late Oscar Wilde of none too fragrant memory.[1] Much of this matter is, as might be expected, in execrable taste. Now is this Life? Is human aspiration indeed to be circumscribed by the walls of some garishly bejewelled temple of the Dionaean Eros; its air oppressive with the exotic fumes of strange incense, and its altar lit with weirdly coloured radiance from mystical braziers? Must we forever shut ourselves in such an artificial shrine, away from the pure light of sun and stars, and the natural currents of normal existence?

It seems to The Conservative that Miss Gidlow and Mr. Mills, instead of being divinely endowed seers in sole possession of all Life's truths, are a pair of rather youthful persons suffering from a sadly distorted philosophical perspective. Instead of seeing Life in its entirety, they see but one tiny phase, which they mistake for the whole. What worlds of beauty—pure Uranian beauty—are utterly denied them on account of their bondage to the lower regions of the senses! It is almost pitiful to hear superficial allusions to "Truth" from the lips of those whose eyes are sealed to the Intellectual Absolute; who knows not the upper altitudes of pure thought, in which empirical forms and material aspects are as nothing.

The editors of Les Mouches complain very bitterly of the inartistic quality of amateur journalism; a complaint half just and half otherwise. The very nature of our institution necessitates a modicum of crudity, but if Miss Gidlow and Mr. Mills were more analytical, they could see beauty in much which appears ugly to their rather astigmatic vision.

EDITOR'S NOTE FP: Conservative 4, No. 1 (July 1918): 7–8 (unsigned). HPL expatiates on the "extreme literary radicalism" of the Canadian amateur journal of the title, edited by Elsie Alice Gidlow and Roswell George Mills. For another and much more pungent squib against Gidlow, see the brief section "A Conjecture" in "Lucubrations Lovecraftian" (p. 277).

Notes

1. The reference is to Wilde's conviction for homosexuality in 1895, resulting in his spending two years in Reading Gaol.

---

# DEPARTMENT OF PUBLIC CRITICISM

(September 1918)

The Dabbler for July upholds the commendable standard established by the two issues of last year, and forms one of the pleasantest literary treats of the season. Mr. Frank C. Reighter, editorially announced as the "only 'dependable' contributor", furnishes a substantial part of the contents, incidentally paying his respects to this critical bureau for what he deems a harsh estimate of one of his poems. Since the present critic is not the one who penned the offending review, an impartial comment is perhaps possible in this place. Our colleague very mildly charged Mr. Reighter with "didacticism", and in doing so did not err. When a writer endeavours to harness his Muse to bald truisms and obvious aphorisms, bidding for the reader's attention with wholly superficial devices and expressions instead of genuine artistry and aesthetic subtlety; he may well be called "didactic". Poetry in its most exalted sense makes no effort to inculcate its precepts directly. Beauty is the one essential aim, with truth and morals only as natural concomitants. Mr. Reighter again (and admittedly) proves his preference for didacticism above art in his present "unreligious sermon" on the human mind. This brief essay is marked by much common sense, even if lacking in thorough insight and creative imagination. A philosopher would doubtless object to Mr. Reighter's blithe assurance in giving the infinitely complex intellect of man an empirically neat septempartite division, but as a mere critic we shall confine our objections to the excessive use of capitals and heavy-faced type in emphasising outstanding points. The skilled artist would accomplish with his flow of rhetoric what Mr. Reighter seeks to accomplish by mere mechanical means. Mr. Reighter's essay on poetry betrays many of the faults which appear in his other work—imperfect training in the niceties of composition, and defective restraint of expression. But all this is atoned for by the author's critical acuteness in defining the province of poesy and analysing the defects of what commonly passes for poesy. We are inclined to classify Mr. Reighter as a keen critic above all else, and to encourage him to study the style of the best essayists; that he may invest his articles with an accuracy and elegance better fitted to command the consideration of the fastidious reader. Mr. Reighter's current verses, "Wishes" and "Success", display much metrical facility; but are too lacking in ethereal beauty to fulfil his own definition of poetry. Prosaic adherence to fact rather than fancy robs them of the elusive Aonian touch. The only technical error we notice—an error found in an alarming amount of current amateur work—is the use of the dissyllable *re-al* as a monosyllable.

As a concrete illustration of the fanciful and really poetic touch missing in Mr. Reighter's verse, we may turn to the compositions of Miss Voelchert and Mrs. Jordan. The former, in her "Silhouette of a Belgian Forest", achieves a high poetic level without resorting to verse, whilst the latter presents a conventional quatrain of delightful polish and delicacy.

Further versified contributions are those of Mrs. Jennie M. Kendall and Dr. O. M. Blood. Mrs. Kendall's ballad is marked by attractive animation and commendable correctness, but Dr. Blood should exercise more care in his use of rhyme and metre. The latter bard's lines are uneven, his final stanza lacking in uniformity with the rest, and one of his rhymes (*appear-disappear*) false because of identity of rhyming syllables.

Editor Lindquist is represented by some pleasing comment, whose sole fault is a tendency toward slang and undue informality. His achievement in publishing *The Dabbler* is an unusual one, and we hope to behold many future issues of this entertaining magazine.

*The Silver Clarion* for June opens with a forceful and well-chosen arraignment of the Huns, copied from a contemporary. We commend the *Clarion* for its espousal of the virile views therein expressed.

"To Mother", a poem by John Milton Samples, is a tribute of much fervour and felicity, marred only by the incorrect use of an archaic verb-form in the third stanza. The final line of this stanza might be amended to read:

"Cast the pure mantle of God's truth."

Another poem of Mr. Samples' is "To a Child with Flowers", which is cast in trochaic triplets—a rather unusual medium. If there be any weakness about this piece, it is in a certain obviousness of conception and Ambrose Philips saccharinity of expression. Mr. Philips, it will be remembered, was that contemporary of Pope from whose name and style of child verse the term "namby-pamby" arose.[1] In justice to Mr. Samples, be it said that this latter quality is not here present in any exaggerated degree, but merely suggested by certain passages.

"Needs", by Mrs. W. V. Jordan, is in its author's didactic vein; and is animated by a harmony and beauty which lend strength to its precepts.

Both timely and noble are Theodore Draper Gottlieb's lines "It is Not Death to Die". Mr. Gottlieb reveals a richness of thought and facility of technique which entitle him to a conspicuous place amongst the bards of amateurdom.

"I Have Dreamed and Called and Longed", by Eugene B. Kuntz, is an emotional lyric of much warmth and depth, which proves its author a poet of high rank.

Of the prose features Sarah Story Duffee's airy little sketch elicits a word of praise for its grace, whilst Mr. Norcross' short biography of Milton shews all the terseness, accuracy, and lucidity of an encyclopaedia article.

The Silver Clarion for July is distinguished by a most acceptable poem of virile cast, "Alone in the Desert", by Harry E. Rieseberg. Its style and sentiment remind us somewhat of the honest homespun verse of the last century, and we believe Mr. Rieseberg will find his audience increasingly appreciative if he continues to cultivate this popular appeal.

"The Murmur of Roots", by Anne Tillery Renshaw, possesses the power and subtlety we are accustomed to expect from its celebrated author, and presents a vivid picture indeed.

"A Lullaby", by Agnes Richmond Arnold, is not without technical irregularities and overworked rhymes, but as a whole displays a quaint sweetness which recommends it to the discerning reader.

"About the Fireside", by W. Frank Booker, is a lyric of great promise and smoothness, which makes us anxious to peruse its author's work in larger quantities.

"The Sweet Today", by Winifred Virginia Jordan's, is a characteristic bit of wholesome optimism, redeemed from commonplaceness by apt and attractive poetical imagery.

Editor Samples furnishes two poems, "An O. K. World" and "My Heart Is Over There", both of which are correct in structure and appealing in idea.

"Under a Spreading Chestnut Tree", by Sarah Story Duffee, is a two-part story of the type which Mrs. Duffee generally produces. Opinions may differ regarding this somewhat juvenile style, but there is no gainsaying its present popularity amongst large numbers of readers. The narrative has a certain charm which strikes the lover of innocuous simplicity, and its dainty pathos doubtless titillates many a tender tear-duct. It appears to us as a tale which might find ready reception in the professional press.

The Spectator for July exceeds the preceding number in size, and easily equals it in merit. Rev. William Wallace Burton is a definite thinker, and does not hesitate to discuss his views in print, hence his attractive journal has all the piquancy of personality. The opening article is autobiographical; relating Editor Burton's career from early days to the present, and affording an interesting chronicle of progress. Following this is the usual array of editorials, all well written and for the most part sound in opinion. In "Studies along the Path of Nature", Mr. Burton writes pleasantly of the birds and animals which have come under his observation, ending with a bit of philosophy.

"Maid April", by Winifred Virginia Jordan, is the principal non-editorial contribution. It is sufficient praise to say that Mrs. Jordan here maintains the same high standard which brought her the Verse Laureateship last July.

The United Amateur for July is a fitting climax to a year of excellence which knows no precedent in amateur journalism. Any number of this volume incomparably surpasses even the best official organs of past years; yet the July number, with its contributions from laureate-winners and honorary members, is clearly the best of the six.

In "Rewards", Mr. Edmund Vance Cook gives more than a hint of that genius which has brought him professional literary renown. The theme is a peculiarly appropriate one for an amateur journal, and is clothed in verse of faultless form. If trite, it is only because all major truths are often told.

"The Relationship of Poetry to Music", by Blanche Blood, is a smoothly written essay emphasising a fundamental condition which has affected aesthetic development since the dawn of culture.

William Marion Reedy, in the sermon headed "The Amateur", pays a deserved tribute to the artist who labours only for the sake of his art, and incidentally offers some valuable advice to the aspirant.[2]

"A Cremona Speaks", by Perrin Holmes Lowrey, is a poem of such extraordinary merit that more than one reader has singled it out for enthusiastic commendation. Mr. Lowrey has already attained professional poetical success, and is now preparing to widen his horizon by volunteer service in the aërial navy of his country. The congratulations of amateurdom attend this valiant and gifted soldier-poet in his new military career.

"At the Root", an essay by H. P. Lovecraft,[3] sets forth without sentimentality the facts concerning mankind's attitude toward war, and the folly of pacifism both present and prospective. Many readers, accustomed to religious extravagances and philanthropic theorising, will not relish such plain truths; but since these contentions are practically no more than a reflection of the authoritative views of America's greatest man, Col. Roosevelt, their accuracy cannot be lightly attacked. We regret, however, that Mr. Lovecraft did not choose a less hackneyed theme for his article.

"The Burden That Six Men Bore", by Arthur Goodenough, is a piece of sober verse which none but a true-born New Englander and a genuinely inspired poet could write. The grim spirit of the sandy seacoast breathes subtly through these well-wrought lines. Certain members of last year's critical bureau would censure the imperfect rhyme of *man* and *again* in stanza three, but since it is authorised by Walker's Dictionary we shall not do so.[4]

"Hope and Expectation", an essay by Paul J. Campbell, reveals the mental vigour and forceful style of its gifted author, and draws most cleverly an important philosophical distinction.

"Only a Singer" is a poem of much merit by our Literata Olive G. Owen. The only discordant note is the second line of the third stanza, which presents a hopelessly unpoetical effect. The term "captain of finance" is a stock phrase having no place in poetry, and its use here is hard to explain.

"His Little Candle", by Eleanor Barnhart Campbell, is one of the few really brilliant short stories appearing lately in the amateur press. In plot, incidents, and atmosphere the tale conforms to standard requirements; whilst the sentiments expressed are noble ones. The character-drawing is particularly natural, all the motives bearing the stamp of verisimilitude.

"When the Sun Is Blazin' Hot", by Frank G. Morris, is in rather striking contrast to the brief war lyrics we have been receiving from its author's pen. Mr. Morris here gives a bit of Nature in Western rural dialect, garnishing his homely picture with a multitude of graphic and colourful details. The internal rhyming plan is not sustained perfectly throughout the poem, though all the end rhymes are satisfactory. From the ability shewn in this fragment, we predict for Mr. Morris a bright poetical future.

Another vivid summer picture is furnished by Beryl L. Mappin, whose prose sketch, "A Somerset Combe", attracts the reader with a succession of graceful descriptions. Considering Miss Mappin's youth, the merit of this sketch is quite unusual.

*The Voice from the Mountains* for July is one of the most remarkable first ventures we have ever beheld. Fired by the splendid achievements of W. Paul Cook, his fellow-townsman and business associate, Mr. James Joseph Moloney of Athol, Mass., has inaugurated his amateur career with the publication of an illustrated magazine whose size and elaborateness would do credit to any veteran member of the fraternity. The dominant note sounded in the July *Voice* is patriotism, cover and contents alike reflecting this noble spirit; but besides the matter of national interest, we are treated to a representative and unbelievably copious display of amateur talent.

"Man and the Supernatural", a philosophical essay by Alfred Galpin, Jr., is the outstanding feature. Mr. Galpin, a scintillant youth whose mental development has far outrun his years, here unfolds a train of metaphysical ratiocination which places him at once amongst the few genuinely deep thinkers of amateurdom, and establishes his fame as a student independent of popular delusions and pragmatical limitations. A fellow-critic has predicted a great future for this remarkable young author, who has not yet turned seventeen, and to his opinion we add our own. Minds of such keenness and calibre are very rare. Mr. Galpin's versatility is well illustrated by the "Sonnet to Poetry" which appears farther on in the magazine. Here the philosopher becomes the aesthete, and beautifully expresses the power and function of the Pierian art.

"On a Battlefield in France", by Howard Phillips Lovecraft,[5] is a Pindaric ode containing one or two vivid pictures despite its now hackneyed theme. We are of the opinion that the author might have conveyed his thought more effectively in a different metre. Mr. Lovecraft is also responsible for "Ver Rusticum", a Nature-poem in heroic couplets.[6] This is what one member of our bureau calls "Pope-try", and has little to recommend it save a certain smoothness of metre and fidelity to the classical models. The most serious misprint is in line 9 on page 21, the word *Whereon* being rendered *Whereupon.*

Winifred Virginia Jordan is in this issue represented by two contributions, both poems of great merit, exhibiting opposite phases of their author's genius. "That I Might Be the Cool Blue Wind" is a graceful lyric of light felicity, whilst "When I Sail on the Sea" shews a deeper power. The internal rhymes in the latter piece are especially deserving of praise.

"The Spirit of Sacrifice", by Ethel L. Stratton, is a short story by a new member, and though perhaps unambitious in theme, is pleasant and wholesome; easily equalling many of the lighter semi-didactic tales found in popular professional periodicals.

"The Monarch of the World", by Agnes Richmond Arnold, is a poem of merit, containing vivid images despite a lack of technical polish. Practice will remove from Mrs. Arnold's style the slight imperfections which are now apparent.

"A Haunted House" by Maude Kingsbury Barton, is correct in rhyme and metre, and graphic in atmosphere, though its effect is weakened by the somewhat anticlimactic last line. The use of the expletive *"did"* in several places is perhaps excusable on account of the intentional quaintness of the poem.

"A Southern Sunset", by Edwin Gibson, is a prose-poem of great beauty, representing the work of a young author likely to succeed in literature.

Kate L. Humphrey contributes two poems, "A Vision" and "The Juggernaut". Both shew much promise, albeit faulty construction. We are still trying to figure out the meaning of the final line of "A Vision"—"To the boy in the West who drums"— our present opinion being that the necessities of rhyme had much to do with it.

"That the Light May Shine Again", by Julia R. Johnson, is a didactic poem of much grace, though perhaps shewing a few traces of that stiffness which will disappear from its author's style in the course of time.

"In My Dreams Unbroken" is a delightful surprise from the pen of Rev. Eugene B. Kuntz. Though long devoted to Alexandrine pieces, the author here shews his adaptability by presenting an airy trochaic specimen, whose delicious melody is as sprightly as any critic could wish. The many contributions of Dr. Kuntz form one of the most acceptable ingredients of amateur literature.

Arthur H. Goodenough contributes four poems, all of that merit and distinction which his celebrity causes us to expect. To us, "The Hills" seems the best of the quartette, since it possesses a bounding animation and soaring spirit which forcibly impress its strength and sincerity upon the reader. How few bards of our amateur circle have approached the enviable record of Mr. Goodenough, who this autumn celebrates the 30th anniversary of his first appearance in print as a poet!

"There's No Place Like Home", by Rose Neyman, is the work of a juvenile author, hence must not be judged by the severest classical standards. Its plot lacks the coherence and continuity necessary to successful fiction, being almost totally without logical sequence or development toward a climax. The dream incident is an intrusion upon the unity of the theme, and should be eliminated. Stock phrases of the Sunday-school book type are another objectionable element. There is something unconsciously comic in such a super-trite moralising conclusion as "My darling parents, you are right! There is no place like Home, Sweet Home!"

"A Stormy June", by Wilfred Kemble, is one of this gifted author's typical sonnets, and is especially rich in that *sine qua non* of lyrical verse, the "simple, sensuous, and impassioned" quality whose absence from another amateur's style is lamented by a brother critic.

"Pad and Pencil on the Mohawk Trail", by Jonathan E. Hoag, is one of its author's most delightful pieces. Mr. Hoag's tuneful reflectiveness stamps him as a thinker and singer of rare endowments, and we hope his contributions to the amateur press may be frequent and long continued.

Mrs. Helene H. Cole's review of the Curran hoax, "A Sorry Tale", is marked by considerable critical acuteness, and appreciation of a plot whose cleverness is altogether out of the ordinary. It is unfortunate that the author of "A Sorry Tale" should have cheapened her really excellent work by attributing it to a supernatural creator, yet this harmless attempt to achieve notoriety should not prejudice the reader against the novel itself. As Mrs. Cole clearly shews, it is far from contemptible as a literary production. Mrs. Curran's case is singularly like that of Macpherson of Ossianic fame.

"If I Could I Would", by James Joseph Moloney, is a bit of very light verse whose success is commensurate with its design. Mr. Moloney needs only practice to become a witty and pleasing adept in versification.

The editorial in this number, written by W. Paul Cook, displays the usual skill of that capable writer. In the next issue we hope that Editor Moloney may himself address us, a privilege to which his splendid initial achievement most emphatically entitles him.

EDITOR'S NOTE FP: *United Amateur* 18, No. 1 (September 1918): 3–8 (unsigned). HPL resumes his customary role as Chairman of the Department of Public Criticism. However, one lengthy section of this column (pp. 5–6; not included here) was signed "A[lfred] G[alpin], Jr.," consisting of a substantial review of the July 1918 issue of the *Vagrant* and including a long discussion of HPL's poem "The Poe-et's Nightmare."

*Notes*

1. Actually, the epithet was attributed to British poet Ambrose Philips (1674–1749) in Henry Carey's play *Namby-Pamby* (1725).
2. William Marion Reedy (1862–1920) was a well-known American journalist, publisher of *Reedy's Mirror* (1913–20) and owner of other newspapers.
3. See CE5.
4. See n. 7 to DPC (June 1916).
5. See AT 416. First published (*National Enquirer*, 30 May 1918) as "On a Battlefield in Picardy."
6. See AT 293–95. The poem is a revision of a work entitled "Rural Springtime" (ms., JHL; dated 25 March 1918).

---

# DEPARTMENT OF PUBLIC CRITICISM

*(November 1918)*

*The Hazel Nut* for October is devoted to the commendable purpose of encouraging the sale of Liberty Bonds, and contains some stirring verse and prose of a patriotic nature. "Buy Bonds—More Bonds", by A. M. Adams, reveals that metrical and rhetorical vigour for which its author is so distinguished. Mr. Adams shews great power in the composition of that kind of poetry which modern critics like to describe as "gripping", and occupies a niche of his own in the Aonian galaxy of amateurdom.

The prose article "Buy More Bonds" is unsigned, but is presumably by the editor. In its command of facts and presentation of arguments it is a model of forceful and laconic style. Altogether, *The Hazel Nut* has shewn itself to be the most practically patriotic publication connected with the association, with the possible exception of Mr. Moloney's magnificent *Voice* of last July, whose elaborate cover and apt quotations placed it in a class by itself.

*The Martian* for October introduces to the public amateurdom's latest prodigy, Edward Sherman Cole, who at the tender age of twenty-six weeks has produced a leaflet worthy to rank in quality with the best accomplishments of our circle. Mr. Cole, viewing the world from a remarkably unprejudiced angle, finds much to commend in the race amongst whom he has so recently taken up his residence; and altogether displays himself as a remarkable optimist in preserving so cheerful an outlook amidst chaotic conditions. Most philosophers would derive a certain melancholy if suddenly introduced to this planet at so dark a period in its affairs. However, the bright aspect of Mr. Cole's beliefs is rapidly being justified by the defeat of the Hun and the establishment of an armistice; hence we may regard him as a young man of poise and farsightedness, rather than as one whose optimism is based solely on unsubstantial idealism. We hope to see many future issues of *The Martian*, and trust that Mr. Cole may coöperate with Mr. Galpin in bringing fame to the United's infant element!

*The Silver Clarion* for August contains Mrs. Winifred V. Jordan's delectable poem, "Afar and Near", whose melody and imagery are equally attractive.

"The Scourge", by John Milton Samples, is a fervid religious poem whose most conspicuous defect is the attempted rhyme of *nations* and *creation* in the first and last stanzas. Another fault is the rhyme of *brothers* with itself in the fourth stanza.

"To Her", by James Laurence Crowley, marks the return to amateurdom of a somewhat well-known poetical contributor of two years ago. Mr. Crowley's style exhibits little change, and we must again urge upon him a wider range of themes, a greater accuracy of technique, and a closer attention to the rhetorical proprieties of standard poetry.

"Mercy", by John Osman Baldwin, seems at first to consist of eight lines of free or nearly free verse, followed by a single octosyllabic couplet. On second perusal we discover that such is not the author's intention, but that the lines vary irregularly from trimeter to pentameter, therefore we will not try to guess at the true design. We will merely urge Mr. Baldwin to exercise a greater care in composition, since his theme deserves better presentation. He is, as we have before remarked in these columns, a genuine poet of more than usual endowments.

"Phaeton", by Howard Phillips Lovecraft,[1] is the author's metrical protest against those pragmatical critics who have termed his verse too ethereal in subject and deficient in human interest. The rhymes are correct and the prosody smooth, though as a purist we must protest against the rhetorical enallage whereby the adverb or preposition *beyond* is made to serve as a noun.

*The Silver Clarion* for September gains distinction from its leading article, a subtle and artistically written allegory by Alfred Galpin, Jr., entitled "Nolens Trahitur". In this fatalistic protest against individualism and seclusion, our young author displays to a notable degree his wide vocabulary and command of language, as well as that indefinable mysticism which marks him as a fabulist of power and skilled expression.

"Somewhere in France", a poem by Arthur Goodenough, well sustains the high reputation of that author, investing a contemporary theme with suitable grace and solemnity.

"Night Lights on San Francisco Bay" exhibits the increasing poetical skill of Joseph Thalheimer, Jr., and is technically flawless save for the use of fire as a dissyllable in the final stanza.

"The Soldier's Reply", by Eugene B. Kuntz, is equally acceptable in sentiment and construction, and represents a genuinely inspired poet at his best.

"I Cannot Understand", by editor Samples, is a truly delightful poem of unusual form and perfect execution, which promises well for the future of our gifted poet-publisher.

Mr. Samples' editorial, "The Morning Cometh", treats of the approach of victory in lofty and inspired style, revealing its author as a poet despite his prose medium.

*The Silver Clarion* for October opens with "An American Creed for Patriotic Citizens", by Mrs. Louise H. Collins. This creed, written last winter, has been widely reprinted in the professional press, and has elicited from President Wilson a personal note of grateful appreciation to the author. Its polished paragraphs reveal not only an exalted sentiment, but a literary skill and Biblical scholarship which reflect the highest credit upon Mrs. Collins.

"Immortality", a poem in blank verse by Jonathan E. Hoag, is almost Miltonic (if one may employ so overworked a comparison) in reach and technique. Its artistic workmanship is equalled only by its philosophical insight and noble optimism.

"To My Love", by Henriette Posner, is a pretty piece of heroic verse revealing much native ability and a good ear for metre, yet lacking evidences of mature scholarship and poetical practice.

"Monos; An Ode" is a pleasantly meaningless philosophical Pindaric by an author more accustomed to iambic pentameter.[2]

"The Darkest Hour", by Sarah Story Duffee, is a very meritorious poem in a short metre with double rhymes. Our only criticism is that the first and second and fourth and fifth lines of the stanzas should be rhymed. Lines of such brevity cannot convey the best effect till they have the added ornament of rhyme.

"Twilight", by Anne Tillery Renshaw, is a poem thoroughly delightful and adequate in conception, atmosphere, and execution, as the author's name indeed guarantees.

"Thou Knowest, Lord", by John Milton Samples, is a religious poem of commendable fervour, whose only doubtful point is the rhyme of *sin* and *again*. Also by Mr. Samples is "Yonderland", whose metre moves a little haltingly in places, but whose general idea is genuinely poetical. The first line of stanza four contains two censurable points; the false accentuation of "*con*-fines", used as a noun, and the use of *did* as an expletive. Mr. Samples should remember Mr. Pope's classic advice regarding expletives and their "feeble aid".

"A Lesson", by Mrs. Mamie K. Samples, displays marked crudity in rhyme and metre, yet reveals a truly poetical attitude. The accent and syllabification of the lines require attention, as does the false rhyme of *while* and *child*. The phraseology at times becomes exceedingly prosaic, as in the first line of stanza four: "My attention next the lily held." The choice of metre and rhyming plan is ingenious and artistic; in fact, we believe that Mrs. Samples will rank among our best poets after a preliminary course of practice and reading of standard authors—especially authors of the older school.

*The Spider* for July is the product of Mr. Wheeler Dryden, our erstwhile East Indian member, who is now about to take up his residence in the United States.[3] This tiny sheet, measuring only about three and a half by four and a half inches, is a good example of the intensity of purpose which causes amateur journalists to maintain their activity despite the most adverse conditions, such as constant travelling and the vicissitudes of a tropical climate. The present issue, being given over mainly to a discussion of certain amateur affairs, is scarcely representative of the magazine's usual merit; and we may hope for more literary issues after the editor's settlement in America.

*The United Amateur* for September, delayed and rendered typographically heterogeneous by conditions arising from the influenza epidemic, surmounts all obstacles and presents to us a meritorious array of contributions. In number these are not many, since the inevitable presence of official matter somewhat restricts space.

"Mountain-Wonder", by Anne Vyne Tillery Renshaw, is a delicate nature-poem whose correctness and artistry recommend it to the reader.

"Greek Literature", a brief essay by Verna McGeoch, gracefully and capably handles a theme of highest interest to all lovers of culture. Not only is the language well chosen and the development skilful; but the whole displays its author's keen sympathy with the artistic spirit of classical antiquity.

"Hellas", a piece of rather obvious hack-writing by H. P. Lovecraft, is even in metre and correct in grammar, but falls flatly beneath the level of inspiration its subject causes us to expect.[4]

"Nostalgia", by Samuel Loveman, is a supremely artistic lyric of pensive cast, well worthy of its celebrated author.

Another powerful poem is Mr. T. D. Gottlieb's elegy on the late Quentin Roosevelt, a composition whose nobility is not unworthy of its supremely noble subject.

EDITOR'S NOTE  FP: *United Amateur* 18, No. 2 (November 1918): 29–32 (unsigned). HPL wrote only selected sections of the column (only these sections are here included); two other sections—on p. 29 and pp. 29–30—were written by "A[lfred] G[alpin], Jr." HPL's segments give much space to the *Silver Clarion*.

*Notes*

1. See AT 435–36.
2. The poem is by HPL. See AT 436–37.
3. Wheeler Dryden was half-brother to Charlie Chaplin. He met HPL in New York on several occasions in 1924–25.
4. See AT 124.

---

# NEWS NOTES

*(November 1918)*

Sergeant Alfred Pingel, former treasurer of the Appleton Press Club, and U.A.P.A. member, was gassed in action July 15th, while fighting on French soil with the 150th Machine Gun Battalion, according to casualty reports. No word from "Mike" has been received since his injury, save a short letter stating that he had been so injured, but making no mention of his present condition. He was a volunteer member of the company before the outbreak of the war, and served on the Mexican border.

Consul Hasting, who may be remembered as the author of the inimitable burlesque, "Two Loves", in the July *Conservative*, is the latest potential recruit to amateur journalism. Mr. Hasting, though of mature mind, is yet of a somewhat reticent disposition, fearing publicity so much that he has declined to enter either association. He has a place on an Outagamie County, Wisconsin, newspaper, and divides his labours between editorial work and furnishing mental diversion for the other hard-worked members of the staff. Publishers wishing to encourage Mr. Hasting's leaning toward A. J. should send all papers and communications to Consul Hasting, care of Alfred Galpin, Jr., 779 Kimball St., Appleton, Wisconsin.[1]

The first issue of *Intowin*, the magazine issued by the U. S. Ordnance Department, is graced by a poem from Mrs. Renshaw's pen, entitled "It's Up to You".

EDITOR'S NOTE  FP: *United Amateur* 18, No. 2 (November 1918): 38 (unsigned). Although the Official Editor of the UAPA for 1918–19 was Verna McGeoch, HPL appears (by internal evidence) to have contributed this section, which directly follows a section of his essay "The Literature of Rome" (CE2).

*Notes*

1. "Consul Hasting" was a pseudonym of Alfred Galpin. Prefacing the poem "Two Loves" in the *Conservative* 4, No. 1 (July 1918): 8, HPL has written: "The Conservative, in order to forestall conjecture, desires to state that 'Consul Hasting,' signed to the following parody, is not a pseudonym for himself. The *nom de plume* cloaks one of our most brilliant new members, a young man of great attainments and infinite promise."

---

# [LETTER TO THE BUREAU OF CRITICS]

To the Honourable Bureau of Critics,
    National Amateur Press Ass'n.,
        Athol, Mass., U.S.A.

Gentlemen:—

Having lately observed the just and manly protests of Messrs. F. C. Reighter and J. Osman Baldwin against the biased and inhuman tone of your published reviews; we, the undersigned, desire to add our voices to this chorus of wronged and aggrieved merit.

Are you not aware, gentlemen, that you have no right to pronounce judgment upon the effusions of genius greater than your own? What if we poets do occasionally overlook the inconsequential minutiae of such trivial things as rhyme, metre, and good taste? We would have you know, that these things are but trifles to great souls, and that if you fail to forget them in admiration of our larger impressionistic efforts, you forthwith convict yourselves of deficient super-aestheticism.

Mr. Reighter has very acutely observed, that there is only *one* (the italics are his own) truthful side of every question. We are impelled to add, that of course a poet always *knows* (these italics are ours) when he has hit upon the truth; and that consequently when we bards say a thing, it is invariably above criticism. Why waste your ink, gentlemen of the bureau, in these days of conservation?

Now, gentlemen, we rise to protest against some of the *de*-structive criticism we have received at your hands. One of us some years ago wrote a poem containing the eminently correct rhyme of *brown* and *ground*, and one of your brutal department had the effrontery to say it was erroneous, *despite the fact that he offered no substitute.* Members of the National, I appeal to you against this tyranny oligarchy of littlewit reviewers! Think of this case; a critic protesting against a rhyme, *when he is incapable of making any rhyme whatsoever himself!* We declare this to be an outrage against the citizens of a free country, and a violation of the constitution and the Magna Charta! Let the critic seek, as our fellow-sufferer Mr. Reighter suggests, the sanctified privacy of his chamber; and in solemn accents utter repeatedly the words *brown* and *ground*, passing over the final consonant of *ground* as a non-essential, and giving the whole a most sonorous and resounding roll. We say to you, that if you do this you will find our—that is, Mr. Softly's—rhyme absolutely "A-1 Perfect".

Now while of course we care naught for the cruel things you have said of our work—we are above such petty censure, since we belong to the "so-few"—we must intervene in Mr. Reighter's behalf concerning the "widow's cruse of oil" allusion. Evidently your ancestors are not Roman, else you would have recognised the simile as referring to the inexhaustible bowl of Baucis and Philemon, in Ovid—you all know the passage.

> "———haustum cratera repleri
> Sponte sua, per seque vident succrescere vina."[1]

The "widow" reference was a trivial *lapsus calami*, or figure of speech.

[N.B. My friend Mr. Softly is in error; I am of opinion that Mr. Reighter alluded to the very pretty incident in the history of Elisha, the Semitic Prophet, as related in the fourth chapter of Second Kings. However, deem me not an Hebrew because I am familiar with the legend. Neither is Mr. Softly, who quoted Ovid, a Roman!—
*Ward Phillips.*]

My—or rather *our*—sympathy goes out abundantly to Mr. Baldwin. As he says, the fiendish malignancy of the critics of amateurdom has deterred all of our beginners from exhibiting their embryonic but inspired products to the world. In fact, we *never* see any crude products in amateur papers nowadays. Gentlemen, you are discouraging incipient genius by attempting to assist writers.

Infant poesy must never be vexed by the precepts of a guide or *de*-structive critic. Like a delicate flower it must blossom of itself, assisted only by gentle showers from the benevolent watering-pot of polite panegyric.

Far be it from us to take umbrage at what is said of our own work; we are, as we said before, steeled against the darts of envy, and appreciative of any genuine attempts at *con*-structive criticism; but we cannot bear your unjust and heinously harsh estimates of our recent poetry in *The Tryout*. Mr. Softly is most contemptuous of your ill-timed censure against his serious artistic attempt entitled "Damon and Delia",[2] and vows you shew vast ignorance in declaring it 'not always successful, too long, and sometimes awkward and unmusical'. He spent several years in the composition of this masterpiece, and has been told by his landlady's cousin (a graduate of grammar-school) that it surpasses even the best of the "Love-Epistles of Aristaenetus", as translated in 1771 by Halhed and Sheridan.[3]

As for Mr. Phillips's "Eidolon"[4]—he maintains an haughty silence at your ungenerous strictures, but wants information as to why you dare call the piece lacking in those contrasts necessary to produce full horror, *when you do not offer an improved version yourself.* I am not—that is, Mr. Phillips is not—egotistical in the least; but we consider "The Eidolon" one of the most graphic and impelling Poe-ems to appear in the amateur press since the dawn of our hobby; one whose beauties are desecrated by the earthly appraisal of a mere critic.

As we terminate this friendly communication, we entreat of you not to deem us in the least incensed or even mildly perturbed. Our remarks, we assure you, are but philosophical observations—altogether impersonal—designed to assist you in conquering the grave faults of criticism which have made your bureau an object of detestation amongst all sensitive members of the so-few, and all disciples of the obscurely beautiful in poesy.

Permit us to subscribe ourselves as your devoted and obedient servants,

Ned Softly,
Ward Phillips.

P.S. Mr. Softly desires that you will look up what Mr. Addison, a *real* critick, said about his lines "To Mira"; in No. 163 of the *Tatler.*[5]

EDITOR'S NOTE FP: *National Amateur* 41, No. 3 (January 1919): 93 (as by "Ned Softly" and "Ward Phillips"; in section titled "The Members' Forum"). HPL satirically takes the side of two amateur writers offended at the severity of the criticism directed against them in the NAPA's Department of Public Criticism. HPL tended to regard the NAPA's department as being far too lenient on mediocrity than the analogous department in the UAPA. HPL here provides the source of his pseudonym "Edward Softly" (see n. 5).

*Notes*

1. From Ovid, *Metamorphoses* 8.679–80: "They saw that the mixing-bowl, as often as it was drained, kept filling of its own accord, and that the wine welled up of itself" (tr. Frank Justus Miller).
2. HPL, "Damon and Delia, a Pastoral," *Tryout* (August 1918), as by "Edward Softly"; *AT* 118–21.
3. *The Love Epistles of Aristaenetus* (1771), tr. from the Greek by Richard Brinsley Sheridan and Nathaniel Brassey Halhed. Aristaenetus (d. 358 C.E.) was a Greek grammarian; the letters are probably attributed to him falsely.
4. HPL, "The Eidolon," *Tryout* (October 1918), as by "Ward Phillips"; *AT* 38–40.
5. In *The Tatler* No. 163 (25 April 1710), Addison (under the pseudonym "Isaac Bicker-staffe") pretends to praise a poem, "To Mira on Her Incomparable Poems," by "Ned Softly," calling it "a little nosegay of conceits, a very lump of salt: every verse has something in it that piques. . . ."

---

# DEPARTMENT OF PUBLIC CRITICISM

*(January 1919)*

*T*he *Brooklynite* for November boasts as its leading feature a patriotic and appealing sonnet by Editor Kleiner, entitled "Ready though Uncalled". In considering this piece, the reviewer is compelled to do something not often done in Mr. Kleiner's case—to call into question the accent of a word. In line 9, we find the word *can*-tonment erroneously accented on the second syllable, though in justice to the author it must be pointed out that this particular perversion has wide recent precedent; *canton*-*ment* being one of several military terms to suffer through hasty usage since the outbreak of the great war.

"O Tempora, O Mores!", by Katherine B. Collier, is a correct and pleasing bit of verse which adds much to the magazine.

Of the two impromptu effusions labelled "Picnic Poetry", and composed under adverse circumstances, that from the pen of James F. Morton, Jr., is incomparably the better. Mrs. Isaacson's similar piece is marred by a certain sordidness or earthiness which has no place in verse, and which not even the frivolity of the theme can excuse. In light verse, elusive delicacy is the *sine qua non*, and we defy any critics, however lenient, to justify a quatrain so utterly nauseating as the following:

> "I ate and ate and ate again,
>     And nothing made me sick
> Until Daas gave me a dirty bun,
>     And that thing did the trick."

Miss Pearl K. Merritt's "essay" on the recent Blue Pencil picnic is fluent and entirely grammatical; though like many other pieces of its author's work, of no particular literary interest or exaltation. Miss Merritt is undoubtedly an ideal informal letter-writer, but evidently oversteps her province when attempting more ambitious productions. This verdict, however, is given without a wide knowledge of her earlier work; which many competent critics praise highly.

Mr. A. M. Adams is more successful as an essayist, and manages to infuse some real, glowing, and practical patriotism in his colloquial discourse on "Halloween Pranks". We are glad to see so virile a piece at this particular time; when through the reaction brought about by the return of peace, a great deal of sneaking Hun and pacifist propaganda is likely to be circulated either openly or in decorously camouflaged style.

Owing to his recent bereavement and ill health, Mr. Kleiner's editorials are necessarily brief; but they are none the less of a quality which makes us hope that his occupancy of the editor's chair will be of long duration.

*Pine Cones* for December is the first issue of a new and very meritorious paper published on the duplicator by Rev. J. Clinton Pryor. As an old-time amateur of the highest type, Mr. Pryor needs no introduction to our fraternity; and his enterprise needs no recommendation other than the assurance that it is fully up to the best Pryoristic standard.

The magazine opens with "Earth and Sky", a piece of verse in *ottava rima* by H. P. Lovecraft.[1] In metre and general form this production seems tolerable, though its intellectual rather than emotional appeal would in the opinion of many critics debar it from classification as poetry.

By far the most important feature of the issue is the long essay on "Conduct" by the editor. In this masterly piece of sociological analysis, Mr. Pryor displays a keen insight, sound reasoning, and lucid expository style, which mark him as a close thinker and powerful writer.

"Comment Pryoristic" touches varied themes; one of the most interesting being that of amateur criticism, a thing so widely discussed of late in both associations. Mr. Pryor here displays a broad and intelligent attitude; though we might point out in possible defence of a brother critic, that the strictures on his recent story may have been merely hints as to a tendency, rather than actual censure of a defect. Surely no one could misinterpret or lose track of the plot in "After the Curtain Falls", but a critic might fancy that the artistic obscurity (in itself valuable) shewed signs of transcending the limit which must be heeded in all such cases.

Altogether, *Pine Cones* is a splendid achievement, and we make no attempt to conceal our delight at the fact that we are to see six issues each year. May it last forever, or until a permanent printed *Dryad* from Mr. Pryor's parsonage supersedes it.

*The Silver Clarion* for November opens with "Wishes", a poem of great power by Anne Tillery Renshaw. The slightly impressionistic atmosphere, being carefully restrained, is wholly pleasing; and the lines reflect a sentiment which upon reflection will be found to be universal.

"November Days", by John Osman Baldwin, is a poem of real merit; an opinion we give in defiance of the less than lukewarm generalisations of another critic concerning Baldwin verse. Mr. Baldwin need only give himself a course in intensive technical training, in order to cast off the crudities which cause so many otherwise acute reviewers consistently to underestimate his work. This Department, for one, stands ready to aid him in every way possible.

"The Value of Travel", by C. A. Shattuck, is a not unacceptable justification of the traditional "rolling stone", in essay form. As a piece of literature it has decided limitations; being marked by an all-pervading didacticism, crudity, and immaturity, which alienate the cultivated reader.

"The Sacrifice", a poem by Agnes Richmond Arnold, is correct and appealing. How well have the Allied arms now vindicated the prophecy, that "Usurpers' flags shall soon be furl'd!"

"Death", a poem by Jonathan E. Hoag, was suggested by a sermon, and represents at his best a venerable bard who will next month celebrate his 88th birthday. Especially striking is the passage:

> "What bard with grace could ever sing
> The cloying charm of endless spring,
> Or praise eternal day?"[2]

Very short, but very powerful, is "Blindness", a poem by Winifred Jordan. To the religious enthusiast, a passage like the following must appeal strongly:

> "The flow'r-strewn sod
> Must speak, within life's dark,
> Of God!"

"We Shall Triumph If We Wait", by Arthur Goodenough, is an inspirational piece in every way worthy of its justly renowned author. In passing, however, that in *couplet* verse it is not customary to indent alternate lines. By the same hand is the equally meritorious poem, "There Blooms a Rose in Paradise", whose conception and execution attract praise.

The final feature of this issue is Editor Samples' classically correct poem entitled, "The Soil of France". Our only possible objection to this is the extreme inversion in line 4 of the second stanza:

> "That glory new imparts".

Mr. Samples is obviously increasing in technical skill, and will prove a factor to be reckoned with in the poetical annals of amateurdom.

*The Silver Clarion* for December bears on its cover a rather long and somewhat mediocre Christmas poem by John Osman Baldwin. This piece, both in thought and technique, is indubitably below Mr. Baldwin's best level. Specifically, we may mention the poetical inappropriateness of such a word as *phenomena*—which, by the way, is used where the singular form *phenomenon* should be—as well as the manifest incorrectness of such a rhyme as *Flag* and *glad*. The difference of final consonants here involved should be very obvious; even to a bard as "easy-going" as Mr. Baldwin.

"Where Willows Drowse", a poem by Dr. Eugene B. Kuntz, is of a grace and merit characteristic of its author. Dr. Kuntz never fails to achieve a high standard, few other amateur poets being able to boast an equal intensity and sincerity in their worship of the Nine. One remarkable idiosyncrasy is to be noted in Kuntz poetry; namely, that when using iambics the author never varies his metre with trochees, spondees, and amphibrachs, after the fashion of most bards. In thus renouncing variety, however, he seems happily immune from that monotonousness which might be expected under such conditions.

"The Phantom", by John Milton Samples, is a pious and pleasing poem in anapaestic metre; whose defects, purely technical, are probably all due to the novelty of this measure in the hands of an author more accustomed to iambics. Missing syllables are the chief fault. The anapaest is by no means so easy to use correctly, as appears from its external fluency. True, syllabification is vastly more flexible than in iambic and trochaic feet; but the variations must all be within certain limits determined by the taste and metrical ear of the bard. Thomas Moore is an excellent poet to read in order to obtain familiarity with anapaestic composition.

"To the American Flag", by J. E. Hoag, is a spirited patriotic piece; here marred by a couple of exasperating misprints. The third and fourth lines of the second stanza should read:

> "As in noble rank increasing,
> Each new *ray* outshines the last."[3]

"Thistles", by Winifred Virginia Jordan, is a didactic poem of much grace and thoughtfulness; whose moral should be universally heeded.

"Along the Marne Tonight", by Anne Tillery Renshaw, is a meritorious military poem. Unfortunately, the present text was printed from an early version which does not incorporate latest revisions.

"My Faith", by Arthur Goodenough, is the equal of any poem in this issue as regards thought; and the only technical point open to question is the rhyme of *death* and *faith*. Walker does not explicitly sanction this combination, yet there are many considerations which deter us from denouncing it as mere assonance.

Mr. Samples' editorial is a timely one, and bears the heading "Victory and Peace". Though the practical observer may be pardoned a mental reservation as to the increasingly godlike soul of man, and the approaching cessation of all warfare; none can deny the unimpeachable nobility of the author's ideals.

*The United Amateur* for November opens with an essay by H. P. Lovecraft on "The Literature of Rome".[4] So far as we can see, the facts are authentic and the style correct; though of course such a composition calls for little more than a fairly good memory and a reasonable knowledge of the subject. In the final paragraph a misprint mars the sense. The word *as* should occur between *enjoyment* and *of*. Through the process of editorial abridgment, much of the original essay was relegated to the back of the volume in the form of supplementary notes. Here misprints are especially numerous; the worst being "*Heroids*" for *Heroides*, "*Thistia*" for *Tristia*, *A. Livius* for *T. Livius*, "*Rumianus*" for *Am-*

*mianus,* and *"Severinno"* for *Severinus.* We hope the article may serve its purpose in turning more than one amateur to the study of a subject whose importance can hardly be overestimated.

An essay of kindred type is "M. Tullius Cicero—'Pater Patriae'", by Helene H. Cole. In this brief article the merits of Ciceronian thought and style are well displayed, and treated in a somewhat subjective manner.

A third prose piece (though according to ultra-modern conceptions it might be termed poetry) is "Aunt Prissy's Red Cross Prayer", by Heinrich (alias Mary H.) Lehr. This homely sketch has a distinct appeal in its delineation of pathos and wistfulness, and displays much knowledge of human nature on the author's part.

Turning to the poetical selections, we must give particular mention to "Dusk", by Perrin Holmes Lowrey, which would take high rank in any magazine, amateur or professional. In liquid melody of sound, Mr. Lowrey excels most of his fellow-amateurs; and his choice of unusual metres is almost always strikingly felicitous.

"Nearing Winter", by Winifred Virginia Jordan, is reprinted from the august and impressive *Boston Transcript,* and certainly fulfils the best traditions of that classic journal. As we have had occasion to remark before, Mrs. Jordan is peculiarly at home in handling rural New England themes.

Another of the group of reprints so well selected by the editor is "Bulgaria's Surrender", by Rheinhart Kleiner; written just after the collapse which commenced the series of enemy surrenders. Mr. Kleiner is here at his best, displaying a fervour for the right which contrasts advantageously with the weak-kneed pacifism of certain other bards.

"To Alan Seeger", by H. P. Lovecraft,[5] prolongs the military strain by celebrating the memory of a young American hero of the French Foreign Legion, who, had the fortunes of battle spared him, would have been one of our country's greatest poets. Seeger was a bard of the broadest and keenest vision, and in his verses hailed as his greatest fellow-citizen that mighty leader of men for whom the whole world is in recent mourning as these paragraphs are penned. As the martyr-poet said in his "Message to America":

> "You have a leader who knows—the man
> Most fit to be call'd American,
> A prophet that once in generations
> Is given to point to erring nations
> Brighter ideals toward which to press
> And lead them out of the wilderness.
>
> I have been too long from my country's shores
> To reckon what state of mind is yours,
> But as for myself I know right well
> I would go through fire and shot and shell
> And face new perils and make my bed
> In new privations, if ROOSEVELT led!"[6]

"To Towne's Volcanic Mount", by Jonathan E. Hoag, is a graceful and dignified tribute in verse to a geological wonder near the author's home. Mr. Hoag is an acknowledged master of subjects of this kind, and the reader will gain from this pleasing poem many reminders of his earlier work in a similar vein.

The editorial section is especially strong this month, beginning with some pertinent reflections on civilisation's recent victory, and ending with a merited rebuke to that element in the National Amateur Press Association which is responsible for the fatuous and insolent "absorption" resolution presented at the Chicago convention. We are glad to see our influential and impartial Official Editor go on record so forcibly and unequivocally.

In concluding our remarks on this thoroughly excellent issue, we must not overlook W. Paul Cook's sympathetic and well-written obituary of the late Henry G. Wekhing. Amateurdom could not ask for a more tasteful and appropriate tribute to one whom it mourns so deeply.

The United Co-operative for December marks the beginning of a publishing enterprise which should help in remedying the present paucity of papers. Financed jointly by a large group of editors, its production involves but few individual sacrifices.

The present number opens with a "rough and ready" army camp poem, written by Mrs. Jordan and dedicated to her enlisted cousin, entitled "Have You Met My Buddy?" Despite a profusion of slang, the piece is distinctly captivating; and vastly above the majority of verses lately written by persons who try to reflect the rugged army spirit. It rings true, which cannot be said of many military poems by non-military authors. More obviously Jordanian is "Days of Laughter", a haunting, tuneful, and delicate bit of poetical pensiveness, especially consoling and appropriate at a time when all the world is wrapped in gloom and uncertainty.

Miss Maryetta (alias Mary H.) Lehr is likewise represented by two poems; one of which, "The Unfathomed Sea of Pain", is particularly thoughtful and profound. "Forgive My Heart, Too Numb to Love" throbs with real emotion, which is not lessened by the questionable accentuation of "on-slaught" on the last syllable.

A third bard is Ward Phillips, Esq., whose heavy lines on "Ambition" reveal his usual attitude concerning the insignificance of man and the futility of things in general.[7]

The first prose piece is an essay on "The Simple Spelling Mania", by H. P. Lovecraft.[8] The vagaries and underlying fatuousness of orthographical "reform" are here displayed for the benefit of amateurdom, some of whose younger adherents have occasionally shewn a lamentable tendency to use some of the pernicious current "simplifications".

"In Days of Childhood" is a witty collection of juvenile anecdotes by J. Clinton Pryor, who vouches for the truth of each one. These breezy glimpses of carefree and ingenuous infancy introduce a delightful note into a magazine which might otherwise earn the epithet of "heavy". Mr. Pryor's column of comment is as always of sound sense and great interest. His praise of the United Amateur is certainly deserved; and many of his strictures on a certain critic (ourself, to be candid!) are probably merited as well. However, we must remind him that in criticism it is often the reviewer's duty to point out superficialities in reasoning, a procedure which necessitates a trifle of the attempted refutation whereof he complains.

EDITOR'S NOTE FP: United Amateur 18, No. 3 (January 1919): 53–59 (unsigned). Certain portions of the column (not included here) were not written by HPL; these include pp. 53–54 (signed "W. P[aul] C[ook]") and pp. 55–56 (signed "A[lfred] G[alpin], Jr."). Galpin's segment discusses the December 1918 issue of the Pippin (a paper issued by the Appleton

High School Press Club), about which HPL wrote the poem "To the A. H. S. P. C., on Receipt of the Christmas *Pippin*" (AT 346–47).

*Notes*

1. See AT 108–9. The poem was first published in the *Little Budget of Knowledge and Nonsense* (July 1917).
2. The poem was once attributed to HPL; possibly it was revised by him. See S. T. Joshi, "Two Spurious Lovecraft Poems," *Crypt of Cthulhu* No. 20 (Eastertide 1984); 25–26.
3. This poem has also been attributed to HPL. See n. 2 above. The correction here indicated by HPL may suggest that he revised the poem.
4. See CE2.
5. See AT 417–18.
6. Alan Seeger, "A Message to America" (1916), in Seeger's *Poems*, ed. William Archer (New York: Scribner's, 1916), pp. 164, 165.
7. The poem is by HPL. See AT 124–25.
8. See CE2.

---

# DEPARTMENT OF PUBLIC CRITICISM

*(March 1919)*

*T*he *Coyote* for October–January is a "Special War Number", dedicated to Cpl. Raymond Wesley Harrington, the editor's valiant soldier brother, and having a general martial atmosphere throughout. Among the contents are two bits of verse by the gallant overseas warrior to whom the issue is inscribed, both of which speak well for the poetic sentiment of their heroic author.

"Lord Love You, Lad", a poem by Winifred V. Jordan, is the opening contribution; and deserves highest commendation both for its spirit and for its construction.

"The Paramount Issue", by William T. Harrington, is a somewhat ambiguous attempt to trace the responsibility for the great war to alcoholic liquor and its degenerative effect on mankind. The author even goes so far as to say that "had man been represented in true and noble form, then war would have been impossible". Now, although the present critic is and always has been an ardent prohibitionist, he must protest at this extravagant theory. Vast and far-reaching as are the known evil effects of drink, it is surely transcending fact to accuse it of causing mankind's natural greed, pride, and combative instincts, which lie at the base of all warfare. It may, however, be justly suggested that much of the peculiar bestiality of the Huns is derived from their swinish addiction to beer. Technically, Mr. Harrington's essay is marked by few crudities, and displays an encouraging fluency. Other pieces by Mr. Harrington are "A Bit of My Diary", wherein the author relates his regrettably brief military experience at Camp Dodge, and "Victory", a stirring editorial.

"Black Sheep", by Edna Hyde, is an excellent specimen of blank verse by our gifted laureate. Line 14 seems to lack a syllable, but this deficiency is probably the result of a typographical error.

A word of praise is due the general appearance of the magazine. The cover presents a refreshing bit of home-made pictorial art, whilst the photograph of Corporal Harrington makes a most attractive frontispiece.

*The Pathfinder* for January is easily the best issue yet put forth by its enterprising young editor. "Hope", which adorns the cover, is a poem of much merit by Annie Pearce. The apparent lack of a syllable in line 2 of the third stanza is probably due to a printer's error whereby the word *us* is omitted immediately after the word *for*.

"How and Why Roses Are White", by Margaret Mahon, is a fairy legend of much charm and decided originality, which argues eloquently for its author's imaginative scope and literary ability.

"Happiness in a Glove" is a very facile and pleasing rendering of a bit of Spanish dialogue. Through a mistake, the authorship is credited to the translator, Miss Ella M. Miller, though her own manuscript fully proclaimed the text as a translation.

"Welcome, 1919" is a brief contemplative essay by Editor Glause; in spirit admirable, but in phraseology shewing some of the uncertainty of youthful work. Mr. Glause might well pay more attention to compact precision in his prose, using as few and as forceful words as possible to express his meaning. For instance, his opening words would gain greatly in strength if contracted to the following: "Now that a new year is beginning." Farther down the page we find the word *namely* in a place which impels us to question its use. Its total omission would strengthen the sentence which contains it. Another point we must mention is the excessive punctuation, especially the needless hyphenation of *amateurdom* and *therefore*, and the apostrophe in the possessive pronoun *its*. The form *it's* is restricted to the colloquial contraction of "*it is*"; the similarly spelled pronoun is written solidly without an apostrophe. Additional notes by Mr. Glause are of equal merit, and his reply to a recent article on travel is highly sensible and commendable. He is a writer and thinker of much power, and needs only technical training in order to develop into an essayist of the first rank. As an editor he cannot be praised too highly for his faithfulness in publishing his welcome and attractive quarterly.

*Pine Cones* for February well maintains the high standard set by Mr. Pryor in his opening number. "Life, Death and Immortality", by Jonathan E. Hoag, is a brief but appealing piece from the pen of a gifted and venerable bard, and thoroughly deserves its place of honour on the cover. On the next page occurs a metrical tribute to this sweet singer on his 88th birthday, written by H. P. Lovecraft in the latter's typical heroic strain.[1]

"The Helpful Twins", a clever child story by Editor Pryor, is the prose treat of the issue. It would, indeed, be hard to find more than one or two equally interesting, human, and well-developed bits of fiction in any current amateur periodicals. Not only are the characters drawn with delightful naturalness, but there is real humour present; and the plot moves on to its climax without a single instance of awkwardness or a single intrusive or extraneous episode. In short, the story is almost a model of its kind; one which ought to prove a success in a professional as well as an amateur magazine. Mr. Pryor's humour is more broadly shewn in the smile-producing pseudo-anecdotes of "The Boy Washington".

The bit of unsigned verse, "A New Year Wish", is excellent, though we question the advisability of having an Alexandrine for the final line.

"Comment Pryoristic" is always interesting, and that in the current *Pine Cones* forms no exception to the rule. The appearance of this vigorously alive and intelligently edited publication is proving a great and gratifying factor in amateurdom's post-bellum renaissance.

*The Recruiter* for January marks the advent to amateurdom of a new paper, which easily takes its place among the very best of recent editorial enterprises. Edited by Misses Mary Faye Durr and L. Evelyn Schump in the interest of the United recruits whom they are securing, its thoroughly meritorious quality speaks well for the new members thus added to our circle.

The issue opens auspiciously with a lyric poem of distinguished excellence by Helen McFarland, entitled "A Casualty". In depth of sentiment, fervour of expression, and correctness of construction, these melodious lines leave little to be desired; and seem to indicate that the United has acquired one more poet of the first rank.

"Billy", a character sketch by L. Evelyn Schump, introduces to the Association a light essayist of unusual power and grace, whose work is vividly natural through keen insight, apt and fluent expression, and mastery of homely and familiar detail. The present sketch is captivatingly life-like and thoroughly well-written, arousing a response from every lover of children.

"Winter", a brief poem by Hettie Murdock, celebrates in a pleasant way an unpleasant season. The lines are notable for correctness, spontaneity, and vitality, though not in the least ambitious in scope.

Martha Charlotte Macatee's "Song of Nature" reveals its 12-year-old creator as a genuine "Galpiness" (if we may coin a word which only amateurs and Appletonians will understand). Mistress Macatee has succeeded in infusing more than a modicum of really poetic atmosphere and imagery into her short lyric, and may be relied upon to produce important work in the coming years of greater maturity. The chief defect of her present piece is the absence of rhyme, which should always occur in a short stanzaic poem. Rhyming is not at all difficult after a little practice, and we trust that the young writer will employ it in later verses.

"Tarrytown", by Florence Fitzgerald, is a reminiscent poem phenomenal strength, marred only by a pair of false rhymes in the opening stanza. Assonance must never be mistaken for true rhyme, and combinations like *boats—float* or *them—brim* should be avoided. The imagery of this piece is especially appealing, and testifies to its author's fertility of fancy.

"Shades of Adam", by Mary Faye Durr, is an interesting and humorously written account of the social side of our 1918 convention. Miss Durr is exceptionally gifted in the field of apt, quiet, and laconic wit, and in this informal chronicle neglects no opportunity for dryly amusing comment on persons and events.

"Spring", by L. Evelyn Schump, is a refreshingly original poem in blank verse, on a somewhat familiar subject. For inspiration and technique alike, the piece merits enthusiastic commendation; though we may vindicate our reputation as a fault-finding critic by asking why alternate lines are indented despite the non-existence of alternate rhymes.

*The Recruiter's* is brief and business-like, introducing the magazine as a whole, and its contributors individually. Amateurdom is deeply indebted to the publishers of this delightful newcomer, and it is to be hoped that they may continue their efforts; both toward seeking recruits as high in quality as those here represented, and toward issuing their admirable journal as frequently as is feasible.

*The Silver Clarion* for January comes well up to the usual standard, containing a number of pieces of considerable power. In "The Temple of the Holy Ghost", Mr. Arthur Goodenough achieves his accustomed success as a religious poet, presenting a variety of apt images, and clothing them in facile metre. The only defect is a lack of uniformity in rhyming plan. The poet, in commencing a piece like this, should decide whether or not to rhyme the first and third lines of quatrains; and having decided, should adhere to his decision. Instead, Mr. Goodenough omits these optional rhymes in the first stanza and in the first half of the third and fourth stanzas; elsewhere employing them. The result, while not flagrantly unharmonious, nevertheless gives an impression of imperfection, and tends to alienate the fastidious critic. Mr. Goodenough possesses so great a degree of inspiration, and so wide an array of allusions and imagery, that he owes it to himself to complete the excellence of his vivid work with an unexceptionable technique.

"The Cross", a sonnet by Captain Theodore Draper Gottlieb, is dedicated to the Red Cross, with which the author is serving so valiantly. In thought and form this piece deserves unqualified praise.

"Death", by Andrew Francis Lockhart, exhibits our versatile Western bard in sober mood. The poem contains that unmistakable stamp of genuine emotion which we have come to associate with Mr. Lockhart's work, and is technically faultless.

"Destiny", by W. F. Pelton, is a sonnet of smooth construction and thorough excellence by one whom we know better as "Wilfred Kemble".

The lines "To My Pal, Fred" present Mr. Harry E. Rieseberg, a new member of the United who has for some time been a regular *Clarion* contributor. In this piece Mr. Rieseberg falls somewhat below his usual standard; for though the sentiment is appropriate, the metre is sadly irregular. Mr. Rieseberg should count the syllables in his lines, for he is a young poet of much promise, and should allow his technique to keep pace with his genius.

"Faith", by Winifred V. Jordan, enunciates a familiar doctrine in melodious and original metaphor, and well sustains the poetical reputation of its celebrated author.

"The Song Unsung", by W. F. Booker, is a war poem in minor key, which deserves much praise.

"You're Like a Willow", by Eugene B. Kuntz, is marked by that warmth of fancy and wealth of imagery for which its author is noted.

"Thoughts", a courtly offering from the quill of James Laurence Crowley, winds up the poetical part of the magazine; this month a very amble part. In rhyme and metre this sentimental gem is quite satisfactory.

The only prose in this issue is Mr. Samples' well-written editorial on "The Passing Year". Herein we find some really excellent passages, savouring somewhat of the oratorical in style.

*The Silver Clarion* for February is of ample size and ample merit. Opening the issue is an excellent poem in heroic couplets by Mrs. Stella L. Tully of Mountmellick, Ireland, a new member of the United. Mrs. Tully, whose best work is in a lyric and religious vein, is one endowed with hereditary or family genius; as the Association no doubt appreciated when reading the poetry of her gifted sister, Mrs. S. Lilian McMullen of Newton Centre, in the preceding issue of *The United Amateur*. The present piece by Mrs. Tully, "The Greatest of These Is Love", is based upon a Biblical text, and sets forth its ideas very effectively, despite a few passages whose stiff construction betrays a slight inexperience in the traditions of heroic verse.

"The Two Crosses", by Capt. Theodore Gottlieb, is also in heroics, and graphically compares the most holy symbols of today and of nineteen hundred years ago.

More of the religious atmosphere is furnished by John Milton Samples' trochaic composition entitled "The Millennium"—from whose title, by the way, one of the necessary *n*'s is missing. In this pleasing picture of an impossible age we note but three things requiring critical attention. (1) The term "super-race" in stanza 5 is too technically philosophical to be really poetic. (2) The rhyme of *victory* and *eternally* is not very desirable, because both the rhyming syllables bear only a secondary accent. (3) There is something grotesque and unconsciously comic in the prophecy "Then the lamb shall kiss the lion". Such grotesqueness is not to be found in the original words of Mr. Samples' predecessor and source of inspiration, the well-known prophet Isaiah (vide Isaiah, xi:6–7).

"Nature Worship", by Arthur Goodenough, is one of the most meritorious poems in the issue, despite some dubious grammar in the first stanza, and an internal rhyme in the final stanza which has no counterpart in the lines preceding. The first named error consists of a disagreement in number betwixt subject and verb: "faith and form and . . . mazes which perplexes, dazes".

"'The New Order", an essay by John Milton Samples, is an eloquent but fantastically idealistic bit of speculation concerning the wonderful future which dreamers picture as arising out of the recent war. To us, there is a sort of pathos in these vain hopes and mirage-like visions of an Utopia which can never be; yet if they can cheer anyone, they are doubtless not altogether futile. Indeed, after the successive menaces of the Huns and the Bolsheviki, we can call almost any future Utopian, if it will but afford the comparative calm of pre-1914 days!

"No Night So Dark, No Day So Drear", by Mamie Knight Samples, is a poem which reveals merit despite many crudities. The outstanding fault is defective metre— Mrs. Samples should carefully count her syllables, and repeat her lines aloud, to make sure of perfect scansion. Since the intended metre appears to be iambic tetrameter, we shall here give a revised rendering of the first stanza; shewing how it can be made to conform to that measure:

> "No night so dark, no day so drear,
> But we may sing our songs of cheer."
> These words, borne from the world without,
> Cheer'd a heart sick with grief and doubt.
> O doubting soul, bow'd down so low,
> If thou couldst feel, and only know
> The darkness is in thee alone,
> For grief and tears it would atone.
> "No night so dark, no day so drear,
> But we may sing our songs of cheer."

Let the authoress note that each line must have eight syllables—no more, no less. For the trite ideas and hackneyed rhymes, nothing can be recommended save a more observant and discriminating perusal of standard poets. It must be kept in mind that the verse found in current family magazines and popular hymn-books is seldom, if ever, true poetry. The only authors suitable as models are those whose names are praised in histories of English literature.

W. F. Booker's "Song" is a delightful short lyric whose sentiment and technique deserve naught but praise.

"When I Am Gone", a poem in pentameter quatrains by James Laurence Crowley, contains the customary allotment of sweet sentiment, together with some really commendable imagery. Mr. Crowley's genius will shine brightly before long.

"The Path to Glory", by Andrew Francis Lockhart, is perhaps the poetic gem of the issue. In this virile anapaestic piece Mr. Lockhart sums up all the horrors of the trenches in such a way that the reader may guess at the extent of the sacrifice undergone by those who have given all for their country.

In "Coconino Jim, Lumberjack", Mr. Harry E. Rieseberg shews himself a true and powerful poet of the rugged, virile school of Kipling, Service, Knibbs, and their analogues.[2] The present piece is entirely correct in rhyme and well developed in thought, wanting only good metre to make it perfect. This latter accomplishment Mr. Rieseberg should strive hard to attain, for his poetry surely deserves as good a form as he can give it.

A word of praise should be given Mr. Samples' editorial, "The Professional in Amateur Journalism", in which he shews the fallacy of the plea for a cruder, more juvenile amateurdom, which often emanates from members of the older and less progressive associations. As the editor contends, intellectual evolution must occur; and the whole recent career of the United demonstrates the value of a purely literary society for genuine literary aspirants of every age and every stage of mental development.

EDITOR'S NOTE FP: *United Amateur* 18, No. 4 (March 1919): 79–82 (unsigned). The entire column was written by HPL. He continues to devote considerable space to the *Silver Clarion*.

*Notes*

1. "To Jonathan Hoag, Esq., on His 88th Birthday, February 10, 1919" (AT 348–50).
2. The references are to the poets Rudyard Kipling (British; 1865–1936), Robert W. Service (Anglo-Canadian; 1874–1958), and Henry Herbert Knibbs (American; 1874–1945).

# WINIFRED VIRGINIA JORDAN: ASSOCIATE EDITOR

Commencing with this issue, *The Silver Clarion* adds to its editorial staff one of the most celebrated poets and most prominent workers in Amateur Journalism— Mrs. Winifred Virginia Jordan, of Newton Center, Mass.

Mrs. Jordan, a writer of poetry since 1910, joined the United in October, 1915, as one of the many recruits of select grade then being secured by Mrs. Anne T. Renshaw. Her poetry, which was eagerly sought and voluminously published by all amateur editors from the very first, soon became famous throughout the fraternity, and earned the unstinted panegyric of nearly every critic both official and unofficial. Beginning with the exquisite yet wonderfully dissimilar poems, "List to the Sea" and "The Song of the North Wind", Mrs. Jordan's verse has appeared in unlimited quantity in practically every one of the amateur papers, till it is a familiar saying, that no journal is really complete without a specimen. Unforgettable to the discriminating reader are such rare lyrics as the "Morven's Mead" series, the "Songs from Walpi", "April", "Insomnia", "Dear", "'Tis Maytime in the Pine Tree State", and "Nearing Winter." Realising the sustained merit and inspiration displayed in such a vast and diverse array of poetry, Amateurdom was not surprised when, last summer, Dr. Henry T. Schnittkind, of the Stratford Publishing Co., Boston, awarded Mrs. Jordan the Verse Laureateship of the United.

But Mrs. Jordan's success has not been altogether confined to Amateurdom. *Weekly Unity, The Newton Graphic, The National Magazine,* and *The Boston Transcript* are among the professional publications to which she contributes, and she has received at least one spontaneous offer from a book publishing company, with a view to issuing a volume of her collected works.[1]

Officially and editorially Mrs. Jordan has achieved almost as much distinction as she has achieved in the poetical field. Immediately upon joining the Association, she became an active worker on the Ladies' Auxiliary Recruit Committee, and in 1917 was elected Second Vice-President by an overwhelming majority. Her success in office led to her renomination and equally brilliant re-election in 1918, her present term being marked by such constructive work as the restoration of printed stationery for the Association, and the establishment of the United Women's Press Club of Massachusetts, a local body whose instant success gives promise of a Boston convention before many years elapse. Of this club, whose first official organ is soon to appear, Mrs. Jordan has naturally been elected President. As a publisher, Mrs. Jordan is celebrated for *Eurus,* issued in February, 1918, and dedicated to our venerable bard, Mr. Hoag, on his eighty-seventh birthday. In quality this journal is surpassed by none, and it has everywhere led to the wish that future numbers might appear.

Mrs. Jordan's serious literary work is all poetical, and her poems may be roughly grouped in six classes: Lyrics of ideal beauty, including delightful Nature poems replete with local colour; delicate amatory lyrics; rural dialect lyrics and vigorous colloquial pieces; poems of sparkling optimism; child verse; and poems of potent terror and dark suggestion. Varied as may seem this range, it is all pervaded by a fresh and original individuality which gives it a certain homogeneity and makes it characteristically and unmistakably Jordanian. No poet, indeed, is less a copyist or follower of models than Mrs. Jordan. Though refreshingly and musically conservative in choice of metre, and never inclined toward the vagaries of imagism, she gives her products, of whatever kind, a distinctive stamp of scintillant and ethereal fancy. With her, sordid realism has no place; and her poems glow with a subtle touch of the fanciful and the supernatural, which is well sustained by tasteful and unusual word-combinations, images, and onomatopoetic effects.

The genuine excellence of Mrs. Jordan's work, as contrasted with average amateur poetry, cannot too strongly be emphasised. In her the United possesses a poet of real depth and inspiration, now at the beginning of a literary career which will take her far beyond the limits of Amateurdom. Altogether, the *Clarion* has reason to congratulate itself upon its new Associate Editor.

EDITOR'S NOTE FP: *Silver Clarion* 3, No. 1 (April 1919): 9–11 (as by "El Imparcial"). A brief biography of Jordan, some parts of which were later expanded into a critical article on her verse, "Winifred Virginia Jackson: A 'Different' Poetess" (*United Amateur,* March 1921; CE2). This is the last article by HPL written under the "El Imparcial" pseudonym.

*Notes*

1. Jackson published only two volumes in her lifetime, *Backwoods: Maine Narratives, with Lyrics* (1927) and *Selected Poems* (1944; with Major Ralph Temple Jackson).

# HELENE HOFFMAN COLE—LITTERATEUR

Of the various authors who have contributed to the fame of our Association, few can be compared in sustained ability and breadth of interests to the late Helene Hoffman Cole. Represented in the press as a poet, critic, essayist, and fiction-writer, Mrs. Cole achieved distinction in all of these departments; rising during recent years to an almost unique prominence in the field of book-reviewing. Her compositions display a diversity of attainments and catholicity of taste highly remarkable in one of so relatively slight an age, familiar knowledge of foreign and archaic literature supplying a mature background too seldom possessed by amateur authors.

It is as a poet that Mrs. Cole has been least known, since her verse was not of frequent occurrence in the amateur press. A glance at the few existing specimens, however, demonstrates conclusively that her poetical gifts were by no means inconsiderable; and that had she chosen such a course, she might easily have become one of the leading bards of the United. Verse like the unnamed autumn pieces in *Leaflets* and *The Hellenian* possess an aptness and cleverness of fancy which bespeaks the true poet despite trivial technical imperfections.

In fiction the extent of Mrs. Cole's genius was still further revealed, nearly all her narratives moving along with impeccable grace and fluency. Her plots were for the most part light and popular in nature, and would have reflected credit on any professional writer of modern magazine tales. Of her stories, "The Picture", appearing in *Leaflets* for October, 1913, is an excellent example. More dramatic in quality is "Her Wish", in the August, 1914, *Olympian*. This brief tragedy of a Serbian and his bride is perhaps one of the very first tales written around the World War.

But it is in the domain of the literary essay that this authoress rose to loftiest altitude. Of wise and profound reading, and of keen and discriminating mind, Mrs. Cole presented in a style of admirable grace and lucidity her reactions to the best works of numerous standard authors, ancient and modern, English and foreign. The value of such works in amateurdom, extending the cultural outlook and displaying the outside world as seen through the eyes of a gifted, respected, and representative member, scarce needs the emphasis of the commentator. He who can link the amateur and larger spheres in a pleasing and acceptable fashion deserves the highest approbation and panegyric that the United can bestow. Notable indeed are Mrs. Cole's sound views of Sir Thomas Browne's "Hydriotaphia" in *The United Amateur*, of "Pelle, the Conqueror" in *The Tryout*, and of numerous South American works but little known to Northern readers. Of equal merit are such terse and delightful essays as "M. Tullius Cicero, Pater Patriae", where the essayist invests a classical theme with all the living charm of well-restrained subjectivity. The style of these writings is in itself captivating; the vocabulary containing enough words of Latin derivation to rescue it from the Boeotian harshness typical of this age. All that has been said of Mrs. Cole's broader reviews may be said of her amateur criticism, much of which graced the columns of *The Olympian* and other magazines.

The exclusively journalistic skill of Mrs. Cole now remains to be considered, and this we find as brilliant as her other attainments. As the editor of numerous papers during every stage of her career, she exhibited phenomenal taste and enterprise; never failing to create enthusiasm and evoke encomium with her ventures both individual and coöperative. Her gift for gathering, selecting, and writing news was quite unexampled. As the reporter *par excellence* of both associations, she was the main reliance of other editors for convention reports and general items; all of which were phrased with an ease, urbanity, and personality that lent them distinctiveness. Not the least of her qualities was a gentle and unobtrusive humour which enlivened her lighter productions. Amateurdom will long remember the quaint piquancy of the issues of *The Martian* which she cleverly published in the name of her infant son.

During these latter days nearly every amateur has expressed a kind of incredulity that Mrs. Cole can indeed be no more, and in this the present writer must needs share. To realise that her gifted pen has ceased to enrich our small literary world requires a painful effort on the part of everyone who has followed her brilliant progress in the field of letters. The United loses more by her sudden and untimely demise than can well be reckoned at this moment.

EDITOR'S NOTE FP: *United Amateur* 18, No. 5 (May 1919): 92–93. A tribute to a deceased amateur, the wife of HPL's close friend Edward H. Cole. HPL himself does not seem to have had a close association with Mrs. Cole, even though it was under her presidency (as Helene E. Hoffman) that HPL joined the UAPA in April 1914. In his carelessness regarding the rendering of French words, HPL habitually omitted the acute accent in the word *littérateur*.

# DEPARTMENT OF PUBLIC CRITICISM

*(May 1919)*

*The Arizonian* for March represents the older rather than the newer type of amateur journalism, being largely composed of amateur notes and comments, and having a supplement exclusively devoted to such matter. Papers of this kind undoubtedly have their place in the Association, serving to stimulate a healthy interest in our affairs and problems; though one cannot help regretting that they do not reserve more space for pure literature, which is after all the foundation and motive for our various activities.

Mr. Thalheimer's publication, however, by no means neglects the higher side of amateurdom; since it contains a short story by the editor, entitled "Danny Kenyon and the Horseless Carriage", which ranks among the best humorous efforts of the season. The situations and development are everywhere replete with true humour, whilst the style and dialogue harmoniously sustain the general effect and emphasise the Western atmosphere.

"To J. A. M.", by Harry E. Rieseberg, is the solitary poem in this issue. In this amatory effusion, Mr. Rieseberg loses some of his poetical potency without gaining any compensating technical correctness, wherefore the effect is not all what one might expect from so gifted a bard. Aside from the all-pervading commonplaceness, the chief faults are metrical and grammatical. Line 1, stanza 1, lacks a syllable. In the last line of the same stanza the word *thee* is used where *thou* is required. Mr. Rieseberg should remember that in a comparison the nominative case is used. In stanza 2 the final rhyme is unjustifiably omitted—unless we are to believe that the author intended *Navajo* and *thee* as a rhyme, in which case we may merely say that the would-be rhyme is very incorrect indeed. The last stanza is easily the gem of the piece, since besides being correct, it contains several turns of thought and expression which are poetical.

*The Brooklynite* for January is rather prophetic and political in tone, devoting much of its space to roseate dreams of a future Utopia a la Wilson.

Mrs. Lewis leads the poetical procession with her "Thoughts for the New Year", in which a high level of inspiration is maintained save for a very few passages such as

> "Labour shall play a mighty part
> In governing the State."

The defect of a passage like this is its prosaic quality, due to the unimaginative and un-adorned presentation of a plain statement in the ordinary language of conversation or written prose. If a poet desires to eschew the use of ornate expression, it behooves him to see that his images are all truly symbolic and metaphorical. Bare facts and bare lan-guage make prose and nothing more, even when cast in the most approved metrical forms. A slight technical error in Mrs. Lewis' piece is the inharmonious second line of the last stanza, which contains a redundant syllable. It is not permissible to introduce these irregular lines when the bulk of the verse is perfectly regular, as in this case.

Another well-wrought poem is Mr. Morton's "Prophecy for 1919", which is alto-gether free from errors of taste or of technique. The only criticism which one might offer, is that the sentiment shews a bit of overconfidence in the reality of things yet unproven. Mr. Morton's second contribution, "The Wilson Colossus", is in a lighter vein, and was (as we may infer from the third stanza) written before the self-appointed dictator of creation attempted the block the aspirations of Italy. Since then the tide has turned, as we may judge by the act of Genoa in changing the newly named "Wilson Street" to "Fiume Street".

Another albeit cruder specimen of Wilsonism is afforded by Mr. Knack's lines, "Wilson and I". In this piece occur frequent examples of imperfect familiarity both with the finer rules of technique, and with the best traditions of poetic thought. Mr. Knack should read the standard poets closely and analytically, in order to grasp their spirit, and acquire command of their methods.

The lone essay in this issue is by A. M. Adams, and is entitled "What Shall We Do with the Kaiser?" Mr. Adams advocates subtlety, and would confront Herr Hohen-zollern with sights and sounds well calculated to remind him of the misery his minions have wrought. If Wilhelm be really as humane and soft-hearted as his erstwhile press-agent Rosner would have us believe, this punitive programme ought to be at least fairly effective!

*Corona* for March is in many respects the most unique manuscript magazine ever issued, for despite its humble form its contents place it emphatically in the very front rank of high-grade literary journals. Edited by Mrs. Eleanor Barnhart Campbell, it con-sists entirely of her work, and represents her in the four fields of poetry, fiction, essay, and editorial.

"White Logic", the opening contribution, is a philosophical poem of great force and perfect construction, touching upon the ultimates of truth in a manner far re-moved from the common.

"The Loafer" exhibits Mrs. Campbell in her best-known domain, that of the short story, and amply justifies her eminence as the sole wearer of supreme fictional laurels in the United. Here we find the same mastery of detail, verisimilitude of atmosphere, and keen analysis of human acts, which other work of the same author has taught us to ex-pect. Not many writers can equal Mrs. Campbell in intelligent sympathy for lower-class types. In this tale a dull, crude, vulgar, unappealing, and even repellent old labourer is made manifest as the possessor of dreams, impulses, and aspirations toward liberty, which few would associate with one of his kind. The superficial observer would pass "Bill Hawkins" by as one too primitive to study, but Mrs. Campbell seeks and discovers the dormant individuality which not even low life can wholly efface from the human animal.

"The Charmed Life" is an essay on the evolution of the vigorous mind, following an expanding mentality with great skill and vividness through its successive experiences and disillusionments. The artistry is finished and convincing; nor would the philosophy be less so, were it not for the incongruously romantic optimism of the conclusion. This final burst of conventional soul-satisfaction suggests a concession to the popular demand for a "happy ending", or a substitution of some particular case for the general lot of mankind.

Mrs. Campbell's editorials are all notable for good taste and sound sense, though ranging in subject from literary criticism to summer vacations. Especially to be endorsed is the appeal for a wider issuance of manuscript magazines by those who are otherwise unable to enter the publishing field. The technical structure of *Corona*, which was typed on the machine whose name it bears, deserves a particular word of praise. Neatness and ingenuity appear in equal proportions, and the collection of foolscap sheets is made to take on a dignity well befitting the distinguished merit of its literary matter.

*The Hazel Nut* for April is as patriotic as other recent issues, being very largely devoted to Victory Loan and War Savings Stamp propaganda. This propaganda, largely composed of professional newspaper syndicate matter, forms a supplement and occupies the four inner pages of the magazine; leaving the four outer pages for typical amateur uses. The leading feature of the issue is A. M. Adams' well-written article, "Reminiscences of Ante-Bellum Days". We must not infer from this heading that the author's memory extends beyond 1861, for the term "The War"—with accent on the article—has now come to mean a greater and later conflict than the "late unpleasantness" in which our grandsires fought. Mr. Adams, indeed, is dealing with his experiences in Paris and London at the very beginning of the world conflagration. His impressions form highly interesting reading, being related with just enough detail to lend vividness and personality.

*The Hellenian* for Autumn imparts to the reader both pleasure and regret; pleasure from the intrinsic worth of its contents, regret from the sad fact that its gifted editor, publisher, and printer, Mrs. Helene Hoffman Cole, is no longer among the living. This new journal, commencing so auspiciously, would undoubtedly have become one of the brightest lights of amateurdom had Mrs. Cole lived; as it is, only one more number will appear, that being completed by Mr. Edward H. Cole as a memorial to his wife.

In the present issue, all the contents come from the pen of Mrs. Cole. The opening feature is an unnamed autumn poem, one of the very few metrical compositions which the author presented to the amateur public. Though not absolutely perfect in the finer points of technique, this piece reveals a fertile mind, ripe culture, and developed taste which would have made of Mrs. Cole a distinguished poet had she chosen the field of verse instead of that of prose.

"The Eleventh Hour" is a brief but powerful sketch dealing with the close of the great war, and possessing a tragical and highly dramatic conclusion. The climax comes adequately after a well-developed series of images.

"Two Americans" is a joint review of the published reminiscences of Brander Matthews and Hamlin Garland.[1] Here Mrs. Cole exhibits all that taste, observation, and reflectiveness which made her an ideal reviewer; creating an absorbing parallel between her two subjects, and calling up the atmosphere in which each lived and worked.

The editorials in *The Hellenian* are all of the merit harmonious with that of the other parts. Amateurdom is the dominant theme, and the advice offered is of a soundness which should cause every reader to accept it unreservedly. As the farewell message—though not consciously so—of one of amateur journalism's most valued and capable leaders, it has indeed a double claim to attention and compliance.

*The Junior Amateur* for April is a new and patriotic enterprise conducted in behalf of the War Savings Stamp campaign by Mr. Raymond P. Adams, aged one and one-half years. Mr. Adams, like other young amateurs, is a forceful writer; and much may be expected of him in the future. A prominent contributor to this issue is the editor's cousin, Miss Florence P. Schliep, who is considerably his junior—that is, as considerably as his limited years permit. These two geniuses have produced in collaboration a piece of excellent verse about themselves, which opens the magazine and forms the principal feature. In thought and technique this piece is thoroughly excellent—let our older writers do as well!

*The Martian* continues to uphold the high literary reputation of Edward Sherman Cole, incidentally presenting us with a portrait of that remarkable young editor. In the first of the two recent numbers Mr. Cole's interpreter is his mother; but in the latest issue he has secured the collaboration of his brilliant and erudite father, who served at his particular request for a co-editor "with brains in his feet". Mr. Cole's progress will be watched with additional interest now that he has a rival in the person of Mr. Raymond Adams, for the competition between these youthful literati is likely to be keen indeed. Amateurdom's best wishes attend them both.

*Pine Cones* for April is notable for its well-selected contributions, a meritorious variety of which are present. "Ingratitude", a poem in blank verse by James F. Morton, Jr., is a highly artistic protest against deforestation in America, and reveals a mastery of sound and rhythm which only a writer of genius and scholarship can achieve.

"Oh, Winds of Balmy Touch", by Eugene B. Kuntz, is one of its author's typical poems; replete with striking and original images, and animated by a consistently melodious felicity.

"A Mutual Awakening", by Willis Tete Crossman,[2] is an exceedingly well-developed piece of light fiction, whose smoothness is unmarred by hitch or lapse. From the first word to the significant last line its technique is impeccable. The only charge a critic might bring against it is triteness, but that is a charge applicable with equal justice to most of the light fiction in the better grade of professional magazines.

"When the Snow Is on the Hill", by Jonathan and Meredith Hoag, represents the result of collaboration betwixt grandsire and grandson; for Meredith is the grandchild of our noted Greenwich poet—79 years the junior of that gifted lyrist. In this piece a short trochaic metre is handled to advantage, and a rural coasting scene graphically and vividly described. Other short poems here are the didactic and religious verses of Annie Pearce and Clara Lizette Bell. Both of these bards display deep and genuine poetic feeling, and err but slightly on the technical side. To mention a doubtful instance or two—Miss Pearce in "To a Wild Rose" repeats the same rhyme too soon, and in "Sunshine" somewhat falls short of the ideal in attempting double rhyme.

The Pryoristic comment in this issue is of unusual interest; since it deals with the length of amateur literary efforts and refutes the conclusions of those who preach undue brevity. Mr. Pryor points out very well the necessity of giving the writer free scope, and the disastrous effect of excessive abbreviation.

The Silver Clarion for March is largely devoted to the memory of its late associate editor, Mrs. Sarah Story Duffee, who died late in January. Tributes of great appropriateness are paid by the surviving editors, the poem by Mr. Samples being especially fervent and graceful. In this piece, the only flaws are the super-trite expression "briny tear" in the fifth stanza, and the rhyme of delight and light, involving identical syllables, in the sixth stanza. Another piece of Mr. Samples' verse is entitled "In Flanders Field My Laddie Sleeps". Here the main defect is an undesirable internal rhyme in the first line of the third stanza. Still more verse by the chief editor appears in the form of a tribute to Mr. J. E. Hoag, author of some excellent poetry on death and immortality which has appeared in the Clarion. This piece is exceedingly well conceived and phrased, and would be flawless but for the unfortunate attempt to rhyme wealth and death.

The Clarion has recently enlarged its staff, adding as an associate editor the brilliant author and poetess, Winifred Virginia Jordan. Future issues will undoubtedly reflect the spirit of artistic improvement now astir.

The United Amateur for January is a wholly meritorious edition, well maintaining the usual standard.

"The Rime", a graceful and musical sonnet by Wilfred Kemble, opens the issue. Mr. Kemble's work is of a very high order, and is justly gaining increased representation in amateurdom.

"A New Year and a New Era", by Maurice Winter Moe, is a timely bit of prophetic optimism containing a valuable exhortation to amateur journalists.

"The Literature of England", an essay by Henry Clapham McGavack, reveals to us a capable writer's experiment in an abrupt impressionistic style savouring somewhat of Thomas Carlyle and the Boston Transcript's weekly war review. While the present critic's attitude toward such a style can hardly be one of warm sympathy, it must yet be admitted that the difficulties of surveying the whole of our literature in less than three pages excuses much, and that Mr. McGavack has striven most intelligently and cleverly to expound the fundamentals whilst eliminating needless detail.

"An Unwrit Poem of the West", by Eugene B. Kuntz, shews the tuneful Colorado bard in a measure whose brevity detracts not at all from its pleasing effect.

"In Sunset Land", a reflective essay by L. Evelyn Schump, presents many attractive pictures and displays a prose style of phenomenal grace, vividness, and correctness.

The airily lilting lyric entitled "My Mistress, Music", introduces to the United Mrs. S. Lilian McMullen, a poetess destined to rank among the foremost of amateur singers. Both in thought and in execution this piece is eminently successful; the quaint and original metre being admirably adapted to the sense.

"Beauty", an essay by Annie Pearce, is remarkable for its reflective insight and apt development. Miss Pearce is especially skilled in dealing with spiritual abstractions, and is here plainly in her element.

"Thoughts", by Stella L. Tully, is a highly meritorious poem in a somewhat unusual metre, and is distinguished by a rare lyrical fervour.

In the pair of sketches headed "As Genius Views Genius", we behold the mutual biographies of Misses Margaret Trafford and Beryl Mappin, bright stars of the United's semi-juvenile element. Both pieces are interesting and well phrased.

The editorial department in this issue is as strong and as convincing as usual, matters of more than amateur interest being discussed. The editor's tribute to Col.

Roosevelt is graceful and appropriate, prefacing an elegiac poem of greater length from the pen of H. P. Lovecraft.[3]

The Reading Table presents a wisely chosen array of extracts from standard English poets, ranging from Chaucer to Browning. It is well that amateurs should thus be confronted with classic specimens; for there has been of late a growing tendency among young poets to slight the past, and to grow egotistical for want of the sobering effect of a representative background.

EDITOR'S NOTE FP: *United Amateur* 18, No. 5 (May 1919): 99–103 (unsigned). HPL wrote the entire column, with the exception of one section (p. 102; not included here) signed "W. P[aul] C[ook]," covering Kleiner's *Piper* (April 1919). This is the last such column HPL wrote for the UAPA; henceforth, his critical duties were performed solely for the NAPA (1922–23 and 1931–36).

*Notes*

1. Brander Matthews (1852–1929), *These Many Years* (1917); Hamlin Garland (1860–1940), *A Son of the Middle Border* (1917).
2. A pseudonym of W. Paul Cook.
3. "Theodore Roosevelt: 1858–1919" (AT 425–27).

---

# TRIMMINGS

## Our Bow to the Public

In presenting to the amateur world this first number of our publication, we solicit the charitable judgment of critics and contemporaries. The United Women's Press Club of Massachusetts is the newest of local organisations, and can therefore scarcely be expected to act with the mature assurance of those older clubs to which experience has brought the gift of mellowness.

We hope, nevertheless, that our efforts shall not be found unworthy of perusal; since it is our sincere aim to cultivate what small gifts we may possess, in a serious and diligent fashion. Our ideals may perhaps be expressed most succinctly by those of Elizabeth Stuart Phelps which we have chosen as our motto: "*Begin humbly. Labour faithfully. Be patient.*"

## Our Candidate—Anne T. Renshaw

The United Women's Press Club of Massachusetts is primarily a literary rather than political society, but it will endeavour to wield whatever influence it may possess for the good and efficient management of the Association with which it is affiliated. Just now the most important duty of United members is to see that Mrs. Anne Tillery Renshaw of State College, Pennsylvania, is elected next month to the Official Editorship.[1]

Recent events have proved beyond a doubt that the Official Editorship is the most essential and responsible office in the Association. *The United Amateur* is the centre and core of all our activities; that to which we feel impelled to live up, and that by which we are judged in the outside world. Indeed, one may almost say that we are never better or worse than our official organ. The splendid intellectual progress which we have made since the summer of 1917 is almost conclusively attributable in the main to the tireless and tasteful enterprise and consistently uplifting influence of Miss Verna McGeoch, who brought to amateurdom an altogether new and radically higher standard of editorship.

Our duty, then, is to see that this standard is maintained; and fortunately there is available a candidate who perhaps alone of amateur journalists is able to parallel the McGeoch achievements—Mrs. Anne Tillery Renshaw. To recite the glowing record of Mrs. Renshaw is almost superfluous. Entering amateurdom in 1914, she at once became a dominant figure; building up the membership with a greater influx of really cultivated recruits than had ever before been known to the United. To her exclusively is due the foundation on which Miss McGeoch later built. As a poetess and constructive journalist, Mrs. Renshaw has few equals; and it would be impossible to name any other person connected with the society so thoroughly able and disposed to continue the official organ at the McGeoch level. She is at present an Instructor in an important State University, and can well command the time, culture, and resources necessary for the task.

The most pitiful experience in life is a relapse to primitive beginnings at a time when the goal is almost in sight; and relapse occasioning the total loss of all the fruits of progress. How lamentable to slip to the bottom when the summit is almost within reach! Such would be the United's experience next year if an editor of defective culture were elected. The work of many years would be destroyed, and the Association would undoubtedly settle back into those old plebeian ways which once gave our rivals ground for ridicule. Let us bestir ourselves and ensure by our votes the Official Editorship of Anne Tillery Renshaw!

In the half-year of its existence the United Women's Press Club of Massachusetts has grown to satisfying proportions. At this rate, what will it not be a year hence? We have confidence in our future, and are willing to demonstrate it by inviting the United's 1920 Convention to our nuclear point—the city of Boston. Of the joys of a Boston convention, those Nationalites who have gathered here so many times in the past can well testify. Rich in traditions and objects of interest to the literary student, Boston may without exaggeration be termed the ideal spot for an author's assemblage. *Vote for Boston as the 1920 Convention Seat.*[2]

EDITOR'S NOTE  FP: *Bonnet* 1, No. 1 (June 1919): 10–12 (unsigned). This is the editorial column of the *Bonnet*, the Official Organ of the United Women's Press Club of Massachusetts. Winifred V. Jordan was Official Editor; HPL (as well as Maurice W. Moe) was listed as Official Critic. HPL's authorship of this editorial—as well as the poem "Helene Hoffman Cole: 1893–1919: The Club's Tribute" (*AT* 352–53)—has been determined by internal evidence. No other issue of the *Bonnet* is known to exist.

*Notes*

1. Anne Tillery Renshaw was in fact elected Official Editor of the UAPA for 1919–20.
2. The UAPA convention of 1920 was held in Columbus, Ohio.

# FOR OFFICIAL EDITOR—ANNE TILLERY RENSHAW

Associational politics, happily dormant since the sordid period of 1916, has once more raised its sinister head to challenge the achievements of those who have laboured in behalf of the United's evolution; and distasteful though the subject may be to the true friend of amateur literature, prompt discussion is necessary if the work of recent terms is not to be undone. Out of its native darkness after a welcome absence of three years comes the turbulent Cleveland element (apologies to Mr. Samuel Loveman—shining exception!) with its attending train of blatant vulgarity and innuendo, bent on seating in the Official Editor's chair a candidate of such conspicuous unfitness for power that his defeat becomes a public duty on the part of those who cherish the progress and paramountcy of the United.

Direct comment on *The Cleveland Sun* and what it represents is obviously impossible in these columns, because of the boorishly sneering attitude which that contemporary has chosen to adopt toward The Conservative and his efforts in amateurdom. Comment, under these circumstances, could not but reflect a certain amount of personal disgust and purely subjective opposition. But no such inhibitions of good taste restrain the pen which would point out reasons why one William J. Dowdell of *Bearcat* notoriety must not be allowed to acquire the enormous—almost supreme—influence as a moulder of policy which goes with the Official Editorship of the United Amateur Press Association.

Mr. Dowdell, ever since he became old enough to entertain opinions of his own, has consistently favoured the cruder and less desirable side of amateur journalism. His bitter and puerile hostility to those improvements of 1915–16 which placed the United upon its present cultural basis, and his very singular oversights as Secretary in mailing proxy ballots, are too well known to require citation; while his more recent complete devotion to the National speaks for itself. The absurd anti-Campbell outbursts appearing in the *Bearcat* three years ago worked greatly to the detriment of the United, and gave the National ground for one of its illiberal attacks upon us. As a publisher—and it is as a publisher par excellence that he makes his appeal for votes—no one can fail to see that Mr. Dowdell's claims far exceed his accomplishments. He is, indeed, a veritable Prince of Broken Promises. Members of the United who contributed cash for the coöperative paper he was to issue in 1916 are still awaiting the arrival of that paper; meanwhile wondering why their literary matter was pirated by Mr. Dowdell's personal *Bearcat,* and why their money has not been refunded!

Mr. Dowdell glibly pledges himself to a continuance of the McGeoch editorial policy if elected. Do his past and present performances warrant such a prediction? Since actions speak louder than words, it appears to The Conservative that the election of Mr. Dowdell would result in an abrupt drop in the official organ from classical to plebeian standards. Mr. Dowdell is clever, and could go far in literature if he chose; but up to now he has shewn no inclination to succeed except on a very low cultural plane—the plane of commercial "yellow" newspaper journalism. His artistic birth has not yet taken place. It is probably no exaggeration to say that the *Bearcat* and *Sun,* as now conducted, are fair specimens of the grade of official organ which Mr. Dowdell would give us—when he might condescend to give us any. Need more be said? Forewarned is forearmed!

The vote of every well-wisher of the United Amateur Press Association should be cast for Mrs. ANNE TILLERY RENSHAW as Official Editor. Mrs. Renshaw, now an Instructor in Pennsylvania State College, and a reciter and poetess of repute, needs no introduction to amateurs. Her work as a recruiter has been the greatest constructive force in the United during recent years, and of available candidates she alone is able to maintain the McGeoch editorial standards. Under her guidance the official organ can continue to act as a nucleus for the intellectual activities of the Association; without it, the organ must inevitably lose prestige, and the best elements of our membership become dormant or disappear entirely from amateurdom. Few realise how much of next year's programme hinges absolutely upon Mrs. Renshaw's election.

It would be interesting to analyse the motives of those "dark forces" which have set up a candidate in opposition to Mrs. Renshaw. Significant indeed is their close connexion with the rival society—Mr. Dowdell is now a National member only, and has not been in the United for a period of more than two years. These Clevelandites come to us from the National with plans which if successful will tend to submerge our Association and restore to the senior organisation its long-coveted ancient supremacy. Shall we not rally to the defence of the United with votes for Mrs. Renshaw as Official Editor?

EDITOR'S NOTE  FP: *Conservative* 5, No. 1 (July 1919): 11–12 (unsigned). Another piece advocating Renshaw as Official Editor. This was the only issue of the *Conservative* to appear in 1919, just as the issue of July 1918 was the only issue of that year. HPL would not publish another issue of his paper until 1923, although he stated repeatedly both in print and in letters that he was ready to publish another issue as early as 1921; financial difficulties evidently prevented his doing so.

## AMATEURDOM

Judging from the quality of most of the United papers which have lately reached The Conservative's desk, amateur journalism has now attained a cultural level not before touched since the later 'eighties and early 'nineties. At what other period in recent years has the space of six months afforded such a display of wit and intellect as is included in the journals appearing since the dawn of 1919? To mention *The United Amateur* would be redundant. Under the McGeoch regime that organ is wholly beyond praise; a model which our competitors both envy and emulate. But the uniformity with which individual publications maintain high standards is as remarkable as it is encouraging. In steady succession have arrived *The Recruiter*, *Pine Cones*, *The Hellenian*, *Corona*, and *The Piper*; the last named of which comes just in time for admiring recognition in these columns.

*Pine Cones* and *Corona* represent a departure from conventional typography which establishes an excellent precedent. Too much importance has been attached to the printing-press in modern amateurdom, and it is gratifying to observe that editors are beginning to realise the more basic object of literature—the diffusion of thought irrespective of medium. It is noteworthy that these non-printed journals occupy the highest rank, intellectually, amongst the season's products. If this worthy example is followed as it should be, our circle will be enriched by the utterances of many learned and cultural members hitherto inarticulate through inability to issue printed papers.

The untimely death of Mrs. Helene Hoffman Cole is a source of lamentation throughout amateurdom. In the loss of so gifted and diligent a worker, the cause suffers immeasurably. United members perused with melancholy interest the May official organ, which contained numerous tributes to Mrs. Cole, and which forms a literary monument to her honoured memory. Of corresponding value will be the forthcoming *Hellenian*, commenced by Mrs. Cole but shortly before her demise, and completed by Mr. Cole as an affectionate memorial.

That amateurs of intelligence are not indifferent to man's chief solace and source of inspiration, is well demonstrated by the almost simultaneous appearance of two poems in praise of *books*; one by Mr. Kleiner in *The Piper*, the other by Mr. Goodenough in these columns.[1] Both pieces represent genius of a high order, and both will awaken an universal response from those readers who have weighed carefully the relative value of life's various blessings.

Mr. John Milton Samples' regularly issued monthly, *The Silver Clarion*, is an amateur journal whose progress and development should be watched with interest. At present censured by certain critics for its atmosphere of sanctity and unsophistication, it has lately enlarged its editorial staff and embarked upon a course of steady artistic development. Its policy, however, will not be altered; and it will remain as a sturdy exponent of honest Anglo-Saxon virtue in an age tainted with degeneracy and continental ideals.

EDITOR'S NOTE FP: *Conservative* 5, No. 1 (July 1919): 12 (unsigned). A discussion of contemporary activities and issues in the UAPA.

*Notes*

1. Arthur Goodenough, "The Joy of Books," *Conservative* 5, No. 1 (July 1919): 6.

# LOOKING BACKWARD

## I.

If cultivation in literature and literary imagination teaches anything, it is that Time is a purely physical phenomenon; powerless to affect the mind and personality of him who consciously resists its changes. The eternal youth of Endymion is more a striking allegory than an idle tale, for does not the dreamer escape the engulfing current of years, remaining ever able to perpetuate or re-create whatsoever age or scene he wills? We speak superficially of "obsolete" and "modern" things, fatuously fancying that the latter are different and superior; yet will not reflection prove that all are of one essential nature, occupying an equal place and importance in an eternity which has neither beginning nor ending? The abstract and independent mind belongs to no particular age or period: it can dwell for an hour within the walls of Nineveh, and in the next hour sport with Pan on Maenalian slopes. It can exchange thoughts with Ben Jonson at the Mermaid and with Samuel Johnson at the Mitre; or, narrowing down suddenly to the microcosm of amateur journalism, can with suitable material live over again the *Dies Halcyonei* which so great a throng lament as lost.

Such is the train of reflection awakened by hours of browsing amongst the yellowed amateur papers of long ago, a privilege which lately befell the writer through the unfailing kindness of our indispensable *Tryout*. Confronted with this array of journals, none could fail to visualise the early days from which they have survived; and at the desire of the editor this visualisation will be shared as far as possible with *Tryout's* readers. If our backward glance seem to the elder generation to contain any irreverence toward tradition, or to betray any grievous ignorance of old-time conditions and motives, our excuse must be the necessarily limited data at hand. *Ex pede Herculem*[1] is a proverb rather inapplicable to an institution as heterogeneous as amateur journalism. But it may none the less be of interest to revive old scenes for the eyes of a later age, and to arrange our fabled past by the side of the present for a comparison, be it ever so imperfect.

Our curtain rises in 1882 upon a nation freshly mourning the martyred Garfield[2] and still vigorous and optimistic despite certain vague shadows of socialism, foreign immigration, and other forms of decadence. Telephones and electric lights are novelties, the automobile is undreamed of. Horse cars still jingle over the streets. Letter postage is three cents, soon to descend to two (unconscious counterpart of Great War conditions), but amateur papers can be mailed at second class rates.

Amateurdom is taking itself seriously—more seriously than the future age of 1920 can conceive of. It is a group of ardent souls, mostly young men and youths, who have apparently concentrated all their recreational facilities in this one field; living therein their whole non-professional lives, and lavishing upon it a devotion which in 1920 hardly four members will be able to shew. Their seriousness is a part of the spirit of the age; of an America yet young, simple, and hopeful; fundamentally unvexed with the sophistication, cynicism, and doubt of value which are later to creep in. There is great confidence—abounding faith in the external forms of life and demeanour. Mid-Victorianism is in the air, and trifles often loom large.

Papers are large and exceedingly numerous, and in many cases of substantial literary merit. As in the later times, controversies rage endlessly. Here a hater of the late Professor Longfellow[3] carps about the poet's tameness or dependence upon foreign literature; there an idolator lauds to the skies his polished and musical mediocrity. The beginnings of rationalism are appearing, and clear thinkers are waging unequal combats against legions of the dully orthodox. Activity and prosperity abound, and one member deems the institution so important that he records in book form his "Career and Reminiscences".[4]

But there is a darker side to the picture. It must be admitted that not all of our members are litterateurs. Unpleasant official controversies are numerous, and interest in vapid politics is tremendous. Contests for empty offices, involving not a single literary issue, are conducted with incredible earnestness and sometimes doubtful scrupulousness. Political animosities and ballot scandals ring disagreeably above the general turmoil. Frequently the law is invoked in the form of affidavits with notarial seals. Obviously, as it will in 1920, amateurdom contains many persons of marked commonness, whose objects are far from scholarly. Convention reports do not always chronicle a very high type of diversion, and the future generation would be reluctant to follow the New York delegation of '83, whose sociological research took them to such places as McGlory's dance hall, the Empire saloon, and Allen's dive. Later we shall see the reaction which naturally arose from such intrusions of lower standards.

In this age activity centres in the National Amateur Press Association, the United standing over a decade in the future. Sectional associations, however, are abundant from north to south, and east to west. Conventions of these associations are often of more importance than those of the National itself, that of N.E.A.P.A. at Gardner, Mass., in 1883 being especially memorable.[5] Gardner is the seat of much local activity, including high-school activity—being in a sense the Appleton of its time. New England amateurdom, it may be remarked, seems to have a tone more uniformly high than that of any other section.

The great names of the day for the most part will be familiar to later ages as those of "Fossils". Willard O. Wylie, Brainerd Prescott Emery, George Edward Day, C. A. Watkyns, Joseph Dana Miller, Truman J. Spencer, and J. Rosevelt Gleason are but a few of the luminous beacons who shine above the majority. In 1883 appears a "marvelous little tot" named Edith May Dowe, who writes realistic analytical fiction with a pen unsurpassed. Some day she will be known as the successful authoress, Mrs. Edith Miniter. This year also introduces us to Ernest A. Edkins, poet, critic, and fantaisiste, who is to become what is without a doubt the greatest figure in amateur literature.[6]

A conspicuous feature of this and the preceding period is the actual payment of authors for their products. In later years our writers will consider themselves fortunate in having their manuscripts printed without remuneration, but the amateur of the 'eighties frequently inserted in the press such "professional" cards as the following:

> "BRAINERD P. EMERY, *Sketch Writer Laureate* of amateurdom, is prepared to contribute sketches and poems at low rates to first-class papers only. For rates, etc., address Lock Box 150, Newburgh, N.Y."

To complete the professional atmosphere, many of the papers charge subscription rates and handle paid advertising.

## II.

An old-time amateur of the highest type, still active, has classified the amateurs of the past into three distinct species: the literati, the plodders, and the politicians. That classification undoubtedly holds good today, although we are fortunate enough to have the third class much less numerously represented.

The literatus was the true apex of amateur development. He and he alone upheld the highest ideals of our institution, and upon him alone the credit for our intellectual achievements must rest. At the same time, however, the plodder must not be slighted. To him is due in great measure the existence of the amateur press; for although many of the literati were active publishers, the real impetus for publication undoubtedly arose amongst a more unliterary class who preserved to a large extent their boyish love of print and publicity. Many of the so-called plodders possessed much native taste; and although not active as authors, were in a sense genuine patrons of letters. Certainly they are to be commended above the type of person who, failing to acknowledge a want of artistic inspiration, perversely scribbles on without it.

Of the politicians it is difficult to speak without a smile. Many of them were recruited from the two other classes, and when coming from the literati, they often conferred substantial benefits upon amateurdom. But in all too many cases they were a distinct set of bright, shrewd, and none too patrician youths, with much skill in handling fellow-men, but with little or no aesthetic interest or inspiration. They sought office for its own sake; and their ideals and triumphs were of tinsel only. They had no issues to champion, and their standard of success was merely the ability to sway those about them. Office to them was not an opportunity to serve, but a mere prize to be captured for its own intrinsic value as an advertisement of cunning and popularity. The politicians saw in amateurdom an easy field for the exercise of cheap subtlety on a small scale; and they do not seem, on the whole, to have realised very clearly its artistic ambitions. On the other hand, many of them served faithfully and well, and relieved the literati of the dull drudgery of routine administration. Such politicians regarded amateurdom with affection and gratitude, because it had conferred upon them the things they sought.

Raising the curtain once more upon the bygone scene, we are confronted by a pleasing and varied array of papers. Of these Mr. Louis Kempner's *Union Lance* claims particular attention; not so much for a uniformly high literary tone, as for size, enterprise, and regularity. In 1884 the *Lance* was awarded a prize as the best edited amateur journal of its time; and in 1889 it received the editorial laureateship. Before the writer lie a number of copies extending from the first issue of the second series, October 1883, onward; through which a steady improvement can be traced. The first paper is unpromising, since it contains little besides those provoking and impertinent personalities so frequently found in the older amateurdom. Such things may interest the vulgar for an hour, but they are not literature. They lay emphasis on exactly the wrong aspects of our work, and contribute nothing to our intellectual progress.

But in the second issue, edited by Joseph Dana Miller, an abrupt rise is discernible. The opening feature, a poem by Mr. Miller entitled "The Dead City", is clearly the promising utterance of one who will become a genuine poet. Faults indeed are present—strained rhythm, doubtful rhymes, and stiff phraseology; but beneath the crudities of youth repose unmistakable evidences of real poetic feeling, elicited by contemplation of Cordova's vanished glory and beauty. Also by Mr. Miller is an excellent critique of Longfellow; a reply to an attack made on that poet by other amateurs. The attack itself, appearing in the *Bay State Brilliant* under the pseudonym of "Python", is no mean achievement, but is obviously unjust; and marred by a certain bitter prejudice which impairs its critical value. Mr. Miller indisputably goes too far in his admiration of the Charles River bard, yet shews in his defence a much greater degree of taste than the composite "Python". In his remarks on the essential borrowings of authors from the thoughts and imagery of the past, and in his citation of precedents to prove his case, he reveals an enviable literary background. Any shortcomings in the prose style of this essay, such as excessive italicisation, or overliteralism in refuting Pythonic assertions, may be laid to the author's youth alone. Another of Mr. Miller's pieces is an exquisite fable on religion, which might profitably be perused at the present time by such super-pietists as Mr. John Milton Samples. This allegory concerns an hypothetical pink elephant in a far country, beheld by none yet the subject of infinite speculation and antagonism. The orthodox believed his trunk was blue, whilst heretics insisted it was as pink as the rest of him. Finally a traveller suggested that there might not be any pink elephant at all, since no proof of his existence had ever been discovered. But the natives burned alive this impious disturber of their hereditary faith.

The later issues of this series of the *Union Lance* contain splendid bits of criticism and discussion, despite a definite leaning toward political affairs. It affords us, perhaps, the clearest of all pictures of amateurdom's inner life. One notes the commendable breadth of reading of most of the leaders, a breadth perhaps greater than that prevailing today, yet detects the immaturity inseparable from the tender age of the various authors. In the 'eighties youth held sway unopposed, and our present mature membership would feel quite lost in such a galaxy of semi-adolescence. From this circumstance arose the still existing prejudice of the "Fossils" against grown-up amateurs.

In the remarkable *Granite State Amateur* of a year ago we were treated to a reprint of a very effective short story—missing from the files before the writer—which originally appeared in the *Lance* for July 1884. "Mr. Dean", by Joseph Dana Miller, was founded upon a posthumously discovered synopsis of Nathaniel Hawthorne's; and its development does credit to his age of amateurdom. The imaginative atmosphere and gruesomely suggestive conclusion are handled in a manner which certainly cannot have caused Mr. Hawthorne's shade any marked dissatisfaction.

The third and last series of the *Lance* falls within the province of a future article, and forms a very bright page in amateurdom's history. Meanwhile we will be consistent chronologically, and survey other products of the early 'eighties. New England, and Massachusetts in particular, produced many excellent journals; typical specimens being the *Northern Breezes* of Masters Heywood and Green—two almost Galpinian youths— the *Bay State Press* of H. K. Sanderson, the neat *Our Compliments* of Willard O. Wylie and Mr. Sanderson, and the *Bay State Brilliant* of Finlay A. Grant and A. A. Stewart. Mr. Grant was a publisher and political leader of unusual merit, fidelity, and prominence, who will receive more extended mention later.

Of these Massachusetts journals, *Northern Breezes* easily takes the lead. Appleton itself could not produce two brighter boys than the cousins Charles Heywood and Frank H. Green of Gardner, whose mature language and instinctive final choice of amateurdom's most worthy side placed them on an equal footing with the older youths about them. Like other persons of ability, they had enemies. Their genealogical researches led to their denunciation as "aristocrats", yet who in these days of democratic decadence will condemn their just pride of lineage?

The brilliant and incisive critical articles of these young editors are a delight to the lover of literature and of precocity. Not always are they entirely just, as witness the overzealous attack on Mr. Edkins, then a new recruit; but they are always candid, observing, and honestly analytical, drawn from a satisfactory fund of culture and solid reading. Master Green's defence of the classics against the clumsy strictures of a practical soul who declared that "Greek and Latin never help a man make a living" ought to be republished today.

Other parts of the country furnished such journals as Mr. Watkyns' *La Critique*, New York; Mr. Metcalf's *Pandora*, Adirondack, N. Y.; Mr. Steele's *The Amateur*, Buffalo, N. Y.; Mr. Antisdel's *Qui Vive*, Detroit, Mich.; Mr. Harrison's much-discussed *Visitor*, Indianapolis, Ind.; Mr. Emery's brilliant *Sentinel*, Newburgh, N. Y.; and Mr. Hastings' witty *Chic*, Berkeley, Cal. Besides these papers, of course, were a vast number not included in the collection under consideration. *Chic* was a particularly sprightly undergraduate affair by a student at the University of California. A large sheet boasting a decorative cover, it was profusely illustrated with clever cartoons, and afforded a bright example of college journalism. The facetiae, all original, were occasionally of richly comic quality.

### III.

Amateur journalism has always been particularly rich in striking contrasts. Side by side have flourished the most exclusive and meritorious, and the most primitive and barbaric, of publications. Yet the latter are not always to be condemned, since they frequently represent the first faltering steps of young editors who will one day stride with the gods. In the early 'eighties no better example of literary contrast can be found than that afforded by Mr. Brainerd Emery's *Sentinel,* and Mr. Finlay Aaron Grant's *Young Nova Scotia.* With one member purely literary, and the other frankly juvenile and popular, this pair furnish a typical case of extremes.

The *Sentinel,* edited by Mr. Emery in conjunction with one or more associates, bore the motto "*Fidelis et Suavis*",[7] and on the whole lived up to it. It was a large sheet, eight by eleven and one half inches in dimensions, and possessed a tasteful neatness of typography and arrangement which assisted in impressing the reader with its quality. It may be remarked in passing, that at this age of amateurdom there was none of that standardisation in the size of journals which we notice today. The rather awkward pages of the *National Amateur* furnish the only notable survival.

The *Sentinel* evidently strove to occupy the front rank among the really literary journals of its day, and without a doubt succeeded. The substantial articles, good stories, acute critical paragraphs, and really inspired poetry, all attest its excellence; and the political remarks which at first sight seem intrusive were probably necessary phases of the editor's constant warfare on the sordid and commonplace side of amateur journalism. Among the foremost features were the poems of Mr. Emery himself, advancing from effusions which shew unmistakable traces of juvenile inexperience, to work of a grade forecasting his future fame as a bard. Mr. Emery touched the heights in poetry, though never losing a certain carelessness and laxity in technique which prevented his verse from competing in uniform musical grace with the haunting passages of an Edkins or (to digress into the present) a Samuel Loveman. The best Emery poem in the *Sentinel* file before us is "A Serenade" (April–May 1884), in which a decorative sense of rare delicacy is displayed.

Other notable *Sentinel* poets are J. Rosevelt Gleason, James J. O'Connell, George Edward Day, J. Bascom Sherrill, and Joseph Dana Miller. In many cases these writers reached an enviable level, their work being marred only by such minor technical flaws as we find in the best amateur poetry of today. For example—Mr. Gleason contributes an exquisite sonnet "To a Young Poet" (Sept.–Oct. 1883), yet mars its melody by accenting *vagaries* on the first syllable, and apparently misplacing the accent of *vibrates* as well. On the whole, Mr. Miller is probably the leader of the Aonian band. A more genuinely meritorious poem than his "Gnomic Verses" (May 1885) would be hard to find in the files before the writer. There were several *Sentinel* poets of what might be called the second order—Harry E. Batsford, "Bertha", Clarence E. Stone, and others. Among these we find the same characteristic errors which affect certain amateur bards today—the symmetrical stanzas, false rhymes, and similar jarring details so familiar to our abused and hard-working critical bureau.

The essays in the *Sentinel* are commensurate with the poetry. Ascending from such transcribed high-school lessons as the serial, "Progress of the English People and Language", we come upon work of the first quality; including Shakespearian analyses by Truman J. Spencer, the greatest student of the Sweet Swan of Avon whom amateurdom has ever produced. In the essay class may perhaps be grouped some of the brilliant critical paragraphs of the editor. One of the best of these critiques, touching on the poetry of George Edward Day, was reprinted last December in the *Tryout,* hence is probably familiar to contemporary readers.

The *Sentinel's* fiction, like the fiction of modern amateurdom, was a weak point. Conspicuous for its utter, unrelieved crudity, was a serial by one Georgie H. Raymond, entitled "Butterfly Villa". Certain esteemed contemporaries sedately censured Mr. Emery for publishing a piece representing such vulgar manners and boorish conduct; but the average critic's censure is necessarily anything but sedate. For an equally absurd yet seriously intended picture of social life, one must look to such narratives as "The Young Visitors". Miss Raymond seems to have been a school-girl devotee of the popular dime novels of her time, for surely she could nowhere else have derived such a grotesque set of artificial stock characters and situations. Perhaps the most completely hilarious feature is the impossible and unpronounceable pseudo-Cockney dialect placed in the mouth of one evidently meant to be an English gentleman of birth and cultivation; though the Pamela-like[8] epistolary conclusion, wherein all stray ends are gathered up, is a close second. But let it not be thought that "Butterfly Villa" is typical of *Sentinel* fiction. The short stories of the pseudonymous "Stuyvesant", who was Poet Laureate as well as a fiction writer, possess much merit; whilst the single tale of William F. Buckley, "Doctor Challys" (April–May 1884), is entitled to the sincerest praise.

As a representative of amateurdom in the early 'eighties, the *Sentinel* perhaps takes first place. It does not, however, represent Mr. Emery at the zenith of his career; for it is in the later age of *Athenia* that this brilliant amateur comes into his own. We shall subsequently have occasion to note that later age—which forms the real Halcyon period of amateur journalism—but at present let us consider the sharp contrast afforded by the popular amateur journals of *Sentinel* days, journals of which *Young Nova Scotia* is a typical specimen.

Published by Mr. Finlay Aaron Grant, a faithful and diligent worker who served as the National's president in 1882–3, *Young Nova Scotia* was probably the most ambitious exponent of semi-professional juvenile journalism which amateurdom has ever known. At various times Mr. Grant also edited several real amateur journals, notable the *Boys' Folio*; but the remunerative venture seems to have been his most elaborate enterprise. Published at New Glasgow, N. S., and charging a subscription rate of 60 cents a year, Mr. Grant's magazine paralleled in size and probably in merit most professional boys' papers of the second order; and in addition occupied a much higher ethical plane. Its contents were the usual melange of verses, fictional thrillers, puzzles, jests, philately, numismatics, curiosities, and bits of general information. Most of its contributors were amateur journalists, and it always remained more or less within amateurdom's circle. Occasionally this amateur connexion would give it a piece of real merit, such as "Forgotten", by James L. Elderice, "A Chequered Career", by James J. O'Connell, or "The Pantheist's Hymn", by Joseph Dana Miller. The puzzle department is especially to be noted because of the popularity of this pastime among the amateurs of the period. "The National Puzzlers' League" was practically a branch of amateurdom, and evidently furnished mild mental recreation for more than one tired litterateur as well as for the less serious element. The writer is quite sure that there was no irony in Mr. Grant's offer of a copy of Webster's Unabridged to the person making the best puzzle during the first six months of 1882.

Naturally, the poetry in so juvenile a paper must not be expected to attain an Heliconian level. In the January 1882 number occurs an effusion of 24 eight-line stanzas—"Lucian and Lydia; a Spanish Legend, by Max J. Lesser, A. B." Judging from his technique and phraseology, one fancies that Mr. Lesser's alphabetical appendage must have been of maritime rather than academic significance. We will herewith reproduce a typical stanza and let our readers judge for themselves:

> "'Twas her father's wish some proud hidalgo
>     Should his daughter to the alter (sic) lead,
> That with him to his proud home she shall go,
>     And their heir his titles shall succeed;

> But his hope to be attained was never
>     'Twas alas but a frail and fleeting dream—
> How the hand of fate the same did sever
>     Is the subject of the poet's theme."

"The poet" was a very romantic gentleman, and wrote many prize "poems" entitled "Zante", "Thule", and other exotic things.

The popular variants of mid-Victorian romanticism are well shewn in some of the short stories. "How It Happened", by Edwin Burdock, is a gem of purest ray serene, containing the usual "gentlemanly, handsome, dark-eyed stranger". Another exquisite bit of fictional sentiment—four chapters squeezed into three pages—is "Lois; or Righted at Last", by Edwin B. Lowe. This time we find a "bold handsome stranger" later called a "pretty, brave sailor lad". The affection of this comely nautical youth for the beauteous heiress of Castlewold, whom the had valiantly rescued from a direful death, provokes the ire of the fair one's stern father, but honest Robert Lennox proposes none the less ardently. Say he:

> "Marry me, darling! If your proud parent will not give us pardon and take us to his home, I will take you to America, and there make you a home less luxurious, surely, but one where love shall reign supreme!"

Later we hear the raving of Lord Herbert Castle, the proud Norman baron whose "original ancestoral (sic) home had been but a massive stone mansion with a single tower", though "succeeding generations had in time added to it until it covered an immense space". Lord Herbert is really pained at his daughter's mesalliance, and does not hesitate to say so:

> "She must go from my house. The beggar she has wed must take her and care for her—henceforth I have no daughter. I do not wish her name to be ever again spoken in my presence—I never wish to look on her again. She shall never—if I know it—receive another farthing of my wealth . . . and Lord Castle arose and walked haughtily across the room."

But all is well by the end of Chapter Four, so our readers need not worry.

The advertisements in *Young Nova Scotia* are of the sort generally found in boys' papers of thirty or forty years ago. Such things as chromos, stamps, acquaintance cards, popular songs, lovers' garlands, and printing materials seem to be in great demand; exhibiting the versatility of the journal's youthful clientele.

Before leaving this publication the writer cannot refrain from noting one feature of the "Curiosity Corner"—verses which read backward as well as forward. One specimen is especially appropriate in these days:

> "Mind and body, soul depraves;
> Mankind ruins, filled are graves;
> Near and far diseases spread;
> Beware, oh, beware! Cup is red!
>
> Red is cup! beware, oh, beware!
> Spread diseases far and near!
> Graves are filled, ruins mankind;
> Depraves soul, body and mind!"

## IV.

The amateurdom of the 'eighties affords no character more quaintly interesting than Thomas G. Harrison of Indiana, whose popular *Visitor*, previously called the *Welcome Visitor*, falls within our period of research. Honest, industrious, and intensely devoted to the cause of amateur journalism, Mr. Harrison deservedly received the highest honours the institution could bestow; and perpetuated his name through the authorship of a 330-page volume of mixed amateur history and personal memoirs, entitled, "The Career and Reminiscences of an Amateur Journalist".[9]

Mr. Harrison, though the author of several passable bits of literary prose and verse, belonged essentially to the plodder-politician type of amateur. As a politician, however, he was animated by an ideal of genuine service which robs the designation of its implied reproach. This earnest worker was one of those delectable souls from whom boyhood never departs. Though never hostile to art and advancement, it is much to be doubted if he often worried greatly about these things. For him amateurdom was largely a glorious playground or fraternal order, wherein he could "play editor" to his heart's content, enjoy the pleasure of friendship with many youths of different types, feel the exhilaration that comes with wielding power over other men in even the most restricted spheres, and gratify that naive, harmless, and entirely open vanity which was the amusement of his contemporaries. Mr. Harrison candidly sought fame, and considered his amateur celebrity as a definite asset which it was his duty and pride to enhance and display as much as possible.

Of the *Visitors* before us, the first is the issue of April 10, 1883, and the last that of August 13, 1884. Through the file are discernible the various elements that contributed to its strength and weakness; the fearless and often genuinely witty comment on amateurs and amateur affairs which made it prominent, and the crudity, plebeian tone, and egotistical atmosphere which deprived it of a higher standing. Mr. Harrison often had co-editors who conducted personal columns; but these were never of a literary type, so that the magazine remained fairly homogeneous. Occurring in nearly every issue is a full-column advertisement of the editor's book of reminiscences—an advertisement which is in itself a work of art; containing such highly original words as "chronologous", and such delicious passages of self-praise as this:

> ". . . the most valuable addition to the annals of Amateur Journalism ever published . . . interesting to every one who is or will be or has been a member of the amateur press."

Oddly enough, subsequent events seem actually to have justified this statement. The book, though couched in faulty and abominable English and filled with mere personal matter toward the end, seems to have embodied in its strictly historical section a selective judgment which renders it the best single chronicle of the amateur movement in existence.

The most unique and widely discussed feature of the *Visitor* was the wholesale reprinting by Mr. Harrison of the various comments on him and his work which appeared in other papers. Though received by the public as a sign of vanity, the habit was probably the joint offspring of vanity and humour, for the reprints were as often adverse as favourable, and were set off by laconic headlines whose clever sarcasm and occasional brilliancy would do credit to any modern "colyum" artist of the F. P. A. or B. L. T. school.[10] Adverse criticism merely confirmed Mr. Harrison in his practice; and at one time he reminded his critics that most editors could not find so many comments about them to reproduce, naively adding that he did not even begin to reprint all that was written about him. The Harrisonian wit may be fairly well shewn by one or two specimens of the famous reprints with their *Visitor* headlines:

## "O'CONNELL POLITICALLY DEAD.

The fight between Harrison and O'Connell is a very melancholy affair. Melancholy because neither show signs of killing the other.—*Tomahawk.*"

## "WHAT!

Where is that Western candidate hinted at some time ago by Harrison? Has Harrison played him false, or—what?—*The Nugget.*"

Mr. Harrison's polemical prowess was well displayed in an elaborate controversy with Eugene A. Brewster of the *Sentinel* staff. Cleverly arranging the attacks of his adversary as chapters of a novel, Mr. Harrison gave each chapter a satirical heading and called the whole "A Twice-Told Tale". It is pleasant to note that this controversy terminated in a particularly warm and thorough reconciliation.

Of Mr. Harrison's real attitude toward fame and his critics, much is revealed in a frank letter to Mr. Kempner published in the *Union Lance*. Who shall say that the *Visitor's* unashamed pursuit of glory was more than the open expression of strivings and wishes felt by all, yet usually repressed? He wrote:

"In truth, much of my conceit is *assumed,* for I realise *assertion* is a necessary ingredient to fame, so I practice it."

Mr. Harrison attended the New York Convention in July 1883—the famous convention at which the destruction of proxy ballots caused so great a sensation—and published his experiences in a serial narrative entitled "A Midsummer Ramble". This serial at once brought added notoriety to the *Visitor*, a notoriety resulting from the nature of some of the events chronicled. At that period the fastidious artist was not the typical amateur, and much of the convention sightseeing consisted of the sort of "slumming" so popular among certain visitors to the metropolis thirty or more years ago. To the raw, lively young Westerner the sordid dens and bar-rooms of the great city were a fascinating novelty, and in his article he dwelt upon them with such evident zest and ardour that the more refined amateurs protested quite emphatically. However, it is to be doubted if Mr. Harrison was disturbed by the criticism. He and his convention associates had had what they considered a "good time"; and their very enjoyment of the sport of "seeing the seamy side of life" argues a temperament not especially sensitive to the reproaches of good taste.

This underworld convention has a singularly amusing echo in the amateurdom of thirty-two years later. Many readers of *Tryout* will recall the attack upon active amateurs made by members of "The Fossils" five years ago, when the latter were so anxious to drive from amateurdom anyone over the age of twenty. One of the chief Fossil spokesmen at that time was a certain Charles C. Heuman, who seized upon the delegates at the 1915 convention (Brooklyn) as his especial prey, and prepared an article in which he denounced with virtuous and vehement ire the harmless excursions of these folk to a few of the insipid "Bohemian" haunts where curious bourgeois observers are shewn what is supposed to be the atmosphere of real aestheticism. Mr. Heuman's eloquence against such abysmal iniquity was really touching—one may find it in the December 1915 *Fossil*—and he was especially thankful that his son, the offspring of so spotless a sire, had never been contaminated by contact with modern amateurs. Now the humour of Mr. Heuman's position comes from a comparison of his 1915 utterances with his part in the 1883 "Midsummer Ramble" so vividly delineated in the *Visitor*. The ensuing parallel columns tell their own story, and point their own moral.

| Thomas G. Harrison | Charles C. Heuman |
| In *The Visitor*, November 8, 1883. | In *The Fossil*, December 1915. |

"As yet we had seen but little of New York by night, but we commenced going the rounds. Charley Heuman (!!), whom we hunted up, escorted Reeve and ourself one evening, and we were taken to a number of resorts on Fourteenth street, Sixth avenue, Prince street, and others. Of these the "Haymarket" was the most interesting. This used to be a famous theatre, but is now a dance house some grades better than McGlory's. It is the home of the Dude, and the ablest representatives of this class can always be found there. The women who frequent it are better looking and better dressed than at any other place we were in. At the "Empire saloon" Heuman fell in with an old friend who introduced us to an interesting specimen of the London Cockney, fresh from Britain; a genuine London 'Array, who dropped his h's most elegantly. He wouldn't reciprocate the numerous "treats," however; in revenge for which we got in a mash on his girl, about which the two men came near quarrelling. About the worst place we were in was The Allens, which is a most disreputable dive, the loafing place of pickpockets, cracksmen, and all classes of thieves and criminals."

"It was my fondest wish that my boy follow in my footsteps (!!!), and I looked forward year after year to his initiation (into amateurdom). He is fifteen now, and ripe for it; but there is school, there is football practice, there are his bicycle, his camera, his wireless. Besides, he has a sufficient outlet for his literary yearnings through his school paper. But even if one of the barker's vulgar appeals to send a dollar and become 'literary' should escape my censorship, would I permit him to mingle with a crowd of sophisticated men and women, who would try to drag him to chop-suey dives, cheap cabarets, and the like at convention time and try to teach him to insult his father's life-long friends? Not that I have any fear of the boy—he is only fifteen, and it wouldn't take him fifteen minutes to discover that he had ventured into the realm of humbug, and that these people were not the kind of people with whom he was accustomed to associate." (?)

*Vale, Heumane, censor moralium!*[11]

## V.

It is characteristic of human nature that every age should look back upon former times as a period of happy superiority. Today amateur journalists recall as the "halcyon era" any and all eras beyond the scope of their experience. Forty years ago it was the same, as we learn from the advertisement of Harrison's "Career", where the author says: "Every amateur who wishes to read about the halcyon days should not fail to read this book." But it is nevertheless possible for one who surveys amateur history as a whole to point out a definite age which in combined literary tone and publishing activity stands out above all others. This is the decade of 1885–1895, during which the amateur press attained practically the same cultural level that it possesses today, yet boasted a quantitative superiority but little below the standard of former times. It concludes the most celebrated journals and magazines ever produced by amateurdom, including Mr. Emery's *Athenia,* Mr. Spencer's *Investigator,* and Mr. C. W. Smith's well-beloved *Monthly Visitor,* forerunner of our present *Tryout.*

During this period amateur literature developed a polish and urbanity hitherto lacking. The younger members were growing up, and the artistic and intellectual influence of the literati was asserting itself to a degree which quite overshadowed the cheap machinations of the politicians. In 1886–7 the cultivated and uncultivated factions met in a sharp struggle; which, though resulting in a nominal victory for the uncultivated, really aroused amateurdom to a sense of its shortcomings, and spurred the majority on to higher types of endeavour. The opening number of *Athenia,* dated October 1886, contained some stirring arraignments of amateurdom's cruder side. In his "Letter from an Amateur of Nowhere, who is visiting the United States, to his Friend Lorenzo, Grand Scribe of the Amateur Authors' Association of Nowhere", Mr. James J. O'Connell of Brooklyn touched drastically and intelligently upon the dulness of politicians, the pompous emptiness of officialdom, the commonness of conventions, and the inanity of over-puffed authors; whilst in the editorial columns Mr. Emery vigorously advocated the radical regeneration of the National. These capable and cultured writers minced no words, and their utterances appear to have created a profound stir in amateurdom. But discouraging replies from the "Philistine" element poured forth plentifully, so that the reformers finally decided on separation as the only dignified course. Accordingly there was announced in *Athenia* for January 1887 a secession of amateurdom's best element from the recognised associations, and the formation on a vastly higher plane of the "The Literary Lyceum of America". The Lyceum, under the leadership of Mr. Emery, planned to "draw only its nucleus from amateur journalism". Further recruiting was to proceed on a more select basis, and to embrace elements with literary rather than journalistic or fraternal interests. This design, in theory, was admirable, but it involved practical difficulties well-nigh insuperable. To cut loose from the amateur world, with its far-reaching ramifications and stimuli to publishing activity, was an extreme step; and it soon became apparent that the despised "plodder" with his commonplace ideas is the real mainstay of the amateur press. It is sounder policy to form alliances with dulness when it is not antagonistic, than to reject all ties with the crude. The safety of amateurdom can be sufficiently ensured by war on only the active and malignant opponents of progress. So we find that many literati, notably Mr. Spencer, refused to leave the associational world; and that in the end the Lyceum seceders returned to the fold with recantations of their separatist doctrine. But to assume that the movement was a failure is a mistake. The crudity of the older amateurdom had been held to the light, and henceforward the element of pure literature occupied a larger place.

*Athenia* is perhaps a perfect type of the select amateur journal of the halcyon age. Edited by Brainerd Prescott Emery, its contents were selected with commendable care, and included the best contributions of the amateur writers, as well as the editor's own keen criticisms. The heading of the first number was pleasingly classical with its well-drawn portrait of the patron deity, and its ingeniously Greek-looking rendering of the title. In this issue we find a short story somewhat below the general standard, some criticisms of unexceptional brilliancy, a powerful poem by Charles Heywood (editor of *Northern Breezes*) entitled "In Praesentia Mortis", and a supremely artistic bit of weird genius by Ernest A. Edkins—a bit of night-black poetical fancy so arresting in its sombre power that we cannot refrain from reproducing it here in full, as a specimen of the older amateur literature at its best.

## THE SUICIDE

By *Ernest Arthur Edkins.*

O what is abroad in the night, in the night,
That I needs must awake from my dreams,
And seek the lone bridge, and the sight, and the sight
Of a sullen deep river that rolls in its might—
Of a humble river that seems
Like the treacherous tide of my dreams?

I lean over the rail in the toils of the trance
And the tide flees away from my face,
But in its broad breast I encounter the glance—
The wild ghastly glance of two eyes that advance
Not an inch in the current's swift face—
That stare blankly up at my face.

Long shuddering swords of resilient light
From the furthermost sinuous shore,
Trail over the waters or bury their bright
Keen blades in the tide—but they point to a sight
On the glistening, watery floor
That freezes my heart to its core.

For the eyes, the calm beautiful unseeing eyes
That hold me enthrall'd in their spell—
No longer are mortal—their swift vision flies
Up a moon-riven path thro' the Stygian skies,
And away from this earthly hell
Where the spirit disdain'd to dwell.

O delicate form down there in the dark,
O pitiful sight that I see—
Thy golden hair cruelly caught in the bark
Of a half-sunken tree, and thy body a mark
That the world of tomorrow, by thee,
May its own inhumanity see!

Can any reader declare that a higher level of amateur achievement has ever been reached? Some of these lines and images are strokes of nothing less than pure genius, and it is doubtful if any contemporary writer can more than approach them. Mr. Edkins was one of the brilliant coterie of young poets devoted to the exquisite and the

exotic; a coterie which, though occasionally derided as "affected", did much to inculcate the importance of literary form in the amateur world.

Later numbers of *Athenia* were more evenly balanced; with better stories, even
with less striking verse. It is regretted that the file before the writer is so incomplete.

Another splendid and typical paper of this brilliant age is Mr. Louis Kempner's revived *Union Lance*, edited in collaboration with Mr. Norbert Heinsheimer. As in the
earliest series, amateur social and political discussion is not absent; but it is now so well
subordinated to pure literature that it fails to be obtrusive. Among the regular contributors we find Brainerd Prescott Emery, Joseph Dana Miller, Geo. Edgar Frye, Harriet C. Cox, Truman J. Spencer, and Mr. Heinsheimer; all submitting work that will
redound to amateurdom's credit as long as the institution exists. Mr. Emery's column
of reviews, "With Critic's Quill", is perhaps the best critical department amateur journalism has ever known; though no doubt it was as severely attacked in its day as are
the critical departments of the present.

Before us lie copies of the *Lance* extending from January 1889 to January 1890,
and in this brief year we find crowded a multitude of excellencies. The first number
gives us within the confines of a single page a clever translation from Bion by Mr.
Heinsheimer and a sentimental poem of genuine worth (rare phenomenon) by Fanny
Kemble Johnson, while subsequent numbers reveal such treasures as J. Rosevelt Gleason's review of "Robert Elsmere",[12] Mr. Spencer's Shakespearian study, "The Regicides
Inverness", and the remarkable composite critique of Ernest A. Edkins' poetry by Norbert Heinsheimer and J. J. Mack. Truly it is not difficult to determine amateurdom's
real "halcyon days".

In 1891 Truman J. Spencer successfully brought forth the most ambitious work
ever undertaken by an amateur—his celebrated 520-page *Literary Cyclopedia of Amateur Journalism*,[13] which included specimens from the pens of all the best amateur authors, together with critical and biographical introductions by the editor. No more
fitting culmination to a Golden Age could have been devised, for here was arrayed and
introduced the whole galaxy of genius which had made amateurdom an institution to
be proud of. Of that galaxy most still are living, yet regrettably enough only one or two
remain active in our little world. Mr. Spencer was editor of the *Investigator*, one of the
most artistic journals of its time, and deserved a high place among those whose activities he chronicled.

Our survey has now brought us to a stage where the beginnings of the present may
be discerned. Familiar names such as Arthur Goodenough, James F. Morton, Jr., and
C. W. Smith begin to be met with in the amateur press, whilst all unknown to fame
many leaders of today are born or are perpetrating their first literary attempts with
ruled pad and faltering pencil. Here the file before us ends; and here, though we may
some day record our impressions of later ages, our present task is done.

We have viewed the most prosperous period of a hobby which will probably never
expire, though it may undergo many modifications. Amateur Journalism is a pastime,
but it is more than a common pastime. It is at bottom a spontaneous striving for untrammelled artistic expression on the part of those unable to speak as they choose
through the recognised literary channels; and as such it possesses the fundamentals
which make for permanent endurance.

EDITOR'S NOTE  FP: *Tryout* 6, No. 2 (February 1920): [3–6]; 6, No. 3 (March 1920): [1–8];
6, No. 4 (April 1920): [3–10]; 6, No. 5 (May 1920): [3–10]; 6, No. 6 (June 1920): [3–10].

Published as a booklet, *Looking Backward* (Haverhill, MA: C. W. Smith, [1920]). The booklet is merely a kind of offprint of the pages of the *Tryout* serialization. The date of the pamphlet's issuance is supplied by Edwin Hadley Smith, who in a prefatory note to an excerpt from "Looking Backward" entitled "Dr. Jekyll and Mr. Hyde" (*Boys' Herald* 63, No. 1 [1 January 1934]: 7) declares: "In 1920 C. W. Smith published a 36-page booklet called *Looking Backward.*" The article was then reprinted in two parts in Ernest A. Edkins' amateur journal, the *Aonian* 2, No. 3 (Autumn 1944): 146–51; 2, No. 4 (Winter 1944): 177–86 (this appearance rpt. Necronomicon Press, 1980). The essay is a survey—based upon journals provided to him by C. W. "Tryout" Smith—of the so-called halcyon days (approximately the period 1885–1895) of amateur journalism, although HPL begins his survey in 1882 and does not proceed much beyond 1890. HPL was, of course, personally acquainted with few of these old-timers, although in the 1930s he came in touch with Ernest A. Edkins and persuaded him to resume amateur activity. In the late essay "Defining the 'Ideal' Paper" (1937; see p. 411) HPL affirmed that "the amateurdom of 1885–1895 towered mountainously above the amateurdom of today."

*Notes*

1. Literally, "from the foot, Hercules"; i.e., one can identify Hercules from the length of his footprint; in other words, one can identify anything great by the traces it leaves behind. The anecdote goes back to Herodotus (*Histories* 4.82). See also Aulus Gellius, *Noctes Atticae* 1.1.

2. President James A. Garfield was shot by Charles J. Guiteau on 2 July 1881; he died on 19 September.

3. Henry Wadsworth Longfellow (1807–1882) died on 24 March 1882.

4. See n. 9 below.

5. The events in "The Colour out of Space" (1927) begin in 1882. Although the town of Gardner (in north-central Massachusetts) is not mentioned in the story, the central characters are the Gardner family.

6. HPL became acquainted with Edkins only in 1932, when the two were working on the critical bureau of the NAPA. Edkins then became one of HPL's closest late correspondents. See also Section V below.

7. "Faithful and smooth."

8. The reference is to Samuel Richardson's sentimental epistolary novel *Pamela* (1740–41).

9. Thomas G. Harrison (1860–?), *The Career and Reminiscences of an Amateur Journalist, and a History of Amateur Journalism* (Indianapolis: Thomas G. Harrison, 1883).

10. "F. P. A." refers to Franklin P. Adams, author of the long-running column "The Conning Tower" (see n. 8 to DPC [May 1917]). "B. L. T." refers to Bert Leston Taylor (1866–1921), American journalist and author of the "A Line o' Type or Two" column in the *Chicago Tribune* (1909–21).

11. "Farwell, Heuman, guardian of morals!"

12. *Robert Elsmere* (1888) by Mrs. Humphry (Mary Augusta) Ward (1851–1920), a best-selling and controversial novel about a clergyman's loss of faith.

13. Truman J. Spencer, *A Cyclopedia of the Literature of Amateur Journalism* (Hartford, CT: Truman J. Spencer, 1891).

# FOR WHAT DOES THE UNITED STAND?

It is [not] easy to comply in 500 words with a request for an article on what the United represents. An amateur journalistic association is generally too democratic to have any one object for long; it is rather a battle-ground between the proponents of opposed ideals.

I think, however, that since the dawn of the Hoffman administration, when the best elements were automatically sifted out through the secession of most of the confirmed politicians, we have been gradually acquiring a policy and a tradition which will endure. The printing-press, political, and frivolous phases have been passed through; and our aspirations seem to be crystallising into a form more worthy than any of our past aspirations.

Judging from the majority of our truly active members, the United now aims at the development of its adherents in the direction of purely artistic literary perception and expression; to be effected by the encouragement of writing, the giving of constructive criticism, and the cultivation of correspondence friendships among scholars and aspirants capable of stimulating and aiding one another's efforts. It aims at the revival of the uncommercial spirit; the real creative thought which modern conditions have done their worst to suppress and eradicate. It seeks to banish mediocrity as a goal and standard; to place before its members the classical and the universal and to draw their minds from the commonplace to the beautiful.

The United aims to assist those whom other forms of literary influence cannot reach. The non-university man, the dwellers in distant places, the recluse, the invalid, the very young, the elderly; all these are included within our scope. And beside our novices stand persons of mature cultivation and experience, ready to assist for the sheer joy of assisting. In no other society does wealth or previous learning count for so little. Merit and aspiration form the only criteria we apply to our members, nor has poverty or primitive crudity ever retarded the steady progress of any determined aspirant among us. We ask only that the goal be high; that the souls of our band be seeking the antique legacy of verdant Helicon.

Practically, we are aware of many obstacles; yet we think we are in the main fulfilling our functions. Naturally, we do not expect to make a Shelley or Swinburne of every rhymer who joins us, or a Poe or Dunsany of every teller of tales; but if we enable these persons to appreciate Shelley and Swinburne and Poe and Dunsany, and teach them how to shed their dominant faults and use words correctly and expressively, we cannot call ourselves unsuccessful. Only genius can lead to the heights; it is our province merely to point the way and assist on the gentler, lower slopes.

The United, then, stands for education in the eternal truths of literary art, and for personal aid in the realisation of its members' literary potentialities. It is an university, stripped of every artificiality and conventionality, and thrown open to all without distinction. Here may every man shine according to his genius, and here may the small as well as the great writer know the bliss of appreciation and the glory of recognised achievement.

EDITOR'S NOTE FP: *United Amateur* 19, No. 5 (May 1920): 101. HPL's most concise statement as to what amateurdom (specifically the UAPA) means to him. He sees it as a vital tool in education and in the development of literary talent in a non-remunerative setting, where more experienced writers help their cruder colleagues to gain literary polish.

# THE PSEUDO-UNITED

Recent developments make it interesting to observe the pathetic progress of a very mediocre amateur press association which bears the name of our own, and which professes to derive its title through just inheritance. It is also interesting to investigate the origin of this body, and to ascertain why it attempts to lay claim to our own part.

The so-called "United Amateur Press Association of America", which has from time to time favoured our society with amusing displays of puerile animosity, is the result of a political revolt which occurred in 1912 at the La Grande, Oregon, convention. The presidential election on that occasion was a hotly contested one, the candidates being the late Helene Hoffman Cole and one Harry Shepherd of Bellingham, Washington. So close was the result, that considerable examination of ballots had to be made before the victor could be announced; but finally it was determined to the satisfaction of all impartial observers that the then Miss Hoffman was safely and lawfully elected. Here the matter should have ended, but the followers of Mr. Shepherd did not bear the defeat of their candidate with good grace. Instead of acquiescing and accepting the Hoffman administration—which, by the way, was one of the brightest in our history, and was extended over a second term—the Shepherdites insisted on proclaiming their candidate elected, and withdrew from our activities; paradoxically calling themselves the "only United" and ostentatiously hailing the United itself as an "outlaw" or "rebel" association.

Little was gained by this coup d'etat. The most cultivated members took no part in the secession, and the separatist faction has since maintained its existence only through the support of a few powerful irreconcilables in and near the city of Seattle. Its cultural tone has steadily declined, until today the majority of its members are of extreme crudity—mostly superficial near-Bolsheviki and soulful plumbers and truck-drivers who are still at the moralising stage. Their little schoolboy compositions on "Individualism", "The Fulfilment of Life", "The Will", "Giving Power to the Best", and so on, are really touching. One would like to introduce them to Voltaire, Haeckel,[1] James Branch Cabell, or some other real thinkers! In material prosperity the intellectual condition is well matched. Official organs are few and far between except when the Erford purse is generously open, and of the artistic quality of the various publications the less said the better. Such is the grandiose association which detests us so thoroughly, yet which we have always suffered to jog along unnoticed, as an always harmless and sometimes helpful medium for the energies of the very crude.

The present remarks are inspired by the peculiarly insulting manner in which some of the ungrammatical secessionists have received our amicable attempts to recruit pseudo-United members for the U.A.P.A. Recognising that many of the "pseudos" are far from hopeless educationally, we this year sought to give them the benefits of real amateur journalism, and to bring them into the United without conflicting in any way with their allegiance to their humbler yet worthy faction. We adopted the very reasonable notion that the world contains room for both associations, each of which has its own particular object. At first, our overtures seemed to be met in a rational manner. One very well-meaning Flatbush gentleman, after asking if he could join the United without the knowledge of his fellows in the pseudo-United, almost decided to affiliate; when conscience—or the word of a superior officer—caused him to suffer the malady known as "cold feet" and back out at the last moment, exclaiming in the "reverse English" which has made him a common laughing-stock for five years:

> "For one to do this step, regardless of time or circumstance, I would be inflicting an injustice to myself. Under these circumstances, I have reconsidered my previous step, and therefore decline to affiliate with your body, and I wish you to take steps to rectify the statement erroneously circulated. . . . This letter is not written at the request of Mr. Erford, or anyone else connected with our staff, or private information circulated to us. This action is entirely voluntary on my part."

Others of the pseudo-United have proved ungrammatical but less vacillating. Our latest gem is from a person somewhere in Michigan, who says:

> "Under no conditions could I consider membership in your association as prevailing facts, which I have no doubt as to their truth, prove that your association is not the real United but only a discontented faction who withdrew from the La Grande Convention in 1912. . . . Your *activities* in our association to deprive us of some of our members *is* wholly unfair to us and we can see your motive in doing so."

Had this Michigan litterateur learned to read, he would have noted in our letter to him the paragraph:

> "My purpose is to invite you to affiliate with us as well. There will be no conflict of opportunity or loyalty, since there is no warfare between the two branches now. Many of your officers are members of both branches, just as many of our members are also affiliated with the older association—the National."

Perhaps it is a waste of time to take notice of affairs as trivial as this, but we desire to forestall any remarks from our esteemed contemporaries to the effect that we have been seeking to disrupt a weaker and humbler association. We have borne no malice toward our sometimes peevish "little brother", but have merely tried to give some of its members a chance for improvement. We still think that the pseudo-United has a useful and legitimate place as a primary school to form a stepping-stone to the United, and we hope that its temper will improve as it grows further and further beyond the dominance of its intransigent leaders. Meanwhile we shall do the simplest and most widely acceptable of all things—leave our pseudo-United friends unmolested amidst this native barbarism!

EDITOR'S NOTE FP: *United Amateur* 19, No. 5 (May 1920): 106–8 (unsigned). The article can be safely attributed to HPL, as it won the Editorial laureateship award for the 1919–20 term, and HPL was listed as the author at that time. This is one more of HPL's screeds against the United Amateur Press Association of America (see "The Morris Faction,"

p. 33), this one considerably sharper in tone than the others because HPL was rebuffed in his attempts to persuade some members to join his UAPA.

*Notes*

1. HPL was greatly influenced by naturalist and philosopher Ernst Haeckel (1834–1919), whose *Welträthsel* (1899; Eng. tr. as *The Riddle of the Universe*, 1900) significantly affected his materialist thought.

# THE CONQUEST OF THE HUB CLUB

On July 5, 1920, occurred one of the most momentous events in the history of the well-known Hub Club of Massachusetts; the capture of the organisation by the United Amateur Press Association. The attack was deeply premeditated, having been planned by the notorious political boss and politician, H. P. Lovecraft, alias L. Theobald, Jr., and abetted by the thrice re-elected second vice-president, Mrs. W. V. Jordan, and the newly converted and already vociferously active United propagandist, George Julian Houtain, Esq.

Of this political ring one member, Mrs. Jordan, had been working among the Hubites for some time; Mr. Houtain arrived on July 3, laying the last stones of the foundation of this gigantic coup d'etat. Mr. Lovecraft did not arrive until the day of the event, but had prepared to relieve the victims of their cash and to complete the work of devastation.

The first Nationalite to fall into the snare was Mrs. E. Dorothy MacLaughlin, who was rapidly followed by Mrs. Laurie A. Sawyer, and slightly less rapidly by Mrs. Miniter. The first genuine obstacle to be encountered was J. Bernard Lynch, Esq., who manfully resisted the bandits on the ground that an ancient feud had forever alienated him from the United. When, however, it was demonstrated that the United he remembered was not the genuine society of that name his defence proved inadequate and he passed over to the conquered majority. M. Oscar White did likewise.[1]

But the career of the boldest highwaymen must come to an end at last. When Mr. Charles A. A. Parker was attacked he proved the rock on which the bark of banditry was wrecked; for his frigid attitude of refusal dispelled the charm which had held the victims inert and helpless. No more recruits to *real* amateur journalism were secured.

But out of the raid three important results remain to affect the future of amateurdom. After thirty years of darkness the Hubites have been blessed with the light of the United; at last the United has secured for its ranks the cream of Boston's intellectual elite; and more than all this, there has sprung into being a new association destined to eclipse all the associations of the past—the immortal and classical society of the EPGEPHIANS.

EDITOR'S NOTE FP: *Epgephi*, September 1920, pp. 13–14 (as by "54 & 7–8THS§"). HPL's contribution to an amateur journal (the only issue ever issued) devoted to a convention held in the Boston area on 2–12 July 1920. HPL attended the convention for the period 4–5 July, sleeping in the home of Alice M. Hamlet in Dorchester (with two chaperons), this comprising the first time HPL had slept under a roof other than his own since 1901. The piece can be attributed to HPL because the pseudonym in question is identified on p. 1 of *Epgephi* as belonging to "How—P—lip L—e—ft." The Hub Club was a celebrated amateur press club (chiefly associated with the NAPA) in Boston; from this point onward HPL made regular visits to it until his departure to New York in March 1924. Epgephi apparently refers to a couch in the home of Edith Miniter and Charles A. A. Parker at 20 Webster Street in Allston, MA, where many amateurs reposed on overnight stays.

*Notes*

1. For HPL's later tussles with Michael Oscar White over the merits of Samuel Loveman's poetry, see "In the Editor's Study" (*Conservative*, July 1923; CE2).

# NEWS NOTES

*(September 1920)*

The United welcomes the reinstatement of George Julian Houtain, its first Laureate Recorder, and prominent member of the past. His revived *Zenith* will be the Association's leading news and editorial sheet during the coming year, and we hope that its issuance may be frequent. Mr. Houtain is a successful attorney, and recently occupied new offices at 206 Broadway, New York City.

The Woodbees recently held a successful rummage sale which surpassed all expectations and solved the club's financial problems in a manner quite surprising in this age of altitudinous printers' prices. $25.00 of the proceeds was most generously contributed to the Official Organ Fund, thus ensuring the successful publication of the November *United Amateur*. Were other clubs to assist in this liberal fashion, the unbroken issuance of the Official Organ throughout 1920–21 would be assured. The United feels itself greatly in the Woodbees' debt, and delights to behold such an example of associational loyalty. Coming numbers of *The Woodbee* are eagerly awaited by our members.

Miss Margaret Abraham, our new Treasurer, was valedictorian last June at Appleton High School, and has now entered the University of Chicago, where she has every reason to expect a brilliant and successful career. Her present address is 49 Kelly Hall, U. of C., Chicago, Ill.

Much pleasure is felt by the United at the advent of many members of the celebrated Hub Club of Boston, Mass., an organisation heretofore connected exclusively with the National. This society has a history extending over thirty years, and its official organ, *The Hub Club Quill*, was founded in 1901. Among the members joining the United are Mrs. Edith Miniter, famous not only in Amateurdom but in the outside world of letters; Mrs. Laurie A. Sawyer, Amateurdom's premier humourist; Mrs. E. Dorothy MacLaughlin, editor of *The National Tribute*; Michael Oscar White, renowned for clever light verse; and Joseph Bernard Lynch, professionally prominent as a short-story writer of the "human interest" type. Mr. Lynch's advent is a reinstatement, since he was among our earliest United members. Credit for this distinguished recruiting belongs to Mrs. W. V. Jordan and George J. Houtain, himself but newly reinstated.

Amateurdom will remember 1920 as the year when three conventions, instead of the usual two, were held. The third was the unofficial gathering at Boston during the week of July 4, which has been perpetuated by the deliciously whimsical magazine *Epgephi*. Besides the local amateurs, there were present W. Paul Cook, Rheinhart Kleiner, George Julian Houtain, and H. P. Lovecraft, all ex-Presidents of the United or the National.

News items concerning amateurs are solicited from our members. Send them to the Official Editor.

EDITOR'S NOTE  FP: *United Amateur* 20, No. 1 (September 1920): 16 (unsigned). With HPL's election as Official Editor for the 1920–21 term (he would be re-elected for 1921–22, 1923–24, and 1924–25), it became his responsibility to write the "News Notes" in the *United Amateur* as space permitted. This column is quite brief, but several later ones were of substantial length, frequently discussing HPL's own close associates.

# AMATEUR JOURNALISM:
# ITS POSSIBLE NEEDS AND BETTERMENT

It is with great humility that I respond to an invitation to speak on Amateur Journalism: Its Possible Needs and Betterment, to an audience most of whose members are far better equipped to speak than am I. In the presence of our cause's most honoured and able veterans, the remarks of one active for only six years must necessarily lack authority. However, in case the opinions of a relative novice may possess some slight spark of value, I will not decline the proffered opportunity for discussion.

Had I devised the title of this address myself, I should have introduced a transposition, saying "amateurdom's *needs* and *possible betterment*". For our needs are certainties, while it is our betterment which contains the element of doubt. That we are imperfect, we know well; that we can find a mode of improvement, is problematical in view of the long existence of our hobby at practically the same level. There is less progress in the world than idealists affect to believe. It is, nevertheless, our duty to give constant attention to the state of amateur journalism; that its best traditions may not be obliterated, nor its literary quality impaired by carelessness or the dominance of unworthy political groups. Symposia like the present gathering are invaluable in their tendency to renew interest and permit of an exchange of views and plans for resisting decadence.

The present needs—or I might say the perpetual needs—of amateurdom are naturally divisible into two classes; qualitative and quantitative. The first class may be exemplified by many conspicuous phenomena, such as crude, flamboyant, and inartistic papers, papers of lax literary standards, and official criticism so puerile that its appearance in an official organ is almost an insult to amateur letters. All these qualitative evils are traceable to the lack of some centralised authority capable of exerting a kindly, reliable, and more or less invisible guidance in matters aesthetic and artistic. Such an authority must obviously be unofficial, since official recognition of literary capability is impossible, and should preferably consist of a small group of members representing various phases and ideals. It can never be created by any formal process, but must be born spontaneously out of the aspiration of amateurs in general; existing through tradition and tacit recognition by the majority. The important thing is to have such a group enthroned apart from the political processes of the various associations, like the learned academies of the Latin countries, surviving all changes of official boards and exerting its sway in a spirit of coöperation rather than of dictatorship. Lest I seem to deal in vague abstractions, let me suggest how such an academic authority might be composed, and how it might discharge its functions. Its beginning must be purely voluntary—an offer of services on the part of those qualified to render them. Certain qualified members must undertake the entirely new burden of offering help to both writers and publishers. They must approach crude authors whose work shews promise, and crude publishers whose papers appear to possess the spark of aspiration; offering a revision and censorship which shall ensure the publication of the articles or journals in question, free from all the main errors in taste and technique. That a majority of the crude authors and publishers will accept this aid has already been proved by concrete instances; so we can state with safety that if literary leaders can be found, a fairly high standard can be established at once, and maintained in a majority of the current amateur publications. In brief, it is possible to create a standard of correct writing and editing by forming a voluntary board of censorship and revising practically all the products of the cruder amateurs. The good effects of such a standard are not far to seek. When a majority of the amateur journals shew a proper degree of polish, whether natural or artificial, writers and editors will no longer be content with crudeness. The pitiful self-complacency of the inveterate dunce will necessarily vanish, so that his kind will be forced either to improve or to quit organised amateurdom; whilst the worthy ambition of the real aspirant will be encouraged by the aid extended, and the recipients of revision and censorship will learn correctness from their unofficial preceptors. One consequence of this policy would be the raising of standards on the part of careless editors. Many good papers are at present hampered by certain crude contributions which appear interspersed among the meritorious matter. These contributions should be either revised or eliminated, for they furnish a discouraging setting for the better work; and they would be attended to if amateurdom demanded it. The paramount object should be to outlaw the imperfect. Not to discourage the aspirant in his first stages, but to give nothing but the best the stamp of final approval; to fix the goal unalterably high. It is the creation of a sentiment which we need; a sentiment of endeavour which shall spurn conscious laxity and satisfied mediocrity. Here the question of official criticism enters. I do not think that it is my own United affiliation which impels me to say that much of the criticism in the *National* is not only worthless but harmful. The inability of the best qualified critics has left the field open to others, and a majority of the current reviews in *The National Amateur* have become highly reprehensible in their failure to point out flaws and recommend improvements. Such laxity is harmful because it is a tacit endorsement of crudity. If faults be left uncensured, there will be no spur to set the novice onward toward his goal. With an official "little senate" to determine literary standards and revise amateur matter adequately, such feeble reviews would not be tolerated. Authors and editors who failed to conform to the standard would be given the impetus needed—their deficiencies would be noted and singled out. Of course, no unofficial authority could remedy poor criticism without coöperation from the official board. Only a higher sense of discrimination and responsibility on the part of those who appoint critics could prevent the publication of such humiliatingly inane things as the recent attack on Samuel Loveman's exquisite lyrics on the ground that they do not belong to the "cheer-up" penny-a-line school. To recapitulate on the subject of qualitative improvement and centralised authority, let me say that in my opinion there should be correspondence between the literary leaders of amateurdom on the subject of wholesale revision and censorship. The few who start the movement should strive to interest other capable leaders, with the purpose of creating a board of practical service to offer aid to all writers and publishers willing to accept it. This board should work unselfishly, unceasingly, and almost unrecognised, for the good of amateurdom; until very soon it would be recognised as a permanent arbiter of taste, above and apart from the political machinery of any association. If any idealistic and ultra-conscientious person object to the plan on account of its possible oligarchical tendencies, let him consider the lessons of history. All brilliant periods of literature have corresponded with the existence of dominant coteries, from Pericles to Augustus, and down through the ages to the coffee-house circles of Dryden and Addison and the literary club of Dr. Johnson. In truth, the ideal of utter democracy in the arts is a false and misleading one; which though zealously cherished by many persons, ought to be discarded in the interest of truth and progress. Centralised authority has existed for many years and with marked success in the United Association, raising that organisation to a literary supremacy which even its worst enemies hesitate to challenge. That the principle should be more widely extended, is both logical and desirable.

I fear I have not left myself space to speak at length regarding quantitative improvement, but I will make the most of my limited opportunities. This problem is both psychological and financial, involving the enthusiasm of the membership on the one hand, and the difficulties of printing on the other hand. The first phase, I confess, baffles me somewhat. The public mind seems to have been adversely affected by the force of the present crisis in world affairs, so that a dampening spirit of lassitude and futility envelops everything. Spontaneity and buoyancy such as we knew before 1914 are impossible to achieve nowadays, when the very foundations of society and government seem in jeopardy. That cannot be improved. If I knew how to remedy world psychology I should not be speaking before amateurs, but in the councils of state and the parliaments of the powers. However, I can at least suggest that the more ardent few do what they can to arouse greater interest by pointing out the advantages of amateurdom over other hobbies and diversions. I would especially recommend the deliberate creation of interesting controversies, either on subjects of worldwide general interest, or on purely literary topics; avoiding only amateur politics, which presents unsuspected potentialities of evil. Above all, let mutual comment be encouraged. We should make it virtually a rule to see that as many articles as possible receive printed replies. The controversies and comments in Master John Milton Heins' *American Amateur* furnish an ideal example of what is needed.

The financial problems are, when one comes to consider them at close range, almost as baffling as the psychological problems. That the increase in printers' rates must greatly curtail the volume of published matter is a foregone conclusion, and we may only urge with redoubled force that every owner of a home press publish to the very extent of his capacity—as a duty to the institution which has given him so much of pleasure and profit in the past. C. W. Smith is a model whom every press-owner should keep constantly in mind—that is, as regards intent and volume, not typographical accuracy. Then we must investigate to the full the possibilities of the mimeograph. John Clinton Pryor and Horace L. Lawson have shewn us what can be done without a printing-press,[1] and we must encourage the extension of this kind of activity by ceasing to harbour any prejudices in favour of printing. Let us remember that print is only a form—only a medium. The important thing in literature is the transmission of thoughts, so that no writer should hesitate to send his best work to the non-printed magazines. If these periodicals cannot command the coöperation of our authors, they can never flourish. Manuscript magazines, while manifestly far behind printed and duplicated magazines in utility, should be encouraged in every known way. Of these, Mrs. Eleanor B. Campbell's *Corona* is the logical model. This paper was circulated by typing as many carbon copies as possible and setting each of them along a designated route to be passed around. None of the circulation lists was unwieldy, yet a large territory was covered. The fatal obstacle to success in this field is the negligence of those who receive magazines. I myself attempted to circulate one two years ago, yet it disappeared before it could leave New England.[2] Another magazine, which I circulated for the editors, started on its rounds in April, 1919; and has only just reached New York State! The only remedy for this reprehensible state of things is in-creased conscientiousness, which I hope the pressure of hard times will develop in most of us. In leaving the subject of papers, I will again repeat what I have so often said else-where—that coöperative publishing should be encouraged as widely as possible. It may soon be the only feasible method of issuing a printed journal, and all objections against it should be overruled in the shortest possible order.

Increase in revenue in all associations is now practically a necessity, and should be adopted as quickly as possible. That we should still charge only pre-war dues is mani-festly absurd. But even these increases can hardly ensure suitable official organs. Both associations have kept their official organs alive only through individual philanthropy, and for this unorganised charity some more equitable system of endowment should be substituted. Finally, we must reflect upon the waste of dual organisation. The sepa-rateness of the United and National is regrettable, and if consolidation could be ef-fected according to the Morton plan we would be amply repaid for laying aside small prejudices and subordinating minor differences.

So, to my mind, stands the present situation. Roseate dreams are futile, yet our in-stitution cannot but benefit from intelligent and concerted endeavour.

EDITOR'S NOTE FP: *The Dark Brotherhood and Other Pieces* (Sauk City, WI: Arkham House, 1966), pp. 82–87. Text based upon the TMS (JHL). The essay is an address HPL was asked to deliver at the Hub Club gathering in Boston on 5 September 1920 (see Joshi, *Life* 180–81 and 664n.7). It is one of his most trenchant discussions of the deficiencies in amateur jour-nalism, and it becomes clear that HPL is increasingly irritated at the slow literary progress exhibited by many members; he now proposes a kind of "centralised authority" that would correct the grossest lapses in style, taste, and content in amateur writing prior to publica-tion. This plan—similar to but even more oligarchic than his earlier proposal for a "De-partment of Instruction"—was of course never adopted.

*Notes*

1. Pryor's *Pine Cones* and Lawson's *Wolverine* were mimeographed magazines.
2. The reference is to *Hesperia.* See SL 1.68, 136 and n. 1 to DPC (January 1918).

---

# EDITORIAL

*(November 1920)*

Editorial comment upon amateur journalism generally falls within one of two classes; complacent self-congratulation upon a mythical perfection or hectic urging toward impossible achievements. It is our purpose this month to indulge in neither of these rhetorical recreations, but to make one very prosaic and practical appeal which springs solely from realistic observation.

This appeal concerns the official situation in the United. For several years our foes have reproached us for excessive centralisation of authority; asserting that the control of our society is anything from oligarchical to monarchial, and pointing to the large amount of influence wielded by a very few leaders. Denials on our part, prompted by the conspicuous absence of any dictatorial ambitions in the minds of our executives, have been largely nullified by the fact that while power has not been autocratically usurped and arbitrarily exercised, the burden of administrative work has certainly been thrust by common consent on a small number of reluctant though loyal shoulders. A few persons have been forced to retain authority because no others have arisen to relieve them of their burdens, until official nominations have come to mean no more than a campaign by one or two active spirits to persuade certain patient drudges to "carry on" another year. Nor does the formal official situation reflect all of the prevailing conditions. Much of the Association's most important activity, such as recruiting, welcoming, and criticism, verges into the field of unorganised effort; and here the tendency to leave everything to a narrow group is overwhelming.

Obviously, this condition demands a remedy; and that remedy lies in one direction only—an acceptance of potential official responsibility by all of those members who possess the time and experience to act as leaders. As the fiscal year progresses, the season for candidacies draws near; and amateurs who feel competent to sustain their share of the administrative burden should come forward as nominees, or at least should respond when approached by their friends. That office-holding involves tedious work, all admit, but this tedium is a small price to pay for the varied boons of amateurdom. In unofficial labour an unequal willingness should be shewn. Why is it that all the private revision in the United is performed by about three men at most, despite the presence in our ranks of a full score of scholars abundantly capable of rendering such service? If the *literati* as a whole will not awaken to the needs of the day, one of two things will occur. The United will stagnate quietly under the perpetual dictatorship of a limited group of unwilling but benevolent autocrats, or it will succumb to the onslaught of some political clique of vigorous barbarians who will destroy in a month what it has taken the United over ten years to build up. Memories of 1919 should prove to us the reality of such a danger of sudden relapse.[1]

Our appeal, then, is for responsible candidates for high office, and for volunteers in the work of maintaining interest and lending literary aid. We know that executive energy and enthusiasm tend to be more abundant in the Goth than in the Greek; that those best qualified to serve are generally least moved by political ambition. But we are sure that the needs of our society should arouse enough sense of duty among its cultivated membership to draw to the front a new generation of leaders. We ask for new presidential and editorial candidates who are prepared to serve faithfully and independently if elected; for new critics and recruiters who understand our traditions and are willing to expend energy in upholding and diffusing them. Shall 1921 bring them to light?

EDITOR'S NOTE  FP: *United Amateur* 20, No. 2 (November 1920): 29. The only editorial written in the 1920–21 term. HPL notes complaints by some members of "excessive centralisation of authority." HPL rebuts the charge, but grumblings of this sort eventually gained strength and led to the ouster of HPL and his colleagues in the election of July 1922.

*Notes*

1. The reference is to William J. Dowdell's failed quest to become Official Editor of the UAPA. See "For Official Editor—Anne Tillery Renshaw" (p. 237).

# NEWS NOTES

*(November 1920)*

George Julian Houtain on June 12 addressed the annual convention of the National Institute of Inventors in New York City. His able speech, widely featured in the daily press, described the crusade made against the fraudulent patent attorneys who prey upon inventors. At the banquet in the evening he acted as toastmaster. Mr. Houtain will this autumn participate in the publication of a magazine devoted to the interests of inventors; a new type of enterprise which shall present the problems and personalities of these practical geniuses in a manner calculated to bring them closer to the public.

Maurice Winter Moe is receiving felicitations on his return to the teaching profession, for which he is so conspicuously well fitted.[1] He now fills a post at the West Division High School, Milwaukee, Wis., where his success is already notable; and in addition conducts much valuable work in connexion with boys' clubs and the Y. M. C. A. Mr. Moe should now be addressed at 751 Farwell Ave., Milwaukee. (Since this item was written, Mr. Moe's address has been changed to 2431 Cedar St., same city.—Publisher.)

Our brilliant young member Jay Fuller Spoerri pursued a summer course at the University of Chicago, and was prominently connected with the University Players, taking part in the professional presentation of Augustus Thomas' "Witching Hour" in Gary, Ind.[2] His portrayal of "Lew Ellinger" was well received. Mr. Spoerri has now returned to Washington to his regular course at George Washington University, and is again to be addressed at 304 House Office Building in that city. He will figure prominently in the centennial celebrations of the University, having been elected President of the Junior Class.

In the September number of the *National Magazine* appears a long and interesting article on the work and personality of Mrs. W. V. Jordan, the United poetess, from the pen of no less a biographer than our newly reinstated member J. Bernhard Lynch. A note by the editor on Mr. Lynch gives additional interest. Accompanying the article and note are excellent portraits of both Mrs. Jordan and Mr. Lynch. Such outside recognition of our members give us the keenest of pleasure, and a renewed conviction of the worth of amateur journalism.

Our new Second Vice-President, Miss Alice M. Hamlet, is taking a post-graduate course at the New England Conservatory of Music, and bids fair to become one of Boston's most accomplished musical instructors.

Miss Bertha Lee Hempstead, whom the old-timers will remember as an amateur writer and publisher, but who has been a professional newspaper special writer for the last twelve years, contracted pulmonary tuberculosis while engaged in patriotic service in the A. E. F. overseas under the Y. M. C. A., and died October 1, 1920, at Albuquerque, N. M., after a brave but unavailing fight for life.

Prof. N. A. Crawford, managing editor of *The Industrialist*, organ of the Kansas State Agricultural College, writes: "Bertha's death was a great loss, not only to those of us who knew her well, but to the state as a whole. She was easily the most effective and influential newspaper woman in Kansas."

Edward F. Daas, leader in United affairs, is now on his way to South America. He is travelling slowly and stopping at various places of interest, which will probably include St. Petersburg, Fla., winter residence of ex-Official Editor McGeoch. He is now in New Orleans, whose quaint and exotic sights he is exploring as thoroughly as possible. With Mr. Daas is Eugene C. Dietzler, prominent in the Washington club last year. Both should henceforward be addressed at 1717 Cherry St., Milwaukee, where arrangements for forwarding mail have been made.

Mr. and Mrs. Paul J. Campbell entertained Messrs. Daas and Dietzler at Prairie Queen Grange during December. After the publication of Mr. Campbell's *Liberal*, they will start for Florida on a tour.

Horace L. Lawson of *Wolverine* fame, who spent last year at sea in the merchant service in quest of local colour, will shortly reward the expectations of his admirers with a series of interesting and realistic marine tales entitled "Tales of the Lake Turain".

Frank Belknap Long, Jr., youthful author of some very "gripping" *contes cruels*, is now pursuing journalistic studies at New York University.

In a recent number of the professional magazine *Class* appeared a highly sensible and interesting article by Prof. Philip B. McDonald, entitled "Empties in the Train of Thought".

*The Arbitrator* for November contains some valuable argumentative matter by James F. Morton, Jr., on the subject of the taxation of church property.[3]

Joseph Bernard Lynch's short story masterpiece, "Making Good on the Props", has been republished in the *National Magazine* and syndicated for publication in smaller cities. This tale was included in Edward J. O'Brien's annual list of best stories when originally published.

A new recruit likely to be of great prominence is Miss Myrta Alice Little (Colby A. B., Radcliffe A. M.) of Hampstead (Westville P. O.), N. H. Miss Little is, like our leader Mr. Moe, a high-school English teacher; and she is in addition a professional author of increasing success. She is pursuing a systematic course in short story construction, and will probably be numbered among the successful writers of the future.[4]

Mrs. Maude Kingsbury Barton achieved a spectacular success on October 28, when she produced at the Baker Grand Theatre, Natchez, Miss., a cycle of fairy plays entitled "Once Upon a Time". The performance was conducted under the auspices of the order of the White Shrine, and was staged with local talent. Mrs. Barton's supervision, directing, costuming, and setting were praised enthusiastically on every hand, and the enterprise formed the subject of the *Natchez Democrat's* leading editorial on the following day. A matinee and evening performance were given, both playing to S. R. O. The United congratulates its gifted Mississippi representative upon so great a triumph.

Mrs. Anne Tillery Renshaw, with characteristic energy, has transferred her interests from State College, Pa., to Washington, D. C. During the autumn she was circulation manager of *The Suffragist*, a large illustrated monthly, whose subscription department she practically revitalised with her efficient management. She has now accepted a chair at Research University, becoming head of the English Department with the title of Professor. Mrs. Renshaw receives the sympathy of the Association upon the death of Mr. Renshaw in November, and upon the illness of her mother at the same time.

*El Dorado*, literary organ of the Penn State Press Club, has evolved into *The Blue and White*, which represents State College as a whole. The first number, now before us, contains contributions of excellence from J. Gordon Amend, Sarah E. Croll, and Edna M. Sell, United members.

John Milton Samples, our Poet-Laureate, has recently suffered from poor health, including a severe ocular trouble which only rest could relieve; but has nevertheless successfully pursued his studies at Mercer University, where he lately passed some difficult examinations with flying colours. Mr. Samples' excellent *Silver Clarion*, suspended on account of the rising cost of printing, will be resumed if arrangements can be made for the purchase of a press.

Publishers are urged to be sure to include on their mailing lists Mr. Harry N. Lehmkuhl, 688-32nd St., Milwaukee, an especially enthusiastic new recruit of Mr. Moe's.

The professional success of our young member Eric McLean of Altrincham, England, is highly gratifying. Mr. McLean's juvenile tales are now appearing in some of Great Britain's leading junior publications, and are marked by a merit not always found in boys' fiction. "Madmen's Gold", in *Chums*, is especially noteworthy.

Miss Annie Pearce has lately assumed charge of a weekly Children's Column, writing about 1200 words of prose each week, besides contributing frequent short poems.

Among the possibilities of the near future is a book of poems by our beloved and brilliant bard Jonathan E. Hoag, who celebrates his 90th birthday on February 10th.[5]

Ex-President Rheinhart Kleiner recently joined a organisation of professional authors in New York, and will probably become a figure of increasing prominence in the outside poetical world.

The Boston "Epgephian Convention" of July 4th and after proved such a success that subsequent gatherings were held in August, September, and January. The August gathering coincided with the Hub Club's Annual Picnic, and was held at the home of Nelson Glazier Morton in Melrose Highlands; one of the features being a trip into the beautiful Middlesex Fells. The September conclave was held at Allston headquarters, and was adorned by the presence of a number of notable old-timers including Mrs. Harriet Cox Dennis, Leonard E. Tilden, and James F. Morton, Jr. In January the assemblage took place at Charles Parker's home in Maplewood. A Boston sub-convention of more formal and elaborate nature will take place at the Quincy House on February 22nd, and is expected to draw a notable attendance from all over the East.[6]

Rev. David V. Bush, Pastor of the Central People's Church of St. Louis and former member of the United, received as a welcome Christmas gift the degree of D. D. Dr. Bush has amateurdom's congratulations on his new and well-earned honour.

Amateurs are advised to extend an especially thorough welcome to a new member whose enrolment will appear in our next issue, Dewey S. Patton, Ph. D. (U. of C. '20), an instructor of mathematics in a college at Muskogee, Okla. Mr. Patton is now publishing a book of his essays,[7] and a review of Ibanez' "La Catedral" from his pen will soon appear in the amateur press. This important new member was proposed by Jay Fuller Spoerri.

News items concerning amateurs are solicited from the members. Send them to the Official Editor.

EDITOR'S NOTE  FP: *United Amateur* 20, No. 2 (November 1920): 30–32 (unsigned). HPL surveys amateur activity in recent months, concentrating on such of his associates as George Julian Houtain, Maurice W. Moe, David Van Bush, and others.

*Notes*

1. In commemoration of the event, HPL wrote the poem "On the Return of Maurice Winter Moe, Esq., to the Pedagogical Profession" (*Wolverine*, June 1921; *AT* 145–46).

2. *The Witching Hour*, by American playwright Augustus Thomas (1857–1934), was produced in 1907 and published in 1916.
3. Morton, at this time an atheist, had earlier published a pamphlet on the subject, *Exempting the Churches* (1915). See also *Shall Church Property Be Taxed: A Debate*, with Lawson Purdy (1921?).
4. HPL visited Little twice in the late spring and summer of 1921; see *SL* 1.139–40, 183–84.
5. *The Poetical Works of Jonathan E. Hoag* (New York: Privately printed), edited by HPL, did not appear until 1923.
6. HPL attended the meetings in July, August, and September 1920 and on 22 February 1921. See Joshi, *Life* 196–97, 201.
7. No such volume has been located.

---

# NEWS NOTES

*(January 1921)*

Alfred Galpin, Jr., is proving an Executive worthy of the traditions of our society. His December *Philosopher* is the most notable paper of recent years in point of quality, the maturity and thoughtfulness of the editorials constituting something quite exceptional in amateurdom.

Thanks to President Galpin, the United will this year shine again in the matter of distinguished Laureate Judges. As Judge of Editorials we shall have the services of no less a celebrity than H. L. Mencken,[1] greatest of American literary critics, and perhaps the sole champion of purely artistic standards on this continent.

Winifred Virginia Jackson, foremost amateur poetess, has lately added to a collection of laurels already great. Besides placing much work in the professional press, she has gained distinction from the publication of some of her verses on wall cards, the latter attaining much popularity and ready sale. The delightful "River of Life" may be obtained in this form at 25 cents per card from the Old South Press, 830 Washington St., Boston, Mass. In January, Miss Jackson was honoured by an interview from the *Boston Sunday Post* regarding her work, the article appearing in the issue of January 30, with an excellent portrait.

At a recent meeting of the Woodbees, the following official board was elected: President, Arthur Ziegfeld; Vice-President, Edith W. Fowler; Secretary and Treasurer, Henriette Ziegfeld; Literary Director, Norma Sanger; Official Editor, Ida C. Haughton; Assistant Editor, Leo Fritter. Plans have been made for a repetition of former dramatic successes, two one-act plays being on the club's schedule for May. Another coming event is a rummage sale like that which succeeded so well last year. At the present writing, another *Woodbee* is in press.

George Julian Houtain, editor of *The Zenith*, was in Washington in March, and attended an interesting meeting of the Pen and Ink Club.

Among our newest members is Dr. Joseph Homer, of Boston, who has to his credit a volume of verse which may be found in the Boston Public Library.[2] Dr. Homer has scientific as well as poetic interests, and will undoubtedly form a party to that extensive philosophical discussion which has become a feature of the United. Credit for this brilliant recruit belongs to Winifred V. Jackson.

John Milton Samples, Poet-Laureate, was recently the subject of a special article in the *Macon Sunday Telegraph,* which told interestingly of his amazing range of activities. It is hard to believe that one poet can simultaneously engage in five distinct occupations, yet such is the feat of our versatile *Clarion* editor, who holds two positions with the post-office department, conducts a card-writing business, and often acts as a clergyman, while constantly studying at Mercer University. Such an ambitious programme, followed by a man of ample family responsibilities, should serve to put to shame those less strenuous workers who complain that they have "no time"! A recent number of the *Mercer Cluster,* organ of Mr. Samples' college, contains so much of his work that we are reminded of the *Clarion*—which latter, we are glad to note, will make a reappearance in May under the joint editorship of Mr. Samples and Julian T. Baber.

Miss Myrta Alice Little, of Westville, N. H., is a new member of particular distinction, having compressed a phenomenal number of academic honours into a surprisingly short period. Entering Colby University at sixteen, she graduated with honours and became a high-school teacher of English, French, and German before attaining her majority. Then, having pursued a brilliant post-graduate course at Radcliffe which gained her the degree of A. M., she became at once the head of the English department of Alfred University. After a period there, and at Temple University, Miss Little contemplated a position in Constantinople; but was prevented from carrying out this plan by the opening of the war. Subsequent academic connexions were with the Rhode Island College of Education, and Wheaton College; followed by a Y. W. C. A. Educational Secretaryship in California. Very recently Miss Little decided to turn from the scholastic field to creative authorship, and has already achieved encouraging results in literature, both amateur and professional. Her principal products are fictional and poetical, and are of such a quality that success seems assured. With new members of this type, the United need never fear for its future supremacy. For securing Miss Little as a member, credit is due to our energetic Second Vice-President, Alice M. Hamlet.

Amateurs will learn with regret of the sudden and untimely death of Julian J. Crump, former United member and brother of our distinguished poetess, Daisy Crump Whitehead. Mr. Crump was instantly killed on February 20, 1921, at Seffner, Fla., his home, while crossing the railway tracks in his automobile. The sympathy of the Association is extended to his widow, and to his sister, Mrs. Whitehead.

Messrs. Edward F. Daas and Eugene C. Dietzler, last mentioned as sojourning in New Orleans, are continuing their southward progress. In January they reached St. Cloud, Fla., the winter home of the Campbells; and thereafter all four enjoyed a pleasing succession of automobile trips, embellished with the various diversions peculiar to Florida's genial climate. Among their excursions was one to Orlando, another to St. Augustine, where they beheld America's oldest house and drank from the fountain of youth, and one to St. Petersburg, where on March 5 they called at the home of our former Official Editor, Miss Verna McGeoch. Later in March the party proceeded to Melbourne and descended the east coast to Palm Beach and Miami, at which latter place Messrs. Daas and Dietzler entrained for Key West on their way to Havana. We await with interest the news which our migratory members will send from Latin-America.

Mr. and Mrs. Paul J. Campbell spent the winter in Florida, whither they went by motor in January. Their journey through the "black belt" was marked by several adventures, including an attempted hold-up; while their later excursions through the southern peninsula were enlivened by such incidents as becoming lost in the night and encountering a five-foot snake. On their return trip they plan to visit several of the Southern amateurs, including John Milton Samples, Mrs. M. Almedia Bretholl, James Larkin Pearson, and Chester Pierce Munroe. Mr. Campbell's *Liberal,* appearing early in

March, has proved to be one of the most interesting, meritorious, and widely discussed publications of the season.

British amateurdom continues to manifest activity in as great a degree as economic conditions allow. The *Free Lance* has been followed by two more manuscript magazines of merit—the *Northumbrian* of Mr. McKeag, and the *Aspirant* of Misses Pearce and Mahon. American amateurs unable to issue printed journals would do well to emulate the zeal and diligence of these faithful publishers.

The United takes pride in the new laurels of its scintillant and versatile member, Mrs. S. Lilian McMullen (Lilian Middleton), who is now writing songs for professional publication with the music of Ernest Harry Adams. The latest of these to appear is "The Bumble Fairy", a dreamily exquisite piece already sung by several vocalists of note.

Prof. Philip B. McDonald is rapidly becoming a familiar figure in the general literary world, his peculiarly piquant style finding favour with an increasing number of publications. He is already a *Literary Digest* fixture, and his reviews of Wells' "Outline of History" and Reade's "Martyrdom of Man" have pleased the readers of the *New York Times* and the *Springfield Republican*, respectively. In *Chemical and Metallurgical Engineering* for February 9, Prof. McDonald has a brilliant unsigned editorial on the value of conceit, while a recent *Texas Review* contains a detailed political article from his pen. He is the author of the anonymous article, "The Ignorance of Science", in the *Literary Digest* of March 19.

Misses Annie Pearce and Margaret Mahon are to be congratulated upon the publication of many of their verses in booklet form. Poetry lovers may obtain these booklets at sixpence each from the publisher, F. Warren, 45 Selhurst New Road, South Norwood, S. E. 25, England.

The Boston Amateur Conference of February 22, held at the Quincy House, was successful from every point of view, reflecting the greatest credit upon Mrs. Edith Miniter, who led in arranging it. The event was divided into two major sessions—an afternoon symposium under the chairmanship of Nelson G. Morton, and a dinner, with the renowned "old-timer" Willard Otis Wylie as toastmaster; both evoking a representative display of wit and wisdom from the numerous delegates and visitors. A musical programme featuring Mrs. McMullen's "Bumble Fairy" proved a delightful interlude. Among those present, aside from the local members, were Mrs. Bertha York Grant Avery, George Julian Houtain, Mrs. K. Leyson Brown, Mrs. E. Dorothy MacLaughlin, W. Paul Cook, and H. P. Lovecraft.

The annual Convention of the United Amateur Press Association will take place in Washington, D. C., July 8, 9, and 11, 1921. A large attendance is desired and expected; for the advantages of an amateur gathering in so interesting a city, and under the auspices of a club as capable as the Pen and Ink, are too obvious to be ignored by any member able to make the journey.

An exceptionally promising recruit who deserves special attention from the welcoming committee is James F. Abel, Bureau of Education, 5th and G Sts., N. W., Washington, D. C. Mr. Abel will be a prominent figure at the Convention, and should prove a permanent acquisition of great value.

Adam Harold Brown, our new Canadian member,[3] and a writer of notable humorous stories, sends the following item regarding the new Canadian Authors' Association:

"All literary societies will welcome the recently formed Canadian Authors' Association, in which are most of the best-known novelists, poets, playwrights, essayists, and short-story writers in the Dominion, besides many who reside in the United States. Its first President is John Murray Gibbon, the novelist; Secretary, B. K. Sandwell, of Montreal; Treasurer, W. S. Wallace, of Toronto; while its ten Vice-Presidents (one for each branch) and its thirty members of the council bear names distinguished in the life of arts and letters. The new association plans to strengthen and advance the cause of literature not only in Canada, but throughout the English-speaking world."

The Woodbee Club has postponed its next rummage sale until autumn. Judging from the results of the first, it should prove a substantial aid both to the club and to the United as a whole. *The Woodbee* has now attained to the dignity of a twelve-cent magazine, such being the actual cost per copy of the latest and widely welcomed issue. On May 27 the club gives a drama, "Aunt Maggie's Will", which will be noted with interest by those who have witnessed the previous dramatic successes of the versatile members.

C. W. Smith, beloved editor of *The Tryout*, has now fully recovered from the nervous breakdown which has caused his inimitable journal to be missed of late. He attributes his recovery to the policy of keeping in the outdoor air. A new *Tryout* will soon be in the mails, followed by an issue covering the conventions.

John Milton Samples and family, of *Silver Clarion* renown, entertained Mr. and Mrs. Campbell at Macon during the northward migration of the latter tourists. The representatives of orthodoxy and liberalism found one another highly congenial.

Frank Belknap Long, Jr., recently won a prize for a short story in an interesting competition connected with his college—New York University.

James J. Hennessey, old-time United member, is now returning to the fold and delighting his correspondents with some artistic penmanship second only to the Samples brand. Mr. Hennessey is to be addressed, Care of General Delivery, Pittsburgh, Pa.

Messrs. Daas and Dietzler are at present sojourning in Havana, where they expect to stay for more than three months. They may be addressed at Lagunas 38 Altos.

EDITOR'S NOTE  FP: *United Amateur* 20, No. 3 (January 1921): 43–44 (unsigned). HPL discusses the activities of current amateurs, including Myrta Alice Little, whom he would visit in New Hampshire later in the year (see "The Haverhill Convention," p. 289).

*Notes*

1. H. L. Mencken (1880–1956), celebrated American journalist and critic.

2. Joseph Homer, *Post Poems* (Boston: Bailey Press, 1920), a pamphlet of 7 pages.

3. Brown was a member of the Transatlantic Circulator, a group of Anglo-American amateurs who exchanged manuscripts and commented on them. HPL, a member for much of 1921, circulated several poems and stories through the organization, and in response to criticisms of them wrote the three essays now titled *In Defence of Dagon*.

# THE UNITED'S POLICY 1920–1921

The ideal of pure literature paramount and unalloyed.

The conduct of the official organ as an exponent of the best in amateur writing, conservative but representative, and impartial in all controversies.

Assimilation of existing recruits rather than intensive recruiting. Promotion of local clubs according to the principles of earlier administrations, especially the Hoffman administration. Closer binding of clubs to the general association, and greater notice for the detached member.

Encouragement of open discussion of all matters concerning the amateur public, save that political contentions be avoided as far as possible. An impartial and receptive attitude toward all literary questions and disputes.

Encouragement of publishing both individual and coöperative, and recognition of mimeographed and circulated magazines on a basis of equality with printed magazines.

Recognition of the vital distinction between public and private criticism. Greater notice and enlarged personnel for the private bureau. Gradual development of the public bureau into a general topical review of important representative, current amateur literature. (Acknowledgment of current literary tastes as significant if only ephemeral. A. G. Jr.) (Preservation of sound literary ideals in defiance of contemporary decadence. H. P. L.)

Removal of verse and study laureateship classes, and removal of all restrictions regarding the number of entries necessary to ensure awards. Retention of the Literatus title and restrictions connected therewith.

Consolidation of Secretaryship and Treasurership into one appointive office, and consolidation of the two manuscript bureaux into one.

Elevation of entrance fee to one dollar, and dues to two dollars annually.

Maintenance of a special endowment fund for the official organ.

Attitude of amity toward other associations, neither proselyting nor permitting others to proselyte amongst us.

(Signed)
ALFRED GALPIN, Jr., Pres.
H. P. LOVECRAFT, Official Editor


EDITOR'S NOTE FP: *Zenith*, January 1921, p. [1]. A statement of the UAPA editorial policy, cowritten by HPL and Alfred Galpin, provided presumably at the request of George Julian Houtain, editor of the *Zenith*. In a note following the item, a note headed "The National's Policies: 1920–1921" reads: "The Editor regrets to state that President Moitoret and Official Editor Outwater were both indifferent to his request for a statement of the policies of the National Amateur Press Association for the current year. THE ZENITH trusts they will show more interest in the proper performance of their official duties."

# WHAT AMATEURDOM AND I HAVE DONE FOR EACH OTHER

I entered Amateur Journalism late in life—at the age of nearly twenty-four—so that I cannot justly attribute all my education to its influence. This lateness was, however, most emphatically not of my choosing. The instant I heard of amateurdom's existence I became a part of it, and count among my deepest regrets the fact that I did not discover it some seventeen years earlier, when as a youth of seven I put forth my first immortal literary product, "The Adventures of Ulysses; or, The New Odyssey".[1]

Upon joining the United Amateur Press Association I spent the first few months in an attempt to discover just what Amateur Journalism is and just what it is not. My notions had been rather nebulous, and I was not sure whether delight or disillusion awaited me. Actually, I found both; but delight was so much in the majority that I soon realised I was a permanent amateur. That was in 1914. In 1921 I can report unchanged sentiments.

What I have done for Amateur Journalism is probably very slight, but I can at least declare that it represents my best efforts toward coöperating in a cause exceedingly precious to me. As I began to perceive the various elements in the associational sphere, I saw that heterogeneity and conflict were, as in all spheres, the rule. Trying to judge impartially, I concluded that at that particular time the purely literary element stood most in need of support. Fraternalism and good cheer are largely self-sustaining. Politics, in my honest individual opinion, is an evil. What required fostering was the very object which amateurdom professes to hold supreme—aid to the aspiring writer. Accordingly I decided that while sharing in all the general responsibilities of active membership, I would chiefly lend whatever small influence I might have toward the encouraging of mutual literary help.

My chance to do something tangible came sooner than I expected. In the fall of 1914 I was appointed chairman of the Department of Public Criticism in the United,[2] and was thus provided with a bimonthly medium of expression, together with a certain seal of officialdom on my utterances. What I did was to commence a definite campaign for the elevation of the literary standard—a campaign attempting on the one hand a candid and analytical demonstration of prevailing crudities, and on the other hand a tireless flow of suggestions for improvement. I abandoned altogether the policy of praising crude papers and articles because of obscure considerations connected with their standing in amateurdom, and insisted that writers and editors at least choose a goal of urbane correctness. Knowing that such a demand entailed an obligation to help personally, I undertook a fairly extensive amount of private criticism, and offered my services to any person wishing the revision of manuscripts or magazine copy. There were many responses to this offer, and I immediately found myself very busy reconstructing prose and verse and preparing copy for various amateur journals. I met with a certain amount of opposition and made many enemies, but believe that on the whole I may have accomplished some good. The standard of correctness in the United certainly rose, and most of the writers and editors I helped soon began to take pains on their own account; so that my aid became less and less necessary. This, however, is due only in part to my efforts. My successors in the critical bureau have been decidedly better, and the work was at the outset facilitated by a change in recruiting policy, established by others, whereby our new members were drawn from sources involving more extensive previous education.

In other fields I fear I have done all too little for amateur journalism. From 1915 to 1919 I issued an individual paper called *The Conservative*, but circumstances have since forced me to suspend its publication.[3] I have helped in coöperative publishing enterprises, though never with very brilliant results. As official editor of the United this year I am trying to issue a paper of the best quality, but am able to make little headway against the quantitative limitations. I have, I hope, done my share of administrative drudgery both official and unofficial. Despite a distaste for office holding I have accepted various posts in the United whenever my services seemed desirable, and have tried to be useful in substituting for incapacitated officials.

As a writer, the field in which I should like to serve most, I seem to have served least. When I entered amateurdom, I unfortunately possessed the delusion that I could write verse; a delusion which caused me to alienate my readers by means of many long and execrably dull metrical inflictions. An old-fashioned style at present out of favour added to the completeness of my failure. Since emerging from the poetical delusion I have been almost equally unfortunate, for in following my natural inclination toward fantastic and imaginative fiction I have again stumbled upon a thing for which the majority care little. My attempts appear to be received for the most part with either coolness or distaste, though the encouragement of a few critics like W. Paul Cook, James F. Morton, Jr., and Samuel Loveman has more than compensated for the hostility of others. The Cleveland-Chico clique,[4] seeking by ridicule to drive me from the amateur press, is well offset by any one of the gentlemen just named. Only time, however, will shew whether or not my effusions possess any value.

Happily, I can be less reserved in stating what amateurdom has done for me. This is a case in which overstatement would be impossible, for Amateur Journalism has provided me with the very world in which I live. Of a nervous and reserved temperament, and cursed with an aspiration which far exceeds my endowments, I am a typical misfit in the larger world of endeavour, and singularly unable to derive enjoyment from ordinary miscellaneous activities. In 1914, when the kindly hand of amateurdom was first extended to me, I was as close to the state of vegetation as any animal well can be—perhaps I might best have been compared to the lowly potato in its secluded and subterranean quiescence. With the advent of the United I obtained a renewed will to live; a renewed sense of existence as other than a superfluous weight; and found a sphere in which I could feel that my efforts were not wholly futile. For the first time I could imagine that my clumsy gropings after art were a little more than faint cries lost in the unlistening void.

What Amateur Journalism has brought me is a circle of persons among whom I am not altogether an alien—persons who possess scholastic leanings, yet who are not as a body so arrogant with achievement that a struggler is frowned upon. In daily life one meets few of these—one's accidental friends are mostly either frankly unliterary or hopelessly "arrived" and academic. The more completely one is absorbed in his aspirations, the more one needs a circle of intellectual kin; so that amateurdom has an unique and perpetual function to fulfil. Today, whatever genuine friends I have are amateur journalists, sympathetic scholars, and writers I should never have known but for the United Amateur Press Association. They alone have furnished me with the incentive to explore broader and newer fields of thought, to ascertain what particular labours are best suited to me, and to give to my writings the care and finish demanded of all work destined for perusal by others than the author.

After all, these remarks form a confession rather than a statement, for they are the record of a most unequal exchange whereby I am the gainer. What I have given Amateur Journalism is regrettably little; what Amateur Journalism has given me is—life itself.

EDITOR'S NOTE FP: *Boys' Herald* 46, No. 1 (August 1937): 7–8 (as by "Harold P. Lovecraft"). According to the introductory note by Edwin Hadley Smith (editor of the *Boys' Herald*), the speech (the manuscript of which Hadley apparently owned) was dated 21 February 1921. It was delivered at the Boston Conference of Amateur Journalists the next day. The lecture is HPL's most concise and poignant account of the manner in which his entry into amateur journalism allowed him to emerge from a five-year period (1908–13) of seclusion and introspection, so that HPL does not exaggerate when he states that amateurdom has given him "life itself."

*Notes*

1. More properly, "The Poem of Ulysses; or, The Odyssey." The existing text is a "second edition" dated 8 November 1897; the "first edition" probably predated HPL's seventh birthday (20 August 1897).
2. HPL replaced the previously appointed Chairman, Ada P. Campbell; his first column appeared in November 1914 (see p. 14).

3. Two further issues appeared in March and July 1923.

4. The reference is to hostility to HPL's official editorship of the UAPA expressed by William J. Dowdell of Cleveland and others, which ultimately led to HPL's defeat in the election of July 1922.

# NEWS NOTES

*(March 1921)*

President Alfred Galpin, Jr., was this year honoured by the Charles Champion trophy, awarded at Lawrence College for conspicuously meritorious work on the staff of the college weekly, *The Lawrentian*. The United congratulates its youthful executive on such well-deserved laurels.

On Friday evening, May 27, the Woodbees presented with great success their play "Aunt Maggie's Will", with a cast of amateurs well known in the United. The leading lady, as may be imagined, was Miss Norma Sanger, who well sustained her reputation for histrionic ability. Particular mention is due the comedy characters—Miss Elizabeth Ballou as an eccentric housekeeper, and Mrs. Frances Hepner Fritter as an Irish servant, both of whom elicited unbounded applause and approbation. The play was the second and major feature of a pleasant evening entertainment, the first part of which included musical and elocutionary features by prominent Woodbees, beginning with an address by Leo Fritter. The affair was a financial as well as artistic success, and will ensure an ample *Woodbee* later in the season.

An announcement of interest to amateurs is that of the engagement of Miss Verna McGeoch, former Official Editor, to James Chauncey Murch, Esq., of Chicago. Miss McGeoch has achieved amateur immortality as editor of the official organ for two years during the trying war period,[1] and as the virtual regenerator of the paper from a qualitative point of view. Her double volume will in later years be eagerly sought as one of the finest achievements of amateur journalism. Mr. Murch is the son of Rev. F. B. Murch, a prominent Presbyterian clergyman, and has won distinguished success in commercial endeavour. To the future Mr. and Mrs. Murch, the United extends its warmest and most widespread congratulations.

On June 27, Second Vice-President Alice M. Hamlet left her summer home in New Hampshire, and is to be addressed until August 1 at Box 68, Bradford, N. H.

Mrs. Anne T. Renshaw plans a Northern trip for the month of August, during which she will confer with the amateurs of New York and Boston. One June 8, at the 100th Commencement of George Washington University, she received the degree of A. B., together with a Bachelor's Diploma in Education.

EDITOR'S NOTE FP: *United Amateur* 20, No. 4 (March 1921): 60 (unsigned). An unusually brief column, focusing on the Woodbees of Columbus, OH.

*Notes*

1. McGeoch was Official Editor of the UAPA for 1917–19.

# THE VIVISECTOR

*(March 1921)*

Amid the echoes of the many controversies on criticism which are raging throughout Amateur Journalism Mr. Lawson has had the temerity to furnish new material for abuse. Beginning with this number *The Wolverine* will contain a department wherein some of the current papers and popular authors of our world will be treated with frankness according to their merits. It will not, despite its formidable name, be a department of cruelty; but it will be called so by its enemies—hence the title. No amateur ever was or ever will be satisfied with what is said of him, and any critic who expects appreciation will be disappointed. However, there have been flaws in former critical departments which The Vivisector will try to avoid. Criticism in *The National Amateur* is often densely ignorant and occasionally absurd, the only sensible reviews recently being those of Rheinhart Kleiner and Nelson Glazier Morton in 1918, and that of Samuel Loveman in 1920. Others have included gross errors, laughable flattery, defective background, and pitiful want of appreciation. In *The United Amateur* there has been less crudity but so much more prejudice that the score is nearly even. Antique opinion and obtrusive moralising, both out of place, have deformed reviews which might have been scholarly. Since March 1920 there has been an improvement—let it continue.

Opportunely enough, the first paper before us for review opens with an article on criticism by E. Dorothy MacLaughlin. Needless to say, we refer to George Houtain's January *Zenith*, which despite some discouraging boisterousness is the best amateur newspaper to appear for a long time. Mrs. MacLaughlin's article is the soundest thing on its particular subject which we have seen in the current press, and might be read with profit by some of the unnamed gentlemen referred to above. But the "big feature" of the *Zenith* is Houtain's own account of his summer travels, entitled "20 Webster Street".[1] Without claiming to be a writer in the literary sense, Houtain has really achieved a singular felicity in the art of telling about his experiences; and surpasses with his perfectly spontaneous rambling the studied effects of many more scholarly narrators. His artless digressions and interjections are refreshing, though it would do him no harm to regulate a little his flow of sentimentalising at the start, and to think twice about what to include and what to exclude in the way of personal details and opinions. We are not sure how much some of his subjects may appreciate his "write-ups". The *Zenith's* "Art Department" merits a word by itself. The double-page cartoon is very cleverly conceived and deserves a somewhat better artist to carry out Houtain's ideas.[2] Of its kind, the *Zenith* is a joy.

One of the best of recent papers is Wesley H. Porter's *Toledo Amateur*, the leading feature of which is a remarkably effective short story by Edna Hyde, entitled "Ferenza's Girl". Miss Hyde's reputation as a poet has caused her few stories to receive less attention than they deserve. In point of fact, they are among the best in the amateur press—the supply never being abundant. In this particular story the realism is the salient thing.

William J. Dowdell's "Last Clew" might be almost equally successful if properly developed, but as it is no attempt is made to expand it beyond a mere synopsis. The economy of the newspaperman, which differs from the economy of the story-writer in many ways, is too apparent. It would pay Dowdell to devote more time to the study of the story. He has ideas and methods which are lacking in many writers of more finished but less natural effusions.

Mrs. Dora Moitoret, always a pleasing writer, has limitations as a critic. Her "Rambling Reviews" are much too opinionated and too little analytical to claim first rank. We feel that the writer has distinct prejudices, but are not told much about the real strength or weakness of the articles passed upon.

The unfailing good sense of W. Paul Cook appears in everything he writes, and the "Amateur's Mailing List" is no exception. Sometimes one fears that the amateur public, in admiring the deeds of Cook as a publisher, may not fully appreciate the quiet grace and forcefulness of expression which mark him as a gifted writer despite a few solecisms.

Mrs. K. Leyson Brown's poem shews an excellent idea suffering from imperfect form. The metaphor of the "pearl" is weakened by the reference to a "pearl's dying". In writing poetry one must think not only of the subject but of the consistencies and precedents to be followed. There is an immense fund of lore for every poet to live up to, and he who neglects it fails.

As an editor, Wesley H. Porter is growing, but has not yet reached full stature. Little, though, need be said by the critic, for care and experience will do more than advice. The news notes shew good news sense, and the editorials are pertinent, if plain. The sketch "Lonesome" is evidently from life, and thus deserves respect, but many would question the taste of parading family affairs before the public even for the sake of securing a good piece of "sob stuff". And "sob stuff" is far from the highest form of art.

In form and appearance *The Toledo Amateur* takes a high place among recent home-brewed papers—the cover is very tasteful and the hand-set title page leaves little to be desired unless one harks back to *Olympian* or *Lucky Dog* standards. Mr. Porter has done well.

EDITOR'S NOTE FP: *Wolverine* No. 9 (March 1921): 12–16 (as by "Zoilus"). The first of five columns (four of which were written by HPL) written under the pseudonym of "Zoilus," referring to the Greek critic (fl. 4th century B.C.E.) who gained notoriety by sharply criticizing the Homeric poems. However, "The Vivisector" columns are actually quite mild and even flattering to most of the amateur writers they discuss. Authorship of the columns is confirmed by examination of correspondence between Horace L. Lawson (editor of the *Wolverine*) and HPL, surviving at JHL. An undated letter (probably written in early 1921) by Lawson to HPL states: "As for your 'Zoilus' article, it reads about like a review of *The Cleveland Sun.*" This appears to refer to the present column.

*Notes*

1. One section of this article, entitled "Lovecraft," discusses Houtain's meeting with HPL at the "Epgephi" convention in Boston on 20 September 1920. See Peter Cannon, ed., *Lovecraft Remembered* (Sauk City, WI: Arkham House, 1998), pp. 86–89.

2. One segment of the cartoon features a caricature of a dour-looking HPL with the caption, "Lovecraft Laughing."

# [LETTER TO JOHN MILTON HEINS]

I shall vote for E. Dorothy MacLaughlin for President of the National because of her individual fitness for the post, as well as her representation of the elements devoted to honest literary endeavour. The encroachment of factions dealing only in personal malice and debased and scurrilous journalism should be resisted at the polls for the good of the whole amateur cause.

EDITOR'S NOTE  FP: *American Amateur* 2, No. 5 (April 1921): 153. An excerpt from a letter in which HPL supports Dorothy MacLaughlin for president of the NAPA. Under her married name E. Dorothy Houtain, she was in fact elected president for the 1921–22 term at the NAPA convention in Boston in July 1921, which HPL attended.

# LUCUBRATIONS LOVECRAFTIAN

## The Loyal Coalition

Of the various unsolved mysteries of the American public mind, none is more baffling than the persistent failure of the people to awaken to the menace of Irish rebel propaganda. Proud as this nation seems to be in most matters respecting its independence, it has again and again suffered seditious minorities of Hibernian malcontents to affront its dignity and imperil its tranquillity through their criminal attempts to use it as a tool in effecting their own selfish ends. We have condemned in terms of unmeasured scorn the Germans, both citizens and non-citizens, who abused our hospitality by plotting in our midst and seeking to exploit us to Germany's advantage. These vipers we called "hyphenates", and denounced as un-American, justly abhorring their service of a foreign master whilst enjoying the advantages of residence here. We said much, in fact, concerning the impossibility of a divided allegiance. Yet through it all we have supinely tolerated a serpent a thousandfold more hateful than the Prussian hydra; a monster which owes us more loyalty because of longer American heritage, yet which gives us, if anything, less—the odious dragon of Fenianism and its successors;[1] which has for over sixty years crouched in the United States, never accepting Americanism or placing our interests first, but working stealthily and unceasingly to employ our giant strength in fomenting rebellion in that alien and distant Ireland which it values so much more than the America which has given its adherents protection and prosperity for so long.

The bare facts of the case hardly need re-stating in these columns. We have all viewed with disgust the tactics of the Fenian organisation and of the more recently formed Sinn Fein;[2] the subtle campaigns of hatred against our Mother Nation, whose friendship is so important to us and to the world's equilibrium; the creation of a solid and unscrupulous "Irish Vote" to intimidate our weaker politicians into passing legislation favouring Irish rebellion and endangering Anglo-American harmony; the open and unashamed employment of every sort of power, civil and ecclesiastical, to fill our public offices with disloyal Irishmen; the aid, both tacit and unconcealed, given to Germany at a time when war with that country was a duty of honour on our part; and the open insults to a friendly power which have compelled our Secretary of State to tender needed apologies to its ambassador. Such things cannot be endured forever, for they are increasingly dangerous. If our personal pride of Anglo-Saxon blood and American nationality is not enough to stir us to resentment against the trouble-makers who defame the one and seek to use the other as a lever for foreign political manoeuvres, we must at least concede that action is necessary when these malefactors approach the point of actually embroiling us in a nefarious war with our British kinsfolk over a question which concerns us not at all. Let us not be deceived. A small but darkly potent Sinn Fein minority in America is striving day and night to commit America to an endorsement or recognition of the mythical "Irish Republic" which cannot but strain Anglo-American friendship to the utmost.[3] It is striving to place America in the anomalous position which England would have occupied had it recognised the Confederate States over half a century ago. Is America ready to be plunged into a new war; a war in which she will b. in the wrong, and which her decent inhabitants will loathe and wage only with the leaden heart and consciousness of error which spell defeat? If not, let her crush with iron heel the noxious head of the thing that has crawled upon her soil since 1858, and dismiss in everlasting disgrace the political forces whose eyes, focussed on Ireland, see the United States only as a pawn.

Who shall awake us? Around what standard shall we rally in our combat against the foe within our gates? An answer to these questions, so long wanting, has at last been supplied by an organisation formed at Boston a year ago, and known as *The Loyal Coalition*. Growing out of the Boston committee formed to receive the Ulster clergymen who lectured on the truth about Ireland in 1919–20, the Coalition has crystallised into permanent form and national scope; conducting an educational campaign both through printed matter and public speakers, and seeking to found branches in every part of the United States. Sponsored by patriotic men and supported by voluntary contributions from loyal American citizens of every kind and belief, it is giving organised utterance to the hitherto inarticulate majority who demand that foreign agitators—foreign by allegiance if not by birth—keep their hands off the American government. In supporting the Loyal Coalition, the members of the United Amateur Press Association should take a prominent part. As beneficiaries of an undivided Anglo-Saxon civilisation, it is our particular duty to advance its interests and oppose its enemies; and we should not regard contributions to the Coalition's treasury as any less important than the contributions which we made so cheerfully to the various war activities three or four years ago. Our enemies are contributing freely to the "bond issue" of the scoundrel De Valera;[4] shall we be less loyal to the right, than they are to the wrong? The address of the Loyal Coalition is 24 Mount Vernon St., Boston 9, Massachusetts. Membership may be secured by any contribution of a dollar or more, and this dollar entitles the donor to a goodly amount of Coalition literature for distribution. Several of the best-known members of the United are already active Coalitionists, and it is to be hoped that the majority will emulate their example; joining the new society, spreading its doctrines, and if possible forming local branches. Let us play our part in this silent war—a war in many ways as significant in its potentialities as the horrible cataclysm from which we are just emerging.

Though the actual facts of the Irish problem do not concern us as Americans, and could not, even if justifying rebellion in Ireland, justify interference by our country, it may be well for us to glance at the situation and appreciate the utter emptiness of the

Sinn Fein's claims. Ireland, never a separate nation, has been part of the British dominions since 1172; prior to which time it was merely a battle-ground of half-barbarous chiefs. It is as integral a part of our Mother Land as Texas is of our own land. The early "English oppression" over which Sinn Feiners wax so eloquent and incoherent was never as severe as is popularly stated, and was not so much an isolated case as a type of all provincial government in the somewhat distant past. Ireland suffered no more "wrongs" than dozens of provinces which are today staunchly loyal to their respective governments, and in modern times there has been nothing even remotely resembling oppression. Ireland is today the spoiled child of the British Empire, and the political repressions now practiced by the government are merely temporary emergency measures designed to meet a sedition indescribably flagrant. The Sinn Feiners in Ireland are criminals of nearly the lowest type—traitors, slackers, pro-Germans, murderers, maimers, rioters, and cattle-thieves—and in dealing with them the British authorities are as lenient as they can be. Here in America such creatures would be lynched by an indignant citizenry. These are the folk who talk of their legendary "republic", and make themselves absurd by comparing their island to the various subject nationalities of the Continent which are now undergoing repatriation. Ethnically and linguistically Ireland is not a separate unit, but a part of the British fabric. Its race-stock in the East and North is as Teutonic as that of England and Scotland, and its only real language is English. The effort of the Sinn Feiners to learn and speak the nearly obsolete Gaelic jargon of the ancient tribes adds a comical touch to a grave situation. And when the spectre of "self-determination" is brought up, we are forced to smile again; for perhaps the most complete conceivable negation of this much-discussed principle is that contained in the secessionist Sinn Fein's attitude toward loyal British Ulster. Ulster, says the Sinn Fein, must secede whether it wants to or not! Ireland is not a separate nation, and could not exist apart from the Empire. Only a fatal defect in the reasoning powers of some of its people keeps alive the tradition of Anglophobia and secession. Sooner or later the Sinn Fein must calm down and accept the advantages afforded by a section of the British Empire which is not only free from all persecution, but especially blessed with favours.

Perhaps a final word on Ireland as a world problem may not be amiss, as a hint why this troubled region can never safely be set adrift as a separate "nation". To approach this matter, we must brush aside the deliberately and maliciously circulated lies of William R. Hearst and other poisonous publicists concerning England's alleged acquisitiveness, and recognise frankly that the whole maintenance of the far-flung civilisation we know depends absolutely on the power and integrity of the British Empire, sustained by the strength of our own kindred nation. We Anglo-Saxons have founded a civilisation undoubtedly greater than any other in existence. In justice, morality, progressiveness, and general effectiveness, that civilisation leads all others so conspicuously that comparison is useless. Only a keen imagination can picture the deplorable state of the world if such an immense and beneficent influence were to weaken, be dethroned from world-wide supremacy, and suffer replacement by another culture. It is a calamity which we cannot really visualise, since we instinctively accept Anglo-Saxonism as something to be taken for granted; something natural and eternal. Yet the secession of Ireland would in an instant enfeeble the whole body of Anglo-American power by placing at England's very gate a separate and dangerous enemy; one which has by past actions proved itself ready to intrigue and ally itself with the worst foes of civilisation.[5] Given complete independence, a Sinn Fein republic would prove the ready weapon and strategic base of any alien power operating against Great Britain, America, or both. The safety of our enlightened ideals and institutions, the safety of the civilised world itself, depends upon the retention of Ireland within the British Empire. The Sinn Fein seeks to use America as a tool toward the destruction of the widespread cultural edifice of which America is itself a part; seeks to use the great national exponent of law and order as an abettor of chaos and disintegration. Let its answer come in unmistakable accents from the Loyal Coalition!

## Criticism Again!

It would be futile for the United's Department of Public Criticism to reply to most of the querulous complaints levelled against it. In nine cases out of ten the circumstances are very simple—one mediocre and egotistical author plus one honest review equals one plaintive plea that the bureau, or part of it, is engaged in a diabolical plot to suppress incipient genius. The complainer, as a type, is one who candidly opposes any attempt at genuine constructive criticism, but who expects the department to mince along as a medium of flattery. He feels that his dollar dues entitle him to a certain amount of praise irrespective of merit.

But there is another sort of complaint which must be received very differently—a calm, balanced sort prompted by intelligent difference in opinion, and connected only subconsciously with personal feelings anent reviews. This sort of censure comes from cultivated scholars with fixed and rigid theories regarding the province and limitations of literary criticism. As a rule, they have never been adversely criticised by the bureau they attack; and therefore make their objections with unquestionably detached and disinterested intent, in the name of abstract justice and conventional art. Only close analysis would reveal the slight personal animus—perhaps some trifling instances wherein the bureau's evident prejudices clashed with the complainants' equally cherished prejudices. This is pardonable, because it is human—but it explains why many deem it their duty to attack the relatively inoffensive critics whilst permitting real associational menaces to flourish unrebuked. Lest my observation seem to carry a hidden sting, let me hasten to say that I do not speak as one holier than the majority. I felt it a "sacred and impersonal obligation" in 1919 (although my plaint never saw the light) to express my disapprobation when the National's reviewer made some hasty remarks on my "Earth and Sky"; chiding me for emphasising man's insignificance in the *infinite universe* when he is so clearly the supreme being of *this one tiny globe* (reward for discovery of critic's logic!) and stumbling over my use of the intransitive verb *to south*, which he could have found with ease in the Farmer's Almanack or Webster's Unabridged. No, the writing public cannot be blamed for keeping a sharp lookout for the sins and blunders of the critic—but the critic himself must not be left undefended.

As an ex-critic in the United, and one of those who stand in the path of the darts which Messrs. J. Clinton Pryor and W. Paul Cook are hurling from the pages of *The United Co-operative* and *The Vagrant*,[6] respectively, I will venture to speak a word in behalf of myself and my former colleagues. It is with reluctance that one opposes two amateurs of such sterling quality as those just named, especially since one must deeply respect their attitudes whilst refuting their conclusions; but such opposition is necessary if the board of critics is to work unhampered. Man is an imitative animal, and the regrettable concentration of hostile attention on the critical bureau will cause a legion of dunces to emulate irresponsibly what Messrs. Cook and Pryor have done responsibly; the result being a pandemonium which these gentlemen will relish as little as will any other serious scholars.

The one leading protest of Messrs. Pryor and Cook is that personal opinions on various subjects have been expressed in the official critical reviews. They argue that such a practice is harmful, in that it causes the views of individuals to be published as the official views of the United as a body. This contention, forming indeed the whole crux of Mr. Cook's elaborate indictment in *The Vagrant*, surely sounds weighty and plausible enough when carelessly stated; yet may be thoroughly exploded almost at the very outset.

*Official criticism is "official" only so far as it concerns the relation of the work criticised to the artistic standards recognised as universal.* This may be accepted as axiomatic, since the official functions of the board cannot be held to extend beyond the province assigned to it; and by Messrs. Cook and Pryor's own admission, that province is art only. Most critics are far from stolid and unimaginative, and naturally tend to view a theme humanly rather than mechanically. They behold a subject in all its lights and relations, and in many cases round out their reviews by including trains of suggested thoughts and opinions which are decidedly individual. It may be that this habit is sometimes carried to excess—our critics are not unearthly paragons—but whatever one may think about it, this fact remains: *no personal opinions are given the stamp of officialdom, because officialdom does not extend beyond art.* Suppose, to quote an instance brought up by Mr. Pryor over a year ago, a critic is reviewing an amatory poem. He points out its excellence of rhythm, its beauty of sound, and its cleverness of conception—then adds that in his opinion amatory verse is "old stuff" at best, and hardly worthy of the poet's powers. Has he exceeded his province? Not in the least. He has, if anything, made himself clearer by honestly stating his own position instead of concealing it—for all critics really have views of their own—and in adding this personal touch he has in no way involved the United officially. Seldom have our critics failed to separate general and personal views. The expressions of political and philosophical opinion to which Messrs. Pryor and Cook object so violently, are of course entirely outside the question. Such expressions, from their very nature, cannot possess official authority; so that the Association is well aware that the critics speak individually. When a critic adds to his conventional dictum a view of his own, he does not impair the force of the dictum in the least. The addition is often necessary to produce a human and interesting review, and its worst possible fault is space consumption. It may be taken for granted that the average critic will neither usurp large amounts of space for his views, nor air opinions subversive of the public interest. A survey of *The United Amateur* fails to disclose anything alarming, and often reveals that both sides of a question are espoused with equal vigour by different critics.

Often the objectors reveal distinct and amusing prejudices of their own. Mr. Pryor—a clergyman—complains of the uttered views of a rationalist reviewing an orthodox essay, yet passes over in significant silence an equally polemical review of a rationalistic essay by an orthodox critic! In passing, it may be remarked that in this particular case both critics were not altogether outside the field of their duty. They were analysing the reasoning of the essays they were dissecting, and proving rather well that the essayists were not grappling with the cores of their respective problems at all.

In the present *Co-operative* Mr. Pryor repeats his error. Disliking a plainly worded criticism of *The Lingerer*, he forgets to note the critic's admiring concessions and distinctions. Even more strongly disliking the utterly impersonal *Clarion* review, a review far milder than many unofficial critiques of the same paper, he condemns the critic for merely repeating the ordinary rules of taste prevailing in the cultivated world—presumably because they conflict with the obsolete theories of Puritan theocracy. Mr. Pryor also—curiously enough—objects to a comment on one of his own articles which was actually made in his defence! When a man writes seriously of having an open mind toward spiritualism, most hard-headed readers will tend to smile; but the abused critic took pains to emphasise the real truth that the author expressed—that spiritualism must not be condemned dogmatically *by those who believe in immortality.* Surely, the critic remarked, the one idea is no more absurd than the other.

Mr. Cook's encyclopaedic article in *The Vagrant,* aside from the fundamental fallacy previously noted, contains more than one vulnerable spot. In his anthology of critically uttered opinions, the compiler sets down many things which could be culled from almost any series of reviews extending over a space of two and a half years; besides calling up as questionable at least two points about which nobody concedes room for debate at all. He indicates, accusingly enough, that one critic "believes in the principles of heredity". Really! We know a critic who believes that the earth is round! He also shews that a critic "does not believe any of the tales of supernatural phenomena told by soldiers on the European battlefields".[7] How strange! It is also rumoured that there were really no witches in Salem! There is not a single view cited by Mr. Cook which is not held by millions of intelligent average citizens. The Association as a whole, despite the complainant's gratuitous assumption, stands behind none of the extraneous topics; though the questions of Greenwich Village decadence and *vers libre,* being wholly artistic, do border on the critic's legitimate province and involve our aesthetic policy more or less. But in these matters the majority are now powerless. Just as soon as they wish to favour modern corruption, they may elect a President pledged to appoint a sympathetic Critical Chairman. Which leads one to inquire why more elections are not conducted on literary issues?

From Mr. Cook's really wild condemnation of anti-Wilson matter, one would hardly be surprised to discover that he is or has been rather a Wilson partisan. Surely he seems more spontaneously indignant at anti-Wilson than at pro-Wilson utterances—a strange attitude indeed for an absolutely dispassionate observer! As a matter of fact, he has declared that his Wilson idolatry ceased in that fateful spring of 1917, *for reasons just opposite to those which cause the average patriot to oppose the arrogant theorist.*[8] I hesitate to suggest the two or three more obvious interpretations, for I hardly think them true. Mr. Cook likes subtlety, mystery, and "diplomacy", and one may read his preferences in several ways. At any rate, I know that he has never been pro-German. But it remains a fact that he passionately hates the point of view of the ordinary Wilson critic, who opposes that politician on conservative patriotic grounds. One may wager safely that our gifted *Vagrant* is no Republican! I freely affirm that I am the anti-Wilsonite whose sins Mr. Cook deems "more than unpardonable"—to quote the least hectic of his fervid expressions—yet I must plead, with many others, that *facit indignatio versus.*[9] History will rightly adjudicate the question. Since I am the "offender", I cannot but smile at my opponent's too great readiness to read a subtle anti-Wilsonism into the casual critical reference to Colonel Roosevelt, before his decease, as "America's greatest man".[10] True, the anti-Wilsonism might have been there; yet when I wrote that passage I was thinking not of the smallness of any man, but of the greatness of Theodore Roosevelt—and what American of the present age can be classed with him? Does Mr. Cook fancy that the title of President necessarily raises a man to supreme greatness, and that to call anyone but the President our "greatest man" is *lèse majesté?* Was it considered an insult to President Adams in 1798 to call General Washington our "greatest man"? Of course, Colonel Roosevelt was against the late Wilson administration—as the truest patriots were—but general praise of an anti-administrationist does not necessarily imply a special condemnation of the opposite party.

In censuring the critic who congratulated the United on its escape from the Dowdell menace of 1919, Mr. Cook is ostentatiously combating a shadow. It is true that this congratulation might be rather out of place if coming from the pen of any person connected with the campaign; but as it happens, *every* reference to the Cleveland ring was left to other hands. The criticism in question was the work of a young man totally inactive during the first half of 1919—who, although a candidate for office, took no part in the real campaign, and had scarcely any communication with the campaigners prior to the election. Mr. Cook knew this—which makes one doubly sorry. In commenting on the whole unfortunate political contretemps, Mr. Cook somewhat surprises his readers by his cold reference to the work of those who have striven to advance the United's cause. It is to be hoped that his own truly titanic efforts and almost incredible generosity will not be similarly unappreciated by others—as they certainly are not by those whom he seems in this reference to slight ever so subtly.

Mr. Cook, I have not a doubt, honestly considers himself absolutely impersonal—a superman, as it were. Surely he *is* a superman in his services to the amateur cause! But why can he not perceive the plain truth that any assumption of godlike impersonality is for the most part a species of unconscious egotism and petty vanity?

Summing up the entire criticism situation, I cannot repress a certain discouragement at the trend of affairs. The recent labours of our reviewers have with few exceptions been ungratefully minimised and subjected to withering and injudicious tirades which devitalise the whole critical fabric. As objectors multiply the restrictions with which they would fain fetter the bureau members, all the usual incentives for service gradually disappear, and it becomes increasingly difficult to induce really qualified persons to serve. These self-constituted reformers are really doing an irreparable damage to the public criticism of the United.

It seems to be the duty of both critics and objectors to exercise forbearance. Realising the prevalent prejudice against frankness, the reviewer must unselfishly strive to adopt an artificially opinionless style as completely as possible. He must not hesitate to acknowledge occasional past instances of extremism and intolerance, or fail to sympathise as best he can with his opponents' point of view. And upon the thoughtful objector rests a reciprocal obligation. He must not expect more than mortal perfection from the critic, or seek to hamper him by the imposition of too many arbitrary limitations. He must observe closely before drawing conclusions. Frequent informal exchanges of ideas between the critics and those who have suggestions to make, would be of great mutual aid.

So great is my confidence in the lofty motives of Messrs. Cook and Pryor, that I should like nothing better than to see them appointed to the bureau at some future time; with one of them as Chairman. Mr. Cook, at least, has had much experience in this field; and I trust that he and Mr. Pryor may seriously consider such an arrangement. To the amateur public it would bring two valuable reviewers in an age when good critics are scarce. To Messrs. Cook and Pryor it would bring a chance to develop their original theories, and to obtain a full idea of the contemporary critic's province "from the inside", as it were.

The experiment is worth trying.


## Lest We Forget

Mr. Gibson's brief article in this issue of the *Co-operative* affords an excellent example of the idealistic reaction of the recent war. Sickened with blood, injustice, and cruelty, the sensitive soul recoils from the thought of another conflict, and preaches a peace based on rational remembrance of what has been.

And yet how futile is every aspiration of mankind! The same causes which have made men forget the lessons of past wars, will make them forget the lessons of this war; and none can tell how soon another menace may rise from the lands beyond the Rhine, where power is held more precious than life. When that menace takes bodily form, what remembrance of ours will defend us from its aggressions? So to our list of things not to be forgotten we must add one more item—vigilant strength! Let us indeed remember the horrors of war, but let us remember that those horrors are greatest for the nation least prepared. Let us seek no conflict, but let no conflict find us weak and unready. The hand which rises forbiddingly, or the voice which cries "No!" to war, must have the physical force to master those who do not acknowledge its authority.

## A Conjecture

In the July *American Amateur,* the precocious Miss Elsie (alias Elsa) A. Gidlow of *Les Mouches* fame refers with admirable courtesy to "Mr. Lovecraft with his morbid imitations of artists he seems not even able to understand". Possibly Mistress Elsie-Elsa would prefer that the amateurs follow her own example, and perpetrate morbid imitations of morbid artists whom nobody outside the asylum is able to understand.

EDITOR'S NOTE  FP: *United Co-operative* 1, No. 3 (April 1921): 8–15 (unsigned). HPL's lengthiest contribution to the cooperative paper of which he was coeditor; the title makes one wonder how previous bibliographers failed to attribute the work to HPL. Its two largest sections discuss Irish-American relations and the function of personal opinion in official UAPA criticism. The latter issue was of great importance to HPL, as he conceived official criticism (as embodied in the Department of Public Criticism) as a central tool in educating amateurs to proficiency in writing. HPL's screed is perhaps the more heated because one of his critics is W. Paul Cook, one of his closest amateur associates.

*Notes*

1. The Fenian movement had its origins among the Irish immigrants in New York and Chicago in the 1850s, as a means of combating anti-Irish prejudice, chiefly stirred up by the Know-Nothing Party. It is canonically dated to 1858 (a date cited below by HPL), when the Irish Republican Brotherhood was established.

2. Sinn Fein was organized as a political party in Ireland in 1905. In 1919 it elected Eamon de Valera (1882–1975) president of the party.

3. Ireland was granted partial independence from Great Britain when the Irish Free State was established on 6 December 1921.

4. De Valera came to the United States in May 1919 to elicit financial support for Irish independence. Over the next eighteen months he raised $6 million.

5. The reference is to attempts by Irish rebels to solicit German assistance in the independence movement, leading to the Easter Rebellion of 1916, during which 450 Irish citizens and 100 British soldiers were killed.

6. See John Clinton Pryor, "Comment Pryoristic," *United Co-operative* 1, No. 1 (December 1918): 6–7; "Comment Pryoristic," *United Co-operative* 1, No. 3 (April 1921): 7; W. Paul Cook, "Official Criticism," *Vagrant* No. 11 (November 1919): 31–35.

7. The most celebrated of these was Arthur Machen's short story "The Bowmen" (1915), which was widely believed to be the narrative of a real event in which angels came to the assistance of beleaguered British troops at Mons. HPL may or may not have been familiar with "The Bowmen" at this time, but he did not discover the bulk of Machen's weird writing until 1923.

8. HPL is suggesting that Cook abandoned his support for Wilson when the latter—defying his campaign promise of 1916 to keep America out of the war—declared war on Germany in April 1917. HPL had criticized Wilson for not declaring war sooner.

9. "Indignation produces [my] verses." Juvenal, Satires 1.79 (versum [verse] in Juvenal).

10. The comment was made in DPC (January 1919); see p. 220.

---

# NEWS NOTES

*(May 1921)*

President Alfred Galpin, Jr., is taking a summer course at the University of Wisconsin, where he will no doubt duplicate his usual Lawrence honours. The season's last *Lawrentian*, a large and elaborate "Booster Issue", was published entirely under his editorship; and does distinguished credit alike to him and to the college.

Edward F. Daas returned from Cuba in time to participate in the recent United convention. He is at present visiting Mr. and Mrs. Paul J. Campbell at Ridgefarm, Ill., and will later return to his home in Milwaukee. Mr. Dietzler, his companion on the southward journey, will return at a later date.

At a meeting held at Rock Creek Park during the convention, the Pen and Ink Club elected the following officers for the coming year: President, Amy D. Putnam; Vice-President, Martin G. Stecker; Secretary, Birdie Harris; Treasurer, Edna B. Vincel; Official Editor, Jay Fuller Spoerri. It is likely that a *Blotter* may be issued during the coming months; a publication which the United will heartily welcome.

An especially gifted new member of the United is Mrs. Stella V. Kellerman, 1741 Lanier Pl., Washington, D. C., who lately won first prize in the poetical contest conducted by *American Ambition*. Mrs. Kellerman's winning poem, "Life Triumphant", was selected as the best in nearly forty thousand; and her other works shew a corresponding merit. The poetess is the widow of the late Prof. Kellerman of Ohio State University, who lost his life if 1908 whilst on a scientific expedition in Guatemala; and in former years she was herself active in the world of science. She was a charter member of the Ohio Academy of Science, and twice elected to its Vice-Presidency, and likewise belonged to the Kansas Academy of Science. Mrs. Kellerman's poetry shews traces of the scientific influence, being mainly of somewhat philosophical and didactic cast. It is to be hoped that the bard's Washington residence will cause her to be active in the Pen and Ink Club. Credit for this brilliant acquisition belongs to that distinguished recruiter Paul J. Campbell.

An engagement of great interest to the United is that of our members George Julian Houtain and E. Dorothy MacLaughlin, the latter newly elected to the Presidency of the National. The congratulations of all amateurs attend these diligent workers in the cause.

Rheinhart Kleiner, in company with James F. Morton, Jr., and Ernest A. Dench, recently completed an interesting walking trip through northern New England. The route lay through three states—Massachusetts, New Hampshire, and Vermont—and included the celebrated home of *The Vagrant* at Athol, Mass.

W. Paul Cook, who has just completed twenty-five years as an amateur journalist, was presented with a silver loving-cup at the recent National convention. Singularly enough, this convention was the first he had ever attended.

A prospective member of unusual merit, who deserves attention from our recruiters, is Mr. T. Francis, 819 Hartley Hall, Columbia University, 1124 Amsterdam Ave., New York City.

An especially enthusiastic new member and fictional beginner, with whom our expert writers of stories are urged to get in touch, is Miss Helen Clark, Care of Memorial Hospital, Pawtucket, R. I. (Home address, 37 Walnut St., Watertown, Mass.)

United members will learn with regret of the dangerous illness of Miss Annie Pearce, of Scarborough, England, who is about to undergo a trying operation with no anaesthetic other than cocaine. Miss Pearce urges tolerance for her failure to answer letters during this critical period, and hopes to renew amateur activities with doubled vigour after emerging from the ordeal.

Among the major bereavements which have afflicted amateurs during recent months are those of H. P. Lovecraft, whose mother, Mrs. S. Lovecraft, died on May 24, and of Mrs. Daisy Crump Whitehead, whose husband, Edward L. Whitehead, died on July 10. Especial sympathy is due Mrs. Whitehead, since this is the second sudden blow to befall her this year; her brother, Mr. Julian J. Crump, having been instantly killed February 20.

Members who enjoyed our "Jackson issue" for March will be pleased to hear that a similar "Loveman issue" is planned for the coming year. In this coming number, we shall present the portrait and poetry of Amateurdom's premier classicist and fantaisiste, and hope to secure a somewhat exhaustive critique of his work from a sympathetic and competent pen. Amateurdom deserves to know more about its few real colossi than was possible under the old policy of general criticism.

On Saturday, July 2, 1921, peace was formally established between the United States and Germany, and between William J. Dowdell and H. P. Lovecraft. The latter treaty was signed at 9 p.m. at 20 Webster St., Allston, Mass., and was confirmed by a joint photograph taken at 2 p.m., July 5, by George Julian Houtain. Pictorial evidence will be found in a coming *Zenith*.

Among the most desirable recruits of the year is Miss Margaret M. Sullivan, 1281 Melbourne Rd., East Cleveland, O., a teacher in the Cleveland Central High School. Copies of the school paper attest her ability to a marked degree, as does also the following extract from a letter written by her to Mrs. Ida C. Haughton, her distinguished sponsor to the United:

"I shall do my best to uphold the work of the United Amateur Press Association. I am proud to belong to an organisation so dear to your heart, and doubly proud to have its next President for my own dear friend. . . . I have been teaching at Central High since June 20 from 8:00 to 11:05 a.m., and have really enjoyed the work; feeling that I have accomplished more than in the regular school year. I have two classes in second-year English, each period comprising an hour and a half. A new problem confronted me in dealing with numbers of Jewish pupils. They are very quick and bright, in marked contrast to my regular stolid Bohemians and Poles. I really catch a wonderful vision of America in it all, and glorify the public schools more each day. One morning last week I went into my class-room, which is used for literary societies during the year, and which consequently has a piano, and found a regular musicale in progress. At the piano was a very light, refined coloured girl, accompanying a talented, handsome Jewish boy who was playing a violin. After their number they played for Bettina Colombi, a charming Italian girl with a wonderful lyric soprano voice. Their audience included negroes, Jews, Poles, Bohemians, Welsh, and Americans. Truly the Melting-Pot!"

Members anxious to advance the United's cause are invited to communicate with Mr. A. C. Dorr, President, Montana State Industrial School, Miles City, Mont., regarding the advantages of the Association. The boys of Mr. Dorr's school edit a paper, and have expressed a desire to enter our ranks and taste the pleasures of organised amateur journalism.

EDITOR'S NOTE FP: *United Amateur* 20, No. 5 (May 1921): 66–67 (unsigned). It is evident that this issue of the *United Amateur* appeared several months after its date, perhaps as late as late July, since HPL in these notes discusses events relating to amateurs as late as July 10. He includes a brief and wry note about the NAPA convention of early July ("On Saturday, July 2, 1921 . . .").

# THE VIVISECTOR

*(June 1921)*

Recently there has been much discussion as to the "futility" of amateur journalism, and a glance at some of the current output—undiluted politics—goes far to uphold this idea. But now and then there comes one of those rare joys which cause us to revise our opinions and admit that the trash is worth enduring for the sake of the diamonds. Such a diamond, flawless and polished, is *The Philosopher*, issued by Alfred Galpin, Jr., of Appleton, Wis. Galpin is probably the most remarkable youth who ever entered amateur journalism. A prodigy in his boyhood, he is at nineteen the possessor of that exceptional mental maturity which suggests Edward H. Cole, and has in addition a searching quality of analysis and iconoclasm which marks him for prominence as a critic in the Mencken manner. Few would believe that *The Philosopher* is a first paper, yet that is exactly the nature of this brilliant emanation from the President of the United Amateur Press Association.

*The Philosopher* is not merely a collection of the work of the best amateur writers, though it is indeed that to start. That level is in the opinion of too many amateurs the supreme level toward which to strive, yet in fact it makes for tediousness and lack of distinctiveness. It is quite amusing to note how much alike all our best papers are, no matter who the editor. Graeme Davis escaped this pitfall in his *Lingerer*, which bore the indelible imprint of character and individuality, and now Alfred Galpin has accomplished the same thing in a less marked and more conservative way. *The Philosopher*, despite a few exceptions, is filled with matter representing the same essential mood— that questing view of the universe which forms a meeting-place for imagination and disillusion. Such a mood tends to be cosmic and catholic—to admire a pretty trifle in one moment and to brush away a popular fad in the next; to dream of wonder and beauty, yet to admit the consequences of a mechanistic universe. Underlying it is a deep, subtle essence of humour, though it is not always recognised as such because it is never clownish or obvious.

The cream of *The Philosopher* is undoubtedly its editorial department, which is Galpin on paper. The three sections—Modern Poetry, Spoken English, and World Situation—display three distinct angles of a many-sided personality whose development is truly phenomenal considering his youth. The quality of analysis and sincerity, seldom found in juvenile work, is the dominant note. Where most young men are disposed to moralise and repeat platitudes, Galpin plunges in desperately—perhaps falling short of his mark occasionally, but always winning distinctiveness by being tremendously *real*. It was once said of another fairly young editor that he lived in a "play world". This can never be said of Galpin. The idealism and superficiality of youth are not for him, and the reader cannot help recognising that all his words represent genuine ideas, not casually picked up, but worked out originally from close and accurate thinking. He is conservative in manner, but ruthlessly free from tradition in thought. With an artist's faculty for choosing the right word, he is yet most of all a thinker—a *philosopher*, if you please.

But Galpin's many contributors should not be neglected. Quite notable is the trilogy of imaginative stories, in which our editor makes a pseudonymous appearance as his own contributor. Each of these tales has a quality all its own. Ira A. Cole, in "A Vision of the Plains", achieves the level of true genius; joining observation and imagination in exactly the right proportion. He keeps his feet on the ground and adheres to Nature in a way which cannot be recommended strongly enough to some of our amateur Poes and Maurice Levels, yet in places his fantasy is a poem. The only fault of Cole is that he does not contribute to the press often enough. Howard Phillips Lovecraft's "Polaris" shews an excess of imagination over observation, and finds its main strength in images rather than details. There is a Baudelairian quality of gloom not found in Mr. Cole's work, and rising to noticeable proportions at the beginning and end of this piece. The most marked defect of "Polaris" is its plot basis, which involves scientific elements beyond the popular range. To base an essentially impressionistic tale on prosaic science is an artistic mistake.

The strength of Galpin's, or "Consul Hasting's", own "nightmare"—"Marsh-Mad"—is rhetorical.[1] The use of exactly the right word in the right place is its salient quality, and only in places does this verge on preciosity. The anticlimactic ending is a mistake, since it mars the tensity of the preceding parts, but it is doubtless in accord with the spirit of its author, whose keynote is sophistication rather than wonder. Of the three stories Cole's is undoubtedly the greatest. It has a simplicity which Lovecraft's lacks, and is free from the sudden disillusionment which marks Galpin's

Of the two philosophical studies which justify the magazine's name, Galpin's allegory "Stars" seems to take first rank. In this brief fragment the author has summarised human aspiration and the quest of life, yet he has done so without once becoming formal, schoolmasterish, or platitudinous. Miss Durr's "As Ye Judge" is marked by distinguishable sanity and good sense—the ideal liberalism of a thoughtful mind—and lacks only originality of presentation to be remarkable. Not that it is in any sense unoriginal, but that it states in unornamented way truths which are universal among progressive students today.

We come now to the poetry, and here find a feast of varied nature and merit, though none of the pieces is lacking in the latter quality. To pick a favourite is hard, but we believe that the reader who gets through the paper without preconceived notions will linger longest over two bits of exquisite pathos which arouse their effects by means of quiet art rather than sensational phrases—"Old Man", by Lilian Middleton, and "When I Wake", by Winifred Virginia Jordan. Perrin Holmes Lowrey is widely known professionally as well as in amateurdom, and no light haunting lyrics could surpass in felicity his "Autumn' and "For a Lady". However, he is challenged seriously by Rheinhart Kleiner and Daisy Crump Whitehead in their delicious trifles "Alas!" and "Roses". This art of concise exquisiteness is refreshing—we wish there were more of it among us. Clerical verse is represented by the contributions of Wilfred Kemble and Eugene B. Kuntz, both of whom are ministers. Each succeeds admirably in creating atmosphere, though we find no novel images or arresting phrases. Their verse is rather of the kind that captivates subtly by presenting pictures which age and tradition have made haunting and magical. "The House", by Ward Phillips, is Poe-esque and not especially notable.[2] The phrases sound impressive, but it does not take long to see that they conform to a well-worn pattern and follow a distinct school. The author has done little more than repeat a mood he has already expressed in Mr. Cook's Vagrant—in a piece called "The City", if we remember rightly.[3] "The Christmas Spirit", by Helen Patterson, is smooth and musical, but little else. "The Critic", written by Galpin under his now familiar nom de plume of "Consul Hasting", is a veritable gem of vers de société. We have had altogether too little of this sort of thing in the associations since the period of Spencer's Cyclopedia, and would urge other writers to try their hands at it. Let no one, however, fancy it is easy. It demands deft thought, a sure metrical touch, and above all else sophistication.

Such is The Philosopher—a paper which we predict would instantly take rank among the "Five Best Papers" if it were a National product. It is, in a sense, a landmark; may many such flourish!

EDITOR'S NOTE  FP: Wolverine No. 10 (June 1921): 11–14 (as by "Zoilus"). HPL's authorship of the column is confirmed by a letter from Horace L. Lawson to HPL (20 March 1921; ms., JHL): "May I have the next instalment of 'The Vivisector' soon? I must start preparation for the May number immediately." As there was no May number, the issue Lawson is referring to must be the issue for June. The entire column is devoted to Alfred Galpin's Philosopher (December 1920), although HPL characteristically denigrates his own contributions, the story "Polaris" and the poem "The House."

Notes

1. The story was written in 1918, and caused HPL to delay the writing of his story "The Tree" (1921) because he felt that Galpin had so well utilized the "living tree" conception.
2. The poem is by HPL. See AT 45–46.
3. See AT 46–48.

# THE HAVERHILL CONVENTION

Of the various shrines renowned in the annals of amateur journalism, none surpasses in importance that which bears the title of 408 Groveland St., Haverhill, Mass. It is here that Tryout is issued faithfully from month to month, and here that C. W. Smith, leader in publishing enterprise since 1889, presides like a patron deity over an Arcadian domain.

Yet notwithstanding these things, 408 Groveland St. still remains a terra incognita to most amateurs. Like the forbidden city of some royal dynasty, it is sacred ground, trodden only by the elect. Now and then some favoured mortal makes the pilgrimage and returns, but the number of such pilgrims is not great. It is therefore scarcely to be wondered at that a pardonable pride fills the souls of those who, on the afternoon of Thursday, June 9, participated in the unofficial Haverhill convention.

This convention was, in truth, not large; consisting only of the host, his learned and brilliant author-neighbour, Miss Myrta Alice Little, A. M., of Hampstead, N. H., Historian-Elect of the U.A.P.A., and the undersigned; together with Thomas Tryout, the Official Cat,[1] and small Annette, the Official Mascot. In enthusiasm, however, it atoned for its slender attendance; for, as may be imagined, there is amateurical inspiration in every cubic inch of the atmosphere of *Tryout* office. Each delegate is eager for a repetition of the event on a longer scale.

My own credentials for admission to this conclave were those of a servitor and scribbler. For some years I have been attached to the *Tryout* staff as rhymester, rhyme-collector, historian, and proofreader (of limited sections only), and had naturally acquired an increasing desire to behold with the physical eye my benevolent "boss" and his publishing plant. Was not my one and only "book", "Looking Backward", here given the immortality of print?[2] Now the hour had arrived, and guided by the new lettered luminary whose kind invitation had brought me north, and whose delightful family had royally entertained me at Little Towers in Hampstead, I entered the Elysian meads and groves of *Regio Tryoutiana*. Haverhill, let me add, is the most delectable of disappointments. Prepared to behold a dingy manufacturing town, the traveller is astonished by a city of beautiful homes, lawns, trees, and gardens; in taste and attractiveness second to none. Amid such an environment, it is not strange that *Tryout* should possess its delightfully Doric air of pastoral grace.

Flanked by fertile flower and vegetable gardens, and blessed with a background of mystical faun-peopled woods dear to the editor's heart, stands the pleasant cottage numbered 408 Groveland St. In the rear, reached by a broad verdure-bordered path, is the Holy of Holies—*Tryout* office. Here, within walls made colourful by pictures, stamps, buttons, post-cards, and countless other accumulations of delightful nature, rests the faithful *Tryout* press with its type-cases, piles of paper, files, and other accessories, the whole establishment ruled by the genial editor.

To do justice here to Mr. Charles W. Smith is impossible, since it is he who will put these remarks into type; so I will content myself by describing *Tryout's* creator as a slender, wholesome, outdoor-looking man. He claims to have been born many centuries B.C., but in aspect and carriage nothing but youth is suggested. From his trim iron-grey hair and beard, and erect, well-proportioned form, one might pronounce him forty-five or fifty; yet he vows that this is a gross underestimation. Mr. Smith is a shining embodiment of those doctrines which teach the blessings of contentment and rural retirement. As Mr. Pope hath it:

> "Happy the man whose wish and care
> A few paternal acres bound;
> Content to breathe his native air,
> In his own ground.

> \* \* \* \*

> Sleep by night; study and ease,
> Together mix'd; sweet recreation;
> And innocence, which most does please
> With meditation."[3]

Gifted with health, our Tryout is never idle or listless; but spends his days as Nature intended, at once pleasing himself and conferring pleasure on others. He is a monarch in his fair domain; a spirit ever youthful, constantly revivified by his quiet pursuits—editing, printing, walking, exploring "Whittierland",[4] stamp-collecting, and conversing with his grandchild-mascot and playful nine-year-old Thomas cat. He recalls the familiar lines of the Mantuan swain:

> "Tityre, tu patulae recubans sub tegmine fagi
> Silvestrem tenui Musam meditaris avena;
> Nos patriae finis et dulcia linquimus arva;
> Nos patriam fugimus: tu, Tityre, lentus in umbra,
> Formosam resonare doces Amaryllida silvas."[5]

Mr. Smith's own writing reflects much of this Arcadian colour in inimitable fashion, and it is to be regretted that he does not allot a large portion of magazine space for such quaint and unforgettable essays as "Anent the Melancholy Days", and "Scared? No-o-o!"

Two hours is all too brief an interval for a full-sized convention, but much can be compressed therein amidst an atmosphere as saturated with amateur tradition as is that of Tryout office. Files of Tryouts and Monthly Visitors were produced, old convention photographs studied, and vain inquiries made as to the identity of "Lester Kirk" and "Dame Gossip".[6] The meeting of two Merrimack Valley leaders like Miss Little and Mr. Smith, representing the newest as well as the oldest traditions of the amateur world, should augur well for future local activity, especially since another gifted Haverhill litterateur is about to join the ranks of the United.

Altogether, the Haverhill convention was a decided success. Washington and Boston may furnish imitations impressive in point of numbers, yet neither can command so central a position in the ocean of amateur efforts. Tryout is the social lifeblood and nervous system of the fraternity today; if any doubt it, let him try to picture an amateurdom devoid of this indispensable bond and inspiration.

EDITOR'S NOTE  FP: Tryout 7, No. 4 (July 1921): [21–25]. An account of HPL's visit (with Myrta Alice Little) to the home of Charles W. Smith, editor of the Tryout. The trip occurred on June 9, less than three weeks after the death of HPL's mother, Sarah Susan Lovecraft.

Notes

1. HPL would later write an elegy on the cat's demise: "Sir Thomas Tryout: Died Nov. 15, 1921" (Tryout, December 1921; AT 147–49).

2. See p. 253.

3. Pope, "Ode to Solitude" (1717), ll. 1–4, 13–16.

4. John Greenleaf Whittier (1807–1892) was born and spent his early years in Haverhill.

5. Vergil, Eclogues 1.1–5: "In peaceful Shades, which aged Oaks diffuse, / You, Tityrus, enjoy your rural Muse; / We leave our home and (once) our pleasant fields; / The native swain to rude Intruders yields, / While you in Songs your happy Love proclaim, / And every grove learn Amarillis' name" (tr. John Caryll [1684]).

6. Two pseudonymous contributors to the Tryout.

# News Notes

*(July 1921)*

The United Convention, July 8–11, was quiet but very pleasing; a successful business and social programme being followed with great harmony. The following officers were elected for 1921–22: President, Ida C. Haughton; First Vice-President, Frank Belknap Long, Jr.; Second Vice-President, Eleanor Beryl North; Official Editor, H. P. Lovecraft; Manuscript Manager, Grace M. Bromley; Laureate Recorder, Howard R. Conover; Historian, Myrta Alice Little; Directors, Paul J. Campbell, Anne T. Renshaw, and Jay Fuller Spoerri. State College, Pa., was selected for the 1922 convention. Of the Constitutional amendments voted on, only that affecting the Secretary-Treasurer's bond failed to pass. This means that we have once more only our two Vice-Presidents, that the Secretaryship and Treasurership have been consolidated into one appointive office, that the Manuscript Bureaux have been reduced to one, that all dues and fees have been doubled, and that sundry changes have taken place in the Laureateship conditions. The usual full report of the Convention will occur in these columns in September.

Several United members were present at the National's successful Boston Convention, July 2–5, and report a highly interesting programme.[1]

President Alfred Galpin, Jr., has returned to Appleton after a highly profitable six weeks at the University of Wisconsin's summer school, and reports progress in a heartening variety of subjects, including Baudelaire, Nietzsche, de Gourmont, Huysmans, Anatole France, Dreiser, Dostoyefsky, Max Stirner, le Comte de Gobineau, painting, sculpture, Hellenistic-Roman civilisation, organic evolution, anthropology, and the special branch of the latter which he denominates the "ology of the studens Americanus"! A pleasing array of snapshots testifies to the last-named acquisition, and future articles in the amateur press will no doubt confirm the evidence regarding the others.

Miss Dorothy Roberts, Fourth Vice-President, has graduated with brilliant success from the Marietta High School, and will this autumn enter the University, where she will take an ambitious course including English, trigonometry, French, Livy, Greek Drama, psychology, ethics, logic, ancient history, and Renaissance history, leading to the degree of B. A. The United is proud to see its best traditions so nobly upheld by the rising generation.

The latest delightful surprise for Amateurdom is the masterly mimeographed *Apprentice* of our sterling leader Maurice Winter Moe. Those who study out the clever technique of its make-up will realise the vast possibilities of the duplicated sheet; and will be converted to that school of thought which holds that the mimeograph is the ultimate solution of the high cost of printing. Mr. Moe, having finished a successful school year, is now at his summer home on Cedar Lake, and should be addressed at Route 6, West Bend, Wis. After September 1st he will be at his new and permanent home, a very desirable flat at 2812 Chestnut St., Milwaukee, Wis. Amateurs should note this new address with care.

The attention of amateurs is invited to the new conditions in the Laureate department. We have now gone back to our four original classes, poem, story, essay, and editorial only; and have dispensed with the need of a certain number of competitors. We have, on the other hand, imposed a restriction on the number of pieces any one member may submit in each class, choosing three as a reasonable limit. Entries may be changed, but only three in a class from each member will be allowed. Members are urged to study these requirements, and not to be backward in submitting entries during the coming year. Laureate awards for 1921 are not yet announced, though most of the judges have been secured. Editorials will be judged by H. L. Mencken, stories by Prof. McPheeters of Lawrence, essays by Prof. Percy Ward of Chicago, and poems probably by our former member Perrin Holmes Lowrey, who is a professor of English and a magazine bard of established position.

Mr. Wheeler Dryden is now appearing with great success at the Savoy Theatre, San Francisco, in an Irish musical play entitled "Peggy Machree". Among a notable cast, he occupies a prominent position.

Miss Anna H. Crofts is taking a summer course at Columbia University, where she is delving deeply into the technical secrets of pedagogy.

A revival of *The Conservative* is to be expected in the near future, at least two numbers being likely to appear during the official year. The first will contain a notable group of poems likely to win the approval of the discriminating.[2]

The Woodbee picnic of August 6 was somewhat hampered by poor weather, though the supper was a success. Business and literary features have been postponed till the next regular meeting, and a compensating picnic is likely to be held at the Frazier Farm on Labour Day. A *Woodbee* is to be expected soon, much of the work being performed by Assistant Editor Fritter, on account of the Presidential duties of Mrs. Haughton.

EDITOR'S NOTE  FP: *United Amateur* 20, No. 6 (July 1921): 73–74 (unsigned). The issue came out at least a month late, as HPL recounts the Woodbee picnic of August 6. HPL also supplies brief accounts of the UAPA and NAPA conventions in July.

*Notes*

1. HPL attended the convention. See "Within the Gates" (p. 293) and "The Convention Banquet" (p. 295).
2. The poems in the March 1923 *Conservative* were "To Satan" by Samuel Loveman (pp. 1–2); "The Crock o' Gold" by Lilian Middleton (p. 4); "The Storm" by John Ravenor Bullen (pp. 9–10); "Fause Murdoch" by James F. Morton, Jr. (pp. 12–16); "Song XVIII Cent." by Lilian Middleton (pp. 20–21). Betty Earle's "I Will Lead Thee" (pp. 16–19) is a compendium of verse and prose.

# WITHIN THE GATES

## by "One Sent by Providence"

Mr. Toastmaster, Ladies, Gentlemen, and Politicians:—

Although not called upon by name, I have been informed that the reference to Providence is my cue; hence believe that this is the proper time to make myself ridiculous by attempted oratory. Providence is notable as a dispenser of both blessings and afflictions; the former to be hailed with gratitude, the latter to be borne with patience. I am one of the latter, and can but hope that your patience will prove adequate. Remember, at least, that this oration is not voluntary; and visit your wrath upon Providence—or the Toastmaster—rather than upon me!

The subject of my sermon is announced as "within the gates"—presumably referring to the presence of a strictly United man in the midst of the National's Babylonish revelry—more or less "alien and alone", as it were, to quote from a famous poem dear to the heart of the *Zenith's* scholarly editor.[1] Accordingly I have taken as my text that not unknown line about a gate which appears in the celebrated epic of my fellow-poet Dante—

"All hope abandon, ye who enter here."[2]

I will omit the context—not only because I do not remember it, but because it would perhaps offend some loyal Nationalite by suggesting a certain comparison which I have with truly Heinsian[3] delicacy suppressed.

Having thus introduced my remarks as artistically and verbosely as possible, let me dispense with further preliminaries and confess that I have not the slightest idea of what I should say this evening. This, however, is probably nothing unusual for a postprandial Cicero or Demosthenes, hence it need cause me no anxiety. I may add, in extenuation, that this is only my second public oration. Having escaped alive after my first, in February,[4] I may venture to hope for similar clemency now—in spite of the representation of the "Sun Group" on the jury.[5]

Since I have nothing in particular to say, it behoves me to say it as tastefully as possible—allowing the appropriateness of my remarks to compensate for their vacuity. Within the gates of—the National, what could be more appropriate than a reference to that institution's chief interest—politics? I could say much of politics, but in a Puritanical city might not be able to say all that recent politics deserves; hence will confine myself to one point—a defence against a recent attack upon me, basely launched by an exceedingly eminent and heretofore respected amateur.

In *Views and Reviews* there appears an outrageous accusation, which although mentioning no names, affects me too obviously to permit of doubt. It is charged that I, as so-called Rhode Island Chairman of some "intensive recruiting drive", employed the backs of National application blanks to write "poetry" on.[6] I take this opportunity to refute so unjust a charge, relying for absolute vindication on Mr. Dowdell; who will, as in the past, assure you all that I never could and never can write a line of genuine poetry! But I will go even further, and vow on my own responsibility that I did not even *attempt* to write verses on those blanks. My waste-basket contains the proof—for what I did write on them was a descriptive prose article for *Tryout*, which you may read for yourselves in the very next issue—if you are good at puzzles.[7]

Mr. Houtain, noting my weight and elevation, once wrote in *The Zenith* that my voice is seemingly out of keeping with my size.[8] This may or may not be true. If, however, I do not soon conclude, these remarks are likely to be sadly *in* keeping with my elephantine magnitude. I could say much of the honour and pleasure I feel at being present at this momentous conclave, but am reluctant merely to repeat the obvious.

As a text for this long and sonorous intellectual silence I quoted an epic. Let me, therefore, follow the example of the epic poets, and instead of tapering off with a grandiloquent peroration, cease abruptly and dramatically. I have held you within the gates of infernal dulness.

"Thence issuing, we again behold the stars!"[9]

EDITOR'S NOTE FP: *Lovecraft Studies* No. 10 (Spring 1985): 29–30. A humorous speech written for the NAPA convention in Boston in early July 1921. It was delivered—along with speeches by James F. Morton, William J. Dowdell, and Edward H. Cole—at the NAPA banquet on July 4 at the Hotel Brunswick, directly following the opening remarks by toastmaster Willard O. Wylie. HPL pokes fun at his very presence at the convention, since in his previous published writings he had declared himself so firmly a loyal member of the UAPA.

*Notes*

1. George Julian Houtain. The quote is from Rudyard Kipling, "Possibilities" (1886), l. 28.

2. From Dante's *Inferno* 3.9 (*lasciate ogne speranza, voi ch'intrate*). HPL uses the translation of Henry Francis Cary (1805–14; *LL* 218–19).

3. A reference to Charles W. Heins, a leading figure in the NAPA.

4. "What Amateurdom and I Have Done for Each Other" (p. 271). HPL appears to have forgotten his earlier lecture, "Amateur Journalism: Its Possible Needs and Betterment" (p. 259).

5. The reference is to William J. Dowdell (editor of the *Cleveland Sun*) and his associates.

6. "The 'intensive recruiting drive' organized by the present National board was certainly started with 'pep, vigor and vim.' In fact, with everything except judgment! The chairman for Massachusetts is a resident of Maine, the chairman from New York has resigned from all amateur organizations, and the chairman for Rhode Island is using the backs of blanks for writing poetry on!" Edith Miniter, "*Crumpets*, Supplementing *The Muffin Man*," *Views and Reviews*, 25 June 1921, p. [3].

7. "The Haverhill Convention" (p. 289). HPL alludes to the notoriously poor typography of the journal.

8. See the section "Lovecraft" in "20 Webster Street" by George Julian Houtain: "Lovecraft honestly believes he is not strong—that he has an inherited nervousness and fatigue wished upon him. One would never suspect in his massive form and well constructed body that there could be any ailment. To look at him one would think seriously before 'squaring off.'" *Zenith*, January 1921, p. 5; rpt. *Lovecraft Remembered*, p. 87.

9. Dante, *Inferno* 34.139 (tr. Henry Francis Cary [*beheld* for *behold* in Dante/Cary]).

# THE CONVENTION BANQUET

The 46th Annual Banquet of the N.A.P.A. was held at the Hotel Brunswick, Boston, on July 4 at 8 p.m., and presented many pleasing and unique features. Its culminating event was the gift of a silver loving-cup to amateurdom's "strong man" and benefactor, W. Paul Cook, and in every detail it proved a credit to those who arranged and enlivened it.

Tasteful programmes printed by Charles A. A. Parker, artfully concealing the names of the speakers, were found by the guests as they entered the hall; and when each of the banqueters was seated, Toastmaster Willard O. Wylie led the assemblage in the singing of "America"—a patriotic tribute appropriate not only to the day but to the occasion, since its words were written by the grandfather of the prominent amateurs James and Nelson Morton.[1]

The attendance was large; and in order that none might remain strangers, the Toastmaster arranged a method of progressive introduction whereby each feaster was named by the person on his right. Entertainment was not deferred until after the feast, but commenced with the very first of the toothsome courses. Joseph Bernard Lynch regaled his auditors with his perennial musical classic, "On a Starry Night in Ireland", whilst Misses Elinor Parker and Gladys Frye furnished pleasing humorous recitations, some of them in Hibernian dialect. James F. Morton, Jr., lent a climactic touch with some inimitable stanzas on the pronunciation of English as practiced in various centres of culture, including Kalamazoo.

The regular speaking also began before the end of the repast. Toastmaster Wylie headed the list with some introductory remarks of unusual felicity, and presented each speaker with a grace which his subjects found hard to equal and impossible to excel.

Mr. Lovecraft, assigned the subject "Within the Gates" and announced as "One Sent by Providence", spoke in humorous vein. Following him was Mr. William J. Dowdell of Cleveland, "A Live Wire Amateur Journalist" who spoke ably on his "Favourite Recreation". In his well-received remarks Mr. Dowdell emphasised the paramount need of publicity for the activities of amateurdom.

Ex-President Edward H. Cole next spoke in his capacity of "A Leader of the Past", having the subject "Fleeting Years" and touching upon the changes wrought by time in our circle. His tributes to the departed were of especial beauty and interest. Then, turning from the past to the present, Mr. Cole began to celebrate the virtues of a leader of today whose services are hard to parallel. None save the modest subject of the eulogy himself could mistake the trend of the speech; and the wildest applause and spontaneous cheering arose when Mr. Cole, in the name of the National Association, presented the symbol of supreme service—a silver loving-cup—to that indefatigable leader and worker W. Paul Cook. Mr. Cook, too overwhelmed to speak at length, thanked the Association as best he could; and resumed his seat amidst admiring yells of "What's the matter with Cook? He's all right! Who's all right? W. Paul Cook!" Never was a loving-cup more justly bestowed than upon this tireless and brilliant author, editor, printer, and executive; to whose credit stands the greatest of all volumes of The National Amateur.[2]

George Julian Houtain, billed without political insinuation as "A Repeater", spoke with notable wit and subtlety on various topics administrative and otherwise, and shewed himself a magnanimous victor in the amateur fray. He announced, amidst vociferous congratulations, his engagement to Pres. E. Dorothy MacLaughlin.

Ex-President Cook, after an interval for recovery from his grand ovation, disclaimed his programme title of "Convention Dodger", and explained why this convention was his first, despite his full quarter-century as an amateur.

Mrs. Sawyer, with a "Dooley Paper" entitled "20 Webster St.", furnished the keenest humour of the occasion, and emphasised the supremacy of the "Temple Epgephi" as an amateur shrine.

"The Man with the Stick", scheduled to speak on "Volume XLIV", proved to be none other than ex-President Charles W. Heins; who told many interesting anecdotes of the newly elected Official Editor—his own thirteen-year-old son.[3]

A brilliant unannounced speaker was the forceful William W. Lapoint, whose patriotic orations made him prominent in war work a few years ago. Mr. Lapoint sensibly and vigorously urged a greater positive patriotism in amateurdom, and received a "curtain call" when he had concluded.

The question of "Riches, What Are They?" was answered with great eloquence by "A Certain Rich Man"—ex-President James F. Morton, Jr., who justly and felicitously named the boons of knowledge and friendship as the greatest wealth.

Ex-President Edith Miniter spoke briefly on absent amateurs under the heading "The Vacant Chair", rendering a tribute to that leading pillar of our hobby—the unseen but never-active Tryout.

Last on the programme came the newly elected President, E. Dorothy MacLaughlin, who received a magnificent floral tribute, and responded with much felicity.

Immediately upon the close of the speaking, ex-President Cole called a short business meeting, during which Mr. Dowdell commenced the collection of a fund for publicity and official organ purposes, heading the subscriptions with a generous $15.00. Most of the National leaders present proved generous donors; so that the year will commence with a very encouraging prosperity.

EDITOR'S NOTE Unpublished (ms., JHL). It is surprising that this account of the NAPA convention in Boston in July 1921 did not appear in an amateur paper, but no publication of it has been located. The mere fact that the ms. exists helps to confirm that the essay is unpublished, as HPL would in all likelihood have destroyed the ms. if any published version existed.

*Notes*

1. The words to the song "America" (based on the tune of "God Save the King," the British national anthem) were written by Samuel Francis Smith (1808–1895) in 1831.
2. Cook was Official Editor of the NAPA for 1918–19, although his final issue of the *National Amateur* (dated July 1919) was not distributed until early 1922 (see "News Notes" [March 1922]). That issue contained HPL's essay "Idealism and Materialism—A Reflection" and the story "The Picture in the House."
3. John Milton Heins.

# EDITORIAL

*(September 1921)*

In the excellent October *Woodbee*, Mr. Leo Fritter criticises with much force the attempt of the present editor to conduct *The United Amateur* on a tolerably civilised plane. He points out that the appearance of a journal representing a fairly uniform maturity of thought and artistic development may perhaps tend to discourage those newer aspirants who have not yet attained their full literary stature, and thus defeat the educational ends of the Association.

Mr. Fritter gathers his material for complaint from the opinions of certain amateurs with whom he has held communication, and on this basis alleges a "widespreading dissatisfaction" with the present editorial policy. We have ourselves received numerous and enthusiastic assurances of an opposite nature, especially since the Fritter attack, so that we must rebut at least his charge that we are ignoring the membership's wishes and 'trying to conform them to a mould we have arbitrarily cast according to ideas of our own'. To adopt a lower standard would, indeed, be affronting a more influential element than that which may at present be dissatisfied; an element which has possibly gained higher claims to consideration through the *continuous* nature of its services to the Association during trying times when others were silent and inactive.

But in determining the question of editorial policy, the abstract merits of the case are more important than the act of pleasing this or that person or group. Were we convinced that the existing order hampered the sincere novice, we would abandon it without pride or ceremony. That we do not, is because we are certain that retrogression and decadence would constitute a fatal mistake. The public we serve is assumed to be a genuinely progressive one, a group bent upon attaining some measure of proficiency in that sincere self-expression which is art. If it were not, it would have joined some other association of different purposes—the defiantly crude Erford pseudo-United or the complacently social and stationary National. What justifies the separate existence and support of the United is its higher aesthetic and intellectual cast; its demand for the unqualified best as a goal—which demand, by the way, must not be construed as discriminating against even the crudest beginner who honestly cherishes that goal. With these objects in mind, it will be seen that the self-satisfied exaltation of the superficial, the obvious, the commonplace, and the conventional, would form the greatest possible tactical error. The goal would be unjustifiably obscured, and the aspiration of the membership stunted, through the enshrining of a false and inferior goal—a literary Golden Calf. We must envisage a genuine scale of values, and possess a model of genuine excellence toward which to strive. It would pay better to work toward a high standard oneself, than to seek to drag the standard down to fit whatever particular grade of ignorance one may happen to have at a given moment. With proper effort any member may eventually produce work of the *United Amateur* grade, and such work will be certain of a cordial welcome in this office. The official organ is not so narrow as it seems; if more of our capable members would favour it with their literary contributions, the range of authors represented would not be so restricted. It is not the editor but the body of our *literati* who must bear responsibility for the constant reappearance of certain names. This issue is headed by the same poet who headed the last two—but only because another eminent amateur, so far unrepresented during the present regime, utterly ignored our repeated requests for a contribution.

Mr. Fritter—who, I fear, wrongs etymology in his acceptance of the word *amateur* as meaning a tyro rather than a genuine and disinterested artist—forgets that a relapse to cruder standards would totally unfit the United for serving that staunch element which has contributed most to its present welfare. Many would find a society of the lower grade intolerable; certainly it could not hope to hold the very ones who have given this organisation its existing distinctiveness and preëminence.

Yet in the arguments of Mr. Fritter there is an underlying soundness which misapplication should not obscure to the analytical reader. He is right in lamenting, as we believe he does, the absence of a suitable publishing medium for the work of our younger writers. It is not in a spirit of affront to him that we give preference to the plan of President Haughton, as outlined in her opening message, for the re-establishment of a special magazine for credentials. We should be glad to curtail the official organ in the interest of such a magazine, as indeed we offered to do at the beginning of the term.

*Frustra laborat,* says the old proverb, *qui omnibus placere studet.*[1] We regret that any one policy must of necessity displease a few members, yet do not see how any improvement could be effected by making a change which would merely shift the displeasure to another and even more continuously industrious group. It is significant that the Gothic party have no editorial candidate of their own to offer, so that the thankless and toilsome office has been forced upon one whose indifferent health makes it an almost unbearable burden to him. The question is one which should ultimately be decided at the polls, each party putting forward a nominee who can be depended upon to fulfil its mandates. Meanwhile the present editor, whose sincere beliefs and policies were fully known long before his unopposed election, stands ready to resign most cheerfully whenever a suitable successor can be found. Bitterness, division, and personalities must be avoided at any cost, and we may be reckoned as a supporter of *The United Amateur* under any editor and policy.

EDITOR'S NOTE FP: *United Amateur* 21, No. 1 (September 1921): 7–8 (unsigned). HPL continues to combat accusations that the editorial policy he has instituted for the *United Amateur* has alienated many members whose work is judged insufficiently literary for inclusion in the official organ. HPL must have been particularly galled at being criticized by Leo Fritter, whom he had supported for several UAPA offices in previous years.

*Notes*

1. "He who strives to please everyone toils in vain."

# NEWS NOTES

*(September 1921)*

The United takes pride in the distinguished recognition just accorded its premier poetess, Winifred Virginia Jackson; recognition of a degree hitherto gained by no other amateur journalist. Four poems of Miss Jackson's, "Fallen Fences", "Miss Doane", "The Farewell", and "Cross-Currents", have been selected by the eminent critic and editor, William Stanley Braithwaite, for publication in his 1921 "Anthology of Massachusetts Poets", whilst another notable group has won the supreme distinction of inclusion in Mr. Braithwaite's authoritative general "Anthology of Magazine Verse" for 1921, to be published in November.[1] We may appreciate the honour thus reflected upon the United when we consider the exclusive standards and classical reputation of the Braithwaite anthologies, as published by Small, Maynard & Co. of Boston. These anthologies, says the *New York Times*, are "signs of the times and milestones upon the way". According to the *Atlantic Monthly*, they "show the vigorous state of American poetry". Of Mr. Braithwaite the late William Dean Howells said: "Mr. Braithwaite is a critic very much to our mind, and is the most intelligent historian of contemporary poetry we can think of." The United indeed has reason to congratulate its poetical luminary, and indirectly itself, as the first and continued field of Miss Jackson's efforts.

One of the most brilliant and important of recent recruits to the United is Mrs. Sonia H. Greene, 259 Parkside Ave., Brooklyn, N. Y. Mrs. Greene is a Russian by birth, and descended from an illustrious line of artists and educators. Coming at an early age to the United States, she acquired a remarkable degree of erudition mainly through her own initiative; being now a master of several languages and deeply read in all the literatures and philosophies of modern Europe. Probably no more thorough student of Continental literature has ever held membership in amateurdom, whilst our many philosophical members will note with interest her position as a former Nietzschean who has at present rejected the theories of the celebrated iconoclast.

On July 4 Mrs. Maude Kingsbury Barton directed with brilliant success the pageant "The Fireman's Dream", a phantasy in six scenes, composed by herself and acted by a cast of three hundred persons in the interests of the firemen of Natchez. The production aroused great enthusiasm, and was highly praised in the *Natchez Democrat* for July 17.

The Woodbee Club, now doubly prominent in amateurdom through its possession of both the Presidency and the Secretary-Treasurership, continues to be the most active of local bodies. On Labour Day, September 5, a successful corn roast was held on the Frazier Farm, whilst on September 24 the third annual rummage sale took place. Of the proceeds of the latter, $25.00 will be very generously donated to the Official Organ Fund in five-dollar instalments. The latest event is a farewell party to Miss Henriette Ziegfeld on the eve of her departure for India. *The Woodbee* for October has appeared with its usual vigour and a new and pleasing typographical dress. Henceforward this publication will be under the editorship of Leo Fritter. Much renewed activity is expected as a result of the return of Mrs. Dora H. Moitoret, the club's founder, for a winter's visit with her parents in Columbus.

Ernest Lionel McKeag, our versatile British member, has joined a theatrical repertory company of high grade in Huddersfield, where plays by Shakespeare, Shaw, Ibsen, Maeterlinck, and others will be presented. The experience will be a useful one in view of his ambitions as a dramatic critic, and the good wishes of the United attend him during his Thespian days.

An example of amateur devotion and enthusiasm which should be heeded by all members as an inspiration to renewed activity is afforded by our new recruit, Mrs. Sonia H. Greene of Brooklyn, N. Y. Mrs. Greene, immediately upon receipt of a bundle of United papers and before the arrival of her membership certificate, sent the following phenomenal pledge to the Official Organ Fund; a pledge eloquent of a real and self-sacrificing interest which, if shared by the majority of our workers, would bring about at once that amateur renaissance so long desired, yet always so prone to retreat into the future. Mrs. Greene writes:

"So much do I appreciate the efforts of all those who contribute to the sum total of this pleasurable experience, that I, too, wish to do my meagre 'bit' . . . I shall consider it a special privilege to be permitted, each month, to contribute with a modest portion of my earnings; so that those who have not the financial means may make use of mine in advancing the noble cause of amateur journalism. I hereby pledge myself to contribute fifty dollars ($50.00) for the season 1921–22."[2]

Wish such new members, the United's future need give no anxiety to its warmest well-wishers.

Amateurdom will be pleased to hear of the recovery of Miss Annie Pearce from the dangerous indisposition previously mentioned in these columns.

Beyond a doubt, the leading amateur publication of the season is Mrs. Sonia H. Greene's resplendent October *Rainbow*. The editor is anxious to have this magazine reach every member of the United, and hopes that all who have been accidentally overlooked will notify her at 259 Parkside Ave., Brooklyn, N. Y., that the omission may be repaired.

On the evening of July 29, the Woodbees tendered a surprise party to Mrs. Ida Cochran Haughton, to congratulate her upon her unanimous election to the United's Presidency. During the festivities the appointment of the new Secretary was announced; this official being Miss Alma Sanger, 667 Lilley Ave., Columbus, Ohio, to whom all future applications and renewals should be addressed.

EDITOR'S NOTE FP: *United Amateur* 21, No. 1 (September 1921): 8, 12 (unsigned). HPL introduces Sonia H. Greene to UAPA members; he had first met her at the NAPA convention in Boston in July. He makes especial note of her unprecedented contribution of $50 to the Official Organ Fund (for which see p. 418).

*Notes*

1. The volumes referred to are *Anthology of Massachusetts Poets* (Boston: Small, Maynard, 1922) and *Anthology of Magazine Verse for 1921* (Boston: Small, Maynard, 1921). The latter volume included Jackson's "The Cobbler in the Moon," "Finality," "The Tricksy Tune," "Eyes," "Deafness," "Hoofin' It," and "The Purchase." All these poems are identified as having appeared in the *Conservative*, but none of them did so, no issue having appeared in 1921. According to George T. Wetzel and R. Alain Everts (*Winifred Virginia Jackson—Lovecraft's Lost Romance* [Privately printed, 1976]), Jackson carried on a long-term affair with Braithwaite.
2. See further *SL* 1.143.

---

# A SINGER OF ETHEREAL MOODS AND FANCIES

The accompanying lines were prepared in 1919 at the request of C. W. Smith for a booklet to be dedicated to Mrs. Dowe's memory. Since the writer was not personally acquainted with the poet and had seen but a limited amount of her work at the time, the piece was offered under a pseudonym; thus appearing in *The Tryout* after the plan for a booklet was abandoned.

It is with gratification that the stanzas are now presented for reprinting; for while the writer is conscious of his total want of merit as a bard, he is glad of the opportunity to express, under his own signature, his appreciation of a rare poet. Mrs. Dowe was a poet in the highest sense—a singer of ethereal moods and fancies, who never confused her art with lesser arts, or allowed it to break up into abnormal fragments in the modern manner. Hers was the delicate fancy from which real images are born, and in her death literature lost an exponent who can never be replaced.

EDITOR'S NOTE FP: *In Memoriam: Jennie E. T. Dowe*, ed. Michael White (Dorchester, MA: [W. Paul Cook,] September 1921), p. 56. A brief essay to accompany a poetic tribute ("In Memoriam: J. E. T. D."; *AT* 350) to Jennie E. T. Dowe (1841–1919), an old-time amateur and mother of Edith Miniter.

---

# NEWS NOTES

*(November 1921)*

An important new member of the United is Mr. Washington Van Dusen of Philadelphia, a poet of unusual power and felicity.[1] Mr. Van Dusen has to his credit a pleasing book of collected verses, "Songs of Life and Love", published by the J. B. Lippincott Co.;[2] poems which the *Baltimore World* compared to "delicate wild flowers that surprise us with their fragrance and beauty when we are least expecting them". The activity and success of Mr. Van Dusen may be judged by the fact that in 1918 he had 25 poems accepted by standard publications, including the *Boston Transcript, Springfield*

*Republican, Philadelphia Public Ledger, Chicago Tribune, New York Evening Post, Book News Monthly,* and several others.

Mr. Van Dusen is prominent in the American Literary Association, Browning Society of Philadelphia, and Philadelphia Society of Arts and Letters; in all of which his work has won signal honours. He is Chairman of the Programme Committee of the Society of Arts and Letters, and in the Browning Society was recently selected to prepare a paper on Browning. A member of the Class of 1889, University of Pennsylvania, he is a contributor to its piquant publication, *The Nudge.*

Commercially, Mr. Van Dusen is prominent in the affairs of the extensive United Gas Improvement Company, of whose pleasing illustrated magazine, *The Circle,* he is Associate Editor. Credit for obtaining this distinguished recruit belongs to that staunchest of United leaders, Paul J. Campbell.

Our former Fourth Vice-President, Miss Dorothy Roberts, is proving her brilliancy as a Freshman at Denison University, Granville, Ohio, where she is already a member of the staff of the college weekly, *The Denisonian.* During her high school days she was Editor-in-Chief of the Marietta H. S. *Weekly Original.*

The United welcomes to the ranks of its publishers that energetic young Woodbee, Mr. Arthur F. Ziegfeld, of 1471 Oak St., Columbus, Ohio, whose pleasingly printed *Follies* has made such a favourable impression on the membership. Mr. Ziegfeld—who in the title makes clever employment of the celebrated name he bears[3]— does his own typographical as well as editorial work, and provides an amateur newspaper of a sort very welcome to the United. "Act I, Scene II" is admirably neat, and we wish for the production of a record run, played to standing room only!

The attention of our poets is called to a comparatively new organisation especially suited to their needs, to which many United members already belong. This flourishing contemporary, the American Literary Association, has its headquarters at 308-35th St., Milwaukee, Wis., where it publishes a bi-monthly official organ of pleasing size and appearance, the *American Poetry Magazine.* The magazine, which is not sold to the general public but furnished free to members, contains a selected variety of the members' work; together with helpful and appropriate articles and departments. Membership of the ordinary sort is obtainable through payment of $2.00 annual dues ($1.00 for the first year to United members only), though Supporting Membership at $10.00 per year, and Life Membership at $100.00, may also be secured. An expert bureau of criticism, skilled in the difficulties of the average new poet, furnishes constructive advice to members at the rate of $1.00 per 30 lines or less.

Information concerning the society may be obtained from its headquarters, and for the sum of 20 cents a sample of its year-book and its magazine can be procured. Among the United members also belonging to the American Literary Association are John Ravenor Bullen, Myrta Alice Little, Washington Van Dusen, Effie Alger Allen, and Elizabeth Cheney-Nichols.

The marriage on August 30 of George Julian Houtain and E. Dorothy MacLaughlin is of much interest to United members. Mr. and Mrs. Houtain plan the issuance of a professional monthly magazine of piquant cast, to be entitled *Home Brew,* among whose contributors will be our members Rheinhart Kleiner and H. P. Lovecraft.[4]

The continued successes of our Poet-Laureate, Mrs. S. Lilian McMullen (Lilian Middleton), cast additional lustre on the United as amateurdom's chief source of authentic creative artists. Poetry by Mrs. McMullen appeared on the editorial page of the *New York Times* for October 15; a distinction which can be appreciated by those familiar with the standards of that celebrated publication.[5]

With vast regret we learn of the loss of awards in the Editorial Laureateship contest. Mr. Mencken generously made his decision, and promptly mailed all data to President Galpin; but through an accident to the envelope, most of the material—including the letter of award—failed to reach its destination. It being inadvisable at this late date to reassemble the entries and impose again on Mr. Mencken's good nature, Mr. Galpin has decided to omit the award for 1921; a very generous decision, since it is almost certain that he himself would be the winner.

On October 12 our former Official Editor, Miss Verna McGeoch, was united in marriage with Mr. James Chauncey Murch of Pennsylvania. Mrs. Murch may be addressed after November 9 at 144 S. 4th St., Easton, Penn.

Ex-President Alfred Galpin, Jr., is distinguishing himself at the University of Wisconsin, whose "Lit" recently published a brilliant essay from his pen, an essay later reviewed in the college *Daily Cardinal*. On October 26 Mr. Galpin attended a meeting of the exclusive literary club of the University, "The Stranglers", where he read his "Picture of a Modern Mood,", published last May in these columns, and selections from the poetry of our superlative artist Samuel Loveman. His entire programme was favourably received.

Miss Henriette Ziegfeld of the Woodbee Club on November 12 sailed for India, where she will be engaged in missionary work at Nagercoil, Travancore, in the southernmost part of the peninsula.

Mrs. Maude K. Barton's latest achievement in tableau and pageantry is the entertainment "Books and Memories", given in Cathedral Hall, Natchez, November 2. It was in ten scenes, and received exceedingly favourable mention. Mrs. Barton was on the Artistic Committee of the recent Natchez Cotton Carnival, an event of much local importance.

Honours come rapidly to our poets. On November 5 *The Literary Digest* reprinted a poem of Mrs. McMullen's from the *New York Times*,[6] while the *Boston Transcript's* annual poetic summary by William Stanley Braithwaite featured Miss Jackson, giving selections, photographs, and a brief biography. In the *Boston Sunday Herald* for December 18 the work of Miss Jackson is treated in an illustrated article, and during the same month *The Outlook* has used this author's poetry.[7]

Mrs. Rosa A. Hayden, who dwells in Shakespeare's native town of Stratford-on-Avon, has had a gratifying amount of professional literary success. To her credit are three volumes of verse, including one of war poetry whose proceeds were devoted to the succour of war prisoners in Germany, and several illustrated poetical post-cards, mainly relating to Shakespeare and Stratford. She is now preparing a post-card of Sulgrave, Northamptonshire, ancestral home of the Washingtons, whose verses have elicited grateful recognition from ex-President Wilson.

Paul Graham Trueblood, our youthful poet-member, turned sixteen last October. He is a high-school student of great brilliancy, representing his class in debate and having a general reputation for scholarship. Besides literature, which claims his prime devotion, he is deeply interested in the musical and forensic arts. His ultimate ambition is to become a writer and journalist.

EDITOR'S NOTE  FP: *United Amateur* 21, No. 2 (November 1921): 21–23 (unsigned). HPL discusses Washington Van Dusen, Alfred Galpin, and other amateurs.

*Notes*

1. HPL met Van Dusen (1857–?) in Philadelphia in November 1924.

2. Washington Van Dusen, *Songs of Life and Love* (Philadelphia: J. B. Lippincott Co., 1899). Van Dusen also published *Immortelles and Other Poems* (Philadelphia: J. B. Lippincott Co., 1890) and *Sonnets on Great Men and Women and Other Poems* (Philadelphia, 1929).

3. HPL refers to Florenz Ziegfeld (1869–1932), founder of the Ziegfeld Follies, one of the most celebrated vaudeville acts of the period.

4. HPL's contributions to *Home Brew* were "Herbert West—Reanimator" (as "Grewsome Tales"; February–July 1922) and "The Lurking Fear" (January–April 1923).

5. Lilian Middleton, "In the Tender Irish Weather," *New York Times* (15 October 1921): 12.

6. "In the Tender Irish Weather" was reprinted in *Literary Digest* 71, No. 6 (5 November 1921): 30.

7. Winifred Virginia Jackson, "The Northwest Corner," *Outlook* 129, No. 13 (30 November 1921): 527.

---

# [LETTER TO JOHN MILTON HEINS]

[c. November 1921]

My dear Mr. Heins:—

Permit me to thank you most sincerely for the attractive silver medal which your Association has been so kind to award me. The honourable mention is as gratifying as any ordinary laureateship, since my superior is no less a person than James F. Morton, Jr. The idea of the medals, for which I believe your Association is indebted to you alone, is certainly a most desirable one; since it stimulates in the contests a keen interest otherwise lacking. I regret that my prime allegiance to the United Association forbade me to contribute to your medal fund in these lean times, but am sure you can appreciate the principle involved. If you ever join the United and start such a fund, you may depend upon my fullest coöperation!

It was not without a qualm of conscience that I accepted the medal when informed of it by Mr. Houtain—it seemed to some degree unethical to step into another Association, grab a valuable prize, and then step out again with only a brief word of thanks. My qualms were overruled, however, and I now tender the thanks with as much contribution as the occasion demands.

Thanking you again—both you and your association, in fact—and assuring you to have any part of this letter published if you so choose,

Believe me,

Most sincerely yours,

H. P. Lovecraft

EDITOR'S NOTE FP: *National Amateur* 44, No. 3 (January 1922): 27. HPL acknowledges an award as runner-up in the essay laureateship in the NAPA for 1921; the laureateship was won by James F. Morton. It is not clear which essay by HPL (published in the 1920–21 term) received the award.

# EDITORIAL

*(January 1922)*

Amidst the prevailing efforts of a small but pugnacious group to "liven" up the United through attacks on the Official Organ, a few basic principles should be remembered by those who stand in bewilderment.

Our constitution does not define the functions of *The United Amateur* beyond making imperative the publication of certain official documents. The rest is left to an unwritten combination of tradition and editorial judgment. Any editor, once elected, is absolutely in control of the magazine aside from the essential official matter; his only external obligation being a tacit recognition of the prevailing objects of the Association. In the present case a narrow circle of agitators seems to be seeking political capital by accusing the editor of placing too high an estimate on the membership and purposes of the United.

Since the whole development of the Association is involved in this matter, it is important that a prompt and perfect understanding be reached. The opinions of all members should be known, and if the editor finds that he has been in error, he will be glad to arrange for the accommodation of the Organ to the wishes of the majority. Up to the present time, despite the florid overstatements of the few who are trying to work up a new and wholly artificial dissatisfaction, this office has received *not so much as one complaint* as to policy save from the two politicians who are seeking to lower the United's standards. Endorsements as to the existing policy have been many, and as long as these remain so tremendously in the majority, it would be a betrayal of trust to make a change to please a tiny group. If there are those who differ, why do they not speak?

Since truth is the only perfect clarifier when politics seeks to becloud, it is necessary that the editor state his policy here and now with the utmost candour. Shorn of all irrelevant things, that policy is simply the maintenance of those standards established in the United by the departure of the chronically political element in 1912. Prior to that time the Official Organ was mainly a bulletin of reports; not, as the present agitators would imply, a repository for indiscriminate amateur writings. The standard developed since then is the creation of no one person, but a logical outgrowth of the rising calibre of a vital and progressive society. It is neither one of favouritism nor one of autocracy; but merely one of *stimulation*. It is an embodiment of the United's desire to let the Official Organ exemplify the members' progress by using the best available material. No genuine aspirant has ever been frowned upon, or so far as we know given any ground for discouragement. The Organ is a beckoner and encourager, designed to inspire the members to renewed efforts to produce work worthy of symbolising the United. Would anyone so far insult the Association as to wish its official exponent to cater to that type of mediocrity which neither improves nor wishes to improve? Our columns are open to all who toil for the fruits of art, and statements to the contrary cannot be interpreted as other than irresponsibly ignorant or craftily misinterpretative. While insistence on a certain degree of merit is of course necessary, it is not true that *The United Amateur* makes any arbitrary restrictions. The Organ was not designed for the publication of various members' work, nor is access to its columns one of the special objects of membership, as certain agitators are artfully intimating. But notwithstanding these technical points, all proficient writers are welcome. It is illuminating, in view of the prevalent loose statements, to reflect that throughout the present editor's service *not more than three manuscripts have been rejected;* and that even these three were or will be elsewhere placed. Those seeking an Associational disturbance will not scruple to take advantage of every outward appearance which seems to favour them— unavoidable delays, spatial limitations, and other things interfering with prompt publi- cation of all matter to this office. The present editor will be denounced as a "tyrant" by elements attempting to degrade standards which he did not establish!

The life and well-being of the United are at stake, and it is imperative that the membership exercise the most careful and independent reflection before accepting the views of radicals bent on retrogressive experiments.

EDITOR'S NOTE FP: *United Amateur* 21, No. 3 (January 1922): 36 (unsigned). HPL laments the decline of amateur activity in the UAPA and again defends himself against charges that he is publishing only the work of his own close colleagues in the *United Amateur*. This was the last editorial HPL would write for this term; he would lose the election of July 1922 and not be reinstated to the Official Editorship until 1923.

---

# NEWS NOTES

*(January 1922)*

United poets are rapidly rising to fame in the outside world through popular antholo- gies. Arthur H. Goodenough, our only surviving Literatus in his field, has four po- ems in the current "American Anthology of Newspaper Verse", and had three in the pre- ceding issue.[1] Such honour to our veterans is gratifying to the whole Association.

Edward J. O'Brien's review of the Braithwaite Anthology in *The Boston Transcript* gives especial distinction to the United leader, Winifred Virginia Jackson. Mr. O'Brien, in sifting out the twenty-five best poems in the Anthology, chooses five by Miss Jack- son; although most authors are represented by only one, and no other by more than three. In the course of his review, the critic says: ". . . America has produced two new poets of great significance this year in Winifred Virginia Jackson, with her stark disin- terested portraits of a spiritually rotting New England full of sterile tragedy and dusty death, and in Elinor Wylie, with her dynamic gospel of Blake in a modern setting. . . ."

Wheeler Dryden, having moved southward, has participated in several film pro- ductions in Los Angeles. Recently he took an important part in the community pro- duction of "Fanny's First Play", an honour of no slight magnitude. A further honour consists of a "write-up" in the community publication, *Holly Leaves*, where is described Mr. Dryden's curious walking-stick with silver handle and sacred buffalo ferule, the gift of an Indian prince during our dramatic member's travels through the Orient.

Our brilliant young fantaisiste, Frank Belknap Long, Jr., is just convalescing from a severe illness including an operation for appendicitis, which kept him for a long pe- riod at the Roosevelt Hospital. He has been forced to resign the First Vice-Presidency, but will soon be an active literary factor again.

One of our most distinguished new accessions is Mrs. Renshaw's recruit, Edward Lloyd Sechrist, of Washington, D. C., whose powerful essay on Columbus will intro- duce him to United readers. Mr. Sechrist is studying advanced literature at Research

University, and promises to be heard from in the future. He is a traveller and philosopher, with strong predilections for the more genuine side of Nature; and has spent much time in such remote places as South Africa and Polynesia.[2]

Mr. and Mrs. Paul J. Campbell are among this year's migratory members. After a holiday trip to Chicago, during which all of the city's literary and artistic delights were sampled, they are now settled for a season at Mahomet, Ill., where they will delight amateurdom with a *Liberal* and *Corona*—both from the Campbell Press—before returning to Prairie Queen Grange to construct their new bungalow.

Honours come fast to our luminous young member, Jay Fuller Spoerri. He has now been elected President of the Enosinian Society, the venerable and exclusive literary organisation of George Washington University, which this year celebrates its centennial. The society has in its day been addressed by speakers as eminent as the Marquis de Lafayette, John C. Calhoun, Daniel Webster, William Cullen Bryant, and James Russell Lowell.

Samuel Loveman's new *Saturnian,* just emerging from the press of W. Paul Cook, is without a doubt the artistic event of the year. No magazine of even approximately equal aesthetic merit has appeared for many months. The exorcism against modern verse is a thing to remember, and the translations from Baudelaire and Verlaine are things to chant and admire.[3]

The United has recently added to its ranks the pleasing and well-beloved poet, Mrs. K. Leyson Brown, who, like Mr. C. W. Smith, possesses the secret of eternal youth. Two of Mrs. Brown's recent patriotic poems, "America Forever" and "Columbia Triumphant", were sent to President Harding and Chairman Hughes of the Armament Conference,[4] both eliciting appreciative recognition.

A new poetical recruit of great promise and ability is Fred Keller Dix, of Prospect, O., recently brought into the fold by Mr. Fritter. Mr. Dix is a newspaper man connected with *The Marion Daily Star,* and has studied extensively in the field of *belles lettres.* Last year his collected poetry was issued in book form, the volume containing all types of verse from the homely Rileyesque to specimens whose melody and universality lift them close to the sky. The United welcomes so gifted an addition, and will watch with pride his future journey up the green Parnassian slope.

James F. Morton, Jr., has outdistanced all other amateurs by attaining the dignity of sculpture. This year he has been immortalised by a bust of heroic size, the work of a promising young New York artist, Louis Keila, who has also made a bust of President Harding.[5]

The recent memorial to Mrs. Jennie E. T. Dowe, issued jointly by W. Paul Cook and Michael Oscar White, is a landmark in amateur history.[6] Most notable of all the contents is the long sketch by Mrs. Dowe's daughter, Mrs. Edith Miniter, which is perhaps the finest specimen of affectionately humorous biography ever evolved by an amateur. Elaboration of this sketch to novel length and setting is under discussion. The Memorial was reviewed in *The Boston Transcript* by William Stanley Braithwaite.

The Woodbee Club continues to form a little amateur world whose many social activities are of interest. In January a reception was held for the high-school editors of Columbus, and from the enthusiasm there developed many recruits may be expected. A new *Woodbee* is out, and likely to attract notice because of its systematic attacks on the Official Editor and existing literary regime in general. Mr. Ziegfeld has ably staged the Third Scene of his *Follies,* in which is continued the local barrage against the Official Organ, and in which is also a very just censure of the National for its relapse to recruit-snatching methods. On December 24th the Club received the pleasing news that Miss Henriette Ziegfeld had safely reached her destination in India, despite two threatened onslaughts of *mal de mer* during the voyage; onslaughts which were cleverly defeated by means of judicious pedestrianism.

Readers who noted Mr. Galpin's friendly review of "The Crawling Chaos"[7] will be interested to know that the opinions of the learned often differ. A prominent politician with a distaste for the "wild, weird tales" of H. P. Lovecraft mistakenly credited this whole narrative to him,[8] and during a denunciation of Lovecraftian stories remarked: "We can hardly go them. That Crawling Chaos is the limit. His attempts at Poe-esque tales will land him—— Did you know he was on the staff of 'The Houtain Home Brew' to furnish six of his worst——" Mr. Lovecraft awaits his landing with keen interest.

Arthur F. Ziegfeld bids fair to become one of the few genuine humourists of the United. The following epigram, modestly buried in the inner columns of the *Foliies,* deserves reprinting: "I have often thought that if all amateur journalists were put into one building, it would surely be a 'survival of the fittest'. From what is written in letters, it certainly would create some bedlam."

William Dowdell has rejoined the United, and plans an excellent issue of *The Bearcat* for the near future. Recently he was appointed Official Editor of the National, and has given our esteemed contemporary a strikingly meritorious organ. *The Cleveland Sun* has been launched professionally as a Sunday afternoon newspaper, and has achieved a circulation mounting high into the thousands. Mr. Dowdell has a rare gift of energy, visible in whatever direction he exercises it.

*Home Brew,* the professional magazine of Mr. and Mrs. George Julian Houtain, has met with striking success; so that the second edition will consist of two and a half times more copies than the first. The United's best wishes attend its enterprising publisher-members.

Ernest Lionel McKeag, our able British journalist-member, is again in Germany gathering data for the press. Mr. McKeag's new *Northumbrian* has just started on its American rounds, and will be welcomed by all its recipients.

Robert D. Roosma-Le Cocq, veteran British amateur, has lately joined the United. In his magazine, *Le Cocq's Comment* for January, this energetic member parries the attacks of his foes with pyrotechnic results.

United papers are now appearing with a somewhat more encouraging frequency. Mr. Lawson's November *Wolverine* forms a notable event, as will the Culinary *Vagrant* about to rise above the horizon of Athol. Mr. Harrington's new *Coyote* lacks nothing in energy and sincerity, whilst the Kleinerian *Piper* lives up to all its traditions of urbane sophistication. Meanwhile the east is luminous with promise—for a second *Rainbow* of surpassing iridescence will soon span the heavens.

Master Leon Stone's *Austral Boy* reveals the brilliant presence of an amateur spirit at the antipodes. We urge our readers to write Master Stone in an effort to bring him into the United—his address is 3 Stamford St., Parkside, South Australia.[9]

J. Bernard Lynch, our gifted writer of light fiction, was represented in the *Boston Post* Sunday Magazine for March 19 by an interesting specimen of his well-known street-car stories, entitled "The European Trip".

This office had a delightful interesting caller on the afternoon of March 25, in the person of Mr. Leonard E. Tilden, the distinguished "Old-Timer" who is working so valiantly to secure second-class postal rates for amateur journals.

The editor wishes tearfully to disclaim both authorship and censorship of the four concluding items of the November News Notes.[10] These gems of composite origin were "slipped" in without the austere approval of our (usually) eagle eye; and that eye now becomes moist and saline because of the conspicuous use of the impossible concoction *"thusly"*, which we hope no discerning reader will lay at our modest door!

EDITOR'S NOTE FP: *United Amateur* 21, No. 3 (January 1922): 31–33 (unsigned). HPL discusses the doings of many amateurs, and includes a wry account of a hostile reaction to his own collaborative tale, "The Crawling Chaos."

*Notes*

1. Actually, Goodenough had three poems in *Anthology of Newspaper Verse for 1921*, ed. Franklyn Pierre Davis (Enid, OK: Frank P. Davis, 1922): "Restlessness," "As I Walked Out One Day," and "Red Ireland." He had four in the previous volume, *Anthology of Newspaper Verse for 1920*, ed. Franklin [sic] Pierre Davis (Enid, OK: Frank P. Davis, 1921): "An August Cricket," "Card Houses," "Death's Poverty," and "The Smoke of Chimney Cottages."

2. HPL met Sechrist (1873–1953) in Providence in February 1924 and in New York on 3 November 1924. It was Sechrist's accounts of the ancient African city of Zimbabwe that led to HPL's writing of the poem "The Outpost" (1929).

3. HPL refers to contributions by Samuel Loveman in the *Saturnian* 1, No. 3 (March 1922): "Modern Poetry (An Exorcism)," an essay (pp. 1–3); "Translations from Baudelaire" (pp. 3–11); "Translations from Verlaine" (pp. 12–15).

4. HPL refers to the Washington Naval Conference (1921–22), led by Secretary of State Charles Evans Hughes (1862–1948), which led to treaties among major powers restricting the use of naval armaments.

5. HPL to Maurice W. Moe, 18 May 1922 (AHT): "At length descending, we set out for the studio of Louis Keila, where rest in imperishable marble (plaster) the sculptured (modelled) features of our James Ferdinand. . . . Keila is a tough guy from the slums—half Greek and half Jew. He has no manners or refinement, but is unmistakably gifted in sculptural art. He has done Pres. Harding's bust, and sports a framed acknowledgement and autographed portrait from His Normalcy. Morton likes the fellow immensely, and is trying to civilise him. The Morton bust is very good indeed—shewing Jim in a characteristic and quizzically smiling mood. Keila was going to make some small replicas for sale, but gave up the idea. It was interesting to see statue and model side by side—both bore the test very well."

6. Michael White, ed., *In Memoriam: Jennie E. T. Dowe* (Dorchester, MA: [W. Paul Cook,] 1921). HPL contributed the essay "A Singer of Ethereal Moods and Fancies" (see p. 301) and the poem "In Memoriam: J. E. T. D." (both p. 56).

7. "Glancing a trifle backwards, I recall the attention of amateurs to the most important story recently published, 'The Crawling Chaos,' pseudonymously written by Winifred Virginia Jackson and H. P. Lovecraft. The narrative power, vivid imagination and poetic merit of this story are such as to elevate it above certain minor but aggravating faults of organisation and composition." Alfred Galpin, "Department of Public Criticism," *United Amateur* 21, No. 2 (November 1921): 21.

8. It was a collaboration between Lovecraft and Winifred V. Jackson.

9. Stone went on to do pioneering biographical and bibliographical work on HPL in the 1940s. See his column, "Lovecraftiana," *Koolinda* No. 5 (April 1948): 11–13; No. 6 (December 1949): 14–15; Nos. 7/8 (1950–51): 15–16; No. 9 (December 1952): 11–14.

10. These items have been omitted in the present edition.

## *RAINBOW* CALLED BEST FIRST ISSUE

Easily the foremost of all the current amateur output, and unquestionably the most brilliant first issue of any paper within the present critic's recollection, is the October *Rainbow*; edited and published by Mrs. Sonia H. Greene. Mrs. Greene, though a very recent recruit, has absorbed the amateur spirit with amazing speed; and possesses a very high conception of the duty of the individual to the institution. As a result she has become almost at once a leader, and has put forth a publication not only distinguishing her but assisting substantially in the advancement of amateur letters.

Unlike the average amateur paper, *The Rainbow* is not a haphazard collection of all the available manuscripts of the period, or yet a weary chronicle of trivial gossip and social insipidities. Mechanically dazzling and impeccable with its iridescent cover, numerous illustrations, and pleasing paper and typography, it nevertheless derives its chief claim to notice from its intellectual policy and carefully chosen contents. *The Rainbow,* in a word, represents a genuinely artistic and intelligent attempt to crystallise homogeneously a definite mood as handled by many writers. The mood is that of enlightened liberalism and civilised honesty and independence of thought; nor is its atmosphere lost even for a moment, despite several agreeable interludes of lighter nature. From the briefest item to the longest article and most ambitious poem there is uniformly sustained a tone of freedom and revolt against the stultifying lies, stupidities, hypocrisies, and mental narcotics of the conventional age which we are only now beginning to shake off.

In appraising the contents of the paper, we find first honours quite evenly shared in different fields, by Alfred Galpin, Jr., with his essay on "Nietzsche as a Practical Prophet", and by Samuel Loveman with his magnificent cry in verse, "A Triumph in Eternity". Mr. Galpin, though at this writing but twenty years of age, is beyond a doubt the greatest and most corrosive intellectual force in amateur journalism. It is easy to overpraise a precocious lad, but the term "precociousness" is a mild one to apply to a mentality infinitely searching, widely informed, phenomenally inclusive, and analytical to the point of genius. Alfred Galpin, a scholar and a sceptic from childhood, brings to the problems of philosophy a mind vibrant with energy and unencumbered with illusions. Totally devoid of the usual prejudices and superficialities of adolescence, he weighs the evidence about him with a judgment at once unspoiled and mature, and scales it against a background of erudition even now great, but constantly increasing with prodigious rapidity. "Nietzsche as a Practical Prophet" is almost an ideal essay; the subject being approached with clearness, developed with vigour and with a gratifying recognition of origins, and driven home with a compelling logic and series of concrete illustrations which bespeak the utmost skill and sophistication. The tone is admirable throughout; one of appraisal and appreciation, always inquiringly impersonal and never descending to mere hero-worship.

Mr. Loveman's poem is something to read in a mood of admiration bordering on awe. That the author stands at the head of our poetical band today is too obvious to require emphasis; it remains only to survey the radiant world of wonder he creates, and to trace as far as we can the sources of its splendour. Samuel Loveman is the last of the Hellenes—a golden god of the elder world fallen among pygmies. Genius of the most poignant authenticity is his, opening in his mind a diamond-paned window which looks out clearly upon rarefied realms of dream and scenes of immortal beauty seldom and dimly glimpsed by the modern age. He is the living negation of dull-grey contemporary realism and sordidness; the faithful standard-bearer of the beautiful and the universal as men knew these things in happier times. To the reader of limited background his work is obscure—obscure because it brushes aside the cobwebs of the commonplace and returns to that pure ecstasy and passion on which all art is founded—obscure because it touches greatness. It is not in the power of even the most appreciative critic to analyse fully the beauty he so keenly feels and so enthusiastically proclaims. Of Mr. Loveman's poetic vision we may only say that it involves to the highest degree that selective quality which is genius. The poet looks upon life, and with his own peculiar magic detects those elements most closely connected with the essentials of beauty; combining these instinctively in the most effective manner, and arranging them to best advantage against the background of the universe. Here, perhaps, is his secret—his basically cosmic rather than local point of view; a point of view which opens his fancy to sublime and terrible vistas reaching out beyond the stars and the aether we know. With all infinity for a temple, the trivialities of life lose their false claim to worship; and the hierophant shews his few followers a sight which the vulgar may never see—a cosmos of irradiate dreams and splendid shadows, with forces never less than Titanic and figures never less than Olympian. There are old, ivied walls, distant perfumed groves, columns of veined marble and alabaster that reach to the clouds, and shapes of wistful loveliness which are at once human and divine. And over all is the shadow of eternal tragedy—the shadow of pathos and disappointment that is all of life, shot through by the one pale violet beam of pity. This, then, is the art of Samuel Loveman—to distil from life's verities all that there is of beauty, re-creating the rarefied spectacle in breathless sublimity and investing it with an atmosphere snatched

> "From an ultimate dim Thule—
> From a wild, weird clime that lieth, sublime,
> Out of Space—Out of Time." [1]

"A Triumph of Eternity" is typically Lovemanic, though written five years before publication.

"Nietzscheism and Realism", by H. P. Lovecraft, is a set of cynical observations extracted from letters and arranged in aphoristical form.[2] Not written for publication, they demand some leniency of judgment; though their general purport is not likely to be denied by the contemporary thinker.

Mr. Kleiner's verse is here, as always, pleasing. The two brief amatory lyrics lack nothing of music, delicacy, and grace; and confirm the impression that their author is amateurdom's foremost exponent of the lighter and more courtly forms of his chosen art.[3]

James F. Morton, Jr., departs from the realm of profound scholarship long enough to provide some tuneful and captivating stanzas on the next convention.[4] As might be expected, he is urbane and correct; though so familiar a theme offers many pitfalls in the way of commonplaceness and insipidity.

Mrs. Greene's own contributions to The Rainbow are of varied and representative nature. "Mors Omnibus Communis" is a poem vital with the tragedy and mockery of existence.[5] "Amateurdom and the Editor" is a graceful editorial column in which the objects of amateurdom are re-stated with much power and piquancy. "Idle Idyls" and kindred personalities exhibit the editor as a brilliant and fraternal commentator, while the column headed "Philosophia" displays a vision and sense of proportion gratifying in an age as unsettled as this. Mrs. Greene is a thinker with much to say, and with a fast-growing power to say it effectively.

EDITOR'S NOTE  FP: *National Amateur* 44, No. 4 (March 1922): 44–46 (unsigned). A paean to the first issue of Sonia H. Greene's *Rainbow* (No. 1 [October 1921]). The article is part of the "Bureau of Critics" column (equivalent to the UAPA's Department of Public Criticism), and is HPL's first such contribution to the NAPA; he would write many "Bureau of Critics" columns in 1931–36. HPL is listed, with Samuel Loveman (chairman) and Edward H. Cole, as one of the Bureau of Critics for this NAPA term, although he would not contribute any further columns. HPL's enthusiastic tribute to Loveman's poetry would later embroil him in a dispute with Michael Oscar White (see "Bureau of Critics," p. 328).

*Notes*

1. Edgar Allan Poe, "Dream-Land" (1844), ll 6–8.
2. Elsewhere (HPL to the Gallomo, 21 August 1921; AHT) HPL states that the essay was extracted from two letters to Sonia H. Greene.
3. Kleiner's contributions to the issue were "To ———" (p. 12) and "Oh, If the Gods" (p. 14).
4. James F. Morton, "How I Would Like to Be Entertained at the Next National Convention" (p. 8).
5. HPL states (HPL to Rheinhart Kleiner, 21 September 1921; AHT) that he "set ['Mors Omnibus Communis'] aside for revision"; from internal evidence, the poem does appear to be revised by HPL.

# NEWS NOTES

*(March 1922)*

A recent literary offering of unusual worth is "Singers of the Crowd", an anthology of poems by members of our valued contemporary The Quill Club of London. Among the contributors we find John Ravenor Bullen, whose work has long been a source of pride to the United.

The level of literary achievement represented in this collection is a high one, no piece falling below substantial merit, and many rising to exceptional distinction in thought, imagery, or sheer lyrical harmony and intensity. Gratifyingly enough, free verse is entirely absent; shewing a commendable balance and perspective on the part of the committee of selection.

Most frequently recurring of all notes is that evoked by the simple loveliness of Nature as set forth in the English landscape; a circumstance not without significance to those intent on tracing genius to its source. That England has produced the best poetry of modern times, few will deny; and whilst much of this excellence is doubtless due to racial qualities, still more is perhaps to be associated with the always fresh beauty with which the English eye is surrounded from infancy. Certainly, British poets both amateur and professional, recognised and unrecognised, have possessed an exceptional responsiveness to that May-morning rural loveliness so characteristic of our ancestral island, and so strongly emphasised in Chaucer, the illustrious father of them all.

Mr. Adam Harold Brown, our interesting Canadian member, sends the following item as a sequel to a recent article of his:

"Apropos of my article, 'Pleasing Yourself', in *The United Amateur*, I recently heard another anecdote of O. Henry, which I have never seen in print. About 1909 some of his work was taken in advance by a certain New York magazine; but, as was sometimes the case, the story came in piece by piece. As the ending failed to appear on the last day when the presses were waiting, the editor had the bright idea of running the tale as it was, and offering a cash prize to readers who could supply the missing 'twist'. The plan was a great success. Many writers and non-writers boldly—and perhaps vainly—tried their hands. Probably their efforts evoked an amused and tolerant smile from O. Henry himself—that whimsical Knight of 'Bagdad-on-the-Subway'."

The amateur papers of the season are brilliantly justifying the hopes of those who looked forward to a prosperous year. W. Paul Cook's titanic *National Amateur*, issued as a conclusion to his volume of three years ago and dated July 1919, is an epoch in history; whilst his *Vagrant*, mailed shortly before, again sets the pace for individual papers. From the Campbells come a *Liberal* and *Corona*, contributing importantly to our intellectual activities, and on every hand we descry the Apollonian radiance which streams from Samuel Loveman's magnificent *Saturnian*.

Mrs. K. Leyson Brown, having spent over two months at her brother's home in Los Angeles, Calif., has now returned to her home in Bloomfield, N. J. Mrs. Brown intends to be increasingly active in the affairs of the United.

Early in April, New York was favoured by a visit from Samuel Loveman, our Prince of Poets, to whom the local amateurs were proud to do homage. He was the guest of Mrs. Sonia H. Greene, brilliant editor of *The Rainbow*, who magnanimously turned over her entire apartment to Mr. Loveman and to H. P. Lovecraft, who made a pilgrimage to meet him; herself stopping with neighbouring friends.[1] On Sunday, April 9, a gathering was held at the Greene residence in honour of Mr. Loveman; this event marking also the first personal appearance among the local members of Frank Belknap Long, Jr., distinguished young prose-poet and former First Vice-President of the United. Paul Livingston Keil, new recruit and student of Nature lore, likewise lent his presence. During the visit many of the New York amateurs generously guided Messrs. Loveman and Lovecraft to sundry points of interest; and it will be long before either will forget such sights as the skyline from Manhattan Bridge, shewn by Rheinhart Kleiner, or the bust of James F. Morton, Jr., shewn by the well-beloved original model himself. *Home Brew* office was visited, and a well-arranged musicale heard at the home of the former United member, Adeline E. Leiser, and the unique Russian spectacle "Chauve-Souris" witnessed at the 49th Street Theatre under the benignant guidance of Mrs. Greene. Other high lights are the visit to the Metropolitan Museum of Art, participated in by Messrs. Loveman and Lovecraft, and the pilgrimage to Poe's Cottage in Fordham, made by Messrs. Loveman, Morton, Long, Keil, and Lovecraft.[2] In that shrine of America's greatest literary artist, a brooding atmosphere lingers, and unseen wings seem to brush the cheek of the worshipper. It may be expected that many poetic echoes of the journey will resound on Mr. Loveman's lyre in the near future.

Miss Jennie E. Harris, whose exquisite poetry appears under the pseudonym of "Betty Earle", is now teaching English to a class of 150 in Plainsville, Kans. That the scene is an attractive one is proved by her mention, under date of April 1, of "fields just turning green, and level plains as far as the eye can see. . . . Space, far reaches, waiting fields, golden grain." Such a panorama should prove a decided stimulant to the Muse.

Word reaches us that our valued South Dakota member, Andrew Francis Lockhart, is a candidate for the United States Congress. His election is ardently hoped for, alike by those who admire his poignant poetry, and by those who respect his intrepid battles against adverse social and political conditions in the past.

Important additions to the United's younger generation are Edgar J. Davis,[3] age 13, a gifted bard of Merrimac, Mass., whose soul is with the good old gods of Asgard, Thor, Woden, and Freyr; and Paul Livingston Keil of New York, an arrow-head expert and student of Indian lore who Indianises his name to the pleasing and colourful dissyllable "Pauke". Both Norseman and Manhattan Sachem are highly welcome to our ranks, for there is no amateur material like enthusiastic youth.

Mr. Raymond J. Jeffreys of Columbiana, O., a National member of some prominence, and now brought into the United by Mr. Fritter, departs on June 10 for a honeymoon tour of great uniqueness; nothing less than a circumnavigation of the entire globe in an automobile.

During this trip, said to be the first of its kind ever undertaken, Mr. Jeffreys will write feature newspaper stories; while readings before the leading families of the principal cities will be given by his bride, Miss Pauline Mayo, now a national figure in Lyceum and Chautauqua circles. Appointments with dignitaries have already been arranged, and it is hoped that the expenses of the journey may be largely defrayed by the talents of the adventurous couple. The event will cover nearly three years, and will include about fifty nations. Surely Mr. Jeffreys, who is a World War veteran and newspaper man, may be reckoned as our premier cosmopolitan!

E. Edward Ericson, Official Publisher of the United, has sustained a painful accident involving a fracture of a rib and other injuries; which may necessitate some additional delay in the appearance of several papers. The sympathy of the Association is extended to the sufferer.

The Woodbees on April 29 held a successful rummage sale, obtaining over twenty dollars as their net profit. On July 13, 14, and 15 the club will entertain the United convention, which has been moved to Columbus on account of the lack of members at State College, Pa., the site originally chosen. All amateurs who can attend the convention are urged to do so; excellent entertainment and spirited political activity being likely.

Charles A. A. Parker, old-time amateur, has recently announced his willingness to help solve the problem of printers' rates. He is at present ready to use his augmented press outfit, the largest non-professional outfit in amateur journalism, in printing papers for amateurs at reasonable rates. United members are urged to get in touch with him at 30 Waite St., Maplewood, Malden, Mass., as a possible incentive toward a renaissance of the individual paper.

EDITOR'S NOTE  FP: *United Amateur* 21, No. 4 (March 1922): 43–45 (unsigned). HPL discusses, among other subjects, his own first visit to New York in early April 1922. The mere fact that this event (along with the Woodbees' rummage sale on April 29) is discussed here shows that this issue of the *United Amateur* appeared at least two months after its cover date.

*Notes*

1. This was HPL's first visit to NYC. See *LVW* 93–106.

2. Keil took the celebrated photograph of HPL, Long, and Morton in front of the Poe cottage. (Loveman was not in the picture.) See Keil's article, "I Met Lovecraft," *Phoenix* 3, No. 6 (July 1944); 149.

3. HPL met Davis the following year, as the two of them explored Newburyport, MA, in April 1923.

# THE VIVISECTOR

*(March 1922)*

If a critic should seek to appraise amateur poetry without the usual blinders of prejudice and partiality, he would probably find that among all our much-puffed rhymers there are just three real artists of the first magnitude; artists who besides having the necessary technique and cultural background, have in addition the unique perspective, the heightened faculty of comparison, and the innate sense of song which form actual poetic genius. These three are Samuel Loveman, Winifred Virginia Jackson, and S. Lilian McMullen (Lilian Middleton). The first two are already well known, but the latest of the triad, and present Laureate of the United Association, deserves an analytical appreciation which she has not before received from the press.

Mrs. McMullen, of Irish birth and musical training, is the most genuine *lyrist* in amateur journalism. Her poems are songs, and not less so because there are no visible notes. Throughout their range they shew a sincere individuality—an authentic style—which gives them a kind of unity despite their varied themes. Such distinctiveness of style bespeaks the presence of real genius, because it necessarily proceeds from a special and individual point of view and quality of vision. It is something original and uncopied, resulting from the poet's personal insight.

The charms of "Middleton" verse, though elusive and hard to define, are very potent, obvious, and unique. The poetry is thoroughly conservative, and woven of the lighter and more etherealised moods of the fancy, but it fascinates with its delicately sketched pictures and flawlessly musical structure. While the commonplace and the sordid are assiduously shunned, a large number of the poems revolve around the simpler scenes of life—the plainer characters and sentiments which in unskilful hands become hackneyed and tiresome, but which with the touch of genius gain a delicate and unforgettable radiance. There is a brooding spirit of quaintness and witchery, overlying a subtilised perception of the eternal tragedy of all things, which results in a kind of dainty pathos expressed more by a sigh than a storm of futile tears. We see this clearly in such verses as "Over the Hilltops and Far Away" and "The Tender Irish Weather".

But if pathos be one leading aspect of "Middleton" poetry, piquancy is another. French models have strongly influenced Mrs. McMullen, and a strain of Gallic verse will be found running through all her work. This is perceptible not only in the many poems like "Marie-Louise", where numerous French phrases are introduced, but in other pieces where the influence works indirectly to produce an incomparable tripping lightness—a dancing, sparking quality shewn both in the vivacious anapaestic metre and in the mercurial, whimsical imagery and handling.

Even in her most serious poetry, Mrs. McMullen never descends to mere emotional intensity—that mushy "slopping over" of the modern bard which Edward J. O'Brien denounces as a 'sterile sentimental waste'. No matter how ordinary the theme, the poet manages to view it with an original bias and describe it with a selective skill attesting to her artistic mastery. Who can forget "Desireé Logier"? And who, no matter how "fed up" on amatory effusions he may be, can deny the individual charm of "My Name"?

Another critic has spoken of the "serenity" of McMullen verse. This is only apparent. It is true that the imagery of childhood, home, and friends figures largely, but the analyst will find that these pictures are painted intelligently, and with a correct sense of proportion. There is a concomitant realisation of the limitations and insipidity of life which bursts forth meteorically now and then in such Byronic protests as "In Rein", or such fragments of despairing realism as "Behind the Swinging Door".

"Middleton" verse occupies a prominent and distinctive place in amateur literature. It represents a well-defined attitude toward life, and a highly individualised mood of aesthetic awareness. Its lyrical excellence would alone make it notable, but it has additional imaginative elements which contribute much and promise still more. It is the reflection of a rich and cultivated personality, and vibrant with the outdoor freshness of a rural May morning. Such poetry cannot help having the dual appeal of classicism and familiarity; so that we need not wonder at Mrs. McMullen's universal popularity among all classes of readers. Amateurdom is honoured in having such an artist as a member.

EDITOR'S NOTE  FP: *Wolverine* No. 12 (March 1922): 10–13 (as by "Zoilus"). An account of the poetry of Lilian Middleton. Although HPL speaks highly of her work, she never became a close colleague. The essay is a condensed version of an unpublished work, "The Poetry of Lilian Middleton" (14 January 1922; CE2). HPL's authorship of this column has been established only by internal evidence. The previous column (November 1921) was written by Alfred Galpin, as confirmed by Horace L. Lawson's comment in a letter to HPL (19 September 1921; ms., JHL): "I enclose Galpin's review of *The Wolverine*, written at your request."

# NEWS NOTES

## (May 1922)

Dr. David V. Bush, introduced to the United in 1916 by Andrew Francis Lockhart, is rejoining this year and observing the progress lately achieved. Dr. Bush is now a psychological lecturer, speaking in the largest cities of the country and drawing record-breaking crowds wherever he goes. He is the author of several published volumes of verse and prose, the latter mainly psychological in nature, and has been rewarded by phenomenally extensive sales. This year Dr. Bush has established a large psychological magazine, *Mind Power Plus*, which sells for 35 cents per copy and has already attracted a remarkable amount of favourable attention.[1]

On April 15 our dependable young member Horace L. Lawson, editor of *The Wolverine*, was united in marriage to Miss Marjorie Congdon, of Pontiac, Mich., also an amateur journalist, and President of the Michigan Amateur Journalists' Association. The United extends its heartiest felicitations upon this auspicious combination of literary forces.

Amateurdom's pleasing and perennially youthful poet, Mrs. K. Leyson Brown, is spending the summer in Massachusetts, and should during that time be addressed in care of Mrs. Harriet Vaupel, R. F. D., Pleasant St., Framingham Centre, Mass.

Mrs. Haughton and other assemblers of the recent *New Member* deserve much credit for providing a sorely needed outlet for the work of the recruit. The United should have further numbers of this or an analogous publication, and it is to be hoped that such can be made feasible. The editorial note in the present issue would gain strength and pertinence if more closely connected with the subject-matter and less fertile in accidental misstatements.

Without a doubt the greatest publishing event of the season is the second number of Mrs. Sonia H. Greene's magnificent *Rainbow*. It is difficult to imagine either mechanical lavishness or excellence of contents carried to a greater extreme, and the United may well be proud of having such an exponent. The editorial tone is a stimulating one, forming an influence in just the proper direction at this trying juncture of amateur history. A special word is due the excellent portraits of eminent amateurs, among which is the first likeness of our poet-laureate, Mrs. S. Lilian McMullen (Lilian Middleton) ever published in Amateur Journalism. Amateurs failing to receive *The Rainbow* are urged to notify the editor at 259 Parkside Ave., Brooklyn, N. Y.

EDITOR'S NOTE FP: *United Amateur* 21, No. 5 (May 1922): 55–56 (unsigned). A brief column discussing David Van Bush, Sonia H. Greene, and others.

*Notes*

1. HPL wrote an article, "East and West Harvard Conservatism," for some unidentified issue of *Mind Power Plus*. See CE5.

# [LETTER TO THE N.A.P.A.]

November 30, 1922

Board of Executive Judges,
National Amateur Press Association,
Mrs. E. D. Houtain, Chairman,

Dear Mrs. Houtain:—

I am in receipt of your communication of the 27th inst., notifying me of the Board's appointment of myself as President of the National Amateur Press Association.

In reply I take pleasure in giving my acceptance, with the assurance that no matter how inadequate my efforts may seem, I shall at all times endeavour to discharge my duties to the satisfaction of the membership and the best interests of amateur journalism.

Appreciating the Board's confidence in my qualifications, and its offer of administrative support, I am

Most cordially and fraternally yours,
H. P. Lovecraft

EDITOR'S NOTE FP: *National Amateur* 45, Nos. 2/3 (November [1922]–January 1923): 6. HPL officially accepts his appointment as interim president of the NAPA for the duration of the 1922–23 term, upon the resignation of William J. Dowdell. Truman J. Spencer, in his *History of Amateur Journalism* (New York: The Fossils, 1957), reports that Dowdell resigned because of "changes in his business life" (p. 70), but HPL's remark in a letter that Dowdell "ran off with a chorus girl in 1922" (HPL to Lillian D. Clark, 27 July 1925; ms., JHL) may have had something to do with the matter. Rheinhart Kleiner notes that "The amateur world rocked with the sensation when Lovecraft's name was announced as that of the new president" ("Howard Phillips Lovecraft," *Californian* 5, No. 1 [Summer 1937]: 6), given his well-known allegiance to the UAPA.

---

# PRESIDENT'S MESSAGE

*(November 1922–January 1923)*

January 11, 1923

To the Officers and Members of the National Amateur Press Association:—

In assuming the office to which I have recently been appointed, it would perhaps be superfluous to remark that I shall do my utmost to discharge the duties and meet the responsibilities assigned me. Entering at a discouragingly low tide of interest, activity, and administrative efficiency, it will be my endeavour both to put in motion the clogged official machinery and to arouse some measure of that literary and publishing vitality which best justifies the existence of amateur journalism. Too much time has been lost to ensure perfect success, but concerted action by all the membership will accomplish much toward the needed restoration.

## Officers

Public thanks are due our Official Editor, Mr. Harry E. Martin, for his consent to continue service in his all-important capacity amidst so many obstacles. Whatever good results the coming months may bring must be attributed in a great measure to his faithful coöperation. Mr. William T. Harrington is taking steps to qualify as Treasurer and by the time this is read will probably be fully installed in the office to which he was elected. Meanwhile he has served ably in printing and mailing the notices of executive change. Ex-Treasurer Lawson, by retaining and administering the funds until Mr. Harrington's formal induction, has proved an appreciated benefactor.

Mr. Wesley H. Porter, because of professional editorial burdens unforeseen at the time of his election, has been obliged to resign as Secretary. It is hoped that his successor can be appointed in time for announcement elsewhere in this issue. A kindred situation exists in the case of Mr. Elgie A. Andrione, who has tendered his resignation as Second Vice-President. I have myself, in view of the executive burden, deemed it best to withdraw from the Bureau of Critics; and I am pleased to announce Chairman Loveman's appointment of Mr. Edward H. Cole in my place. No action has been taken regarding the Bureau of Publicity, since a fully working administration must necessarily precede any efforts at expansion.

## The National Amateur

An experience of nine years in amateur journalism has convinced me that the nucleus of an amateur press association is the official organ. By this animating central spark its whole activity is paced and its whole tone and atmosphere determined; so that it would be no exaggeration to call the official editor the actual head of all constructive work. Accordingly, I would select as the keynote of this entire message the one urgent and earnest plea—support *The National Amateur*. Fortunately, a constitutional amendment permits more liberal appropriations for the organ than have hitherto been allowed; and I hope that all the members will rise to the occasion by contributing as much as their purse and judgment may dictate. Contributions may be sent to me, and I will in later messages include reports as custodian of the fund. At present I may report donations of $2 from Mr. Leonard A. Merritt, $5 from Mr. and Mrs. H. L. Lawson, and $10 from myself; besides the pledge here listed:

| | |
|---|---|
| Harry E. Martin | $30 |
| William Dowdell | 25 |
| Mr. and Mrs. G. J. Houtain | 15 |
| Howard Jeffreys | 8 |
| William R. Murphy | 5 |
| Harry R. Marlow | 10 |
| W. Alvin Cook | 1 |
| Dr. Edwin B. Swift | 1 |
| Orvan T. G. Martin | 1 |
| Edward F. Suhre | 1 |

The payment of these pledges within a reasonable time may be depended upon.

*The National Amateur* for July, 1922, is still in type and will be issued as soon as possible by Mr. Dowdell, it having been decided that a normal number this year is more needed than a de luxe brochure at some future time, as planned last September.

### Publishing Activity

Next to my plea for a well-financed official organ, I would place an appeal for as many individual papers as the membership can possibly publish. There can be no genuine and sustained amateur enthusiasm without such channels of universal communication as a vigorous amateur press provides, especially when a period of unusual lethargy and misdirected energy looms behind as an added handicap. Therefore, it seems clear that if we ever intend to issue papers, now is the urgent time. I shall strive to set an acceptable example with *The Conservative*, and am greatly encouraged by the similar promises which appear from many sources. It is less difficult than formerly to secure printing at reasonable rates, and prospective publishers might advantageously consult such printer-members as Charles A. A. Parker, William B. Tracy, Howard Jeffreys, and W. W. Burton. Those who possess presses should use them now if ever, taking as an example the titanic amateur devotion of our beloved veteran C. W. Smith, who is continuing to issue his indispensable *Tryout* though forced to house his press in a cramped and sand-choked cellar.

Hints of a renaissance are conveyed by some of the current publishing prognostications. The Hub Club, through Editor Sandusky, will issue a *Quill*, while a coöperative journal is planned by Mrs. Miniter. Mr. Paul Livingston Keil has an illustrated paper in press and First Vice-President Townsend will continue ably with his *Oracle*. More *Coyotes* are to be expected from Treasurer Harrington, nor will Mr. Lawson's *Wolverine* be either less frequent or less excellent. Rumours of a *Liberal* from Mr. Paul J.

Campbell, of *The Scribbler* from Cleveland, of a new paper from Mr. Michael White, of a coöperative paper from Mesdames Hazel P. Adams and Ethel M. J. Myers, and of a club paper from the new Gotham Club, are all received with keen pleasure. Meanwhile the faithful *Brooklynite* and *Scot* continue to teach us lessons in unremitting effort.

Coöperative publishing should be considered by all who cannot bear the burden of an individual paper. The expense is relatively small, yet the results are surprisingly gratifying. Those now interested should consult with Mrs. Miniter who is at present planning a coöperative paper. At a later date I hope to undertake the issuance of a *National Co-operative*, like my *United Co-operative* of former years.

## General Activity

Just as the sole justification of amateurdom is an amateur press, so is the sole justification of an amateur press a suitable amateur literature. It is, therefore, urged upon all our author-members to see that no editor remains unsupplied with literary matter of merit. Particularly to be desired is that vital material forming the sincere and original self-expression of vigorous personalities; prose and verse written because it cannot help being written, rather than mechanical efforts to repeat hackneyed patterns for the sake of having something to sign. Truly creative work of the sort desired is the most effective stimulant of that intelligent discussion and comprehensive criticism which should form the life of an amateur press association. Members will contribute much to our cause by noting and criticising the outstanding literary products of the current amateur journals; commenting in print when possible, or in any case writing to the authors and editors in question. Such exchange of ideas often gives rise to the most interesting debates and intellectual diversions, things which not only serve amateurdom and the National, but which give to the participants an unexampled pleasure and inspiration for renewed effort. Sincere thanks are due those who have, by pledges of support to the reconstructive plans of the new administration, signified their willingness to engage in these fundamental and essential activities. A gratifying state of mental alertness among us is shewn by the outside achievements of many of our members; among which we may mention the books published and in preparation by Samuel Loveman, the new patriotic magazine *Citizen Sovereignty* edited by James F. Morton, Jr., the highly successful stories of J. Bernard Lynch in the *Boston Sunday Post*, the interesting magazine articles by Luella H. Belden, the increasingly featured verse of Rheinhart Kleiner, the fantastic prose-poetry of Frank Belknap Long, Jr., and the countless other examples of like import.

## Criticism

There is in my mind no doubt but that informal criticism is the most important function of amateur journalism; hence I would urge the members to take the fullest possible advantage of the private revision, advice, and correction offered by the Bureau of Critics. This service of the National has been sadly neglected, probably because it is a growth of custom not mentioned in the constitution. The literary aspirant should feel that he has at his disposal a source of instruction which will never neglect his particular needs and should frequently send his cruder products for constructive and analytical criticism by the chairman or other members of the Bureau. At the same time, the more proficient members are requested to serve as volunteer auxiliaries in the work of private criticism, sending their names to Chairman Loveman and indicating the quantity and nature of the revision they feel best able to undertake. Those who cherish the National Association as oldest of its kind should not allow a continuance of the recent complaints that it fails in performing its primary function—the development of the novice.

## Goals and Policies

In sharing an effort to lift the National from its present stagnation, I am acutely aware that opinions differ widely as to the proper sphere of the organisation. There are those who wish to preserve exactly the atmosphere of the founders, laying principal stress upon the mechanical exercise of typography and the wit-sharpening regimen of political manoeuvring. Such conservatives are to be respected, though I cannot help feeling that the social changes of the period have largely removed the needs and conditions which created and sustained the Association in that special form. That state of things postulated a wholly youthful membership with mainly practical ambitions, and it can hardly be denied that the present age has given such youngsters too many alternative activities to leave a clear field for amateurdom as then conceived. Much more effective and desirable, as I view it, is the later conception developed by experience and exemplified in the golden age of the 'eighties and 'nineties, whereby literary advancement and liberal culture through mutual aid were recognised as paramount.

Since about 1885, it has apparently been the National's policy to combine the original with the newer conception in proportion varying with the nature of the administration in power. Such, no doubt, will be indefinitely the case; and I shall not seek to meddle with custom beyond expressing my opinion that the future would be the brighter for a decided stand on the side of literature.

What has brought the Association to its present plight is a flagrant disregard of its highest objects and an almost criminal cultivation of false standards whereby the empty tinsel of official position was deified into the glittering goal of a hundred greedy and shameless scrambles. It is only with profound humiliation that we can survey recent activities—activities in which every proper value has been subordinated to a brazen exaltation of vulgar personal publicity.

We will, no doubt, continue to be told that a middle course is soundest; and the mechanical, social, and political elements must of historical necessity accompany the literary element. This is perhaps true to a certain extent, but I cannot repress the conviction that our greatest prosperity, usefulness, and enjoyment will not arrive till we shall have inclined toward that literary and educational field where we are really unique, and shall have recognised that our genuine honours are those not of the presidency but of the laureateship or critical chairmanship.

## Clubs

An increase in local club activity augurs well for our general reconstruction. I have been privileged to see for myself the vigorous advance of the Hub and Blue Pencil Clubs, and I am informed encouragingly of the new Gotham Club of New York City and the sturdy organisation of Akron. Word, moreover, reaches me that a new and substantial Cleveland club has been organised under the brilliant leadership of Messrs. Loveman, Martin, and Carroll, the latter a new member of the Association, thus indicating a successful convention next July. Papers from all these societies would do much to promote the National's welfare.

## Vitality

The success of the year depends on a general acceleration of all these currents whose flow has recently been so sluggish. Let us read more books of provocative originality, whether classics that are always fresh or modern products which challenge accepted standards, that we may have a greater and more insistent spur to authentic, dynamic expression. What sort of a torpor does it argue, when amateurdom crawls placidly on with apparently unshaken faith in Longfellow, Tennyson, and the other bourgeois idols, at a time when Ben Hecht, James Joyce, James Branch Cabell, T. S. Eliot, and their fellows are besieging the very citadel of orthodox aesthetics? We must raise the blinds. How can we be active and write if we fail to read and think? Subject-matter is what we need; subject-matter so vital that we cannot possibly keep silent about it! And having read, reflected, and written, we must see that our matter is published, criticised, and discussed; see that it reaches the Second Vice-President or some editor for placement, the First Vice-President for laureateship entry, and the Bureau of Critics for review. Let us resolve that whenever we feel tempted to write an insipid personal paragraph or perpetrate a wearisome reminiscence of some gathering which has no possible interest or significance, we will instead read a significant book, poem, or article until a real theme presses within us for utterance. That is the secret of the flaming spontaneity which is art. Nor should we forget that in order to materialise our world of heightened cerebral life, we must liberally support a good-sized official organ and a flourishing array of individual and coöperative papers.

## Recruiting

The subject of recruiting and publicity is one which can be appreciated only at a later stage. Be it now sufficient to say that I hope to see a very limited campaign for members, and one centreing in novices of high-school age whose principal interest is literature rather than politics, radio, stamp-collecting, or making money by mail. We need offer no affront to the practical type when we say that the aesthete is the type most in need of what we have to offer, and the type which we are least liable to acquire without particular solicitation.

Appreciating to the utmost the generous support so spontaneously accorded me since my appointment, I am

Most faithfully yours,
H. P. LOVECRAFT, President

## Addition to the President's Message

I am pleased to announce that Miss Juliette Haas of Brooklyn has accepted the Secretaryship, and that Mr. W. T. Harrington, R. F. D. 4, Box 72, Vermillion, S. D., has qualified as Treasurer, and dues should be sent to him promptly.

EDITOR'S NOTE FP: *National Amateur* 45, Nos. 2/3 (November [1922]–January 1923): 1–3. An exhaustive summary of the current state of the NAPA and a plea for renewed amateur activity. HPL's devotion to the amateur cause is indicated by his contribution of $10 to the NAPA's fund to publish the National Amateur, a prodigally generous donation given his chronic poverty.

## PRESIDENT'S MESSAGE

*(March 1923)*

Providence, R. I.
March 7, 1923

To Officers and Members of
The National Amateur Press Association:—
Considering the obstacles created by the inactive months preceding, we may reasonably take some satisfaction in the National's progress since the writing of the January message. A certain amount of interest has been awakened, literary discussion is on the increase, and a full official board has been successfully been assembled. It is to be hoped that by July we shall have achieved a momentum sufficient to give the new administration an auspicious start.

### Officers

Mr. Harrington has now fully qualified as Treasurer, and is actively discharging the functions of his office. Miss Juliette Haas, originally Historian, has accepted appointment as Secretary, and is prepared to receive applications or furnish blanks. To fill the Historianship thus vacated, it is a pleasure to announce the appointment of Mrs. Edith Miniter, whose long amateur experience and extensive literary background will ensure a record free from trivialities and offensive personalities. Mrs. Mary A. Kennedy of Allston has consented to act as Second Vice-President, while as Secretary of Publicity we have that proved master in his field, Mr. William Dowdell, whose former publicity work speaks volumes for what he will accomplish now that he is again able to offer active service.

Mr. Dowdell, acutely realising the present associational crisis, asks no funds whatever; but will generously act as a self-financed committee of one. Before July he will issue not only the final number of his official organ volume, but an individual *Bearcat* or *Cleveland Sun* as well. He is now general press representative for William J. Vail, owner of numerous theatres in the middle west and four travelling productions and chairman of the Publicity Committee of the Ohio Constitutional League.

### The Official Organ

Mr. Martin's excellent November–January *National Amateur* may be regarded as a harbinger of still better issues to come, if the members will conscientiously see that the fund is kept at a suitable level. Responses to the mimeographed appeal have been gradual, but sufficient to relieve the acutest phases of the situation. If those who have not already contributed will now do so, we shall be able to complete the year with a volume of creditable size. Contributions since the last report are, besides Editor Martin's payment of $23 on the September issue, as follows:

| | |
|---|---:|
| Mr. and Mrs. G. J. Houtain | $15.00 |
| Horace Freeman | 5.00 |
| Nelson Glazier Morton | 5.00 |
| Albert A. Sandusky | 5.00 |
| Howard Jeffreys | 5.00 |
| Harry E. Martin | 5.00 |
| Mrs. Hazel P. Adams | 2.00 |
| Louis J. Cohen | 1.00 |
| Wheeler Dryden | 1.00 |
| Ella A. Merritt | 1.00 |
| Mary Morgan Ware | 1.00 |

To all these generous donors the Association extends its deepest gratitude.
Pledges or parts of pledges still unpaid are as follows:

| | |
|---|---:|
| William Dowdell | $25.00 |
| Harry R. Marlow | 10.00 |
| Howard Jeffreys | 3.00 |
| William R. Murphy | 5.00 |
| W. Alvin Cook | 1.00 |
| Orvan T. G. Martin | 1.00 |
| Edward F. Suhre | 1.00 |
| Edwin B. Swift | 1.00 |

Besides these sums actually pledged, which we are certain of securing, many other contributions have been promised informally by various members.

### Laureateships

Announcement of the laureate judges must be postponed till the next message. Meanwhile attention is called to the alarmingly small number of entries in all the classes, a condition which in some cases may actually prevent award. Insufficient publishing media may be taken as one major cause for this deficiency, and we hope that all our editors will realise their duty in the matter of providing space for those writers who desire to compete. Closest coöperation with First Vice-President Townsend is essential if we are to make a good record in this important branch of our activities. Any appeals which he may issue should be heeded with the greatest alacrity and seriousness.

### The Convention

The vigorously reorganised Scribblers are working hard toward the success of the coming convention, which will be held in Cleveland on July 2, 3, 4, and 5.

As members of the Convention Reception Committee the following capable amateurs have been appointed: William Dowdell, Samuel Loveman, Alfred Fingulin, Richard R. Kevern, George Kirk, and Charles G. Kidney. Mr. Dowdell will serve as chairman, and our members may justly look forward to a gathering of ample size and inspiring quality. As Custodian of Ballots, Mrs. Amanda E. Thrift has been appointed.

## Publishing Activity

The present and the predicted future, though by no means all that could be desired, nevertheless denote a definite emergence from the recent total stagnation of publishing activity. *The Hub Club Quill, The Alabama Amateur,* and the January *Brooklynite* have duly appeared; and all promise superior issues to come. As an illustration of what really enthusiastic amateurs can do even when without facilities for a printed journal, we have the piquant *Dubuque Amateur* of Messrs. Cohen and Klinker, prepared on the typewriter with a maximum of carbon copies. This sheet deserves to be remembered and emulated by others who have something to say yet feel unequal to a more elaborate effort; for a similar process could be used in conducting many a literary discussion among members. Such discussions are now forestalled or checked by the sheer inability of the parties to get their arguments before the amateur public. Hard as it may seem to that elder generation bred in the tradition of fine typographical handicraft, the present amateur age demands first of all ideas; and no mechanical medium should be considered too humble or inappropriate for their conveyance. If you have anything to say, say it; and never mind how! At the same time, our artistic printers are urged to maintain the highest possible standards, since we cannot afford to slight any form of beauty. Among the papers to come are those forecast in January, plus an individual venture from Miss Edna Hyde and a coöperative product of the entire Merritt-Dench clan, from Mr. Leonard Merritt down to the bungalow cat at Sheepshead Bay. To stimulate still more publishing, which we need so desperately, Mrs. Hazel Pratt Adams has unselfishly offered to assume complete charge of the issuance of any paper which any member may care to publish, attending in full to the arrangement, printing, addressing, and mailing, at a charge of only $20 for eight pages or $12.50 for four pages the size of the recent *Brooklynite*. This opportunity is so marvellously favourable, and so easy for even the newcomer, that we see no excuse for the lack of a striking revival of individual publishing.

## General Activity

Much encouragement may be derived from the apparently genuine shift of interest toward those aesthetic and intellectual matters which form the legitimate province of amateurdom. Papers like *The Wolverine* and *The Oracle* promote this healthy development in a manner reflecting much credit upon their editors; and their far-reaching influence for good is now strikingly shewn by the rapidly ramifying literary controversy precipitated by an *Oracle* critique, and probably destined to culminate in a thorough comparative explosion of the conventionally English and the freely universal artistic traditions. Additional impetus to the upward movement will be furnished by Mr. Campbell's *Liberal*, now well under way, and containing an immensely valuable continuation of the "Experience Meeting" feature, which has already been so notable.

Important above all else in rebuilding amateurdom is the thorough inculcation of the principle of expression for its own sake. Now and then we hear of persons or groups who could be active but who refrain because such and such an official or administration is in power. This is sheer childish sulking, and is based upon a theory of amateurdom so puerile that it is almost absurd to discuss it seriously. The real amateur is not active for the sake of promoting somebody's administration or rewarding this or that flatterer, nor is he inactive to punish certain enemies or harm certain victims. The activity of the true devotee is based solely on his mind; he is active when he has something to say and the time to say it, and inactive only when one or both of these elements may be absent. It does not matter who the political officers of the Association are, so long as they perform their mechanical functions with reasonable fidelity. The president is an office-boy or man-of-all-work, and the official editor is a drudging Atlas who bears a world of care with very little glamour or reward. What does matter is the general intellectual life as carried on by the rank and file of the members independently of the political scaffolding; a life which depends on individual papers, correspondence, and discussions, and which should not be affected in the least by the annual changes of routine officials.

The inactivity of last autumn, caused by a non-functioning board, bespeaks a dependence which ought to be remedied as soon as possible. Allied to this need for intellectual independence is the need for drastic extirpation of pernicious personalism. It is time we served notice on the sordid and worldly-minded that, if they will not leave amateurdom, they must at least keep their vulgar and trivial quarrels out of it. Some weeks ago a member expressed apprehension lest some official appointee attack him under cover of a business report. He was assured that personal satire of this kind would, under this administration, meet first with merciless censorship and next with instant removal of the offender. The present executive will do his best to spread a custom which he has always been careful to observe—that of tearing in small pieces any paper of personal or political gossip and slander as soon as its nature is revealed by the opening paragraphs. Fortunately, recent months have furnished practically nothing which demands this Spartan treatment; and it is to be hoped that the eradication will prove complete and permanent. There are other spheres than amateurdom for the cult of intrigue, vindictiveness, and ethical espionage. All we are interested in is literary expression, and interfering influences must be vigorously excluded if our institution is to amount to anything.

In outside activities our members have continued to distinguish themselves. Mr. Wheeler Dryden is co-author of "Suspicion", a drama of more than ordinary success in which he has also been acting, while Mr. Frank Belknap Long, Jr., has sold an important poem besides winning special honourable mention in the *New York Globe's* prize contest with his lines "Exotic Quest".[1] Mr. J. Bernard Lynch has had much work syndicated recently, and the letters of Messrs. A. M. Adams and James F. Morton, Jr., frequently delight the readers of the *New York Tribune*. Mr. James Larkin Pearson has founded a new magazine of wide appeal, and recently issued a brief but fascinating autobiography in pamphlet form.

## Criticism

How many of the members have awakened to the need and paramount value of our critical department? It is to be hoped that no aspirant has failed to submit his work to

Chairman Loveman, and that no literary expert has shirked the duty of undertaking some share of the private criticism or revision. If in any case delay has been unavoidable, now is the time to awaken and to coöperate in the year's programme. Address Mr. Samuel Loveman, 1537 East 93rd Street, Suite 2, Cleveland, Ohio. The public work of the Bureau of Critics has been admirable and every member should honour the example set by Mr. Edward H. Cole, who contributed 3000 words while suffering from painful illness.

## Recruiting

Secretary of Publicity Dowdell is now ready for business, and should be sent not fewer than 25 copies of each new paper published. We should also be alert in sending him the names of all possible recruits for the National, keeping in mind that the qualities in demand are real intellectual brilliancy and a sincere literary aspiration of the disinterestedly artistic rather than the professionally journalistic sort. We want more Lovemans, Mortons, Longs, Martins, and Coles, rather than budding Hearsts, Robert W. Chamberses, or Edgar A. Guests.

Thanking the membership for its sincere and unselfish coöperation in an arduous reconstructive task, I remain

> Fraternally yours,
> H. P. LOVECRAFT,
> President

EDITOR'S NOTE FP: *National Amateur* 45, No. 4 (March 1923): 4–5. Another extensive report on current amateur activity in the NAPA.

*Notes*

1. See Long's *In Mayan Splendor* (Sauk City, WI: Arkham House, 1977), p. 65.

---

# BUREAU OF CRITICS

*(March 1923)*

## The Oracle

In the December *Oracle* Mr. Clyde G. Townsend has proved the sustained excellence of his editorial talent by providing a magazine of admirable taste and balance. Not only in the range of contributions, but in the editor's own column of pointed remarks, we find strong evidence that Mr. Townsend is becoming an amateur leader of the very first order.

Poets, as is usual in amateur journalism, are most numerously represented in the current issue. This omnipresence of the Muse is not without its mechanical reason, a restriction of space which does not permit the most advantageous development of prose forms. Could we but ensure a more voluminous amateur press, it is certain that we should have a prose literature equal in quality to our poetry.

Fred Keller Dix is a bard wholly new to our circle, and a very welcome addition if "The Nymph of the Waterfall" is typical of his work. It is true that this specimen shews many signs of immaturity, such as occasional triteness of imagery, stiltedness of language, and suggestions of tawdriness like the line, "Fair, queenly maid, attired as for a ball"; but on the whole it represents a vividness of vision and sincerity of expression which lead us to expect notable development on Mr. Dix's part.

"August 19, 1922", by Edna Hyde, is a war elegy of the sort most typical of its author. Its merit, which is great, lies in its sincerity and simplicity, qualities which give it the combined attributes of perfect form and perfect naturalness of diction.

Another war poem, yet of very different kind, is "The Last Charge", by Ada Elizabeth Fuller. Here we have a less perfect technique, as revealed in a few stanzaic irregularities and in certain unmelodious lines like "An unspoken soldier-prayer"—an anapaest where a dactyl is demanded. But such trifles sink to unimportance when we consider the quality of the whole. In conception and imagery this poem is admirably powerful and removed from the commonplace, many of the passages evoking strongly limned pictures of the most authentic artistry. The spectral atmosphere broods grimly and ghoulishly as the phantom riders gallop on under a sickly, dying moon—

> "A phantom host on a phantom charge,
>     A horrible, endless thing."

Miss Fuller is undoubtedly a poet of substantial attainments, whose work should be watched with interest.

Of the other poems it may be said that none lacks a pleasing touch of familiar sentiment, though all hint a need for escaping from the obvious and the superficial. In every case the authors shew a susceptibility to progress which opens up pleasing avenues.

Prose fiction has had exponents in this number, the longer and more ambitious being by a new author among us, Miss Eleanor B. North. "Fleur-de-Lis", the piece in question, is a smooth and excellently handled narrative, though handicapped by the artificiality and sentimentality which young writers can seldom escape. The characters and situations are of a stereotyped sort; and hardly represent the kind of fiction which a person of Miss North's ability will give us after years and wider reading have supplied a richer background.

"Abandoned", by E. Dorothy Houtain, is a clever light sketch of the "surprise" order, very short, but wholly to the point and with a decidedly ingenious and original climax. The details of language alone demand criticism, and here one might suggest that less abrupt sentences and greater grammatical symmetry would enhance the general effect.

The solitary essay is Mr. Michael White's attempt the analyse the verse of Samuel Loveman, the third article of a critical series whose earlier members were rather more successful in their estimates.[1] Against Mr. White's style there is little to be said; for it displays a clearness, fluency, and kinship to the more obvious literary tradition, which other amateur essayists would be fortunate in possessing. Where our essayist succeeds less, is in his roughshod trample over fields of imagination necessarily beyond the scope of the concrete, practical, witty, and purely physical mind; subtle and delicate regions of shadowy images and associated ideas whose romances make no dent on the case-hardened iconoclast with earth-planted feet and taste attuned to the common-sense of the superficially visible.

Mr. White is not to be censured or depreciated for an aesthetic limitation shared by critics as illustrious as the pyrotechnical H. L. Mencken. All that could reasonably be asked is that he recognise it himself, as he would the analogous phenomenon of colour-blindness or tone-deafness; and beware of the temptations which a caustic humour and love of stinging deflation are apt to supply. So frankly revealed is Mr. White's equipment, especially in his bafflement before certain Lovemanic passages not at all cryptical, his unconsciously humorous gropings for literal equivalents of intensely colourful images, and his citizenly insistence on moral purposes, Christian piety, and brotherly absorption in the commonplace "folks" just across the way, that we hardly fancy his strictures can harm a poet of Mr. Loveman's endowments. The sufferer is the icono-clast himself, who naturally would gain more power from an intense cultivation of those regions where he is perfectly at home.

Many of Mr. White's remarks are distinguished by rare shrewdness, and we cannot but agree with him in rebuking the floridness of the critical article he so violently dis-likes. The article in question did indeed shew a lamentable tendency toward "fine-writing", though that fact hardly bears on the question of Mr. Loveman's merit, which has been pretty well settled in amateurdom for the past fifteen years. It is, by the way, to the credit of Mr. White's discernment that he duly recognises the inexhaustible background and fine artistry of Loveman's verse. He may be depended upon until the elusive element of imagination creeps in to set all his sensible practicalities awry; not verse, but poetry, is his Waterloo.

Mr. White makes a highly interesting analysis of the spirit of modern poetry, though here, as elsewhere, the ultimate essence seems to prove troublesome. It would, for example, be easy to shew the inconsistency of recognising modern trends and at the same time advocating a homely purposefulness and condemning a 'blasphemousness', which involve conceptions long ago discarded by the aesthetic pioneers of today. But such hyper-criticism would be largely futile, and would tend to minimise the many genuine merits of Mr. Michael White's review. For after all, our essayist has given us exactly what we need at this stage of amateur affairs, clear and coherent utterance of purely literary nature, enriched with commendable scholarship and certain to provoke a wide and spirited discussion of artistic fundamentals.

EDITOR'S NOTE FP: *National Amateur* 45, No. 4 (March 1923): 1–3 (signed "Contributed"). Although Samuel Loveman was chairman of the Bureau of Critics, internal evidence sug-gests that HPL wrote this segment. HPL devotes much of the column to a somewhat super-cilious criticism of Michael White's censorious article on Samuel Loveman, a topic to which he would return in an untitled note in the last issue of the *Conservative* (see CE2).

*Notes*

1. Michael White, "Poets of Amateur Journalism: III. The Poetry of Samuel Loveman," *Oracle* 3, No. 4 (December 1922): 12–17. See further HPL's "In the Editor's Study" (*Con-servative*, July 1923; CE2).

## RURSUS ADSUMUS

Again the dispensations of fortune permit The Conservative to appear before the public in wonted guise; mellowed perhaps by the passing of time, yet in essence as unchanged as his title would indicate. In the world around, the spectator beholds a multitude of mutations; as younger minds arise to impugn the values and discard the manners of former days. With such bold adventurers The Conservative will contend less bitterly than of yore, for with age he hath grown mindful of the spirit of originality; yet for himself he will crave the reciprocal indulgence of his juniors, and assert on their own ground of individuality the right to cling to his accustom'd periwig and small-clothes. Whilst they, in hectic style, dissect the smallest particles of thought and invade the remotest recesses of consciousness; it may perhaps be permitted to an old gentleman to view the world as a natural whole without the microscope of modernity, and to express himself in a fashion which, if stilted, is scarce more so than the fashions of youth with their misused words and pertly artificial affectations.

EDITOR'S NOTE  FP: *Conservative* No. 12 (March 1923): 5 (unsigned). Part of the "In the Editor's Study" column. HPL announces the resumption of the *Conservative* after nearly a four-year hiatus. The rest of the column is HPL's celebrated condemnation of T. S. Eliot's *The Waste Land*, titled "Rudis Indigestaque Moles" (see CE2).

## THE VIVISECTOR

*(Spring 1923)*

Among the most pleasing and versatile masters of light verse who have graced amateur journalism in recent years, is the favourite bard of the Blue Pencil Club, Reinhart Kleiner. Mr. Kleiner's verse is marked by a sureness of technique and a daintiness of touch distinctly his own. Never startling or garish, content with the use of a few simple metres and with no temptation to emulate the eccentricities or even the legitimate experiments of the *vers librists* whose vogue is already passing, avoiding the expression of the tenser emotional attitudes, it never lapses into prosaicism or banality. Least of all is Mr. Kleiner ever inclined to be didactic. He has no sense of an urgent mission, no vast moral or religious lesson to convey to his readers. While fully capable of appreciating all types of poetry and all the poets who have enriched our language, he is personally ambitious of achieving excellence only in the single field of *verse de société*. Let others write to teach; he is satisfied to please, and to please worthily, by adding something to the grace and beauty of existence. In Praed and Prior, Dobson and Locker,[1] he finds precursors in one of the most charming of the many phases of poetic expression.

As may be inferred, humour in its most delicate form is seldom wanting in Mr. Kleiner's flowing measures. Sometimes, as in "Snackin' Around", it is colloquial and almost boisterous. Again, in "Dangerous Ages", it is of a subtle and evanescent order. Always it is somehow felt in the background or as a faintly sensed undercurrent, even when the theme is avowedly of a serious order, for sentiment and humour are more closely akin than is commonly realised.

Mr. Kleiner is extremely fortunate as a writer of occasional verse. Happy indeed are his intimates, who have found certain events of their lives fittingly adorned by the work of his facile pen, when loyal friendship or affection has kindled his ready imagination. "Good Wishes" and "To Charles LeRoy Adams" are examples of this phase of Mr. Kleiner's work, which will be prized as permanent treasures by those affected.

His power in the treatment of graver themes, where the imagination penetrates into the deeper realities of life, and for a moment the smiling humour of his more frequent moods is forgotten, is the mark of the genuine poet. It evidences the fact that his usual choice of subject is not due to mental triviality or to a Muse capable of inspiring him only in the minor aspects of life, but is self-imposed and deliberate. His laureate poems, "Evening Prayers" and "A Mother's Song", the last named being declared by himself to be his own favourite and that by which he would rather be judged than by any other, are assuredly authentic poetry of no mean order. Nor do they stand alone. Underneath his light moods there always broods a spirit of profound emotion, which at times insists on coming to the surface. It may be predicted that in spite of himself Mr. Kleiner will in the years to come find the urge to the production of lyrics of an intenser type growing more surely irresistible.

In his present phase, however, his main delight is in toying with the lighter moods of life, and bringing to our overtense lives the relief of which none can doubt the need. It is no unworthy mission to teach us to relax our minds, and to taste the exquisite charm of entering into the play of a gifted fancy and a fine imagination. He brings the spirit of beauty into the field of common life; and those gifted children of song who thus lighten the daily burden render a service incalculably great. Mr. Kleiner's dainty love-lyrics, infinitely varied in picture and in melody, add greatly to the charm of our recent amateur literature. We shall continue to prize Mr. Kleiner as a poet dear alike to poets and to the common reader, even if his work shews little change from that which he has already achieved. Yet we cannot help feeling and hoping that still more is to follow, and that so indubitable a talent will in the future unfold itself along even broader lines.

EDITOR'S NOTE  FP: *Wolverine* No. 14 (Spring 1923): [11–13] (as by "Zoilus"). The last "Vivisector" column. HPL's authorship has been determined by internal evidence. HPL writes a genial account of the poetry of Rheinhart Kleiner. About this time he also wrote a poetic tribute, "To Rheinhart Kleiner, Esq., upon His Town Fables and Elegies" (*Tryout*, April 1923; AT 151–53).

*Notes*

1. HPL refers to the British poets Winthrop Mackworth Praed (1802–1839), Matthew Prior (1664–1721), Austin Dobson (1890–1921), and Frederick Locker-Lampson (1821–1895). He owned works by Prior (*LL* 707), Dobson (*LL* 254), and Locker-Lampson (*LL* 540–41).

# PRESIDENT'S MESSAGE

*(May 1923)*

Providence, R.I.

May 3, 1923

To the Officers and Members of the National Amateur Press Association:—

It is a pleasure to record the steady growth of activity in the Association which the past two months have revealed. Gradual though the progress has been, the actuality and solidity of the revival are no less manifest; so that we may now look ahead with a genuine optimism hardly possible a half-year ago.

## Officers

The only official change since March is the regretted but unavoidable resignation of our Recorder, Mr. Arthur Kline, whose outside work made amateur service impossible. In his stead has been appointed Mr. Rowan R. White of Warren, Ohio, former Boy Scout Representative, an enthusiastic member who needs no introduction. Mr. White is now busy determining the activity of our voting public, and it is to be hoped that all the membership may display some token of creative existence for inclusion in his report.

## The Official Organ

The March *National Amateur* brilliantly justified our confidence in Editor Martin and gives us high hopes for May and July. At the same time, meagre finances kept the size much below the desired level. Additional fund contributions are imperative if quantity is to be in any way commensurate with quality, and we trust that the remaining months of the fiscal year may shew a reascending donation curve. In recording past contributions and pledges, the administration owes apologies to several members who made cash payments at the New York convention, but who have hitherto been set down as merely pledged. This matter has now been straightened out through the efforts of several interested parties, so that the following record of donations either previously overlooked or made since the March report is probably correct in all details:

| | |
|---|---:|
| Harry R. Marlow | $10.00 |
| William G. Snow | 10.00 |
| W. Alvin Cook | 7.00 |
| Sonia H. Greene | 7.00 |
| Edward H. Cole | 5.00 |
| William R. Murphy | 5.00 |
| Anonymous | 2.00 |
| Orvan T. G. Martin | 1.00 |
| Edward F. Suhre | 1.00 |
| Edwin B. Swift | 1.00 |

The amount of the overlooked contributions, those of Messrs. Murphy, Martin, Swift, and Suhre, and $1 of Mr. Cook's contribution, will have been turned over to the fund by the time this record appears. In expressing gratitude for the generosity of the several donors, a particularly large share should be allotted to Mr. W. G. Snow, President of the Fossils, whose ample gift testifies not only his individual liberality but the increasing good will of his society as well. Improved relations with this organised body of amateurs of the past are much to be desired and will probably be achieved through better mutual understanding.

Pledges still unpaid at the date of writing are as follows:

William Dowdell ........................................................................ $25.00
Howard Jeffreys ............................................................................. 3.00

Early receipts will facilitate a successful completion of the year.

## Laureateships

The following judges of Laureate Awards, men eminently qualified in their respective provinces, have been appointed for the present year: Poetry, Nixon Waterman, celebrated New England poet and "colyumnist" of the *Boston Traveller*; Story, Herman Landon, master of plot, author of successful mystery and detective tales, and official of the Writers, New York's congenial band of professional litterateurs; Essay, Chester Noyes Greenough, Professor of English, Harvard University; History, C. A. A. Parker, leading amateur and student of N.A.P.A. history.[1] Every effort will be made to ensure proper awards by prolonging the period of permissible entry as much as possible, in order to accommodate those whose productions have been kept from print through the dearth of amateur papers. In return, we urge the members to do their part in freely entering their work, as recently requested by First Vice-President Townsend in the letter he so generously issued.

## The Convention

The gathering at Cleveland, sponsored by an active local group, and further supported by enthusiastic clubs in neighbouring cities, promises to be an exceedingly brilliant affair; and wide attendance is advised. Among the delegates will be amateurs as famous as Maurice Winter Moe, who has just rejoined the National, and Albert A. Sandusky, whose linguistic originality and super-Sheridanesque repartee are the pride of one or more hemispheres.

## Publishing Activity

Nothing could be more encouraging for amateurdom than the recent increase in papers, both individual and coöperative. Let it but continue, and the institution will find itself once more on its feet in a definite way. Special notice is due the sumptuous, brilliant, and delightfully unexpected *Dennisonian*, which marks the return to activity of Mrs. Harriet Caryl Cox Dennis, a dominant figure in the National during the later 'eighties and the 'nineties. This felicitous reawakening of the faithful should serve as an example to scores of other old-time leaders who, if they but knew it, would still find in their youthful hobby a diversion and intellectual outlet not unworthy of their tastes and powers. What would we not give to restore to our firmament such orbs as Ernest A. Edkins and his contemporaries, many of whom are yet physically and aesthetically among the living?

Other new papers of interest are Mrs. Adams' recent ventures, *The Hazel Nut* and *The Old Timer*, Mr. Harrington's *Coyote*, Mr. Townsend's March *Oracle*, and the splendid new official organs of the Gotham, the Hub, and the Scribblers clubs. Among prospective papers are a Dowdell paper, Mr. Parker's *L'Alouette*, Mr. Lawson's *Wolverine*, another *Conservative*, a June *Clevelander*, and many items predicted in previous reports. Again we urge all the members to publish to the very fullest extent of their capacity, lest the present revival lose its momentum.

## General Activity

Certain contemporary tendencies probably mark an actual beginning of that renaissance of intelligence in amateurdom whose need is so visibly shewn by Mr. Cole in his March official criticism. It is a hopeful sign when the outstanding topic of discussion in our press is not the executive calibre of this or that individual, or the hilarity of this or that club meeting, but the basic artistic qualities of our poets and the schools they represent. The Philistine and Dadaist and all who stand between such extremes are gradually defining and comparing their positions; and the existence of such things as ideas is at least hinted at. Intelligent controversy will shortly receive a stimulus from the appearance in our microcosm of Mr. H. A. Joslen, the first thorough "young modern" we have had since the Gidlow-Mills days. This vigorous newcomer has already circulated his journal, *The Gipsy*, among a few Nationalites.

Recent outside activities of our members are eminently deserving of mention. Besides his regular editorial duties, James F. Morton, Jr., has just finished the editing and publishing of a full-size book; the complete poetical works of the venerable amateur journalist, Jonathan E. Hoag, which contains tributes in verse and prose by many National members.[2] Samuel Loveman has nearly finished his book of critical appreciation of the late Edgar Saltus, something which should attract notice in the general literary world.[3] Arthur Goodenough is again represented in the annual "American Anthology of Newspaper Verse", this time by three selections; he frequently contributes to *The Springfield Union*, *Rutland Daily Herald*, and *Brattleboro Reformer*. John Ravenor Bullen, in the 1923 contests of the Philadelphia Society of Arts and Letters, has made a phenomenal sweep of prizes, capturing first and second awards for lyrics, second award for stories, and third award for sonnets. Rheinhart Kleiner's poem on Brooklyn, printed in *The New York Evening Post* and spontaneously reprinted by the weekly publication of the Brooklyn Chamber of Commerce as a front-page illustrated feature, has received comment in F. P. A.'s famous "Conning Tower". And Geo. Julian Houtain, after delivering an eloquent oration on "Vampires" before the Morons of Greenwich Village, gained a very laudatory illustrated writeup in *The New York World*.

## Criticism

The high quality of the current critical work, for which we are chiefly indebted to Messrs. Edward H. Cole and Samuel Loveman, scarcely needs mention or demonstration; and it is especially gratifying to learn that many members have awakened to the true nature, objects, and advantages of amateurdom sufficiently to send their manu-scripts to Chairman Loveman for private criticism. What is now the prime desideratum is that a corresponding proportion of literarily proficient members volunteer their criti-cal and revising services to supplement the Lovemanic labours. Had we a selective ser-vice act, it is probable that quasi-pedagogical demands of this sort would be made on such capable figures as Rheinhart Kleiner, Maurice W. Moe, James and Nelson Mor-ton, John Ravenor Bullen, Frank Belknap Long, Jr., Edith Miniter, W. R. Murphy, George Kirk, or W. Paul Cook. Lacking that high-handed authority, we must be con-tent to let these potential recommendations stand as hints of greater or less subtlety.

## Clubs

The growth of local activity is one of the season's most encouraging signs; and it is only with satisfaction that we can view the revivified amateur organisations in Boston, Brooklyn, New York, Cleveland, and Akron. Still more pleasure is afforded by reports of a new club in Warren, Ohio, founded by Messrs. Rowan R. White, Fred G. Ritezell, and Harry R. Marlow. Warren will be the seat of the Memorial Day convention of the Ohio Amateur Journalists' Association.[4]

## Recruiting

If the National is to achieve a proper influx of new and vital material, Secretary of Publicity Dowdell's campaign for recruits must be backed to the limit by the member-ship. Opportunities for securing the affiliation of capable and congenial material must not be overlooked, and everyone is advised to send for a stock of blanks and booklets, which he may have on hand for immediate use whenever a person of suitable tastes and talent is encountered. Likewise, it is again urged that publishers conscientiously supply Mr. Dowdell with copies of their journals. All things considered, there is proba-bly no recruiting argument nearly so good as a prepossessing specimen paper.

But two months of the current official year now remain. We have done much to recover our flagging impetus, yet no thought of cessation should cross our minds. The precepts promulgated by Editor Martin in the March *National Amateur* are as good for next year as for this; and only by continuing to follow them can we be sure of the un-broken and spontaneous prosperity which we all desire so keenly.

Fraternally and appreciatively yours,

H. P. LOVECRAFT,
President.

EDITOR'S NOTE  FP: *National Amateur* 45, No. 5 (May 1923): 5–6. The third of HPL's re-ports during his interim presidency of the NAPA.

*Notes*

1. See n.2 to "A Voice from the Grave" (p. 423).
2. See n. 5 to "News Notes" (November 1920). Six of HPL's birthday poems to Hoag ap-peared in the volume.
3. The work was never published, although HPL continues to discuss it in letters of 1924–25.

4. See "Lovecraft's Greeting" (p. 336).

---

## LOVECRAFT'S GREETING

As President of the National Amateur Press Association to the members of the Ohio Amateur Journalists' Club in convention at Warren, Ohio, Decoration Day, 1923.

It will give me pleasure if this greeting can reach you in time for reading at your annual banquet; for, as I can honestly say without the speaker's usual insincerity, I have a particularly high regard for the amateur journalists of Ohio.

Your state has developed the greatest aesthete ever known to our hobby—Samuel Loveman, of Cleveland—and in William Dowdell of the same place has produced a publicity worker without a peer. For organised activity no other, to my knowledge, has so much to shew; since you can point to local clubs in Cleveland, Akron, Columbus, Warren, and Lorrain—the latter only just established. Ohio contains the president and official editor of the United Association—Messrs Conover and Fritter—and the gifted Official Editor of the National—Mr. Harry E. Martin. Both the *United Amateur* and *National Amateur* are published within its borders by Mr. Howard Jeffreys of Columbiana.

But I cannot attempt to catalogue all the amateur glories of Ohio—they are too numerous. I can only commend in a general way the genuine and healthy literary spirit of the state as I have found it, as attested by the contents of *The Clevelander* and the rise of such new figures as Dudley Carroll and Carroll E. Lawrence.

The past is altogether too broad a field to cover, one to which an amateur recruit of 1914—as I am—cannot do thorough justice. But here also I seem to find evidences of Ohioan eminence, for the names of Thrift, Brodie, Sinclair, and the Cincinnati circle of some thirty-five years ago are things to conjure with.

With such long-standing and well-diffused activity, it is only natural that Ohio should today have the only sectional association in existence. To this association the National extends its sincerest congratulations and good wishes, together with a hope that it may by increasing its usefulness and in a period of reconstruction serve as a model and inspiration for the foundation or revival of others of like nature in various parts of the country.

As an individual and as a representative of the National I salute you. Would that I were present that the cordiality of my words might be the more manifest.

EDITOR'S NOTE FP: *Buckeye* 3, No. 1 (June 1923): 3. A letter (dated 29 May 1923) to the Ohio Amateur Journalists' Club on the occasion of an amateur gathering there on Memorial Day.

# PRESIDENT'S MESSAGE

*(July 1923)*

Providence, R. I.
June 9, 1923.

To the Officers and Members of the
National Amateur Press Association:—

The ending of the present official year, a period so inauspiciously begun, affords us some opportunity for pride and thankfulness, for whatever we may have failed to accomplish, it is at least true that we have emerged from our nadir of depression and embarked upon a course of intellectual consciousness and increasing activity in all departments. The enduring vitality of amateur journalism has been proved, and only some unexpected disaster can check the heightened creative impulse which promises so much for the coming twelve-month!

## Officers

For all that has been administratively achieved since the reorganisation of the official board in November and the weeks following, supreme credit must go to the effective coöperation extended the executive by his associates. The presence of able minds at strategic points has obviated blunders of the grosser sort, and prevented breakdowns by a judicious distribution of burdens. No praise is too high for Editor Martin, Vice President Townsend, Secretary Haas,[1] and the active workers on the Bureau of Critics; as for those workers outside the formal board of 1922–23 who have been pillars of proved strength—Mr. Horace L. Lawson, always ready to help in tight places, and the various veterans whose advice has done much toward making the administration the smooth-running inconspicuous mechanism it should be.

## The Official Organ

Despite financial obstacles *The National Amateur* has maintained a high qualitative and quantitative standard, achieving the normal number of issues save for the one curtailment necessitated by the autumnal hiatus in activity.

Mr. Martin has performed a titanic labour in spite of many hindrances, and our sincerest gratitude is due to him and to those whose financial contributions made his work possible. Since the May list of donations one more has arrived: a generous offering of five dollars from the returning old-timer, George W. Macauley. Nearly all pledges are paid up, and to those who have been delayed in paying we would urge a payment as soon as possible to the new administration in order that the *Amateur* for 1923–24 may have a thoroughly favourable beginning.

## Laureateships

By the time these words appear, the Laureate judges will be in possession of a full quota of entries, so that complete awards may be expected. It is hoped that results may be announced at the convention, and in any case the September *National Amateur* will reveal the decisions.

## The Convention

In an eleventh-hour appeal, we again urge convention attendance upon all whose health, finances, and business may permit it. The gathering at Cleveland on July 2, 3, 4, and 5 promises to prove an event of extraordinary importance, with the local clubs of three or perhaps four Ohio cities participating virtually en masse, and with a phenomenal array of illustrious visitors from remoter spheres. The purely literary nature of Cleveland's recent activity should lend an atmosphere of charm rarely found at a wholly social gathering, while the social side itself will, of course, lack nothing in vigour and piquancy. Communications to Mr. Dowdell, the alert and capable arbiter elegantiarum, will ensure satisfactory arrangements.

## Publishing Activity

Vast encouragement is to be derived from the pleasing shower of individual and coöperative papers amidst which the official year is expiring. The majority of publishing promises now stand redeemed, while many an unannounced journal adds its inspiration.

The impressive *Dennisonian* has been quickly followed by *L'Alouette*, in which Mr. Parker and several colleagues dispense wit and wisdom; and a third *Hub Club Quill* may be in the members' hands before this message. Mr. Jeffreys' stimulating *Sketch* and a delightful new *Brooklynite* are out, and the Merritt-Dench project has materialised magnificently in *Odd Seconds*. The second *Conservative*, we hope, is also among those present.[2] Mr. Campbell's *Liberal*, always an event, once more is with us; while the July *Oracle* further stimulates genuine thought. The new *Wolverine* offers exceptional literary and critical matter, and in a briefer way Mr. Keil's *Pauke's Quill*, Mr. Labovitz's *Stick O'Type*, and Mr. Tracy's *Type Clicks* help to banish dulness and lethargy. The *Clevelander* sets a new standard in the form of a strictly literary club organ, and achieves real notability from its Lovemanic contributions. Still other papers will probably be abroad by the time these lines are read; among them a second *Clevelander*, a *Buckeye* from the Ohio Amateur Press Association, whose successful convention occurred Memorial Day, and an official organ from the newly organized club in Lorain, Ohio. For generously facilitating the publishing programme, vast credit should be accorded to Mr. Charles A. A. Parker, whose charitably low printing rates have made possible many a paper which would not otherwise have existed.

Such is our enviable impetus. It now behooves us to maintain unslackened the pace we have achieved. A few papers published at the end of a season, however desirable intrinsically, have no permanent meaning unless they signify our general determination to become and remain articulate and aesthetically alive for the sake of these qualities themselves; persevering under all conditions and through every conceivable change of political administration. The great desideratum is a sincere and spontaneous literary life utterly independent of mechanical or executive matters.

## Local Clubs

Not for many years have local club prospects seemed so bright as at present. The Hub Club, oldest of all, has achieved a new and surpassing vigour through reorganisation and now treads unaccustomed heights with its vivacious paper and elaborately planned convention.

The Blue Pencil Club in its latest organ displays a strengthened and systematic policy, and a determination to confine leadership in its unique field of intelligent and piquant relaxation and fraternal stimulus. The Scribblers of Cleveland, though founded or reincarnated only last January, are already conspicuous for the fearless singleness their devotion to strictly literary aims; while the Gotham and Rubber City clubs hold their own admirably. Especially gratifying is the report of new clubs in Warren and Lorain, Ohio, the former sponsored by Messrs. Rowan R. White, Harry R. Marlow, and Fred G. Ritezell, and the latter by Mr. Raymond Fletcher and Mr. and Mrs. F. C. Gonder. On Memorial Day was held the convention of the Ohio Amateur Press Association, our only surviving sectional organization. The success of this event convinces us that a revival of the type would work for the benefit of all amateurdom.

On considering local clubs, it strikes one as singular that only two—the Hub and Blue Pencil—should have weathered the storms of long years. It would pay the newer societies to study their secrets and follow in their footsteps rather than join the silent majority in the Valley of Nis.[3]

Especial care should be taken in the quest for new members; care that the acquisitions be not mere social friends of indeterminate tastes, but always actual literary enthusiasts whose love of aesthetics is sincere, intense, and unmixed with mediocre professional ambitions. The best pattern for a local club is the sort of circle of aesthetes found around the major book shops of our more alert cities—groups to whom beauty and ideas are the greatest interest in life.

## Criticism

There is ground for considerable satisfaction in the progress of criticism this year, especially as regards the private revision of manuscripts. Messrs. Loveman and Cole command our deepest gratitude for upholding a sound artistic standard leaning neither toward Victorian dulness and insipidity nor toward modernistic chaos and extravagance. This matter of critical standards is so liable to become an acute official issue in the near future, that we believe it ought to be thrashed out while still in the unofficial stage, as it is likely to be in the course of the controversy started by Mr. White's *Oracle* critique. The important thing is to ensure a critical bureau so impartial that no writer may find himself condemned or ridiculed merely for following a tradition at variance with that of his reviewer. Individual differences of opinion are inevitable and desirable, but we must, if possible, discourage the dogmatic arrogance which impels a critic of one particular school to judge by his own narrow values the authors who follow other schools, and to deal out supercilious censure or condescending shreds of faint praise on the puerile and grandiloquent assumption that these other schools have no background, standing, or authentic existence. Ultra-conservatives and ultra-radicals err equally in this respect; indeed, we hardly know which is the more provokingly pitiful, the unimaginative fossil who scarcely realises that William Blake, Nietzsche, Huysmans, Remy de Gourmont, and George Santayana have been born, or the feverish Freudian who speaks patronisingly of Homer and Milton, and knows Dryden only by name. Both of these extreme types must curb their personal prejudice, acknowledging on the one hand that the continuous stream of traditional art can never be despised, and on the other hand that the growth of sophistication and psychological knowledge has added to the general body of art many new and unaccustomed forms and points of view which are none the less genuine because they involve shifting values and apparently enigmatic subtleties of thought.

What we must seek to destroy is the clownish snickering of the half-educated at the products of both conservative and radical; a snickering which, if not checked, will end by discouraging all sincere artistic effort of any kind.

## Recruiting

Secretary of Publicity Dowdell is to be congratulated on what he has done in the brief time at his disposal. His successor next term should receive equal support, for a campaign once commenced possesses a momentum which should not go to waste. Recruiting should be increasingly discriminating, and credentials should be more than nominal formalities. We cannot hope for internal harmony unless we confine admission to persons in sympathy with our aims—persons truly enamoured of beauty and eager for self-expression for its own sake. In the writer's opinion, assimilation is even more valuable than acquisition; so that our very first and strongest efforts should be spent in interesting persons already on the membership list, and in introducing them to all the various phases of our work and associational life. There is really very little reason why amateurdom should consist of an active inner circle surrounded by a penumbra of transient members who never learn our inmost counsels or share our essential spirit. Another important matter is the inclusion in the National Association of many local club members who at present either fail to belong to the country-wide body or else remain as inactive "fillers" on its list. The inactivity of these persons in the National constitutes in many cases a reprehensible waste of fine material, and we would urge that the local clubs encourage their members not only to join the National but to participate to the fullest extent in its general correspondence, discussion, and publishing activities. It is unfortunate that there should be so many half-amateurs.

## General Activity

There is little reason to complain of the state of activity among our members, if achievements both inside and outside the National be reckoned. Messrs. James F. Morton and A. M. Adams continue to enrich the "colyums" of the daily press, an especially clever poem of the former's appearing in Don Marquis's "Lantern" in the *N. Y. Tribune* not long ago. Mr. Morton is also busy with scholastic lecturing. Mr. Samuel Loveman will shortly publish a book on the late Edgar Saltus, while poems of Mr. Frank Belknap Long, Jr., are due for early featuring in prominent places.[4] A highly important linking of amateur and outside literary worlds is foreshadowed by Mr. Charles

A. A. Parker's plan to issue in book form the collected works of certain amateur poets, beginning with the late Mrs. Jennie E. T. Dowe and later including such celebrated figures as Samuel Loveman, Edna Hyde, Nelson Glazier Morton, Edith Miniter, and Michael Oscar White.[5] If the consent of the authors and the coöperation of the amateur public can be secured, this design will ultimately materialise in the form of "Ye Handwerke Series"—whose archaic title is inspired by the contemplated manner of publication, hand-work on Mr. Parker's own private press. No more laudable design for the preservation and popularization of meritorious amateur verse has ever been put forward, and it is to be hoped that our authors and readers may assist Mr. Parker in this Herculean move toward an amateurdom of increased dignity and permanent value.

With such activities and prospects, the members are urged with sincerest fervour not to let the coming year witness a petering out or relapse to trivial and unliterary conditions. For the socially and commercially inclined there are plenty of congenial organizations—Elks, Rotarians, Y. M. C. A., Boy Scouts, Mutual Welfare League, and what not. Let the Babbitts seek their level. But let us keep amateur journalism attuned to that unique minority who need it most—the lonely "Lucian Taylors" of the world,[6] who possess personalities and individual minds, live rather than vegetate, thrill at beauty and shrink from tawdriness, and demand a selected fellowship because they must express themselves yet cannot among the commonplace, self-satisfied, uncomprehending bulk of mankind. These are the real amateur journalists—sensitive and artistic minds that see in the universe more than the atoms and molecules, food and clothing, dollars and cents, and patterns and platitudes of the throng. They deserve consideration because there are so few of them, and because the mediocre monotonies of the diurnal treadmill have so little to offer them. Grant them at least one haven from the maddening greyness, sameness, tameness, hypocrisy, and emptiness of the crude and futile puppet-show called life; one haven on earth *"ubi saeva indignatio ulterius cor lacerare nequit!"*[7]

It is not learning or proficiency which determines the amateur; these indeed are often the remote goals he seeks. What does determine him is the possession of a real individuality, be it cultivated or uncultivated, and this moves us to realise that the supreme banes of our circle are the obvious and the commonplace. These are the facile and insidious foes that creep unawares into our most pretentious counsels—these elusive atmospheric drugs which subtly stifle our aspirations and debase our efforts. Sometimes they masquerade as wit, sometimes as great wisdom or erudition; but always they retain the same stultifying qualities—supine acceptance of conventional externals and illusions, sottish absorption in repetitious details and meaningless practicalities, stupid and ephemeral mock-values, and a gleeful infantile exultation in the stereotyped, glamourless, and painfully predicable routine of the common, cowed, inhibition-ridden, habit-ruled multitude. In such drab Philistinism is a negation of every sincere and genuine value in life; a repudiation of every faculty which distinguishes men from one another and from the presumably lower animals. It is a servile and cowardly resignation of real humanity; a sale of each soul's individual birthright of beauty and intellect for a watery collective anaesthesia and sheep-like system of wholesale ____try[8] and rote action. What depths of mental poverty and aesthetic paralysis yawn in the simple fact that hordes of people, each supposedly endowed with individual perceptive faculties and a responsive imagination, vary not a whit in their stolid, incurious reactions to the world's wonders, and glimpse not a vision beyond the bare, material, geometrical outlines of the scene before them. One patient herd; one conglomerate mind; one universal coma! This every-day, beauty-void point of view, or absence of a point of view, is a kind of death to the individual personality. It is a darkness of mediaevalism—a repression and a resignation. Life is an escape from it, and only the real thinker or the real artist lives. Art and Thought form a sort of resurrection—a sort of glorious pagan renaissance of some half-fabulous golden antiquity of freedom, beauty, intensity, and individuality. From one grey world the artist escapes to a colourful cosmos of hundreds of brilliant worlds—for does not an awakened imagination shatter all barriers and empower the mind to shape the impressions it receives? Nor must any two artists see exactly the same kaleidoscope of worlds; for do not the sensitive fancies of men differ as much as their faces? Truly, artists exchange a hideous common sepulture in shadow through spheres irradiate and iridescent. To give such liberty and adventures to aspiring spirits capable of receiving them, modern amateur journalism exists. Can even the stoutest defender of unimaginative mediocrity tell us why the institution should be held back to accommodate bovine Philistines who do not crave these peculiar benefits? Let the National rise above the surly, dog-in-the-manger psychology whereby so many of its contemporaries have suffered wreckage at the hands of their unprogressive substrata!

## Conclusion

As the writer lays down the insignia of office after seven months' tenure, he is conscious of a vast surge of relief. The burdens have been many, but will not be regretted if they prove instrumental in redeeming and preserving amateur journalism as a genuinely artistic force. Of the gratitude owed to the many officers and members whose coöperation has been so indispensable, words cannot tell. It is possible only to hope that one's own efforts have been worthy of such valiant and generous support. Our Association's future lies with others, and to these it is a pleasure to wish success in unbounded proportions. May a creditable past of nearly half a century serve as an earnest of still brighter years to come.

Valete!

H. P. LOVECRAFT, President.

EDITOR'S NOTE FP: *National Amateur* 45, No. 6 (July 1923): 4–6. HPL's final message, although it would be followed by a summation, "The President's Annual Report" (see p. 344). Its comprehensive summary of amateur activities during the period of HPL's presidency concludes with an eloquent plea for amateur journalism as the haven for the sensitive aesthete.

*Notes*

1. The references are to Harry E. Martin, Clyde G. Townsend, and Juliette Haas.

2. HPL refers to the *Conservative* of July 1923, following the issue of March 1923. No more issues would be published.

3. HPL appears to be referring to his own story "Memory" (*United Co-operative*, June 1919), which begins: "In the valley of Nis the accursed waning moon shines thinly . . ." The phrase "the valley Nis" also appears in Poe's poem "The Valley of Unrest" (1831), ll. 7 and 15.

4. Long's poems were issued three years later as *The Man from Genoa and Other Poems* (Athol, MA: W. Paul Cook, 1926).

5. The project never materialized, although Parker did publish Edna Hyde's *From Under a Bushel: A Book of Verse* (Saugus, MA: C. A. A. Parker, 1925), with an introduction by Samuel Loveman.

6. HPL refers to the introspective hero of Arthur Machen's *The Hill of Dreams* (1923). He had read the novel around June 1923 (see *SL* 1.233).

7. "Where savage indignation can lacerate his heart no more." The epitaph on the grave of Jonathan Swift (1667–1745) in St. Patrick's, Dublin.

8. In all copies consulted, broken type has rendered this word illegible.

# [UNTITLED NOTES ON AMATEUR JOURNALISM]

Mr. Charles A. A. Parker, with characteristically sprightly wit, remarks on the loyalty shewn toward royalty in distress. At least, this is what we believe he means, although the colloquial operation of Grimm's philological law has somewhat enriddled the text. He is to be congratulated upon his able exemplification of his paragraph, as shewn by a nobly satiric scorn of all foes of the snowy Archangel Michael.

---

Mr. H. A. Joslen's *Gipsy* is an unique and by no means unwelcome addition to amateur journalism, supplying the place of the long-departed *Les Mouches Fantastiques*. In his valiant attempt to break away from mediocrity and imitative stupidity, the editor shews a healthy artistic instinct. It must now be his care to avoid the excess of sheer revolt for revolt's sake, and the vulgarity sometimes resulting from an anti-Puritanism itself Puritanical in seriousness. Beauty, lightness, delicacy, and just a touch of irony— these are the marks of a true art independent of social or ethical barnacles, and founded on a just conception of life's essential triviality and futility.

---

The appearance of a book by an amateur is always an occasion for legitimate rejoicing in our circle; and when the author can count no less than 92 years to his credit, we may be pardoned something like positive jubilation. Such is the case this month, which brings to view the complete Poetical Works of Jonathan E. Hoag, carefully edited and fittingly bound.[1] Since Mr. Hoag is still writing with undiminished fecundity, we may expect another volume from him as he becomes a centenarian.

---

Few literary recommendations are more apt than that of Mr. Edward H. Cole in the *Hub Club Quill*, whereby we are advised to read the periodical essayists of the eighteenth century. In many respects this glittering, cynical, rational period is closer to our own disillusioned time than any other; for it represents a dominant intellectualism and critical and analytical spirit exactly paralleling this era of Anatole France, Cabell, and the columnar sophisticates. Just as the post-Renaissance world as a whole is nearer classical antiquity than the Middle Ages, so is our twentieth century much nearer the eighteenth then the intervening nineteenth century. It has long been the opinion of The Conservative that the eighteenth century marked a glorious apex of many kinds of taste; notably that in prose style and in all ordinary forms of architecture, furniture, and decoration. The correctness of this view seems rather pleasingly confirmed by the return to Colonial patterns now practiced by American home-builders and city-planners, and we may hope for further confirmation in the literary field.

---

Unusual interest attaches to the prospective volume of the late Mrs. Jennie E. T. Dowe's collected Irish verse, to be issued next autumn by Mr. Charles A. A. Parker for sale at a dollar and twenty-five cents per copy.[2] It is possible that this may be the fore-runner of many similar volumes of the work of amateur poets; an event of the greatest possible benefit to amateurdom, and one which would enshrine Mr. Parker as a Prince of Pioneers.

---

A news note of more than passing amateur interest is furnished by Mr. Alfred Galpin Jun.'s receipt of a Graduate Service Scholarship in the University of Chicago, for the year 1923–24. Our erstwhile infant prodigy will not only study, but teach 80 hours per quarter; thus early arriving at an academic distinction always predicted by those who unqualifiedly consider him the greatest intellectual ever connected with amateur journalism.

---

The subtly mirthful commentator E. M., in *L'Alouette*, curiously mistakes a Swin-burnian *scream* for a *groan;* and expresses doubt as to the identity of the "Amateur Humorist" described in Frank Belknap Long's recent critical phantasy.[3] Speaking of doubt, The Conservative presumes it is Mr. White's scholarly article which E. M. means, in alluding to something whose value equals "ooOOOO" minus the rims.

EDITOR'S NOTE FP: *Conservative* No. 13 (July 1923): 24–28 (unsigned). HPL discusses the activities of various amateurs, including Jonathan E. Hoag and Edward H. Cole.

*Notes*

1. See n. 5 to "News Notes" (November 1920). No other book by Hoag ever appeared.
2. No such volume appears to have been published.
3. Frank Belknap Long, "An American Humorist," *Conservative* No. 12 (March 1923): 2–5. The article is an attack on Michael Oscar White for his criticism of Samuel Loveman's po-etry. HPL's comment relates to the conclusion of Long's piece: "When Swinburne read any-thing of that sort he emitted a low scream, and vanished."

# THE PRESIDENT'S ANNUAL REPORT

Providence, R.I.,
July 1, 1923.

To the Officers and Members of the National Amateur Press Association, Assem-bled in Cleveland, Ohio:—

The dominant sentiment which I feel at this moment is—notwithstanding my intense relief at official emancipation—one of regret at my absence from the convention. To have participated in this gathering would have culminated in ideal fashion seven months of executive effort, besides renewing for me some of the most valued ties in the amateur world; but since circumstances—which should be spelled with vertical lines through the S's—have defeated my wish, I may only report at a distance in an effort to fulfil the constitutional requirement.

My report will not be a brilliant one, because I have no brilliant achievements to record. It will not be a formally business-like one, because I am not blessed with the commercial and statistical sort of mind. All that I shall strive to do is to outline the Association's general trend, leaving details to the Recorder, Historian, and others whose province it may be to chronicle them.

Upon accepting appointment Nov. 30, 1922, I found the Association in a state of considerable disorganisation and inactivity. There existed a reaction from the preceding year of strenuousness, and the official board was handicapped by unfortunate outside distractions. At the same time stagnation was by no means absolute; the five months from July to December shewing a total of ten papers published, and $34.00 donated to the Official Organ Fund.

## Officers

The first task of the new administration was to put in order a working official board. This was not as easy as might be expected, since nearly all qualified members were retarded by some drawback or other; ill health or business, or infelicitous combinations of both. The functioning of the Treasury has suffered from the lateness of the incumbent in qualifying, and from his subsequent difficulty, on account of illness, in maintaining continuous activity. For supplementary work as acting Treasurer at various times, Mr. Horace L. Lawson deserves the unstinted thanks of all the members. Second Vice-President Elgie Andrione, Secretary Wesley H. Porter, and Recorder Arthur Kline all found it impossible to serve through the year, and have been replaced respectively by Mrs. Mary A. Kennedy, Miss Juliette M. Haas (previously Historian), and Mr. Rowan R. White. Gratitude is due these appointees for what they have accomplished, particularly Miss Haas, whose capable management of complex records doubly complex through previous chaos was a task of formidable magnitude. As an historian, after the Secretarial transfer of the original incumbent, Mrs. Edith Miniter was appointed and will shortly demonstrate her capability. As Secretary of Publicity Mr. William Dowdell is making up for unavoidable inaction which compelled him to resign the Presidency. And as a Critic, Mr. Edward H. Cole has brilliantly justified his appointment by striking the heaviest blows for an amateurdom of genuine taste and intelligence.

For the officers who continuously "carried on", no praise is too high. Mr. Harry E. Martin has met every difficulty single-handed and produced through all the turmoil of changing regimes a highly creditable *National Amateur* with only one number omitted. Mr. Clyde G. Townsend has furnished a pattern for all future Vice-Presidents to follow, publishing an enterprising paper and conducting the laureate department with almost unparalleled clearness, accuracy, and efficiency. At the head of the Bureau of Critics, Mr. Samuel Loveman has exerted a salutary influence on the whole aesthetic policy of the administration; accomplishing valuable results in private revision as well as public reviewing.

## Publications

According to the data at my immediate disposal, there have been 46 papers, representing 28 different names, since my assumption of office. Of these one is a deferred *National Amateur,* while perhaps five (four different names) are products of the present political campaign; but the general mass does much to sustain the belief that we are entering upon a spontaneous literary renaissance. The average quality is refreshingly high, and we should take particular delight in the determination of our younger editors—Messrs. Townsend, Lawson, Joslen, and others—to preserve a strictly literary policy. In our local club organs we are decidedly fortunate. The individuality of each is strongly marked—*Brooklynite* for social and associational interests, *Gothamite* for piquancy and anti-Puritanism, *Buckeye* for fraternal informality and good will, *Hub Club Quill* for maturely professional affiliations, and *Clevelander* for disinterested aesthetic endeavour. De luxe publications have been wholly absent, so that one hesitates to acclaim any single issues as notable. We need not hesitate, however, in selecting one publication as supreme in the service it does our cause through the maintenance of diffused interest and the presentation of timely news. That universal link and quaintly appealing inspiration is the faithful and modest *Tryout,* published in defiance of every obstacle which time and space, the earth or the waters thereof, may send. Long live the [one and] only C. W. Smith!

Combining data for the entire year 1922–23 we may count 56 papers, representing 31 different names.

## Finances

It is now an established fact that, at the present printing rates, no amateur press association can finance its official organ on existing dues. Consequently my first financial move as President was to appeal in a mimeographed circular for contributions to the *National Amateur* fund. Responses, while by no means approaching the level of the previous year, have been substantial; so that an official organ of reasonable size has been maintained. The total amount contributed by all donors since my appointment was $98.00, all of which has been used in printing the *National Amateur.* Counting the sums contributed during Mr. Dowdell's presidency, the fiscal year 1922–23 has brought a total of $132.00 in donations.

## Recruiting

Unquestionably the weakest spot of this administration has been in recruiting. I can find no record of an applicant before my appointment and since then the number has not been great. Technical difficulties make it impossible to secure exact figures, but I believe that up to the last advices our total of applications is 27, of which 8 are reinstatements. Much of this poor showing is due to the impossibility of securing a Secretary of Publicity until the latter part of the year, while another factor is the slowness with which many of the local clubs promote the affiliation of their personnel with the National.

## Laureateships

First Vice-President Townsend deserves exclusive personal credit for the fine array of laureate entries now in the hands of the judges. Arousing the membership with a circular appeal at a time when the contests were in the greatest peril, he has assembled about thirty competitors in the various classes, so that the general success is assured. At this writing only two verdicts have reached me. One is that of Charles A. A. Parker, Judge of Histories, who awards the Laureateship to James F. Morton, Jr., and Honourable Mention to Mrs. Edith Miniter. The other is from Prof. C. N. Greenough, Dean of Harvard University, who awards the Essay Laureateship to H. P. Lovecraft[1] with Honourable Mention to Frank Belknap Long, Jr. If any new results reach me in time, I will transmit them immediately to the convention.

## Local Clubs

The present year has been preëminently one of revival in local club activity, with several thriving new societies, some notable reincarnations, and at least one case of spectacular rebuilding and expansion. Nor has there been any essential decline in those organisations whose continuous activity is of longer standing. Among the newly founded clubs are those at Warren and Lorain, Ohio, and possibly the new Gotham Club also, since its connexion with the older body of that name is a matter of atmosphere and locale rather than personnel. Reincarnations are led by the Scribblers of Cleveland, who last January entered upon a new—and I hope a permanent—lease of life with an evident policy of pure literature for its own sake. The florescence of the Hub Club under Mr. Lynch has been striking indeed, and with its enormous membership, ample publications, semi-professional personnel, and elaborate entertainments, is now a somewhat dazzling phenomenon. Akron, we sincerely trust, is approximately normal, though *The Rubber Band* is missed of late. And the Blue Pencil Club, always distinguished for mellow friendliness and wholesome entertainment, has quite surpassed itself in clever programmes and unique pedestrian excursions. The primary aim of all these clubs should now be to assimilate their new material into the fabric of the National as a whole, rather than drift farther and farther away from organised amateurdom. Many do not need this admonition, but it is perhaps not out of place in view of the wide and regrettable tendency of local branches to become wholly absorbed in their own activities.

## Intellectual Life

I have said so much in my bi-monthly messages on the subject of purely literary amateurdom, that I doubt if any extended additional remarks are needed here. I will repeat, however, that I believe every effort should be made to keep the National to its proper goal of aesthetic and intellectual encouragement. Our primary purpose, if we are able to claim a place of unique merit in the world, must be to promote artistic self-expression for its own sake; for the moment we cater to the would-be commercial writer, or depart into the realms of the merely social, fraternal, and political, we find that we are not only deserting a field that needs us intensely, but encroaching upon domains already served by other organisations far more specialised and efficient in their respective lines.

If the present year can be looked back upon as one of literary revival, I shall not feel that I have laboured entirely without reward. Signs of such a revival have not been wanting, and it is a wholesome symptom that Mr. Michael White's practical, devout, and civic-minded criticism of Mr. Samuel Loveman's gorgeous and exquisite poetic traceries should have precipitated a spirited, widening, and increasingly impersonal aesthetic controversy which is yet in its infancy, and which bids fair to become the leading topic of conversation and debate in the amateur journals and salons of the coming year. Aided by the vigorous prodding of Mr. Edward H. Cole, ideas are coming into their own; and we may not have to endure much longer the desiccated husks of commonplaceness and conventionality which have been so annoying in the past. New writers are coming up—writers who create actual images of the beauty that haunts their minds, instead of scribbling mediocre trash for the sake of cheap praise, small change, or the sight of their own names in print.

Let us beware of discouraging them at the outset by a coarse and ill-timed ridicule or disparagement which would merely reveal our own clownishness and ignorance, and let us likewise avoid that stony silence and neglect whose result is almost equally murderous to art. It would profit us to adopt that aesthetic awareness which prevailed in the "Hal-cyon Days" of the 'eighties or 'nineties, when the dawn of a new author among us was the signal for boundless comment, criticism, and enthusiasm of utmost spontaneity. Not long ago an old-timer expressed wonder at the apathy of modern amateur journalism toward its artists. In 1888 a virtual cyclone of attention was precipitated by the advent of the youthful and iconoclastic short story genius, Edith May Dowe, the present Mrs. Miniter. What comparable demonstration today attends such notable newcomers as Frank Belknap Long, Jr., master of poetic phantasy and ironic modernism, or Dudley Carroll, psychological fictionist *par excellence?* We must awake, and remain awake. We must read—and read not alone the hackneyed high-school standby and newsstand booboisie-bait, but the vital intellectual and artistic products of all the manifold cultural streams which unite to form our strange, complex, disillusioned, scintillant, and almost exotic post-war civilisation. We shall not be without leaders—torch bearers of the new age are already with us in the persons of Mr. Long and of Messrs. H. A. and Olin L. Joslen of Ohio, whose utterances will puzzle the backward into study and debate, and arouse the alert to comment varying from acquiescence to challenge. Certainly, we have incentives in plenty—and we on our part should resolve not to let them pass by unheeded or to re-lapse tamely and flabbily into the lethal banality of other days; prattling puerile personali-ties in journals either pitifully frivolous or disgustingly venomous, or tangling our faculties in the trivial red tape and small beer of official pomposities and electoral publicity-seeking. Let us vow before the altars of all Pegāna's Gods that the present break in our mental slumbers shall not be a mere turning over in the night, but a true awakening to a morning of properly directed activity.

## Conclusion

The official year is over, and the present board will not be sorry to lay down its re-sponsibilities. To the effective coöperation of my colleagues I owe whatever level short of failure my executive striving may have reached, and for that coöperation I wish to thank them as we retire. I have encountered no intentional obstacles and have found so much encouragement at every turn that I am forced to look outside the National in order to maintain my cosmic attitude of perfect cynicism. I believe that the coming year holds brilliant developments, and hope that the newly elected board may receive as undivided a support and as active a background as the members can give it. I for one shall not be half-hearted in my endeavours.

It occurs to me that I was supposed to write an annual report. Possibly something of the sort may be found buried amidst the eight preceding pages of miscellaneous verbiage. At any rate I am done.

Sharing your thankfulness at that circumstance, and wishing that I might have read—or tried to read—these remarks in person before you, I take my leave to become

H. P. LOVECRAFT,
Ex-President N.A.P.A.

EDITOR'S NOTE  FP: *National Amateur* 46, No. 1 (September 1923): 1–3. HPL's summary of his interim presidency of the NAPA. A report of this type was apparently de rigueur for the NAPA, although UAPA presidents rarely if ever wrote them. HPL takes proper pride in his role in reviving amateur activity during a period of confusion and apathy. In letters HPL notes that Edward H. Cole had begged him to run for NAPA president for the 1923–24 term, but he declined (see HPL to Edward H. Cole, 23 and 24 February [1923]; mss., JHL).

*Notes*

1. HPL won the essay laureateship for "In the Editor's Study" (*Conservative*, March 1923), containing the sections "Rursus Adsumus" (see p. 330) and "Rudis Indigestaque Moles" (CE2), his celebrated attack on T. S. Eliot's *The Waste Land.*

# TRENDS AND OBJECTS

The essential question before us today is—what is the National now aiming at, and how far is it actually conscious of its inmost aims? Last year that question, so far as official policy was concerned, was excessively easy to answer. The president, official editor, and critical department were solidly agreed in making a very thorough trial of pure literature and literary creation as an object; so that by the end of the term the atmosphere was clearly one of disinterested aesthetic analysis and endeavour. At this point the motive forces rested to some extent, wishing to see what natural response might result from the original momentum.

As the lapse of months begins to reveal what actually is occurring, it is impossible to avoid the conclusion that pure artistry has not extensively "taken" as a dominant policy. To a period of aesthetic interest has succeeded a period of associational reminiscence and familiar discussion, with attention centred not upon abstract beauty and expression, but upon the history and mechanical operation of the amateur circle.

Another contender for notice has also appeared and assumed extensive proportions—the trade-writing in which so many Nationalites are engaged, and which has become such a leading issue with them. More and more do we notice a drift toward the ideal of commercial writing and trade journalism—an ideal wholly dissociated from artistic authorship, though not to be scoffed at in its own sphere.[1]

It appears, then, that the natural bent of the society when not subjected to concerted guidance in a given direction is mainly practical and non-imaginative. Not of their own volition do the members devote themselves utterly to the worship of austere beauty for its own sake, nor do they find supreme satisfaction in the capture and idealisation of vivid images without ulterior reward. The operations of the human taste and intellect, as such, are insufficient to interest them sincerely.

And what of all this? Shall we complain and seek to restore the aesthetic goal, or shall we acquiesce and relinquish the allegiance of the aesthetes among us? To my mind, neither alternative is necessary, for I believe that it will be possible to continue the National as an historical and inclusive movement—social, political, and practical—whilst providing for the artistic sympathiser a special and congenial field.

This special field is the re-born United Amateur Press Association; now emerging from its wreckage by the anti-literary party, and prepared to resume its functions as an exponent of aid and encouragement for the aesthetic amateur—an inviolate haven for the sensitive artist, in no way encroaching on the activities of the National, but rather stimulating them by forming an aesthetic rallying-point and removing the tension caused by unsatisfied spirits. In this United rebirth many loyal Nationalites are happily coöperating so that altogether the stage seems set for a notably useful division of such energies as must be divided.

Here, then, is the natural future for our hobby. Let the National maintain its traditional place as centre of general and practical activity; rallying recruits around our standards, lending the colourful social atmosphere which so many demand, and forming our bond of linkage with the past and with our valued alumni. To the United leave the specialised cultivation of pure beauty which in the National so many resent, yet without which so many lose interest. Who shall set limits to the results obtainable for an alliance so friendly and felicitous?

EDITOR'S NOTE FP: *National Official* (March 1924): 6. HPL ponders on his continual goal of making amateurdom a haven for disinterested literary expression, but realizes that the NAPA is probably not the ideal forum for the fulfilling of such a goal; he instead sees the "re-born" UAPA in that role.

*Notes*

1. See further HPL's essay "The Professional Incubus" (*National Amateur*, March 1924; CE2).

---

## EDITORIAL

*(May 1924)*

Once more the United, well-nigh asphyxiated by the tender ministrations of those who sought to shield it from the rude winds of literature, commences the long and arduous climb "back to normalcy". One is tempted to dilate upon the theme of "I-told-you-so", and draw various salutary morals from the utter disintegration following the revolt against high standards; but in sober fact such gloating de luxe would be supremely futile. The situation teaches its own lesson, and we are not yet far enough out of the woods to indulge in leisurely exultation. The future is in our own hands, and the downfall of the anti-literati will avail us nothing unless we are ready to rebuild on the ruins the edifice they demolished in 1922.

Rather does it become us to pay our foes the tribute they deserve, and to concede the honestly beneficent intention which animated their work of destruction. They sought sincerely to do that which could not be done, and the toil of their leaders was none the less admirable and unselfish because it was mistaken. To Mr. Fritter is due a world of respect for the energy with which he laboured, and the sacrificing perseverance with which he carried through his publishing programme unaided in the face of every obstacle. He fought boldly and well, and if we can serve our opposite ideal as creditably as he served his, we shall account ourselves fortunate.

Reconstruction is now the supreme desideratum in the United, and suggestions of every kind are welcome. As an opening gun in the campaign for survival and development, we publish in this issue a paper by the universally known amateur leader, James F. Morton, Jr., who now actively enters the Association for the first time in his amateur career of thirty-five years. Mr. Morton, conscious of the suicidal waste entailed by the existence of several smaller associations, yet equally aware of the overwhelming and universal sentiment against consolidation, proposes a just and rational division of functions among the three existing societies; whereby each may supplement the others in an amicable way, and none have occasion to encroach upon ground preëmpted by any other. In brief, Mr. Morton would have the Erford association cover in a general way the western region of the United States, where other associations are sparsely represented; would have the National represent amateurdom's historical tradition and diverse activities social and political; and would leave to the United that field of pure and constructive literary effort which it has itself adopted since the reorganisation of 1912.

So far as the United is concerned, the present editor cannot do otherwise than endorse Mr. Morton's plan without reservation. It has long been our opinion that the United should confine itself to literary work of serious intent, and this later commentator adds nothing to what we maintained before. Given a friendly rapport with other organisations which can take care of such members as rebel against strictness of policy, we would be far less likely than now to experience internal dissensions, or to impress casual dilettanti as wishing to discourage beginners.

Where we differ from Mr. Morton is in the detail touching on the Western or Erford association. Mr. Morton would make this society regional, but we believe that its existing trend disposes it to a function still more valuable—that of providing a field for the numerous writers who, though disinclined to expand to severely artistic proportions, nevertheless find in writing and argument their chief interest, and do not wish to participate in the complex social-political tradition of the National. Here is a province promising rich rewards—such a province as our own misguided anti-literati desired so ardently in 1922, yet could not engraft upon an association as alien to it as the United.

Regional associations, it seems to us, are not desperately needed; for any of the major societies can with proper recruiting become national in scope. What we do need is a tripartite division of the whole amateur field; in which the National shall attend to the social and historical end, holding the conventions, keeping the records, and binding together the local clubs; the Erford handle the casual writing end, serving those who wish a medium of publicity unfettered by rules of exact taste and punctilious rhetoric; and the United devote itself undividedly to the encouragement, instruction, criticism, and inspiration of such whole-hearted aesthetes as aspire to genuine self-expression and the creation of verbal beauty for beauty's sake.

In line with the policy of a purely literary United is the tentative decision of the President to hold a mail election instead of a convention next July.[1] The present editor would enlarge upon that idea to the extent of abolishing the annual convention altogether, and sticking to artistic and intellectual correspondence whilst the National attends to the social side. With provinces defined and rivalries removed, there is no sound reason why the National, as the social-political body, should not be the fraternal nucleus of all amateurdom, or why its conventions should not form the yearly meeting-point of United and Erford members as well as of its own personnel. We would welcome communications on this subject, in order that the sentiments of all may be known before any formal amendment is introduced.

EDITOR'S NOTE  FP: *United Amateur* 23, No. 1 (May 1924): 10–11. HPL's only editorial (and the only issue of the *United Amateur*) in the 1923–24 term. HPL had been re-elected Official Editor, a year after being ousted by what he referred to as the "anti-literary" party; but recalcitrance from the outgoing official board had prevented funds from being transferred to HPL, so that a United Amateur could not be issued until almost the end of the term. HPL expresses more weariness than bitterness at the turn of events, and as a remedy he finally acknowledges that the UAPA might have to merge with the NAPA—an eventuality that would have been unthinkable to him five or even two years previously. In the event, HPL's branch of the UAPA collapsed from apathy and inactivity in 1926 or 1927. The "other" UAPA (the United Amateur Press Association of America) continued until 1939.

*Notes*

1. The mail election, conducted by HPL and his wife Sonia from their apartment at 259 Parkside Ave. in Brooklyn, resulted in the re-election of Sonia as President and HPL as Official Editor.

# NEWS NOTES

(May 1924)

On March 3, 1924, occurred the wedding of Sonia H. Greene, President of the United Amateur Press Association, and H. P. Lovecraft, Official Editor of that society.

The marriage is the culmination of nearly three years of acquaintance, beginning at the Boston convention of the National in 1921, and ripened by a marked community of tastes and parallelism of interests. It may quite justly be added to the long list of amateur journalistic romances which our social chroniclers delight to enumerate and extol.

The ceremony, performed by the Reverend George Benson Cox, took place at historic St. Paul's Chapel, New York; a noble colonial structure built in 1766 and dignified by the worship of such elder figures as General Washington, Lord Howe, and that Prince of Wales who later became successively the Prince Regent and King George the Fourth.

Following the wedding, the bride and groom departed on a brief tour of the Philadelphia region, whose venerable and historic landmarks accorded well with the scene of the ceremony itself. On Sunday, March 23, after their return to New York, Mr. and

Mrs. Lovecraft entertained members of the Blue Pencil Club at their home, 259 Parkside Avenue, Brooklyn, where, needless to say, amateurs will always be welcome.

Mr. and Mrs. Lovecraft plan a continued career of amateur activity, which will begin with a vigorous attempt to resuscitate the United. Already in harmony as to plans and policies, the union will not alter or modify their programme as previously announced; but will add the final touch of cohesiveness to their concerted efforts.

Ex-President Rheinhart Kleiner was recently honoured by the inclusion of three of his light verse products in Christopher Morley's anthology "The Bowling Green", which comprises choice bits culled from Mr. Morley's late "colyum" of identical name in the *New York Evening Post*.[1] John V. A. Weaver, reviewing the book in the *Brooklyn Daily Eagle*, further honours Mr. Kleiner by choosing one of these pieces for the unique distinction of quotation in full; adding that this specimen—"Brooklyn, My Brooklyn"—should find a place in every Brooklynite's scrap-book.

Noah F. Whitaker, celebrated in the United as editor of the piquant *Pegasus*, was lately made the subject of an illustrated feature article in the *Springfield (Ohio) Sunday Sun*. Views of Mr. Whitaker and his home-made press, and accounts of his mechanical vocation and literary avocation, combine to produce a picture of the keenest interest and fascination. Mr. Whitaker, whose advanced education is due largely to his own efforts, is a prolific bard of the old school; following to a great extent the Byronic tradition. His work embraces descriptive, narrative, lyrical, didactic, and satirical poetry, and extends frequently into prose, in which medium he is an effective critic and castigator of modern free verse and the background which produces it.

The United receives a striking and auspicious accession in the advent to membership of Clark Ashton Smith, California poet, artist, and fantaisiste. Mr. Smith, who embodies both in poetry and in pictorial art the haunting satanism and grotesquerie of Poe, Baudelaire, John Martin, Doré, Sime, Arthur Machen, and their like, is the author of three volumes of verse,[2] and conducts a column of poetry and epigrams in the *Auburn (Cal.) Journal*. The merit of his work is universally hailed by the literati of the west coast, and George Sterling has written two eulogistic prefaces for his published verse.[3] Mr. Smith's latest book, "Ebony and Crystal", is dedicated to no less a kindred spirit than our own United product Samuel Loveman.[4]

In the professional poetical magazine *L'Alouette*, Mr. Charles A. A. Parker has sought once more to break down the barriers betwixt amateurdom and the professional world. The first issue is of ample size and distinguished merit, including contributions by some of the foremost amateurs of the past and present. Mr. Parker's editorial associates in this venture include W. Paul Cook, H. P. Lovecraft, Edith Miniter, Maurice Winter Moe, James F. Morton, Jr., William R. Murphy, Ada Borden Stevens, and Michael Oscar White.

Miss Grace M. Bromley, formerly connected with the U. S. Department of Agriculture, has recently accepted a position as Assistant Secretary of the District of Columbia Bankers' Association, being the first woman ever elected to serve in that capacity. Washington newspapers have taken considerable notice of the event, making it the basis of several illustrated articles.

Stella V. Kellerman, California United member, was selected by the San Diego Writers' Club to prepare an ode to the solar eclipse of last September. So successful was her work that it gained publicity in printed and illustrated form, being used as a souvenir of the "Fete of the Sun" at Coronado.

EDITOR'S NOTE  FP: *United Amateur* 23, No. 1 (May 1924): 7–8 (unsigned). HPL gives an account of his own wedding to Sonia H. Greene (then president of the UAPA), along with the activities of other amateurs.

*Notes*

1. Three poems by Kleiner—"To Pyrrha in the Poconos," "To Lalage [On Her Resignation as File Clerk]," and "Brooklyn, My Brooklyn"—were included in *The Bowling Green: An Anthology of Verse*, ed. Christopher Morley (Garden City, NY: Doubleday, Page, 1924), pp. 97–102.
2. *The Star-Treader and Other Poems* (1912), *Odes and Sonnets* (1918), and *Ebony and Crystal* (1922). HPL had come into contact with Smith in August 1922, and they quickly became close colleagues.
3. Sterling (1869–1926) wrote prefaces to the latter two volumes cited in n. 2.
4. HPL reviewed the volume in *L'Alouette* (January 1924; *CE2*).

---

# EDITORIAL

(July 1925)

The amateur inactivity of 1924–'5, in which the United has played so lamentably great a part, forms a striking warning of the oblivion which will shortly overtake us unless something drastic and energetic is done. Lack of funds has made impossible the systematic issuance of this official organ—and lack of public spirit has prevented any spontaneous protest or attempt to remedy the condition. Illness of the President and of the Secretary-Treasurer[1] has retarded executive work in two vital departments—but only sheer indifference has stalled the replacement machinery which should have risen to the occasion in each case. What can we say, indeed, when a whole annual election is omitted, and an entire official board suffered to groan under its lightly taken burdens a second year?

In this matter the present editor is doubtless as much to blame as anybody else. It is true that a multiplicity of outside duties have drained his head, hand, and schedule of nearly all available time and energy; but it is also true that when a member finds his duties unfeasible he ought to retire and make way for younger blood. Such the editor now purposes to do, as he sends forth this concluding word of a barren and discouraging period. Efforts are already under way for a briskly conducted campaign of revival by certain of the newer amateurs; and our readers are urged to heed diligently and conscientiously any circular appeals for activity which may in the near future arrive under not very familiar signatures. A mail election is in the air, for which genuinely effective candidates have been sought with the greatest and most unbiassed assiduity. By the time these lines are read a new and determined official board of young leaders may be seated in power—and it will henceforward be our part, as privates in the ranks, to sustain them with every needed act of loyalty and coöperation.[2] The intense labour entailed in actively managing and administering an amateur press association can be understood only by one who has been through it. There is planning, financing, letter-writing, and adjusting beyond all belief; so much, in truth, that old-timers are forced to drop out willingly or unwillingly when external matters begin to demand a prime share of their energy. If, then, our leaders in their heyday are willing to serve the cause with this extreme of devotion; the very least we can do is to play faithfully our easier parts as cogs in the mechanism which their cerebral muscle-power must keep in motion.

Consolidation is again abroad on men's tongues, and this time with much better excuses than formerly; since the current inactivity of all existing amateur associations would surely suggest a tightening up through the assemblage of any remaining real workers under one administrative system. Mr. C. W. Smith, of *The Tryout,* has been foremost in advancing this plan, and his editorial observations are uniformly marked by the soundest sense. Consolidation, while undoubtedly impairing the special features which each association possessed in the palmy days, is the logical course for a divided amateurdom which must confess itself moribund. With a chance for independent survival and retention of its particular characteristics, any association would be well justified in objecting to the design; but when the choice is between extinction and merging, one's point of view is necessarily changed. Such a choice, indeed, leaves the special qualities as little possibility of endurance on the non-merging side as on the merging side—and since one cannot have them in any case, why not save what one can from the wreck?

At the same time, haste in this or any other serious step would be a profound mistake. For the present our only task is to restore our own society to something like coherence, consciousness, and articulateness, that it may take stock of itself and decide what it can most profitably do. It may be that the new board, by crusading far afield for youthful, energetic, and superior membership, will be able to inaugurate a new era of active writing, criticism, stimulation, and discussion in the traditional United manner; in which case it would of course again become ridiculous to consider amalgamation with other bodies of less definite and constructive policies. But the question is debatable. Let us keep it in mind as we work steadily toward the rebuilding of the United we used to know. If we can have that United again, well and good. If not, it is at least better to have some sort of amateur journalism than none at all.

EDITOR'S NOTE FP: *United Amateur* 24, No. 1 (July 1925): 8–9. The only editorial written (and the only issue of the *United Amateur* to be published) in the 1924–25 UAPA term. HPL acknowledges partial responsibility in the inactivity of the UAPA, given his own busy schedule of work outside amateurdom, and hopes for renewed activity with a coming mail election.

*Notes*

1. Sonia had taken ill in November 1924 with acute gastric pain, and she was forced to stay at a sanitarium in New Jersey for a week. By the end of the year she had left New York to seek employment in the Midwest. The Secretary-Treasurer was Edgar J. Davis. On his illness see "News Notes" (July 1925).
2. The UAPA's official board for the 1925–26 included Edgar J. Davis, President; Paul Livingston Keil, Vice-President; Victor E. Bacon, Official Editor; and Frank Belknap Long, Chairman of the Department of Public Criticism.

# NEWS NOTES

(July 1925)

Arthur H. Goodenough, United Literatus, is again represented in the American Anthology of Newspaper Verse; the 1924 issue containing two of his recent productions, "The Brightest Crown" and "The Apparition".

George Willard Kirk, one of our newer members and a rare book dealer of note, has settled in New York and associated himself with a former fellow-Clevelander in an extremely tasteful shop at 97 Fourth Avenue. Amateurs visiting the metropolis would do well to make this establishment their headquarters and rendezvous—looking for the sign of "Martin's Book Store".

James Larkin Pearson, prominent North Carolina amateur for the past quarter century, has just published on his own press a volume of his collected poetry, amounting to 374 pages. It is entitled "Pearson's Poems", and contains his complete verses from 1891 to 1923.[1] Some are reprinted from the amateur press, others from professional newspapers and magazines. All are distinguished by a genuine poetic vision and a touch of humanness which brings up the Robert Burns comparison to most of the reviewers who have studied the book. Mr. Pearson, whose address is Boomer, N. C., is selling the volume personally at a price of $2.10 post-paid. So preëminently a product of amateur journalism is this author, that no United member should fail to include the new publication in his library.

Mr. and Mrs. C. F. Bretholl, prominent former amateurs of Chicago and St. Louis, have settled on a rich and spacious orchard farm near the summit of Brushy Mountain in the heart of the North Carolina fruit belt. Their address is Pores Knob, N. C.

Early last November Mr. Edward Lloyd Sechrist of Washington spent some time in New York, absorbing many of its museums and antiquities under the guidance of the Official Editor.[2]

Mrs. Anne T. Renshaw, former Official Editor and supreme leader in the reconstruction work of 1914–1916, is now enjoying marked celebrity in Washington, D. C., as a teacher of oratorical and dramatic method. She is prominently connected with the School of Expression in Boston, founded and long conducted by the late Samuel S. Curry, who at one time was a United member.

To Washington Van Dusen, our Philadelphia member, has fallen the honour of a double first award in the recent poetical contest of the Philadelphia Society of Arts and Letters; his lyric and sonnet both standing at the head of their respective departments.

Edgar J. Davis, our keen young Secretary-Treasurer, is now convalescing from a severe attack of typhoid fever which kept him confined at the Peter Bent Brigham Hospital, Boston, during the greater part of the spring.

Ex-President Alfred Galpin, having been married in June, 1924, last autumn accepted a post as Instructor in French at the Rice Institute, Houston, Texas, perhaps the leading university of the Lone Star State. His interests are veering more and more away from literature toward music, and after suitable years of study he hopes to be recognised as a pianist and composer.

Samuel Loveman, premier amateur poet, sojourned in New York from September, 1924, to the last of May, 1925, and intends returning permanently before the coming autumn. While there he inhabited a picturesque old house on the heights of Brooklyn, his spacious bow-window overlooking the harbour, with its focus of all the world's commerce, and the fairy-like sky-line of Manhattan with its aerial pyramids and pinnacles.

Paul J. Campbell has been exceedingly busy with agricultural pursuits during the past year, but has found time to make several highly interesting motor trips, and to complete the manuscript of the novel, "The Pursuit of Happiness", on which he had long been working. A *Liberal* is now in the press.

Former Laureate Rheinhart Kleiner continues to advance in standing as one of New York's cleverest light versifiers. Scarcely a week now elapses without the appearance of something from his pen in the vivacious "colyums" of the better metropolitan dailies.

H. P. Lovecraft, Official Editor, on January 1st moved from Flatbush to the old Brooklyn Heights section, where he may be found at 169 Clinton Street, amidst rows of venerable brick and brownstone. In November he made a somewhat leisurely trip to Philadelphia, staying at the Y. M. C. A., and studying at length the colonial antiquities of the city and its suburbs. In April, accompanied by George W. Kirk, he paid a hurried visit to Washington and its Virginia environs; where the benevolent and expert guidance of Mrs. Renshaw and Mr. Sechrist enabled him to see much in a sadly abbreviated time.

To James Ferdinand Morton, Jr., staunchest of amateurs, has come an honour and opportunity which elicits our warmest congratulations. Early in the year, after an examination in which sheer merit was the only possible criterion, he received appointment as Curator and absolute head of the newly-founded Municipal Museum at Paterson, N. J., where his wide artistic and scientific knowledge will be employed in the most fitting fashion. He has entered with zest upon his arduous duties, and when the Museum opens we shall have a chance to behold very tangibly the fruits of his genius and labour. He is now to be addressed at The Museum, care Free Public Library, Paterson, N. J.

Frank Belknap Long, Jr., is achieving considerable prominence as a fantastic fictionist through work featured in the professional magazine, *Weird Tales*. The December issue chose one of his stories, "Death Waters", as a theme for the cover design, and few subsequent issues have been without his work. It is interesting to note that the editor of this piquant publication, Farnsworth Wright, is a former United member; having been one of us when a resident of San Francisco.

Mrs. Edith Miniter, whose articles on antiquarian and other themes form a steady and well-known ingredient of current professional letters, has returned to Allston, where she may be addressed at 21 Imrie Road.

Among the amateurs and former amateurs represented in the poetic Bookfellow Anthology for 1925 are Frank Belknap Long, Jr., Washington Van Dusen, May M. Duffee, Bertha Grant Avery, and the Rev. J. Herbert Bean.

Albert A. Sandusky, Cantabrigian expert in contemporary colloquialism, spent the Memorial Day holidays in New York; discussing amateur matters with Official Editor H. P. Lovecraft.

President Sonia H. Lovecraft, having last January spent some time in Cincinnati, has just returned from Saratoga Springs where her health received substantial benefit.

Victor E. Bacon, former Hub Club member, is now settled in St. Louis and about to take a leading part in an unprecedentedly strong movement for the full revival of United activity.

EDITOR'S NOTE  FP: *United Amateur* 24, No. 1 (July 1925): 7, 11–12 (unsigned). HPL's last such column for the UAPA, discussing the activities of Alfred Galpin, Samuel Loveman, and other amateur colleagues.

*Notes*

1. James Larkin Pearson (1879–?), *Pearson's Poems* (Boomer, NC: Published by the Author, 1924). A volume of this title had been published in 1906.
2. See n. 3 to "News Notes" (January 1922).

---

# A MATTER OF UNITEDS

There has recently been pointed out to me in an issue of Mr. Erford's *United Amateur* an editorial note concerning the other branch of the United and its Official Editor which really requires a word of rectification among the few who have received the paper. It seems impossible that Mr. Erford's information can be as meagre as would appear from his remarks, so I can only conjecture that his attitude is one of shrewd effect, as frequently practiced in the legalistic pleading of special causes.

The existence of two Uniteds since 1912 has been so well known a phenomenon that only the very newest members can be deluded by statements such as Mr. Erford makes in his excessive though well-intentioned zeal; but for the sake of these novices it ought to be pointed out that the United duplication is the result of no deliberate creation or imposture on either side. In 1912, at which time the United was living up to its name in spite of more than one previous division, a very hotly contested election took place at the annual convention; the final vote being so close and so dependent on a technically accurate interpretation of the voting status of many members that no one can say even now with absolute finality which side gained the legal victory. Unfortunately, much recalcitrance was displayed in both camps; and in the end each group of adherents claimed the shade of preference necessary to a decision. Since both parties considered their respective candidates elected as President, each naturally viewed the candidate of the other in the light of an usurper; and in the end a general cleavage occurred, each division realigning its membership and official board in conformity with its conception of who was President, and regarding itself as the authentic continuation of the original society.

Now although I did not join amateurdom until two years after these events, they were still recent enough in my time to make it very plain to me that both sides were equally sincere in their conflicting positions. The branch which I happened to join was that opposed to Mr. Erford's, and I naturally have a bias in its favour; but at no time have I been disposed to brand the other branch as illegal or unjustified, or to do other than regret that continuance of ill-feeling on both sides which makes recombination impossible. Opinionated "die-hards" in either faction are really playing with amusing unconsciousness into the hands of the National when they perpetuate this United division; for with a friendly and coöperative use of half the energy which they spend in calling each other "rebels" and "pro-National traitors" they could undoubtedly reorganise a solid and compact body of literary aspirants which, because of its essential difference of aim from the fraternal National's, would need to fear no competition from that august and archaic body.

The question of United-National relations has always been obscured by error—though probably through misconception rather than through deliberate misstatement. Neither branch of the United owes anything to the National, and all attempts to make the non-Erford branch appear an ally of the older body are fallacious—probably based on the purely accidental circumstance that its President at the time of the "split" was in social touch with some National members through membership in the Blue Pencil Club of Brooklyn.[1] At the present time, of course, when the very existence of all amateurdom is menaced by indifference and decadence, the subject of consolidation for mutual strengthening has been freely broached; but never except on terms of the most unquestioned equality. The very notion that either United could ever form a National tributary of any sort is so amusing that only ignorance or deliberate obscurantism could ever cause it to be suggested. The National has no more interest in one of our branches than in the other—and if it has ever contributed toward the creation or support of any volume of the *United Amateur,* I am in a position to know that the volume in question is not one published by the non-Erford branch.

Both Uniteds have existed continuously though with varying fortunes since the time of their "split", each developing certain individual characteristics peculiar to itself. My own branch—the non-Erford one—has specialised in serious literary upbuilding more than in social or fraternal features, and has consequently sacrificed some of the fanatical *esprit de corps* which makes its rival so violently and picturesquely in evidence at times; but I can give assurance that its continuity through various ups and downs is no less absolute. We have not taken gaps in the visibility of Mr. Erford's society as evidence of its final cessation, and we doubt very much the seriousness of Mr. Erford when he so blithely interprets similar gaps of our own as evidence of our definite death and burial. Only the extreme novice, as we have said, can possibly be deceived by rhetorical efforts such as this.

Mr. Victor E. Bacon, the object of Mr. Erford's ill-considered and ill-informed attack, was Official Editor of the United before he ever heard of the existence of the Erford branch. He was persuaded to assume this responsibility, much against his own inclinations, by those anxious to bring about a revival of literary amateur journalism; taking office at a time when scant funds and adverse conditions had limited *The United Amateur* to a single annual number for the two years preceding. His sole object was a renaissance and maintenance of the United's best traditions, and he has continued to discharge his duties with the highest credit; slighting no task because of the National office thrust upon him by those who had watched his valiant fight in the United. His policy has been in no way affected by his discovery that Mr. Erford's branch exists, and he has indeed exchanged many friendly letters with Erfordites since coming in contact with the rival branch.

It is quite time that vestigial feuds and naive poses of assumed ignorance be dropped on both sides of the United controversy. Years enough have elapsed since 1912 to make United members realise the smallness of the original difference; and to cause all sensible partisans to wish for a concerted drive toward a greater strength, rather than for a perpetuated squabbling over issues which less than a hundredth of the present personnel of either branch knows or cares anything about. Both Uniteds are a fact, and both will continue to be such until someone has the breadth, courage, and diplomacy to effect a reunion. Neither has enough in common with the National, as a careful survey has developed, to make consolidation with that body practicable; so that good sense and a liberal desire for amateurdom's general welfare would seem to dictate an amicable and tolerant reunion as the only decently rational course to follow in a depressed period when every waste of energy in duplicated organisation and internecine strife is a direct blow at the existence of the amateur institution itself.

The thing about the United which distinguishes it from the National is the fact that for a majority of its members in both branches the art of writing itself, as distinguished from social and fraternal features only loosely connected with writing, forms the dominating interest. This is a characteristic which ought to override all inherited acrimonies and bring about a coalescence of forces in which both branches might recombine on equal terms; each recognising the claims of the other, and frankly admitting the ambiguous nature of the 1912 election, where the possibilities of error in either direction were so great. Both branches carry an alert and interested membership of considerable size, none of whose individuals is deriving the fullest benefits of his affiliation so long as this mutually exclusive division continues. In the Erford society localisation produces a very unfortunate twist, and in the other there is a diffuseness forming an almost equal evil. It is time to pool strengths and weaknesses, welding all elements into one compact body in which a sane and effective average can be struck between the narrow and literalistic chauvinism on one side, and the loose organisation and apathy-breeding politicalism on the other. With a nation full of young and active persons anxious to write and still unable to find a place in the larger literary world, it is absurd that no adequate society should exist at this moment for their coördination and arrangement in channels of mutual helpfulness. To this purpose the United was originally dedicated; and that the energy which ought to go toward its realisation should be squandered in vapid personal prides and meaningless rivalries, is an eternal reflection on the cultural quality and administrative competency of amateur journalism.

Let there be no more cheap abuse, then, in an age when more worthy tasks demand performance. Leaders of both Uniteds ought to confer as soon and as seriously as possible on a recombining move whereby the dual membership can expand its energies toward one object instead of two; and this would indeed be no difficult task in the eyes of anyone whose vision is not clouded by obsolete and irrelevant issues. The recognition of both official boards on equal terms between 1912 and the date of reunion would involve no prohibitive sacrifice for any rational partisan, and would solve a problem whose continued existence saps wickedly and inexcusably at the vitality of an institution which all factions equally cherish. Of course, the appropriate leaders for such a conference are the younger rather than the older members. Veterans long identified with arbitrary bitternesses are no persons to inaugurate a forward-looking policy of concession and compromise, but they can shew their breadth of vision by abstaining from obstructionist tactics. Slander leads nowhere save backward, and if both sides are wise there will come in the near future a very alert and determined analysis of the situation by amateurs of the present generation—not by the bygone period to various phases of which both Mr. Erford and I belong—whereby there may be born again a United Amateur Press Association justifying every word and syllable of its long-belied yet well-beloved title.

EDITOR'S NOTE FP: *Bacon's Essays* 1, No. 1 (Summer 1927): 1–3. HPL's final, and most balanced, account of the split in the UAPA resulting from the disputed election of 1912. The article was published in an amateur journal edited by Victor E. Bacon.

*Notes*

1. The President of the UAPA (non-Erford branch) in 1912–13 was Helene E. Hoffman, later Helene Hoffman Cole.

## THE CONVENTION

Belying all fears anent the decay of Amateur Journalism, and overcoming individual handicaps which made its arrangement doubly difficult, the 1930 convention of the National Amateur Press Association was a brilliant success, and must be regarded as the most satisfactory amateur gathering of recent years. Again Boston has proven its ability to rise to the heights of hospitality; praise for the varied, perfectly functioning programme being due to the heroic volunteer efforts of Mrs. L. A. Sawyer, Mrs. Mary Kennedy, and Mr. J. Bernard Lynch—[as well as] others who stepped into the gap and ensured wise planning and financing when the regularly appointed committee found service impossible for various reasons.

Seldom has the atmosphere of a convention been so charged with renewed activity and constructive effort. Drawing a remarkable attendance of old-timers of the most solid sort, the event took on the aspect of a genuine renaissance; and left its participants with a sense of fresh concentration and energy which will be hard to shake. For this unusual attendance much credit must be given to Edwin Hadley Smith's *Convention Amateur,* which stirred up interest in advance of this well-planned event.

Of the veterans present at one or more sessions may be mentioned Mr. and Mrs. Edwin Hadley Smith of Washington; Louis Charles Wills, Brooklyn; Vincent B. Haggerty, Jersey City, who came with his wife and sister; Leonard E. Tilden, Washington; E. F. Suhre, St. Louis; W. O. Wylie, Beverly; William R. Murphy, Phila.; James F. Morton, Paterson; H. P. Lovecraft, Providence; Mr. and Mrs. George A. Thompson, Fairhaven. Among the local amateurs E. H. Cole, A. A. Sandusky, Laurie A. Sawyer, Mary A. Kennedy, and Mr. and Mrs. J. Bernard Lynch.

The younger generation, less visible numerically, made a strong qualification through the presence of editor Spink of Washington, Ind., and of the promising new recruit, Francis B. Richardson, of Newark, N. J., who has already issued a paper.

The effectiveness of the three-day programme was ensured in the absence of ranking officers by choosing James F. Morton as presiding officer at the business sessions. He filled the post with his keen ability and made possible a considerable speeding up of the routine work, ably assisted by Laurie A. Sawyer as recorder.

With the Hotel Statler as headquarters, and a parlour on the mezzanine floor provided for the business sessions, the convention opened at 10 a.m. on Thursday, July 3d, with an address of welcome by James F. Morton. At 2 p.m. a business session disposed of committee reports, and later the delegates enjoyed a festive dinner at "Nan's Kitchen", a quaint basement restaurant in a Back Bay byway. The evening was consumed by the meeting of the proxy committee, and by a caucus which lasted until very late.

On Friday, July 4th, the principal business session and general election [took place] at 10 a.m. The proxies were counted with remarkable judgment and harmony. The election of President Bacon and the re-election of Official Editor Spink and Secretary Haggerty, the liberalisation of the size of the Official Organ, and the choice of St. Louis as the 1931 convention seat, all mark a serious and intelligent attitude and a firm determination to set amateurdom on a practical way to recovery. Plans were outlined for securing the interest of the boy printer of the sort who originally founded the National, and planning for an alumni association for the National members who no longer are active, yet wish to keep ties in the association.

At noon a recess was declared, and the entire delegation had lunch in the Statler's dining room as guests of Mr. Wills. The afternoon session disposed of several important points, and after the adjournment a long informal discussion was held regarding the proposed alumni association, leading spirits in the latter movement being Messrs. Smith, Haggerty, Wills, and Lynch.

After another recess the delegates reconvened at six o'clock at Seville Restaurant in Boylston St. for the 55th Annual Banquet, with James F. Morton as Toastmaster. The large attendance made the event highly successful, and at nine o'clock the celebrants adjourned to the convention parlour at the Statler for a round of informal and impromptu speechmaking. Mr. Morton's ceremonial oratory appeared to advantage, as always. Other applauded speakers were Miss Saunders and Messrs. Smith and Spink, the latter young man concluding the exercises with a bit of notable sentiment. Unorganised discussion continued late in the evening, and several of the delegates were visible on the mezzanine until the small hours of the morning.

The convention's final day, Saturday, July 5th, opened with a residual business session, at which resolutions, committee reports, and other loose ends of administrative details were disposed of. The closing movements, involving a successful attempt to defer the time of official disbandment till precisely "high noon", were marked with considerable humour and whimsicality introduced by Messrs. Murphy and Cole, and carried the delegates far into the maze of syntax, lexicography, and parliamentary niceties. The climax was a hearty and spontaneous vote of thanks to Mr. Morton for the vast part his service as presiding officer had played in the success of the sessions.

After lunch the delegates reconvened at the Berkeley Sq. landing for a trip up the Charles River to Sunset Bay, and the circulation of the Charles River Basin, on the large motor launch "Flo and Ruby", operated by that delightful marine-lecturer Capt. Charles H. Munroe. Capt. Munroe, a living mine of river folklore and an orator of ingenuous fluency and grace, provided an unceasing stream of descriptive and illustrative comment throughout the voyage; greeting each sight along the bank with appropriate anecdotes and poetical extracts, and occasionally enlivening the atmosphere with comic stories of familiar but always acceptable content. This time the Captain had an eager and responsive audience worthy of his talents, and Mr. Morton distinguished himself as a cheer leader when it came the time for shouting beneath the stone arches of the Charles's many bridges. The river itself needs no description, hence one may simply say that the entire party seemed to appreciate its varied beauties—the skyline of Boston, still relatively unspoiled by tall buildings; the Georgian grace of the new Harvard buildings along both the Cambridge and Brighton shores; the spires of Cambridge as seen in Old World fashion, across stretches of riverside pasture land; and the mystical glory of Sunset Bay glimpsed through a summer haze with the tower of Perkins Institute for the Blind outlined against the west. On the return trip an added attraction was provided in the form of a marine rescue—Mr. Lynch's eagle eye espying a befuddled drowning man near the Harvard Bridge. Capt. Munroe's cool, quick response to the situation was typical of a Yankee skipper, and that helpless struggler—whose liquid confusion was not entirely aqueous and external—was soon taken aboard and delivered at the nearest wharf. Toward the end of the voyage the captain gave a keenly interesting description of the Charles's change from a salt estuary to a fresh-water basin, and of the clever system of locks now providing access to the ocean outside. Last impressions concerned the famous West Boston Bridge, on whose wooden predecessor Longfellow once stood at midnight, and a clever floating reproduction of the ship "Arbella", on which in the year 1630 the ancestors of more than one convention delegate performed a memorable transatlantic voyage. Credit for this memorable trip is due to Mr. Lynch.

After a return to the Statler, where some early-leaving delegates were given reluctant farewell, and late-arriving Mr. Suhre accorded a hearty welcome, the convention proceeded en masse to the Sawyer house at 20 Imrie Road, Allston, a place celebrated in later years as unofficial headquarters of the Hub Club and all Boston-residing and - visiting amateurs. The gathering on this occasion assumed an aspect of a happy reincarnation of the old days, beginning with one of Mrs. Sawyer's old-fashioned New England bean suppers; in the serving of which delightful feast much assistance was rendered by Mrs. Kennedy and the youthful Mr. Richardson. It was symbolic of the spirit of reincarnation and propitious renaissance that the 1921 convention napkins, properly surcharged for 1930 purposes, were provided for use at this function.

The evening, with the group of amateurs discoursing on the well-remembered porch and in the well-remembered rooms of this amateur shrine, brought back the festive spirit of 1920 to such an extent that the lapse of a decade seemed almost mythical; and it was freely prophesied by all present that an enthusiasm so aptly re-created could not really decline. Those who recalled the old Hub days thought of the whimsical lore of the "Temple Epgephi"[1] and half imagined that the wild tiger forming the present reigning [feline] was no other than the wild, well-known "Tat" or "grey brother" of beloved memory.[2]

At a late hour the visitors adjourned to the Statler, saying final farewell in front of the now historic edifice. The sign, [sic] spirit of the convention, so happily contrasting with other gatherings of recent years, formed almost a surprise to those who attended, and heartened everyone with the feeling that amateurdom's vitality is not so far and hopelessly spent as many are wont to assume in these days. Virtually all the features excelled expectations, and the smoothness of the programme pleased and encouraged the volunteer emergency workers who had made such a sudden impromptu conquest of grave obstacles. Not a delegate failed to express his keen enjoyment; everyone carried away a sense of stimulus and renewed activity which can, with proper encouragement and coöperation, be made to accomplish [much] in amateurdom. Coincident with this [was] the news that St. Louis is looking upward and already planning for a lively and fruitful convention in 1931. Sincere regret was occasioned by the absence of several faithful workers who had been expected to attend this year; Edith Miniter, President-elect Victor E. Bacon, W. Paul Cook, Michael White, retiring President Marlow, among others. A Boston convention without Mrs. Miniter is almost unthinkable, and great sympathy was expressed concerning the bronchial illness which kept her away from the event.

As usual, the post-convention dispersals were not instantaneous; and many pleasant reunions and excursions followed the gathering. On Sunday, July 6, Messrs. Morton and Suhre visited Nantasket Beach and braved a spectacular thunderstorm, while on Monday Messrs. Spink, Suhre, and Lovecraft explored the antiquarian intricacies of Salem and Marblehead. Mr. Suhre extended his travels as far north as Portland, Maine. Mr. and Mrs. Smith made a thorough and appreciative tour of Cape Cod, beginning with a boat trip to Provincetown. The convention season, most assuredly, has been one of old-time fulness and festivity. May its aftermath as measured by papers published and ideas exchanged sustain this flattering parallel.

EDITOR'S NOTE FP: *Tryout* 13, No. 8 (July 1930): [3–11] (as by "Theobald"). HPL writes enthusiastically of the NAPA convention in Boston in July 1930, the second and last national convention he would attend. It is ironic, given HPL's devotion to the UAPA, that the only two such conventions he attended were those for the NAPA (the other being the 1921 convention in Boston). HPL's enthusiasm heralds his re-entry into amateur activity, as he served on the NAPA's Bureau of Critics for much of the period 1931–36.

*Notes*

1. See "The Conquest of the Hub Club" (p. 257).
2. A cat belonging to Edith Miniter; see "Mrs. Miniter—Estimates and Recollections" (p. 381).

---

# BUREAU OF CRITICS

*(December 1931)*

## Verse Section

An attempt to survey the recent poetry of our writers reveals first of all the astonishing reality of the National's renaissance. No less than twenty-four verse-containing publications have been submitted, and these represent only part of the output of the amateur press for the last few months. Clearly, the prophets of disaster have erred for once.

It would be unjust to judge amateur verse by the rigorous standards of the academic literary world, yet it would be equally wrong to suspend all truly artistic standards. While the amateur poet need not be expected to produce work fit for publication in *Harpers* or the *Saturday Review*, it is certainly not too much to expect him to strive in the right rather than in the wrong direction; that is, to bear in mind what poetry really is, and to try to produce something which shall be genuine poetry (even though on a very modest scale) rather than seek for merely imitative effects or indulge in the hackneyed and insincere didacticism or sentimentality typical of popular newspaper verse.

What, then, is genuine poetry in the first place? How shall the beginner know what to emulate and what to avoid among the mixed models that occur in the course of his study and ordinary reading? There are plenty of definitions of poetry, most of them almost valueless because of conventional perspective and empty romanticism. The old reliable *Encyclopaedia Britannica* is probably about as sensible as any authority in attempting an estimate when it says that "absolute poetry is the concrete and artistic expression of the human mind in emotional and rhythmical language".[1] This means that the subject-matter of real poetry is simply the thought and feeling naturally contained in a sensitive personality, uttered for the sake of emotional relief in a manner conforming to the principles of harmony in sound and imagery, and conveyed in tangible pictures, symbols, suggestions, or comparisons rather than in direct statements.

A real poem is always a mood or picture about which the writer feels very strongly, and is always couched in illustrative hints, concrete bits of appropriate pictorial imagery, or indirect symbolic allusions—never in the bald declarative language of prose. It may or may not have metre or rhyme or both. These are generally desirable, but they are not essential and in themselves most certainly do not make poetry. The usual content of popular syndicate doggerel—trite metrical moralising about virtue and vice or stale jingling about love, home, and mother—is merely rhyming prose. Sincerely felt emotion and concrete indirectness or symbolism of utterance are the essential features of poetry, and the latter characteristic—the concrete indirectness or symbolism—is its absolute mark of distinction from that which is essentially prose.

But the expression must be artistic as well as concrete, and to this end the poet must select his words and forms very carefully for their value in the fields of sound and meaning. The language, whether in verse or otherwise, must be fluid and musical; and the words must be chosen not only for their dictionary meaning but for those more delicate overtones of exact associative meaning and symbolic significance which they have picked up through centuries of familiar use in common speech and literature. One must learn by wide reading and practice how to choose the exactly right word; the word whose presence magically makes a sentence real poetry instead of prose.

This most emphatically does not mean, however, that the outmoded romanticisms and archaisms regarded by Victorian and earlier rhymers as "poetic language" are desirable or even permissible in the poetry of today. Simplicity is the chief requisite of sincere emotional expression, and only the vital forms of common speech, intelligently managed, are able to convey emotion without a sense of pompous emptiness and insincerity. Absurd tinsel trappings like *hath, o'er, yclept, ope, 'gainst, 'twixt*, and so on can be ruled out at the start. Much in same class are the stock phrases or "clichés" beloved by popular poetasters. These, of course, are to be shunned as ignominious devices wholly incompatible with original expression. The poet must speak in his own language and not in any ready-made jargon compounded of *dewy morns, golden tresses, cloud-capped peaks, babbling brooks*, and the like.

Now how well have our National bards succeeded of late in aiming at the right target? A glance at the recent papers shews many very heartening performances both in the domain of serious poetry and in that parallel domain of clever light versifying which raises metrical prose to a dignity all its own. The Spring–Summer *Ripples from Lake Champlain* is especially rich in material which rings true. Roger Rush, in "Disappointment", finely exemplifies the principle of symbolism in a brief image which dispenses altogether with the externals of form.

> "The wind
> whistles through the trees
> down to the sea and ships
> only to find the ships no longer
> need it."

Here is a simple concrete image which tells more of the essence of disappointment, and of the author's genuine perception and feeling, than any amount of literal statement or hackneyed allusion to "cups dashed from one's lips" could even begin to convey. This image is the poet's own, and its originality and simplicity give it a very poignant power. "Nocturne", by Ray H. Zorn,[2] has something of the same kind of originality, though in a less compact form. Of a smoother and more conventional cast, albeit of undeniably less vigour, as "A Wish", by Sue Howard, "For a Day", by Marie Tello Phillips, "When Phyllis Comes to Tea", by Bessie Margot Cassie, and "Pansies", by Marjorie Tullar. These specimens shew the definiteness of mood and command of language typical of mature and cultivated verse, and at no point do they sink to the medium of literal statement which is the negation of all real poetry. "The Writer's Prayer", by Pearl Adoree Rawling, and "Comrades", by Florence Grow Proctor, fall below this standard because they state things instead of depicting or symbolising them. "Sunset", by George H. James, has the true method but suffers from lack of originality of conception and imagery. "The Rhymester's Plight", by Walter Rice Davenport, is spirited light verse without pretensions to more mystical levels. It may be said on the whole that none of the current *Ripples* verse is devoid of merit.

Another publication achieving a high verse average is the cleverly modernistic *Now*. "Landscape in Shadow", by Frances Henderson, has marked distinction, for its pictorial images all transmit a strong and authentic mood, while its language fully sustains the atmosphere. Bits like "pale gold corn, swept by shades of phantasy" are memorable. "Mud Pies", by Angela Contrera, is authentic in mood but escapes poetic perfection by following the linguistic method of philosophic prose.

The file of *Tryout* contains some splendid recent specimens, notable among which is Leland B. Jacobs' sonnet "Dolores", in the June issue. Sincerity and musical form join finely in this pensive retrospection. "Winter Moonlight Reverie", by Erma Eaton, in the July issue, is less assured, yet possesses a convincing pictorial quality. In the September issue George W. Roberts' "Forgotten Ships" deserves especial praise because of the spontaneous adaptation of the rhythm to the theme and images. The work of Arthur Goodenough and Eugene B. Kuntz, represented in each issue, seldom sinks to banality, though it sometimes falls into usual patterns and employs statement instead of symbolism.

Scattered through the other current journals are many poems of very substantial worth. "Night River", by David H. Cade in the April *Portage*, shews a rich and powerful poetic vision which occasionally succeeds in achieving poignant expression, but which is handicapped by an unwillingness to exercise care and selectiveness in language and rhythm. In the summer *Ink Spots* "Remembrance", by Margaret Richards, has an original imagery altogether commendable; but "God's Gifts", by F. Earl Bonnell, contains the conventionality and didacticism which exclude actual poetic feeling. *Leisure Hours* for August has a very felicitous though not boldly novel poem by Mr. Goodenough entitled "The Heritage". Dr. Kuntz, in "I Sang a Song", unfortunately employs more conventional images than are found in the splendidly sincere mountain poetry forming his most distinguished work.

A bit of good light verse of the popular sort is Harry L. Swan's "Nebraska Spring" in the April *Goldenrod*. Smooth, though lacking the essence of original thought, feeling, and expression, are several pieces scattered through other magazines—"Found—Happiness", by Caddie M. Whitsitt, and "A Night in June", by Morris G. Weinstein, in the June *Search-Light;* "The Summer Walk", by Scot Bovlan in the June–July *Hullabaloo;* and "Kootenai River", by Doris H. Huffman in the April *Portage*. Verse of this kind is frequently very pleasant, and always argues a degree of accomplishment which may produce more solid material when directed inward and steered away from hackneyed prettiness and commonplace reflection. A greater amount of progress, however, would be required of versifiers as wholly conventional as Anita M. Wheeler in "The Fairy Dance" (August *Scribbler*) or Myrtle Evelyn Gonyeau in "Spring" (June–July *Hullabaloo*).

Among the season's products are two pamphlets of verse published by their respective authors, "Only a Red, Red Rose and Other Poems" by Victor A. Berry (32 pp.), and "Echoes", by Katherine Kennon Rucker (24 pp.). Neither of these is at all extreme in point of immaturity, though Mr. Berry's offering is thoroughly permeated with the well-worn sentimentality suggested by its title. Miss Rucker's "Echoes" are several steps in advance of this state, though their Millay-like lyricism does not often escape accustomed patterns and unsophisticated language and symbolism. The best poems are "Premeditation", with its real originality of conception, and "Silver Chips", which has the striking image:

> "The silver shavings of the moon
> Were curling everywhere."

On the whole, there is no reason to complain of the present state of amateur verse, or to feel that its average is greatly below that of any remembered period.

EDITOR'S NOTE FP: *National Amateur* 54, No. 2 (December 1931): 2–3, 6 (dated 21 October 1931). HPL's first Bureau of Critics column since the column of March 1923. He served as verse critic for much of the period 1931–36, and (as his letters to Edward H. Cole attest) was constantly soliciting the assistance of other amateur critics to handle other aspects of the Bureau of Critics (e.g., prose, typography, etc.). HPL's reports embody his revised thinking on verse form and technique as a result of his abandonment of literal adherence to eighteenth-century prosody; it is no surprise that such verse as *Fungi from Yuggoth* (1929–30) also embody these new principles.

*Notes*

1. The defintion comes from the article "Poetry" by British critic Theodore Watts[-Dunton] (1832–1914) in the 9th edition of the *Encyclopaedia Britannica*, which HPL owned (LL 299).

2. Zorn later joined the fantasy fandom movement and became an early commentator on HPL. His *Nix Nem Quarterly Review* in the late 1930s featured reviews of early HPL volumes, and his three issues of the *Lovecraft Collector* (January, May, and October 1949) contain much interesting matter.

---

# CRITICS SUBMIT FIRST REPORT

## H. P. Lovecraft and Helm C. Spink Turn In Criticisms

### Verse Section

Good verse has by no means been wanting in the National during the past six months, and more than one specimen has attained the grade of real poetry through its apt use of symbolism and imagery in conveying its message.

"Finis", by Ray H. Zorn in the June *Sea Gull*, is an example of modernism marked by figures as unusual as "The antimony chalice of quarter moon" and "My feet walk faithfully and disinterested as a horse at the shelling-mill." However one may regard the extreme forms of this studied avoidance of traditional poetic language, it cannot be denied that the fashion has a wholesome tendency to discourage dependence on stock phrases and imagery. It is the first duty of the poet to take his symbols directly from observation and experience rather than from mere literary usage, and this is what the moderns are trying most emphatically to do. It remains to be judged whether they overdo the principle badly in their occasional use of language and rhythms belonging distinctly to prose, and in their frequent concoction of obviously strained and attenu-ated similes and metaphors. Mr. Zorn, in this specimen, is more unconventional in ex-ternals than in essence; some of the figures—like the notably felicitous "Sand lies dead at the bottom of the glass"—being largely in the main tradition. That the intended mood is successfully created, no unbiased reader can doubt.

The Spring number of *Ripples from Lake Champlain* contains a number of authen-tic poems. In "The Singing of Spring", Charles Malam conveys a genuine picture with images of carefully chosen commonplaceness whose first-hand derivation gives them solid value. "Swamp Dusk" by Gordon Platt, and "Mood" by Bettie Margot Cassie, also possess a vivid pictorial and mood-suggesting quality. "Vanity" by Mary Katherine Newton, "Forsythia" by Frances Ball Coolidge, and "Rebirth" by Marjorie Tullar, are all effective examples of the allegorical rhetoric which finds symbols of human emotion in the phenomena of Nature. Another excellent poem by Miss Tullar, "Inspiration", appears in the Spring *Ink Spots*.

*Tryout* presents us with many pleasing specimens of verse from month to month, and it would be impossible to comment on every attractive poem in its pages. One of the most distinctive of its recent items is "Frontiers", by George W. Roberts, in the May issue, which despite a few structural awkwardnesses holds a very arresting poign-ancy and imaginative reach. Another short lyric of undoubted force is "Silence", by Sylvia Edith Comstock, in the Summer *Interim*.

Echoes of Mr. Orton's unusual sonnet, "Pension", continue to reverberate. The latest exercise in this vein is by the breezy editor of *Masaka*, who airs his opinion of the soul-tortured school of poets in an extremely clever bit of untitled light verse.

A new metrical voice in Amateurdom is that of Mr. Charles Finney Copeland, editor of *The Headlight*, who expresses a somewhat philosophic temperament in neatly turned verse with apt and vivid rhetoric which now and then raises it to considerable heights of pleasing forcefulness. Mr. Copeland likes to give his utterances a homely, every-day cast, and the tone of most of his reflections tends toward the practical and popular rather than toward the abstract, the complex, or the metaphysical. Of the specimens at hand, the most interesting is a rhymed soliloquy of the "Spirit of Trans-portation", in which the author displays a notable sense of pageantry and scope of imagination despite the sometimes prosaic and commonplace nature of his vocabulary, diction, and images. The trim, old-fashioned metre with its clever internal rhymes is a pleasure to scan, although we must admit that the handling of the subject as a whole is a trifle too scientific and factual, and too little dependent on pure symbolism and ec-stasy, to form actual poetry in the strictest and narrowest sense. Keenly poetic flashes, however, are gratifyingly abundant.

EDITOR'S NOTE FP: *National Amateur* 55, No. 2 (December 1932): 1–2. HPL discusses re-cent verse contributions to the NAPA, especially those of Ray H. Zorn.

---

# VERSE CRITICISM

The Summer–Autumn *Ripples from Lake Champlain* does not disappoint those who have come to expect an ample quota of genuine poetry from that publication. Charles Malam contributes two especially notable poems, "Silhouette of Trees", with its vivid pictorial and symbolic elements, and "The Waters Recede", with its quiet tragedy and authentic Vermont psychology. "Old House", by George Scott Gleason, transmits a sombre mood with admirable fidelity, but could be considerably smoother in metre—especially as regards the last line. Other distinctive items in the magazine are "Small Home", by Elizabeth Warner Merill; the sonnet "Evergreens", by Lillian Thayer Stoddard; and the thoughtful though metrically irregular "Hereafter", by Vera Doyle Willard.

Rugged verse of the sort which hovers precariously between poetry and epigram is exemplified in recent papers by the clever work of Sesta Matheison, whose "Vanity" in the Fall *Ink Spots,* and "Contrast" in the November *Empire,* are thoughtful and well phrased. "Desire", a bit of regular verse by the same author, has less originality.

The current work of Katherine K. Rucker maintains its author's increasingly high standard, with "Fragility" in the Fall *Goldenrod,* and the rather originally modelled "Jazz" in the November *Empire,* as salient specimens.

Considerable good material by Margaret Nickerson Martin appears in the autumn and winter journals. "Indian Summer", in the November *World Contact,* has a fine pictorial quality despite the doubtful use of "wove" as a participle. "Wanderlust", in the same paper, is too much of a catalogue to possess the same imaginative appeal.

The sonnets of Malvin B. Plunkett are generally smooth and thoughtful, though their purely poetic quality is often marred by obvious didacticism. Excellent recent samples are "Jewels" in the December *Tryout* and "Psychology" in the November *World Contact.*

Of the very youthful generation, Arthur Cantor is a figure of unusual promise; his "Solitude", in the November *Empire,* being a delightful bit of imagery and mood despite some of the obvious rhymes and expressions common to early work. These touches of the trite (such as "breeze-trees" and "clod-God" rhymes) are by no means obtrusive or bound up with the thought; indeed, most of the text is commendably free from stock phraseology. "Serenade", in the December *Tryout,* is highly musical in metre, but somewhat awkward in phraseology. Expressions like "Song of the serenade" are plainly tautological, while there is an inescapable awkwardness and lack of real meaning in such an attempted comparison as "putting opera in the pale". These flaws will undoubtedly disappear as the author's familiarity with the best poetry grows wider, more intimate, and more analytical. Likewise, he will later on choose themes less secondhandedly "literary" than the unmistakably hackneyed nightingale. "Inspirations", in the Fall *Goldenrod,* exhibits Mr. Cantor in a lighter mood, and is quite adequate except for certain vague flatnesses of diction (such as use of the essentially cheap expression "galore") which further experience will certainly remove.

Other promising youthful work includes "Bits", by Mary Mosher in the *Garden State Amateur,* which shews a keen appreciation of beauty. "Wintry Days", by Anna Feinberg in the December *Aberations,* is vivid and fresh despite the outworn stock phrases (like "grand and glorious") and other immature touches (like "frost *so* gray" and "clouds float by *so* lazily") characteristic of beginners' products. The concluding stanza is rather forced in its language and falls below the level of the rest. "Life", by the same author in the same paper, is a little too obviously sententious to form poetry in the strictest sense.

EDITOR'S NOTE FP: *National Amateur* 55, No. 3 (March 1933): 3. A brief account of NAPA verse during the previous months.

# REPORT OF BUREAU OF CRITICS

### Verse Criticism

Mr. Edward J. O'Gara, in the February *Sunapee Echoes*, brings a new and welcome voice to amateur poetry. While not altogether free from certain stock characteristics of traditional verse—such as an occasional "mayhap", "oft and again", "pearly morn", and "starry night"—he tends to possess a very gratifying command of his medium, and at no point falls into crudity. Mr. O'Gara's current specimens all display a decidedly genuine poetic fire and vision, and an unmistakable ability to communicate these things in apt, vivid, and concrete images. "Autumn" splendidly captures the spirit of the declining year, and contains a succession of graphic sound impressions which sink in as effectively as the visual ones. "Sunapee Harbour" conveys the essential feeling of a landscape with delightful directness and potency. "Impatience", an experiment in the modern manner, is far from feeble; yet leaves one with the opinion that traditionalism is really better suited to the author.

The Spring *Ohioan* has more than one poem worthy of note. "My Dream Castle", by Alfred L. Mooney, follows an odd and original pattern—unrhymed but regular— which fits itself very well to the plan of detached images. Of these images most have a hint of freshness and vigour which promises well for the poet's development. Ray H. Zorn's "Faithlessness", in the same issue, is cast in free verse of adequate strength and rhythm, though its mode of attaining its effect is perhaps primarily intellectual rather than imaginative. "Radio Brings Your Voice", by Pearl A. Rawling, is smooth and acceptable, even if unmarked by especial distinctiveness. Katherine K. Rucker's two poems in the April *New Amateur* are both full of charm, as is Arthur Goodenough's "April" in the same paper.

In *The Flying Quill* for January, Earl Henry has a simple little poem, "The First Snow", whose net effect is curiously appealing despite an apparent excess of naiveté and a hint of the unconsciously comic in the lines: "Heed not the rabbits, little boy, they call thee but to slay." The April *Sea Gull* contains, very appropriately, Rev. Eugene B. Kuntz's poem "Sea Gulls", whose fresh and graphic imagery produces a lasting picture.

The season's juvenile verse is well represented by the stanzas "My Dog", by Fay Master, aged 9, in the February *Watch Tower*. The extremely youthful poetess writes with a smooth, sprightly correctness which many of her elders might well envy, and the material is wholly free from the usual ponderous didacticism of tender years. Another youthful product is "Evening on the Ocean", by Anna N. Feinberg in the February 11th *Manettism*. While the metre is very uncertain, the obviously fresh and vigorous imaginative approach to the subject marks the poem as one of distinct promise.

Light verse, of which really excellent specimens are not very common in amateurdom, receives an unusually clever exemplification in James F. Morton's "The Weather", in the March *Brooklynite*. Joined to a genuinely witty handling of the subject is a fluent heroic measure employing double rhymes throughout.

The balance of the season's verse appears to be largely of a somewhat didactic or homiletic nature; illustrating the tendency of the young, and of the beginner in general, to use metre for the reiteration of obvious ethical or philosophical truths rather than for that expression of moods or crystallisation of pictures which forms the essential province of poetry. This, however, does not prevent many of the specimens in question from being highly ingenious in conception and smooth in technical form.

"Three Verses", by Florence Grow Proctor in the February *Printer's Pet,* have all the felicity of polished epigrams. "Happiness", by John W. Miller in the same paper, is equally smooth and correct, but perhaps a little closer to prose in spirit. "Kind Words", by Chester A. Rhodes, is more amateurish; containing, in addition to very trite subject-matter and phrases, the false rhyme of "name" and "vain". One of the first tasks of the poetic novice should be to learn just what word combinations are actual rhymes, and what are not. However, the metre of this piece is correct throughout.

Margaret Nickerson Martin is represented by several excellent specimens; one of which—"Rendezvous" in the March *Spare Time*—escapes the author's prevailing didacticism. This promising poem is marred by one false rhyme ("this"—"tryst") and by a full line of painful inversions—"And seek, to fact with fancy meet". "Dross", in the February *Sea Gull,* would be better if the last stanza did not fail in metre. The line "You may dishonor give, for true" is especially in need of emendation—not only in metre, but in syntax and meaning. Grammatical inversions such as occur here are no longer tolerated in serious verse. "Footsteps", in the February *Spare Time,* is good except for the attempted rhyme of the syllable "self" with itself. Identical syllables do not make a true rhyme, a difference in the opening consonant (coupled, of course, with absolute identity in the final consonant) being required. "Hope", in the March *World Contact,* has excellent passages, though the metre of certain lines seems to be unnecessarily rugged.

"Youth and Old Age", by Edith Buckminster in the February *Spare Time,* is smooth and pleasing despite some exceedingly trite stock phrases.

EDITOR'S NOTE  FP: *National Amateur* 55, No. 4 (June 1933): 8. HPL discusses the verse of Edward J. O'Gara, Margaret Nickerson Martin, and other amateurs.

---

## BUREAU OF CRITICS COMMENT ON VERSE, TYPOGRAPHY, PROSE

### Verse

Amidst the generous summer and autumn flood of amateur verse one may scarcely do more than select a few representative specimens for comment. Much of the current material, it must be granted, is frankly metrical rhetoric rather than that intense, symbolic, and largely pictorial form of emotional expression properly called poetry; but this is only to be expected in a realm where novice and initiate meet on equal terms. Good metrical rhetoric in itself forms an accomplishment far from trivial; and the statement that a certain rhymed composition is not actual poetry must not be considered as an inherent slight.

Of the season's metrical output, the most notable items are without doubt two poems by Rev. Eugene B. Kuntz—"The Carlsbad Caverns", in *Leisure Hours* for January 1933, and "A Sunrise in Pecos Valley", in the Spring *Goldenrod.* Both of these specimens have slight touches of cumbrousness in phraseology, yet each is none the less emphatically a true poem, conveying with remarkable richness a genuine imaginative picture fully envisaged and poignantly felt by the poet. The lines on the great caverns have many images clearly springing from the poet's own vision and appreciation, such as:

> "Magenta floating in the golden sea,
> And purple bubbling up from pools of blue"

and other conceptions of singular geometrical and chromatic effects. In the sunrise poem the sense of pageantry is marvellously simulated despite a few admittedly trite passages. Even where the language is well-worn, it is impossible not to recognise the clearness of the stupendous picture in the author's mind. He sees a thing definitely, feels it strongly, and manages to transmit something of his feeling to the reader. That is what poetry is. Dr. Kuntz is a poet in the most authentic sense, a thing we must not allow his voluminous newspaper verse—which naturally has a different object and follows different traditions—to make us forget.

Another bard to whom honours are due is the very youthful but remarkably precocious Arthur Cantor, whose improvement month by month argues the laying of a solid poetical basis. "Awakening", in the Spring *Goldenrod*, triumphs over a hackneyed vernal theme. Its sprightly use of ballad metre is admirably suited to its airy material, indicating that the young poet realises a secret of his craft which all too many amateurs ignore—namely, that the mood and atmosphere of a poem ought to be reflected in the sound and accent, as well as in the dictionary meaning, of the words. Most beginners adopt a metre and vocabulary without much consideration of their express relevance to the given theme; merely trying to have the syllables count correctly, and selecting words for cold meaning alone instead of pausing to decide whether the spoken sound contributes to the force of the ultimate impression. This is probably a result of the virtual ignoring of oral in favour of written expression—a tendency which the prevalence of the radio will in time tend to counteract. "Solitude", in the April *Leisure Hours*, is a rather remotely titled lyric on the autumn wind; involving a brisk and capable use of that rugged semi-modern metre which wavers between the dactyl and the anapaest. The varied imagery of the lines suggests a fertile imagination increasingly capable of expressing itself through symbols, pictures, and associational devices rather than through tame prose statement.

A new singer of much grace and smoothness is Mr. Frank Bailey, whose sonnet "The Rose", in the April *World Contact*, and whose quatrains entitled "Fickle" in the July *New Amateur*, display a gratifying level of taste and metrical accomplishment.

In the May *Sunapee Echoes* Mr. Edward J. O'Gara's "Sunset" contains a pleasing flight of fancy but is marred by a somewhat anticlimactic and tritely conceived last stanza. The contraction of *handiwork* to *handwork* for metrical convenience is hardly a felicitous or even permissible liberty. The same paper contains two not unpromising verses of more amateurish calibre by Mrs. Fred Martin, and an appealing juvenile bit called "Wishing", by Helen Beal, aged 10.

"Friendship", by Eleanor A. Chaffee in the May *Leisure Hours*, is commendable for well-handled ideas and correct and tasteful diction. Ray H. Zorn's "Incident" in the July *Watch Tower* has undeniable vigour, yet contains the quite inexcusable false rhyme of *pass* and *last*. In the May *Spare Time* is Edith M. Buckminster's "Spring", which has vivid touches of fancy despite essential triteness of theme and wavering uncertainty of metre. The various issues of the *Granite State News* contain several verses by Doris M. Johnson, apparently a juvenile poetess. Underneath the irregular metre and rather sketchy grammar ("All wish he could *of* lived more") there occur many hints of a quite encouraging degree of imagination, especially in "The Brook" and "To a Pine Tree".

A very interesting poem—containing perhaps as much of the sheer poetic spirit as any other piece of the season's verse yet handicapped by a somewhat elementary style which includes awkward inversions like *tower high* and artificially archaic contractions like *'neath*—is "The Window", by Frances Heatley Hoskins in the May *Sea Gull*. This brief vignette, while weighted by a somewhat trite and conventional allegorical touch in the last couplet, contains one of the very few really bold poetic pictures found in amateur verse—a window looking down from a high tower

> "Just half way up between the earth and . . . the vaulted sky;
> By it roars the winter wind, black hair streaming free,
> And Little Lady April's feet come dancing from the sea.
> A white bird soars sublimely, the planets meditate . . ."

This—we may remind those exponents of flat rhyming prose who seem so unable to grasp the kind of imagination which makes actual poetry—is undoubted poetry, though obviously of a developing sort whose linguistic framework is not yet fluent and assured. It is the nimble fancy manifest in striking visual imagery which here forms the essence of the poetic feeling. Further work of the author will be worth watching closely.

Another piece much smoother in technique and almost as boldly poetic in its imagery is "Sanctuary", by Ralph Allen Lang in the October *Americana*. This graceful and musical sonnet is of splendidly correct craftsmanship, and has a pictorial vividness which never flags or trickles into empty rhetoric. On the whole, it probably forms the most thoroughly satisfactory single poem of the season's assortment. The only possible point to criticise is the slight conventionality manifest in such a hackneyed allusion as "Aurora", and such a well-worn compound as "dew-drenched".

Other items in *Americana* well attest the good judgment of its poetry editor, Mr. Alfred L. Mooney. His own lines "Admonition to Love" are especially effective, as is "The Lady Poverty", by Evelyn Underhill.[1]

Of current examples of free verse Rychard Fink's "Swim" in the June *Molecule* contains more of the true concrete sensation which is poetry than does the philosophic, reflective "My Mind", by Angela Gertrude Smith in the April *Leisure Hours*. In structure, however, it is less finished; there being very little to justify its division into lines. While Miss Smith's line-units seem at least partly motivated, nearly all of Mr. Fink's cleavages appear to be quite arbitrary and capricious, serving only to chop up a rather good piece of impressionistic prose-poetry. It is very probable that more than half of the existing specimens of so-called free verse would be much better off if left in connected prose form. Wilde, Dunsany, and many of the French symbolists illustrate the heights to which genuine prose-poetry can rise.

In the several issues of *Hodge Podge* before us we behold what seems to be a semi-professional broadside very usefully devoted to versification and kindred interests. Unfortunately the aesthetic standard of the enterprise—aside from such elementary and academic matters as rhyme and scansion—is of a rather indiscriminate liberality, so that a great deal of obviously flat material and strained expression is steadily featured. Mr. Frank Baldwin's "Ballade of New York" in the July issue has occasional passages of potent suggestion, but is marred by such awkward lines as these:

> "From present back to old Dutch time"
> "To days of graft, probes, towers, crime"

and at least the following grammatical slip, where a singular verb tries to match with a plural subject:

> ". . . . where *doth* chime
> Strange medleys, vile curses, obscene rhyme."

Incidentally, the metre of the last-quoted line would bear emendation.

EDITOR'S NOTE  FP: *National Amateur* 56, No. 2 (December 1933): 1–2. HPL discusses the verse of Eugene B. Kuntz, Arthur Cantor, and other amateurs.

*Notes*

1. Evelyn Underhill (1875–1941) was a British writer on religion most celebrated for her study *Mysticism* (1911). One assumes that the poem in question is a reprint from some standard magazine.

---

# BUREAU OF CRITICS
*(June 1934)*

## Verse

In examining the recent poetic products of the National one is moved to wish that the standard of technical skill might be built up a little more generally than it is at present. Several observers have pointed out how great a bulk of amateur verse ignores all or many of the laws of rhyme, metre, and verbal or rhetorical appropriateness; remaining essentially on the level of hit-or-miss doggerel, with its message presented in lines of uncertain length, accent, and rhyme, and in phrases either lifelessly trite or clumsy with a dominantly prose vocabulary and manner. The chief complaint against this type of writing is not that it is not poetry, but that it is not forcible or effective expression of any kind.

Indeed, we sometimes find a definitely poetic mood or conception imbedded in lame verse of this sort, its vigour hopelessly sapped and its point hopelessly blunted by the stumbling immaturity of its medium. Of course, it would be absurd to censure the real beginner for being in a crude stage through which everyone must pass at the outset. The trouble is that too many casual bards are content to stay beginners, never bothering to learn the rules and styles which transform shapeless feebleness into pointed and graceful utterance.

The process of learning the various metres or fixed arrangements of accents essential to good verse is not in the least difficult. There are not many of these metres, and to grasp and recognise each of them is an extremely simple matter. It is also extremely simple to understand that any one unit of verse must stick to the same arrangement of accents in each line instead of stammering on in an unbalanced and unguided fashion and producing amorphous results like the following—an actual recent example:

> "When it must continually grind
> On one thing particularly in mind."

Rhyme, too, is not a complex thing. There are certain easily recognised types of sound-arrangement which form true rhymes, and certain types which do not. The laws of the case are very clear, so that we need only study a few simple rules in order to avoid the painful false rhymes (like *rain-name, pass-last,* etc.) with which amateur verse is so badly cluttered.

Nor is appropriate wording—though admittedly a harder subject than mere metre and rhyme—by any means as formidable a study as most suppose. An alert and copious course of reading in the standard poets—plus a steadfast ignoring of cheap newspaper and pulp magazine jingles—will soon teach any average person what general forms of language are appropriate to verse and what are not.

Altogether, it would seem that the failure of certain amateurs to advance beyond the cruder stages of versification is caused mostly by a sheer lack of easy information which might quickly be obtained if the right facilities were at hand. We cannot too strongly urge the novice not to rest satisfied until he has read some elementary book or article on the rules of metre and rhyme, and on the right sort of models to follow. There are many excellent things of the kind—an especially concise, dependable, plainly worded, and inexpensive specimen being the booklet by George E. Teter entitled "An Introduction to Some Elements of Poetry". This brochure may be obtained from The Kenyon Press, Wauwatosa, Wisconsin, for a very nominal sum.[1]

Of current metrical specimens a number deserve notice either for force and aptness of imagination or for grace of structure. In "Mountain and Man", in the October *Watch Tower,* James F. Morton employs a stately, traditional blank verse medium to present some concepts of peculiar grandeur and impressiveness, whose cosmic scope amply atones for any suggestions of heaviness or didacticism. Milder aspects of Nature find potent symbolic embodiment in Eugene B. Kuntz's "Aspen in Autumn", in the December *Tryout.*

A new voice in the National is that of Mrs. Natalie Hartley Wooley,[2] whose brief, wistful lyrics strike one's fancy with singular sharpness through certain faint overtones subtly suggesting magical vistas and dim regions beyond the confines of daylight reality. "Western Night", in the Summer *Goldenrod,* has great charm and power; while "Flight", in the October *Sea Gull,* unites with its general elfin quality a poignant human pathos.

Katherine K. Rucker continues to contribute pleasingly and generously to the amateur press, and displays an increasing power in eschewing the trivial and conquering metrical obstacles. Close attention to metre, and the cultivation of a sharp discrimination between different kinds of poetic "feet", are the chief things one might at present recommend to Miss Rucker for consideration. Of her recent contributions "A Sad Good Bye", in the November *Bookmark,* deserves especial notice for its imagery. Its possible points of improvement are purely technical—such as a stricter preservation of the original iambic metre, which falters somewhat in the second stanza, and a stricter attention to verbal accuracy in order to avoid lapses like the employment of *pierce* in a passive sense, and the use of *reply* without a preposition as if it were the word *answer.*

George H. Coffin, in the October *Eaglet,* presents several bits of imagery in both free and regular verse which speaks well for his poetic sensitiveness. The verses of Edith M. Buckminster in the August *Spare Time* also show a highly promising ability to speak in symbols. In *The Headlight* for October Mr. Charles Finney Copeland presents several samples of straightforward didactic verse in metre of gratifying accuracy.

An especially distinctive bit of recent poetry is Frances Davis Adams's powerful and macabre sonnet "Taloned Night", in the January *Hodge Podge.* Genuine emotion and extremely vivid imagery stamp this piece as far removed from the average—passages like the following being particularly effective:

"Where winking stars unceasing whirl and shed
Their whittled points within a primrose arc."

"This is the hour to climb the thunder's back
And race before the talons of the night."

Among juvenile products, honourable mention should be given to "Christmas Night", by Mary Jane Thomas (age 9) in the Christmas *Manettism*, and "Christmas Day Tragedy", by Nancy Black (age 11) in the December *Pen Point*.

EDITOR'S NOTE FP: *National Amateur* 56, No. 4 (June 1934): 7–8. HPL prefaces his discussion of amateur verse with remarks on what constitutes verse as opposed to prose—an issue also broached in such other essays as "Notes on Verse Technique" and "What Belongs in Verse" (both in CE2).

*Notes*

1. George E. Teter, *An Introduction to Some Elements of Poetry* (Wauwatosa, WI: Kenyon Press, [1927]; *LL* 868). HPL may have revised this work, as he appears to have been doing some revision work for the Kenyon Press at this time.
2. Wooley, about whom little is known, became a late correspondent of HPL. She wrote to HPL both individually and as part of the late correspondence group, the Coryciani.

# CHAIRMAN OF THE BUREAU OF CRITICS REPORTS ON POETRY

Lovecraft Finds Much Good Verse; Commends Improvement Campaign

Recent months have brought out an unusual amount of good verse in the National, auguring well for the qualitative renaissance to which the new administration is committed. Very welcome, too, are the current efforts to improve and popularise the work of the members—the admirable set of poetic hints by Maurice W. Moe in the Summer *Perspective Review*, the friendly exploitations featured in recent issues of *The Tryout*, and the verse contest instituted in the *Review* by our present Official Editor, Mr. Bradley.

Notable amongst the contemporary output are the two sea-poems by George H. Coffin in the February *Eaglet*: "Islands" and "The Difference". Here we find vivid concrete pictures, and comparisons which are apt if not altogether novel, set in a verbal medium of smooth construction and satisfying rhythm. Verse like this is obviously the gifted expression of sincere emotion; in other words, real poetry.

Equally genuine is the poetic quality of Earl Henry's prize-winning "Winter Hut" in the April *Perspective Review*. The wistful pensiveness of these lines is not merely a matter of words, but something echoed in the metrical structure as well. Another distinguished and adequate bit of pensiveness is Stewart Atkins's well-turned sonnet "Request", in the May *Bookmark*. The same mood redeemed at the end by a compensating glow of cheer is very gracefully portrayed in Richard A. Thomas, Jr.'s "Song for a Winter Night" in the February *Bookmark*.

Margaret Nickerson Martin continues to enrich amateurdom with a steady stream of excellent work, of which "Sea Fever" in the Summer *Perspective Review*, and "Request" (a curious parallel in theme and title to Mr. Atkins's sonnet!) in the undated *Rose*, are especially fine specimens. Another lyrist of growing power is Miriam Bralley, whose "To Daphne" in the April *Bookmark* and "Rain Dress" in the March 3 *Manettism* display a very promising combination of sprightly fancy and clever image-making. And of a kindred lyric grace, enhanced by a strongly musical quality, is the poem "Summer Night", by Alida Grenelle in the Summer *Eaglet*.

John Steindler's "Pot Pourri" in the Spring *Voyageur* presents some unusually poignant images in irregular form. In the Winter 1933 issue of the same magazine John Tangney conveys an impression of power through more conventional channels in "Sea Prayer". A similar air of genuineness, though coupled with a slight juvenility manifest in well-worn phrases like "tree-tops on high" and in such a "poetic" contraction as "'Tis", pervades Sally True's appealing lines on "The Forest Trees" in the June *Encinal*.

One of the most deeply excellent poems of the season is "Sanctuary" by Natalie Hartley Wooley in the March *Sea Gull*. Rhythm and language unite to convey a subtle impression of dreamy unreality, as in the lines

> "Lie in a drowsy quietude beneath the swinging stars"

and

> "And life a strange dim echo of the song the ages sung."

"Finis", by Jack Sellers in the February *Hodge Podge*, is a grave and excellent sonnet. In a lighter vein of wistfulness is Myrtle Olive Strang's bit of anapaestic verse, "Lost Dreams of a Vagabond", in the Summer *Perspective Review*. Margaret L. Richards ably continues the pensive strain in "Shooting Stars", in the June *Empire*.

Among the more lilting lyrics of the season may be noted Ben H. Smith's tuneful "Lilac Time" in the May *Tryout*. "Melody", by Russell L. Paxton in the Summer *Californian*, has an undeniable sprightliness despite the handicap of hackneyed lines like "singing, dear, of you" and "Tears the heart of me".

In the domain of thoughtful, unrhymed verse, J. David Adams's "The Acid Test" in the Summer *Eaglet* deserves mention for its analytic seriousness. Possibly the same ideas might be expressed in a more symbolic way, less in the manner of prose, but such added subtleties are things which can be acquired gradually and unconsciously through practice and the reading of the best poets. In "A Path Beside the Sea" Robert S. Wilson displays marked promise. There are naive and prosy passages, where bold statement and essentially unpoetic expression tend to jar on the sensitive reader—for example:

> "Where schoolboys from the nearby town delight to take a swim"

and

> "Some man has called this Chapman's point. I call it paradise."

But in spite of these defects there are present a keen observation and a zestful type of concrete description which mark the author as a true poet and indicate that further study and practice would amply repay him.

EDITOR'S NOTE FP: *National Amateur* 57, No. 1 (5 September 1934): Sec. 2, p. 3. HPL discusses current NAPA verse.

# MRS. MINITER—ESTIMATES AND RECOLLECTIONS

## I.

It would be an interesting if invidious task to attempt a classification of amateur journalists past and present on a basis of sheer quality. The process would not be simple; for to be a "great amateur" one must not only possess absolute intellectual or aesthetic talent, and excellence in scholarship and letters, but must successfully devote a substantial part of his energies to the furtherance of what is really best in the amateur cause. Fame founded on political prowess and purely social activity in amateurdom, or on triumphs—literary or otherwise—in the outside world, would not count. Only high-grade thinkers and creators serving amateurdom in a high-grade way would be eligible for exaltation. The number of the "great" as reckoned by such a standard would probably be smaller than we like to think—but in their very front rank, acclaimed without a dissenting voice, would undoubtedly be placed the late Edith Miniter.

Mrs. Miniter was the daughter of a poetess and a mathematician, and in her own personality and work as a fiction-writer the diverse strains clearly shewed. She had, while disavowing poetry as a major interest, a sense of the soil, and of the pageantry of life and visible forms, which amounted to a poet's symbolism. Yet at the same time her keen faculty for observation, analysis, and comparison forbade her to view mankind and the world through a poet's sentimental haze. Her eye for the minutiae of human conduct, speech, and manners was almost preternaturally sharp; and this, coupled with her extreme sensitiveness to incongruities and comic contrasts, marked her out early as a natural humourist and ironist. She was a sworn and consistent foe of the pompous, the extravagant, and the romantic. A born deflater, she scorned the stupid optimisms, violent, overcoloured situations, false emotions and motivations, and artificial "happy endings" which cluttered up the dominant fiction of her earlier years.

In short stories and novels alike she chose to draw the ordinary people she knew in the ordinary situations most common to them. With her tremendous command of detail, she built up characters so life-like that our memories confuse them with persons we have met. All their traits and foibles stand out before us, and we watch their groping progress through the familiar every-day world toward that impasse of unsatisfying inconclusiveness which forms the goal of most human pilgrimages. We see their fatuous, practical, or greedy springs of action without the varnish of conventional sentiment and mendacious melodrama; we follow their gestures, idioms, accents, and typical absurdities, till each figure becomes utterly individualised and unforgettable. The satire is never heavy or violent. Always subtle, it peeps forth slyly as an integral part of the description and perspective. Addison and Jane Austen, especially the latter, are comparisons which naturally occur to one. And yet there is at times a certain grim realism which vaguely suggests something more—perhaps the objective school of Flaubert and de Maupassant, despite Mrs. Miniter's conscious rejection of all influences and subjects outside her own ancestral stream.

For above all things, Mrs. Miniter was an unalloyed outgrowth of her hereditary soil. It was supremely appropriate that, though her childhood home was in Worcester and the scene of her mature activities as writer and newspaper woman was Boston, she chanced to be born in her grandfather's farmhouse on Wilbraham Mountain in Central Massachusetts, amidst fields and groves that her forbears had known for generations. New England's rock-strown countryside, its great elms, its stone walls and winding roads, its white-steepled villages, and its curious moods, phrases, and folkways formed the core of her inheritance; and upon this most of her interests and art was built.

The books, records, and tangible objects connected with the long continuous stream of local life fascinated her profoundly, so that eventually her antiquarianism reached a professional status. As a collector of old china she was notable, and readers of the Boston Transcript and Springfield Republican will not soon forget her articles on antiques, old schoolbooks, local history, and bygone customs of which she was almost the last first-hand reporter. Her zeal in research and her memory for ancient things were fully as sharp as her observation of details around her. No more indefatigable collector of quaint epitaphs ever lived.

Nor was she ever long out of touch with the ancestral scene. Nearly every summer or autumn found her in the shadow of Wilbraham Mountain—while, with a symbolic aptness rivalling that of her birth, the last nine years of her life were spent on the ancient soil, in the rambling, antique-filled farmhouse of a close friend and extremely distant cousin. With such a programme, her detailed, coördinated knowledge and basic, sympathetic comprehension of Central New England character, speech, legends, manners, and customs became those of a profound specialist. The field was worthy of her devotion, for the Connecticut Valley's backwaters present typical and tenacious phases of life not to be found elsewhere; phases contrasting sharply with the brisk, well-ordered, seaward-gazing, and often adventurous life of coastal New England and its vivid old ports.

In the first Puritan days this region was a trackless wilderness covered with black woods whose depths the settlers' fancy peopled with unknown horrors and evil shadows. Then the Bay Path was hewn through to the settlements on the Connecticut, and after King Philip's War thin streams of pioneers began to trickle along it and branch off from it; cutting faint roadways and clearing meagre farmsteads on the silent rocky hillsides. Grim, low-pitched, unpainted farmhouses sprang up in the lee of craggy slopes, their dim, small-paned windows looking secretively off across leagues of loneliness. Life was hard and practical, and contact with the world very slight. Old tales and thoughts and words and ways persisted, and people remembered odd fancies which others had forgotten. There was less breadth and changing of ideas; less response to new times; than on the coast, where links with Europe were many, and where prosperity and "book-l'arnin'" had fostered a more flexible mentality.

The years passed, and modern influences stole into the Wilbraham country. Springfield's proximity began to be felt, and a stately brick academy arose in the village on fields above the sleepy, elm-shaded street. Farmers throve in a modest way, and took on a literacy and taste clearly reflected in the general life. Finer houses were built. But always the undercurrent of isolation and ancient whispers persisted. One of Mrs. Miniter's ancestresses in the early nineteenth century was a suspected witch; and people talked about the queer sounds in the air each evening at the pasture bars where the road bends north of the mountain.

Then the cityward tide set in, and some of the most vigorous stock vanished—to return only for burial in the spectral cemeteries near the village. Funerals, Mrs. Miniter once wrote, came to form Wilbraham's chief industry. Deserted houses grew common, and some of the humbler farmers began to shew queer softenings of morale and queer vagaries in their standards. Foreigners appeared—the typical Connecticut Valley Poles whom the keen realist so faithfully depicted in her novel "Our Natupski Neighbors".[1] A new element of sombreness was added to the old background of persistent legend— the sombreness of decay, desolation, and impending change. Even in its late phases the ancient land cannot lose its distinctiveness! All this Mrs. Miniter caught as clearly as she caught the ancestral heritage. She was, from first to last, a realist; and in her the brooding countryside had a voice and an historian.

But in no sense was Mrs. Miniter a rustic, provincial, or one-sided artist. Side by side with her reflection of old backgrounds was a mature, cosmopolitan scholarship and general culture which always made her see her chosen field in its true perspective. Her interests were as wide as those of any other urban litterateur, as all who knew her stories, book-reviews, and brilliant conversation can well attest. In taste she followed the nineteenth-century main stream, though constantly transcending it in unexpected ways. None excelled her in social accomplishments and organising genius; qualities which made her for over thirty years the natural leader of Boston amateurdom and the originator of the most typical touches of wit and distinctiveness in the Hub Club's programmes and publications. No mere coincidence caused the death of the club only a few months after her final departure from Boston.

## II.

The details of Mrs. Miniter's long career—a career inseparable from amateur journalism after her sixteenth year—will doubtless be covered by writers well qualified to treat of them. Reared in Worcester, taught by her poet-mother and at a private school, and given to solid reading and literary attempts from early childhood onward, the erstwhile Edith May Dowe entered amateurdom in 1883 and was almost immediately famous in our small world as a fictional realist. Controversies raged over her stories—so different from the saccharine froth of the period—but very few failed to recognise her importance. After 1890 she was engaged in newspaper and magazine work in the larger outside world, though her interest in amateur matters increased rather than diminished.

From 1894 onward she dominated the historic Hub Club of Boston, and was foremost in ensuring the success of amateur conventions in her city. In 1895 she was official editor of the National, and in 1909 she became its president. Her occasional editorship of *The Hub Club Quill*, and of various individual papers, gave repeated proof of her peculiar charm as a humorous commentator, and of her skill and effectiveness in meeting amateurdom's diverse issues. Especially famous was her *Aftermath*, published after the conventions she attended and touching on their salient features with inimitable humour and acuteness. The same qualities of wit and observation animated all her letters, so that she was highly valued as a correspondent. Her home, whatever its location, was always a recognised headquarters of amateurs—its charm enhanced by the presence of her gifted mother, Mrs. Jennie E. T. Dowe, from 1896 until Mrs. Dowe's death in 1919.

In 1916 appeared Mrs. Miniter's novel "Our Natupski Neighbors", the sequel to which has unfortunately never seen publication. Her short stories had meanwhile gained a substantial foothold in many standard magazines, while her reviews and antiquarian articles enjoyed more than a local fame. Actually, she deserved even more recognition than she received. It was her misfortune to follow a middle course in an age of abrupt transition—so that in youth her work was far in advance of its time, while in later life it failed to keep pace with the decadent and abnormal interests of modernism. It was in the "Natupski" period that she and her environment most closely coincided, and that she received the enthusiastic praise of William Lyon Phelps and other critics.[2] At no time could she have been an idol of the masses, since her work was too honest for vitiated popular taste. Her integrity as an artist was absolute. She did not cater to the low-grade demands of the herd, and probably could not have done so had she wished.

My own direct acquaintance with Mrs. Miniter dates only from the summer of 1920, when I first attended gatherings of the Boston amateurs. She was then inhabiting the memorable halls of 20 Webster St. in Allston—"Epgephian Temple" of cryptic amateur lore—and was, as always, surrounded by a home-like array of antiques and family possessions, and attended by a faithful feline bearing the various names of "Grey Brother", "Grey Bother", and "Tat".

The festive July conclave marking my introduction is still fresh in memory.[3] Though of diminutive stature, and given to choosing a low and inconspicuous seat amidst an assembly, Mrs. Miniter did not fail to dominate more or less imperceptibly every event at which she was present. Her piquant conversation and constant humour gave a vividness to the most ordinary happenings, and vastly enlivened an all-day trip to Castle Island. My own bias toward the archaic made me especially appreciative of her interests in that direction. Later I enjoyed the spirited and hilarious comments on the gathering which she published—both under her own name and as the amanuensis of "Tat"—in that short-lived but unforgettable journal *Epgephi*.

For the next few years I saw Mrs. Miniter quite often at meetings and festivals of the Hub Club, and always admired the effectiveness with which she devised entertainment and maintained interest. In April, 1921, her quaintly named and edited paper *The Muffin Man* contained a highly amusing parody of one of my weird fictional attempts . . . "Falco Ossifracus, by Mr. Goodguile"[4] . . . though it was not of a nature to arouse hostility. Notwithstanding her saturation with the spectral lore of the countryside, Mrs. Miniter did not care for stories of a macabre or supernatural cast; regarding them as hopelessly extravagant and unrepresentative of life. Perhaps that is one reason why, in the early Boston days, she had declined a chance to revise a manuscript of this sort which later met with much fame—the vampire-novel "Dracula", whose author was then touring America as manager for Sir Henry Irving.[5]

It was in September, 1921, that W. Paul Cook issued his ample brochure in memory of Mrs. Dowe,[6] for which Mrs. Miniter furnished a magnificent tribute in the form of a biographical sketch of her mother. This sketch, in which the ancestral Wilbraham background is described with great piquancy and detail, and in whose later parts the fortunes of the household are traced with keen dramatic humour, contains not a little self-revelation, and forms one of the most adequate records of its writer's personality now available.

Throughout the N.A.P.A.'s Boston convention of 1921 Mrs. Miniter's guidance and inspiration were manifest. In the breezy *Aftermath* describing this event I was quite overwhelmed to find the chapter headings dedicated to me—each being a quotation from Dr. Samuel Johnson, as was fitting in commemorating an eighteenth-century devotee. Late in 1922 Mrs. Miniter was prominent in reorganising the Hub Club and broadening its personnel. Her abode was then the pleasant white house in Maplewood where the still-flourishing *L'Alouette* held forth. Here her library and her many antiques were displayed to especial advantage. Throughout 1923 she stood behind the club, aiding in its expansion campaign, and lending her wit to its banquet and convention programmes, and to its official organ.

At this period a heated controversy regarding schools of poetry was raging in amateurdom—the disciples of Victorian placidity being arrayed against the followers of Swinburne, Baudelaire, and the Symbolists. As an anti-Victorian, I published among other things an editorial with distinctly cool references to the soulful Messrs. Longfellow and Tennyson.[7] Mrs. Miniter, on the other side, countered with a long column of comment whose paragraphs were separated by alternate quotations from the two gentlemanly versifiers in question.

This, too, was the time when explorers of the old Massachusetts coast towns had the benefit of Mrs. Miniter's antiquarian knowledge. I recall a trip to old Marblehead with its tangled ways and brooding gambrel roofs, in which Edward H. Cole also participated.[8] Mrs. Miniter supplied many legends and particulars which no guide-book could furnish—and it was on this occasion that I first heard of the rustic superstition which asserts that window-panes slowly absorb and retain the likeness of those who habitually sit by them, year after year.[9] To Boston also Mrs. Miniter was an ideal guide. All the historic sites and literary landmarks were at her tongue's tip—including many which would otherwise have been very difficult to find. No one could surpass her in explaining the various minor domestic objects of the past—betty lamps, sausage-guns, potato-boilers, tinder-wheels, clock-jacks, plate-warmers, smoking-tongs, and the like—which are found in such abundance in antique collections, and around the kitchen fireplaces of old houses open as museums.

## III.

1924 and 1925 brought many changes, and before the close of the latter year Mrs. Miniter's permanent return to her native countryside was effected. The seat of her residence was Maplehurst, "back of the mountain" in North Wilbraham; a large, rambling farmhouse, once an inn, which lies just across the marsh-meadows from Wilbraham Mountain, at a bend and dip of the road where giant maples form a green, mystical arcade. This is the ancestral domain of the Beebes—with whose surviving representative, the locally famous antiquarian and antique collector Miss Evanore Olds Beebe, Mrs. Miniter combined household forces.

Miss Beebe—now unfortunately an invalid—was then virtually the leading spirit of Wilbraham; a kind of feminine village Pooh-Bah who held, among numberless other offices, the posts of Superintendent of Schools and member of the town council. She was a stout, capable, kindly, and quietly humorous gentlewoman then about seventy years of age, and was looked up to as an oracle by all the surrounding population. Her telephone rang constantly with requests for information and advice—political, social, historical, domestic, or otherwise—from citizens and town officials, and her voice in civic affairs was one of almost supreme authority. Though of straitened finances, she was the owner of most of the land in sight, including a good part of Wilbraham Mountain. An old friend of the family, and a distant kinswoman of the Olds line, she had been Mrs. Miniter's hostess on many a summer sojourn; so that the returning native's immediate milieu was by no means a strange one.

The house, of early nineteenth-century date, was spacious and attractive; and was literally choked to repletion with the rare antiques inherited or assembled by its owner. The ancient tables, secretaries, and chests which crowded the large rooms were covered and piled high with lesser antiques of every conceivable sort—china, glassware, candlesticks, snuffers, sand-boxes, whale-oil lamps, and all the other typical legacies of the past. Venerable paintings and samplers in close array all but hid the centuried paper of the walls, while the archaic fireplaces formed a setting for innumerable warming-pans, foot-stoves, sets of bellows and fire-irons, and less recognisable household appliances of yore. Amidst this antiquarian's paradise there moved—with a truly miraculous lack of evil consequences—a retinue of seven cats and two dogs, each with a distinct personality of his own.[10]

"Printer" (whose name was a corruption of "Prince of Orange"—this in turn based on the colour of his eyes) was the dean of the felidae, and had seen nearly seventeen winters in this world. He was a tiger of friendly disposition, and last of the Beebe mousers to know or avail himself of the old-fashioned "cat-ladder"—a series of brick steps inside the great chimney—which led from the ground floor to the realms above. "Old Fats" was a bluff, brusque, plumpish outdoor cat of golden hue and great martial prowess, whose primary ambition seemed to be to become a dog. He would curl up beside the dogs as if one of their clan, and would follow his human friends all over the farm—trotting caninely at their heels. His three brothers "Tardee", "Pettie", and "Prince of Wails" (so named for his vocal attainments) were likewise of aureate colouring. Pettie was the most affectionate and gentlemanly of the household, while the Prince's chief fame arose from his ability to thread his way among and over the furniture without the least damage or even peril to the labyrinth of fragile antiques. Their sister "Little Bit" was a tiger, and fond of sleeping in a tripod-suspended kettle on the lawn. Her young daughter "Tiger Ann" (later renamed Marcelle) completed the feline roster at the period of the present writer's census. Of the two dogs "Stitchie" was an aged collie of aristocratic lineage and impeccable courtesy, beginning to suffer from deafness and dim sight while "Donnie" was a boisterous and clumsy puppy in the process of growing to Gargantuan proportions.

The farm still existed as such, though operated on a reduced scale by the time of Mrs. Miniter's advent. Very little ground was really cultivated, but haying was conducted with local talent seasonally engaged—and with the more or less languid coöperation of the one hired boy, a sentimental vocalist whose melodic enthusiasm rivalled that of the Prince of Wails. Of livestock there remained some poultry, two lowing kine, and two patriarchal equines. The barn was a huge, spectral place with an immense hayloft. Picturesque sloping meadows stretched off in every direction, and just down hill at the road's bend there brooded the pasture bars where strange nocturnal influences were said to linger. Between the highway and the mountain the marsh spread out—half traversed by the grass-grown remnants of a never-finished road. On summer nights the throngs of dancing fireflies above the marsh—and above the pasture of the haunted bars—were of a strange multitudinousness and brilliancy which well justified the rustic whisperings attached to them.[11]

Into this congenial environment Mrs. Miniter fitted admirably and instantaneously. It was her own country, and here she remained till the end; though a vague idea of a possible return to Boston caused her to keep some of her possessions stored there. More and more of her articles dealt with Wilbraham folklore—articles which she wrote at intervals between work on two still unpublished novels. Material was plentiful at hand, and not far away dwelt the colourful Polish family around which her "Natupski" novel had been written. Through her pen the reading public came to know of Lieut. Mirick, whose killing of a "pizen sarpient" in a hayfield on Wilbraham Mountain in 1761 gave rise to the name "Rattlesnake Peak" as applied to the principal summit. In other articles she told of the mysterious murders of travellers, of the man who moved a schoolhouse to his own neighbourhood to accommodate his children, of the inn whose floor shews the marks of stacked Revolutionary muskets, of the ensign who in 1744 could carry six bushels of salt on his back all at one time, and of kindred choice bits from Wilbraham's long annals.

An eight-day visit to the household at Maplehurst in July, 1928, formed my last personal glimpse of Mrs. Miniter. I had never seen the Wilbraham region before, and was charmed by the vivid vistas of hills and valleys, and the remote winding roads so redolent of other centuries. No better hierophants of the local arcana than Mrs. Miniter and Miss Beebe could possibly have been found, and my knowledge of Central New England lore was virtually trebled during my short stay.

I saw the ruinous, deserted old Randolph Beebe house where the whippoorwills cluster abnormally, and learned that these birds are feared by the rustics as evil psychopomps. It is whispered that they linger and flutter around houses where death is approaching, hoping to catch the soul of the departed as it leaves. If the soul eludes them, they disperse in quiet disappointment; but sometimes they set up a chorused clamour of excited, triumphant chattering which makes the watchers turn pale and mutter—with that air of hushed, awestruck portentousness which only a backwoods Yankee can assume—"They got 'im!"[12] On another day I was taken to nearby Monson to see a dark, damp street in the shadow of a great hill, the houses on the hillward side of which are whispered about because of the number of their tenants who have gone mad or killed themselves.

I saw the haunted pasture bars in the spectral dusk, and one evening was thrilled and amazed by a monstrous saraband of fireflies over marsh and meadow. It was as if some strange, sinister constellation had taken on an uncanny life and descended to hang low above the lush grasses. And one day Mrs. Miniter shewed me a deep, mute ravine beyond the Randolph Beebe house, along whose far-off wooded floor an unseen stream trickles in eternal shadow. Here, I am told, the whippoorwills gather on certain nights for no good purpose.

I was taken over the sightly Beebe acres by my hostess, Old Fats trotting dog-like at our heels; and beheld some of the silent, uncommunicative, slowly retrograding yeomanry of the region. Later the aged, courtly Stitchie and Mrs. Miniter were my joint guides to neighbouring Glendale and its ancient church and churchyard. Still another trip was up old Wilbra'm Mountain, where the road winds mystically aloft into a region of hushed skyey meadow-land seemingly half-apart from time and change, and abounding in breath-taking vistas. Through the haze of distance other mountains loom purple and mysterious. A line of fog marks the great Connecticut, and the smoke of Springfield clouds the southwestern horizon. Sometimes even the golden dome of the Hartford state house, far to the south, can be discerned. Though the slopes were much as Lieut. Mirick must have known them in his day, I saw no "pizen sarpients". On the way Mrs. Miniter pointed out the home of the "Natupskis" immortalised in her novel.

A subsequent day was devoted to a long walk around the mountain, over roads which included some of quite colonial primitiveness. On this occasion, for the only time in my life, I saw a wild deer in its native habitat. Wilbraham village, under the mountain's southern slope, is a drowsy, pleasant town with a quiet main street and giant elms. Mrs. Miniter displayed the moss-grown graveyards of the place—one of which, The Dell, includes a dank wooded declivity beside a stream that is said to wash away the earth and expose curious secrets at times. The old brick Academy, built in 1825 and still surviving after many vicissitudes, was another interesting sight. The return trip, beginning in the wild and picturesque woodlands behind the Academy, led over unspoiled colonial roads on the mountain's side, and revealed many of the brooding, unpainted houses of other generations. At one stage of the journey I saw the house where Mrs. Miniter was born—built in 1842 by her grandfather, Edwin Lombard Tupper, and still inhabited by his direct descendants. Among the varied and exquisite prospects along this route is one of a strangely blasted slope where grey, dead trees claw at the sky with leafless boughs amidst an abomination of desolation. Vegetation will grow here no longer—why, no one can tell.

Toward the end of my visit Mrs. Miniter gave directions for a walk too long for her to attempt, and I followed an ancient road—full of striking vistas—to the pleasant village of Hampden. The town lies at the bend of a stream, and all the houses are strung at length along a road winding up the side of a mountain from the valley. Here the traditional white-steepled church building shelters a thriving grocery store—one of those humour-fraught contrasts in which Mrs. Miniter always delighted. Here, also, stands a World War memorial in the most flamboyant taste (or lack of taste) of Civil War times—the gift of an aged local magnate who remembered the past and knew what he wanted!

The hours spent at Maplehurst among the old books and antiques, with Pettie and Tardee and the Prince weaving dexterously through the narrow lanes of navigation and venerable Printer often drowsing, purring, or sneezing in my lap, will not soon be forgotten. Mrs. Miniter and Miss Beebe formed unsurpassable hosts, and the impromptu course in folklore which they gave me was illustrated at every turn by volumes, pictures, and actual objects from the local past. The fireflies at evening—the distant, wind-borne strains of melodious Chauncey[13] tramping homeward across the fields—the delightful agricultural-pedagogical household next door, whose kindly proffered Model T helped to solve many problems of distance—the tales of other days brought forth by Mrs. Miniter from her inexhaustible store of erudition—all these varied recollections spring up at mention of the name of Wilbraham.

During the final years Mrs. Miniter was harassed by illness—largely an increase of the asthmatic tendency which had long troubled her. Letters, though always cheerful and overflowing with wit, became fewer and fewer. It was hoped that she might attend the Boston convention of the National in 1930, but her health was unequal to the trip. Just after that conclave the brilliant young western amateur Helm C. Spink, who had been a leading delegate, paid her a memorable visit at Wilbraham; and I still treasure the jointly written sheet of humour which hostess and guest sent me—a mock-journal whose title, The Dog-matic Cat-egory, was based on my keen interest in Maplehurst's furry fauna.

After 1931 came the illness and ultimate invalidism of Miss Beebe, which placed upon Mrs. Miniter new burdens and responsibilities. There were likewise accidents—two falls involving fractures—affecting Mrs. Miniter herself. And always the anxieties and retrenchments attendant upon the depression hung in the offing. Work, however, went bravely if intermittently on; and the unpublished novels doubtless bear myriad touches made almost at the last.

Messages from the outside world shed many a heartening beam—and the familiar countryside itself, of which she was so wholly and innately a part, must have been a potent balm in its way. Never was she separated from the old things and ancestral influences that she loved so well. Her health gave way bit by bit; but the cherished books and favourite china and home-like confusion of andirons and crickets and warming-pans were always around her, while from her front windows age-old Wilbra'm Mountain always loomed up across the eerie marsh-meadows. She died on June 4, 1934—late enough, perhaps, to have seen the year's first fireflies dancing over the pasture grasses. And now she rests among the time-crumbled headstones of her forefathers in the old graveyard below the mountain—The Dell, with its trees, its shadows, and its spectral stream.

It is difficult to realise that Mrs. Miniter is no longer a living presence; for the sharp insight, subtle wit, rich scholarship, and vivid literary force so fresh in one's memory are things savouring of the eternal and the indestructible. Of her charm and kindliness many will write reminiscently and at length. Of her genius, skill, courage, and determination her work and career eloquently speak. Though a lifelong antiquarian, she was not one to yearn vainly for the past or bewail the present and future—her staunch mood of acceptance being admirably summed up in one of her rather infrequent specimens of verse, a sonnet entitled "1921", appearing in the pages of the clever *Muffin Man*. There is no better way of closing this tribute than to quote that sonnet complete—for in it so much of its author stands revealed:

> "Dear dreams of youth—could one seek your return,
> Ask glamour of an earlier spring to glow,
> Or clothe in verdure trees now lying low,
> In ashes dull cause wonted fires to burn,
> Still life's best lessons would be left to learn.
> Of many brooks is made one river's flow;
> From yesteryears tomorrows thrive and glow;
> The future nothing of the past may spurn.
>
> "Nor is aught forfeit. In its course the stream
> Denotes accretion, gain for evermore;
> So ripples life with joy beyond the dream,
> When mellow hues of autumn tinge the shore.
> I would not call you back, dear dreams of youth,
> So much you're bettered by the present truth!"

EDITOR'S NOTE  FP: *Californian* 5, No. 4 (Spring 1938): 47–55. Text based upon the AMS (JHL), as the printed text is frequently erroneous and omits a section toward the end. The essay was written 16 October 1934, as part of a proposed tribute volume to Miniter, who had died 4 June. Although HPL spent many months assembling contributions to the volume (to have been published by W. Paul Cook), he never managed to prepare the book for publication. The article is one of HPL's finest biographical portraits and one of his best essays, expressing sincere affection and admiration for Miniter as an amateur, a writer, and a human being, and providing valuable insights into his own encounters with Miniter, one of which (in the summer of 1928) was instrumental in his writing "The Dunwich Horror." Miniter was indeed one of the greats of amateurdom. Kenneth W. Faig, Jr., has assembled two large collections of her amateur writing, *Going Home and Other Amateur Writings* (1995) and *The Coast of Bohemia and Other Writings* (2000), both published by Moshassuck Press (Glenview, IL).

*Notes*

1. See n. 3 to DPC (January 1918).

2. William Lyon Phelps (1865–1943) was a leading American critic of the time. His review was apparently published in a newspaper and has not been located. *Natupski* was also reviewed favorably by another well-known critic, H. W. Boynton, in the *Nation* (30 November 1916).

3. See n. 6 to "News Notes" (November 1920).

4. Edith Miniter, "Falco Ossifracus: By Mr. Goodguile," *Muffin Man* (April 1921): n.p.

5. This anecdote has not been confirmed by Stoker scholars or biographers.

6. See "A Singer of Ethereal Moods and Fancies" (p. 301).

7. HPL refers to his essay "Rudis Indigestaque Moles" (*Conservative*, March 2923; CE2).

8. The trip evidently occurred in the early months of 1923. See Joshi, *Life* 293.

9. The legend is cited in "The Unnamable" (1923; *D* 201–2).

10. Around 1930 HPL wrote a series of poems on Miniter's cats and dogs, "Veteropinguis Redivivus" (*AT* 177–79).

11. Fireflies are briefly cited in "The Dunwich Horror" (1928; *DH* 156), much of whose topography is taken from HPL's 1928 visit to Miniter at Wilbraham. HPL admitted that the town of Dunwich is located roughly in the area of Wilbraham, Monson, and Hampden (*SL* 3.432–33).

12. The legend of whippoorwills as psychopomps figures prominently in "The Dunwich Horror."

13. Cf. the character Chauncey Sawyer in "The Dunwich Horror" (*DH* 177f.).

---

# REPORT OF THE BUREAU OF CRITICS

*(December 1934)*

## Verse Department

Some of the most interesting of the National's current poems are concentrated in the first issue of Messrs. Baker and Adams' *Literati*, a venture which deserves the warmest encouragement of all the members. "The Alien", by Natalie Hartley Wooley, has a flowing rhythm and delicate suggestion of unknown vistas which combine to produce a very potent effect. "Wind Song", by Miriam Bralley, likewise has a strong hold on the imagination, though the technique is less sure, and the evident attempt to rhyme *candle* and *mantle* is scarcely successful. A third bit of authentic and original fancy is Margaret Lockerbie Richards' "Homesick"—a piece which could, however, be improved by a smoother and better correlated development. There is a certain sense of deficient continuity between the third and fourth lines, while the omission of articles in the second line gives an impression of laborious metrical straining. It would have been better to find another wording which could conform to the dominant pattern without the sacrifice of perfectly idiomatic language. "Tequila", by Alida Grenelle, is full of vivid images, but has an unfortunately prosaic line at the start. If the phrase

"Tequila—the name has a musical sound"

could be de-literalised to read

"Tequila—the name is music"

—or something equally removed from bald statement—the ends of poetry would be better served. In the realm of prose-poetry the pseudonymous "Ong Kee Seh" succeeds very well with the two fragments "Drouth" and "High Summer". Both achieve a gratifying synthesis of sensory images and symbolised emotions. As poetry editor, John D. Adams has clearly demonstrated his ability to distinguish genuine imagination from spurious sentiment and empty and imitative rhetoric.

Honours for light verse go to the ever-tuneful veteran Rheinhart Kleiner, whose "Before and Behind the Scene", in the September *Brooklynite,* reflects human nature with mingled fidelity and grace. One might wish that more in the younger generation would approach the problem of versified expression with something of Mr. Kleiner's sureness and thoroughness; laying a firm foundation of deeply ingrained technical mastery and accuracy, and thereafter being able to sing with perfect spontaneousness, yet with a smooth beauty and unconscious skill made instinctive by adequate preparation.

"For a Summer Excursion", by Andrew Hewitt in the August *Bookmark,* has a lilting grace, unexpectedness of phrase, and fertility of imagery which move one to a second reading. There is something of real creativeness in pictures like these:

> "—roads that dream between the hills
> And break off in the lovely sky."

> "Brown husks that blue moons burn into."

Margaret Nickerson Martin's "Three Faces", in the April *Eaglet,* achieves a sincere poignancy with an unrhymed metre of studied irregularity. "Orchids", by E. Leslie Spalding in the Summer *Pied Typer,* is more regular in form and a bit more artificial in its perfervid sentiment. "Perplexed", by Jack Greenberg in the August *Hodge Podge,* is unusual in its keen imaginative power and graphic symbolism. The structure as a whole is somewhat uncertain and groping, but the most valuable element of all—originality—is there.

In the September *Tryout* the ever-faithful Arthur Goodenough finely reflects a mood with his sombre and almost stately "Voices of the Night".

EDITOR'S NOTE FP: *National Amateur* 57, No. 2 (December 1934): 1. HPL reports briefly on current amateur verse.

---

# REPORT OF THE BUREAU OF CRITICS

*(March 1935)*

## Verse Department

The current movement toward better poetry in the National is well exemplified by Ray H. Zorn's page of advice and criticism in the Winter *Perspective Review.* The questions and analyses put forward by Mr. Zorn cover a wide array of typical and important points, and deserve the careful study of all our beginners—actual or perennial.

Of the season's metrical products only a few can be mentioned in detail. "On Mountain Trails at Night", by Eugene B. Kuntz in the Winter *Goldenrod,* presents a series of moods, images, and impressions derived from landscape values and having an unusual power of suggestion despite certain touches of heaviness, prose diction, and possible triteness. The pictorial vividness of some of the lines is especially marked.

*Americana,* reappearing after a long absence, contains an ample verse quota, among which may be cited Alfred Leland Mooney's smooth and musical rondeau, "Rainy Night". This piece has some excellent lines and cadences, but suffers from an obvious straining to conform to the highly artificial rhyme-scheme. Expressions like "sameness that's bizarre", "thunder to its mate attends", or "where aught one wends" are so remote from clear-cut imagery and straightforward language as to suggest at once their purely mechanical motivation. There is also an erroneous use of *fire* as a dissyllable. *Unleased* for *unleashed* is doubtless a misprint.

The verses of Albert Chapin, scattered through many of the recent journals, display a dependable degree of fluency and correctness and occasionally attain substantial power. "To Mother", in the October *Presque Isle Trail*, contains a very apt conception;[1] while "Memory", in the Autumn *Pied Typer*, and "Funeral March", in the Spring *Enterprise*, also merit notice.

Natalie Hartley Wooley has rapidly become one of the most frequent versifiers in the association, and is well represented in current papers. Some of her recent specimens are light and essentially casual, but virtually all possess the wistful, half-whimsical, half-eerie note characteristic of the author. "Lines to Cleopatra" in the December *Tryout*, and "Mountain Pool" in the Winter *Goldenrod*, are among the best of Mrs. Wooley's contemporary offerings.

Another mainstay of amateur verse is Margaret Nickerson Martin, of whose recent poems "A Different Way", in the Fall *Californian*, and "These Have I Seen", in the December *Printer's Pet*, are particularly good.

A distinctly unusual and grimly powerful bit of verse is "Ivan Kovitch", by Marion van Laningham in the Autumn *Pied Typer*. Earl Henry's "Song of an Aged Bard" in the Christmas *Manettism* is excellent except for the *been-men* rhyme and the rather forced contraction *man's* (for *man has*) in the final line.

"Flame and Songs and Other Poems", by Marion Lee, is a brochure of extreme excellence and tastefulness just issued from the private press of Will Bates Grant, Greenwood, Massachusetts. It comprises twelve very brief poems in Mrs. Lee's characteristically quiet, reflective style, and likewise embodies some of the finest typography and bookmaking lately seen in amateurdom. Most of the contents has previously appeared in such magazines as *Spirit*, *Nebulae*, and *The Circle*, and every item is apt and vivid in its particular direction. "Departure" leaves an especially lasting, wistful impression. Something of the author's cleverness in imagery can be illustrated by the final piece, "Transposing":

> "Only the pine of all the trees
> Has caught the murmur of the seas,
> Whisp'ring it softly o'er and o'er
> For ears that cannot reach the shore."

An announcement of vast interest to old-timers concerns the prospective appearance of a volume of collected lyrics by Samuel Loveman,[2] probably the National's greatest poet of the last twenty years, by Caxton Printers of Idaho, noted as the original publishers of the works of Vardis Fisher.[3]

EDITOR'S NOTE FP: *National Amateur* 57, No. 3 (March 1935): 1. HPL writes of the verse of Ray H. Zorn, Albert Chapin, Natalie H. Wooley, and other amateurs.

*Notes*

1. HPL discusses this poem further, quoting it in full, in "What Belongs in Verse" (*Perspective Review*, Spring 1935; CE2).

2. *The Hermaphrodite and Other Poems* (Caldwell, ID: Caxton Printers, 1936).
3. Vardis Fisher (1895–1968), American novelist and poet.

---

## LOVECRAFT OFFERS VERSE CRITICISM

One of the younger amateurs, himself a poet of no small attainments in the modern manner, recently commented despairingly on the relatively small amount of really good poetry to be found amidst the associations' large verse output. We may sympathize with his wish for higher standards without sharing his extreme pessimism. Through its very nature as a medium of beginning, experiment, and encouragement, amateur journalism is bound to present work of extremely varied quality. If among this a certain amount possesses merit, while other specimens shew a steady growth toward merit under the influence of practice, suggestions, and comment, it cannot be said that the associations have failed in their purpose.

So far as verse is concerned, it is our business to point out what poetic utterance really is, and what it is not; to urge the intense, sincere, original, symbolic, concrete recording of moods, pictures, and impressions in suitable language and cadences, and give warnings against false or feeble sentiment, cheap second-hand platitudes, trite moralisings, chaotic images, prose psychology and presentation, inappropriate form, clumsy, inept, incorrect, or incoherent diction, and bad rhyme and metre. This, in an ideal association, would probably be done in several ways: the public reviewing of typically good and typically poor published verse in the official organ, with as much illustrative, explanatory, and constructive comment as possible; the private furnishing of advice and revision, when requested, on individual verses, published and unpublished; the publication of general articles on poetic problems; the listing of helpful outside articles, manuals, and reading courses; and the fostering of a sense of taste and proportion through the exhibition and analysis of typical verses of varying excellence, mediocrity, and defectiveness, and perhaps through some system of tabulation and concise grading printed in the official organ and covering all work published by members—a system likewise useful in the prose field.

Admittedly, the National as yet meets these ideal requirements only in part. We have public reviewing and private criticism, but neither is as thorough or universal as it might be were more space and more critics available. We have general articles on poetry, but these might well be longer, more numerous, and more directly aimed at the specific problems revealed by the actual run of amateur verse. We have reference suggestions, but they tend to be sparse and sporadic. And finally, our facilities for illustrating typical merit and demerit in verse are limited largely to casual remarks in the course of official reviews, and do not embody any form of all-inclusive grading and tabulation.

There is thus plenty of room for improvement on our part. That such a course of improvement is at least tentatively launched, the present policies of such papers as *The Bookmark, The Literati, The Perspective Review,* and *The Californian* would seem to indicate. One hopes that the new administration will heartily support these policies, and supplement them through the appointment of larger critical boards, the revival of typical amateur work of more brilliant periods, the consideration of innovations such as inclusive tabulation and grading, and the publication of some very carefully selected reference lists and instructive and illustrative articles.

Regarding the last-named matter it might be suggested that the association make some effort toward securing the issuance, serially or otherwise, of "Doorways to Poetry",[1] an almost ideal compendium of illustrative, analytical, and taste-forming poetic information written by Maurice Winter Moe and so far unpublished. All who have read this work in manuscript agree that it forms a more helpful summary of poetic precept, advice, illustration, and demonstration than any other single manual; and it is a veritable tragedy that it has so far remained inaccessible to the amateur and general public.

Turning to current verse, we find *The Literati* well sustaining its policy in the second number. "Ask Me Not", a bit of free verse by Frances Davis Adams, presents a highly unusual image in a thoroughly original way. "Which Heart to Break", by "Ong Kee Seh", represents a very graceful type of poetic prose, though having subject-matter of a rather familiar species. In "Stars", by Dorothy Huddleston Balch, there is much poetic feeling and originality—robbing even the notion of "an angel's tear" of the triteness it would otherwise possess. John D. Adams, in "Old Man Turn Away", captures much of the spirit of the Indian. "A Mountain Spoke to Me", by Jack Starkweather, is full of poetic suggestions.

Unrhymed verse appears to be gaining prominence in amateurdom, whether because of the energy saved in not looking for rhymes, or because of the authors' belief that their moods can better be presented without such aural devices. Two samples possessing unusually clever imagery are "The Perfect Thing", by Sophia Alexander Wittman in the Winter *Ink Spots*, and "Love", by Margaret Nickerson Martin in the January *Sea Gull.*

In a more traditional vein, and of substantial power and grace, are "Saint Martin's", by Edna Hyde McDonald in the Spring *Californian*, and "Tradition", a sonnet by Eleanor Wood in the March *Brooklynite*. The attempted rhyming of *sun* and *young* in the latter piece is distinctly unfortunate.

The appealing poetry of Miriam Bralley seems to be gaining in smoothness and general excellence. "Tonight" and "Snowfall", both in recent issues of *The Manettism*, contain concepts and images of considerable aptness and freshness, and are agreeably regular in construction.

The Spring *Literati* is full of interesting poetry of varied types. "On the Winding Stair", by Sally Everett, is generally graceful and well-constructed, though the theme is one quite frequently used in verse. Some of the lines might possibly be a trifle more fluent if the accents, emphases, and vowel and consonantal sounds were more carefully manipulated. "Longing", by "Ong Kee Seh", delicately catches the essentials of a mood in apt symbols according to the Oriental manner. A more modern and probably less enduring fashion of expression is admirably satirised by Alida Grenelle in "Darst I?" In "Dawn Peeped In at the Window" Ray H. Zorn expresses poignant emotion in appropriately simple lyric.

Richard A. Thomas, Jr., strikingly demonstrates his capacity for original imagery and symbolism with the intentionally rugged lines called "Pursuit", where the heightened subjectivity of modernism is sought for in the delineation of a mood. The vividness and uniqueness of the result cannot be denied, though it remains to be seen whether a more powerful effect could not have been secured through the cultivation of greater harmony and the use of symbols less individual and abstractly intellectualised. Another bold and effective bit of imagery by Mr. Thomas is the very brief "Pastorale".

Brevity, indeed, seems very much the fashion in the current issues; several capable bards being represented by microscopic specimens of clever imagery and illustration. Jack Hille, in "Speed", gives three exceedingly graphic glimpses of this sort, and other well-pointed examples are "Domesticity", by Lolly Williams, "Soul of Flowers", by Mary Morgan Ware, and "Friendly Rain", by Marion Connelly.

A poetry booklet of unusual excellence in contents and appearance alike is "April", by Katherine R. Rucker, just issued by the Sunnyside Press of Monroe, N. C., as a supplement to *The Bookmark*. This timely and attractive offering consists of three poems on vernal themes, adorned with appropriate decorative illustrations.

"April", the opening lyric, combines a pleasant tuneful lilt with a series of very sensory symbols. "The Lane House" exhibits Miss Rucker's natural aptitude for the involved French patterns of repeated rhyme, and embodies a mood of wistful reminiscence in notably felicitous images. The line "With sunshine timid as a fawn" is especially good, with metre well adapted to the scene.

Orthoepical purists will be inclined to call into question two of the rhymes in these verses—*born* with *dawn* and *gone,* and *abroad* with *regard.* These rhymes, though perfect to the ear in England and the Eastern United States, are theoretically defective—and indeed practically so in Ireland, Scotland, and the Central and Western United States, where the letter "r" is noticeably rolled. It is generally better, in rhyming, to observe this distinction between "r" syllables and similar syllables lacking the "r", even in regions where the actual sound of the two types is identical.

The format and typography of the brochure are exceptionally tasteful in an unassuming way, and the whole venture reflects the highest credit upon author and publisher.

EDITOR'S NOTE FP: *National Amateur* 57, No. 4 (June 1935): 5–6. HPL again urges amateurs to contemplate the difference between verse and prose, and to make sure that their conceptions are such as genuinely deserve embodiment in the former rather than the latter.

*Notes*

1. HPL had been working with Maurice W. Moe on *Doorways to Poetry*, a comprehensive treatise on poetic appreciation, since at least 1928, but, in spite of expressions of interest by Macmillan and other leading publishers, the book was never issued. The ms. does not appear to be extant.

---

# DR. EUGENE B. KUNTZ

The appearance of a new brochure of the poetry of Eugene B. Kuntz is to be welcomed by all lovers of graceful verse and all members of organised amateur journalism. In "Thoughts and Pictures", published in 1932 by C. W. Smith, a pleasing array of Dr. Kuntz's lighter newspaper stanzas was offered in permanent form. The present volume includes material of varied nature from the pages of *Hodge Podge, Cadences, Ivory Tower,* and *The Literary Messenger,* and helps to pave the way for that large volume of serious poetry which one hopes may some day appear.

Dr. Kuntz needs no introduction to followers of current poetry magazines and anthologies, to members of the National Amateur Press Association, to readers of the southwestern dailies and of the Presbyterian denominational press. A clergyman by vocation, he has long been a disciple of the poet's art and has mirrored the grandeur of his beloved mountain scenery and the diverse needs of the human spirit, in lines of spontaneous origin, whose chief specimens represent creation of the most genuine sort.

His nature-poetry forms, perhaps, his prime achievement, but even on the homeliest of themes, his fluency and eloquence are advantageously displayed.

A stately traditionalism, in which freshness and strong emotion ward off triteness, is the keynote of Dr. Kuntz's poetry. Didacticism is only occasional and seldom obtrusive. Few have savoured the mystic beauty of nature more sensitively and appreciatively, or experienced its dramatic or picturesque aspects more widely, than Dr. Kuntz. Reflecting his impressions in verses whose long, sonorous couplets or quatrains teem with vital phrases, apt compound-words, and frequent images of keen originality, he surely earns the right to be considered a poet in the most complete sense.

Eugene B. Kuntz, born in the vineyard-green Rhineland, was brought to America in infancy and reared amidst the mellow influences of the old South. A college mate of Secretary of State Cordell Hull,[1] he turned early to the ministry, and has filled many important pastorates in the West and Southwest. His academic honours included the degrees of Doctor of Divinity and Doctor of Letters, the latter conferred not long ago in recognition of his achievements in poetry. Dr. Kuntz is now a resident of Santa Barbara, California.

EDITOR'S NOTE FP: *Hodge Podge* 5, No. 6 (September 1935): [1] (as "Dr. Eugene B. Kunz"). HPL supplies a plug for a new book of verse by Kuntz, *Poems* (New York: Hodge Press, 1935). HPL had earlier edited (and probably revised the contents of) a previous volume by Kuntz, *Thoughts and Pictures* (1932), for which he wrote a foreword (see CE2).

*Notes*

1. Cordell Hull (1871–1955), secretary of state under FDR (1933–44). Hull attended a normal school in Bowling Green, KY (1886–87), and the National Normal University in Lebanon, OH (1888–89), then read law for five months at the Cumberland Law School in Lebanon, TN. Presumably Kuntz knew Hull from the first of these institutions.

## SOME CURRENT AMATEUR VERSE

*The Lone Wolf*, a new all-verse quarterly issued by Mr. A. Zimmerman and consisting solely of his own metrical work, illustrates the strong hold which the poetic ideal has on our members. The two issues at hand include many short pieces of varying merit; and throughout there is a strength of emotion, and scope and fertility of vision, which attest the genuine poetic leanings of the author.

All the verses, however, are severely handicapped by a lack of linguistic command and an apparent unfamiliarity with English idiom suggesting that the writer was born to another tongue. We see such phrases as *tired to make* instead of *tired of making; tell sad stories their little ones* instead of *tell sad stories to their little ones;* or *throat and heart sings* instead of *throat and heart sing*—and in one place encounter such a mispronunciation (as indicated by rhyme and metrical situation) as *Geth-se-mane* for *Geth-sem-a-ne.*

Mr. Zimmerman needs, first and foremost, a thorough drilling in the essentials of idiomatic English, such as can be obtained from text-books or formal courses of instruction in rhetoric, and from a constant, assiduous, and observant reading of the English classics. Later should come special training in poetry, aided by such manuals as Brander Matthews' "A Study of Versification".[1] Such training would guide the bard in his choice of words for phonetic and associative value as well as for dictionary meaning, and would help him in discriminating between phrases and constructions suitable for poetry, and those which through harshness, literalness, commonplaceness, awkwardness, or inappropriate associations are definitely unsuitable.

It would almost undoubtedly pay Mr. Zimmerman to follow this course of polishing, for he very obviously has something of a poetic character to say. He feels keenly the emotional value of certain objects and experiences, and has a strong sense of the drama inherent in cosmic vastness and indifference. Probably he would succeed best in work of a distinctly modern sort, since his feelings lean markedly toward the social vision, the sympathy with the defeated, and the bold, untraditional imagery typical of contemporary expression. He must realise that he has far to go, but should not let the distance discourage him.

Another venture dedicated mainly to verse and its interests is *Hodge Podge*, with its companion *Cadences*, of which a more or less intermittent file is on hand. While many of the issues feature routine material, and clever trifles involving sprightliness rather than intensity, there are also frequent bits of powerful poetic vision or musical grace which demand close attention. Ben H. Smith's "In Lilac Time", in the April *Cadences*, is an exceptionally tuneful rondeau which justifies the author's ample midwestern celebrity. Less technically finished, but much more original in feeling and treatment, are the various poems by Jack Greenberg, of which "Anxiety" and "Voidness Dispelled" are the salient specimens. The latter in particular embodies a gratifying strength and freshness of imagery despite some very awkward handlings of words and accents—such as the impossible line "And a fortuitous gleam breaking through." "Gypsy-Heart", by Frances Davis Adams, is a poem of genuine distinction in which the tempo, language, and images all contribute to a single ethereal, almost elfin effect. Such a quatrain as this illustrates the elusive magic of the whole:

> "I who know the healing of an hour of rain,
> All the secret places where the stars are strung,
> Know a sickled moon can wield a brittle pain,
> Run the misted sky-way where the clouds are hung."

Still another all-verse offering is the Spring *Voyageur*, which opens with the youthful Arthur Cantor's "Lost and Found". This piece of verse exhibits considerable vigour, but tends more toward a didactic prose atmosphere than toward the symbolic beauty of poetry. The author should be on his guard against unauthorised words like the awkward *someplace*. Mr. Cantor succeeds much better in the vigorous stanzas of "Airmail", in the Summer *Enterprise*—a poem containing such strong lines as "Holes gape in pitted nimbus clouds."

Too many of the verses in *The Voyageur* tend to represent a kind of pleasant mediocrity consisting of rather obvious truths and well-worn sentiments re-stated without any of the fresh twists of perspective, fresh symbols for illustration, fresh modes of expression, or fresh flashes of psychological insight which make poetry vital and original. Before a writer embarks on the composition of a poem, it would be well for him to consider whether he really has anything to say which has not been said repeatedly before. In many cases a frank recognition of his intended theme's commonplaceness will cause him to turn to some new theme concerning which he does possess strong and distinctive emotions capable of reflection in vividly individual expression.

But in all cases the originality must be natural and spontaneous. A mere mechanical striving for new subjects and styles leads only to chaos, awkwardness, and sterility—as a survey of the most self-consciously "modernistic" verse quickly reveals. This overreaching tendency which invites triviality is fairly well illustrated by one by one of the items in *The Voyageur*. The following is glibly onomatopoetic and not especially hackneyed, but is the message worth the number of words expended on it?

### "MIDNIGHT SOLILOQUY

"Rain . . . . . . rain
Pattering rain
Slap-dash rain
Rhythmic, pagan rain!
Your continual pat . . . . . pat . . . . . pat . . . . .
Keeps me awake
But I like it . . . . .
I like your clattering dripping staccato noise
Rain on . . . . . rain on . . . . ."

That poems of ideas—despite the dominantly non-intellectual province of poetry—can succeed if properly sustained by appropriate images, is adequately proved by Richard Alexander Thomas's "Skeleton to Life" in *The Manettism* for March 30. There is grim power in this effort, notwithstanding certain harshnesses of language. Smoother and more delicate, and vivid with elusive suggestion in the traditional manner, is Ronald Walker Barr's "Japanesque", in the June *Americana*. Alfred Leland Mooney's brief contributions to the same magazine—"Storm", "No Challenge", and "Great Poem"—are clever and felicitous fragments, the third of which is especially good.

The wistful and sometimes mystical poetry of Mrs. Natalie H. Wooley is well represented in current journals; "Dream Fantasy" and "Sailor's Child", both in *The Manettism* for May 11, being the choicest specimens. Another potent and delicate transcript of a mood is the autumnal sonnet "Intimations", by Eleanor Wood in the September *Brooklynite*.

Light verse has seldom fared well in amateurdom; most rhymers seeming to have a tendency to become trivial, commonplace, and even cheaply meaningless or unmotivated when they sound the jocund lyre. The average specimen of metrical amateur frivolity is an almost painful thing to quote—for there is something embarrassing in the spectacle of an adult with rattle in hand. Among the happy exceptions is Mr. Rheinhart Kleiner, whose urbanely ironic witticisms reveal a genuine command of the satirist's and humourist's medium. "Prejudice", in the June *Brooklynite*, has a Gilbertian quality well worthy of emulation by other practitioners of the harlequin's art.

EDITOR'S NOTE FP: *National Amateur* 58, No. 2 (December 1935): 14–15 (signed "H. P. L."). HPL's final report as a member of the Bureau of Critics (but see "[Literary Review]" for another, unofficial report).

*Notes*

1. Brander Matthews, *A Study of Versification* (Boston: Houghton Mifflin, 1911). HPL frequently recommended this work for beginners in poetry.

# REPORT OF THE EXECUTIVE JUDGES

Chicago, Illinois,
April 25, 1936.

To the Members of
The National Amateur Press Association:

Although no report has hitherto appeared from the office of the Executive Judges, the year has been a very busy one for the members of the Board. Much of the work placed upon their shoulders has remained unfinished for reasons beyond their control, but of sufficient importance to warrant the delays involved. Reports on these unfinished problems would have been very misleading to the members as well as unfair and unjust to those concerned.

In August, 1935, the Board received the request of Mr. O. W. Hinrichs for permission to increase the number of pages in the September *National Amateur*. Mr. Lovecraft being absent on a vacation, the desired permission was granted on August 23, 1935, by Judges Plaisier and Haggerty.

On October 31, 1935, Edwin Hadley Smith protested the 1934–35 History and Story Laureate awards to Ralph W. Babcock, Jr., and Richard Foster, respectively, for contributions appearing in *The Red Rooster* for May 1935; offering evidence to prove that this number of *The Red Rooster* was actually not completed or published until September 1935. An investigation of the case showed that the disputed entries were printed each in a separate 8-page 6 × 9 advance section of the issue in question, both seen by a limited number of members on or around the first of May. The requirements of the constitution are:

> "Article XI, Section 2: Laureate Title. In order to compete for the title 'Laureate' in any department except that of editorials, an active member must publish his entry in an amateur paper by May 1 and send two marked copies of the paper to the Vice President."

Notice of this protest was at once sent to Mr. Babcock and Mr. Foster, and Mr. Babcock agreed to furnish information on the disputed points upon his return from college at Thanksgiving time. The holiday season being too short to permit Mr. Babcock to make a thorough search through his files for evidence concerning the completion and distribution of the May *Red Rooster*, time was extended until the Christmas vacation. Meanwhile Mr. Babcock relinquished his right to the History Laureateship awarded his article, "The Decline and Rebirth of the N.A.P.A.," which appeared in the History Section of the disputed issue, but requested an extension of time until his spring vacation to furnish proof regarding the date and distribution of the Feature Section containing the story by Richard Foster: "As Fate Wills It," which received the Laureate award.

Mr. Babcock having ultimately furnished sufficient proof of the completion and distribution of the Feature Section in compliance with the requirements of the Constitution, Executive Judges Lovecraft and Plaisier find that the Story Laureate award to Richard Foster for "As Fate Wills It", appearing in Section II (Feature Section) of the May *Red Rooster*, was properly made. Mr. Haggerty declined to rule on this question, having been the Judge of Histories at the time.

In view of Mr. Babcock's withdrawal, and of the doubtful circulation of the History Section, the Board finds that the History Laureateship for 1934–35 devolves upon the winner of the Honourable Mention title, Chester P. Bradley, for his "History of the N.A.P.A. 1933–34" in *The Perspective Review* for Autumn, 1934.

Resolutions adopted by the Oakland Amateur Press Club on December 15, 1935, regarding omissions from President Bradofsky's reports of appointments, changes in official personnel and reappointments, were forwarded to the Judges in January. After careful consideration of the evidence submitted, the Judges unanimously agreed that the omissions in President Bradofsky's messages were without censurable intent. The matter having been called to the President's attention, the explanation was accepted by the Oakland Amateur Press Club without further comment.

On January 8, 1936, President Bradofsky requested a ruling regarding his functions as a member of the Constitution Committee in reconciling apparently conflicting or overlapping amendments submitted by Edwin Hadley Smith and Harold Segal, and an interpretation of the ruling of the previous year's judges (*Nat. Am.* June 1935, p. 14) regarding the general functions of the Committee in relation to the formulation of defectively framed amendments. He was given the necessary information and advised that the Committee is not required to formulate amendments which are submitted merely in outline and without the final text intended.

On January 14, President Bradofsky requested a specific ruling on a case involving the same principle; that of a set of unformulated suggestions for amendments submitted to the Constitution Committee by Victor A. Moitoret and Marion C. Morcom. He was advised that the re-writing of these suggestions as true proposed amendments formed no part of the Committee's duty and that they should be returned to their authors for preparation and re-submission in proper form. The Judges also ruled that the authors, in view of their good faith in submitting the suggestions before the expiration of the time allowed for amendments, should be granted a reasonable period after the official time-limit for the necessary preparation and re-submission.

Also on January 14, Pres. Bradofsky requested a ruling on a complete new Constitution submitted by Ex-Pres. Babcock, and a general ruling on the right of members of the Constitution Committee to propose amendments themselves. He was advised that Mr. Babcock's submission of the new Constitution was legal, and that there is no barrier against the proposal of amendments by members of the Committee. He was, however, further advised to suggest to Mr. Babcock that the proposed new constitution be voluntarily withdrawn and re-submitted in the more logical form of separate amendments. In all three of these constitutional matters President Bradofsky acted promptly in accordance with the Board's rulings.

On March 18, 1936, Edwin Hadley Smith preferred charges to the Board regarding the delay of Ralph W. Babcock, Jr., in printing a set of Laureateship Certificates which had been ordered from him and for which he had received the sum of $15.00 in advance. He showed that in Sept. 1934, $25.00 had been given to the Association by Hyman Bradofsky for the printing of such certificates, and that up to the time of the complaint none of the nine winners of the 1935 awards had been supplied as per agreement notwithstanding the placement of the order with Mr. Babcock and the advance payment to him of $15.00 in October 1934. Exhibits were furnished and the complainant appeared to proceed on the assumption that the order was for a large stock of blank certificates for future use, only a fraction of which were to be used for the nine 1935 winners. Mr. Babcock was notified and sent a preliminary reply scarcely in keeping with the seriousness of the complaint. It later developed that his understanding of the order differed from Mr. Smith's, his impression being that only a single set of nine certificates for the 1935 winners had been ordered; these to have the individual names printed in and to be of a de luxe quality warranting the seemingly high price of $25.00 for a single set. Upon receipt of the flippant preliminary reply, the following resolution was adopted by Judges Haggerty and Plaisier, Mr. Lovecraft not voting:

> "The Board of Executive Judges have received a complaint from Mr. Edwin Hadley Smith that Ex-President Ralph W. Babcock, Jr., received $15.00 in October 1934, for the printing of laureate certificates, and that up to the present time these certificates have not been printed. The Board communicated with Mr. Babcock and received his reply, which was flippant and very discourteous, and which seemed to show no recognition of the gravity of the charges.
>
> "We recognize that Mr. Babcock's absence from home will probably prevent him from printing the certificates, which are so long overdue, until his return from college, and we feel that a reasonable opportunity should be given him. We therefore refer this matter to the incoming Board of Executive Judges, to be elected at the Grand Rapids convention, for such action as the circumstances will warrant at that time."

Since this resolution additional testimony has been received; Mr. Babcock stating his conception of the order, citing other witnesses with a similar understanding and indicating that work on a single set of elaborate certificates had begun long previously; being later halted by the Smith complaint concerning the History and Story awards, which threw into uncertainty the identity of the winners in these classes and rendered the printing of their names impossible. On the other hand, testimony from Mr. Bradofsky indicates that in making his gift of $25.00 he had in mind a large stock of blanks instead of a single set of certificates with printed names; thus sustaining the assumption in Mr. Smith's charges. Obviously there has been a grave and definite misunderstanding in the terms of the printing order, which will have the strongest bearing on the final judgment of the case. If the present Board is unable to arrive at a ruling within its term of office, its successor is urged to apply the most painstaking and liberal consideration to this delicate problem.

On April 10, 1936, the Judges were requested by the President to prepare the form and text of the proxy ballots to be used at the coming election. Since this duty is one not ordinarily required of the Board and not specifically mentioned in the Constitution, the Board referred the matter back to the Secretary, through the President.

All papers covering matters brought before the Executive Judges for the 1935–36 term will be turned over to their successors at the Grand Rapids convention.

Respectfully submitted:

VINCENT B. HAGGERTY
H. P. LOVECRAFT
JENNIE K. PLAISIER
*Executive Judges*

EDITOR'S NOTE FP: *National Amateur* 58, No. 4 (June 1936): 2–3. HPL, as one of the three executive judges for the 1935–36 term, gives his opinion on the debates between Hyman Bradofsky and others (as related in "Some Current Motives and Practices").

## SOME CURRENT MOTIVES AND PRACTICES

In the opening issue of *Causerie* Mr. Ernest A. Edkins touches ably and pointedly upon one case of an evil which, though always present in amateurdom, has formed a particularly offensive nuisance during the past year—the evil of personal malice as a major motive of activity. The time was ripe for such an editorial, and more in the same vein from other pens would be welcome. Good will and a rational attitude cannot be established by force or edict, but widespread pertinent comment can sometimes help to discourage their most senseless and persistent violations.

It is again appropriate, as on many past occasions, to ask whether the primary function of amateur journalism is to develop its members in the art of expression or to provide an outlet for crude egotism and quasi-juvenile spite. Genuine criticism of literary and editorial work, or of official policies and performances, is one thing. It is a legitimate and valuable feature of associational life, and can be recognised by its impersonal approach and tone. Its object is not the injury or denigration of any person, but the improvement of work considered faulty or the correction of policies considered bad. The zeal and emphasis of the real critic are directed solely toward the rectification of certain definite conditions, irrespective of the individuals connected with them. But it takes no very acute observer to perceive that the current floods of vitriol and billingsgate in the National Amateur Press Association have no conceivable relationship to such constructive processes.

The sabotage, non-coöperation, legalistic harrying, published abuse, partly circulated attacks, and kindred phenomena which have lately cheapened the association and hampered its work are of an all too evident nature. Surface inspection and close analysis alike reveal only one motive behind them—the primitive and puerile desire of one individual or another, under the influence of childish caprice or ruffled self-esteem, to inflict pain or humiliation or general harm upon some other individual.

It is impossible to discover any useful purpose behind any example of the recent bickering, notwithstanding the lofty and disinterested motives professed in certain cases. Those who invoke trivial and obsolescent technicalities against others for the noble purpose of 'saving the constitution' are careful to confine their austere crusading to persons whom they do not like; while those who thunder against fancied official blunders are equally careful to let their eagle-eyed alertness and civic virtue find such blunders only among their personal foes. Not in any instance can we trace these attacks and persecutions to an actual wish to help the association—for their authors ignore myriads of opportunities to serve and upbuild in other ways. All the zeal very plainly centres around the more savage process of venting private dislike and vindictiveness, and making somebody else uncomfortable.

Unfortunately the evil is not confined to a riff-raff whom the National could readily repudiate. Like other bad habits, egotism and sadism spread to the useful as well as the useless, and form regrettable weaknesses in otherwise gifted and admirable persons. In the present epidemic we ruefully note a great deal of unmotivated savagery from prominent members who are not only capable of better things but who have accomplished and are accomplishing much for the association. Plainly, the needed campaign of reform must be one against *attitudes and practices* as distinguished from *individuals*.

That the N.A.P.A. can—or should—attempt to control the private ethics and individual taste of its various members is greatly to be doubted. It is the function of other social forces to do whatever can be done toward redeeming this or that person from the sway of paltry emotions, primitive perspectives, blunted group-consciousness, and a distorted sense of proportion. What amateurdom may well attempt is simply to oppose the use of its own facilities and mechanism—its papers, its address-lists, and its administrative organisation—as agents in the exercise of loutish personal rancour and gratuitous small-boy brutality. It does not pay to encourage practices which place the institution in a cheap and contemptible light, and tend to alienate the best type of members and prospective members.

Just what can be done about the matter remains to be seen—but the ampler the public discussion, the sooner a feasible avenue of effort can be found. The problem is not one in which absolute suppression can be aimed at. Rather must we work for the discouragement, restriction, and minimisation of the given evil. A good beginning would be the closing of the mailing bureau, critical columns, historian's and librarian's records, and all other departments of official recognition to a paper containing material manifestly unsuitable for publication. The mailing manager might well be required to secure the approval of the president or executive judges before releasing to the membership anything open to suspicion as personally scurrilous or non-constructively savage, while such officials might also be given the power to declare any offending journal—publicly or privately mailed—invalid and technically non-existent as an activity item or vehicle for laureateship entries. Parallel with such action the executive judges should double their alertness in detecting complaints brought to them in a spirit of personal malice, and should exercise a large measure of discretion in dealing with these efforts to use the association as a feudists' accessory.

The part of individual editors is to attack cheap personalism in their columns, and to ignore—except when giving proper refutation to certain specific lampoonings—such exchanges as habitually transcend good taste and fraternal harmony. For the membership at large there remains the duty of generally backing up the side of decency and reasonable decorum—of voting for remedial measures if given the chance; of going on record, when opportunities come, as friends of good conduct; and of withholding acknowledgment and approval from journals which persistently and consciously lapse below civilised standards. Naturally, it sometimes takes a developed analytical ability and fund of tolerant humour to distinguish really anti-social malevolence from the mere ignorant coarseness and harmless low buffoonery which can so closely resemble it. Mistakes will occur, as in other fields. But most of the offences are too manifest to demand hesitancy.

One especial phase of the evil needs close consideration and possibly separate action—this being the circulation of derogatory material behind the backs of the victims. It seems to be a growing custom to attack or ridicule a person in print, yet to refrain from sending that person a copy of the attack. This is manifestly a double offence—indeed, it makes offensive many perhaps legitimate criticisms which would be above censure if sent openly to their objects. The effect of a lampoon sent to everyone but the victim is obvious. Instant reply is cut off, and the original hostile impression has an unfair chance to sink into public consciousness before it can be combated. A punctiliously honourable fighter gives his foe a chance to see hostile material even *before* publication. Comment on an opposite policy is almost needless. While the partial circulation of ordinary papers is hardly to be controlled by rule (although it should be obligatory to supply certain officers and recognised major workers), the practice of attacking in print without supplying a copy to the victim is so gross an injury that its legal punishment is at least a matter worthy of debate. It would pay amateurs to consider the adoption of some measure penalising editors guilty of this practice, even though such a measure would have to be drawn very carefully to prevent injustice and discourage retaliatory sharp practice (in the form of false denials of receipt) on the part of persons properly criticised and supplied by honourable editors.

So far as concrete instances go, the current evil reaches its grotesque apex in the absurd and fantastic persecution meted out during the past year to President Hyman Bradofsky—a persecution which, however, spreads much more ridicule upon its authors than upon its victim. Just what it is about, no one seems to be aware—indeed, nearly every commentator including Mr. Bradofsky assigns a different ostensible cause. The present executive is probably contributing more to the amateur cause, in effort and in publications, than any of his contemporaries. His *Californian*, with its unprecedented space opportunities, has been the greatest recent influence in stimulating amateur prose writing. His high qualitative ambitions for the National are responsible for Mr. Spencer's present critical chairmanship.[1] His financial support—given at the cost of great personal hardship—has floated a sadly burdened official organ. His generosity and good will have been manifested in a dozen channels to the association's advantage. And most of all, he has been a faithful and conscientious president throughout his term; proving inadequate in no respect, and seeking the proper advice before making any move which might be challenged. His encouragement of a policy of high endeavour has won recruits, stimulated worthy writing, and evoked such brilliant new papers as *Causerie* and *The Dragon-Fly*.[2]

Now Mr. Bradofsky may or may not be a superman. He may not combine in a single person the varied talents and aptitudes of a Morton, a Miniter, an Edkins, a Cook, a Spencer, a Loveman, and so on. His official messages may tend toward diffuseness rather than detail, and his prose rhythms may not compete with those of Flaubert or Dunsany. His fiction—still frankly experimental and pursued for the sake of development—may fall considerably short of Balzac's or Dostoievsky's. His response to criticism may shew a bit too much ethical sensitiveness and a bit too little tough combativeness. . . . It is yet too early to give a complete report on this. His handling of sundry communications may or may not involve the tact of a diplomat and the self-effacement of a Trappist. There is no need to present an imposing brief for Mr. Bradofsky, or to become his particular partisan and defender. But granting all his possible variations from theoretical perfection, and comparing his record with that of each of his nearly seventy predecessors, can we find in his acts and policies any conceivable basis for a campaign of general heckling, hounding, and attempted ridicule even a tenth as virulent and systematic as that which certain individuals and groups in amateurdom have seen fit to conduct against him?

Here, indeed, is merely one more case of the prevailing vicious personalism. Mr. Bradofsky, a sterling amateur and dependable president, has offended a few egos; either through some of his maturely considered official acts—appointments, replacements, etc.—or through his outspoken partisanship of sincere literary striving as distinguished from the slapdash imitation of tenth-rate sensational journalism. Therefore, according to the mode, he becomes an object of personal spleen and infantile nose-thumbing among the select circle upon whose toes he has unintentionally trod. Such cases have occurred before; and we cannot, perhaps, blame the tongue-thrusting circle quite so much as the general tolerance of such tactics. Indeed, it is possible that we ought to be grateful to it for bringing such scurrilousness to a *reductio ad absurdum* and crystallising associational sentiment in favour of a cleanup.

The history of this case is amusingly typical. There may be a dozen points in President Bradofsky's official course—as in any president's—which could justify constructive criticism; but the present Thersitean chorus has, no doubt inadvertently, neglected to mention any of these. What, instead, do we find? Counting out mere spiteful digs at the victim's literary efforts and casual utterances, there remain only a series of completely absurd charges concerning administrative moves—the falsity of many of which must have been known even by the makers.

For a characteristic specimen we may take the shrill hue and cry over Mr. Bradofsky's treatment—as a member of the Constitution Committee—of certain amendments and suggestions for amendments submitted to him last January.[3] Irresponsible editorials have shrieked of his "throwing out" this or that measure for reasons of partisanship. Actually, he did not even lay himself open to the suspicion of so doing. Intent on fairness, he referred every debatable point to the executive judges and acted strictly according to their unanimous decisions. He said as much at the time, and all attempts to make it appear that he tried to pass off the private letters of judges as their official rulings will be revealed as silly when the executive board's report appears in The National Amateur. Mr. Bradofsky "threw out" nothing whatever. In one case he *requested* the author of a proposed new constitution to re-submit its measures as separate amendments, and in another case he asked the authors of some unformulated suggestions to frame the latter as true amendments and send them in again . . . all on the advice of the judges. From this record of thoroughly proper official conduct the wild charges have grown—simply because certain individuals have ceased to hold a personal liking for Mr. Bradofsky.

The mere jeering demands less extensive notice, since it bespatters its sources more than it does its targets. The ethics of publishing a sneer-annotated version of a story received for printing—before the circulation of the story itself, and without the sending of a copy to the victim—may justly excite indignation; but the indignation tends to be lost in amusement (and not at the intended victim's expense) when we note the misspelled words and crude solecisms with which the sneering comment abounds! So, too, do we smile (and not at Mr. Bradofsky) when a viciously meant (and absolutely unmotivated) lashing is headed by a phrase in ungrammatical Latin and riddled with the repeated misspelling of a well-known proper name. Most certainly, Mr. Bradofsky is the last person who needs to worry about such a campaign—and the votes which he will receive next month for major offices will doubtless shew how little this childish vituperation has affected the general membership's appreciation of his really notable services. It is the association as a whole which suffers—in dignity, prestige, ethical tone, and general efficiency—when it tolerates the use of its mechanism as an instrument of personal spleen.

Mr. Edkins started a long-needed movement when he spoke out frankly against the prevailing wave of abusive personalism. One hopes to see that movement grow and bear fruit. If amateurdom is to become a playground for private spite, it can scarcely hope to hold those who are seeking an environment favourable to literary development.

EDITOR'S NOTE FP: Mimeographed sheets issued by R. H. Barlow (De Land, FL), probably in late June 1936. The essay is dated 4 June 1936 on the AMS (JHL). HPL comes to the defence of Hyman Bradofsky, President of the NAPA for 1935–36, who was being attacked by such members as Ralph Babcock and Edwin Hadley Smith for supposed unfairness and irregularities in his conduct of official matters. It becomes evident from HPL's account that several members also had a personal hostility to Bradofsky, for reasons that remain unclear;

HPL never suggests here or in correspondence that one of the reasons for this hostility may have been the fact that Bradofsky was a Jew. Bradofsky weathered the storm and was elected Official Editor for the 1936–37 term, but he resigned shortly after his election.

*Notes*

1. The veteran amateur Truman J. Spencer was Chairman of the Bureau of Critics of the NAPA for the 1935–36 term.
2. The *Dragon-Fly* was an amateur paper issued by HPL's young colleague R. H. Barlow (1918–1951). Two issues (15 October 1935 and 15 May 1936) appeared, although they had no contributions by HPL.
3. On this subject see further "Report of the Executive Judges" (p. 396).

---

## [LETTER TO THE N.A.P.A.]

June 22, 1936

To the Convention of the N.A.P.A.
Grand Rapids, Michigan:—

I keenly regret the circumstances which prevent me from being present on this occasion, and wish to extend my greetings to those who are more fortunate. From what I have heard of local plans, I feel sure that the gathering will prove to be one of the Association's most active and enjoyable conventions.

I shall await very eagerly the results of the election, and hope that they may ensure a continuance of those upbuilding efforts which the retiring administration has so valiantly and on the whole successfully conducted despite the most serious handicaps. The past year has seen a perceptible rise in the Association's standards, as shown in such new journals as *Causerie* and *The Dragon-Fly*, and in the increasingly helpful quality of the official criticisms under Messrs. Spencer and Kleiner. During the year to come there will be great opportunities to build upon these foundations, and to carry out such plans as were blocked by the special obstacles of the past.

Our thanks are due to President Bradofsky, and to the colleagues who have loyally stood by him, for an uphill fight on behalf of progress and quality. I am sure we all appreciate the sacrifices which have made possible the issuance of *The Californian* with its unprecedented chances for our prose writers, and which have kept *The National Amateur* up to its present standard. A high example has been set—and we can ask no more of the new administration than that it preserve the same aim and zeal, and make the most of its more favourable conditions.

It is a matter of much regret to me that my own contributions to the year's activities have been few—an unavoidable result of obstacles outside the Association. But that the N.A.P.A. has been no real loser thereby, will be obvious to all who have studied Mr. Kleiner's critical articles. It is my most earnest hope that the new board will see fir to reappoint Mr. Kleiner to the post of verse critic, which he has filled with distinguished ability and raised to a new level of importance.

The dedication of the Presidents' Field, a memorial which places the Association for ever in Mr. Macauley's debt, will help to make the present convention an historic one. Let us trust that it may prove no less historic in its dedication to the officers and members to a task of continued constructiveness and renewed harmony.

Again, my most cordial greetings and sincere regrets.
Fraternally yours,
H. P. Lovecraft.

EDITOR'S NOTE  FP: *Lest We Forget*, October 1936, p. 28. HPL writes to the NAPA in antici-
pation of the convention to be held the next month, and includes words in support of Hyman
Bradofsky. The letter was included in a one-shot issue of a magazine issued by Bradofsky as a
defense of his presidency against the attacks of other members (see "Some Current Motives
and Practices"), and was filled with accounts by other amateurs in support of Bradofsky.

## [LITERARY REVIEW]

### The Californian

Faithfully and regularly, *The Californian* makes its appearance each quarter; a voluminous haven for contributions short and long, and with pages frequently passing
the hundred-mark in number. The service rendered to amateurdom by this publication, while undoubtedly appreciated by our acutest members, has never been properly
emphasised. It is, in effect, the only influence at hand favourable to good prose-writing;
for of all our magazines no other provides consistently the space needed for the development of serious prose tales and essays. The result of inadequate space has always
been to stunt the cultivation of prose among us, and turn the aspiring writer to the
pursuit of verse, whose spatial requirements are so much less. This one-sided condition
has been repeatedly attacked in the past. Let us now thank Mr. Bradofsky and his publication for having done much toward correcting it.

In the Spring, 1936 issue we behold 103 pages of varied material, including some
of very high quality. Before we criticise the presence of occasional crude or middling
contributions, let us remember that the lack of other ample media makes it necessary
for Mr. Bradofsky to be generous toward the beginner. If the less developed prose aspirant cannot find a practice-ground for full-length items here, where is he to find it?
The utmost one could say is that greater strictness might perhaps be exercised regarding the briefer bits, the most commonplace of which could probably gain lodgement
elsewhere to better general advantage.

Dominating the contents of this issue is the satiric mythological allegory on certain phases of human nature entitled "The God and the Man, a Saga of the Uphri-
gees", by the late Charles D. Isaacson. Here we have grace, brilliancy, and wit of a high
order; clever parallels, gentle irony, and apt imagery clothed in musical and well-
balanced prose. This allegory, we are told, would have appeared some years ago in *The
American Mercury* but for H. L. Mencken's withdrawal from that magazine.[1]

Notable also are the less technically mature but intensely serious and straightforward essays of Howard Thomas Mitchell, whose almost naive vigour, sincerity, and
open-minded earnestness mark him out for high regard as a social thinker and exposi-
tor. Mr. Mitchell's diligent, conscientious scholarship in the economic and political
fields of his choice is at once obvious; and his intense purpose and desire for lucidity
give his style a force and directness of the most commendable sort. An overlying dignity prevails, even when occasional sentimentalities and rhetorical awkwardnesses are

apparent. In the course of time we may reasonably expect the defects to wane—as a very slight amount of care, and assiduous study of the best prose models, would cause them to do. Let Mr. Mitchell learn to be careful in little things—avoiding phrases like *synonymous to* instead of *synonymous with*, and studying balance, symmetry, and economy in the shaping of sentences and paragraphs. Of the essays in the present issue, "The Major Conflict" is perhaps the most solid. "What Lincoln Would Do Today" is also excellent, while "If I Had a Million Dollars" is at least thought-provoking. Judged by the most sophisticated standards, Mr. Mitchell may occasionally be guilty of oversimplification, disproportion, and a kind of unrealistic pietism; but the fact remains that he is the most mature, informed, serious, and intelligent of all the amateurs who habitually unburden themselves on the social and political questions of the day. The present reviewer does not agree with the critics who would banish such issues from amateurdom, but he would like to insist that those who approach their discussion prepare themselves with as thorough a study and as serious a spirit as Mr. Mitchell's.

In poetry, as exemplified by "My Old Ohio Home", Mr. Mitchell is not so successful. Here, despite the unmistakable sincerity and strong feeling, triteness, sentimentality, bad technique, and the pervasive aura of the journalistic "Poets' Corner" run riot with disastrous effect. If the author plans to continue in the metrical field, we would urge upon him an intensive study of really good poetry—of the sort included in "The Golden Treasury"[2]—plus a diligent perusal of some manual such as Brander Matthews' "A Study of Versification" or the newly published "How to Revise Your Own Poems", by Anne Hamilton.[3]

Two widely different but equally interesting and informative essays are the late W. R. Murphy's brief "Reflections on a Restoration Comedy" and Henry Jones Mulford's "The Truth about Mother Goose". The former is almost a model of style; the latter tends toward carelessness and diffuseness. But Mr. Mulford, notwithstanding occasional weak spots, puts us greatly in his debt by emphasising the historical background of our familiar nursery rhymes.

In considering the many less ambitious essays, we are led to remark the superiority of those which deal at first-hand with some concrete experience or character or idea over those which attempt more ponderous, abstract, and sententious themes. Especially fresh and pleasing are "Sounds I Love", by Isabel Vajda, "Nona", by Mary Paicopulos, "Book's Eye View", by Hazel Beaver, "Originality", by Eugene B. Kuntz, and the various bits by Otto W. Ferguson. Albert Chapin's essays always have a charm and individuality of their own, while the reflective observations of Messrs. Ridder and Damgaard deserve much consideration. The assorted reminiscences of old-time amateurs are welcome and appropriate, and Mr. Bradofsky's editorials go ably to the point.

The present *Californian* is less lucky in its fiction, most of the specimens being of a light, conventional sort dealing with stock characters, emotions, and situations in a thoroughly derivative manner. The great lesson which the amateur story-teller should learn is that the only sound source of material is life and human character or mood as studied at first-hand. Unfortunately the most accessible sort of modern fiction—the unctuous, insincere, tailored-to-order stuff appearing in commercial "slicks" like *The Saturday Evening Post*—forms the worst possible model for the beginner, teaching him an infinitude of tricks and mannerisms which he must unlearn if he is to achieve genuine aesthetic expression. As a counteractive, the young writer should read Edward J. O'Brien's "Dance of the Machines",[4] and study the tales appearing in the magazine *Story* and in the various O'Brien anthologies.

Nor is good poetry very abundant in the present issue—at least, so far as range of authors is concerned. Of the bards represented, Eugene B. Kuntz easily leads, and of his verses "Moonlight on the Sea" is richest in charm. Some of Albert Chapin's lines—especially "Stars"—are appealing and full of a certain sincerity which augurs increasingly good work from his pen.

The Summer *Californian* shews a substantial advance in typographical appearance, and has as a very welcome addition a classified table of contents. In the average of its contributions it equals its predecessor, and at least one highly remarkable piece of amateur literature is included.

This piece, it is almost needless to point out, is the long and curiously powerful fantasy by R. H. Barlow entitled "A Dim-Remembered Story".[5] Other recent tales by Mr. Barlow in *The Californian* and in his own *Dragon-Fly* have indicated a rapid advance beyond the stage of his brief "Annals of the Jinns";[6] but even so, the present mature work comes as a surprise. Not only is the flow of fantastic imagination better modulated, and the bizarre, dream-like imagery made more vivid and realistic, but the rhythm and idiomatic grace of the style are infinitely improved. The tale is one of abnormal transference to the future—first to the remote future of this planet, and then to a black and inconceivable gulf beyond the life of the cosmos and of time itself. With such a bold conception, the chances for crudity, absurdity, and unconvincingness are manifold; yet Mr. Barlow has escaped all pitfalls, and has produced something so concrete and coherent that we tend to recall it as an actual nightmare experienced rather than as a story read. Some of the visual touches are brilliant and unforgettable—the great forest with blind eyes, tortuous black limbs, and watching leaves and mosses—the vaulted castle of Yrn—and the globular, vibrating entities of the Outside. Especially well managed is the narrator's *transition* from the present to the alien future—a type of fictional action almost invariably bungled by fantaisistes through lack of adequate emotional treatment. Here we find the narrator's own realisation of the process gradual, bewildered, and at first incredulous and reluctant; effected through the slow perception of subtle strangenesses in flora and fauna. No better method could have been chosen. Certain misprints in this story are highly annoying, but in spite of them it leaves a deep impression. Mr. Barlow, still very young, is well worth watching.

Another important contribution to the Summer issue is Clement F. Robinson's erudite and analytical study entitled "Galsworthy and the Law", which traces the great author's early experience as a barrister and his subsequent treatment of the law and lawyers in his fiction. Of admirable force and clearness throughout, and with sufficient explanatory text to link the incidents treated with the plots of the novels as a whole, this essay really forms an indispensable item for any thorough-going Galsworthian devotee.

Howard Thomas Mitchell is represented by three earnest and thoughtful essays—"The Greatest Menace to Progress", a plea for mental flexibility and adaptability, "Why I Want to Write", a brief summary of the author's objects, and "An American Plan for World Peace". All are forceful and well informed; though in the last-named article the author obviously permits ethical feeling, plus an ingenuously orthodox concept of man's place in the cosmic flux, to colour his ideas of the chances for an "International Federation" amidst a world of antipodally different and basically irreconcilable culture-streams. Even this article, however, displays Mr. Mitchell's constructive legal mind and sympathetic social vision to advantage.

"Pure Fantasy", by Donald A. Wollheim,[7] and "Progress" and "John Randolph", by Hyman Bradofsky, are shorter essays of great force and interest. Mr. Bradofsky's succinct capture of Randolph's complex and stormy personality is especially excellent.

Amateur reminiscences have come to be an expected feature in *The Californian*, and the present issue does not disappoint. Mr. Kleiner's study of the late Frank Denmark Woollen, poet and amateur leader in the Golden Age, is notably graphic despite its small compass.

Fiction, aside from Mr. Barlow's achievement, is hardly the strong point of this number. Mr. Bradofsky's stories, while steadily improving in phraseology and balance of parts, are still troublesomely bound to conventional models which include artificially handled emotions, improbable coincidences, obviously theatrical situations and climaxes, and other evidences of a strictly literary derivation. His primary need is to draw from life rather than from literature; to delineate the complex emotions and inconclusive acts of the people he sees around him or learns about from non-fictional sources rather than to mirror the dramatically heightened and naively oversimplified feelings and acts commonly encountered in popular fiction. One may add that the stories of Eunice McKee, Jean V. La Forge, and John Blythe Michel[8] indicate a not dissimilar need.

The Summer issue is well equipped with poetry, some of which is of considerable merit. "Wild Horses", a sonnet by Frances Davis Adams, presents a clear-cut picture and sense of turbulent motion. Jack Wallace Hille's four snatches of free verse embody sharp and delicate images which speak well for his poetic perception and should encourage him toward more ambitious flights. Frank Ankenbrand, Jr., in presenting similar snatches, should be on guard against a touch of affectation—though his "Lake Pictures" embodies fine imagery. Edna Smith De Ran has a good command of metre and rhyme, but must study the art of imagery very closely in order to avoid effects which are jarring and sometimes unconsciously comic. In "Clouds" she has *creeping* clouds which *stride* with flowing curls, which sometimes hang like *rotten gourds* angrily thrusting out silver *swords*, and which (although just said to wear *swords*) now and then *sheath their spears*. (Query: what is a *spear-sheath* like?) However, the spirit is there, and a little attention to technique and the best poetic models would do wonders toward giving the bard a more assured articulateness.

It remains to commend Mr. Bradofsky on the departments—amateur affairs, book review, and letters to the editor—which seem to be designed as *Californian* fixtures. His editorial comment is just and pertinent, while his tributes to departed amateurs are sincere, sympathetic, and generally adequate.

## Causerie

Superlatives are generally dangerous; but if ever they are justifiable, it is in connexion with Mr. Ernest A. Edkins' *Causerie*. For the past twenty years half of the amateurs have been lamenting the passing of the Golden Age, while the other (and usually younger) half have been trying to deny that it ever existed. Here, in a paper published by one of the high lights of the fabled period and faithfully reflecting its characteristics, we have simultaneous proof that the *dies Halcyonei* really did exist, that their passing was abundantly worth lamenting, and that there is at least a fighting chance of our recapturing something of their spirit and quality.

*Causerie* is the sort of paper which amateurdom ought to produce in far greater quantity. It is the message of a literate mind addressed to other literate minds. While we cannot expect all our publications to reach or even approximate this level—for must not the novice begin somewhere?—we have reason to be ashamed that so few are even within seeing distance of it. Amateurdom is supposed to encourage literary *development*;

but where are evidences that any widespread development to a stage of mature well-readness and cultivated vigour of expression exists today? Shew us more papers like *Causerie* and we shall grow optimistic. Admittedly, Mr. Edkins' work was above the average even in the Golden Age; but old files shew that its present stately solitude was by no means foreshadowed then. *Causerie* gives the newest generation a taste of a grade of expression once commonly found among us. Let it serve as an example as well as a delight!

The June issue is remarkable for its book reviews—graceful and appreciative essays on such N.A.P.A. luminaries as Samuel Loveman, Edna Hyde McDonald, and Eugene B. Kuntz. The critique of Mr. Loveman's recent book of poems[9] is perhaps the most understanding, lucid, and sympathetically interpretative analysis which the Lovemanic Muse has yet received—a brilliant study of a brilliant bard. More criticism—including the helpfully ruthless exposure of mediocrity and ineptitude—may be found in the review of last winter's *Californian* and in many of the shorter notes. Here, indeed, is an answer to the pleas of many members that amateur criticism be made sharper and more penetratingly candid. There are those who will deplore such beneficent birching, but even the tenderest soul can scarcely deny that the general level of modern amateur letters calls for something drastic. We need to be jolted into a realisation of how much lower our standards are than they were in 1885 or 1895.

Yet it is not for its criticism that the June *Causerie* is chiefly notable. Most of all, it is the harmonious expression of an extraordinarily rich and gifted personality. The wit is subtle, spontaneous, and engaging; the style is racy, assured, and piquantly allusive; the reminiscent touches are eloquent and appealing; and at least one editorial, "Rain, Music, and Memories", forms a delicately nostalgic essay of Proustian mood, replete with poignant, elusive charm. Amateurs will unite in congratulating Mr. Edkins on his recent recovery from a serious illness, and in demanding that *Causerie* be made a permanent institution.

## Ahoy!

One of amateurdom's chief advantages is encouragement of distinctiveness and originality—of the direct, sincere personal expression which lies at the base of all good writing, but which is almost wholly suppressed in the conventional, formula-ridden world of popular commercial authorship and journalism. This is amply attested by Mr. Otto W. Ferguson's pleasing journal *Ahoy!*, whose first and second issues (March and April, 1936) are before us. Printed from typewritten pages by a more or less novel process, this magazine follows the "plain, homespun" tradition, yet does not often fall into the rubber-stamp attitudes of professional "rough-diamondism" and culture-baiting. Instead, it reflects an active, acquisitive mind keenly alive to the events and currents of the last half-century and nourished by the soundest and most solid kind of literary diet. If Mr. Ferguson chooses to maintain a "village oracle" attitude, he is at least an oracle who reads Pareto and sees through the mawkish sentimentalities of quack writers like Eddie Guest and Harold Bell Wright![10]

The contents of *Ahoy!* includes pungent personal reminiscences, unhackneyed reflections or reading, and a wide variety of witty and iconoclastic comments on life in general. In all of these departments Mr. Ferguson's shrewd, common-sense personality stands out prominently, and the entire enterprise concretely proves the fallacy of the notion—so sadly popular among some of the younger amateurs—that in order to escape pompousness one must parrot the low-grade leers, flippancies, and impertinences of the tabloids and other purveyors to the illiterate. Mr. Ferguson is often irreverent, but he is never cheap.

It would be unfair to comment singly on the various items in *Ahoy!* The issues must be read as a whole if one is to catch their full flavour. Mr. Ferguson's direct, colloquial style has a captivating unaffectedness, but would perhaps be better for the removal of a few modern "Babbittisms" such as the use of *contact* as a verb. The very recent corruptions of our slovenly machine-and-commerce age have none of the redeeming force and quaintness of those homely informal idioms which are truly traditional and rich with the overtones of long usage. Whether Mr. Ferguson displays an unjustified hostility toward good grammar and correct punctuation, others must decide. Probably his gibes at sterile pedantry are more salutary than otherwise.

The sample article in—and on—international language would seem to indicate that this type of device is improving in effectiveness. Mr. Ferguson's text is in the speech called "Occidental"; and the present reviewer, though lacking previous acquaintance with any dialect of the kind, was able to read it through without difficulty—drawing only on English, some fond memories of Latin, and a perilous dictionary smattering of French and Spanish. Altogether, Mr. Ferguson has brought a vivid and welcome shipment to the storehouse of amateur letters, and we hope that his *Ahoy!* may continue to echo along our coast.

## Pine Needles

The tradition of fine printing and magazine design, brought into our period by Mr. Ralph Babcock's *Scarlet Cockerel,* has now received a fresh recruit in the person of Mr. Robie Macauley, whose Autumn *Pine Needles* is in many ways a remarkable achievement. Mr. Macauley is of the extremely youthful generation, but has learned quickly and competently from a gifted father and other amateur associates; so that his latest number needs no apologies or explanations. In general design, choice of typeface, quality of paper, and grade of workmanship, *Pine Needles* is well fitted to take its place among the high spots of amateur printing. Increasing years will place the young publisher on his guard against any tendencies toward flamboyancy, preciosity, or overdecoration which might develop from a desire for quaint ornateness and extreme sumptuousness. Edward H. Cole's *Olympian,* with its blend of richness and classic simplicity, always stands as a corrective model to guide the aspiring art printer.

In its contents *Pine Needles* includes some items worthy of its format—all being given the aspect of editorials through the omission of titles. Mr. Kleiner's essay on mountain and woodland rambles is piquant and graceful; while Miss Winkelman, despite a few vague sentences, shews much common sense in dealing with "youth movements". In his own remarks Mr. Macauley calls for more drastic amateur criticism, notwithstanding the furious resentment which perfect candour has often aroused in the past. In the main his attitude is sensible, although he probably does not realise just how harshly some of our tender strivers (and non-strivers!) would have to be treated if brutal frankness were universal rule. Rigid academic standards cannot be applied indiscriminately to the primary grades of novices, though some of the extreme leniency of the past six years—exercised because of the need of building up amateurdom's quantitative strength and enthusiasm—should certainly be dropped in future.

In only one detail does Mr. Macauley seem definitely on the wrong track—this being his assumption that the existence of the official bureau of critics is a symptom of decay. As a matter of fact, the critical bureau with its reviews in *The National Amateur* has existed since 1904—long before any spectacular decline in amateurdom took place. It is a necessity because of the lack of any regular and dependable individual press with competent reviewers. *Causeries* do not blossom every day, and there is no possibility whatever that individual papers can at any period adequately cover the general output of the association. What is needed is an ampler critical bureau—with more qualified reviewers to divide the heavy work among them, and more space in the official organ to give individual attention to the various items reviewed. It will be a hard goal to achieve; for some of the best critics in amateurdom find themselves unable to serve, while space is always at a premium. But it is the only sound goal, and one well worth working toward.

## Convention Papers

Among the more important echoes of the Grand Rapids convention *The Wag*, published by Edna Hyde McDonald and Helm C. Spink, stands out prominently. It consists largely of a single article of piquant narrative and anecdote by Mrs. McDonald, detailing more or less connectedly her experiences at last July's gathering. In its pertinent comments, selection of incidents, and spirited personal vignettes and character-studies, this epic of recreation takes a leading place among the published convention stories, and makes one hope that it will have regular successors at subsequent conventions—carrying on the witty tradition of the late Mrs. Minter's *Aftermath*. Mr. Spink has given the paper an admirable format and typography.

Similar enterprises are *Conventiongram* and *Happy Daze*, published respectively by the Misses Jane and Bernice McCarthy, and each wholly given over to its editor's convention story. *Conventiongram* contains perhaps the fullest and most detailed of all the Grand Rapids reports—rivalling the official minutes in scope and accuracy, and adding many agreeable side-lights and descriptive touches. *Happy Daze* emphasises the social side, and is very pleasantly and unaffectedly written. Other convention articles can be found scattered through the various current news sheets—that by Mr. Segal in *The Sea Gull* displaying both the merits and the limitations of his chosen popular-journalistic style. We presume the winged reporter realises that such "words" as "alright" and "appellage" are products of some subterraneous folklore other than the English language.

EDITOR'S NOTE FP: *Californian* 4, No. 3 (Winter 1936): 27–33. The title is probably not by HPL; on the AMS (JHL) no title is supplied. The AMS is dated 23 October 1936. The essay is, in effect, a kind of Bureau of Critics article, surveying the contents of several recent amateur journals in the NAPA (especially the *Californian* itself). Of particular note is HPL's enthusiastic discussion of R. H. Barlow's "A Dim-Remembered Story," implying that he had had little if any hand in its revision. (Letters between HPL and Barlow suggest that he did not even see the story until it had appeared in print.)

*Notes*

1. Mencken founded the *American Mercury* in 1924 and edited it down to the end of 1933. Isaacson died in 1936.

2. Francis T. Palgrave's *The Golden Treasury: Selected from the Best Songs and Lyrical Poems in the English Language* (1861; LL 671) is perhaps the most celebrated anthology of English poetry ever assembled.

3. Anne Hamilton, *How to Revise Your Own Poems: A Primer for Poets* (Los Angeles: Abbey San Encino Press, 1936; *LL* 393).

4. Edward J. O'Brien (1890–1941), *The Dance of the Machines: The American Short Story and the Industrial Age* (New York: Macaulay Co., 1929; *LL* 651). HPL constantly recommended this work—a scathing indictment of the formulaic and market-driven nature of the American short story—after reading it in 1929.

5. The story does not appear to have been revised by HPL, as some of Barlow's other fiction was; HPL would not have praised it as effusively as he does here if he had had a significant hand in its writing. For Barlow's collected fiction and poetry, see *Eyes of the God* (Hippocampus Press, 2002).

6. Nine installments of "Annals of the Jinns" appeared in the *Fantasy Fan* (October 1933–February 1935), one more in the *Phantagraph* (August 1936).

7. Wollheim (1914–1990) was a correspondent of HPL (1935–37) and editor of the *Phantagraph* (1935f.). He later attained celebrity as an author and editor in the science fiction field.

8. Michel later became a fan of fantasy and science fiction and wrote a brief article on HPL, "The Last of H. P. Lovecraft," *Science Fiction Fan* 4, No. 4 (November 1939): 3–7; rpt. *Lovecraft Studies* No. 18 (Spring 1989): 18–19.

9. Ernest A. Edkins, review of *The Hermaphrodite and Other Poems*, *Causerie* (June 1936): 2–4.

10. HPL refers to the poetaster Edgar A. Guest (1881–1959) and the popular novelist Harold Bell Wright (1872–1944).

---

# DEFINING THE "IDEAL" PAPER

Your recent article on The Ideal Amateur Paper is extremely well-written and likely to arouse interest and discussion. That is what we need—material for really substantial debate . . . about issues and standards and literary values instead of political office and election tactics.

As for any criticism of mine—perhaps the most general one would be that I think you do the old-timers just a trifle of injustice in describing their complaint. So far as I have noticed, most Golden Age survivors do not hold up any specific type of paper as a model. They would welcome all types if each journal were excellent *according to the particular standard of its own class.* The complaint of the septuagenarians is that *most* (not necessarily *all,* but the representative majority) of the contemporary papers are not excellent *by any conceivable standard.* Not but what there were many papers just as bad in 1885 and 1895. The point is that these lame and trivial journals were not so prevalent then, and that they were frankly recognised as inferior by the critics and high-grade press of the period. What held the focus of attention in 1890 was not somebody's criticism of somebody's official appointments, or gossip about the colour of some convention delegate's necktie, but a hot debate between James F. Morton and Ernest A. Edkins on certain basic literary principles, and on the merits of certain of Mrs. Miniter's short stories. I have looked over many of the old papers, and cannot escape the conclusion that the amateurdom of 1885–1895 towered mountainously above the amateurdom of today. I speak without personal bias, because this period was wholly before my time. I was born in 1890, when Edkins and Morton were at their height of activity; my own period—that of 20 years ago—was not even comparable to the Golden Age. We tried to raise the standard, and produced isolated things like *The Olympian, The Lingerer,* and *The Saturnian,* but in the main we were only pallid echoes. In my heyday as an amateur—1914–1924—there was only a fragment of the rich, spontaneous, high-grade activity of thirty years before that. Hence I speak from a purely impersonal study of old papers published before I was five years old. That remote past had the secret of first-class effort, and I wish some later generation could recapture it!

And what *was* that excellence which shewed itself in papers of so many different kinds? Well, I imagine it was two-fold. In the first place, the leaders of amateurdom were decently educated young fellows instead of irresponsible school-haters; and the majority—even when they did not have the same education *to start with*—recognised the qualities of these leaders and sought to emulate rather than ridicule them. *The standards were high,* even though many individuals fell short of them; and amateurdom proved a real education to more than one originally crude aspirant. In the second place, *members took amateurdom seriously,* and really put their best work into their papers. They would never have thought of issuing anything which did not at least *aim* high. They respected quality instead of belittling it, and tried their best to achieve it. Sometimes they failed, but their failures were respected. No one blames the editor of a poor paper if he has tried his best *to do his best.*

But to get back to the subject of *varied excellence* and its nature. It ought not to be hard to define. Whatever sort of paper one of the leaders of '85 would issue, it would represent the best efforts of a well-educated person to express himself in his chosen way—or to assist other keen minds to express themselves in their respective ways. It would—no matter what its nature or subject matter—reflect a *clear and well-stored mind* accustomed to reasonably mature and logically disciplined thinking, and sensitive to the difference between quality and trashiness in journalism and literature; and would display in its style the writer's knowledge of his native language and its possibilities. If it were largely a news and editorial sheet, it would display the editor's nature in the quality of the news selected (news above triviality, and of interest to developed rather than undeveloped minds) and in the field and tone of the comment. It would be couched in decent English (not necessarily prim or sober, but correct and tasteful even when light or humorous), and if it copied the professional journalism of its day it would choose the reputable journalism written for gentlefolk rather than the low-grade sensationalism popular with coachmen, servant-girls, and illiterate immigrant ditch-diggers. It knew what it wanted to say, and said it in the civilised and harmonious manner of people born to the language and accustomed to use forks and handkerchiefs. No muddled, indecisive thoughts, assorted references to matters not calling for any especial notice, explosive emotional outbursts in sundry variants of gutter patois, paragraphs of amorphous verbiage betraying ignorance of the language or allusion-backgrounds implying a complete unfamiliarity with the best in human thought and achievement. That is, the *best* of the old papers—and there were enough to give amateurdom its dominant tone—had none of these stigmata of inferiority. Even the lightest and airiest of editorial and news sheets were published by youths of taste and education who knew how to think and write, and who expected their readers to be of the same grade. Of course they knew that there were illiterates in amateur journalism, but they thought it wiser to help those illiterates lose their illiteracy than to lower the logic and taste of their own publications to the level of their crudest possible readers. In other words, they had not acquired that annoying post-war affectation which James Truslow Adams calls "the mucker pose".[1]

Papers were careful rather than slipshod; coherent rather than chaotic; intelligent rather than exuberant or explosive; literate rather than amorphous; highly aimed rather than consciously rabble-slanted. And this held good whether a paper specialised in editorials, stories, articles, verse, typography, or whatnot; whether it was small or large; whether it was plain or deluxe; and whether it featured its editor or his contributors. In other words, excellence, no matter what the field in which it is sought for and displayed. The old-time amateur might publish any kind of a paper, but he wanted it to be *good of its kind*. He saw no reason for deliberately catering to (as distinguished from helping and improving) illiterate and intellectually or imaginatively low-grade readers. Amateurs of this kind are not wholly extinct today, but they tend to be overlooked and drowned out amidst the flood of unrelieved triviality and semi-illiterate pointlessness. What we ought to do is to reverse the order of things—putting the triviality and pointlessness back into the minority position which they occupied in 1890. We are too tolerant of cheap, aimless, careless slush—the slush that doesn't try to be anything else. Certainly we ought to give all possible kindness and encouragement to the crude chap *who is trying to do something worth doing*—who is sincerely striving to express well-formed and balanced ideas in coherent language—but we discourage real quality and progress if we habitually applaud the illiterate clown who has no wish to be other than an illiterate clown.

My chief disagreement with your thesis is that I do not think the individual diversity of amateur papers ought to be discouraged. It would be *impossible* to devise any *one* amateur paper capable of pleasing and interesting *all* the membership. Human beings differ too much among themselves to be thus collectively reachable. The only journal which can please a whole family or city-full of people is the huge Sunday paper—and this does not please because any *one* part of it can satisfy everybody, but because it is composed of so many utterly different parts that each recipient can choose what he likes and ignore the rest. Obviously, no amateur journal could even begin to follow this formula—except perhaps something like *The Californian* (the *same* issue of which contains Mitchell's intelligent articles on Beard[2] and a less thoughtful poetaster's doggerel on "The Constitution")—hence we must expect the amateur press to include many papers which only part of the members will fully enjoy; trusting that the *whole* contents of any month's output (like the *whole* contents of the N. Y. Sunday *Times* or *Herald-Tribune*) will be diverse enough to include *something* for *everybody*. It would take all the spontaneity and zest out of an amateur paper if the editor thought he had to "slant" its contents in some vague, inclusive way calculated to please everybody. He might as well be writing lifeless, artificial editor-dictated fiction for the pulp magazines, or insincere advertising propaganda for the trade journals. The whole object of amateur journalism is to let each member express himself *in his own way, as he likes*. The only restriction—or official recommendation—ought to be this: that everyone do his best and seek the highest possible quality whatever the nature or direction of his effort may be. What would *Causerie* be like if Edkins had held himself in for the benefit of primer-pupils and victims of arrested development?

Thus I differ radically with your first conclusion. I would *not* discourage the highly individual or specialised paper (assuming, of course, that editors have the common taste or sense of proportion not to narrow down inside the field of general culture and publish journals devoted to intra-atomic physics, Indo-Chinese sculpture, comparative histology, or direct-mail advertising!) but would encourage a *wide range of subjects and styles among the different publications—giving variety to the amateur press as viewed collectively*. Regarding your second point, I am more in agreement. While I would tolerate certain special types of paper with a single line of contents, including the all-editorial, I would surely recommend that a pleasing variety of contributions and other features be sought for *in any paper which aims at a general-magazine character*. Also, I agree that extensive quotations and other quasi-boiler-plate material from the outside world should be discouraged. Regarding *quality*—I do not think that the good and bad should be mixed too freely, except in certain cases where an outlet for large numbers of manuscripts is imperative. Let a high-grade paper *be* high grade, and let the editor float another sheet for the strugglers and the stunted if he wishes. Fancy a "poem" by some of our more grotesque metrical offenders in Loveman's *Saturnian!* Your remarks on *timeliness* seem just and sensible so far as papers containing amateur comment (and most of them do) are concerned; although there are several types of literary journal, such as *The Dragon-Fly*, to which this principle would scarcely be applicable. *The composition of the mailing list* forms another live and debatable point. While it would be impracticable to expect the publishers of elaborate home-printed papers to supply every stray deadhead and recruit, there ought to be some unwritten policy concerning the covering of active workers and officers—and all concerned in any controversy which the paper in question may contain. 100% circulation is the ideal—and it certainly ought to be followed with all *professionally-printed* papers—where each additional copy does not mean hard labour for the editor.

There are many other points on which I might touch—but I will limit myself to that concerning the province and objects of amateur journalism. Despite the desirability of good printing and magazine design, I am still convinced that *writing* forms our primary field, and that nothing should be permitted to interfere with the fostering of this art among us to the greatest possible extent. This does not mean that the typographical artist is to be belittled; but simply that the mature and creative literary artist should receive, as in the outside world, that degree of precedence determined by the greater scope, depth, and richness of his chosen aesthetic medium.

What is the ideal amateur paper? It may be almost anything not definitely outside our wide circle of interest. There is no one particular kind. But whatever it is, it must represent the competent and serious efforts of its publisher to excel in the domain he has selected.

—H. P. LOVECRAFT,
Jan. 12, 1937.

EDITOR'S NOTE FP: *National Amateur* 62, No. 3 (June 1940): 10–12. The article included other segments (not included here) written by Ralph Babcock and Ernest A. Edkins. It becomes clear that HPL's segment is a letter written to Babcock in response to his article. HPL begins the discussion with an emphasis on the superiority of the amateur papers of the "halcyon" period (1885–95), then goes on to supply his preferences for the content of an amateur magazine.

*Notes*

1. "The mucker-poseurs do not content themselves with talking like uneducated half-wits. They also emulate the language and manners of the bargee and the longshoreman, although where the profanity of the latter is apt to have at least the virtue of picturesqueness, the swearing of the mucker-poseur is apt to be merely coarse." James Truslow Adams (1878–1949), "The Mucker Pose," in *Our Business Civilization* (New York: Albert & Charles Boni, 1929), p. 196.

2. Charles A. Beard (1874–1948) attained celebrity with *An Economic Interpretation of the Constitution* (1917), *The Rise of American Civilization* (1927, 2 vols.; with Mary R. Beard), and other challenging works on American history.

# APPENDIX

# [MISCELLANEOUS NOTES IN THE *UNITED AMATEUR*]

[September 1920:]

Mr. Paul J. Campbell deserves the most unstinted thanks of the United this year, for besides serving as First Vice-President he has furnished free of charge a supply of recruiting booklets and application blanks, thus relieving us of one of our most onerous burdens. Mr. Campbell's eighteen years of undiminished devotion to amateurdom form a thing worthy of emulation.

[November 1920:]

Will the members kindly regard the Secretary's Report as a Supplementary Membership List? Expense prohibits republication of full list in each issue, but these bulletins will furnish all needed information. All recruits here recorded should be given the fullest welcome of which the Association is capable.

Although the supply of "extras" of any issue of *The United Amateur* is somewhat limited, a duplicate ordinarily can be supplied in cases where the regular copy is not received. This happens occasionally in spite of the special care taken to have each issue reach each member promptly upon publication. Please report instances of missing numbers to the Editor or the Publisher.

[September 1921:]

The fullest apologies are due the membership for the lateness of this issue of *The United Amateur.* A prostrating and overwhelming flood of professional duties, coupled with a state of health permiting only the shortest of working hours,[1] has forced the editor to delay transmission of this copy to the publisher until November 4; a date which should be remembered in justice to the latter official, who is equally handicapped in the matter of conflicting duties.

[November 1921:]

Members who criticised the present editor for severity during his chairmanship of the critical department are invited to take a vicarious revenge this month, observing the uncensored remarks of the present juvenile chairman concerning our pathetic ignorance. Of us Master Galpin says: "when the author approaches involved or technical subjects, he shows clearly the unfortunate circumstance that he has never profited by an advanced education." This certainly should purge us of all suspicion of conducting *The United Amateur* on too Olympian a level, although the critic qualifies his dictum by conceding that we realise our own crudity and are striving in our old age to acquire at least the rudiments of an elementary education. In the couse of a few years we hope to guarantee our readers an official organ practically free from the grosser errors of spelling and grammar; meanwhile, *vivat Galpinius parvulus!*[2]

EDITORS' NOTE  FP: *United Amateur* 20, No. 1 (September 1920): 4 (unsigned); 20, No. 2 (November 1920): 26 (unsigned; titled "Editor's Note"), 29 (unsigned); 21, No. 1 (September 1921): 6 (signed "The Editor"); 21, No. 2 (November 1921): 24 (unsigned). Notes on amateur journalism matters chiefly designed as fillers. Internal evidence, and the fact that HPL was the Official Editor of the UAPA and hence the editor of the *United Amateur* for these issues, establish the items as his.

*Notes*

1. HPL had suffered considerable trauma upon the death of his mother on May 24; as HPL noted in "Final Words" (September 1921), in extenuation of his delay in submitting his contribution to the Transatlantic Circulator: ". . . the pressure of other imperative matters, both in the field of associational amateur journalism and in that of professional revision, has rendered greater celerity quite impossible. Indeed, so manifold are the duties with which I find myself now enveloped, that I fear a relinquishment of Circulator membership will be inevatable after this round" (CE5).

2. "Long live tiny little Galpin!" *Parvulus* is a diminutive of *parvus* ("small"), and is meant whimsically or sarcastically. Galpin's comment on HPL's lack of "an advanced education" (HPL had dropped out of high school before securing his diploma) probably touched a raw nerve, as HPL felt shame at his lack of a college degree.

---

# OFFICIAL ORGAN FUND

[September 1920:]

## RECEIPTS

| | |
|---|---|
| Woodbee Press Club | $25.00 |
| From Treasurer up to October 15 | 23.00 |
| Susie Nelson Furgerson | 6.00 |
| Jonathan E. Hoag | 5.00 |
| Verna McGeoch (for each issue) | 5.00 |
| Howard R. Conover | 3.00 |
| Victor O. Schwab | 3.00 |
| Mr. and Mrs. Fritter (for each issue) | 2.00 |
| Rev. Eugene B. Kuntz | 1.50 |
| Anne Tillery Renshaw | 1.50 |
| Anonymous | .25 |

*One Dollar Each:* Margaret Abraham, Agnes R. Arnold, Elizabeth Barnhart, Grace M. Bromley, Mary Faye Durr, Alice M. Hamlet, Hester Harper.

| | |
|---|---|
| Total on hand November 6, 1920 | $82.25 |

## REMARKS

The doubling of printing rates makes large contributions imperative if the Organ is to approach its customary standard. Acknowledgments are due the Woodbee Press Club for its exceedingly generous contribution, and ex-Editor Renshaw for the mailing of an appeal which has proved most effective in the campaign for funds. Emulation of the Woodbees' generosity by other clubs would save a situation which is very threatening.

[January 1921:]

Providence, R. I., April 1, 1921.

## RECEIPTS SINCE NOVEMBER 6, 1920

From Treasurer, up to April 1, 1921.................................................................$21.50
Verna McGeoch (3 instalments) ...................................................................$15.00
E. Edward Ericson ........................................................................................10.00
Edward F. Daas ..............................................................................................6.00
Howard R. Conover.........................................................................................2.00
Anna H. Crofts ...............................................................................................1.00
Ernest L. McKeag............................................................................................1.00
John Milton Samples........................................................................................1.00
Anonymous ...................................................................................................... .75

Balance on Hand, November 6, 1920 ..........................................................$82.25
Received, November 6, 1920, to April 1, 1921 ............................................58.25
                                                                                                                  ———
Total Receipts .............................................................................................$140.50

## EXPENDITURES

To E. E. Ericson for September U. A....................................................................$48.00
To E. E. Ericson for November U. A. ...............................................................48.00
To E. E. Ericson for January U. A.....................................................................36.00
Total Expenditures..........................................................................................$132.00

Balance on Hand, April 1, 1921 ..................................................................$ 8.50

[March 1921:]

Providence, R. I., July 1, 1921.

## RECEIPTS SINCE APRIL 1, 1921

From Treasurer, up to July 1, 1921 ...............................................................$18.50
Verna McGeoch (2 instalments) ....................................................................10.00
E. Edward Ericson ........................................................................................10.00
Mr. and Mrs. Leo Fritter ................................................................................2.00
John Milton Samples........................................................................................1.00
Balance on Hand, April 1, 1921 .....................................................................8.50
                                                                                                                  ———
Total Receipts .............................................................................................$50.00

## EXPENDITURES

To E. E. Ericson, for March U. A. ................................................................$46.00
                                                                                                                  ———
Balance on Hand, July 1, 1921 ....................................................................$4.00

[November 1921:]

Providence, R. I., December 29, 1921.

On Hand, July 1, 1921 ..............................................................................$ 4.00

## RECEIPTS SINCE JULY 1

Sonia H. Greene..............................................................................$50.00
From Treasury up to Dec. 29, 1921 ..............................................41.60
H. P. Lovecraft ...............................................................................5.40
Mr. and Mrs. Leo Fritter ..............................................................6.00
Howard R. Conover ......................................................................5.00
Woodbee Press Club ......................................................................5.00
Theodore D. Gottlieb......................................................................1.00
Ida C. Haughton ...........................................................................1.00

    Total Receipts................................................................$129.00

## EXPENDITURES

To E. E. Ericson for May U. A. ....................................................$24.00
To E. E. Ericson for July U. A......................................................18.00
To E. E. Ericson for Sept. U. A. ...................................................36.00
To E. E. Ericson for Nov. U. A. ...................................................36.00

    Total Expenditures ......................................................$114.00

Balance on Hand December 29, 1921 ...........................................$15.00

[March 1922:]

Providence, R. I., April 25, 1922.

On Hand December 29, 1921.............................................................$15.00

## RECEIPTS SINCE DECEMBER 29

From Treasury up to April 25 ........................................................$31.00
Woodbee Press Club ......................................................................10.00
H. P. Lovecraft ...............................................................................7.00
Anonymous ....................................................................................5.00
Mr. and Mrs. Leo Fritter ..............................................................2.00
Ida C. Haughton ...........................................................................2.00

    Total Receipts................................................................$72.00

## EXPENDITURES

To E. E. Ericson for January U. A. ........................................................................$36.00
To E. E. Ericson for March U. A. .........................................................................36.00

Total Expenditures ..............................................................................................$72.00

Balance on Hand April 25,1922 ........................................................................None

[May 1922:]

Providence, R. I., June 23, 1922.

On Hand, April 25, 1922 ....................................................................................None

### Receipts Since April 25

From Treasury up to June 23 ..............................................................................$28.00
Alfred Galpin, Jr. ....................................................................................................6.00
Woodbee Press Club ..............................................................................................5.00
Mr. and Mrs. Leo Fritter ........................................................................................2.00

Total Receipts ......................................................................................................$41.00

### Expenditures

To E. E. Ericson, for May U. A. ..........................................................................$24.00

Balance on Hand, June 23, 1922 .......................................................................$17.00

EDITORS' NOTE  FP: *United Amateur* 20, No. 1 (September 1920): 11; 20, No. 3 (January 1921): 42; 20, No. 4 (March 1921): 60; 21, No. 2 (November 1921): 24; 21, No. 4 (March 1922): 46; 21, No. 5 (May 1922): 56 (all signed "H. P. LOVECRAFT, Custodian"). A list of contributions to the UAPA and expenditures in the publication of the official organ, the *United Amateur*. The dates affixed to several of the items indicate that the issues appeared months after their cover dates. HPL's contributions in the November 1921 and March 1922 issues are to be noted. He discusses Sonia Greene's unprecedented donation of $50 (made in August 1921 and recorded in the issue for November 1921) in *SL* 1.143.

# [UNTITLED NOTE ON AMATEUR POETRY]

Some qualified person ought to turn his satiric and analytic gifts to the dispassionate, cold-blooded dissection of half a dozen samples of contemporary amateur verse, selected at random—exploring the deplorable discontinuity of thought, sloppiness of scansion, and poverty of theme. Our poetasters should be taught that a mere disconnected jumble of half-baked ideas and delirious abstractions does not add up as *poetry*, or even as decent prose. It simply arrives at gibberish! You can take any really fine piece of poetry and rearrange it in sentences and paragraphs, preserving the original punctuation, and it *still* makes beautiful sense. The little poetry that I have seen in amateur papers (and from which it is probably not fair to draw any broad conclusions) is rather disheartening. It would seem that the writers have little conception of the basic technique of poetry, to say nothing of its essence. They evince no familiarity with the language, the literature, or the craftsmanship of the poet's art. I have seen much better verse in high-school papers. And the worst feature of all is their yen for a sort of fourth-rate, bastard decadence, in which downright incoherence and maundering silliness is fatuously mistaken for some kind of God-help-us Symbolism. I will illustrate the kind of bilge I have in mind by composing a parody here and now, *currente Corona*,[1] and without apologies to any possible original or originals:

## (WET) DREAM SONG

Homer had the pox,
Sappho had the itch,
But I'm just a vox-
Popular sonofabitch.

Mustard without cress,
Cakes without ale,
Satisfy me less
Than a cat without a tail.

I who loved the light
Of extinguished moons,
Chanted all night
My cacophonous tunes.

For hours and hours
On the arid Atlantic,
The clamour of flowers
Drove me quite frantic.

What should one do
When one's on the blink?
Have an oyster stew,—
Or another drink?

E. A. Edkins

EDITOR'S NOTE  Unpublished fragment (AMS, JHL). An unusually blunt and cynical expression of HPL's impatience with the mediocrity of amateur verse; apparently written in the 1930s, as a byproduct of his work on the NAPA's Bureau of Critics.

*Notes*

1. "With my Corona [i.e., typewriter] running," i.e., composed as HPL was at his typewriter (although the text is a handwritten ms.).

## [ON *NOTES HIGH AND LOW* BY CARRIE ADAMS BERRY]

"All of your verse is of admirable quality. . . . You are to be congratulated on the excellence of your work. I wish for your brochure the success it merits."

EDITOR'S NOTE A blurb appearing on page [3] of a flyer, entitled *Announcing the Publication of Notes High and Low by Carrie Adams Berry*, issued by Charles A. A. Parker (Medford, MA) in 1934. Prefacing the comment appears a heading: "HOWARD P. LOVECRAFT, eminent scholar and critic, Providence." Berry was also the author of a play, *New Trails* (1926).

## A VOICE FROM THE GRAVE

. . . I was approached because I had not the slightest interest in amateur politics except as connected with the maintenance of literary standards. All my activity had been in another association, and I was completely neutral toward all the issues and persons in the NAPA. I never accepted dictation, and had only one object in amateurdom: the increase of literary activity, and the raising of aesthetic standards. Thus I suppose I was a sort of antidote for the politics and personalities of 1920–22. I took the office with great reluctance, because at the time I was not very fond of the National—being a United man first and foremost. However, a hostile and anti-literary faction in Columbus, Ohio, had just (July '22) gained control of the United; so I finally decided that for the time being I could best serve amateur journalism through the "rival" organization—whose somewhat chaotic state made it amenable to moulding. So on November 30, 1922, I accepted the office.

My term was, I fancy, neither brilliant nor spectacular; but I think I did for the time being put a quietus on politics and personalities and stir up some interest in literature. I wrote long presidential messages excoriating the ideals of the immediate past and urging activity in strictly literary fields. Also, I fostered a debate on literary ideals—the more flexible and purely aesthetic school of the present versus the conventional, quasimoralistic school of Victorian times—which ran through all the papers and took the place of politics as a fighting issue. I had excellent support from officers and members alike. The Official Editor, Harry E. Martin, stayed on from the Dowdell regime and did splendidly. Only a few new appointments were necessary. I had been on the Critics Bureau (under Samuel Loveman as Chairman), but resigned and appointed Edward H. Cole in my place. He and Loveman—and J. Clinton Pryor—provided extremely fine reports.

N.B. It must be remembered that during this period, and all through the 1920's, the personnel of the National was much more adult than at present, the average age was perhaps the 30's.

Loveman and Long turned out splendid literature in all departments; and of the 46 papers issued, a goodly quota were of pretty high quality. Horace L. Lawson's *Wolverine*, the Hub Club *Quill*, the *Clevelander* (published by Scribblers Club), H. A. Joslin's *Gypsy*, Clyde Townsend's *Oracle*, Parker's *L'Alouette*, Campbell's *Liberal*, and several others deserve particular mention.

There were four steady local clubs—the Hub, to which I belonged (since Boston is only 44 miles from Providence), the Blue Pencil, the Gotham (then flourishing under Houtain), and the Scribblers in Cleveland (with Loveman as moving spirit). Morton was the strong man of the B.P.C., and Mrs. Miniter (plus J. Bernard Lynch) of the Hub. Others were founded in Warren and Lorain, Ohio—the Warren one later to become politically important. The Scribblers—reorganized in January '23—acted as host for the Cleveland convention of 1923. The Hub Club held a round-up or substitute convention for the easterners unable to get to Cleveland . . . Quite a festive event, with over 100 present, including guests. Lynch, a friend of (the Mayor—later Governor) Curley,[11] got the free use of a municipal boat to take the delegates on a harbor sail!

We had some pretty good laureate judges—Nixon Waterman for verse, Herman Landon for story, Prof. Greenough of Harvard for essay, and C. A. A. Parker for history.[22] Finances were very satisfactory. During my term of office $98.00 was successfully pan-handled (I sent out mimeographed appeals)—all spend on the official organ, which was a creditable volume. The weakest point was the *recruiting*. There we nearly fell down—with a total of only 27 new memberships.

All told, I don't think the year was an absolute failure by any means. We did—for the time being—dispel the chaos into which the NAPA had fallen, and there was certainly quite a literary stir, some good papers, and some invigorating debates on really important subjects. It was a long time before scurrilous politics got back into the National. However, the real credit for any advance belongs to those who co-operated so diligently—Martin, Long, Morton, Mrs. Miniter, Loveman, Lynch, Parker, Cole, Pryor, Campbell, etc., etc., and the various clubs.

EDITOR'S NOTE FP: *Scarlet Cockerel* No. 15 (January 1941): 15–19. Part of a letter to Ralph Babcock (editor of the *Scarlet Cockerel*), probably written in the mid-1930s and discussing HPL's interim presidency of the NAPA in 1922–23. The title was obviously supplied by Babcock.

*Notes*

1 James Michael Curley (1874–1958), mayor of Boston (1914–17, 1922–25, 1930–33, 1945–49) and governor of Massachusetts (1935–37).

2 Nixon Waterman (1859–1944), author of many books of poetry, including *A Book of Verses* (1900) and *Sunshine Verses* (1913). Herman Landon (1882–1960), chiefly a writer of mystery stories, including *The Gray Phantom* (1921) and *The Back-Seat Murder* (1931). Chester Noyes Greenough (1874–1938), professor of English (1899–1907, 1910–20) and dean (1921–27) at Harvard; author of *A History of Literature in America* (1904; with Barrett Wendell). Charles A. A. Parker was a well-known amateur (editor of *L'Alouette*) and professional printer.